THE PAPERS OF ALEXANDER HAMILTON

Alexander Hamilton, 1804. Oil portrait by John Trumbull.

THE PAPERS OF

Alexander Hamilton

VOLUME I: 1768–1778

HAROLD C. SYRETT, EDITOR

JACOB E. COOKE, ASSOCIATE EDITOR

 COLUMBIA UNIVERSITY PRESS

NEW YORK AND LONDON, 1961

ACKNOWLEDGMENTS

IN 1955, after almost two decades of study and planning, Dr. John A. Krout, Vice President of Columbia University, and Mr. Charles G. Proffitt, Director of the Columbia University Press, established a project to collect, edit, and publish the papers of Alexander Hamilton. Since that date they have supervised every stage of the enterprise and have unstintingly supported the editorial staff. They have arranged for the project's financing, provided quarters for the staff, and reacted to the complaints and vagaries of the editors with sympathy, understanding, and humor. In the early stages of the undertaking both men were assisted by an advisory board of which Dr. Krout served as chairman and whose other members were Professor Douglass Adair, Mr. Lyman H. Butterfield, Professor Henry Steele Commager, Professor Joseph Dorfman, Professor Carter Goodrich, Professor Louis M. Hacker, Dr. Philip Hamer, Professor Leonard W. Labaree, Professor Dumas Malone, Professor Broadus Mitchell, Professor Richard B. Morris, Professor Allan Nevins, Professor Robert L. Schuyler, and Professor Harold C. Syrett.

This edition of Hamilton's papers would not have been possible without the financial assistance of Time Inc., and the Rockefeller Foundation, which gave unusually generous grants for research and editing. Both deserve the highest commendation and the gratitude of all students of the American past for their willingness to underwrite a form of historical scholarship that is extraordinarily expensive and that, despite the basic significance of its results for the understanding of our times, has little apparent connection with contemporary events.

In addition to providing much needed financial assistance, Columbia University furnished the staff with quarters in a library that contains one of the best collections of American history in the

United States, and it released both the editor and associate editor from most of their academic responsibilities. Despite ever-increasing production costs, Columbia University Press has drawn heavily on its own resources in meeting publication expenses.

The documents which appear in these volumes are owned by individuals, manuscript dealers, governmental agencies, business firms, libraries, historical societies, and educational institutions. Each document is accompanied by a citation giving the name of the document's owner. Such a citation, however, can never repay the editors' debt to those individuals who took the time and trouble to provide staff members with facsimiles of Hamilton documents. Nor can the editors adequately express their appreciation and gratitude to the directors and librarians of the various institutions who supplied this project not only with facsimiles but also with almost every kind of scholarly assistance. The Library of Congress and the National Archives furnished the bulk of the documents used in these volumes and provided answers to countless questions concerning the life and times of Hamilton. Among the many other institutions that have given inestimable assistance are the American Antiquarian Society, the Bank of New York, the William L. Clements Library of the University of Michigan, Columbia University Libraries, the Connecticut Historical Society, the Chicago Historical Society, the Grolier Society, Harvard College Library, the Huntington Library, the Maryland Historical Society, the Massachusetts Historical Society, the Morristown National Historical Park, the New-York Historical Society, the New York Public Library, the New York State Historical Association, the New York State Library, Parke-Bernet Galleries, Passaic County Historical Society, City of Paterson Plant Management Commission, Pennsylvania Historical and Museum Commission, the Historical Society of Pennsylvania, the Pierpont Morgan Library, Princeton University Library, the Rhode Island Historical Society, and Yale University Library.

Of the many individuals who generously shared their specialized information or provided assistance in locating elusive documents, the editors are especially indebted to

Professor Douglass Adair, Claremont Graduate School
Dr. Wayne Andrews, former Curator of Manuscripts, New-York Historical Society

Miss Dorothy C. Barck, Librarian, New York State Historical Association

Mr. Roland O. Baughman, Head of Special Collections, Columbia University Libraries

Miss Polly Beaton, formerly with the Bank of New York

Miss Mary Benjamin, New York City

Mrs. Dorothie Bobbé, New York City

Miss Alice H. Bonnell, Special Collections, Columbia University Libraries

Professor Julian Boyd, Editor, The Papers of Thomas Jefferson

Professor I. J. Brugmans, Nederlandsch Economisch-Historish Archief, the Netherlands

Mr. Lyman Butterfield, Editor, The Adams Papers

Mr. Alexander P. Clark, Curator of Manuscripts, Princeton University Library

Mr. Curtis C. Davis, Baltimore

Professor Julius Goebel, Jr., School of Law, Columbia University

Dr. Philip Hamer, Executive Director, National Historical Publications Commission

Mr. Alexander Hamilton, Federal Hall Memorial Museum, New York City

Mr. Thompson R. Harlow, Director, the Connecticut Historical Society

Mr. Thomas R. Hay, Locust Valley, New York

Mr. Robert W. Hill, Keeper of Manuscripts, New York Public Library

Mr. Richard C. D. Hunt, Jr., Historian, The American Battle Monuments Commission

Professor William T. Hutchinson, Editor, The Papers of James Madison

Dr. Louis C. Jones, Director, New York State Historical Association

Dr. Ralph L. Ketcham, former Associate Editor, The Papers of James Madison

Professor Milton Klein, Long Island University

Carl J. Kulsrud, Archivist, The National Archives

Mr. Wilmer R. Leech, Curator of Manuscripts, New-York Historical Society

Mr. Kenneth A. Lohf, Special Collections, Columbia University Libraries

Miss Anne McCabe, Columbia University Libraries

Mr. David C. Mearns, Chief of Manuscript Division, Library of Congress

Professor Broadus Mitchell, Hofstra College

Dr. Frank Monaghan, Washington, D. C.

Professor Richard B. Morris, Columbia University

The late Mr. Edward B. Morrison, First Assistant, Manuscript Division, New York Public Library

Mr. William A. Oldridge, New York City

Mr. John de Porry, Manuscript Division, Library of Congress

Mr. Percy Powell, Manuscript Division, Library of Congress

Mr. Stephen T. Riley, Director, Massachusetts Historical Society

Mr. Francis S. Ronalds, Superintendent, Morristown National Historical Park

Mr. Clifford K. Shipton, Director, American Antiquarian Society

Mr. Edward T. Sullivan, First Deputy Secretary of State of the Commonwealth of Massachusetts

Mr. William H. Swan, Hampton Bays, New York

The late Mr. Arthur Swann, Parke-Bernet Galleries

Mr. John N. Waddell, Assistant Reference Librarian, Columbia University Libraries

Mr. R. N. Williams, 2nd, Director, Historical Society of Pennsylvania

Miss Constance M. Winchell, Reference Librarian, Columbia University Libraries

Miss Juliet Wolohan, Senior Librarian, New York State Library

The editors are under particularly heavy obligation to Miss F. Helen Beach, Archivist, National Historical Publications Commission, and Mrs. Vincent L. Eaton, Manuscripts Historian, Manuscript Division, Library of Congress, both of whom answered countless queries, discovered hitherto unknown documents, and voluntarily sent information which they thought would be of use to the staff.

Much of whatever merit these volumes may possess can be directly attributed to the industry, skill, and intelligence of several staff members who for varying periods of time during the past six years have worked on this project. Miss Jacqueline Gren and Mr. John Rommel transcribed more than half the documents in this volume and in the subsequent volumes of this work. Dr. Bernard Mason, who is now an assistant professor of history at Harpur College, served as researcher for some of the earlier volumes and as an assistant editor of the volumes covering Hamilton's first two years in the Treasury Department. Miss Dorothy Twohig, who has transcribed documents, checked footnotes, and has performed countless other tasks, is now serving as an assistant editor for the volumes covering the period from Hamilton's resignation as Secretary of the Treasury in 1795 to his death in 1804. Mrs. David B. Truman and Mrs. Harold C. Syrett have checked the accuracy of all transcriptions, and Mrs. Syrett has checked the proof. There is no phase of the work of assembling and editing the Hamilton papers to which Mrs. Jean

Cooke has not made substantial and significant contributions. She has worked on this project since its inception, and her title of assistant editor cannot possibly indicate the value and variety of her work, the depth and range of her knowledge, and the number of times she has saved her fellow-workers from truly colossal blunders.

PREFACE

THIS EDITION of Alexander Hamilton's papers contains letters and
other documents written by Hamilton, letters to Hamilton, and
some documents (commissions, certificates, etc.) that directly concern Hamilton but were written neither by him nor to him. All
letters and other documents have been printed in chronological
order. Hamilton's legal papers will be published under the editorial
direction of Professor Julius Goebel, Jr. of the School of Law,
Columbia University.

Many letters and documents have been calendared. Such calendared items include routine letters and documents by Hamilton,
routine letters to Hamilton, most of the letters or documents written
by Hamilton for someone else (such as the letters written by Hamilton as George Washington's aide-de-camp during the American
Revolution), letters or documents which have not been found but
which are known to have existed, letters or documents which have
been erroneously attributed to Hamilton, and letters to or by Hamilton that deal exclusively with his legal practice.

The notes in these volumes are designed to provide information
concerning the nature and location of each document, to identify
Hamilton's correspondents and the individuals mentioned in the text,
to explain events or ideas referred to in the text, and to point out
textual variations or mistakes. Occasional departures from these
standards can be attributed to a variety of reasons. In many cases
the desired information has been supplied in an earlier note and can
be found through the use of the index. Notes were not added when
in the opinion of the editors the material in the text was either self-
explanatory or common knowledge. The editors, moreover, did not
think it desirable or necessary to provide full annotation for Hamilton's "Cash Books," the letters which Hamilton wrote as George

Washington's aide-de-camp during the American Revolution, and Hamilton's legal correspondence. Finally, the editors on some occasions were unable to find the desired information, and on other occasions the editors were remiss.

GUIDE TO EDITORIAL APPARATUS

I. SYMBOLS USED TO DESCRIBE MANUSCRIPTS

AD	Autograph Document
ADS	Autograph Document Signed
ADf	Autograph Draft
ADfS	Autograph Draft Signed
AL	Autograph Letter
ALS	Autograph Letter Signed
D	Document
DS	Document Signed
Df	Draft
DfS	Draft Signed
LS	Letter Signed
LC	Letter Book Copy
[S]	[S] is used with other symbols (AD[S], ADf[S], AL[S], D[S], Df[S], L[S]) to indicate that the signature on the document has been cropped or clipped.

II. MONETARY SYMBOLS AND ABBREVIATIONS

bf	Banco florin
V	Ecu
f	Florin
₶	Livre Tournois
medes	Maravedis (also md and mde)
d.	Penny or denier
ps	Piece of eight

£	Pound sterling or livre
Ry	Real
rs vn	Reals de vellon
rdr	Rix daller
s	Shilling, sou or sol (also expressed as /)
sti	Stiver

III. SHORT TITLES AND ABBREVIATIONS

Arch. des Aff. Etr. Corr. Pol., Etats-Unis
Transcripts or photostats from the French Foreign Office deposited in the Library of Congress.

Barrett, *Old Merchants of New York*
Walter Barrett, *The Old Merchants of New York City* (New York, 1885).

Bakeless, *Traitors, Turncoats and Heroes*
John Bakeless, *Traitors, Turncoats and Heroes* (Philadelphia, 1959).

Colls. of N. Y. Hist. Soc. for 1915
Collections of the New-York Historical Society for the Year 1915 (New York, 1916).

Fitzpatrick, *Calendar of the Correspondence of George Washington with the Officers*
John C. Fitzpatrick, *Calendar of the Correspondence of George Washington, Commander in Chief of the Continental Army, with the Officers* (Washington, 1915).

Freeman, *Washington*
Douglas Southall Freeman, *George Washington* (New York, 1948–1957).

GW
John C. Fitzpatrick, ed., *The Writings of George Washington* (Washington, 1931–1944).

Hamilton, *History*
John C. Hamilton, *Life of Alexander Hamilton, a History of the Republic of the United States of America* (Boston, 1879).

Hamilton, *Intimate Life*
Allan McLane Hamilton, *The Intimate Life of Alexander Hamilton* (New York, 1910).

Hamilton, *Life*
John C. Hamilton, *The Life of Alexander Hamilton* (New York, 1840).

Hammond, *Letters and Papers of John Sullivan*

Otis G. Hammond, ed., *Letters and Papers of Major-General John Sullivan* (Concord, New Hampshire, 1930–1939).

Harrington, *The New York Merchant*

Virginia Harrington, *The New York Merchant on the Eve of the Revolution* (New York, 1935).

Hawks, *The Official and Other Papers of Alexander Hamilton*

Francis L. Hawks, *The Official and Other Papers of the Late Major-General Alexander Hamilton* (New York, 1842).

HCLW

Henry Cabot Lodge, *The Works of Alexander Hamilton* (New York, 1904).

JCC

Journals of the Continental Congress, 1774–1789 (Washington, 1904–1937).

JCH Transcripts

John C. Hamilton Transcripts. These transcripts are owned by Mr. William H. Swan, Hampton Bays, New York, and have been placed on loan in the Columbia University Libraries.

JCHW

John C. Hamilton, ed., *The Works of Alexander Hamilton* (New York, 1851).

Journals of the Provincial Congress of the State of New-York

Journals of the Provincial Congress, Provincial Convention, Committee of Safety and Council of Safety of the State of New-York. 1775–1776–1777 (Albany, 1842).

"The Lee Papers," *Colls. of N. Y. Hist. Soc.*

"The Lee Papers," *Collections of the New-York Historical Society* (New York, 1872–1875).

Mitchell, *Hamilton*

Broadus Mitchell, *Alexander Hamilton, Youth to Maturity, 1755–1788* (New York, 1957).

Proceeding of a General Court Martial for the Trial of Major General Lee

Proceedings of a General Court Martial, Held at Brunswick, in the State of New Jersey, by order of His Excellency General Washington . . . for the Trial of Major General Lee (Philadelphia, 1778).

PRO: F.O., or PRO:C.O.	Transcripts or photostats from the Public Records Office of Great Britain deposited in the Library of Congress.
Public Papers of George Clinton	*Public Papers of George Clinton* (New York and Albany, 1900).
Ramsing, "Alexander Hamilton," *Personalhistorisk tidsskrift*	Holger Utke Ramsing, "Alexander Hamilton og hans mødrene stoegt Tidsbilleder fra Dansk Vestindiens barndom," *Personalhistorisk tidsskrift*, 24 cm., 10 Raekke, 6bd. (Copenhagen, 1939).
Stevens, *Colonial New York*	John A. Stevens, Jr., *Colonial New York. Sketches Biographical and Historical. 1768–1784* (New York, 1867).
White, *Beekman Papers*	Philip L. White, ed., *The Beekman Mercantile Papers* (New York, 1956).

IV. INDECIPHERABLE WORDS

Words or parts of words which could not be deciphered because of the illegibility of the writing or the mutilation of the manuscript have been indicated as follows:

1. ⟨– – – – –⟩ indicates illegible words with the number of dashes indicating the estimated number of illegible words.
2. Words or letters in broken brackets indicate a guess as to what the words or letters in question may be. If the source of the words or letters within the broken brackets is known, it has been given in a note.

V. CROSSED-OUT MATERIAL IN MANUSCRIPTS

Words or sentences crossed out by a writer in a manuscript have been handled in one of the three following ways:

1. They have been ignored, and the document or letter has been printed in its final version.
2. Crossed-out words and insertions for the crossed-out words have been described in the notes.

3. When the significance of a manuscript seems to warrant it, the crossed-out words have been retained, and the document has been printed as it was written.

VI. TEXTUAL CHANGES AND INSERTIONS

The following changes or insertions have been made in the letters and documents printed in these volumes:

1. Words or letters written above the line of print (for example, 9th) have been made even with the line of print (9th).
2. Punctuation and capitalization have been changed in those instances where it seemed necessary to make clear the sense of the writer. A special effort has been made to eliminate the dash, which was such a popular eighteenth-century device.
3. When the place or date, or both, of a letter or document does not appear at the head of that letter or document, it has been inserted in the text in brackets. If either the place or date at the head of a letter or document is incomplete, the necessary additional material has been added in the text in brackets. For all but the best known localities or places, the name of the colony, state, or territory has been added in brackets at the head of a document or letter.
4. In calendared documents, place and date have been uniformly written out in full without the use of brackets. Thus "N. York, Octr. 8, '99" becomes "New York, October 8, 1799." If, however, substantive material is added to the place or date in a calendared document, such material is placed in brackets. Thus "Oxford, Jan. 6" becomes "Oxford [Massachusetts] January 6 [1788].
5. When a writer made an unintentional slip comparable to a typographical error, one of the four following devices has been used:
   a. It has been allowed to stand as written.
   b. It has been corrected by inserting either one or more letters in brackets.
   c. It has been corrected without indicating the change.
   d. It has been explained in a note.

ILLUSTRATIONS

THE PAPERS OF ALEXANDER HAMILTON

1 7 6 8

Probate Court Transaction on Estate of Rachel Lavien [1]

[St. Croix, February 19, 1768]

SKIFTE BREV NO. XXIX.

Som udi Skifte-Sessions Protocollen er behandlet under No. XXIV
sc: efter afgangne

Rachael Lewine

James Towers Hands kongelige Majestæts til Danmark og Norge
pp. bestalter Skifte-Forvalter ved Christianstæds Jurisdiction paa
Eylandet St Croix udj America og Jvar Hofman Sevel bestalter
Byefoged ved samme Jurisdiction samt med Skifte-Forvalter Laurence Bladwil og Jsaac Hartman tillige med Johan Henric Dietrichs
bestalter Bye- og Skifte-Skriver sammesteds, giøre witterligt

at

Anno 1768 dend 19de Februarij om Aftenen Klokken 10 slet
indfandt sig Skifte-Rætten udj et Huus her i Byen Thomas Dipnall
tilhørende, hvor der for en Time siden et Fruentimmer Rachael
Lewine ved Døden afgangen for at forseigle hendes Effecter til
videre Registrering. Tilstæde ved Forretningen som Vidner vare
bemelte Thomas Dipnall og Fridcrich Wilhl Larsen, hvor da blev
forseiglet et Kammer, hvor udj var hendes Effecter, samt Koffert
etc., derefter blev forseiglet et Pulterkammer og 2de Magaziner i
Gaarden og da der var intet andet at forseigle undtagen Gryder og
andre smaa Ting som blev uforseiglet til Ligets Brug, hvor udj er
includeret 6 Stoele, 2de Borde og 2de Porcelains-Kummer. Saa blev
Forretningen sluttet.

Saaledes passeret testerer

James Towers   Johan Henric Dietrichs
Som Vidner:
Thomas Dipnall   Friderich Wilhm Larsen

Anno 1768 den 22. Februarij indfandt sig Skifte-Rætten der blev administreret af mig James Towers som constitueret Skifte-Forvalter og af mig Johan Henric Dietrichs som kongl. bestalter Bye- og Skifteskriver ved Christianstæds Jurisdiction paa Eylandet St Croix udj America sig udj Thomas Dipnalls Huus her i Byen hvor Madme Rachael Lewine ved Døden dend 19 hujus er afgangen og hvis Effecter blev forseiglet strax ved Dødsfaldet, for nu samme Afdødes Efterladenskab at registrere og vurdere til en paafølgende Skifte og Deeling imellem dend Afdødes efterladte Børn, som ere 3de Sønner navnlig Peter Lewine [2] født i dend Afdødes Egteskab med John Michael Lewine,[3] som siden skal have været skildt fra hende for gyldige Aarsager (efter hvad Skifte-Rætten derom har underrettet sig) af Høyeste Øvrighed, item 2de Sønner nemlig James Hammilton [4] og Alexander Hamilton, den ene 15ten og den anden 13 Aar gl. og ere samme Slifrigbørn sc. siden den Afdødes Skilsmisse med bemelte Lewine. Bemelte Søn Peter Lewine haver og endnu opholder sig i Syd Carolina og efter Underretning er ungefæhr 22 Aar gammel.

Christianssted Byfogedarkiv Skifteprotokol 1766 12/4–1770 15/2 Fol. 386 v (Gl. Nr. 41), Rigsarkivet, Copenhagen.
    1. The translation reads as follows:
                    "PROBATE COURT TRANSACTION NO. XXIX
"Which in the Probate court protocol is recorded as No. XXIV sc. the case of the deceased Rachael Lewine
"James Towers, by His Royal Majesty of Denmark and Norway duly appointed administrator of estates in the Christiansted jurisdiction on the Island of St. Croix in America, and Ivar Hofman Sevel, appointed bailiff in the same jurisdiction, together with Laurence Bladwil, administrator of estates, Isaac Hartman, and Johan Henric Dietrichs, appointed town and probate court recorder in the aforesaid jurisdiction, make known that
"In the year 1768 on the 19th day of February in the evening at 10 o'clock sharp the probate court met in a house here in town belonging to Thomas Dipnal, where an hour earlier a woman, Rachael Lewine, died, in order to seal up her effects for subsequent recording. Present at this transaction were the aforesaid Thomas Dipnal and Friedrich Wilhl Larsen as witnesses to the sealing up of a chamber containing her effects together with a trunk etc., thereafter were sealed an attic storage room and two storage rooms in the yard, after which there was nothing more to seal up, except some pots and other small things which remained unsealed for use in preparing the body for burial, among them being 6 chairs, 2 tables, and 2 wash-bowls. The transaction was then closed.
    "In witness thereof   James Towers   Johan Henric Dietrichs
                                            As Witnesses
                            Thomas Dipnal   Friedrich Wilhm Larsen
    "In the year 1768 on the 22 of February the probate court administered by

me, James Towers, as acting administrator of estates, and by me, Johan Henric Dietrichs, duly appointed by the King as town and probate court recorder in the Christiansted jurisdiction on the Island of St. Croix in America, met in Thomas Dipnal's house here in town, where on the 19th of this month Madam Rachael Lewine died, and whose effects were forthwith sealed up, in order now to take an inventory of them for subsequent distribution among the decedent's surviving children, who are 3 sons, namely, Peter Lewine, born in the marriage of the decedent with John Michael Lewine who, later, is said for valid reasons to have obtained from the highest authorities a divorce from her (according to what the probate court has been able to ascertain), also 2 other sons, namely, James Hamilton and Alexander Hamilton, the one 15 and the other 13 years old, who are the same illegitimate children sc. born after the decedent's separation from the aforesaid Lewine. The above mentioned Peter Lewine has resided and still resides in South Carolina and according to reports is about 22 years old."

The above translation was made by Mr. Carl J. Kulsrud, archivist in charge of Agriculture and General Services Branch, Natural Resources Records Division, National Archives.

Although this is not strictly an H document, it is printed here because it is the first extant document in which H is mentioned. Both Bancroft (George Bancroft, *History of the United States* [Boston, 1858], VII, 79) and Lodge (Henry Cabot Lodge, *Alexander Hamilton* [Boston, 1899], 283–85) refer to an earlier document dated 1766. Bancroft states: "The first written trace of his [Hamilton's] existence is in 1766, when his name appears as witness to a legal paper executed in the Danish island of Santa Cruz." Lodge elaborates on this statement as follows: "I have carefully examined an exact tracing of this signature. The handwriting is obviously Hamilton's." This document has not been found.

Rachel Lavien, H's mother, was the daughter of John Faucett, a doctor and planter, and his wife Mary, both of the English island Nevis. Either in 1745 or somewhat earlier, Rachel Faucett went to St. Croix where she married the merchant John (Johann) Michael Lavien. In 1746, Peter Lavien was born. The marriage was not a happy one, and in 1750 Rachel left her son, Peter, and her husband and ran away from the island. In 1759, Lavien obtained a divorce from Rachel. Shortly after leaving her husband, Rachel Lavien had met James Hamilton, who was the fourth son of Alexander Hamilton, Laird of Grange in Stevenston Parish in Ayrshire, Scotland. They lived together on St. Kitts as man and wife and had two sons, James and Alexander. In 1765, James Hamilton moved his family to St. Croix. Soon after he returned to St. Kitts, leaving his family on St. Croix. He never saw them again. In February, 1768, Rachel Lavien was taken ill with a fever and died shortly afterwards. For a detailed account of H's parentage and boyhood, see Ramsing, "Alexander Hamilton," *Personalhistorisk tidsskrift*, 225–70.

2. H's half brother, who was the sole heir of his father. In 1764, he went to South Carolina and was living there at the time of his mother's death.

3. Rachel Lavien's former husband and Peter Lavien's father.

4. H's brother. After his mother's death he was apprenticed to a carpenter on the island of St. Croix. Nothing is definitely known concerning the remainder of his life. According to Ramsing, he died in 1786.

1 7 6 9

To Edward Stevens [1]

St Croix Novemr. 11th 1769

Dear Edward

This just serves to acknowledge receipt of yours [2] per Cap Lowndes [3] which was delivered me Yesterday. The truth of Cap Lightbourn [4] & Lowndes information is now verifyd by the Presence of your Father and Sister for whose safe arrival I Pray, and that they may convey that Satisfaction to your Soul that must naturally flow from the sight of Absent Friends in health, and shall for news this way refer you to them. As to what you say respecting your having soon the happiness of seeing us all, I wish, for an accomplishment of your hopes provided they are Concomitant with your welfare, otherwise not, tho doubt whether I shall be Present or not for to confess my weakness, Ned, my Ambition is prevalent that I contemn the grov'ling and condition of a Clerk or the like, to which my Fortune &c. condemns me and would willingly risk my life tho' not my Character to exalt my Station. Im confident, Ned that my Youth excludes me from any hopes of immediate Preferment nor do I desire it, but I mean to prepare the way for futurity. Im no Philosopher you see and may be jusly said to Build Castles in the Air. My Folly makes me ashamd and beg youll Conceal it, yet Neddy we have seen such Schemes successfull when the Projector is Constant I shall Conclude saying I wish there was a War.

I am   Dr Edward   Yours   Alex Hamilton

PS   I this moment receivd yours [5] by William Smith [6] and am pleasd to see you Give such Close Application to Study.

ALS, Hamilton Papers, Library of Congress.

1. Edward Stevens, H's boyhood friend and schoolmate, was the son of Thomas Stevens, St. Croix merchant, into whose home H may have been taken after his mother's death in 1768. H addressed this letter to Stevens in New

York City. Stevens was a student at King's College, New York City, from 1770–1774.

2. Letter not found.

3. William Lowndes, a New York ship captain. An advertisement in *The Royal Danish American Gazette*, October 31, 1772, reads "For New-York, The Sloop Hester, William Lowndes Master; will sail in 10 days."

4. William Lightbourn (Lightborn, or Lightbourne), New York ship captain, who also maintained a store in St. Croix. See Mitchell, *Hamilton*, I, 484, and *The Royal Danish American Gazette*, September 29, 1770.

5. Letter not found.

6. Ship captain, employed by New York and British merchants in the Atlantic trade. See White, *Beekman Papers*, II, 727, 763, 764, 811, 845.

I 7 7 I

To The Royal Danish American Gazette [1]

[St. Croix, April 6, 1771]

To the Printer of the Royal Danish American Gazette.

Sir,

    I am a youth about seventeen, and consequently such an attempt as this must be presumptuous; but if, upon perusal, you think the following piece worthy of a place in your paper, by inserting it you'll much oblige   Your obedient servant,   A.H.

> In yonder mead my love I found
> Beside a murm'ring brook reclin'd:
> Her pretty lambkins dancing round
> Secure in harmless bliss.
> I bad the waters gently glide,
> And vainly hush'd the heedless wind,
> Then, softly kneeling by her side,
> I stole a silent kiss—
>
> She wak'd, and rising sweetly blush'd
> By far more artless than the dove:
> With eager haste I onward rush'd,
> And clasp'd her in my arms;
> Encircled thus in fond embrace
> Our panting hearts beat mutual love—
> A rosy-red o'er spread her face
> And brighten'd all her charms.
>
> Silent she stood, and sigh'd consent
> To every tender kiss I gave;
> I closely urg'd—to church we went,

And hymen join'd our hands.
Ye swains behold my bliss complete;
No longer then your own delay;
Believe me love is doubly sweet
In wedlocks holy bands.—

Content we tend our flocks by day,
Each rural pleasures amply taste;
And at the suns retiring ray
Prepare for new delight:
When from the field we haste away,
And send our blithsome care to rest,
We fondly sport and fondly play,
And love away the night.

Cœlia's an artful little slut;
Be fond, she'll kiss, *et cetera*—but
She must have all her will;
For, do but rub her 'gainst the grain
Behold a storm, blow winds and rain,
Go bid the waves be still.

So, stroking puss's velvet paws
How well the jade conceals her claws
And purs; but if at last
You hap to squeeze her somewhat hard,
She spits—her back up—*prenez garde;*
Good faith she has you fast.

The Royal Danish American Gazette, April 6, 1771.
    1. As the writer gives his age as about seventeen and his initials as AH, it is a reasonable assumption that H was the author.
    The following issue (April 10, 1771) of the same paper printed a piece entitled "Rules for Statesmen," which some scholars have also attributed to H. No conclusive evidence, however, has been found to indicate that H wrote this essay. For the view that H may have been the author of "Rules for Statesmen," see Mitchell, *Hamilton,* I, 28.

From Walton and Cruger [1]

[*Jamaica, October 19, 1771.* On November 27, 1771, Hamilton wrote to Jacob Walton [2] and John H. Cruger: [3] "I have now the pleasure to acknowledge the receipt of your favour dated October the 19th." *Letter not found.*]

1. Sometime between 1766 and 1768, H began work as a clerk for the trading firm of Beekman and Cruger in Christiansted, St. Croix. The firm, dealing in both imports and exports, handled the items common in the trade of a plantation economy. By 1769, the partnership had apparently been dissolved, and the firm was subsequently managed by young Nicholas Cruger, member of a prominent merchant family of New York. Occasionally, he undertook joint ventures with Cornelius Kortright under the firm name of Kortright and Cruger. On October 15, 1771, Cruger went to New York City, and during his five-month absence much of the firm's business was carried on by H.

The Cruger business letters, which are in the Hamilton Papers, Library of Congress, are all letterbook copies and fall into three categories: (1) copies of letters composed by H and in the writing of H; (2) copies of letters written by someone other than H, but in whole or in part in the writing of H; (3) copies of letters not written by H and not in the writing of H. Letters in the first category have been printed in full. Letters in the second category have been calendared. Although those in the third category may conceivably be copies of originals which were in H's writing, there is no evidence that this is the case. As a consequence, such letters have been neither printed nor calendared.

For information on the Cruger family and business activities, see B. D. Hassell, "The Cruger Family in America" (MS, MS Division, New York Public Library, 1892); E. F. De Lancy, "Original Family Records, Cruger," *New York Genealogical and Biographical Record,* VI (April, 1875), 74–80; Henry C. Van Schaack, *Henry Cruger, The Colleague of Edmund Burke in the British Parliament* (New York, 1859); Harrington, *The New York Merchant.*

2. Jacob Walton was a member of a prominent New York merchant family and brother-in-law of Nicholas Cruger. See Stevens, *Colonial New York,* 170.

3. John Harris Cruger was a brother of Nicholas Cruger and factor on the British island of Jamaica. The presence of the Crugers in the West Indies was not unusual, for New York merchants often had agents on the islands. Trade with the French West Indies was carried on through the Dutch and Danish neutral ports, especially St. Eustatius, St. Thomas, St. Croix, and Curaçao.

To Thomas Ashburner [1]

[*St. Croix, October 28, 1771.* On November 20, 1771, Hamilton wrote to Ashburner: "I wrote you the 28th of last Month." He then crossed out this sentence and substituted: "Above is triplicate of mine to you." *Letter not found.*]

1. Merchant of St. Eustatius. See letters to Thomas Ashburner, April 28, May 13, 1772, Hamilton Papers, Library of Congress.

To Nicholas Cruger

Mr Nicholas Cruger ⅌ Codwise [1]   St Croix [October 31, 1771] [2]

Dear Sir

Expecting that Capt Codwise would ⟨have⟩ saild two days ago, I had already wrote & delive⟨red⟩ my Letter [3] to him, but the arrival of Capt Lowndes furnishes me with something more to say. By him I receivd sundry Letters; [4] one from Mr. Henry Cruger, [5] one from Mr. John Cruger, [6] one from Mr. John Harris Cruger, and several from Henry Cruger Junior, [7] which last are all Copies and have been answerd, except one of the 24 June. I now inclose it to you with an abstract of the substance of your last Letters to him, which perhaps will be requisite in returing an answer.

I also send you the Owners last Letter now arrivd & a list of the Bills; all the protests for Non-acceptance are come to hand.

In Mr. John Harris Cruger's Letter, he says that he will remit Mr. Teleman Cruger [8] for his ⅓ part of the Sloops first Cargo of Mules & should depend upon your Honour for the other two, being £400. in advance for you, exclusive of your part of her Cargo out. I therefore just inclose a little state of matters between you that you might be able more clearly to convince him of his Mistake. There is nothing in the other Letters that require or will even admit of an answer from me, especially as you will be on the spot, ⟨in⟩ fact their Content are of but little consequence, etc.

LC, in writing of H, Hamilton Papers, Library of Congress.
1. George Codwise, New York ship captain. H and Codwise knew each other in later life. H served as Codwise's attorney in 1784, and Codwise named his son Alexander Hamilton Codwise. See Mitchell, *Hamilton,* I, 484.
2. Date obtained from transcript in the writing of Elizabeth Hamilton, Hamilton Papers, Library of Congress.
3. Letter not found.
4. Letters not found.

5. Father of Nicholas Cruger and an influential New York merchant. The house of John and Henry Cruger, a shipping firm engaged primarily in trade with Bristol and the West Indies, had subsidiary branches abroad managed by the sons of Henry. Henry Cruger was also for many years a member of the New York Assembly and His Majesty's Royal Council for that province.

6. Nicholas Cruger's uncle, mayor of New York City, member of the Provincial Assembly, and first president of the New York Chamber of Commerce.

7. Nicholas Cruger's brother, a merchant of Bristol, England, who was engaged in trade with the American colonies. He later became a member of Parliament, a defender of the American cause during the Revolution, and a friend of Edmund Burke.

8. Brother of Nicholas Cruger, who handled the Cruger mercantile affairs on the Dutch island of Curaçao. His first name was spelled either Tileman or Teleman. Although H frequently used Teleman, Tileman appears to be the correct spelling.

To Nicholas Cruger

⟨Mr.⟩ Nicholas Cruger   St Croix Nov. 4. 1771
⟨Capts.⟩ Cunningham [1]
⟨and⟩ Lowndes

Dear Sir

I wrote you a few days ago by Capt Codwise [2] to which refer you & should send you Copys by this opportunity but I am so unwell that it is with difficulty I make out to write these few lines. Every thing remains as then advisd. I have sold about 30 bbls flour more & Collectd a little more money from different people.

The Major [3] lies so ill that no one expects he'll live till night.

I receiv'd a Letter from Mr. Thomas Ashburner mentioning that Mr. Thomas Thomas [4] was gone to New York but that he had receivd the money from Mr. A. Heyliger [5] before his departure. Accordingly I have orderd it down in joes [6] which is the only thing that would answer just now. Not a word from Curraica yet, nor no appearance of your New Sloop.

I remain with the most permanent Esteem D. Sir

Your very H Serv

LC, in writing of H, Hamilton Papers, Library of Congress.
1. This is presumably the same Captain Cunningham who is mentioned in the Cruger letter books as early as 1766. No first name, however, is given (John Cruger to Beekman and Cruger, August 2, 1766, "Letter Book of John and Henry Cruger, 1764–1768," New-York Historical Society, New York City). On the other hand, the man in question may be Gustavus Conyngham, who

is mentioned in *The Pennsylvania Gazette*, March 5, 1772, as clearing from Philadelphia for Antigua in early March, 1772.

2. H to Nicholas Cruger, October 31, 1771.

3. This may refer to the Mr. Van Vain, who, H later wrote, was on "the brink of eternity." See H to Nicholas Cruger, November 27, 1771.

4. Merchant of St. Eustatius. See letter to Robert Gibb, July 10, 1772, Hamilton Papers, Library of Congress. There was also a Thomas Thomas, ship captain and merchant of Newburyport, who may have been the same man with stores or offices in the both places (Robert A. East, *Business Enterprise in the American Revolutionary Era* [New York, 1938], 228).

5. Abraham Heyliger, a member of a prominent trading and planting family of St. Croix. For information on the Heyliger family, see Waldemar C. Westergaard, *The Danish West Indies* (New York, 1917), 235; and Waldemar C. Westergaard, "A St. Croix Map of 1766," *Journal of Negro History*, XXIII (April, 1938), 224–28.

6. An abbreviation of Johannes, a Portuguese coin worth at that time about £5.

To Nicholas Cruger

Mr Nicholas Cruger   St Croix Novem. 12 177⟨1⟩

Dr Sir ⅌ Lowndes

I send you herewith Copies of my Letter's [1] ⅌ Codwise & Cunningham, since which nothing has occurd worth writing. Markets are just the same excepting in the price of Butter which is now reducd to 15 & 16 ⅌ a firkin. Your Philadelphia flour is realy very bad, being of a most swarthy complexion & withal very untractable; the Bakers complain that they cannot by any means get it to rise. Wherefore & in consideration of the quantity of flour at Market and the little demand for it I have some thought not to refuse 8½ from any good person that will give it, taking 40 or 50 Barrels. Upon opening several barrels I have observ'd a kind of Worm very common in flour about the surface, which is an indication of Age. It could not have been very new when twas shipd and for all these reasons I conceive it highly necessary to lessen the price or probably I may be oblig'd in the end to sell it at a much greater disadvantage. At 8½ you will gain better than 10 rys [2] ⅌ bbl which is not so bad. [New] York flour of 1 cwt. 3 grs.[3] is gladly sold by every body at 8 ps.[4] at retail & a grea⟨t⟩ part of your Philadelphia weighs but little more so that 8½ by the quantity is more than a proportionable price for the difference of weight.

There is still on hand about 290 barrels. All Lightborns is sold at 9 & near all your Fathers ℔ Draper [5] at 8 ps. As to bread I have sold very little. I dont know what to think of it.

The matter between Mr. Heyliger & Mr. Mahan is still unsettled. M Bastian French [6] who was to have been arbitrator for the former is at portoricco and he pretends he can get no one else to supply his place. Mr. French is minutely expected & it is to be hopd that when he arrives there will be a settlement.

No appearance of the Thunderbolt nor no News from Curracoa. I am with unfeigned Regard, Dear Sir   Your very Hum Serv

LC, in writing of H, Hamilton Papers, Library of Congress.

  1. H to Nicholas Cruger, October 31, November 4, 1781.
  2. Abbreviation for real, a former Spanish silver coin, the equivalent of the Spanish bit, an eighth of a piece of eight. In the 1770's it was the equivalent of about 7 pence. The contemporary sterling equivalent of West Indian currency, here and following, is taken from Edward Long, *The History of Jamaica* (London, 1774).
  3. 1 hundredweight and 3 quarter-hundredweight, the weight of one barrel of flour.
  4. A Spanish piece of eight. The piece of eight was the equivalent of the Spanish dollar, known also as a peso. On St. Croix its value was approximately 6 shillings, 6 pence. H students who have used these letters erroneously have interpreted ps. to mean pence.
  5. John Draper, ship captain of St. Christopher (from information supplied by Miss Jean L. Willis, Rutherford, New Jersey).
  6. The situation alluded to arose from the fact that Nicholas Cruger owed money to Rapzot (or Rapsart) Heyliger, and Cruger, in turn, was owed money by Alexander Mahan of St. Croix. Cruger wished to have this affair straightened out by having Mahan pay the money to Heyliger, but Mahan refused. French was then appointed arbitrator of the dispute. See Nicholas Cruger to John Heyliger, June 10, 1772; Nicholas Cruger to Alexander Mahan, June 18, 1772; Nicholas Cruger to John Heyliger, July 14, 1772, Hamilton Papers, Library of Congress.

To Tileman Cruger

Tileman Cruger Esqr.   St Croix, Novemr. 16. 1771

Sir

In behalf of Mr. Nicholas Cruger (who by reason of a very ill state of health went from this to New York the 15th Ultimo) I have the pleasure to address you by the long expected Sloop Thunderbolt, Capt William Newton,[1] Ownd by Mess[rs.] Jacob Walton,

John Harris & Nicholas Cruger, the latter of whom has written you fully concerning her destination—which I need not repeat.

She has on Board besides a parcel of Lumber for yourself, sundry Articles on Account of her Owners as per Inclosd Bill Lading and when you have disposd of them youll please to Credit each partie for ⅓ of the proceeds. Mr. N Crugers proportion of this and the Ballance of your account hitherto will more than pay for his ⅓ Cost of her first Cargo up, and for the other two I shall endeavour to place value in your hands betimes. I only wait for a line from you to know what will best answer.

Reports here represent matters in a very disagreeable light with regard to the Guarda Costo's [2] which are said to swarm upon the Coast, but as you will be the best Judge of what danger there might be, all is submited to your prudent direction.

Capt Newton must Arm with you as he could not so conveniently do it here.

Give me leave to hint to you that you cannot be too particular in your Instructions to him. I think he seems rather to want experience in such Voyages.

Messrs. Walton & John H Cruger are to furnish you themselves with their respective proportions of the Cost of the several Cargoes.

The Staves on Board if by any means convenient I beg may be returnd by the Sloop. They will command a good price here & I suppose little or nothing with you. Could they be got at I would not send them down, but they are stowd promiscuously among other things.

If convenient please to deliver the Hhds [3] now Contain'g the Indian Meal to the Captain as Water Casks and others should he want them. I supplied him with 20 here. I must beg your reference to Mr. Crugers last Letter of the 2d Ultimo for other particulars & am   Sir Your very H Serv

Our Crops will be very early so that the utmost Dispatch is necessary to import three Cargoes of Mules in due time.

LC, in writing of H, Hamilton Papers, Library of Congress.

1. William Newton, a resident of St. Croix, who later married the widow of Cornelius Kortright, who died in 1773. See Barrett, *The Old Merchants of New York*, III, 21.

2. This is a reference to the Spanish customs officials on the Spanish Main. Schachner mistakenly assumed "Guarda Costa's" to be a place, "where pirates lurked" (Nathan Schachner, *Alexander Hamilton* [New York, 1946], 22).
3. Abbreviation for hogsheads.

To William Newton

Capt William Newton   St Croix Nov. 16. 177⟨1⟩

Here with I give you all your dispatches & desire youll proceed immediately to Curracoa. You are to deliver your Cargo there to Teleman Cruger Esqr. agreeable to your Bill Lading, whose directions you must follow in every respect concerning the disposal of your Vessell after your arrival. You know it is intended that you shall go from thence to the Main for a load of Mules & I must beg if you do, you'll be very choice in Quality of your Mules and bring as many as your Vessell can conveniently contain. By all means take in a large supply of provendor. Remember you are to make three trips this Season & unless you are very diligent, you will be too late as our Crops will be early in.

Take care to avoid the Gaurda Costos. I place an intire reliance upon the prudence of your Conduct & am   Your very Hum Servt

For NC   AH

LC, in writing of H, Hamilton Papers, Library of Congress.

To Thomas Ashburner

Mr. Thomas Ashburner   St Croix Nov. 20. 1771

Sir

Above is triplicate of mine[1] to you ⅌ Capt Henton[2] to which have receivd no answer. I have now to beg the favour of you to pay Mess[rs.] Fraser Grant & Baillie of St Christophers on Mr Crugers Account as soon as convenient £13.4.10 Windward Currency for which Mr. Thomas shall have Credit.

I am Sir   Your Respectful hum Serv

LC, in writing of H, Hamilton Papers, Library of Congress.
1. In the MS of this letter the first line is crossed out. It reads as follows: "I

wrote you the 28th of last Month." The letter of the "28th of last Month" is
probably the "triplicate" to which H is here referring. Letter not found.

2. John Henton, ship captain and resident of St. Croix (RG 55, Records of
the Danish Government of the Virgin Islands, National Archives).

To Fraser, Grant and Baillie

Messrs. Fraser, Grant & Baillie　　　　　　St Croix Nov 20. 177⟨1⟩

Gentlemen

I receivd your favour of the 18th Ultimo in due time & beg pardon
for not having answerd it before. I have by this opportunity desird
Mr. Thomas Ashburner of St Eustatius to pay you the little matter
I owe you, and when he has done it, I will be obligd to you for a few
lines certifying the same.

I am Gentlemen. Your Respectful Serv　　　　for Nic Cruger
　　　　　　　　　　　　　　　　　　　　　　　A Hamilton

LC, in writing of H, Hamilton Papers, Library of Congress.

To John H. Cruger

Mr. John H. Cruger　　　　　　　　　　St Croix Nov. 27. 1771

Sir

Your favour of the 21st. Ulto. ℔ Capt Newton lies now before
me, the Contents of which I have properly noted & beg to refer
you to a Letter [1] just finished to Mess[rs.] Jacob Walton & John
Harris Cruger for everything relative to the Sloop Thunderbolt
which I shall say nothing of here. I receivd the articles sent by her,
agreeable to your memorandum & in good order. The Cost is to your
Credit, together with my ⅓ Cost of the Sloops Cargo out &c. &c.
conformable to the Inclosed Memorandum.

I am Sir　Your most Hum Serv　　　　　　for N C
　　　　　　　　　　　　　　　　　　　　　A Hamilton

LC, in writing of H, Hamilton Papers, Library of Congress.
1. H to Jacob Walton and John H. Cruger, November 27, 1771.

To Nicholas Cruger

Mr. Nicholas Cruger   St Croix Nov. 27. 1771

Dear Sir

I have now the pleasure to acquaint you with the arrival of your new Sloop Thunderbolt commanded by Capt William Newton, a fine Vessell indeed, but I fear, not so swift as she ought to be. However the Capt said he had never had an opportunity of a fair trial and consequently could form no right Judgment yet of her sailing.

This goes by way of St Thomas and I must beg youll peruse the inclosed Letter [1] to Mess[rs.] Jacob Walton & John H Cruger (left open for that purpose) for particulars relative to the Sloop, Mules &c. as my warning was too short to permit a repetition of those matters to you. I shall only add as to what I sent down that therein I acted with the concurrence and advice of both your Attorneys and heartily wish for your approbation. I am convincd if you had been present you would have done just as I did.

There is a large Sloop arrivd from Philadelphia with flour, Bread &c. Mr. Nealls [2] Brig is dayly expected with a quantity of Superfine, & Lightbourn & Pell [3] from New York will be here by and by, so that I must endeavour at all events to get your flour off soon or it will be unsaleable. Every day brings in fresh Complaints against it. I have nothing new to offer on other matters of Business but remain with the closest attachment to your Interest

Your very Hum Serv   A Hamilton

I wrote you last by Lowndes to which refer you.[4] Mr. Van Vain [5] is upon the brink of eternity.

LC, in writing of H, Hamilton Papers, Library of Congress.
  1. AH to Walton and Cruger, November 27, 1771.
  2. John Neall, Christiansted merchant, who dealt chiefly in products of the North American colonies. An advertisement by Neal in *The Royal Danish American Gazette*, September 26, 1770, lists products he had for sale at that time.
  3. John Pell, ship captain of St. Croix. In 1769, he is recorded as the master of the sloop *Sally*, trading with St. Croix (White, *Beekman Papers*, II, 978; *The Royal Danish American Gazette*, September 19, 1770).
  4. AH to Nicholas Cruger, November 12, 1771.

5. No record of a Mr. Van Vain has been found. H may have been referring to John Van Veen (or Van Vein), an employee of Pieter Heyliger's commercial firm. See *The Royal Danish American Gazette,* July 14, August 11, 1770; July 17, 1773. Also, see H to Nicholas Cruger, November 4, 1771.

To Walton and Cruger

Mess[rs.] Jacob Walton & J. H. Cruger

St Croix Novembr. 27. 177⟨1⟩

Gentleman

I have now the pleasure to acknowledge the receipt of your favour [1] dated October the 19th. by Sloop Thunderbolt which arrived here on Wednesday Afternoon the 16th Instant, and on the saturday morning following I cleard her out and gave the Captain his dispatches for Curracoa, but he could not sail till the morning after. She landed here only

23 Hhds Indian Meal

6469 Staves

20 bbls Apples

300 Boards   Inch & half

21 Kegs Bread

& 646 Ropes onions

All the rest of her Cargo (I think) must turn out better at Curracoa than here, or at any rate not worse. Could I have landed the superfine Flour conveniently and without detention I should have done it, but the Captain told me it was stow'd so promiscuously that to get at it, would require some time. Wherefore I have sent it down to take its chance with the rest of the Cargo, there being not a moment of time to spare, our Crops are so forward. As to the 2 Hhds Indian Meal, the kegs of Water Bread, the few Staves, and I may add the Boards that were sent down rather improperly; they could not be got at or I should have landed them.

The price of common NY flour here is 7½ & 8 ps. & I fancy it cant well be less at Curracoa. There has been large quantitys of Rye Meal brought here lately from Copenhagen, barrels weighing 250 nt. have been sold at 3½ & 4 ps. Tis true the quality is somewhat inferior to that of New york, but the difference of Weight is adequate to the inferiority of Quality so that [New] York Rye

Meal would not fetch above 4 ps. ℔ barrel at most & must at least be worth as much below.

This is nearly the case with every other Article sent down, which youll observe ℔ Inclosd price Current. I have desird Mr. Teleman Cruger to return the Staves by the Sloop if they will be no incumbrance to her and to give the 2 Hhds containing the Indian Meal to Capt Newton for Water Casks. I supplied him with 20 here but he thought he should want a few more. I am selling the Indian Meal at 23 ps. ℔ Hhd & expect £ 10 ℔ thousand for the Staves (all for Crop pay). The Apples were in every respect very indifferent. The greatest part of them I sold at 20 rys & the rest at 12. Four Rys ℔ piece is the price of the Boards and ℔ 2 ps.[2] of the kegs of Water Bread. As to the Onions I was glad to get rid of them altogether for 40 ps.

A large Sloop with 70 Mules from the Main arrivd two days ago. The terms of Sale—Joes down—which gives me high hopes that he will be oblig'd to go further, Cash of all kinds being very scarce here. Even Danish bits are not to be had much less Joes.

The Captain talks largely of Dangers & difficultys upon the Coast but no doubt exaggerates a good deal (*by way of Stimulation*).

Excepting this one circumstance (a little unfavourable) every thing has a very promising aspect with regard to the price of Mules this Season & I hope will continue so, but I imagine we are rather too late for 3 Cargoes. This I shall be better able to judge of by and by.

Concerning your Tea, you may depend I shall be strictly observant of your directions.

And conclusively I beg leave to assure you Gentlemen that I gave the Sloop Thunderbolt all the dispatch I could from here. The Articles landed from on Board of her tho triffling were very tedious and always take up more time than other things.

LC, in writing of H, Hamilton Papers, Library of Congress.
1. Letter not found.
2. I. e., two pieces of eight for each keg of water bread.

From Thomas Ashburner

[*St. Eustatius, December 10, 1771.* On January 21, 1772, Hamilton wrote to Ashburner: "I received yours Dated Decemr. 10th." *Letter not found.*]

From Nicholas Cruger

[*New York, December 12, 1771.* On January 10, 1772, Hamilton wrote to Cruger: "Your agreeable Letters of the 12 and 20th Ultimo were yesterday handed me." *Letter of December 12 not found.*]

From Nicholas Cruger

[*New York, December 20, 1771.* On January 10, 1772, Hamilton wrote to Cruger: "Your agreeable Letters of the 12 and 20th Ultimo were yesterday handed me." *Letter of December 20 not found.*]

1772

To Nicholas Cruger

Mr. Nicho. Cruger   St Croix Jan 10th [1772]
via Merryland & Philadelphia [1]

Dear Sir

Your agreeable Letters of the 12 and 20th Ultimo [2] were yesterday
handed me [by] Mr Lynsen [3] and Capt Gibb,[4] who arrivd within
a few hours of each other. Nothing cou'd be more pleasing to me
than to hear of the reestablishment of your Health, and I sincerely
wish you a permanent possession of that invaluable blessing.

The 101 barrils superfine Flour from Philadelphia are just landed,
about 40, of which I have already sold at 11½ ps. ℔ bbl but as tis
probable there will be much less imported than I expected I intend
to insist on 12 for the rest. Capt Napper [5] is arrivd and dld [6] every
thing agreeable to his Bill Lading. He landed all at the Westend.
The Beer I beg'd Mr. Herbert [7] to sell there. The plate Stockings &c.
are deposited in Miss Nancy Di Nullys [8] hands, and the Cheeses in
Number 4 were disposed of thus: two, Mr Beekman and self kept,
and the other two I sent on to Mrs. De Nully.

I called upon Mr Heyns [9] to Day with the Bill on Capt Hunter [10]
but he was at the Westend so that I can say nothing of that matter.
(Mr Heyns I am told is Capt Hunters Attorney.)

Capt Gibbs is landing as fast as possible and you may depend I
will give him all the dispatch in my power but I will not undertake
to determine precisely when he will Sail as he tells me his Cargo is
stow'd very inconveniently and the St Croix part of it rather under-
most. If so he will be detain'd longer than cou'd otherwise be expected. His Cargo will turn out pritty well. Lumber is high £18 ℔
M—and most of the other Articles in Demand enough. But as I am
a good deal hurried just now I beg youll accept this instead of a
more minute detail of these matters which I shall send by the Next
conveyance. I have not time to write your Father.

I shall do as you desire concerning the Brig Nancys Accounts.

Capt Wells [11] Cargo consisted of Lumber, Spermac⟨eti⟩ Candles, Codfish and Ale Wives. All the Hoops he brought ⟨were⟩ sold imediately to Mr Bignall at 70 ps ₩ M. and the Spermaceta Candles to different persons at 6 rys pr. ll.[12] We are selling the Codfish at ps. 6½ pr. C[w]t [13] and the Ale Wives at 5 and 6 ps. pr. barrill. He will return in about 10 Days with Sugar and a few Bales of Cotton.

I have not seen Mr Kortright [14] yet to know the particulars of your contract about the Lumber but I make no doubt it will turn out to your wish. I shall provide for it.

When an Opportunity offers I shall do as you desire about the Fustick. Believe me Sir I dun as hard as is proper. The Tea is not yet arrived but Ill keep it when it dose in Store as you Direct.

I minutely expect Capt Newton from the Main and I think we need not fear geting a good price for his Mules when he arrives. I wrote you fully the 27th Novemr Via St Thomas concerning him and shou'd now send Copies but for my hurry as before mention'd. It is strange I have never receiv'd a line from Curracoa.

I return you many thanks for the Apples you were so kind as to send me and shall carefully deliver the little complimentary articles when landed to the respective persons.

This is all I have time to say now and if I have neglected any thing material I beg youll excuse it being with the closest attention to your Interest and most Sincere regard,   Dear Sir   Your most Obt Servt
Alexander Hamilton

I shall provide the Rum and Sugar for Capt Gibb; the price of Rum now is 2/9.

LC, Hamilton Papers, Library of Congress.

1. Superscription is only part of MS in writing of H.

2. Letters not found.

3. Abraham Lysen, merchant of New York, whose trade was chiefly with the West Indies (Stevens, *Colonial New York*, 147–48). He also maintained a store "opposite the Danish Church" in Christiansted (*The Royal Danish American Gazette*, August 6, 1774).

4. Robert Gibb (or Gibbs), ship captain of New York (Mitchell, *Hamilton*, I, 484).

5. John Napier, ship captain of Christiansted (from information supplied by Miss Jean L. Willis, Rutherford, New Jersey).

6. I.e., delivered.

7. Horatio (or Horatia) Herbert, storekeeper in Fredericksted (*The Royal Danish American Gazette*, January 10, 1776).

8. The correct spelling is De Nully. Anna de Nully, daughter of Town Captain Bertram Pieter de Nully, married Nicholas Cruger on April 15, 1772, soon after his return from New York to St. Croix (Ramsing, "Alexander Hamilton," *Personalhistorisk tidsskrift*, 225–70).

9. Patrick Heyns, St. Croix merchant and attorney (*The Royal Danish American Gazette*, February 16, 1771; December 14, 1774; April 15, 1775).

10. George Hunter, resident of St. Croix (*The Royal Danish American Gazette*, February 16, April 24, 1771).

11. George Wells, ship captain employed by John Neall in trade between North American mainland and West Indies (*The Royal Danish American Gazette*, September 26, 1770).

12. I. e., lb., pound.

13. Abbreviation for hundredweight.

14. Cornelius Kortright, son of the well-known New York merchant of the same name. He married into a prominent plantation family of St. Croix, where he settled. On different occasions he cooperated with Nicholas Cruger in commercial ventures (Barrett, *Old Merchants of New York*, II, 20).

To Willing and Taylor [1]

Messrs. Willing & Taylor   St Croix Janu 10. 1772

Gentlemen   ⚘ *Tony White* [2]

This serves to acknowledge receipt of your favour dated ye. 13 Ulto. covering Invoice & Bill Lading for 101 bbls Superfine flour which were landed in good order. I have Credited you for the Cost of them after rectifying a small error in the addition of Nos. 81 to 84 which youll please to examine & Note in conformity.

I am Gentlemen   Your most obdt. Serv   for N Cruger

                                                        A H

LC, in writing of H, Hamilton Papers, Library of Congress.

1. There is no record of a firm called Willing and Taylor. On the other hand, this may be one of the many temporary partnerships formed in the West Indies by Thomas Willing, the well-known Philadelphia merchant. Taylor may have been the Nicholas Taylor to whom Nicholas Cruger wrote on June 19, 1772.

2. Although several Captain Whites traded in and with the West Indies in this period, there is no record of a Captain White whose first name was Anthony. It is likely, however, that H was referring to the same White to whom *The Royal Danish American Gazette*, September 26, 1770, referred when it wrote "Captain White, from this island, is safe arrived at Philadelphia." Anthony White may have been related to Anthony Walton White, a colonel in the American Revolution. See H to Anthony Walton White, September 23, 1777.

To Thomas Ashburner

Mr Thomas Ashburner   St Croix Janu 21. 1772

Sir

I receivd yours Dated Decemr. 10th [1] in due time & observe what you say. I am much obligd to you for your promise to pay Messrs. Grant & Baillie the small sum I owe them and must beg if it is not done before this reaches you, you'll immediately do it as I wish to have the matter settled. Also please to let me know if I must Credit you or Mr. Thomas for whats paid.

I am Sir   Your very Hum Servt   A Hamilton

LC, in writing of H, Hamilton Papers, Library of Congress.
1. Letter not found.

To Tileman Cruger

Teleman Cruger Esqr.   St Croix Febru 1, 177[2] [1]

Sir

Two days ago Capt Newton deliverd me your favour [2] without date & 41 Mules in such order that I have been oblig'd to send all of them to pasture, and of which I expect at least a third will die. The highest offer made me for 20 of the best was 70 ps., whereas if they had been in good order I could readily have obtain £40 round, which I all along entertaind the most sanguine hopes of. Thus you see how unfortunate the Thunderbolts first Voyage has been. But we must try a second time. Accordingly I have put on Board her some Codfish, Rum & Bread as ℔ Inclosd Bill Lading & wish them to a good Market.

Capt Newton is to supply himself with Grass on his way down & I must beg the favour of you by all means to buy or hire him a few Guns which is agreeable to Mr. Crugers directions to me. I should do it here if it were possible but there are none to be had upon any terms whatever & it would be undoubtedly a great pity that such a Vessell should be lost for the want of them. To hire would be preferable—which Capt Newton tells me may be done at 20 ps ℔ Month for a p[ai]r.

It is thought by Judges that the Sloop Thunderbolt ought to carry 60 Mules. If you think so, please to desire the Capt to do it. I have mentiond it to him, but he insists that 48 are as many as she can conveniently hold. The more she brings the better. But I do not pretend to be a Judge of the matter & therefore leave it to you. But Without the utmost dispatch her second Voyage may miscarry like the first. Please to send by the Sloops return a full state of accounts between you & Mr. Cruger that I may enter all things properly.

LC, in writing of H, Hamilton Papers, Library of Congress.
1. MS is incorrectly dated 1771.
2. Letter not found.

To William Newton

Capt William Newton   St Croix Febru 1. 177[2] [1]

Proceed immediately with the Sloop Thunderbolt to Curracoa & deliver the articles you have on Board agreeable to Bill Lading. Follow Mr Telleman Crugers directions in every Respect thenceforward & I trust I may rely on you to perform your part with all possible diligence & dispatch. Reflect continually on the unfortunate Voyage you have just made and endeavour to make up for the considerable loss therefrom accruing to your Owners. Lay in at least a Months supply for your Mules. Let me beg that if Mr T Cruger does not furnish the Vessell with 4 Guns youll do it yourself before you go to the Main. I mean hire them before you go & leave them when you return, paying the Hire which you shall be repaid here. This is all I think needful to say so I wish you a good passage & am   Your Obdt Serv   for N Cruger
                                                        A Hamilton

LC, in writing of H, Hamilton Papers, Library of Congress.
1. MS is incorrectly dated 1771.

To George Hunter

Capt George Hunter   St Croix February 4. 1772

Sir

Inclosd I send you Letter of Advice to William Gillilands[1] draft on you for £111. 16. 6 New York Currency payable in 10 Days & must beg the favour of an immidiate Answer thereto.

The Gentlemen who send it expect a punctual Compliance with the tenor of the Bill, as they receivd it instead of a Cash payment & I hope it may be in your power to give them satisfaction.

I am, Sir   Your most Hum St   for N C
                                                                              AH

LC, in writing of H, Hamilton Papers, Library of Congress.
1. Merchant of New York City (Harrington, *The New York Merchant*, 60, 147).

To Henry Cruger

Henry Cruger Esqr.   St Croix February 24. 1772

Sir   ⅌ Lightbourn

The 9th Ultimo Capt Robert Gibb handed me your favour dated December 19th 1771 covering Invoice & Bill Lading for Sundrys which were landed in good order agreeable thereto. I sold all your Lumber off immediately at £16 pm, luckkily enough, the price of that article being now reducd to £12, as great quantitys have been lately imported from different parts of the Continent. Indeed, there must be a vast Consumption this Crop, which makes it probable the price will again rise unless the Crops at Windward should fall short, as is said to be the case, whereby we shall stand fair to be over-stocked. The Oats & Cheese I have also sold, the former at 6 rys ⅌ Bushel & the latter at 9 Sti[1] ⅌ 1.[2] Your Mahogany is of the very worst kind or I could readily have obtaind 6 Sti ⅌ foot for it but as [at] present tis blown upon,[3] tis fit only for end work. I inclose you a price Current & refer you thereto for other matters.

Capt Gibbs was ready to sail seven days after his arrival but was detaind two days longer by strong contrary Winds which made it impossible to get out of the harbour. Believe me Sir Nothing was neglectd on my part to give him the utmost dispatch & considering that his Cargo was stowd very Hickledy-pickledy—the proceeding part of it being rather uppermost—I think he was dispatchd as soon as could be expected.

Inclosd you have Invoice of Rum & Sugar shipt in the Sloop agreeable to your orders. I could not by any means get your Casks filld by any of the planters but shall dispose of the Hhds, out of which the Rum was started, for your account from which however will proceed a small loss. Also you have account of Sloop's Port-charges etc. which I hope & doubt not youll find right. Youll be a little surprizd when I tell you Capt Gibb was obligd to leave his freight money behind. The reason is this. Mr Burling [4] could by no means raise his part. Tis true he might have been compeld by Law but that would have been altogether imprudent, for to have enforc'd payment & to have converted that payment into Joes, which were extremely scarce, would have been attended with a detention of at least 10 or 12 days & the other freights were very triffling, so that the whole now rests with me, and God knows when I shall be able to receive Mr. Burlings part who is long Winded enough, Mr. Beekman [5] begs to present his best Respects which conclude Sir

Your very Hum Serv   for N C

AH

LC, in writing of H, Hamilton Papers, Library of Congress.
   1. Abbreviation for stivers, a Dutch coin, the equivalent of about one penny.
   2. Pound.
   3. I. e., waterlogged.
   4. Thomas Burling, a St. Croix merchant and member of the firm of Burling and Van Wyck (*The Royal Danish American Gazette,* July 11, 1770; February 23, 1771).
   5. David Beekman, St. Croix merchant who had formerly been Nicholas Cruger's partner. Although the name has frequently been spelled Beckman, this is incorrect, for David Beekman was a member of the family of prominent New York merchants of the same name. See Philip L. White, *The Beekmans of New York, 1647–1877* (New York, 1956), 215–16, 221–22.

To Nicholas Cruger

Mr. Nicholas Cruger   St Croix February 24 177⟨2⟩

Dr. Sir   ⚕ Lightbourn

Herewith you have duplicate of my two last Letters of the 27 November & 10th Ulto. and I now congratulate myself upon the pleasure of addressing you again, but am sorry I shall be obligd to communicate some dissatisfactory occurrencies.

Your Sloop Thunderbolt arrivd here the 29th of the preceding Month with 41 More Skeletons. A worse parcel of Mules never was seen; she took in at first 48 & lost 7 on the passage. I sent all that were able to walk to pasture, in Number 33. The other 8 could hardly stand for 2 Minutes together & in spite of the greatest care 4 of them are now in Limbo. The Surviving 4 I think are out of Danger, and shall likewise be shortly sent to pasture. I refusd two great offers made me upon their first landing to Wit 70 ps. a head for the Choice of 20, and 15 ps. a Head for the abovementiond Invalids, which may give you a proper idea of the condition they were in. Taking this along with it—that if they had been such as we had reason to hope they would be—I could with pleasure have had £40 round, so unfortunate has the Voyage been. However by sending them to pasture I expect to get £100 round for those now alive. 17 are already gone at that price and as they recruit fast the rest I hope will soon go at the same. I pay 2 ps. a Head Montly for pasturage. The Sloop was 27 days on her passage from the Main—not for want of swiftness, for tis now known she Sails well, but from continual Calms & the little wind she had was quite against her. Capt Newton seemd to be much concernd at his Ill luck tho I believe he had done all in his power to make the voyage Successful. But no Man can command the Winds. The Mules were pretty well chosen & had been once a good parcel. I receivd only a few lines from your Brother: no Sales nor anything else; he excusd himself being Sick. I desird him as directed to furnish the Sloop with a few Guns but she went intirely defenceless to the Main; notwithstanding several Vessells had been obligd to put back to get out of the way of the Launches with which the Coast swarms. When Capt Newton urgd

him to hire a few Guns for the Sloop He replied to this effect—
that I only had mentiond the matter to him but that you had never
said a word about it. This last time I mentiond it again & begd the
Captain to hire 4 Guns himself if your Brother did not which he
has promisd to do. The Expence will not be above 15. or 20 ps., and
one escape may not be followd by a second, neither do I see any
reason to run the risque of it. I sent down on your account 10 Hhds
Codfish, 8 Hhds Rum, 40 Philad. barrels & 8 Teirces[1] Bread. The
Rum Cost 2/7½ & is worth 5 bits a Gallon at Curacoa. I believe those
Articles will answer pretty well.

Upon application to Mr Heyns I found I had been misinformd &
that Mr Hunter has no Attorney here; whereupon I wrote him a
Letter[2] to St Thomas & have sent him three Copys of the Same
without receiving any answer. Mr. Ringger[3] is here and is going
over in a day or two. I intend to give him a Letter & beg he'll ask
for an answer and send it over. I am a good deal surprisd at Capt
Hunters Silence.

Brig Nancys Accounts are inclosd. The Tea is arrivd; it Cost 20¼
Sti, but there is a discount of 4 ₩ Ct. for prompt payment. I shall
send Copy of the Invoice &c. to Mess[rs.] Walton & Cruger. The
Lumber you contracted for is arrivd & I am a good deal puzzled to
fulfil your engagements; it is rather early you know to receivd &
Cash is scarce. Mr Beekman[4] would Ship on freight which would
ease the matter but he can receive none yet. However I must manage
some how or other. It would be a pity to pay dead freight.

As to introducing Wine, it depends upon Circumstances. There is
none here at present and if yours could be brought while the scarcity
continues, it would not be difficult to obtain permission to land it.
Other-wise it will be impracticable, unless our General[5] who is
momently expected should bring any new indulgence concerning
that article. But the whole is a chance.

Many changes of Officers are talkd of; in particular tis said Judge
Sevel[6] will be superceded by Jeger[7] the informer—& the Collector
by the present Comptroler, which is all that occurs to me now.
Therefore Ill conclude wishing you safe passage out.

I am   Sir   Your Obdt Serv   AH

LC, in writing of H, Hamilton Papers, Library of Congress.
  1. H should have written tierce, which is a cask larger than a barrel and
smaller than a hogshead.

2. Presumably H for Nicholas Cruger to George Hunter, February 4, 1772.

3. John Rengger, St. Croix merchant and husband of Nicholas Cruger's sister-in-law (*The Royal Danish American Gazette*, April 29, May 10, 1775).

4. David Beekman.

5. Ulrich Wilhelm Roepstorff, Governor General of St. Croix from June 8, 1771, to April 5, 1773.

6. Evan H. Sevel (or Sevil), judge of the St. Croix Upper Court, who died shortly before this letter was written (RG 55, Records of the Danish Government of the Virgin Islands, National Archives; and *The Royal Danish American Gazette*, September 3, 1774).

7. Hans Jeger, about whom little is known beyond that he was a resident and property owner in St. Croix until 1775, when he sailed for Copenhagen (*The Royal Danish American Gazette*, June 4, 1774; June 7, 1775).

To Thomas Gregg

Mr. Thomas Gregg.   St Croix February 24. 1772

Sir

Capt Robert Gibb deliverd me on your Account 2 Mahogany dining Tables which I paid him the freight of. You may depend I shall do the best I can with them being with Esteem, Sir

Your very Hum Serv   for NC
                                                        AH

LC, in writing of H, Hamilton Papers, Library of Congress.

To Walton and Cruger

Messrs. Jacob Walton & John Harris Cruger
                                          St Croix February 24. 1772

Gentlemen ℔ Lightbourn

Preceding is Copy of my last[1] to you & beg leave to refer you thereto. I have at length the pleasure to acquaint you of the arrival of the Sloop Thunderbolt with her first Cargo of Mules but I am sorry to be obligd to offer you so unpleasing an account of them as I shall. The 2d. Ultimo she took in at the Main 48 very good Mules, most of them large and young. She arrivd here the 30th with 41 in the worst order imaginable. This uncommon passage was occasiond by perpetual Calms and even the triffling breezes she had were directly against her. How unfortunate instead of £40 round of which I had fixd the most sanguine expectations to be mortified with an offer of 70 ps. for the choice of 20. However to make the most of them, I sent all that could walk immediately to pasture and have since sold 17 at 100 ps. a Head, which I make no doubt I shall get for all those now surviving. I pay 2 ps. a head Monthly for pasturage. Four have died since they were landed but I fancy I may venture to pronounce all the rest out of danger. The Sloop went to the Main totally defenceless tho by all accounts a few Guns must have been extremely necessary for several Vessells were obligd to return empty to avoid being taken by the Launches which are plenty enough upon the Coast. I begd Mr. Teleman Cruger to put some force upon her. How he came to neglect it I dont know, but to provide against any danger for the future I desird Capt Newton in case Mr. Teleman Cruger did not do it to hire for the Sloop himself three or four Guns. The common hire is 10 ps. a Month for a p[ai]r. I wish good luck to the next voyage. Inclosd you have Sloop Thunderbolts portcharge &c. & Invoice of 38 Chests Tea in good order & which I have stord till farther orders.

I am Gentlemen   Yours very Hum Serv   for N C
                                                      A H

LC, in writing of H, Hamilton Papers, Library of Congress.
  1. H to Walton and Cruger, November 27, 1771.

Nicholas Cruger to Henry Cruger

St. Croix, March 17, 1772. Announces arrival in St. Croix and describes firm's recent business transactions.

LC, in writing of H, Hamilton Papers, Library of Congress.

Nicholas Cruger to Hans Buus [1]

[St. Croix] March 18, 177[2].[2] Is "glad to find my Clerk in my absence has desird you to take all my affairs in your hands that was in Mr. Hassells,[3] who I am confident has been very negligent in them and triffled away a good deal of money to no purpose." Then discusses various cases for which Buus will be responsible.

LC, in writing of H, Hamilton Papers, Library of Congress.

1. In MS, name is spelled Boos. This is incorrect; see *The Royal Danish American Gazette*, March 9, 1771; July 7, 1773; October 9, 1776; and *St. Croixian Pocket Companion* (Copenhagen, 1780), 5.

2. MS incorrectly dated 1771.

3. There were several Hassells (or Hassels) living on St. Croix at this time. This is probably a reference to Gerhard Hassel, who is mentioned as "procurator" in 1777 (*The Royal Danish American Gazette*, June 25, 1777).

Nicholas Cruger to John H. Cruger [1]

St. Croix, March 19, 1772. Discusses business conditions in St. Croix and asks for certain articles. Also requests "two or three poor boys," and adds: "Have them bound in the most reasonable manner you can. I fancy you cant fail of geting them by applying at the Poor-House. I want them to put on plantations."

LC, Hamilton Papers, Library of Congress.

1. The first third of this letter is in an unidentified handwriting. The remainder is in writing of H.

Nicholas Cruger to George Codwise [1]

Tortola, March 30, 1772. Sends "Invoice and bill Lading for 10 Hhds. Rum, ammounting to ps 473.4."

LC, Hamilton Papers, Library of Congress.

1. Only the summary of Codwise's account with Nicholas Cruger, which is at the bottom of the letter, is in writing of H. Remainder is in unidentified handwriting.

Nicholas Cruger to Tileman Cruger

St. Croix, May 5, 1772. Acknowledges receipt "of your favour of the 6th Ulto. Inclosing me my Account Current and account of Sales. . . . I inclose you a sketch of your account with me. . . . The Ballance of my account when you become in Cash youll oblige me by sending me via St Eustatius. . . ."

LC, in writing of H, Hamilton Papers, Library of Congress.

Ann Lytton Venton's Quittance with Alexander Hamilton [1]

[St. Croix, May 16, 1772]

1059. Ann Ventons quittance ved Hammilton for 45 rdr.[2] contant og et oxehoved sucker af 16de maij 1772.

D, Christiansteds byfogedarkiv skifteprot: 1769–80, no. 50, fol. 324, receipt no. 1059, Rigsarkivet, Copenhagen.
  1. The translation reads as follows: "1059. Ann Venton's quittance of the 16th of May 1772 with Hamilton for 45 rigs-dollars cash and a hogshead of sugar."
  Ann Lytton Venton, the daughter of James and Ann Lytton, was H's cousin. Her mother was the sister of H's mother, Rachel Lavien. In 1759 Ann Lytton married John Kirwan Venton. After his death she married George Mitchell. Ramsing states that a friendship developed between the cousins, and H became her middleman when she cashed the advanced payments of her inheritance (Ramsing, "Alexander Hamilton," *Personalhistorisk tidsskrift*). This document is one of the receipts for these payments. For others see May 23, 1772, and May 3, 28, and June 3, 1773. These documents were found on Thomas Lillie's plantation in a wooden chest that had been sealed on his death. The chest was opened on February 6, 1776, and the documents were registered at that time.
  2. Rixdaller or rigsdaler, a Danish dollar equal in value to a piece of eight.

Nicholas Cruger to Henry Cruger, Junior

St. Croix, May 19, 1772. Regrets inability to pay protested bills and adds: "Believe me my good Brother, nothing in life has ever affected me more than this matter has. I wish to God it was in my power to reimburse you but realy it is not."

LC, in writing of H, Hamilton Papers, Library of Congress.

Kortright and Cruger to Henry Cruger, Junior

St. Croix, May 19, 1772. ". . . Believe us Dear Sir it gives us real pain, that we should be the cause of so much uneasiness to you— and the more as we have it not in our power to replace those damn'd Protested Bills as we propos'd (in time). . . . The only compensation we can make you is to remit you—when those Bills return together with their amounts & Charges with you, the whole of the Interest and Damages here which are considerable. . . ."

LC, in writing of H, Hamilton Papers, Library of Congress.

Ann Lytton Venton's Quittance with Alexander Hamilton [1]

[St. Croix, May 23, 1772]

1060. Ann Ventons quittance af 23de maij 1772 rdr. for et oxe-hovet rum.

D, Christiansteds byfogedarkiv skifteprot: 1769–80, no. 50, fol. 324–25, receipt no. 1060, Rigsarkivet, Copenhagen.
   1. The translation reads as follows: "1060. Ann Venton's quittance of the 23 of May 1772 rigsdollar for a hogshead of rum." For information concerning this receipt, see "Ann Lytton Venton's Quittance with Alexander Hamilton," May 16, 1772.

Nicholas Cruger to Thomas Thomas

St. Croix, May 25, 1772. ". . . you can send me the Ballance [of your account] at your leisure. Rye flour will sell for ps. 7. a barrel here readily but the Duty is 25 ∰ Ct. However we enter it as Corn Meal and give the waiter a fee, which hint you must give the Capt if you send any down, and tell him to see me before he enters. . . ."

LC, in writing of H, Hamilton Papers, Library of Congress.

Nicholas Cruger to Nicholas Taylor [1]

St. Croix, June 19, 1772. "I am happy in the Receipt of yours of the 18th Ultimo [with] . . . an account of the things you were good enough to send me in my absence. . . . I inclose you a sketch of your account. . . ."

LC, in writing of H, Hamilton Papers, Library of Congress.
   1. There is no record of a Nicholas Taylor. He may, however, have been a member of the firm of Willing and Taylor to which H had written earlier. See H, for Nicholas Cruger, to Willing and Taylor, January 10, 1772.

Nicholas Cruger to Rengger and Company [1]

St. Croix, July 18, 1772. ". . . This Vessell of mine is a fine large new sloop. I am sending her to New York and I'll thank you to let me know if there is any one at your Island that would ship about 50 Hhds Sugar on freight or if theres any passengers that want to go to New York. She shall come over for them in about a fortnight. . . ."

LC, in writing of H, Hamilton Papers, Library of Congress.
  1. John Rengger, of St. Croix, headed a trading firm with offices in both St. Croix and St. Thomas (*The Royal Danish American Gazette*, April 29, 1775). This letter may have been sent to the St. Thomas branch of the firm, or it may have been sent to a firm of the same name on one of the other islands in the West Indies.

Nicholas Cruger to Rengger and Company

St. Croix, July 27, 1772. ". . . I'm concerned its not in my power to send you over the provisions you order. . . . In my last I beg'd you to procure me freight for my Sloop which desire I now counterma⟨nd⟩ and will be oblig'd only to know if theres any passengers for New York. . . ."

LC, in writing of H, Hamilton Papers, Library of Congress.

To The Royal Danish American Gazette [1]

St. Croix, Sept. 6, 1772

Honoured Sir,

I take up my pen just to give you an imperfect account of one of the most dreadful Hurricanes that memory or any records whatever can trace, which happened here on the 31st ultimo at night.

The Royal Danish American Gazette, October 3, 1772.
  1. This letter is preceded by the following statement: "The following letter was written the week after the late Hurricane, by a Youth of this Island, to his Father; the copy of it fell by accident into the hands of a gentleman, who, being pleased with it himself, shewed it to others to whom it gave equal satisfaction, and who all agreed that it might not prove unentertaining to the Pub-

The port of Christiansted on the island of St. Croix, pictured here as it was in 1815, was probably little changed from the days when Alexander Hamilton was employed as a clerk by Nicholas Cruger.

It began about dusk, at North, and raged very violently till ten o'clock. Then ensued a sudden and unexpected interval, which lasted about an hour. Meanwhile the wind was shifting round to the South West point, from whence it returned with redoubled fury and continued so 'till near three o'clock in the morning. Good God! what horror and destruction. Its impossible for me to describe or you to form any idea of it. It seemed as if a total dissolution of nature was taking place. The roaring of the sea and wind, fiery meteors flying about it in the air, the prodigious glare of almost perpetual lightning, the crash of the falling houses, and the ear-piercing shrieks of the distressed, were sufficient to strike astonishment into Angels. A great part of the buildings throughout the Island are levelled to the ground, almost all the rest very much shattered; several persons killed and numbers utterly ruined; whole families running about the streets, unknowing where to find a place of shelter; the sick exposed to the keeness of water and air without a bed to lie upon, or a dry covering to their bodies; and our harbours entirely bare. In a word, misery, in all its most hideous shapes, spread over the whole face of the country. A strong smell of gunpowder added somewhat to the terrors of the night; and it was observed that the rain was surprizingly salt. Indeed the water is so brackish and full of sulphur that there is hardly any drinking it.

My reflections and feelings on this frightful and melancholy occasion, are set forth in the following self-discourse.

Where now, oh! vile worm, is all thy boasted fortitude and resolution? What is become of thine [2] arrogance and self sufficiency? Why dost thou tremble and stand aghast? How humble, how helpless, how contemptible you now appear. And for why? The jarring of elements—the discord of clouds? Oh! impotent presumptuous fool! how durst thou offend that Omnipotence, whose nod alone were

---

lick. The Author's modesty in long refusing to submit it to Publick view, is the reason of its making its appearance so late as it now does."

At the time that this letter was written H's father was living on St. Kitts. The "gentleman" referred to in the preceding paragraph was Hugh Knox, a Presbyterian minister who had come to St. Croix in 1772. Knox was also an apothecary and sometime journalist, who edited the local paper when the regular editor had to be absent from the island. See Broadus Mitchell, "The Man Who Discovered Hamilton," *Proceedings, New Jersey Historical Society*, LXIX (April, 1951), 88-114.

2. Original reads "they."

sufficient to quell the destruction that hovers over thee, or crush thee into atoms? See thy wretched helpless state, and learn to know thyself. Learn to know thy best support. Despise [3] thyself, and adore thy God. How sweet, how unutterably sweet were now, the voice of an approving conscience; Then couldst thou say, hence ye idle alarms, why do I shrink? What have I to fear? A pleasing calm suspense! A short repose from calamity to end in eternal bliss? Let the Earth rend. Let the planets forsake their course. Let the Sun be extinguished and the Heavens burst asunder. Yet what have I to dread? My staff can never be broken—in Omnip[o]tence I trusted.

He who gave the winds to blow, and the lightnings to rage—even him have I always loved and served. His precepts have I observed. His commandments have I obeyed—and his perfections have I adored. He will snatch me from ruin. He will exalt me to the fellowship of Angels and Seraphs, and to the fullness of never ending joys.

But alas! how different, how deplorable, how gloomy the prospect! Death comes rushing on in triumph veiled in a mantle of tenfold darkness. His unrelenting scythe, pointed, and ready for the stroke. On his right hand sits destruction, hurling the winds and belching forth flames: Calamity on his left threatening famine disease and distress of all kinds. And Oh! thou wretch, look still a little further; see the gulph of eternal misery open. There mayest thou shortly plunge—the just reward of thy vileness. Alas! whither canst thou fly? Where hide thyself? Thou canst not call upon thy God; thy life has been a continual warfare with him.

Hark—ruin and confusion on every side. 'Tis thy turn next; but one short moment, even now, Oh Lord help. Jesus be merciful!

Thus did I reflect, and thus at every gust of the wind, did I conclude, 'till it pleased the Almighty to allay it. Nor did my emotions proceed either from the suggestions of too much natural fear, or a conscience over-burthened with crimes of an uncommon cast. I thank God, this was not the case. The scenes of horror exhibited around us, naturally awakened such ideas in every thinking breast, and aggravated the deformity of every failing of our lives. It were a lamentable insensibility indeed, not to have had such feelings, and I think inconsistent with human nature.

Our distressed, helpless condition taught us humility and contempt

3. Original reads "despite."

of ourselves. The horrors of the night, the prospect of an immediate, cruel death—or, as one may say, of being crushed by the Almighty in his anger—filled us with terror. And every thing that had tended to weaken our interest with him, upbraided us in the strongest colours, with our baseness and folly. That which, in a calm unruffled temper, we call a natural cause, seemed then like the correction of the Deity. Our imagination represented him as an incensed master, executing vengeance on the crimes of his servants. The father and benefactor were forgot, and in that view, a consciousness of our guilt filled us with despair.

But see, the Lord relents. He hears our prayer. The Lightning ceases. The winds are appeased. The warring elements are reconciled and all things promise peace. The darkness is dispell'd and drooping nature revives at the approaching dawn. Look back Oh! my soul, look back and tremble. Rejoice at thy deliverance, and humble thyself in the presence of thy deliverer.

Yet hold, Oh vain mortal! Check thy ill timed joy. Art thou so selfish to exult because thy lot is happy in a season of universal woe? Hast thou no feelings for the miseries of thy fellow-creatures? And art thou incapable of the soft pangs of sympathetic sorrow? Look around thee and shudder at the view. See desolation and ruin where'er thou turnest thine eye! See thy fellow-creatures pale and lifeless; their bodies mangled, their souls snatched into eternity, unexpecting. Alas! perhaps unprepared! Hark the bitter groans of distress. See sickness and infirmities exposed to the inclemencies of wind and water! See tender infancy pinched with hunger and hanging on the mothers knee for food! See the unhappy mothers anxiety. Her poverty denies relief, her breast heaves with pangs of maternal pity, her heart is bursting, the tears gush down her cheeks. Oh sights of woe! Oh distress unspeakable! My heart bleeds, but I have no power to solace! O ye, who revel in affluence, see the afflictions of humanity and bestow your superfluity to ease them. Say not, we have suffered also, and thence withold your compassion. What are you[r] sufferings compared to those? Ye have still more than enough left. Act wisely. Succour the miserable and lay up a treasure in Heaven.

I am afraid, Sir, you will think this description more the effort of imagination than a true picture of realities. But I can affirm with the greatest truth, that there is not a single circumstance touched upon, which I have not absolutely been an eye witness to.

Our General [4] has issued several very salutary and humane regulations, and both in his publick and private measures, has shewn himself *the Man.*

4. Ulrich Wilhelm Roepstorff, Governor General of St. Croix.

The Soul ascending into Bliss, In humble imitation of Popes Dying Christian to his Soul [1]

[St. Croix, October 17, 1772]

AH! whither, whither, am I flown,
A wandering guest in worlds unknown?
What is that I see and hear?
What heav'nly music fills mine ear?
Etherial glories shine around;
More than Arabias sweets abound.

Hark! hark! a voice from yonder sky,
Methinks I hear my Saviour cry,
Come gentle spirit come away,
Come to thy Lord without delay;
For thee the gates of bliss unbar'd
Thy constant virtue to reward.

I come oh Lord! I mount, I fly,
On rapid wings I cleave the sky;
Stretch out thine arm and aid my flight;
For oh! I long to gain that height,
Where all celestial beings sing
Eternal praises to their King.

O Lamb of God! thrice gracious Lord
Now, now I feel how true thy word;
Translated to this happy place,
This blessed vision of thy face;

My soul shall all thy steps attend
In songs of triumph without end.

The Royal Danish American Gazette, October 17, 1772.

1. Although it is impossible to determine beyond dispute that H was the author of this poem, it is attributed to him by J. C. Hamilton, who refers to it as "a hymn," but ascribes it to the period when H attended school in Elizabethtown, New Jersey (Hamilton, *Life,* I, 10, and *JCHW,* I, 48). In the Hamilton Papers, Library of Congress, there is a copy in an unidentified writing of the first three verses of this poem. At the end of the third verse is written in the same hand: "Written by A. H. when 18 years old." At the bottom of the page in still another handwriting is written: "This is a copy in pencil by Alex: Hamilton, my uncle—P.S." The "P.S." presumably refers to the Philip Schuyler who was the son of George L. Schuyler. George L. Schuyler had married H's granddaughter, Mary Hamilton, daughter of James A. Hamilton. The Alexander Hamilton who copied the poem was probably the son of James A. Hamilton, brother-in-law of George Schuyler and uncle of Philip Schuyler.

Two other poems that appeared in *The Royal Danish American Gazette* at this period may have been written by H. The first, which was signed "Omicron" and appeared in the issue of October 14, 1772, described the author's "thoughts on seeing a fine Grove of Trees destroyed by the late Hurricane." The other, which was printed in the issue of October 17, 1772, was entitled "The Melancholy Hours" and signed "Juvenis." Neither poem has been reprinted in this edition of H's papers, for the evidence that H was the author is far from conclusive.

1 7 7 3

Ann Lytton Venton's Order in favor of Alexander Hamilton [1]

[New York, May 3, 1773]

1045. Ann Ventons ordre paa capitain Lillie [2] af 3die may 1773 i Alexander Hammiltons faveur for 15 oxehoveder sucker for Lyttons boe.

D, Christiansteds byfogedarkiv skifteprot: 1769–80, no. 50, fol. 324–25, receipt no. 1045, Rigsarkivet, Copenhagen.
    1. The translation reads as follows: "1045. Ann Venton's order of the 3rd of May 1773 on Captain Lillie for 15 hogshead of sugar from the Lytton estate in favor of Alexander Hamilton." For information concerning this receipt, see "Ann Lytton Venton's Quittance with Alexander Hamilton," May 16, 1772. H at this time was already in America. Mitchell (*Hamilton*, I, 37, 54–55) concludes that H came to the North American colonies in October, 1772, and began his studies at King's College in the autumn of 1773.
    2. Thomas Lillie was a merchant and planter who had been named, along with John Coakley, executor of the will of James Lytton, Ann Lytton Venton's father.

Ann Lytton Venton's Quittance with Alexander Hamilton [1]

[New York, May 26, 1773]

965. Ann Lyttons [2] quittance ved Alexander Hammilton for 50 rdr. betalt af capitain Lillie dend 26de maij 1773.

D, Christiansteds byfogedarkiv skifteprot: 1769–80, no. 50, fol. 324–25, receipt no. 965, Rigsarkivet, Copenhagen.
    1. The translation reads as follows: "965. Ann Lytten quittance of the 26th of May 1773 with Alexander Hamilton for 50 rigsdollars paid by Captain Lillie." For information concerning this receipt, see "Ann Lytton Venton's Quittance with Alexander Hamilton," May 16, 1772.
    2. Ann Lytton Venton.

Ann Lytton Venton's Quittance with Alexander Hamilton [1]

[New York, June 3, 1773]

994. Ann Ventons quittance til Hammilton, til Lillie, for Lyttons estate, for 25 rdr. af 3die junii 1773.

D, Christiansteds byfogedarkiv skifteprot: 1769–80, no. 50, fol. 324–25, receipt no. 994, Rigsarkivet, Copenhagen.
1. The translation reads as follows: "994. Ann Venton's quittance of the 3rd of June 1773 to Hamilton, to Lillie, for 25 rigsdollars for the Lytton estate." For information concerning this receipt, see "Ann Lytton Venton's Quittance with Alexander Hamilton," May 16, 1772.

Notes on the Book of Genesis [1]

[*Elizabethtown, New Jersey, 1773.*] Quotations and paraphrases of the first three chapters of the Book of Genesis.

AD, Hamilton Papers, Library of Congress.
1. Scholars differ on the year of H's arrival in the North American colonies and the dates of his schooling there. These notes, and those which follow, were presumably made while H attended the school of Francis Barber in Elizabethtown, New Jersey. Evidence (Mitchell, *Hamilton*, I, 37, 54–55) indicates that he came to the North American colonies in October, 1772, and began his studies at King's College in the autumn of 1773. He must have attended Francis Barber's academy, therefore, in the winter and spring of 1773.
There are also in the Hamilton Papers in the Library of Congress in H's writing a set of notes on the geography of North America and another set on the geography of South America. Scholars have inferred that these were made at the same time as the notes printed above. The notes on the geography of North and South America were, however, used as a basis for a brief H prepared for the State of New York in a land controversy between New York and Massachusetts in December, 1786.

Notes on the Book of Revelation

[*Elizabethtown, New Jersey, 1773.*] Quotations and paraphrases of Chapters I–XIII of the Book of Revelation.

AD, Hamilton Papers, Library of Congress.

The Iliad of Homer [1]

[*Elizabethtown, New Jersey, 1773.*] Exercise in Homer's *Iliad*, beginning with Book 12. Discontinuously numbered lines in Greek are followed by one page of English translation and notes in English on the geography of the eastern Mediterranean.

D, Hamilton Papers, Library of Congress.
   1. The authorship of this MS is not known. The handwriting bears only a slight resemblance to that of H. If H did write these exercises, he probably did so at Francis Barber's academy in Elizabethtown or at King's College. Allan McLane Hamilton prints a fascimile of one page of the document, to which he refers as "early Greek exercises" (Hamilton, *Intimate Life,* facing p. 24). Mitchell suggests that the exercises may have been prepared by H's "son Philip at King's with corrections in H's hand" (Mitchell, *Hamilton,* I, 501).

List of Books [1]

[*Elizabethtown, New Jersey, 1773.*] Numbered list of twenty-seven books and subjects on Ancient and Medieval history and philosophy.

D, Hamilton Papers, Library of Congress.
   1. The authorship of this MS is not known. The handwriting is not that of H, but the document may be a copy of a missing original by H. Although MS contains no date, it probably belongs to the period when H was in school or college.

I 7 7 4

["Speech in the Fields"] [1]

[New York, July 6, 1774]

1. According to J. C. Hamilton (*Life*, I, 21–23) H made this speech. Almost all of H's biographers have repeated this story. There is no contemporary evidence, newspaper or other, that H made such a speech or even attended the meeting.

Poem on the Death of Elias Boudinot's Child [1]

[New York, September 4, 1774] [2]

For the sweet babe, my doating heart
Did all a Mother's fondness feel;
Carefull to act each tender part
and guard from every threatning ill.

But what alass! availd my care?
The unrelenting hand of death,
Regardless of a parent's prayr
Has stoped my lovely Infant's breath—

With rapture number Oer thy Charms,
While on thy harmless sports intent,
Or pratling in my happy arms—

No More thy self Important tale
Some embryo meaning shall convey,
Which, should th' imperfect accents fail,
Thy speaking looks would still display—

Thou'st gone, forever gone—yet where,
Ah! pleasing thought; to endless bliss.

Then, why Indulge the rising tear?
Canst thou, fond heart, lament for this?

Let reason silence nature's strife,
And weep Maria's fate no more;
She's safe from all the storms of life,
And Wafted to a peacefull Shore.[3]

D, in writing of Elizabeth Hamilton, Hamilton Papers, Library of Congress.
    1. At the end of this poem, Elizabeth Hamilton wrote: "Written by Mr. Hamilton, when he was residing in new jersey, preparing for College, on the Death of a child of Mrs. Boudinot." While attending Francis Barber's academy in Elizabethtown, H was a frequent guest in the home of Elias Boudinot, a New Jersey lawyer, who became a close friend of H. This poem, however, was written after H had become a student at King's College.
    2. The date is that given by George Adams Boyd, *Elias Boudinot, Patriot and Statesman, 1740–1821* (Princeton, 1952), 23.
    3. On a separate sheet of paper, also in writing of Elizabeth Hamilton, is the following sentence: "Little babe thou enteredst the world weeping while all around you smiled; continue so to live, that you may depart in smiles while [all] around you weep."

Account with Robert Harpur [1]

[New York, September 20, 1774]

1774	Mr. Alexr. Hamilton at £3..4 ℔ Quar. Dr.	Con C
		£ s
Sepr. 20th.	entered with me this day, to Study Mathems.	1783. By Cash recd. from him, now Col. Hamilton, as a present at the close of the War } 5 Guins. = 9—

D, from the original in The New York State Library, Albany.
    1. This entry is from the account book of Harpur, who was a professor of mathematics at King's College.
    In order to accelerate his studies at King's College, H was tutored privately by Harpur. See Mitchell, *Hamilton*, I, 55.

A Full Vindication of the
Measures of the Congress, &c. [1]

New-York [December 15] 1774 [2]

FRIENDS AND COUNTRYMEN,

It was hardly to be expected that any man could be so presumptuous, as openly to controvert the equity, wisdom, and authority of the measures, adopted by the congress: an assembly truly respectable on every account! Whether we consider the characters of the men, who composed it; the number, and dignity of their constituents, or the important ends for which they were appointed. But, however improbable such a degree of presumption might have seemed, we

A Full Vindication of the Measures of the Congress, from the Calumnies of their Enemies; In Answer to A Letter, Under the Signature of A. W. Farmer. Whereby His Sophistry is exposed, his Cavils confuted, his Artifices detected, and his Wit ridiculed; in a General Address To the Inhabitants of America, And A Particular Address To the Farmers of the Province of New-York. Veritas magna est & prœvalebit. Truth is powerful, and will prevail. (New-York, Printed by James Rivington, 1774).

1. H was replying to *Free Thoughts on the Proceedings of the Continental Congress, Held at Philadelphia, Sept 5, 1774: Wherein Their Errors are exhibited, their Reasonings Confuted, and the fatal Tendency of their Non-Importation, Non-Exportation, and Non-Consumption Measures, are laid open to the plainest Understandings; and the Only Means pointed out for Preserving and Securing Our present Happy Constitution: In a Letter to the Farmers and other inhabitants of North America in General, and to those of the Province of New-York in Particular. By a Farmer. Hear me, for I Will speak!* (Printed in the year 1774.) This pamphlet is signed "A. W. Farmer" and dated November 16, 1774. Although its authorship has been disputed, it was probably written by Samuel Seabury, Episcopal rector at Westchester, New York. See memorial by Seabury in *The Magazine of American History,* VIII (January, 1882), 119–21, in which he claims authorship.

There is another edition of Seabury's *Free Thoughts,* also printed in 1774. The only changes appear to be in pagination. The title page is a duplicate of the first printing.

2. On December 8, 1774, in *Rivington's New-York Gazetteer; or, the Connecticut, Hudson's River, New-Jersey, and Quebec Weekly Advertiser,* the following was announced:

"In the Press, and in a few Days will be published, By James Rivington, A full Vindication of the Measures of the Continental Congress . . . To the Farmers of the Province of New-York. The Printer, with humble Deference presumes that this answer will meet with a gracious reception at the hands of every reader who has expressed disapprobation to the Free thoughts of Farmer A. W."

On December 15, 1774, the publication of *A Full Vindication* was announced in *Rivington's New-York Gazetteer.*

find there are some, in whom it exists. Attempts are daily making to diminish the influence of their decisions, and prevent the salutary effects, intended by them. The impotence of such insidious efforts is evident from the general indignation they are treated with; so that no material ill-consequences can be dreaded from them. But lest they should have a tendency to mislead, and prejudice the minds of a few; it cannot be deemed altogether useless to bestow some notice upon them.

And first, let me ask these restless spirits, whence arises that violent antipathy they seem to entertain, not only to the natural rights of mankind; but to common sense and common modesty. That they are enemies to the natural rights of mankind is manifest, because they wish to see one part of their species enslaved by another. That they have an invincible aversion to common sense is apparent in many respects: They endeavour to persuade us, that the absolute sovereignty of parliament does not imply our absolute slavery; that it is a Christian duty to submit to be plundered of all we have, merely because some of our fellow-subjects are wicked enough to require it of us, that slavery, so far from being a great evil, is a great blessing; and even, that our contest with Britain is founded entirely upon the petty duty of 3 pence per pound on East India tea; whereas the whole world knows, it is built upon this interesting question, whether the inhabitants of Great-Britain have a right to dispose of the lives and properties of the inhabitants of America, or not? And lastly, that these men have discarded all pretension to common modesty, is clear from hence, first, because they, in the plainest terms, call an august body of men, famed for their patriotism and abilities, fools or knaves, and of course the people whom they represented cannot be exempt from the same opprobrious appellations; and secondly, because they set themselves up as standards of wisdom and probity, by contradicting and censuring the public voice in favour of those men.

A little consideration will convince us, that the congress instead of having "ignorantly misunderstood, carelessly neglected, or basely betrayed the interests of the colonies," have, on the contrary, devised and recommended the only effectual means to secure the freedom, and establish the future prosperity of America upon a solid basis. If we are not free and happy hereafter, it must proceed from the want of integrity and resolution, in executing what they have concerted; not from the temerity or impolicy of their determinations.

Before I proceed to confirm this assertion by the most obvious arguments, I will premise a few brief remarks. The only distinction between freedom and slavery consists in this: In the former state, a man is governed by the laws to which he has given his consent, either in person, or by his representative: In the latter, he is governed by the will of another. In the one case his life and property are his own, in the other, they depend upon the pleasure of a master. It is easy to discern which of these two states is preferable. No man in his senses can hesitate in choosing to be free, rather than a slave.

That Americans are intitled to freedom, is incontestible upon every rational principle. All men have one common original: they participate in one common nature, and consequently have one common right. No reason can be assigned why one man should exercise any power, or pre-eminence over his fellow creatures more than another; unless they have voluntarily vested him with it. Since then, Americans have not by any act of their's impowered the British Parliament to make laws for them, it follows they can have no just authority to do it.

Besides the clear voice of natural justice in this respect, the fundamental principles of the English constitution are in our favour. It has been repeatedly demonstrated, that the idea of legislation, or taxation, when the subject is not represented, is inconsistent with *that*. Nor is this all, our charters, the express conditions on which our progenitors relinquished their native countries, and came to settle in this, preclude every claim of ruling and taxing us without our assent.

Every subterfuge that sophistry has been able to invent, to evade or obscure this truth, has been refuted by the most conclusive reasonings; so that we may pronounce it a matter of undeniable certainty, that the pretensions of Parliament are contradictory to the law of nature, subversive of the British constitution, and destructive of the faith of the most solemn compacts.

What then is the subject of our controversy with the mother country? It is this, whether we shall preserve that security to our lives and properties, which the law of nature, the genius of the British constitution, and our charters afford us; or whether we shall resign them into the hands of the British House of Commons, which is no more privileged to dispose of them than the Grand Mogul? What can actuate those men, who labour to delude any of us into an opinion, that the object of contention between the parent state and the colonies is only three pence duty upon tea? or that the commotions in America originate in a plan, formed by some turbulent men to erect it into a republican government? The parliament claims a right to tax us in all cases whatsoever: Its late acts are in virtue of that claim. How ridiculous then is it to affirm, that we are quarrelling for the trifling sum of three pence a pound on tea; when it is evidently the principle against which we contend.

The design of electing members to represent us in general congress, was, that the wisdom of America might be collected in devising the most proper and expedient means to repel this atrocious invasion of our rights. It has been accordingly done. Their decrees are binding upon all, and demand a religious observance.

We did not, especially in this province, circumscribe them by any fixed boundary, and therefore as they cannot be said to have exceeded the limits of their authority, their act must be esteemed the act of their constituents. If it should be objected, that they have not answered the end of their election; but have fallen upon an improper and ruinous mode of proceeding: I reply, by asking, Who shall be the judge? Shall any individual oppose his private sentiment to the united counsels of men, in whom America has reposed so high a confidence? The attempt must argue no small degree of arrogance and self-sufficiency.

Yet this attempt has been made, and it is become in some measure necessary to vindicate the conduct of this venerable assembly from the aspersions of men, who are their adversaries, only because they are foes to America.

When the political salvation of any community is depending, it is incumbent upon those who are set up as its guardians, to embrace such measures, as have justice, vigour, and a probabilty of success to recommend them: If instead of this, they take those methods which are in themselves feeble, and little likely to succeed; and may, through a defect in vigour, involve the community in still greater danger; they may be justly considered as its betrayers. It is not

enough in times of eminent peril to use only possible means of preservation: Justice and sound policy dictate the use of probable means.

The only scheme of opposition, suggested by those, who have
been, and are averse from a non-importation and non-exportation
agreement, is, by REMONSTRANCE and PETITION. The authors and
abettors of this scheme, have never been able to *invent* a single argument to prove the likelihood of its succeeding. On the other hand,
there are many standing facts, and valid considerations against it.

In the infancy of the present dispute, we had recourse to this
method only. We addressed the throne in the most loyal and respectful manner, in a legislative capacity; but what was the consequence?
Our address was treated with contempt and neglect. The first American congress did the same, and met with similar treatment. The
total repeal of the stamp act, and the partial repeal of the revenue
acts took place, not because the complaints of America were deemed
just and reasonable; but because these acts were found to militate
against the commercial interests of Great Britain: This was the declared motive of the repeal.

These instances are sufficient for our purpose; but they derive
greater validity and force from the following:

The legal assembly of Massachusetts Bay, presented, not long
since, a most humble, dutiful, and earnest petition to his Majesty,
requesting the dismission of a governor, highly odious to the people,
and whose misrepresentations they regarded as one chief source of
all their calamities. Did they succeed in their request? No, it was
treated with the greatest indignity, and stigmatized as "a seditious,
vexatious, and scandalous libel."

I know the men I have to deal with will acquiesce in this stigma.
Will they also dare to calumniate the noble and spirited petition that
came from the Mayor and Aldermen of the city of London? Will
they venture to justify that unparalelled stride of power, by which
popery and arbitrary dominion were established in Canada? The
citizens of London remonstrated against it; they signified its re-
pugnancy to the principles of the revolution; but like ours, their
complaints were unattended to. From thence we may learn how
little dependence ought to be placed on this method of obtaining the
redress of grievances.

There is less reason now than ever to expect deliverance, in this way, from the hand of oppression. The system of slavery, fabricated against America, cannot at this time be considered as the effect of inconsideration and rashness. It is the offspring of mature deliberation. It has been fostered by time, and strengthened by every artifice human subtilty is capable of. After the claims of parliament had lain dormant for awhile, they are again resumed and prosecuted with more than common ardour. The Premier has advanced too far to recede with safety: He is deeply interested to execute his purpose, if possible: we know he has declared, that he will never desist, till he has brought America to his feet; and we may conclude, nothing but necessity will induce him to abandon his aims. In common life, to retract an error even in the beginning, is no easy task. Perseverance confirms us in it, and rivets the difficulty; but in a public station, to have been in an error, and to have persisted in it, when it is detected, ruins both reputation and fortune. To this we may add, that disappointment and opposition inflame the minds of men, and attach them, still more, to their mistakes.

What can we represent which has not already been represented? what petitions can we offer, that have not already been offered? The rights of America, and the injustice of parliamentary pretensions have been clearly and repeatedly stated, both in and out of parliament. No new arguments can be framed to operate in our favour. Should we even resolve the errors of the ministry and parliament into the falibility [3] of human understanding, if they have not yet been convinced, we have no prospect of being able to do it by any thing further we can say. But if we impute their conduct to a wicked thirst of domination and disregard to justice, we have no hope of prevailing with them to alter it, by expatiating on our rights, and suing to their compassion for relief; especially since we have found, by various experiments, the inefficacy of such methods.

Upon the whole, it is morally certain, this mode of opposition would be fruitless and defective. The exigency of the times requires

3. In *Rivington's New-York Gazetteer*, on December 15, 1774, there appeared the following paragraph listing corrections for *A Full Vindication:* "The Readers of the FULL VINDICATION of the Measures of the CONGRESS," it stated, "are desired to correct the following ERRATA, which in the hurry of copying and printing, have been detected."
"Falibility" is changed to read "fallibility" in the list of "Errata."

vigorous and probable remedies; not weak and improbable. It would therefore be the extreme of folly to place any confidence in, much less, confine ourselves wholly to it.

This being the case, we can have no resource but in a restriction of our trade, or in a resistance *vi & armis*. It is impossible to conceive any other alternative. Our congress, therefore, have imposed what restraint they thought necessary. Those, who condemn or clamour against it, do nothing more, nor less, than advise us to be slaves.

I shall now examine the principal measures of the congress, and vindicate them fully from the charge of injustice or impolicy.

Were I to argue in a philosophical manner, I might say, the obligation to a mutual intercourse in the way of trade with the inhabitants of Great-Britain, Ireland and the West-Indies is of the *imperfect* kind. There is no law, either of nature, or of the civil society in which we live, that obliges us to purchase, and make use of the products and manufactures of a different land, or people. It is indeed a dictate of humanity to contribute to the support and happiness of our fellow creatures and more especially those who are allied to us by the ties of blood, interest, and mutual protection; but humanity does not require us to sacrifice our own security and welfare to the convenience, or advantage of others. Self preservation is the first principle of our nature. When our lives and properties are at stake, it would be foolish and unnatural to refrain from such measures as might preserve them, because they would be detrimental to others.

But we are justified upon another principle besides this. Though the manufacturers of Great Britain and Ireland, and the Inhabitants of the West Indies are not chargeable with any actual crime towards America, they may, in a political view, be esteemed criminal. In a civil society, it is the duty of each particular branch to promote, not only the good of the whole community, but the good of every other particular branch: If one part endeavours to violate the rights of another, the rest ought to assist in preventing the injury: When they do not, but remain nutral,[4] they are deficient in their duty, and may be regarded, in some measure, as accomplices.

The reason of this is obvious, from the design of civil society,

4. "neutral," in "Errata."

which is, that the united strength of the several members might give stability and security to the whole body, and each respective member; so that one part cannot encroach upon another, without becoming a common enemy, and eventually endangering the safety and happiness of all the other parts.

Since then the persons who will be distressed by the methods we are using for our own protection, have by their neutrality first committed a breach of an obligation, similar to that which bound us to consult their emolument, it is plain, the obligation upon us is annulled, and we are blameless in what we are about to do.

With respect to the manufacturers of Great Britain, they are criminal in a more particular sense. Our oppression arises from that member of the great body politic, of which they compose a considerable part. So far as their influence has been wanting to counteract the iniquity of their rulers, so far they acquiesced in it, and are to be deemed confederates in their guilt. It is impossible to exculpate a people, that suffers its rulers to abuse and tyrannize over others.

It may not be amiss to add, that we are ready to receive with open arms, any who may be sufferers by the operation of our measures, and recompense them with every blessing our country affords to honest industry. We will receive them as brethren, and make them sharers with us in all the advantages we are struggling for.

From these plain and indisputable principles, the mode of opposition we have chosen is reconcileable to the strictest maxims of Justice. It remains now to be examined, whether it has also the sanction of good policy.

To render it agreeable to good policy, three things are requisite. First, that the necessity of the times require it: Secondly, that it be not the probable source of greater evils, than those it pretends to remedy: And lastly, that it have a probability of success.

That the necessity of the times demands it needs but little elucidation. We are threatened with absolute slavery; it has been proved, that resistance by means of REMONSTRANCE and PETITION, would not be efficacious, and of course, that a restriction on our trade, is the only peaceable method, in our power, to avoid the impending mischief: It follows therefore, that such a restriction is necessary.

That it is not the probable source of greater evils than those it pretends to remedy, may easily be determined. The most abject slavery, which comprehends almost every species of human misery, is what it is designed to prevent.

The consequences of the means are a temporary stagnation of commerce, and thereby a deprivation of the luxuries and some of the conveniencies of life. The necessaries, and many of the conveniencies, our own fertile and propitious soil affords us.

No person, that has enjoyed the sweets of liberty, can be insensible of its infinite value, or can reflect on its reverse, without horror and detestation. No person, that is not lost to every generous feeling of humanity, or that is not stupidly blind to his own interest, could bear to offer himself and posterity as victims at the shrine of despotism, in preference to enduring the short lived inconveniencies that may result from an abridgment, or even entire suspension of commerce.

Were not the disadvantages of slavery too obvious to stand in need of it, I might enumerate and describe the tedious [5] train of calamities, inseparable from it. I might shew that it is fatal to religion and morality; that it tends to debase the mind, and corrupt its noblest springs of action. I might shew, that it relaxes the sinews of industry, clips the wings of commerce, and introduces misery and indigence in every shape.

Under the auspices of tyranny, the life of the subject is often sported with; and the fruits of his daily toil are consumed in oppressive taxes, that serve to gratify the ambition, avarice and lusts of his superiors. Every court minion riots in the spoils of the honest labourer, and despises the hand by which he is fed. The page of history is replete with instances that loudly warn us to beware of slavery.

Rome was the nurse of freedom. She was celebrated for her justice and lenity; but in what manner did she govern her dependent provinces? They were made the continual scene of rapine and cruelty. From thence let us learn, how little confidence is due to the wisdom and equity of the most exemplary nations.

Should Americans submit to become the vassals of their fellow-subjects in Great Britain, their yoke will be peculiarly grievous and intolerable. A vast majority of mankind is intirely biassed by motives of self-interest. Most men are glad to remove any burthens off them-

5. "hideous," in "Errata."

selves, and place them upon the necks of their neighbours. We cannot therefore doubt, but that the British Parliament, with a view to the ease and advantage of itself, and its constituents, would oppress and grind the Americans as much as possible. Jealousy would concur with selfishness; and for fear of the future independence of America, if it should be permitted to rise to too great a height of splendor and opulence, every method would be taken to drain it of its wealth and restrain its prosperity. We are already suspected of aiming at independence, and that is one principal cause of the severity we experience. The same cause will always operate against us, and produce an uniform severity of treatment.

The evils which may flow from the execution of our measures, if we consider them with respect to their extent and duration, are comparatively nothing. In all human probability they will scarcely be felt. Reason and experience teach us, that the consequences would be too fatal to Great Britain to admit of delay. There is an immense trade between her and the colonies. The revenues arising from thence are prodigious. The consumption of her manufactures in these colonies supplies the means of subsistence to a vast number of her most useful inhabitants. The experiment we have made heretofore, shews us of how much importance our commercial connexion is to her; and gives us the highest assurance of obtaining immediate redress by suspending it.

From these considerations it is evident, she must do something decisive. She must either listen to our complaints, and restore us to a peaceful enjoyment of our violated rights; or she must exert herself to enforce her despotic claims by fire and sword. To imagine she would prefer the latter, implies a charge of the grossest infatuation of madness itself. Our numbers are very considerable; the courage of Americans has been tried and proved. Contests for liberty have ever been found the most bloody, implacable and obstinate. The disciplined troops Great Britain could send against us, would be but few, Our superiority in number would over balance our inferiority in discipline. It would be a hard, if not an impracticable task to subjugate us by force.

Besides, while Great Britain was engaged in carrying on an unnatural war against us, her commerce would be in a state of decay.

Her revenues would be decreasing. An armament, sufficient to enslave America, would put her to an insupportable expence.

She would be laid open to the attacks of foreign enemies. Ruin, like a deluge, would pour in from every quarter. After lavishing her blood and treasure to reduce us to a state of vassalage, she would herself become a prey to some triumphant neighbour.

These are not imaginary mischiefs. The colonies contain above three millions of people. Commerce flourishes with the most rapid progress throughout them. This commerce Great-Britain has hitherto regulated to her own advantage. Can we think the annihilation of so exuberant a source of wealth, a matter of trifling import. On the contrary, must it not be productive of the most disastrous effects? It is evident it must. It is equally evident, that the conquest of so numerous a people, armed in the animating cause of liberty could not be accomplished without an inconceivable expence of blood and treasure.

We cannot therefore suspect Great-Britain to be capable of such frantic extravagance as to hazard these dreadful consequences; without which she must necessarily desist from her unjust pretensions, and leave us in the undisturbed possession of our privileges.

Those, who affect to ridicule the resistance America might make to the military force of Great-Britain, and represent its humiliation as a matter the most easily to be achieved, betray, either a mind clouded by the most irrational prejudices, or a total ignorance of human nature. However, it must be the wish of every honest man never to see a trial.

But should we admit a possibility of a third course, as our pamphleteer supposes, that is, the endeavouring to bring us to a compliance by putting a stop to our whole trade: Even this would not be so terrible as he pretends. We can live without trade of any kind. Food and clothing we have within ourselves. Our climate produces cotton, wool, flax and hemp, which, with proper cultivation would furnish us with summer apparel in abundance. The article of cotton indeed would do more, it would contribute to defend us from the inclemency of winter. We have sheep, which, with due care in improving and increasing them, would soon yield a sufficiency of wool. The large quantity of skins, we have among us, would never let us want a warm and comfortable suit. It would be no unbecoming employment for our daughters to provide silks of their own country. The silk-worm answers as well here as in any part of the world. Those hands, which may be deprived of business by the cessation of commerce, may be occupied in various kinds of manufactures and other internal improvements. If by the necessity of the thing, manufactures should once be established and take root among us, they will pave the way, still more, to the future grandeur and glory of America, and by lessening its need of external commerce, will render it still securer against the encroachments of tyranny.

It is however, chimerical to imagine that the circumstances of Great-Britain will admit of such a tardy method of subjecting us, for reasons, which have been already given, and which shall be corroborated by others equally forcible.

I come now to consider the last and principal engredient [6] that constitutes the policy of a measure, which is a probability of success. I have been obliged to anticipate this part of my subject, in considering the second requisite, and indeed what I have already said seems to me to leave no room for doubting, that the means we have used will be successful, but I shall here examine the matter more thoroughly, and endeavour to evince it more fully.

The design of the Congress in their proceedings, it cannot, and need not be desired,[7] was either, by a prospect of the evil consequences, to influence the ministry to give up their enterprize; or should they prove inflexible, to affect the inhabitants of Great-Britain, Ireland and the West-Indies in such a manner, as to rouse them from their state of neutrality, and engage them to unite with us in opposing the lawless hand of tyranny, which is extended to ravish our liberty from us, and might soon be extended for the same purpose against them.

The FARMER mentions, as one probable consequence of our measures, "clamours, discord, confusion, mobs, riots, insurrections, rebellions in Great-Britain, Ireland and the West-Indies;" though at the same time that he thinks *it is*, he also thinks *it is not* a probable consequence. For my part, without hazarding any such seeming contradictions, I shall, in a plain way, assert, that I verily believe a non-

6. "ingredient," in "Errata."   7. "denied," in "Errata."

importation and non-exportation will effect all the purposes they are intended for.

It is no easy matter to make any tolerably exact estimate of the advantages that acrue to Great-Britain, Ireland and the West-Indies from their commercial intercourse with the colonies, nor indeed is it necessary. Every man, the least acquainted with the state and extent of our trade, must be convinced, it is the source of immense revenues to the parent state, and gives employment and bread to a vast number of his Majesty's subjects. It is impossible but that a suspension of it for any time, must introduce beggary and wretchedness in an eminent degree, both in England and Ireland; and as to the West-India plantations, they could not possibly subsist without us. I am the more confident of this, because I have a pretty general acquaintance with their circumstances and dependencies.

We are told, "that it is highly improbable, we shall succeed in distressing the people of Great-Britain, Ireland and the West-Indies, so far as to oblige them to join with us in getting the acts of Parliament, which we complain of, repealed: The first distress (it is said) will fall on ourselves; it will be more severely felt by us, than any part of all his Majesty's dominions, and will affect us the longest. The fleets of Great-Britain command respect throughout the globe. Her influence extends to every part of the earth. Her manufactures are equal to any: Superior to most in the world. Her wealth is great. Her people enterprizing and persevering in their attempts to extend, and enlarge, and protect her trade. The total loss of our trade will be felt only for a time. Her merchants would turn their attention another way: New sources of trade and wealth would be opened: New schemes pursued. She would soon find a vent for all her manufactures in spite of all we could do. Our malice would hurt only ourselves. Should our schemes distress some branches of her trade, it would be only for a time; and there is ability and humanity enough in the nation to relieve those, that are distressed by us, and put them in some other way of getting their living."

The omnipotence and all sufficiency of Great-Britain may be pretty good topics for her passionate admirers to exercise their declamatory powers upon, for amusement and trial of skill; but they ought not to be proposed to the world as matters of truth and reality. In the calm, unprejudiced eye of reason, they are altogether visionary. As to her wealth, it is notorious that she is oppressed with a heavy national debt, which it requires the utmost policy and œconomy ever to discharge. Luxury has arrived to a great pitch; and it is an universal maxim that luxury indicates the declension of a state. Her subjects are loaded with the most enormous taxes: All circumstances agree in declaring their distress. The continual emigrations, from Great-Britain and Ireland, to the continent, are a glaring symptom, that those kingdoms are a good deal impoverished.

The attention of Great-Britain has hitherto been constantly awake to expand her commerce. She has been vigilant to explore every region, with which it might be her interest to trade. One of the principal branches of her commerce is with the colonies. These colonies, as they are now settled and peopled, have been the work of near two centuries: They are blessed with every advantage of soil, climate and situation. They have advanced with an almost incredible rapidity. It is therefore an egregious piece of absurdity to affirm, that the loss of our trade would be felt for a time (which must signify a short time.) No new schemes could be pursued that would not require, at least, as much time to repair the loss of our trade, as was spent in bringing it to its present degree of perfection, which is near two centuries. Nor can it be reasonably imagined, that the total and sudden loss of so extensive and lucrative a branch, would not produce the most violent effects to a nation that subsists entirely upon its commerce.

It is said, "there is ability and humanity enough in the nation to relieve those that are distressed by us; and to put them into some other way of getting their living." I wish the gentleman had obliged his readers so much, as to have pointed out this other way; I must confess, I have racked my brains to no purpose to discover it, and am fully of opinion it is purely ideal. Besides the common mechanic arts, which are subservient to the ordinary uses of life, and which are the instruments of commerce; know [8] no other ways in time of peace, in which men can be employed, except in agriculture and the liberal arts. Persons employed in the mechanic arts, are those, whom the abridgment of commerce would immediately affect, and as to such branches as might be less affected, they are already sufficiently stocked with workmen, and could give bread to no more; not only

8. "I know," in "Errata."

so, but I can't see by what legerdemain, a weaver, or clothier could be at once converted into a carpenter or black-smith. With respect to agriculture, the lands of Great Britain and Ireland have been long ago distributed and taken up; nor do they require any additional labourers to till them; so that there could be no employment in this way. The liberal arts cannot maintain those who are already devoted to them; not to say, it is more than probable, the generality of mechanics, would make but indifferent philosophers, poets, painters and musicians.

What poor shifts is sophistry obliged to have recourse to! we are threatened with the resentment of those against whom our measures will operate. It is said, that "instead of conciliating, we shall alienate the affections of the people of Great-Britain, of friends, we shall make them our enemies;" and further, that "we shall excite the resentment of the government at home against us, which will do us no good, but, on the contrary, much harm."

Soon after, we are told that "we shall probably raise the resentment of the Irish and West-Indians: The passions of human nature" it is said, "are much the same in all countries. If they find us disposed wantonly to distress them, to serve our own purposes, they will look out for some method to do without us: will they not look elsewhere for a supply of those articles, they used to take from us? They would deserve to be despised for their meanness did they not."

To these objections I reply, first with respect to the inhabitants of Great-Britain, that if they are our friends, as is supposed, and as we have reason to believe; they cannot, without being destitute of rationality, be incensed against us for using the only peaceable and probable means, in our power, to preserve our invaded rights: They know by their own experience how fruitless remonstrances and petitions are: They know, we have tried them over and over to no purpose: They know also, how dangerous to their liberties, the loss of ours must be. What then could exite their resentment if they have the least regard to common justice? The calamities, that threaten them, proceed from the weakness, or wickedness of their own rulers; which compels us to take the measures we do. The insinuation, that we *wantonly* distress them to serve our own purposes, is futile and unsupported by a single argument. I have shewn, we could have no other resource; nor can they think our conduct

such, without a degree of infatuation, that it would be impossible
to provide against, and therefore useless to consult. It is most reasonable to believe, they will revenge the evils they may feel on the true
authors of them, on an aspiring and ill-judging ministry; not on us,
who act out of a melancholy necessity, and are the innocent causes
in self-defence.

With respect to the ministry, it is certain, that any thing, which
has a tendency to frustrate their designs, will not fail to excite their
displeasure; but since we have nothing to expect from their justice
and lenity, it can be no objection to a measure, that it tends to stir
up their resentment. But their resentment (it is often said) may ruin
us. The impossibility of doing that, without at the same time, ruining Great-Britain, is a sufficient security.

The same may be said with regard to the Irish and the West-
Indians, which has been said concerning the people of Great-Britain.
The Irish, in particular, by their own circumstances will be taught
to sympathise with us, and commend our conduct. Justice will direct
their resentment to its proper objects.

It is true self-love will prompt both the Irish and the West-
Indians to take every method in their power, to escape the miseries
they are in danger of; but what methods can they take? "The Irish
(it is said) may be supplied with flax-seed from Holland, the Baltic,
and the river St. Lawrence: Canada produces no inconsiderable
quantity already." And as to the West-Indies, "they produce now
many of the necessaries of life. The quantity may be easily increased.
Canada will furnish them with many articles they now take from us;
flour, lumber, horses, &c. Georgia, the Floridas, and the Mississippi
abound in lumber: Nova Scotia in fish."

The Dutch are rivals to the English in their commerce. They
make large quantities of fine linens, gause, laces, &c. which require
the flax to be picked before it comes to seed; for which reason, it
is not in their power to raise much more seed than they want for
their own use. Ireland has always had the surplus from them. They
could, if they were ever so willing, enlarge their usual supplies but
very little. It is indeed probable they may withold them. They may
choose to improve the occasion for the advancement of their own
trade: They may take advantage of the scarcity of materials in Ireland, to increase and put off their own manufactures.

The Baltic has ever supplied Ireland with its flax, and she has been able to consume that, with all she could derive from other quarters.

As to Canada, I am well informed it could at present afford, but a very inconsiderable quantity. It has had little encouragement, hitherto, to raise that article, and of course has not much attended to it. The instances mentioned, of seed being "bought up there at a low price, brought to New-York, and sold to the Irish factors at a great advance," does not prove there is any quantity raised there. Its cheapness proceeds from there being no demand for it; and where there was no demand, there was no inducement to cultivate it.

Upon the whole, it appears, that the supplies of flax-seed, which Ireland might draw elsewhere, could [9] be trifling in comparison with those received from us, and not at all equivalent to her wants. But if this were not the case, if she might procure a sufficiency without our help, yet could she not do without us. She would want purchasers for her linens after they were manufactured; and where could she find any so numerous and wealthy as we are? I must refer it to the profound sagacity of Mr. A. W. Farmer, to explore them, it is too arduous a task for me.

Much less could the West-Indies subsist independent of us. Notwithstanding the continual imports from hence, there is seldom or ever, in any of the islands, a sufficient stock of provisions to last six months, which may give us an idea, how great the consumption is. The necessaries they produce within themselves, when compared with the consumption, are scarcely worth mentioning. Very small portions of the lands are appropriated to the productions of such necessaries, indeed it is too valuable to admit of it. Nor could the quantity be increased to any material degree, without applying the whole of the land to it. It is alledged, that Canada will furnish them with "flour, lumber, horses, &c. and that Georgia, the Floridas and Mississipi abound in lumber; Nova Scotia in fish." These countries have been all-along carrying on a trade to the West-Indies, as well as we; and can it be imagined that alone, they will be able to supply them tolerably? The Canadians have been indolent, and have not improved their country as they ought to have done. The wheat they raise at present, over and above what they have occasion for themselves, would be found to go but little way among the islands.

9. "would," in "Errata."

Those, who think the contrary, must have mistaken notions of them. They must be unapprized of the number of souls they contain: Almost every 150 or 200 acres of land, exclusive of populous towns, comprehend a hundred people. It is not a small quantity of food that will suffice for so many. Ten or fifteen years diligence, I grant, might enable Canada to perform what is now expected from her; but, in the mean time, the West-Indians might have the satisfaction of starving.

To suppose the best, which is, that by applying their canelands to the purpose of procuring sustenance, they may preserve themselves from starving: still the consequences must be very serious or pernicious. The wealthy planters would but ill relish the loss of their crops, and such of them as were considerably in debt would be ruined. At any rate, the revenues of Great-Britain would suffer a vast diminution.

The FARMER, I am inclined to hope, builds too much upon the present disunion of Canada, Georgia, the Floridas, the Mississippi, and Nova Scotia from other colonies. A little time, I trust, will awaken them from their slumber, and bring them to a proper sense of their indiscretion. I please myself with the flattering prospect, that they will, ere long, unite in one indissoluble chain with the rest of the colonies. I cannot believe they will persist in such a conduct as must exclude them from the secure enjoyment of those heaven-descended immunities we are contending for.

There is one argument I have frequently heard urged, which it may be of some use to invalidate. It is this, that if the mother country should be inclined to an accommodation of our disputes, we have by our rash procedure thrown an insurmountable obstacle in her way; we have made it disgraceful to her to comply with our requisitions, because they are proposed in a hostile manner.

Our present measures, I have proved, are the only peaceable ones we could place the least confidence in. They are the least exceptionable, upon the score of irritating Great-Britain, of any our circumstances would permit. The congress have petitioned his Majesty for the redress of grievances. They have, no doubt, addressed him in the most humble, respectful and affectionate terms; assured him, of their own loyalty, and fidelity and of the loyalty and fidelity of his American subjects in general; endeavoured to convince him, that we have been misrepresented and abused; and expressed an earnest desire to see an amicable termination of the unhappy differences now existing. Can a pretext be wanting, in this case, to preserve the dignity of this parent state, and yet remove the complaints of the colonies? How easy would it be to overlook our particular agreements, and grant us redress in consequence of our petitions? It is easy to perceive there would be no difficulty in this respect.

I have omitted many considerations, which might be adduced to shew the impolicy of Great-Britains, delaying to accommodate matters, and attempting to enforce submission by cutting off all external sources of trade. To say all the subject allows, would spin out this piece to an immoderate length; I shall, therefore, content myself with mentioning only three things more. First, it would be extremely hurtful to the commerce of Great-Britain to drive us to the necessity of laying a regular foundation for manufactories of our own; which, if once established, could not easily, if at all, be undermined, or abolished. Secondly, it would be very expensive to the nation to maintain a fleet for the purpose of blocking up our ports, and destroying our trade: nor could she interrupt our intercourse with foreign climes without, at the same time, retrenching her own revenues; for she must then lose the duties and customs upon the articles we are wont to export to, and import from them. Added to this, it would not be prudent to risk the displeasure of those nations, to whom our trade is useful and beneficial. And lastly, a perseverance in ill-treatment would naturally beget such deep-rooted animosities in America, as might never be eradicated; and which might operate to the prejudice of the empire to the latest period.

Thus have I clearly proved, that the plan of opposition concerted by our congress is perfectly consonant with justice and sound policy; and will, in all human probability, secure our freedom against the assaults of our enemies.

But, after all, it may be demanded why they have adopted a non-exportation; seeing many arguments tend to shew that a non-importation alone would accomplish the end desired?

I answer, that the continuance of our exports is the only thing which could lessen, or retard the efficacy of a non-importation. It is not indeed probable it should do that to any great degree; but it was adviseable to provide against every possible obstruction. Besides this, the prospect of its taking place, and of the evils attendant upon it, will be a prevailing motive with the ministry to abandon their malignant schemes. It will also serve to convince them, that we are not afraid of putting ourselves to any inconveniencies, sooner than be the victims of their lawless ambition.

The execution of this measure has been wisely deferred to a future time, because we have the greatest reason to think affairs will be settled without it, and because its consequences would be too fatal to be justified by any thing but absolute necessity. This necessity there will be, should not our disputes terminate before the time allotted for its commencement.

Before I conclude this part of my address, I will answer two very singular interrogatories proposed by the FARMER, "Can we think (says he) to threaten, and bully, and frighten the supreme government of the nation into a compliance with our demands? Can we expect to force submission to our peevish and petulant humours, by exciting clamours and riots in England?" No, gentle Sir. We neither desire, nor endeavour to threaten, bully, or frighten any persons into a compliance with our demands. We have no peevish and petulant humours to be submitted to. All we aim at, is to convince your high and mighty masters, the ministry, that we are not such asses as to let them ride us as they please. We are determined to shew them, that we know the value of freedom; nor shall their rapacity extort, that inestimable jewel from us, without a manly and virtuous struggle. But for your part, sweet Sir! tho' we cannot much applaud your wisdom, yet we are compelled to admire your valour, which leads you to hope you may be able to *swear*, threaten, bully and frighten all America into a compliance with your sinister designs. When properly accoutered and armed with your formidable hiccory cudgel, what may not the ministry expect from such a champion? alas! for the poor committee gentlemen, how I tremble when I reflect on the many wounds and scars they must receive from your tremendous arm! Alas! for their supporters and abettors; a very large part indeed of the continent; but what of that? they must all be soundly drubbed with that confounded hiccory cudgel; for surely you would not undertake to drub one of them, without knowing yourself able to treat all their friends and adherents in the same manner; since 'tis plain you would bring them all upon your back.

I am now to address myself in particular to the Farmers of New-York.

MY GOOD COUNTRYMEN,

The reason I address myself to you, in particular, is, because [10] I am one of your number, or connected with you in interest more than with any other branch of the community. I love to speak the truth, and would scorn to prejudice you in favour of what I have to say, by taking upon me a fictitious character as other people have done. I can venture to assure you, the true writer of the piece signed A. W. FARMER, is not in reality a Farmer. He is some ministerial emissary, that has assumed the name to deceive you, and make you swallow the intoxicating potion he has prepared for you. But I have a better opinion of you than to think he will be able to succeed. I am persuaded you love yourselves and children better than to let any designing men cheat you out of your liberty and property, to serve their own purposes. You would be a disgrace to your ancestors, and the bitterst enemies to yourselves and to your posterity, if you did not act like men, in protecting and defending those rights you have hitherto enjoyed.

I say, my friends, I do not address you in particular, because I have any greater connexion with you, than with other people. I despise all false pretentions, and mean arts. Let those have recourse to dissimulation and falshood, who can't defend their cause without it. 'Tis my maxim to let the plain naked truth speak for itself; and if men won't listen to it, 'tis their own fault: they must be contented to suffer for it. I am neither merchant, nor farmer. I address you, because I wish well to my country, and of course to you, who are one chief support of it; and because an attempt has been made to lead you astray in particular. You are the men too who would lose most should you be foolish enough to counteract the prudent measures our worthy congress has taken for the preservation of our liberties. Those, who advise you to do it, are not your friends, but your greatest foes. They would have you made slaves, that they may pamper themselves with the fruits of your honest labour. 'Tis the

10. "not because," in "Errata."

Farmer who is most oppressed in all countries where slavery prevails.

You have seen how clearly I have proved, that a non-importation and non-exportation are the only peaceable means in our power to save ourselves from the most dreadful state of slavery. I have shewn there is not the least hope, to be placed in any thing else. I have confuted all the principal cavils raised by the pretended Farmer, and I hope, before I finish, to satisfy you, that he has attempted to frighten you with the prospect of evils, which will never happen. This indeed I have, in a great measure, done already, by making appear the great probability, I may almost say certainty, that our measures will procure us the most speedy redress.

Are you willing then to be slaves without a single struggle? Will you give up your freedom, or, which is the same thing, will you resign all security for your life and property, rather than endure some small present inconveniencies? Will you not take a little trouble to transmit the advantages you now possess to those, who are to come after you? I cannot doubt it. I would not suspect you of so much baseness and stupidity, as to suppose the contrary.

Pray who can tell me why a farmer in America, is not as honest and good a man, as a farmer in England? or why has not the one as good a right to what he has earned by his labour, as the other? I can't, for my life, see any distinction between them. And yet it seems the English farmers are to be governed and taxed by their own Assembly, or Parliament; and the American farmers are not. The former are to choose their own Representatives from among themselves, whose interest is connected with theirs, and over whom they have proper controul. The latter are to be loaded with taxes by men three thousand miles off; by men, who have no interest, or connexions among them; but whose interest it will be to burden them as much as possible; and over whom they cannot have the least restraint. How do you like this doctrine my friends? Are you ready to own the English farmers for your masters? Are you willing to acknowledge their right to take your property from you, and when [11] they please? I know you scorn the thought. You had rather die, than submit to it.

But some people try to make you believe, we are disputing about

11. "how and when," in "Errata."

the foolish trifle of three pence duty upon tea. They may as well tell you, that black is white. Surely you can judge for yourselves. Is a dispute, whether the Parliament of Great-Britain shall make what laws, and impose what taxes they please upon us, or not; I say, is this a dispute about three pence duty upon tea? The man that affirms it, deserves to be laughed at.

It is true, we are denying to pay the duty upon tea; but it is not for the value of the thing itself. It is because we cannot submit to that, without acknowledging the principle upon which it is founded, and that principle is *a right to tax us in all cases whatsoever.*

You have, heretofore experienced the benefit of being taxed by your own Assemblies only. Your burdens are so light, that you scarcely feel them. You'd soon find the difference if you were once to let the Parliament have the management of these matters.

How would you like to pay four shillings a year,* out of every pound your farms are worth, to be squandered, (at least a great part of it) upon ministerial tools and court sycophants? What would you think of giving a tenth part of the yearly products of your lands to the clergy? Would you not think it very hard to pay 10s. sterling per annum, for every wheel of your waggons and other carriages, a shilling or two for every pane of glass in your houses, and two or three shillings for every one of your hearths? I might mention taxes upon your mares, cows, and many other things; but those I have already mentioned are sufficient. Methinks I see you stare, and hear you ask how you could live, if you were to pay such heavy taxes? Indeed my friends I can't tell you. You are to look out for that, and take care you do not run yourselves in the way of danger, by following the advice of those, who want to betray you. This you may depend upon, if ever you let the Parliament carry its point, you will have these and more to pay. Perhaps before long, your tables, and chairs, and platters, and dishes, and knives and forks, and every thing else would be taxed. Nay, I don't know but they would find means to tax you for every child you got, and for every kiss your daughters received from their sweet-hearts, and God knows, that would soon ruin you. The people of England would pull down the Parliament House, if their present heavy burdens were not transferred from them to you. Indeed there is no reason to think the

* i. e. the full price of your farms every five years.

Parliament would have any inclination to spare you: The contrary is evident.

But being ruined by taxes is not the worst you have to fear. What security would you have for your lives? How can any of you be sure you would have the free enjoyment of your religion long? would you put your religion in the power of any set of men living? Remember civil and religious liberty always go together, if the foundation of the one be sapped, the other will fall of course.

Call to mind one of our sister colonies, Boston. Reflect upon the situation of Canada, and then tell me whether you are inclined to place any confidence in the justice and humanity of the parliament. The port of Boston is blocked up, and an army planted in the town. An act has been passed to alter its charter, to prohibit its assemblies, to license the murder of its inhabitants, and to convey them from their own country to Great Britain, to be tried for their lives. What was all this for? Just because a small number of people, provoked by an open and dangerous attack upon their liberties, destroyed a parcel of Tea belonging to the East India Company. It was not public but private property they destroyed. It was not the act of the whole province, but the act of a part of the citizens; instead of trying to discover the perpetrators, and commencing a legal prosecution against them; the parliament of Great-Britain interfered in an unprecedented manner, and inflicted a punishment upon a whole province, "untried, unheard, unconvicted of any crime." This may be justice, but it looks so much like cruelty, that a man of a humane heart would be more apt to call it by the latter, than the former name.

The affair of Canada, if possible, is still worse. The English laws have been superceded by the French laws. The Romish faith is made the established religion of the land, and his Majesty is placed at the head of it. The free exercise of the protestant faith depends upon the pleasure of the Governor and Council. The subject is divested of the right of trial by jury, and an innocent man may be imprisoned his whole life, without being able to obtain any trial at all. The parliament was not contented with introducing arbitrary power and popery in Canada, with its former limits, but they have annexed to it the vast tracts of land that surround all the colonies.

Does not your blood run cold, to think an English parliament should pass an act for the establishment of arbitrary power and popery in such an extensive country? If they had had any regard to the freedom and happiness of mankind, they would never have done it. If they had been friends to the protestant cause, they would never have provided such a nursery for its great enemy: They would not have given such encouragement to popery. The thought of their conduct, in this particular shocks me. It must shock you too my friends. Beware of trusting yourselves to men, who are capable of such an action! They may as well establish popery in New-York and the other colonies as they did in Canada. They had no more right to do it there than here.

Is it not better, I ask, to suffer a few present inconveniencies, than to put yourselves in the way of losing every thing that is precious. Your lives, your property, your religion are all at stake. I do my duty. I warn you of your danger. If you should still be so mad, as to bring destruction upon yourselves; if you should still neglect what you owe to God and man, you cannot plead ignorance in your excuse. Your consciences will reproach you for your folly, and your children's children will curse you.

You are told, the schemes of our Congress will ruin you. You are told, they have not considered your interest; but have neglected, or betrayed you. It is endeavoured to make you look upon some of the wisest and best men in the America, as rogues and rebels. What will not wicked men attempt! They will scruple nothing, that may serve their purposes. In truth, my friends, it is very unlikely any of us shall suffer much; but let the worst happen, the farmers will be better off, than other people.

Many of those that made up the Congress have large possessions in land, and may, therefore be looked upon as farmers themselves. Can it be supposed, they would be careless about the farmer's interest, when they could not injure that, without injuring themselves? You see the absurdity of such a supposition.

The merchants and a great part of the tradesmen get their living by commerce. These are the people that would be hurt most, by putting a stop to it. As to the farmers, "they furnish food for the merchant and mechanic; the raw materials for most manufactures are the produce of their industry." The merchants and mechanics are already dependent upon the farmers for their food, and if the non-importation should continue any time, they would be dependent upon them for their cloaths also.

It is a false assertion, that the merchants have imported more than usual this year. That report has been raised by your enemies to poison your minds with evil suspicions. If our disputes be not settled within eighteen months, the goods we have among us will be consumed; and then the materials for making cloaths must be had from you. Manufactures must be promoted with vigour, and a high price will be given for your wool, flax and hemp. It will be your interest to pay the greatest care and attention to your sheep. Increase and improve the breed as much as possible: *Kill them sparingly*, and such only as will not be of use towards the increase and improvement of them. In a few months we shall know what we have to trust to. If matters be not accommodated by spring, enlarge the quantity of your flax and hemp. You will experience the benefit of it. All those articles will be very much wanted: They will bring a great deal higher price than they used to do. And while you are supplying the wants of the community, you will be enriching yourselves.

Should we hereafter, find it necessary to stop our exports, you can apply more of your land to raising flax and hemp, and less of it to wheat, rye, &c. By which means, you will not have any of those latter articles to lie upon hand. There will be a consumption for as much of the former as you can raise, and the great demand they will be in, will make them very profitable to you.

Patience good Mr. Critic! *Kill them sparingly, I said*, what objection have you to the phrase? You'll tell me, it is not *classical;* but I affirm it is, and if you will condescend to look into Mr. Johnson's dictionary, you will find I have his authority for it. Pray then, for the future, *spare* your wit, upon such occasions, otherwise the world will not be disposed to *spare* its ridicule. And though the man that *spares* nobody does not deserve to be *spared* himself, yet will I *spare* you, for the present, and proceed to things of more importance.

Pardon me, my friends, for taking up your time with this digression; but I could not forbear stepping out of the way a little, to shew the world, I am as able a critic, and as good a punster as Mr. Farmer.[12] I now return to the main point with pleasure.

12. The "Farmer" had written:
"We are ordered *to kill them sparingly:* a queer phrase; however, let it pass. If it is not *classical*, it is *congressional;* and that's enough. And after having killed them *sparingly*, if we have any to *spare*, we must *spare* them to our poor neighbours. But supposing that after *killing them sparingly, and sparing*

It is insinuated, "That the bustle about non-importation, &c. has its rise, not from patriotism, but selfishness;" and is only made by the merchants, that they may get a high price for their goods.

By this time, I flatter myself you are convinced, that we are not disputing about trifles. It has been clearly proved to you, that we are contending for every thing dear in life, and that the measures adopted by the congress, are the only ones which can save us from ruin. This is sufficient to confute that insinuation. But to confirm it, let me observe to you, that the merchants have not been the foremost to bring about a non-importation. All the members of the congress were unanimous in it; and *many* of them were not merchants. The warmest advocates for it, every where, are not concerned in trade, and, as I before remarked, the traders will be the principal sufferers, if it should continue any time.

But it is said it will not continue, because, "when the stores are like to become empty, they will have weight enough to break up the agreement." I don't think they would attempt it; but if they should, it is impossible a few mercenary men could have influence enough to make the whole body of people give up the only plan their circumstances admit of for the preservation of their rights, and, of course, to forfeit all they have been so long striving to secure. The making of a non-importation agreement did not depend upon the merchants; neither will the breaking of it depend upon them. The congress have provided against the breach of the non-importation, by the non-consumption agreement. They have resolved for themselves and us their constituents, "not to purchase, or use any East-India Tea whatsoever; nor any goods, wares, or merchandize, from Great-Britain or Ireland, imported after the first of December, nor molasses, &c. from the West Indies, nor wine from Madeira, or the Western Islands, nor foreign Indigo." If we do not purchase or use these things, the merchant will have no inducement to import them.

Hence you may perceive the reason of a non-consumption agreement. It is to put it out of the power of dishonest men, to break the non importation. *Is this a slavish regulation?* Or is it a hardship

---

as many to my poor neighbours as they want, I should, by reason of *killing them sparingly*, have still more to *spare*—what shall I do with them?" (Seabury, *Free Thoughts*, 20).

upon us to submit to it? Surely not. Every sensible, every good man must approve of it. Whoever tries to disaffect you to it, ought to meet with your contempt.

Take notice, my friends, how these men are obliged to contradict themselves. In one place you are told, that all the bustle about non-importation, &c. has its rise, not from patriotism, but from selfishness, "or, in other words, that it is made by the merchants to get a higher price for their goods." In another place it is said, that all we are doing is instigated by some turbulent men, who want to establish a republican form of government among us.

The Congress is censured for appointing committees to carry their measures into execution, and directing them "to establish such further regulations, as they may think proper for that purpose." Pray, did we not appoint our Delegates to make regulations for us? What signified making them, if they did not provide some persons to see them executed? Must a few bad men be left to do what they please, contrary to the general sense of the people, without any persons to controul them, or to look into their behaviour and mark them out to the public? The man that desires to screen his knavery from the public eye, will answer yes; but the honest man, that is determined to do nothing hurtful to his country, and who is conscious his actions will bear the light, will heartily answer no.

The high prices of goods are held up to make you dissatisfied with the non-importation. If the argument [13] on this head were true, it would be much better to subject yourselves to that disadvantage, for a time, than to bring upon yourselves all the mischiefs I have pointed out to you. Should you submit to claims of the Parliament, you will not only be oppressed with the taxes upon your lands, &c. which I have already mentioned; but you will have to pay heavy taxes upon all the goods we import from Great-Britain. Large duties will be laid upon them at home; and the merchants, of course, will have a greater price for them, or it would not be worth their while to carry on trade. The duty laid upon paper, glass, painter's colours, &c. was a beginning of this kind. The present duty upon tea is preparatory to the imposition of duties upon all other articles. Do you think the Parliament would make such a serious matter of three pence a pound upon tea, if it intended to stop there? It is absurd

13. "arguments," in "Errata."

to imagine it. You would soon find your mistake if you did. For fear of paying somewhat a higher price to the merchants for a year or two, you would have to pay an endless list of taxes, within and without, as long as you live, and your children after you.

But I trust, there is no danger that the prices of goods will rise much, if at all. The same congress that put a stop to the importation of them, has also forbid raising the prices of them. The same committee that is to regulate the one, is also to regulate the other. All care will be taken to give no cause of dissatisfaction. Confide in the men whom you, and the rest of the continent have chosen the guardians of our common liberties. They are men of sense and virtue. They will do nothing but what is really necessary for the security of your lives and properties.

A sad pother is made too about prohibiting the exportation of sheep, without excepting weathers.[14] The poor Farmer is at a mighty loss to know how weathers can improve, or increase the breed. Truly I am not such a conjurer, as to be able to inform him; but if you please, my friends, I can give you two pretty good reasons, why the congress has not excepted weathers. One is, that for some time, we shall have occasion for all the wool we can raise; so that it would be imprudent to export sheep of any kind: and the other is, that, if you confine yourself chiefly to killing weathers, as you ought to do, you will have none to export. The gentleman who made the objection, must have known these things, as well as myself; but he loves to crack a jest, and could not pass by so fair an opportunity.

He takes notice of the first of these reasons himself; but in order to weaken its force, cries, "let me ask you, brother farmers, which of you would keep a flock of sheep, barely, for the sake of their wool?" To this he answers, "not one of you. If you cannot sell your sheep to advantage, at a certain age, you cannot keep them to any profit." He thinks, because he calls you brother farmers, that he can cajole you into believing what he pleases; but you are not the fools he takes you for. You know what is for your own interest better than he can tell you. And we all know, that in a little time, if our affairs be not settled, the demand for wool will be very great. You will be able to obtain such a price, as will make it worth your while to bestow the greatest attention upon your sheep.

14. Variant spelling of wethers.

In another place, this crafty writer tells you, that, "from the day our exports, from this province are stopped, the farmers may date the commencement of their ruin." He asks, "will the shop-keeper give you his goods? will the weaver, shoe-maker, black-smith, carpenter work for you without pay?" I make no doubt, you are satisfied, from what I have said, that we shall never have occasion to stop our exports; but if things turn out contrary to our expectation, and it should become necessary to take that step, you will find no difficulty in getting what you want from the merchants and mechanics. They will not be able to do without you, and, consequently, they cannot refuse to supply you with what you stand in need of from them. Where will the merchants and mechanics get food and materials for clothing, if not from the farmer? And if they are dependent upon you, for those two grand supports of life, how can they withold what they have from you?

I repeat it (my friends) we shall know, how matters are like to be settled by the spring. If our disputes be not terminated to our satisfaction by that time, it will [be] your business to plant large parts of your lands with flax and hemp. Those articles will be wanted for manufactures, and they will yield you a greater profit than any thing else. In the interim, take good care of your sheep.

I heartily concur with the farmer, in condemning all illicit trade. Perjury is, no doubt, a most heineous [15] and detestable crime; and for my part, I had rather suffer any thing, than have my wants relieved at the expence of truth and integrity. I know, there are many pretended friends to liberty, who will take offence at this declaration; but I speak the sentiments of my heart without reserve. I do not write for a party. I should scorn to be of any. All I say, is from a disinterested regard to the public weal.

The congress, I am persuaded, were of the same opinion: They, like honest men, have, as much as was in their power, provided against this kind of trade, by agreeing to use no East-India tea whatever, after the first day of March next.

I shall now consider what has been said, with respect to the payment of debts, and stopping of the courts of justice.[16] Let what will

15. "heinous," in "Errata."
16. The "Farmer" wrote: "all legal processes are to be stopped, except in criminal cases. . . . By whose authority are the courts of Justice to be shut up, in all civil cases?" He then described and illustrated the possible results of

happen, it will be your own faults, if you are not able to pay your debts. I have told you, in what manner you may make as much out of your lands as ever: by bestowing more of your attention upon raising flax and hemp, and less upon other things. Those articles (as I have more than once observed) will be in the highest demand: There will be no doing without them; and, of course, you will be able to get a very profitable price for them. How can it be, that the farmers should be at a loss for money to pay their debts, at a time, when the whole community must buy, not only their food, but all the materials for their cloaths from them? You have no reason to be uneasy on that account.

As to the courts of justice, no violence can, or will be used to shut them up; but, if it should be found necessary, we may enter into solemn agreement to cease from all litigations at law, except in particular cases. We may regulate law suits, in such a manner, as to prevent any mischief that might arise from them. Restrictions may be laid on to hinder merciless creditors, from taking advantage of the times, to oppress and ruin their debtors but, at the same time, not to put it in the power of the debtors, *wantonly*, to withold their just dues from their creditors, when they are able to pay them. The law ruins many a good honest family. Disputes may be settled in a more friendly way; one or two virtuous neighbours may be chosen by each party to decide them. If the next congress should think any regulations concerning the courts of justice requisite, they will make them; and proper persons will be appointed to carry them into execution, and to see, that no individuals deviate from them. It will be your duty to elect persons, whose fidelity and zeal for your interest you can't [17] depend upon, to represent you in *that* congress; which is to meet at Philadelphia, in May ensuing.

The Farmer cries, "tell me not of delegates, congresses committees, mobs, riots, insurrections, associations; a plague on them all. Give me the steady, uniform, unbiassed influence of the courts of justice. I have been happy under their protection, and I trust in God, I shall be so again."

I say, tell me not of the British Commons, Lords, ministry, min-

---

the suspension by the courts of action in civil cases (Seabury, *Free Thoughts*, 15-16).

17. "can," in "Errata."

isterial tools, placemen, pensioners, parasites. I scorn to let my life
and property depend upon the pleasure of any of them. Give me
the steady, uniform, unshaken security of constitutional freedom;
give me the right to be tried by a jury of my own neighbours, and
to be taxed by my own representatives only. What will become of
the law and courts of justice without this? The shadow may remain,
but the substance will be gone. I would die to preserve the law upon
a solid foundation; but take away liberty, and the foundation is destroyed.

The last thing I shall take notice of, is the complaint of the Farmer,
that the congress will not allow you "a dish of tea to please your
wives with, nor a glass of Madeira to cheer your spirits, nor a spoonful of molasses, to sweeten your butter milk with." You would have
a right to complain, if the use of these things had been forbidden
to you alone; but it has been equally forbidden to all sorts of people.
The members of the congress themselves are no more permitted to
please their wives with a dish of tea, or to cheer their spirits with
a glass of wine, or to sweeten their butter milk with a spoonful of
molasses, than you are. They are upon a footing with you in this
respect.

By him! but, with your leave, my friends, we'll try, if we can,
to do without swearing. I say, it is enough to make a man mad, to
hear such ridiculous quibbles offered instead of sound argument; but
so it is, the piece I am writing against contains nothing else.

When a man grows warm, he has a confounded itch for swearing.
I have been going, above twenty times, to rap out an oath, *by him
that made me*, but I have checked myself, with this reflection, that
it is rather *unmannerly*, to treat him that made us with so much freedom.

Thus have I examined and confuted, all the cavils and objections,
of any consequence, stated by this Farmer. I have only passed over
such things, as are of little weight, the fallacy of which will easily
appear. I have shewn, that the congress have neither "ignorantly
misunderstood, carelessly neglected, nor basely betrayed you;" but
that they have desired [18] and recommended the *only* effectual means
to preserve your invaluable privileges. I have proved, that their
measures cannot fail of success; but will procure the most speedy

18. "devised," in "Errata."

relief for us. I have also proved, that the farmers are the people who would suffer least, should we be obliged to carry all our measures into execution.

Will you then, my friends, allow yourselves, to be duped by this artful enemy? will you follow his advices,[19] disregard the authority of your congress, and bring ruin on yourselves and posterity? will you act in such a manner as to deserve the hatred and resentment of all the rest of America? I am sure you will not. I should be sorry to think, any of my countrymen would be so mean, so blind to their own interest, so lost to every generous and manly feeling.

The sort of men I am opposing give you fair words, to persuade you to serve their own turns; but they think and speak of you in common in a very disrespectful manner. I have heard some of their party talk of you, as the most ignorant and mean-spirited set of people in the world. They say, that you have no sense of honour or generosity; that you don't care a farthing about your country, children or any body else, but yourselves; and that you are so ignorant, as not to be able to look beyond the present; so that if you can once be persuaded to believe the measures of your congress will involve you in some little present perplexities, you will be glad to do any thing to avoid them; without considering the much greater miseries that await you at a little distance off. This is the character they give of you. Bad men are apt to paint others like themselves. For my part, I will never entertain such an opinion of you, unless you should verify their words, by wilfully falling into the pit they have prepared for you. I flatter myself you will convince them of their error, by shewing the world, you are capable of judging what is right and left,[20] and have resolution to pursue it.

All I ask is, that you will judge for yourselves. I don't desire you to take my opinion or any man's opinion, as the guide of your actions. I have stated a number of plain arguments; I have supported them with several well-known facts: It is your business to draw a conclusion and act accordingly.

I caution you, again and again, to beware of the men who advise you to forsake the plain path, marked out for you by the congress. They only mean to deceive and betray you. Our representatives in general assembly cannot take any wiser or better course to settle

19. "advice," in "Errata."   20. "best," in "Errata."

our differences, than our representatives in the continental congress have taken. If you join with the rest of America in the same common measure, you will be sure to preserve your liberties inviolate; but if you separate from them, and seek for redress alone, and unseconded, you will certainly fall a prey to your enemies, and repent your folly as long as you live.

May God give you wisdom to see what is your true interest, and inspire you with becoming zeal for the cause of virtue and mankind.

A Friend to America.

A Card

[New York, December 22, 1774]

The Friend to America presents his compliments to Mr. A. W. Farmer, and begs leave to decline making any remarks upon his Examination into the conduct of the Delegates, until he has seen what he may have to offer, in answer to the Full Vindication, &c.[1] His reasons, there is no necessity to communicate. He assures Mr. Farmer, that he never imagined, any thing he could say, would frighten, or disconcert him, or induce him to change his sentiments. He is convinced, that the intellectual eye of every advocate for despotism, is too much blinded to perceive the force of just argumentation: The opinions of such are *generally* influenced by motives to which REASON can furnish no counter-poise. All the VINDICATOR proposed to himself was, to prevent the ill effects of the Farmer's sophistry on others.

With respect to the impropriety of expression, "and his wit ridiculed." [2] The author humbly conceives, it would be no easy task to prove it improper. Wit is, by no means, a positive, or precise term: it has various significations: authors have defined, and applied it in different senses. Genuine wit is used in contradisti[n]ction to *spurious* wit; but if the term wit alone, uniformly conveyed the idea of what we understand by *true* or *genuine* wit, then would those adjectives be superfluous, and improper, and their opposites *false* and *spurious*, when conjoined with wit, would be absurd. If wit be a relative term, as it evidently often is, why may it not be used to signify the *false*, as well as the *true* kind? The VINDICATOR, however, does not pretend to be infallible; he may be mistaken, and is ready to alter his opinion whenever a sufficient reason can be produced. It is confessed, that if wit ought to be understood, in the strictest sense, to which Mr. Farmer seems to confine it, the application of the term to his *feeble efforts*, would be altogether indefensible. Wit, in such a sense, was not to be found in his piece, and of course "the impropriety of the expression, and the impracticability of the attempt," must be conspicuous.

Rivington's New-York Gazetteer, December 22, 1774.

1. Soon after the publication of his *Free Thoughts*, Seabury wrote a second pamphlet entitled: *The Congress Canvassed: or, an Examination into The Conduct of the Delegates, at their Grand Convention, Held in Philadelphia, Sept. 1, 1774. Addressed, to the Merchants of New-York. By A. W. Farmer . . .* (New York, Printed by James Rivington, 1774). It was dated November 28, 1774, and included a postscript directed to H, which read:

"POSTSCRIPT. *FARMER* A. W. *has seen a pamphlet entitled, 'A Full Vindication of the Measures of the Congress, &c.' He is neither frighted nor disconcerted by it; nor does he find any thing in it to make him change his sentiments, as expressed in the* Free Thoughts: *If the author of the Vindication has any teeth left, here is another* file *at his service. A. W. would be well pleased with an opportunity of vindicating both his publications at the same time, and he will wait ten days for this* Friend to America's *Remarks upon the* Examination into the Conduct of the Delegates, *which he supposes will be full time enough for so very accomplished a writer to* ridicule *all the* wit *contained in it. A. W. begs the author of the* Vindication *to consult Johnson's Dictionary, and see whether the expression, 'and his* wit *ridiculed,' be classical or not. He is persuaded that had the* Vindicator *possessed the least spark of genuine* wit, *he would have felt both the impropriety of the expression, and the impracticability of the attempt.* Dec. 16, 1774."

Although Seabury wrote the pamphlet on November 28, 1774, and added the postscript on December 16, 1774, the publication of the pamphlet was not announced until December 22, 1774 (*Rivington's New-York Gazetteer*, December 22, 1774). It probably first appeared sometime between December 16 and December 22, 1774.

2. The expression "and his wit ridiculed," referred to in the "Farmer's" postscript and here, was used by H in the title of the *Full Vindication*. The phrase in which it appeared read: "Whereby His Sophistry is exposed, his Cavils confuted, his Artifices detected, and his Wit ridiculed."

Matricula of King's College [1]

[New York, 1774]

ADMISSIONS ANNO 1774.

David Clarkson.

Schuyler Lupton.

Jacob Shaw.

John Gaine.

John Whitaker. Left College 2d. Year.

Samuel Deall.

Horatio Smith.

Paul Randall.

John Brickell.

Daniel Moore.

Edward Cornwallis Moncrieffe. Left College 2d. Year.

James Stiles. Left the College in His 2d. Year.

James Depeyster.

Tristrim Lowther

Thomas Attwood.

Alexander Hamilton.

Nicholas Romeyn, S. M. [2]

D, Columbia University Libraries. This document is on page 18 of a manuscript volume entitled "The Matricula or Register of Admissions & of Graduations & of Officers employed in King's College at New-York."

1. Although this document is not an H document, it is printed here because it is the only extant MS record of H as a student at King's College.

This document unfortunately does not answer the question of when H actually attended King's College. According to Hercules Mulligan, H entered King's College "in the spring of 75 in the Sophomore Class" ("Narrative of Hercules Mulligan of the City of New York," Hamilton Papers, Library of Congress). Robert Troup, on the other hand, recalled that he had become "acquainted with the General in the year 1773 at Kings, now Columbia College, in New York, where I was a student. . . . When the General entered College, he did it as a private student, and not by annexing himself to a particular class" (Robert Troup to John Mason, March 22, 1810, Hamilton Papers, Library of Congress). In referring to the class list on which H's name appears, Mitchell writes: "The list of this class and others . . . may have been written in the book at a later time, not when the class entered or graduated, which would make room for error. The official roster was carelessly kept; Hamilton was doubtless at King's 'as a private student,' as Troup said, in the academic year 1773–1774, and then formally entered, as per the Matricula, in 1774, perhaps 'in the Sophomore Class' as Mulligan remembered" (Mitchell, *Hamilton*, I, 55).

2. "S. M." is the abbreviation for student of medicine.

1775

The Farmer Refuted, &c.[1]

New-York [February 23,] 1775[2]

Sir,

I resume my pen, in reply to the curious epistle, you have been pleased to favour me with; and can assure you, that, notwithstanding, I am naturally of a grave and phlegmatic disposition, it has been the source of abundant merriment to me. The spirit that breathes throughout is so rancorous, illiberal and imperious: The argumenta-

The Farmer Refuted: or A more impartial and comprehensive View of the Dispute between Great-Britain and the Colonies, Intended as a Further Vindication of the Congress: In Answer to a Letter From A. W. Farmer, Intitled A View of the Controversy Between Great-Britain and her Colonies: Including a Mode of determining the present Disputes Finally and Effectually, &c. . . (New York, Printed by James Rivington, 1775).

1. *The Farmer Refuted* was a reply to Samuel Seabury's *View of the Controversy,* which in turn had been written in reply to H's *Full Vindication.* The full title of Seabury's pamphlet is *A View of the Controversy Between Great-Britain and her Colonies: Including a Mode of Determining their present Disputes, Finally and Effectually; and of Preventing All Future Contentions. In a Letter to the Author of A Full Vindication of the Measures of the Congress, from the Calumnies of their Enemies. . . . By A. W. Farmer, . . .* (New York, Printed by James Rivington, 1774). Seabury's *View of the Controversy* is dated December 24, 1774, but its publication was not announced until January 5, 1775.

2. On January 19, 1775, in *Rivington's New-York Gazetteer,* the first announcement of the proposed publication of *The Farmer Refuted* appeared. At that time it was to be called *A more impartial and comprehensive View of the Controversy Between Great Britain and the Colonies Being A further Vindication of the Measures of the Congress. . . .* On February 16, 1775, the same paper stated that in a few days *The Farmer Refuted or, A more comprehensive View of the Controversy. . .* will be published. Finally on February 23, 1775, the actual publication of this pamphlet was announced. *JCHW,* II, 37, dates the essay February 5, 1775, without documentation.

In the pamphlet, preceding the essay the following prologue is found:

"ADVERTISEMENT. THE WRITER of the ensuing sheets can, with truth, say more, than the generality of those, who either espouse, or oppose the claim of the BRITISH PARLIAMENT; which is, that HIS political opinions have been the result of mature deliberation and rational inquiry. They have not been influenced by prejudice, nor, by any interested, or ambitious motives: They are not the *spawn* of licentious clamours, or popular declamation; but the

tive part of it so puerile and fallacious: The misrepresentations of facts so palpable and flagrant: The criticisms so illiterate, trifling and absurd: The conceits so low, steril[3] and splenetic, that I will venture to pronounce it one of the most ludicrous performances, which has been exhibited to public view, during all the present controversy.

You have not even imposed the laborious task of pursuing you through a labyrinth of *subtilty*. You have not had ability sufficient, however violent your efforts, to try the *depths* of *sophistry;* but have barely skimmed along its *surface*.[4] I should, almost, deem the animadversions, I am going to make, unnecessary, were it not, that, without them, you might exult in a fancied victory, and arrogate to yourself imaginary trophies.

But while I pass this judgment, it is not my intention to detract from your real merit. Candour obliges me to acknowledge, that you possess every accomplishment of a polemical writer, which may serve to dazzle and mislead superficial and vulgar minds; a peremptory dictatorial air, a pert vivacity of expression, an inordinate passion for conceit, and a noble disdain of being fettered by the laws of truth. These, Sir, are important qualifications, and these all unite in you, in a very eminent degree. So that, though you may never expect the plaudit of the judicious and discerning, you may console yourself, with this assurance, that

---

genuine offspring of sober reason. To those, who are inclined to doubt HIS sincerity, HE begs leave to recommend a little more *Charity*. To those, who are possessed of greater candor, and who, yet, may be disposed to ask, how HE can be sure, that his opinions have not been influenced by prejudice? HE answers, because he remembers the time, when HE had strong prejudices, on the side, HE now opposes. His change of sentiment (HE firmly believes) proceeded from the superior force of the arguments, in favour of the American claims.

"Though HE is convinced, there are too many, whose judgments are led captive, by the most venal and despicable motives, yet HE does not presume to think every man, who differs with him, either fool, or knave. HE is sensible, there are men of parts and virtue, whose notions are entirely contrary to his. To imagine, there are not wise and good men, on both sides, must be the effect of a weak head, or a corrupt heart. HE earnestly entreats the candid attention of the judicious and well-meaning, and hopes, that what he has written may be read, with as much impartiality, and as sincere a regard to truth, as the importance of the controversy demands."

3. Changed to "sterile" in "ERRATA in the FARMER REFUTED," *Rivington's New-York Gazetteer*, March 16, 1775.

4. Seabury had written: "You had no remedy but *artifice, sophistry, misrepresentation and abuse*" (Seabury, *A View of the Controversy*, 4).

Fools and witlings "will" ev'ry sentence raise,
And wonder, with a foolish face of praise.

You will, no doubt, be pleased, with this further concession, to wit, that there is a striking resemblance between yourself and the renowned hero of the *Dunciad*. "*Pert dulness*" seems to be the chief characteristic of your genius as well as his. I might point out a variety of circumstances, in which you both agree; but I shall content myself with having given the hint, and leave it to yourself and to your *other* * admirers to prosecute a comparison, which will reflect so high lustre on the object of admiration.

Having thus, briefly, delivered my sentiments of your performance in general, I shall proceed to a particular examination of it, so far, as may be requisite, towards placing it in that just point of light in which it ought to stand. I flatter myself, I shall find no difficulty in obviating the objections you have produced, against the Full Vindication; and in shewing, that your View of the Controversy between Great-Britain and the Colonies, is not only partial and unjust, but diametrically opposite to the first principles of civil society. In doing this, I may, occasionally, interweave some strictures on the Congress Canvassed.[6]

First, then, I observe, you endeavour to bring the imputation of inconsistency upon me, for writing "a long and elaborate pamphlet to justify decisions against whose influence none but *impotent* attempts had been made." A little attention would have unfolded the

* If we may judge from the style and turn of thought, you were pleased to be your own admirer in the *card in reply*.[5]

5. "A Card in Reply," to which H refers, appeared in *Rivington's New-York Gazetteer*, December 29, 1774, and reads as follows:
"A Warm Admirer of A. W. Farmer, presents his compliments to Mr. Vindicator, and begs leave to observe to him, that if *he* thinks it 'no easy task to prove' the *impropriety* of the expression, 'and his wit ridiculed' to be *improper*, he is very sorry that *he* has no more *feeling*. He thinks it would have been best for the Vindicator to have taken the hint from the Farmer, and to have corrected the expression in the next edition of his Vindication. If there was no *wit* in Free-Thoughts, why did he attempt to ridicule what was not there? If there was only *false* or *spurious* wit, why did he not call it so? If the Vindicator has not *taste* enough to perceive the impropriety, I dare say he will have the Farmers free permission to blunder on to the end of the chapter; and in conjunction with the Grand Congress, *to ridicule wit, kill* sheep *sparingly*, and *encrease* their *number*, and *improve* their *breed* by keeping *weathers* [i.e., wethers], till their want of wit and common sense renders them ridiculous to the whole continent."
6. See "A Card," December 22, 1774, note 1.

whole mystery. The reason assigned, for what I did, was, "lest those attempts," impotent as they were in a general sense, "might, yet, have a tendency to mislead and prejudice the minds of a few." To prevent this, I wrote; and if I have been instrumental in preserving a single person, from the baneful effects of your insidious efforts, I shall not regret the time I have devoted to that laudable purpose. To confirm, or to add one friend to his country, would afford a more refined and permanent satisfaction to me, than could, possibly, animate the breast of the proudest ministerial minion, though elevated to the pinnacle of his wished-for preferment, and basking in the sunshine of court favour, as the despicable wages of his prostitution and servility.

You tell me, "I knew that at the bar of impartial reason and common sense, the conduct of the Congress must be condemned; but was too much interested, too deeply engaged, in party-views and party-heats, to bear this with patience. *I* had no remedy (you say) but *artifice, sophistry, misrepresentation, and abuse.* These (you call) my weapons, and these I wield, like an old experienced practitioner."

You ask, "Is this too heavy a charge? Can you lay your hand upon your heart, and, upon your honour, plead not guilty?" Yes, Sir, I can do more. I can make a solemn appeal to the tribunal of Heaven, for the rectitude of my intentions. I can affirm, with the most scrupulous regard to truth, that I am of opinion, the conduct of the Congress will bear the most impartial scrutiny, that I am not interested, more, than as the felicity and prosperity of this vast continent are concerned, and that I am perfectly disengaged from party of every kind.

Here, I expect, you will exclaim with your usual vehemence and indecency; you are now espousing the cause of a party! It is the most daring impudence and falshood to assert the contrary! I can, by no means, conceive, that an opposition to a small herd of mal-contents, among whom, you have thought proper to rank, and a zealous attachment to the general measures of America can be denominated the effect of a party spirit. You, Sir, and your adherents may be justly deemed a faction, because you compose a small number inimical to the common voice of your country. To determine the truth of this affirmation, it is necessary to take a comprehensive view of all the colonies.

Th[r]oughout your letter, you seem to consider me, as a person, who has acted, and is still acting some part in the formation and execution of public measures. You tacitly represent me as a Delegate, or member of the Committee. Whether this be done with a design to create a suspicion of my sincerity, or whether it be really your opinion, I know not. Perhaps it is from a complex motive. But I can assure you, if you are in earnest, that you are entirely mistaken. I have taken no other part in the affair, than that of defending the proceedings of the Congress, in conversation, and by the pamphlet I lately published.[7] I approved of them, and thought an undeviating compliance with them essential to the preservation of American freedom. I shall, therefore, strenuously exert myself for the promotion of that valuable end.

In the field of literary contention, it is common to see the epithets *artifice, sophistry, misrepresentation* and *abuse,* mutually bandied about. Whether they are more justly applicable to you, or me, the public must decide. With respect to abuse, I make not the least doubt, but every reader will allow you to surpass me in that.

Your envenomed pen has endeavoured to sully the characters of our continental representatives, with the presumptuous charges of ignorance, knavery, sedition, rebellion, treason and tyranny; a tremendous catalogue indeed! Nor have you treated their friends and adherents, with any greater degree of complaisance. You have also delineated the mercantile body, as entirely devoid of principle; and the several committees as bands of robbers and petty tyrants. In short, except the few who are of your own complexion and stamp, "the *virtuous* friends of order and good government," you have not hesitated to exercise your obloquy and malevolence against the whole continent.

These things being considered, it is manifest, that, in my answer to your Free Thoughts, I treated you with more lenity than you had a right to expect; and did, by no means, observe the strict law of retaliation. None, but yourself, will think, you can, with the least propriety, complain of abuse.

7. This statement should be contrasted with the assertion of most H biographers that he wrote for *The New-York Journal, or General Advertiser,* generally known as Holt's *Journal,* before the publication of his *Full Vindication.* This claim is based on a statement by Robert Troup (Robert Troup to John Mason, March 22, 1810, Hamilton Papers, Library of Congress), but it has never been substantiated.

I congratulate myself upon the sentiments, you entertain of my last performance. Such is my opinion of your abilities as a critic, that I very much prefer your disapprobation to your applause. But, with respect to the *brilliancy* of thought you speak of,[8] give me leave to inform you, that I aimed at nothing more, than justness of thought. I addressed myself to the judgment, not to the imagination. In works, where fancy is predominant, as is the case with yours, there is a better opportunity for displaying brilliancy of thought, than where reason presides and directs. No wonder, then, if you have excelled me in this particular; since your plan is so much more favourable to it, than mine.

I shall, for the present, pass over to that part of your pamphlet, in which you endeavour to establish the supremacy of the British Parliament over America. After a proper eclaircissement of this point, I shall draw such inferences, as will sap the foundation of every thing you have offered.

The first thing that presents itself is a wish, that "*I* had, explicitly, declared to the public my ideas of the *natural rights* of mankind. Man, in a state of nature (you say) may be considered, as perfectly free from all restraints of *law* and *government*, and, then, the weak must submit to the strong."

I shall, henceforth, begin to make some allowance for that enmity, you have discovered to the *natural rights* of mankind. For, though ignorance of them in this enlightened age cannot be admitted, as a sufficient excuse for you; yet, it ought, in some measure, to extenuate your guilt. If you will follow my advice, there still may be hopes of your reformation. Apply yourself, without delay, to the study of the law of nature. I would recommend to your perusal, Grotius Puffendorf, Locke, Montesquieu, and Burlemaqui.[9] I might mention other excellent writers on this subject; but if you attend, diligently, to these, you will not require any others.

There is so strong a similitude between your political principles and those maintained by Mr. Hobbs,[10] that, in judging from them,

---

8. "If you seldom *sink* into meaness of diction," the "Farmer" had written, "you never *soar* into that *brilliancy* of thought; nor, even with the help of Johnson's Dictionary, into that *classical elegance* of expression which is absolutely necessary for the arduous attempt of *ridiculing wit*." See Seabury, *A View of the Controversy*, 4.

9. "Burlamoqui," in "Errata."   10. "Hobbes," in "Errata."

a person might very easily *mistake* you for a disciple of his. His opinion was, exactly, coincident with yours, relative to man, in a state of nature. He held, as you do, that he was, then, perfectly free from all restraint of *law* and *government*. Moral obligation, according to him, is derived from the introduction of civil society; and there is no virtue, but what is purely artificial, the mere contrivance of politicians, for the maintenance of social intercourse. But the reason he run into this absurd and impious doctrine, was, that he disbelieved the existence of an intelligent superintending principle, who is the governor, and will be the final judge of the universe.

As you, sometimes, swear *by him that made you*, I conclude, your sentiment does not correspond with his, in that which is the basis of the doctrine, you both agree in; and this makes it impossible to imagine whence this congruity between you arises. To grant, that there is a supreme intelligence, who rules the world, and has established laws to regulate the actions of his creatures; and, still, to assert, that man, in a state of nature, may be considered as perfectly free from all restraints of *law* and *government*, appear to a common understanding, altogether irreconcileable.

Good and wise men, in all ages, have embraced a very dissimilar theory. They have supposed, that the deity, from the relations, we stand in, to himself and to each other, has constituted an eternal and immutable law, which is, indispensibly, obligatory upon all mankind, prior to any human institution whatever.

This is what is called the law of nature, "which, being coeval with mankind, and dictated by God himself, is, of course, superior in obligation to any other. It is binding over all the globe, in all countries, and at all times. No human laws are of any validity, if contrary to this; and such of them as are valid, derive all their authority, mediately, or immediately, from this original." BLACKSTONE.[11]

Upon this law, depend the natural rights of mankind, the supreme being gave existence to man, together with the means of preserving and beatifying that existence. He endowed him with rational facul-

11. The quotation is from Blackstone's *Commentaries*, "Introduction," Section II ("*Of the* Nature *of* Laws *in general*"), p. 41. H probably used the American printing of Blackstone which appeared in 1771 (William Blackstone, *Commentaries on the Laws of England*, 4 vols. [Philadelphia, Robert Bell, 1771]). But since the pagination of all editions of Blackstone follow that of the original, H may have used any edition that appeared before 1775.

ties, by the help of which, to discern and pursue such things, as were consistent with his duty and interest, and invested him with an inviolable right to personal liberty, and personal safety.

Hence, in a state of nature, no man had any *moral* power to deprive another of his life, limbs, property or liberty; nor the least authority to command, or exact obedience from him; except that which arose from the ties of consanguinity.

Hence also, the origin of all civil government, justly established, must be a voluntary compact, between the rulers and the ruled; and must be liable to such limitations, as are necessary for the security of the *absolute rights* of the latter; for what original title can any man or set of men have, to govern others, except their own consent? To usurp dominion over a people, in their own despite, or to grasp at a more extensive power than they are willing to entrust, is to violate that law of nature, which gives every man a right to his personal liberty; and can, therefore, confer no obligation to obedience.

"The principal aim of society is to protect individuals, in the enjoyment of those absolute rights, which were vested in them by the immutable laws of nature; but which could not be preserved, in peace, without that mutual assistance, and intercourse, which is gained by the institution of friendly and social communities. Hence it follows, that the first and primary end of human laws, is to maintain and regulate these *absolute rights* of individuals." BLACKSTONE.[12]

If we examine the pretensions of parliament, by this criterion, which is evidently, a good one, we shall, presently detect their injustice. First, they are subversive of our natural liberty, because an authority is assumed over us, which we by no means assent to. And secondly, they divest us of that moral security, for our lives and properties, which we are intitled to, and which it is the primary end of society to bestow. For such security can never exist, while we have no part in making the laws, that are to bind us; and while it may be the interest of our uncontroled legislators to oppress us as much as possible.

To deny these principles will be not less absurd, than to deny the

12. The quotation is from Blackstone's *Commentaries*, Book I ("*Of the* Rights *of* Persons"), Ch. I ("*Of the absolute* Rights *of* Individuals"), p. 124.

plainest axioms: I shall not, therefore, attempt any further illustration of them.

You say, "when I assert, that since Americans have not, by any act of theirs, impowered the British parliament to make laws for them, it follows they can have no just authority to do it, I advance a position subversive of that dependence, which all colonies must, from their very nature, have on the mother country." The premises from which I drew this conclusion, are indisputable. You have not detected any fallacy in them; but endeavor to overthrow them by deducing a false and imaginary consequence. My principles admit the only dependence which can subsist, consistent with any idea of civil liberty, or with the future welfare of the British empire, as will appear hereafter.

"The dependence of the colonies, on the mother country," (you assert) "has ever been acknowledged. It is an impropriety of speech, to talk of an independent colony: The words independent and colony, convey contradictory ideas, much like *killing* and *sparing*.* As soon as a colony becomes independent on the parent state, it ceases to be any longer a colony, just as when you *kill* a sheep, you cease to *spare* him."

In what sense, the dependance of the colonies on the mother country, has been acknowledged, will appear from those circumstances of their political history, which I shall, by and by, recite. The term colony signifies nothing more, than a body of people drawn from the mother country, to inhabit some distant place, or the country it self so inhabited. As to the degrees and modifications of that subordination, which is due to the parent state, these must depend upon other things, besides the mere act of emigration, to inhabit or settle a distant country. These must be ascertained, by

* I find Sir, you take a particular delight in persisting in absurdity: But if you are not totally incorrigible, the following interpretation of the unfortunate *adverb* will secure it from any future stripes. It is taken from Johnson's Dictionary: SPARINGLY, not abundantly, *Bacon;* 2, frugally, parsimoniously; not lavishly, *Hayward,* with abstinence, *Atterbury;* cautiously, tenderly. Substitute *frugally* or *not lavishly,* for *sparingly,* and you must blush at your own conceit. "Kill your sheep *frugally* or *not lavishly,*" Where is the impropriety of this? [13]

13. See H's *Full Vindication* in which he parodies the "Farmer" by inventing puns on the word "sparingly."

the spirit of the constitution of the mother country, by the compacts for the purpose of colonizing, and, more especially, by the law of nature, and that *supreme law* of every society—*its own happiness*.

The idea of colony does not involve the idea of slavery. There is a wide difference, between the dependence of a free people, and the submission of slaves. The former I allow, the latter I reject with disdain. Nor does the notion of a colony imply any subordination to our fellow subjects, in the parent state, while there is one common sovereign established. The dependence of the colonies, on Great-Britain, is an ambiguous and equivocal phrase. It may, either mean dependence on the people of Great-Britain, or on the King. In the former sense, it is absurd and unaccountable: In the latter it is just and rational. No person will affirm, that a French colony is independent, on the parent state, though it acknowledge the King of France as rightful sovereign. Nor can it, with any greater propriety, be said, that an English colony is independent, while it bears allegiance to the King of Great-Britain. The difference, between their dependence, is only that which distinguishes civil liberty from slavery; and results from the different genius of the French and English constitution.

But you deny, that "we can be liege subjects to the King of Great-Britain, while we disavow the authority of parliament." You endeavour to prove it thus,* "The King of Great Britain was placed on the throne, by virtue of an act of parliament; and he is King of America, by virtue of being King of Great-Britain. He is therefore King of America by act of parliament: And, if we disclaim that authority of Parliament, which made him our King, we, in fact, reject him from being our King; for we disclaim that authority, by which he is King at all."

Admitting, that the King of Great Britain was enthroned by virtue of an act of parliament, and that he is King of America, because he is King of Great-Britain, yet the act of parliament is not the *efficient cause* of his being the King of America: It is only the *occasion* of it. He is King of America, by virtue of a compact between us and the Kings of Great-Britain. These colonies were planted and settled by the Grants, and under the Protection of English Kings,

* Vide Congress Canvassed.

who entered into covenants with us for themselves, their heirs and successors; and it is from these covenants, that the duty of protection on their part, and the duty of allegiance on ours arise.

So that, to disclaim, the authority of a British Parliament over us, does by no means imply the dereliction of our allegiance to British Monarchs. Our compact takes no cognizance of the manner of their accession to the throne. It is sufficient for us, that they are Kings of England.

The most valid reasons can be assigned for our allegiance to the King of Great-Britain; but not one of the least force or plausibility for our subjection to parliamentary decrees.

We hold our lands in America by virtue of charters from British Monarchs; and are under no obligations to the lords or commons for them: Our title is similar and equal to that, by which they possess their lands; and the King is the legal fountain of both: this is one grand source of our obligation to allegiance.

Another, and the principal source is, that protection which we have hitherto enjoyed from the Kings of Great-Britain. Nothing is more common than to hear the votaries of parliament urge the protection we have received from the mother country, as an argument for submission to its claims. But they entertain erroneous conceptions of the matter; the King himself, being the supreme executive magistrate, is regarded by the constitution, as the supreme protector of the empire. For this purpose, he is the generalissimo, or first in military command; in him is vested the power of making war and peace, of raising armies, equipping fleets and directing all their motions. He it is that has defended us from our enemies, and to him alone, we are obliged to render allegiance and submission.

The law of nature and the British constitution both confine allegiance to the person of the King; and found it upon the principle of protection. We may see the subject discussed at large in the case of Calvin: The definition given of it by the learned Coke, is this, "Legiance is the mutual bond and obligation between the King and his subjects, whereby subjects are called his liege subjects, because they are bound to obey and serve him; and he is called their liege lord, because he is bound to maintain and defend them." [14] Hence

14. *Calvin's Case*, 7 Coke's *King Bench Reports*, 5.

it is evident, that while we enjoy the protection of the King, it is incumbent upon us to obey and serve him, without the interposition of parliamentary supremacy.

The right of parliament to legislate for us cannot be accounted for upon any reasonable grounds. The constitution of Great Britain is very properly called a limitted monarchy, the people having reserved to themselves a share in the legislature, as a check upon the regal authority, to prevent its degenerating into despotism and tyranny. The very aim and intention of the democratical part, or the house of commons, is to secure the rights of the people. Its very being depends upon those rights. Its whole power is derived from them, and must be terminated by them.

It is the unalienable birth-right of every Englishman, who can be considered as *a free agent* to participate in framing the laws which are to bind him, either as to his life or property. But, as many inconveniences would result from the exercise of this right, in person, it is appointed by the constitution, that he shall delegate it to another. Hence he is to give his vote in the election of some person he chuses to confide in as his representative. This right no power on earth can divest him of. It was enjoyed by his ancestors time immemorial; recognized and established by Magna Charta, and is essential to the existence of the constitution. Abolish this privilege, and the house of commons is annihilated.

But what was the use and design of this privilege? To secure his life and property from the attacks of exorbitant power. And in what manner is this done? By giving him the election of those, who are to have the disposal and regulation of them, and whose interest is in every respect connected with his.

The representative in this case is bound by every possible tie to consult the advantage of his constituent. Gratitude for the high and honourable trust reposed in him demands a return of attention and regard to the advancement of his happiness. Self-interest, that most powerful incentive of human actions, points and attracts towards the same object.

The duration of his trust is not perpetual; but must expire in a few years, and if he is desirous of the future favour of his constituents, he must not abuse the present instance of it; but must pursue the end, for which he enjoys it; otherwise he forfeits it, and defeats his own purpose. Besides, if he consent to any laws hurtful to his constituent, he is bound by the same, and must partake in the disadvantage of them. His friends, relations, children, all whose ease and comfort are dear to him, will be in a like predicament. And should he concur in any flagrant acts of injustice or oppression, he will be within the reach of popular vengeance, and this will restrain him within due bounds.

To crown the whole, at the expiration of a few years, if their representatives have abused their trust, the people have it in their power to change them, and to elect others, who may be more faithful and more attached to their interest.

These securities, the most powerful that human affairs will admit of, have the people of Britain, for the good deportment of their representatives towards them. They may have proved, at some times, and on some occasions, defective; but, upon the whole, they have been found sufficient.

When we ascribe to the British house of commons a jurisdiction over the colonies, the scene is entirely reversed. All these kinds of security immediately disappear; no ties of gratitude or interest remain. Interest, indeed, may operate to our prejudice. To oppress us may serve as a recommendation to their constituents, as well as an alleviation of their own incumbrances. The British patriots may, in time, be heard to court the gale of popular favour, by boasting their exploits in laying some new impositions on their American vassals, and, by that means, lessening the burthens of their freinds [15] and fellow subjects.

But what merits still more serious atention [16] is this. There seems to be, already, a jealousy of our dawning splendour. It is looked upon as portentous of aproaching [17] independence. This we have reason to believe is one of the principal incitements to the present rigorous and unconstitutional proceedings against us. And though it may have chiefly originated in the calumnies of designing men, yet it does not entirely depend upon adventitious or partial causes; but is also founded in the circumstances of our country and situation. The boundless extent of territory we possess, the wholesome temperament of our climate, the luxuriance and fertility of our soil,

15. "friends," in "Errata."   16. "attention," in "Errata."
17. "approaching," in "Errata."

the variety of our products, the rapidity of our population, the industry of our country men and the commodiousness of our ports, naturally lead to a suspicion of independence, and would always have an influence pernicious to us. Jealousy is a predominant passion of human nature, and is a source of the greatest evils. Whenever it takes place between rulers and their subjects, it proves the bane of civil society.

The experience of past ages may inform us, that when the circumstances of a people render them distressed,[18] their rulers generally recur to severe, cruel and oppressive measures. Instead of endeavouring to establish their authority in the *affection* of their subjects, they think they have no security but in their *fear*. They do not aim at gaining their fidelity and obedience, by making them flourishing, prosperous and happy; but by rendering them abject and dispirited. They think it necessary to intimidate and awe them, to make every accession to their own power, and to impair the people's as much as possible.

One great engine, to effect this in America, would be a large standing army, maintained out of our own pockets to be at the devotion of our oppressors. This would be introduced under pretence of defending us; but in fact to make our bondage and misery complete.

We might soon expect the martial law, universally prevalent to the abolition of trials by juries, the *Habeas Corpus* act, and every other bulwark of personal safety, in order to overawe the honest assertors of their country's cause. A numerous train of *court dependents* would be created and supported at our expence. The value of all our possessions, by a complication of extorsive methods, would be gradually depreciated, till it became a mere shadow.

This will be called too high-wrought a picture, a phantom of my own deluded imagination. The highest eulogies will be lavished on the wisdom and justice of the British nation. But deplorable is the condition of that people who have nothing else than the wisdom and justice of another to depend upon.

"Political writers (say a celebrated author *) have established it

---

* HUME, Vol. I. ESSAY 5th.[19]

18. "distrusted," in "Errata."

19. The quotation is found in Essay VIII ("Of the Independency of Parliament"). See David Hume, *Essays and Treatises on Several Subjects* (Fourth

as a maxim, that, in contriving any system of government, and fixing the several checks and controuls of the constitution, *every man ought to be supposed a knave;* and to have no other end in all his actions, but *private interest.* By this interest, we must govern him, and by means of it, *make him co-operate to public good,* notwithstanding his insatiable avarice and ambition. Without this, we shall in vain boast of the advantages of *any constitution,* and shall find in the end, that we have no security for our liberties and possessions, except the *good will* of our rulers; that is, we should have *no security at all.*

"It is therefore a just *political* maxim, that *every man must be supposed a knave.* Though, at the same time, it appears somewhat strange, that a maxim should be true in politics, which is false in fact. But to satisfy us on this head, we may consider, that men are generally more honest in a private than in a public capacity; and will go greater lengths to serve a party, than when their own private interest is alone concerned. Honour is a great check upon mankind. But, where a considerable body of men act together, this check is in a great measure removed; since a man is sure to be approved by his own party, for what promotes the common interest, and he soon learns to despise the clamours of adversaries. To this we may add that every court, or senate is determined by the greater number of voices; so that if self-interest influences only the majority, (as it will always do) the whole senate follows the allurements of this separate interest, and acts as if it contained not one member, who had any regard to public interest and liberty." What additional force do these observations acquire, when applied to the dominion of one community over another!

From what has been said, it is plain, that we are without those checks, upon the representatives of Great-Britain, which alone can make them answer the end of their appointment, with respect to us; which is the preservation of the rights, and the advancement of the happiness of the governed. The direct and inevitable consequence is, *they have no right to govern us.*

Let us examine it in another light. The house of Commons re-

Edition, London, Printed for A. Millar, in the Strand; and A. Kincaid and A. Donaldson, in Edinburgh, 1753), I, 64–65. There are numerous editions of Hume; in the edition H used this probably was Essay V.

ceives all its authority from its electors, in consequence of the right they have to a share in the legislature: Its electors are freeholders, citizens and others in Great-Britain. It follows therefore, that all its authority is confined to Great-Britain. This is demonstrative. Sophistry, by an artful play of ambiguous terms, may perplex and obscure it; but reason can never confute it. The power, which one society bestows upon any man or body of men, can never extend beyond its own limits. The people of Great-Britain may confer an authority over themselves; but they can never confer any over the people of America. Because, it is impossible for them to give *that* to another, which they never possessed themselves. Now, I should be glad to see an attempt to prove, that a freeholder, citizen, or any other man in Great-Britain has any inherent right to the life, property, or liberty of a freeholder, citizen, or any other man in America. He can have no original and intrinsic right, because nature has distributed an equality of rights to every man: He can have no secondary, or derivative right, because the only thing which could give him that is wanting, the consent of the natural proprietor. It *is* incumbent upon you to demonstrate the existence of such a right, or any thing else you may produce will be of little avail. I do not expect you will be discouraged at the apparent difficulty. It is the peculiar province of an enterprizing genius to surmount the greatest obstacles, and you have discovered an admirable dexterity in this way. You have put to flight some of my best arguments, with no greater pains, than a few positive assertions, and as many paltry witticisms, and you become altogether irresistible by adding with a proper degree of confidence, *you know the case to be as I state it.*

When I say, that the authority of parliament is confined to Great-Britain, I speak of it, in its primitive and original state. Parliament may acquire an incidental influence over others; but this must be by their own free consent. For without this, any power it might exercise, would be mere usurpation, and by no means a just authority.

The best way of determining disputes, and of investigating truth, is by descending [20] to elementary principles. Any other method may only bewilder and misguide the understanding; but this will soon lead to a convincing and satisfactory crisis. By observing this method, we shall learn the following truths.

20. "ascending," in "Errata."

That the existence of the house of commons depends upon the people's right to a share in the legislature; which is exercised, by means of electing the members of that house. That the end and intention of this right is, to preserve the life, property and liberty of the subject, from the encroachments of oppression and tyranny.

That this end is accomplished, by means of the *intimate connexion* of interest, between those members and their constituents, the people of Great-Britain.

That with respect to the people of America, there is no such *intimate connexion* of interest; but the contrary. And therefore that end could not be answered to them; consequently the *end* ceasing, the *means* must cease also.

That the house of commons derives all its power, from its own real constituents, who are the people of Great-Britain, and that therefore, it has no power, but what they *originally* had in themselves.

That they had no original right to the life, property, or liberty of Americans; nor any acquired from their own consent, and of course could give no authority over them.

That, therefore, the house of commons has no such authority.

What need is there of a multiplicity of arguments, or a long chain of reasoning to inculcate these luminous principles? They speak the plainest language to every man of common sense; and must carry conviction where the mental eye is not bedimmed, by the mist of prejudice, partiality, ambition, or avarice. Let us now see what has been offered in opposition to them.

But, by the way, let me remark, that I have levelled my battery chiefly against the authority, of the house of commons, over America; because, if that be proved not to exist, the dispute is at an end. The efficacy of acts of parliament depends, upon the due authority of the respective branches, to bind the different orders and ranks of the nation.

It is said, that "in every government, there must be a supreme absolute authority lodged some where. In arbitrary governments, this power is in the monarch. In aristocratical governments, in the nobles. In democratical, in the people, or the deputies of their electing. Our own government being a mixture of all these kinds, the supreme authority is vested in the king, nobles and people; i.e. the king, house of lords and house of commons, *elected by the people*.

This supreme authority extends as far as the British dominions extend. To suppose a part of the British dominions which is not subject to the power of the British legislature, is no better sense, than to suppose a country, at one and the same time, to be and not to be a part of the British dominions. If therefore the colony of New-York is a part of the British dominions, the colony of New-York is subject, and dependent on the supreme legislative authority of Great-Britain."

This argument is the most specious of any, the advocates for parliamentary supremacy are able to produce; but, when we come to anatomize, and closely examine every part of it, we shall discover, that it is entirely composed of distorted and misapplied principles, together with ambiguous and equivocal terms.

The first branch is, that "in every government, there must be a supreme absolute authority lodged somewhere." This position when properly explained, is evidently just. In every civil society there must be a supreme power, to which all the members of that society are subject; for, otherwise, there could be no supremacy, or subordination, that is no government at all. But no use can be made of this principle beyond matter of fact. To infer from thence, that, unless a supreme absolute authority, be vested in one part of an empire, over all the other parts, there can be no government in the whole, is false and absurd. Each branch may enjoy a distinct compleat legislature, and still good government may be preserved, every where. It is in vain to assert, that two or more distinct legislatures cannot exist in the same state. If, by the same state, be meant the same individual community, it is true. Thus, for instance, there cannot be two supreme legislatures in Great-Britain, or two in New-York. But, if, by the same state, be understood a number of individual societies, or bodies politic, united under one common head, then, I maintain, that there may be one distinct compleat legislature in each: Thus there may be one in Great-Britain, another in Ireland, and another in New-York, and still these several parts may form but one state. In order to this, there must indeed be some connecting, pervading principle; but this is found in the person and prerogative of the King. He it is that conjoins all these individual societies, into one great body politic. He it is, that is to preserve their mutual connexion and dependence, and make them all co-operate to one common end the general good. His power is equal to the purpose, and his interest binds him to the due prosecution of it.

Those, who aver, that the independency of America on the British Parliament implies two Sovereign authorities in the same state, deceive themselves or wish to deceive others in two ways; by confounding the idea of the same state with that of the same individual society, and by losing sight of that share which the King has in the sovereignty, both of Great-Britain and America. Perhaps, indeed, it may with propriety be said, that the King is the only Sovereign of the empire. The part which the people have in the legislature, may more justly be considered as a limitation of the Sovereign authority, to prevent its being exercised in an oppressive and despotic manner: Monarchy is universally allowed to predominate in the constitution. In this view, there is not the least absurdity in the supposition that Americans have a right to a limitation similar to that of the people of Great-Britain. At any rate, there can never be said to be two sovereign powers, in the same state; while *one common king* is acknowledged, by every member of it.

Let us, for a moment, imagine the legislature of New-York independent on that of Great-Britain, where would be the mighty inconvenience! How would government be frustrated, or obstructed, by this means? In what manner, would they interfere with each other? In none that I can perceive. The affairs of government might be conducted with the greatest harmony, and, by the mediation of the King, directed to the same end. He (as I before observed) will be the great connecting principle. The several parts of the empire, though, otherwise, independent on each other, will all be dependent on him. He must guide the vast and complicated machine of government, to the reciprocal advantage of all his dominions. There is not the least contradiction in this, no *imperium* in *imperio*, as is maintained; for the power of every distinct branch will be limited to itself, and the authority of his Majesty over the whole, will, like a central force, attract them all to the same point.

The second part of your paragraph is this, "In arbitrary governments, this (supreme absolute) power is in the monarch; in aristocratical governments, in the nobles; in democratical, in the people, or the deputies of their electing. Our own government, being a mixture of all these kinds, the supreme authority is vested in the King,

Nobles, and People, that is, in the King, House of Lords, and House of Commons, elected by the people."

You are mistaken, when you confine arbitrary government to a monarchy. It is not the supreme power being placed in one, instead of many, that discriminates an arbitrary from a free government. When any people are ruled by laws, in framing which, they have no part, that are to bind them, to all intents and purposes, without, in the same manner, binding the legislators themselves, they are in the strictest sense slaves, and the government with respect to them, is despotic. Great-Britain is itself a free country; but it is only so because its inhabitants have a share in the legislature: If they were once divested of that, they would cease to be free. So that, if its jurisdiction be extended over other countries that have no actual share in its legislature, it becomes arbitary to them; because they are destitute of those checks and controuls which constitute that *moral* security which is the very essence of civil liberty.

I will go farther, and assert, that the authority of the British Parliament over America, would, in all probability, be a more intolerable and excessive species of despotism than an absolute monarchy.* The power of an absolute prince is not temporary, but perpetual. He is under no temptation to purchase the favour of one part of his dominions, at the expence of another; but, it is his interest to treat them all, upon the same footing. Very different is the case with regard to the Parliament: The Lords and Commons both, have a private and separate interest to pursue. They must be, wonderfully, disinterested, if they would not make us bear a very disproportional part of the public burthens, to avoid them as much as possible themselves. The people of Britain must, *in reality*, be an order of superior

---

* Mr. Hume, in enumerating those political maxims, which will be eternally true, speaks thus: "It may easily be observed, that though free governments have been commonly the most happy, for those who partake of their freedom, yet are they the most ruinous and oppressive to *their provinces*." He goes on to give many solid reasons for this, and among other things, observes, that "a free state necessarily makes a great distinction (between herself and the provinces) and must continue to do so, 'till men learn to love their neighbours as well as themselves." He confirms his reflections by many historical facts and concludes them thus: "Compare the *pais conquis* of France with Ireland, and you will be convinced of this truth; though this latter kingdom being in a good measure peopled from England, possesses so many rights and privileges, as should naturally make it challenge better treatment." [21]

21. This quotation is from Hume's Essay IV ("That Politics may be reduc'd to a Science"). See Hume, *Essays and Treatises on Several Subjects*, I, 25–28.

beings, not cast in the same mould, with the common degenerate race of mortals, if the sacrifice of our interest and ease to theirs be not, extremely, welcome and alluring. But should experience teach us, that they are only mere mortals, fonder of themselves than their neighbours, the philanthropy and integrity of their representatives will be of a transcendent and matchless nature, should they not gratify the natural propensities of their constituents, in order to ingratiate themselves, and enhance their popularity.

When you say, that "our government being a mixture of all these kinds, the supreme authority is vested in the King, Nobles, and *People*, that is, the King, House of Lords, and House of Commons, *elected by the people*," you speak unintelligibly. A person who had not read any more of your pamphlet, than this passage, would have concluded, you were speaking of our Governor, Council and Assembly, whom, by a rhetorical figure, you stiled King, Nobles and People. For how could it be imagined, you would call any government *our own*, with this description, that it is vested in the King, Nobles and *People*, in which, *our own people* have not the *least share?* If our own government be vested in the King, Nobles and People, how comes it to pass, that *our own* people have no part in it? The resolution of these questions will afford a proper field, in which, to display your ingenuity. You must endeavour to transmute the people of America into those of Great-Britain, or your description will be considered, as mere jargon, by every man of sense. Perhaps you may be able, in imitation of that celebrated sophist Spinosa, to prove, that they are only *modally* different, but *substantially* the same. Or if you please, that syllogism of the schools, by which, a *man* is proved a *horse*, may serve as an excellent model. If I recollect right it is in these words

> *Homo est* animal:
> *Equus est* animal,
> *Ergo, homo est equus.*

Which is rendered thus, a man is an *animal:* an horse is an *animal:* Therefore, a man is an horse. By the same method of argumentation, you may prove, that, as Britons and Americans are *generically* the same, they are *numerically* so, likewise, as your description implies. You may form a syllogism thus:

Britons are men:

Americans are the *same:*

Therefore Britains and Americans are the *same.*

This argument will be as good, as the one, I am next going to examine.

"This supreme authority (you say) extends as far as the *British* dominions extend. To suppose a part of the *British* dominions, which is not subject to the power of the British legislature, is no better sense, than to suppose a country, at one and the same time, to be and not to be a part of the *British* dominions. If, therefore, the colony of New-York be a part of the *British* dominions, the colony of New-York is subject and dependent on the supreme legislative authority of Great-Britain."

By "this supreme authority" I suppose you mean the Parliament of Great-Britain. I deny that it extends as far as the *British* dominions extend, and I have given many substantial reasons for this denial, whereas you have never offered any to prove that it does. You have begged the question, and taken that for granted, which is the very point in debate. As to your general position that there must be a supreme, absolute authority lodged somewhere, I have explained, in what sense, it ought to be understood; and shewn, that the several parts of the empire, may each enjoy a separate, independent legislature, with regard to each other, under one common head, the King.

The seeming proof you have subjoined is entirely fallacious; and depends upon the use of the terms *British* dominions, and *British* legislature, in an *equivocal* sense. The former may, either signify countries subject to the *King,* or to the *legislature* of Great-Britain. When we say French dominions, we mean countries subject to the King of France. In like manner, when we say British dominions, the most proper signification is, countries subject to the King of Great-Britain. At least there is no impropriety in using it, in this sense.*

If, by the British legislature, you mean nothing more, than the Parliament of Great-Britain, it is well; but if you affix a different idea to it, you are not *arbitrarily* to impose it upon others. If there

---

* Or if there is, all your objection amounts to this, that we have adopted an improper mode of expression, and for the future we may in the language of the honorable House of Assembly, call the Colonies his Majesty's American dominions.

be any *chimera* in your fond imagination, which you express by that term, you must allow others the liberty to think it such. In short, if by the term, you mean an authority resident in one part of his Majesty's dominions, to make laws for every other part of them; you ought not to apply it in this sense, 'till you have proved, that such an authority does really exist; especially in a controversy about that very matter.

By the British dominions, I mean the countries subject to his Britannic Majesty, in his royal capacity. By the British legislature, I will suppose you intend, simply the Parliament of Great-Britain. Let us now try whether "to suppose there may be a part of his British Majesty's dominions, which is not subject to the parliament, be no better sense, than to suppose a country, at one and the same time to be and not to be, a part of the British dominions." It is impossible for any thing *to be* and *not to be;* but it involves no contradictions [22] to say, that a country may be in subjection to his Britannic Majesty, and in that sense, a part of the British dominions, without being, at all, dependent on the parliament of Great-Britain.* The colony of New-York, therefore, may be a branch of the British Empire, though not subordinate to the legislative authority of Britain.

Upon the whole, if, by the British dominions, you mean territories subject to the Parliament, you adhere to your usual fallacy, and suppose what you are bound to prove. I deny, that we are dependent on the legislature of Great-Britain, and yet I maintain, that we are a part of the British Empire; but in this sense only, as being the free-born subjects of his Britannic Majesty.

Thus have I fully examined that argument, which is esteemed the bulwark of the doctrine of parliamentary supremacy; and I flatter myself, clearly refuted it. The main pillar being now broken down, the whole structure may easily be demolished. I shall therefore proceed with alacrity in the completion of the work. But it is worthy

---

* I doubt not, you will here be disposed to cavil, by urging, that if we deny the authority of parliament, we also reject his British Majesty; since he composes a part of it; but let it be considered, that the Parliament, as such, is a political institution, not a *physical* being. We may deny his Majesty, in his political capacity, as a part of the legislature of Great-Britain, and yet acknowledge him in a similar political capacity, as a part of the legislature of New-York. This is an obvious distinction, and cannot be contested without an affront to common sense.

22. "contradiction," in "Errata."

of observation, that a cause must be extremely weak, which admits of no better supports.

Your next argument (if it deserves the name) is this, "legislation is not an inherent right in the colonies; many colonies have been established and subsisted long without it. The Roman colonies had no legislative authority. It was not 'till the latter period of their republic, that the privileges of Roman citizens, among which, that of voting in Assemblies of the people, at Rome, was a principal one, were extended to the inhabitants of Italy. All the laws of the empire were enacted at Rome. Neither their colonies, nor conquered countries had any thing to do with legislation."

The fundamental source of all your errors, sophisms and false reasonings is a total ignorance of the natural rights of mankind. Were you once to become acquainted with these, you could never entertain a thought, that all men are not, by nature, entitled to a parity of privileges. You would be convinced, that natural liberty is a gift of the beneficent Creator to the whole human race, and that civil liberty is founded in that; and cannot be wrested from any people, without the most manifest violation of justice. *Civil liberty, is only natural liberty, modified and secured by the sanctions of civil society.* It is not a thing, in its own nature, precarious and dependent on human will and caprice; but is conformable to the constitution of man, as well as necessary to the *well-being* of society.

Upon this principle, colonists as well as other men, have a right to civil liberty: For, if it be conducive to the happiness of society (and reason and experience testify that it is) it is evident, that every society, of whatsoever kind, has an absolute and perfect right to it, which can never be with-held without cruelty and injustice. The practice * of Rome, towards her colonies, cannot afford the shadow of an argument against this. That mistress of the world was often unjust. And the treatment of her dependent provinces is one of the greatest blemishes in her history. Through the want of that civil liberty, for which we are now so warmly contending, they groaned under every species of wanton oppression. If we are wise, we shall

---

* If her practice proves any thing, it equally proves, that she had a right to plunder them, as much as possible. This doctrine, I presume, will not be disagreeable to some ears. There are many who would rejoice to see America plundered, in a like manner, provided they could be appointed the instruments.

take warning from thence; and consider a like state of dependence, as more to be dreaded, than pestilence and famine.

The right of colonists, therefore, to exercise a legislative power, is an inherent right. It is founded upon the right of all men to freedom and happiness. For civil liberty cannot possibly have any existence, where the society, for whom laws are made, have no share in making them; and where the interest of their legislators is not inseparably interwoven with theirs. Before you asserted, that the right of legislation was derived "from the indulgence or grant of the parent state," you should have proved two things, that all men have not a natural right to freedom, and that civil liberty is not advantageous to society.

"The position, (you say) that we are bound by no laws, but those, to which we have assented, either by ourselves, or by our representatives, is a novel position, unsupported by any authoritative record of the British constitution, ancient or modern. It is republican, in its very nature; and tends to the utter subversion of the English monarchy.

"This position has arisen from an artful change of terms. To say, that an Englishman is not bound by any laws, but those to which the representatives of the nation have given their consent, is to say what is true. But to say, that an Englishman is bound by no laws but those to which he hath consented, in person, or by *his* representative, is saying what never was true, and never can be true. A great part of the people have no vote in the choice of representatives, and, therefore, are governed by laws, to which, they never consented, either by themselves, or by *their* representatives."

The foundation of the English constitution rests upon this principle, that no laws have any validity, or binding force, without the consent and approbation of the *people*, given in the persons of *their* representatives, periodically elected by *themselves*. This constitutes the democratical part of the government.

It is also, undeniably, certain, that no Englishman, who can be deemed *a free agent* in a *political* view, can be bound by laws, to which he has not consented, either in person, or by *his* representative. Or, in other words, every Englishman (exclusive of the mercantile and trading part of the nation) who possesses a freehold, to the value of forty shillings per annum, has a right to a share in the legislature, which he exercises, by giving his vote in the election of some person, he approves of, as his representative.

"The true reason (says Blackstone) of requiring any qualification, with regard to property in voters, is to exclude such persons, as are *in so mean a situation*, that they are esteemed to have *no will* of their own. If these persons had votes, they would be tempted to dispose of them, under some undue influence, or other. This would give a great, an artful, or a wealthy man, a larger share in elections, than is consistent with general liberty. If it were probable, that every man would give his vote, freely, and without influence of any kind, then, upon the true theory and genuine principles of Liberty, every member of the community, however poor, should have a vote, in electing those delegates, to whose charge is committed the disposal of his property, his liberty and life. But since that can hardly be expected, in persons of indigent fortunes, or such as are under the immediate dominion of others, all popular states have been obliged to establish certain qualifications, whereby, some who are suspected to have no will of their own, are excluded from voting; in order, to set other individuals, whose wills may be supposed independent, more thoroughly upon a level with each other." [23]

Hence it appears, that such "of the people as have no vote in the choice of representatives, and therefore, are govern'd, by laws, to which they have not consented, either by themselves or by their representatives, are only those persons, who are *in so mean a situation*, that they are esteemed to have *no will* of their own." [24] Every *free agent*, every free man, possessing a freehold of forty shillings per annum, is, by the British constitution, intitled to a vote, in the election of those who are invested with the disposal of his life, his liberty and property.

It is therefore, evident to a demonstration, that unless every *free agent* in America be permitted to enjoy the same privilege, we are entirely stripped of the benefits of the constitution, and precipitated into an abyss of slavery. For, we are deprived of that immunity,

23. This quotation is from Blackstone's *Commentaries*, Book I ("*Of the* Rights *of* Persons"), Ch. II ("*Of the* Parliament"), p. 171.
24. This is a paraphrase rather than an exact quotation from Blackstone's *Commentaries*, Book I ("*Of the* Rights *of* Persons"), Ch. II ("*Of the* Parliament"), p. 172.

which is the grand pillar and support of freedom. And this cannot be done, without a direct violation of the constitution, which decrees, to every *free agent*, a share in the legislature.

It deserves to be remarked here, that those very persons in Great Britain, who are *in so mean a situation*, as to be excluded from a part in elections, are in more eligible circumstances, than she [25] should be in, who have every necessary qualification.

They compose a part of that society, to whose government they are subject. They are nourished and maintained by it, and partake in every other emolument, for which they are qualified. They have no doubt, most of them, relations and connexions, among those who are privileged to vote, and by that means, are not entirely without influence, in the appointment of their rulers. They are not governed by laws made expressly and exclusively for them; but by the general laws of their country; equally obligatory on the legal electors, and on the law makers themselves. So that they have nearly the same security against oppression, which the body of the people have.

To this we may add, that they are only under a conditional prohibition, which industry and good fortune may remove. They may, one day, accumulate a sufficient property to enable them to emerge out of their present state. Or, should they die in it, their situation is not entailed upon their posterity, by a fixed and irremediable doom. They, agreeable to the ordinary vicissitudes of human affairs, may acquire what their parents were deficient in.

These considerations plainly shew, that the people in America, of all ranks and conditions, opulent as well as indigent (if subjected to the British Parliament) would be upon a less favourable footing, than that part of the people of Britain, who are *in so mean a situation*, that they are supposed to have no will of their own. The injustice of this must be evident to every man of common sense.

I shall now proceed to take such a survey of the political history of the colonies, as may be necessary to cast a full light upon their present contest; and at the same time, to give the public a just conception of the profound and comprehensive knowledge you have of the dispute; the fairness and candour with which you have represented facts, and the immaculate purity of your intentions.

25. "we," in "Errata."

But, previous to this, the following observations may not be destitute of utility:

His Holiness the Pope, by virtue of being Christ's Vicegerent upon earth, piously assumed to himself a right to dispose of the territories of infidels, as he thought fit. And, in process of time, all Christian princes learned to imitate his example, very liberally giving and granting away the dominion and property of Pagan countries. They did not seem to be satisfied with the title which Christianity gave them to the next world only; but chose to infer from thence, an exclusive right to this world also.

I must refer it to sounder casuists, than I am, to determine concerning the consistency or justice of this principle. It is sufficient for my purpose to observe, that it is the only foundation, upon which Queen Elizabeth and her successors undertook to dispose of the lands in America. Whatever right, therefore, we may suppose to have existed, it was vested entirely in the crown: The nation had no concern in it. It is an invariable maxim, that every acquisition of foreign territory is at the absolute disposal of the King; and, unless, he annex it to the realm, it is no part of it. And if it be once alienated, it can never be united to it without the concurrence of the proprietors.

Were there any room to doubt, that the sole right of the territories in America was vested in the crown, a convincing argument might be drawn from the principle of English *tenure*. By means of the *feudal* system, the King became, and still continues to be, in a legal sense, the original proprietor, or lord paramount, of all the lands in England.* Agreeable to this rule, he must have been the original proprietor of all the lands in America, and was, therefore, authorized to dispose of them in what manner he thought proper.

The great enquiry, therefore, is concerning the terms on which these lands were really dispensed.

"The first charter, granted by the crown, for the purpose of colonization, is" not "that of King James the first, to the two Virginia companies," as you assert. Previous to that, there was one from Queen Elizabeth to Sir Walter Raliegh, for all the territory he might

* See Blackstone, Volume I.[26]
26. This is a reference to Blackstone's *Commentaries*, Book II ("*Of the* Rights *of* Things"), Ch. IV ("*Of the* Feodal System"), pp. 48–53.

discover and plant, between the 33d. and 40th. degrees of North latitude; which was not actually possessed, by any christian prince, or inhabited by any christian people, to have, hold, occupy, and enjoy the same, to him, his heirs, and assigns for ever, with all *prerogatives, jurisdictions, royalties, privileges, franchises*, thereunto belonging, by sea or land; only reserving, to herself, her heirs and successors, the fifth part of all gold and silver *ore* that might be acquired in those regions.

By this grant, Queen Elizabeth relinquished the whole legislative, and executive power, to Sir Walter, upon no other condition than simple homage, and the abovementioned fifth part of gold and silver ore; which shews, that the crown considered itself, as invested with the absolute and entire disposal of the territories in America; and the passive conduct of the nation, declares its acquiescence in the same.

After many successless efforts to plant a colony in Virginia, this charter was forfeited and abrogated, by the attainder of Sir Walter Raleigh; and then succeeded that of King James the first, to the two Virginia companies, dated the 10th of April, 1606. This was afterwards altered and improved, by a second charter, issued in 1609. There was also a third, dated March 12, 1611–12. The mention of this last would not have answered your purpose, and therefore, you chose to pass it over in silence.

In neither of these three, is there the least reservation made of any authority to parliament. The colonies are considered in them, as entirely without the realm, and consequently, without the jurisdiction of its legislature.

In the first charter from King James, there are the following clauses:

"We do ordain, establish and agree, &c. that each of the said colonies, shall have a council, which shall govern and order all matters and all causes, which shall arise, grow, or happen to, or within, the same; according to such *lavs*,[27] *ordinances*, and *instructions*, as shall be in that behalf, given and signed with our hand, or sign manual, and pass under the privy seal of our realm of England.

"And that also, there shall be a council established here in England, which shall consist of thirteen persons, to be for that purpose

27. "laws," in "Errata."

appointed; which shall have the superior managing and direction *only* of, and for all matters, that shall, or may concern the government of the said several colonies.

"Also, we do for us, our heirs, &c. declare, that all and every the persons, being our subjects, which shall dwell and inhabit within every, or any, the said several colonies, and every of their Children, which shall happen to be born within any of the said several colonies, shall have and enjoy all *liberties, franchises and immunities* within any of our *other* dominions, to all intents and purposes *as if they had been abiding and born within our Realm of England.*"

This latter declaration (to which there is one correspondent or similar, in every American Grant) plainly indicates, that it was not the royal intention to comprize the colonies within the realm of England. The powers committed to the two councils demonstrate the same; for they would be incompatible with the idea of any other than distinct states.

The King could neither exercise himself, nor empower others to exercise such an authority, as was really vested in the council, without a breach of the constitution, if the colonies had been a part of the realm, or within the jurisdiction of parliament. Such an exertion of power would have been unconstitutional and illegal, and, of course, inadmissible; but we find it was never called in question, by the legislature, and we may conclude from thence, that America was universally considered, as being without the jurisdiction of parliament.

The second charter explains and amplifies the privileges of the company, erecting them into "one body or commonalty perpetual," and confirming to them the property of their former territories; with the addition of all the islands, lying within a hundred miles of the shores of both seas; together with all *"commodities, jurisdictions, royalities,* priviledges, *franchises* and *preeminences"* to be held of the King, "his heirs, and successors," in free and common socage. They were only to pay one fifth part of all the gold and silver ore, they might find, in lieu of all *services.*

Their government was vested in a council, first appointed by the King, which, upon every necessary occasion, was to be summoned together, by the company's treasurer. But immediately after the persons appointed are named in the charter, it is declared, that "the said council and treasurer, or any of them, shall be henceforth *nominated, chosen, continued, displaced, changed, altered,* or *supplied,* as death, or other several occasions shall require, *out of* the company of the said adventurers, by the *voice* of the greater part of the said company and adventurers." Every member newly elected, to be sworn into office, by the Lord Chancellor.

This council had "full power and authority to make, ordain and establish all manner of *orders, laws, directions, instructions, forms* and *ceremonies* of government and magistracy, fit and necessary for, and concerning the government of the said colony; and the same to abrogate, revoke, or change, at all times, not only within the precinct of the said colony; but also on the seas, in going or coming to or from the said colony."

This charter is also silent with respect to parliament; the authority of which is evidently precluded, by the whole tenor of it.

You, Sir, took no notice of the circumstance, that the council was to be *nominated, chosen, continued,* &c. *out of* the Virginia company itself, agreeable to the voice of the majority. You omitted this, and gave quite a different turn to the matter; but herein you acted not at all discordant with your usual practice. Nor did you esteem it politic to transcribe the following clause: "that the said company, and every of them, their factors and assigns, shall be free of all subsidies and customs in Virginia, for the space of one and twenty years; *and from all taxes and impositions forever,* upon any goods, or merchandizes at any time or times hereafter, either upon importation thither, or exportation from thence."

The third charter is a still farther enlargement of their territory and privileges, and is that, by which their present form of government is modelled. The following extract will shew the nature of it: "We do hereby ordain and grant, that the said treasurer, and company of adventurers and planters, aforesaid, shall and may, once every week, and oftener, at their pleasure, hold and keep a court or assembly, for the better order and government of the said plantation; and that any five persons of our council, for the time being, of which company the treasurer, or his deputy to be always one, and the number of fifteen persons, at the least, of the generality of the said company assembled together, in such manner, as hath been heretofore used and accustomed, shall be reputed to be, and shall be a sufficient court, for the handling, ordering and dispatching of all such casual and particular occurrences, as shall, from time to time happen, touching and concerning the said plantation. And, nevertheless, for the handling, ordering, and disposing of the matters and affairs of greater weight and importance, such as shall *in any sort* concern the weal public, and the general good of the said plantation, as namely the *manner of government*, from time to time, to be used, the ordering and disposing of the lands and possessions, and the *settling and establishing of a trade there*, or such like, there shall be held and kept, every year *forever*, one great general and solemn assembly. In all, and every of which said great and general courts, so assembled, our will and pleasure is; and We do, for us, our heirs, and successors, forever, give and grant to the said treasurer and company, or the greater number of them, so assembled, that they shall and may have full power and authority, from time to time, and at all times hereafter, to *elect* and *chuse* discreet persons to be of our said council, for the first colony of Virginia, and to nominate and appoint such officers, as they shall think fit and requisite for the government, managing, ordering and dispatching of the affairs of the said company, and shall likewise have full power and authority, to ordain and make such laws and ordinances, for the good and welfare of the said plantation, as to them, from time to time, shall be thought requisite and meet; *So always, as the same be not contrary to the laws and statutes of this our realm of England.*"

By this charter, King James divested himself wholly, both of the legislative and executive authority; but, for his own security, prescribed a model for their civil constitution. Their laws were not to be *contrary* to the laws and statutes of his realm of England; which restriction was inserted into all the subsequent charters, with some little variation, such as, that their laws should be "consonant to reason, and not repugnant, or contary, but *as near as conveniently may be* agreeable to the laws, statues and rights of this our kingdom of England."

This mode of expression, so indefinite in itself, shews that the use made of the clause, by some ministerial advocates, is by no means natural, or warrantable. It could only be intended to set forth the British constitution, as a pattern for theirs, and accordingly we find, that upon the arrival of Sir George Yardly, in Virginia, soon after this patent was procured, the government was regulated, upon a new plan, that it might "resemble the British constitution, composed of two houses of parliament and a sovereign: The number of the council was increased, intending this body should represent the house of lords, while the house of commons was composed of burgesses, assembled from every plantation and settlement in the country."

There might be a great dissimilarity between the laws of Virginia and those of Great Britain, and yet not an absolute contrariety; so that the clause in question is not explicit, or determinate enough to authorize the conclusion drawn from it. Besides, if the colonies were within the realm of England, there would be no necessity for any provision in favour of its laws; and if they were without (as is clearly implied by the clause itself) it must be a contradiction to suppose its jurisdiction could extend beyond its own limits.

But the true interpretation may be ascertained, beyond a doubt, by the conduct of those very princes, who granted the charters. They were certainly the best judges of their own intention, and they have left us indubitable marks of it.

In april 1621, about nine years after the third Virginia charter was issued, a bill was introduced into the house of commons, for indulging the subjects of England, with the privilege of fishing upon the coast of America; but the house was informed by the secretary of state, by order of his majesty King James, that "*America was not annexed to the realm, and that it was not fitting that parliament should make Laws for those countries.*"

In the reign of his successor Charles the first (who granted the Massachusetts and Maryland charters) the same bill was again proposed, in the house, and was, in the like manner refused the royal assent, with a similar declaration that "it was unnecessary; that the colonies *were without the realm and jurisdiction of parliament.*"

Circumstances which evidently prove, that these clauses were not inserted to render the colonies dependant on the Parliament; but only (as I have observed) to mark out a model of government, for them. If then, the colonies were, at first *without the realm and juris-diction of parliament*, no human authority could afterwards alter the case, without their own voluntary full and express approbation.

The settlement of New-England was the next in succession, and was instigated by a detestation of civil and ecclesiastical tyranny. The principal design of the enterprize was to be emancipated from their sufferings, under the authority of parliament, and the laws of England. For this purpose, the Puritans had before retired to foreign countries, particularly to Holland. But Sir Robert Naughton, secretary of state, having remonstrated to his Majesty, concerning the impolicy and absurdity of dispeopling his own dominions, by means of religious oppression; obtained permission for the Puritans to take up their abode in America, were [28] they found an asylum from their former misfortunes.

Previous to their embarkation at Holland, they had stipulated, with the Virginia company,* for a tract of land, in *contiguity* with Hudson's River; but when they arrived in America (by some misconduct of the pilot) they found themselves at Cape Cod, which was without the boundaries of the Virginia Patent. There the season compelled them to remain, and there they have prosecuted their settlements.

They looked upon themselves as having reverted to a state of nature; but being willing still to enjoy the protection of their former sovereign, they executed the following instrument.

"In the name of God, Amen! We, whose names are under-written, the loyal subjects of our dread sovereign Lord *King* James, of Great-Britain, &c. *King*, defender of the faith, &c, having undertaken, for the glory of God, and the advancement of the Christian faith, and the honour of our *King*, and country, a voyage to plant the first colony in the northern part of Virginia, do by these presents, mutually, in the presence of God, and one another, covenant and combine ourselves together into a civil body politic, for our better ordering and preservation and furtherance of the ends aforesaid, and by virtue hereof, to enact, constitute, and frame such just and equal laws, ordinances, acts, constitutions and officers, from time to time, as shall be thought most meet and convenient for the general good

---

* This was after they had received their 3d charter.
28. "where," in "Errata."

of the colony; unto which, we promise all due submission and obedience."

In witness whereof, we have hereunto subscribed our names, at Cape Cod, November 11th, 1620.*

This was the original constitution of New Plymouth. It deserves to be remarked here, that these first settlers possessed their lands by the most equitable and independent title, that of a fair and honest purchase from their natural owners the Indian tribes. King James, soon after, erected a Council at Plymouth, in the county of Devon, "for the planting, ruling, ordering and governing of New-England, in America;" and granted to "them, their successors and assigns, all that part of America, lying and being in breadth from 40 deg. of north latitude from the equinoctial line to the 48th degree of the said northerly latitude, inclusively, and in length of, and within all the breadth aforesaid, throughout all the main land, from sea to sea; together with all the firm lands, soils, grounds, havens, ports, rivers, waters, fishings, mines, minerals, precious stones, quarries, and all and singular other commodities, *jurisdictions, royalties, privileges, franchises,* and *preheminences,* both within the said tract of land, upon the main, and also within the islands and seas adjacent. To be held of his Majesty, his heirs, and successors in free and common socage, and the only consideration to be, The fifth part of all gold and silver ore, for, and in respect *of all and all manner of duties, demands, and services."*

This council was vested, with the sole power of legislation, the election and appointment of all officers civil and military, authority to coin money, make war and peace, and a variety of other signal privileges. The colony of New Plymouth was comprehended within the grant. In consequence of which, its inhabitants, a few years after, purchased the claim of the patentees, with all their rights and immunities, and became an independent state by charter.

The same motives that induced the settlement of New Plymouth, did also produce that of Massachusetts. It was first colonized, by

* This ought to silence the infamous calumnies of those, who represent the first settlers in New-England, as enemies to kingly government; and, who are, in their own opinions, wondrous witty, by retailing the idle and malicious stories that have been propagated concerning them; such as their having erased the words *King, Kingdom,* and the like, out of their bibles, and inserted in their stead, civil magistrate, parliament, and republic.

virtue of a patent from the Council at Plymouth, and in a year after, by a charter from King Charles the first, dated the 4th of March, in the 4th year of his reign, by which, the adventurers and inhabitants were formed into "one body politic and corporate, by the name of the Governor and Company of the Massachusetts-Bay, in New-England," and cloathed with powers and privileges resembling those of the colony of New Plymouth.

It happened some time before this, that there was a dissolution of the Virginia Company, by a royal proclamation, dated 15th of July, 1624, by which the colony became more immediately dependent on the King. The Virginians were greatly alarmed at this, and forthwith presented a remonstrance to the throne: In which they signified an apprehension of "designs formed against their rights and privileges." In order to banish their fears, the Lords of the Council (in a letter dated the 22d of July, 1634) gave them an assurance, by his Majesty's direction, "That all their *estates, trade, freedom* and *privileges*, should be enjoyed, by them, in as extensive a manner, as they enjoyed them before the recal of the company's patent." Agreeable to this, their former constitution was confirmed and continued.

The Maryland charter is the next in order, of which you, Sir, have made no mention. It was granted by King Charles I. to Lord Baltimore, and contains such ample and exalted privileges, that no man in his senses can read it, without being convinced it is repugnant to every idea of dependence on Parliament.

It bestows on him "all the country of Maryland, and the islands adjacent; together with all their commodities, *jurisdictions, privileges, prerogatives, royal rights*, &c. &c. of what kinds soever, as well by sea as land; and constitutes him, his heirs and assigns, true and absolute Lords and Proprietaries of the said country, and of all the premises aforesaid; saving always the faith and allegiance, and the sovereign dominion due to *himself*, his heirs and successors, to be holden of the Kings of England, in free and common socage, by *fealty only*, and not *in capite*, paying two Indian arrows, every year, and also the fifth part of all gold and silver ore, which shall from time to time happen to be found. Granting also full and absolute power to the said Lord Baltimore, his heirs, &c. to ordain, make, enact and publish *any laws whatsoever, by* and *with* the *advice, assent* and *approbation* of the *freemen* of the said province, or the greater part of them, or of *their delegates* or *deputies, whom,* for the enacting of the said laws, when and as often, as need shall require, we will, that the said now Lord Baltimore, and his heirs, shall assemble in such sort and form, as, to him and *them,* shall seem best. Provided nevertheless, that the said laws be consonant to reason, and be not repugnant, or contrary, but *as near as conveniently may be,* agreeable to the laws, statutes, and rights of this our kingdom of England."

In another place it is ordained, that he the "said Lord Baltimore, *may from time to time, for ever,* have and enjoy the customs and subsidies, within the said ports, harbours, &c. within the province aforesaid, payable, or due for *merchandizes* and *wares,* there to be laden and unladen; the said *subsidies* and *customs* to be reasonably assessed (upon any occasion) by *themselves* and the *people there,* as aforesaid, to whom, we give power by these presents for us, our heirs and successors, upon just cause, and in due proportion to assess and impose the same."

I confine myself to these extracts, to avoid prolixity; and pass over the enumeration of those many extensive prerogatives, this charter confers; such as the appointment of all officers, civil and military; the power of making war and peace; the establishment of *boroughs* and *cities,* with all necessary immunities, and the like.

In the 14th year of Charles the second, the two colonies, Connecticut and New-Haven, petitioned the King to unite them into one colony, which was complied with. Privileges, as valuable and extensive, as any that had been before granted, were comprized in their charter. There was only a reservation of allegiance to the King, without the smallest share of the legislative or executive power. The next year, Providence and Rhode-Island procured a charter, with privileges exactly correspondent to those of Connecticut.

You are pleased to assert, "that the charters of Rhode-Island and Connecticut, are simply, matters of incorporation," and produce an extract in confirmation of this assertion.

I should be astonished at so extraordinary a deviation from truth, if there were not many instances similar to it. Not only, the whole tenor of their charters, but their constant practice and form of government, hitherto, declare the reverse of your assertion. But, that I may not unnecessarily prolong this letter, by a quotation of the different parts of the respective charters, give me leave to present you with an account of the constitution of these colonies, which was laid before the House of Lords in January, 1734.

"Connecticut and Rhode-Island (say the Commissioners of Trade and Plantations) are charter governments, where almost the whole power of the crown is delegated to the people, who make annual election of their Assembly, their Councils and their Governors, likewise to the majority of which Assemblies, Councils and Governors, respectively, being collective bodies, the power of making laws is granted; and, as their charters are worded, they can, and do make laws, even without the Governor's assent, no negative voice being reserved to them, as Governors in said charters. These colonies have the power of making laws, for their better government and support; and are not under any obligation, by their respective constitutions, to return authentic copies of their laws to the crown, for approbation and disallowance; or to give any account of their proceedings; nor are their laws repealable, by the crown; but the validity of them depends upon their not being contrary, but, *as near as may be*, agreeable to the laws of England."

As to the expression, as *other* our liege people of this our realm of England, or any *other* corporation or body politic within the same, if any stress be laid upon the particle *other*, it will imply not only, that the colonies were simple matters of corporation; but that the inhabitants of them were considered as being within the realm of England. But this cannot be admitted as true, without contradicting other clauses of the same charters. Thus, in the preamble to that of Rhode-Island, it is said, that the first planters "did, by the consent of our royal progenitors, transport themselves *out* of this kingdom of England *into* America." And in each of the charters, the King stipulates, that all the children born in America, shall enjoy "all the liberties and immunities of free and natural subjects, within any of his dominions, as *if* they and every of them *were* born within the realm of England."

The vague and improper manner, in which this particle is used, in many other places of the several charters, will not allow it the least weight in the present instance. In the 11th article of the third Virginia charter, there is this expression: "All such, and so many of our loving subjects, or any *other* strangers that will, &c." The same rule of inference, that makes Rhode-Island and Connecticut simple corporations, will also transform the King's loving subjects into mere strangers; which I apprehend cannot be done, without some degree of absurdity.

In the 15th year of Charles II. Carolina was erected into a principality. A Patent dated March 24, 1663, was granted to eight lord proprietors, vesting them with all its rights, privileges, prerogatives, royalties, &c. and the whole legislative and executive authority, together with the power of creating a nobility. The form of government was determined, by a compact between the people and the proprietors; which contained one hundred and twenty articles; and, "these were to be and remain the sacred and unalterable rule and form of government in Carolina, for ever." A Palatine was to be elected, from among the proprietaries, who was to govern the Principality during his life; and, at his demise, the surviving lords were to succeed him according to the order of seniority. The legislative power was to reside in the parliament of that country; consisting of the Palatine as sovereign; an upper House, in which the proprietors or their deputies, the Governor and the Nobility were to sit; and a lower House *composed of the Delegates of the People.* There was likewise a court established, the members of which were three Proprietaries, and the Palatine, as president; and in this court, the whole executive authority was lodged.

There were also several other courts: the Chief Justice's, the High Constable's, the Chancellor's, and High Steward's Court. The principal officers of the state, in number, titles and power, resembled those of the realm of England. The proprietors of Carolina considered themselves, as possessed of every requisite, towards forming a separate, independent state; and were always extremely jealous of any encroachments. They even disputed the King's authority to establish courts of Vice Admiralty, within their precincts; though for the examination and punishment of offences, committed without them: and always appointed an Admiral of their own. One of their Governors was deposed for "accepting a commission, under King William, as Judge of the Admiralty, when he had, at the same time, a commission from the Lords proprietaries for the same office."

The Philadelphia Charter was next granted; and contained almost an equality of privileges, with that of Maryland. There was indeed a reserve, in favour of parliament, perfectly singular and unprecedented in any foregoing charter; and which must either be rejected, or the general tenor of the grant becomes unintelligible.

It happened, that the Charter of Massachusetts was vacated, by a decision in Chancery; and a new one was conferred by *William and Mary*. The agent for that colony, did not accept it, 'till they had first consulted the most judicious civilians and politicians, upon the contents of it; and, then drew up an instrument, in which, they assigned the reasons of their acceptance. The following extract will serve to shew their sense of it, "the colony (say they) is now made a province; and the General Court has, with the King's approbation, as much power, in New-England, as the King and parliament have in England. They have all English privileges and liberties; and can be touched, by *no law*, and by *no tax;* but of their own making. All the liberties of their religion are for ever secured."

You say, that "the power to levy taxes is restrained to provincial and local purposes, only, and to be exercised, over such only, as are inhabitants and proprietors of the said province."

They are impowered "to levy proportionable and reasonable assessments, rates and taxes, for our service, in the necessary defence and support of the government of the said province, or territory; and the protection and preservation of the inhabitants there." The defence and support of government, and their own protection and preservation, are the purposes, for which they are to raise supplies; and, in my humble opinion, there are no others, to which any society is under an obligation to contribute its wealth or property.

I shall only make one more observation, upon this charter, which is, that there was a reservation in it of liberty, for the people of England, to fish upon their coasts; which would have been useless and absurd, had that province been a part of the realm, and within the jurisdiction of parliament.

Were it necessary to elucidate, still more, a point which is so conspicuous from the several charters of the colonies, as well as the express declarations of those princes, by whom they were granted, to wit, *"that the colonies are without the realm and jurisdiction of parliament."* I might enumerate many striking circumstances, besides those I have already mentioned. But as the case is by this time suf-

ficiently clear, I shall confine myself to the recital of only one or
two more transactions.

An act of the 25th of Charles the second was the first, that ever
imposed duties on the colonies, for any purpose; and these, as the
preamble itself recites, were simply as a regulation of trade, and
were of a prohibitory nature. Notwithstanding this, it was the source
of great dissatisfaction, and was one of the principal causes of the
insurrection, in Virginia, under Colonel Bacon; which after his death
subsided; and then the province sent agents to England, to remon-
strate "against taxes and imposition being laid on the colony, by any
authority, but that of the General Assembly." In consequence of
this, a declaration was obtained, under the privy seal of King Charles,
dated 19th of April, 1676, to this effect, that "taxes ought not to be
laid upon the proprietors and inhabitants of the colony, but by the
common consent of the General Assembly."

About three years after, when King Charles had occasion to raise
a permanent revenue, for the support of Virginia, he did not attempt
to do it by means of a parliamentary donation; but framed a Bill,
and sent it there by Lord Colepepper, who was, at that time, governor, to receive the concurrence of their legislature. It was *there*
passed into a law, and "*enacted by the King's most excellent Majesty, by, and with, the consent of the General Assembly of the
colony of Virginia.*" If the Virginians had been subjects of the realm,
this could not have been done, without a direct violation of *magna
charta;* which provides, that no English subject shall be taxed without the consent of Parliament.

Thus Sir, I have taken a pretty general survey of the American
Charters; and proved to the satisfaction of every unbiassed person,
that they are intirely, discordant with that sovereignty of parliament,
for which you are an advocate. The disingenuity of your extracts
(to give it no harsher name) merits the severest censure; and will
no doubt serve to discredit all your former, as well as future labours,
in your favourite cause of despotism.

It is true, that New-York has no Charter. But, if it could support
it's claim to liberty in no other way, it might, with justice, plead the
common principles of colonization: for, it would be unreasonable,
to seclude one colony, from the enjoyment of the most important

privileges of the rest. There is no need, however, of this plea: The sacred rights of mankind are not to be rummaged for, among old parchments, or musty records. They are written, as with a sun beam, in the whole *volume* of human nature, by the hand of the divinity itself; and can never be erased or obscured by mortal power.

The nations of Turkey, Russia, France, Spain, and all other despostic kingdoms, in the world, have an inherent right, when ever they please, to shake off the yoke of servitude, (though sanctified by the immemorial usage of their ancestors;) and to model their government, upon the principles of civil liberty.

I will now venture to assert, that I have demonstrated, from the voice of nature, the *spirit* of the British constitution, and the charters of the colonies in general, the absolute non-existence of that parliamentary supremacy, for which you contend. I am not apt to be dogmatical, or too confident of my own opinions; but, if I thought it possible, for me to be mistaken, when I maintain, that the parliament of Great-Britain has no sovereign authority over America, I should distrust every principle of my understanding, reject every distinction between truth and falshood, and fall into an universal scepticism.

Hitherto, I have reasonned against the whole authority of parliament, without even excepting the right we have conceded of regulating trade. I considered it, in its original state, as founded in the British constitution, the natural rights of society, and the several charters of the colonies. The power of regulating our trade was first exercised in the reign of Charles the second: I shall not examine upon what principle: It is enough, we have consented to it. But I shall proceed to consider the argument, you make use of, to establish the propriety of allowing special duties to be imposed by way of tribute, for the protection of our commerce.

You argue thus, "Notwithstanding the large landed estates, possessed by the British subjects, in the different parts of the world; they must be considered, as a commercial, manufacturing people. The welfare, perhaps the existence of Great-Britain, as an independent, or sovereign state, depends, upon her manufactures and trade; and many people in America think, that her manufactures and commerce depend, in a great measure, on her intercourse with her colonies; insomuch, that if this should be neglected, her commerce would decline and die away; her wealth would cease, and her martime power be at an end. If these observations be just, they establish the right of the British parliament to regulate the commerce of the whole empire, beyond possibility of contradiction; a denial of it, would be a denial of a right in the British empire to preserve itself; they prove also, that all parts of the empire must be subject to the British Parliament, for otherwise the trade of the whole cannot be regulated. They point out also, the best mode of raising such a revenue, as is necessary for the support and defence of the government, viz. by duties on imports and exports; because these are attended with the least inconvenience to the subject, and may be so managed, as to raise a revenue, and regulate the trade at the same time."

"When it is considered, that Great-Britain is a maritime power; that the present flourishing state of her trade and of the trade of her colonies depends, in a great measure, upon the protection which they receive from the navy; that her own security depends upon her navy, and that it is principally, a naval protection, we receive from her, there will appear a peculiar propriety in laying the chief burthen of supporting her navy, upon her commerce; and in requesting us to bear a part of the expence, proportional to our ability, and to that protection and security which we receive from it."

The supposition, that a cessation of commerce, between Great-Britain and the colonies, would be ruinous and destructive to the former, is ushered in, as the principal argument, for her right to regulate the commerce of the whole empire. I am willing to allow it its full weight; but I cannot conceive how you can pretend, after making such an use of it, to deny it the force it ought to have, when it is urged, as affording a moral certainty, that our present measures will be successful. If you tacitly adopt the principle, and reason from it, in one case, with what propriety can you reject it, in the other? If the preservation of the British empire depends, in any material degree, upon the right of parliament to regulate the trade of the colonies, what will be the consequence if that trade ceases altogether? You must either acknowledge, that you have adduced a very weak and foolish argument, or that the commercial connexion between Great-Britain and the colonies is essential to her security and prosperity. You have either failed, in proving your point, or you have furnished me, with an ample confutation of all your reasoning against the probability of success, from the restrictions laid on our commerce. If our trade be necessary to the welfare of Great-Britain, she must, of course, be ruined by a discontinuance of it.

But it is granted, that Great-Britain has a right to regulate the trade of the empire. The Congress has acknowledged it, so far as concerned their constituents. You infer from thence, that all parts of the empire must be subject to her. They need only be, so far subject, as is necessary for the end proposed, that is the regulation of their trade. If you require any further subjection, you require *means* that are disproportionate to the *end*, which is unreasonable, and not at all allowable.

With respect to the justice of submitting to impositions, on our trade, for the purpose of raising a revenue, to support the Navy, by which it is protected, I answer, that the exclusive regulation of our commerce, for her own advantage, is a sufficient tribute to Great-Britain for protecting it. By this means, a vast accession of wealth is annually thrown into her coffers. It is a matter of notoriety, that the ballance of trade is very much against us. After ransacking Spain, Portugal, Holland, the English, French, Spanish, Dutch and Danish plantations, for Money and Bills of Exchange, as remittances for the commodities we take from Great-Britain; we are still always greatly in arrears to her. At a moderate computation I am well informed, that the profits she derives from us every year, exceed two millions and a half sterling; and when we reflect, that this sum will be continually increasing, as we grow more and more populous, it must be evident, that there is not the least justice in raising a revenue upon us, by the imposition of special duties.

The right of Great-Britain to regulate our trade, upon the plan it is now acknowledged, is not an inconsiderable matter. It is as much as any free people can concede, and as much, as any just people would require. We are not permitted to procure manufactures any where else, than from Great-Britain, or Ireland. Our trade is limited and prescribed, in every respect, as is most for her interest: This is a plentiful source of wealth to her, as I have heretofore shewn, and shall hereafter confirm, by the testimony of some British writers.

But I have found out an argument, which I imagine will go very near convincing yourself of the absurdity of what you have offered, on this head. It is short, but conclusive, *"the principal profits of our trade center in Great-Britain."* * How can you, my dear sir, after making this confession, entertain a single thought, that is incumbent upon us to suffer her to raise a revenue upon our trade? Are not the *principal profits* a sufficient recompence for protecting it? Surely you would not allow her the whole. This would be rather too generous. However ardent your affection to her, and however much it may be your glory to advance her imperial dignity, you ought to moderate it so far, as to permit us to enjoy some little benefit from our trade. Only a small portion of the profits will satisfy us. We are willing to let her have the *principal* share, and this you acknowledge she already has. But why will you advise us to let her exhaust the small pittance, we have reserved, as the reward of our own industry in burthensome revenues? This might be liberality and generosity; but it would not be prudence; and let me tell you, in this selfish, rapacious world, a little discretion is, at worst, only a *venial* sin. It will be expedient to be more cautious for the future. It is difficult to combat truth; and unless you redouble your vigilance, you will (as in the present instance) be extremely apt to ensnare yourself.

I shall now briefly examine the excellent mode, you have proposed, for settling our disputes, finally, and effectually. All internal taxation is to be vested, in our own legislatures, and the right of regulating trade, by duties, bounties, &c. to be left to the parliament, together with the right of enacting all general laws, for all the colonies. You imagine that we should then "have all the security for our rights, liberties and properties, which human policy can give us."

Here we widely differ in sentiment, my opinion is, that we should have no "security, besides the good will of our rulers, that is no security at all." Is there no difference between one system of laws and another? Are not some more favourable and beneficial to the subject, better calculated to preserve his life, and personal liberty than others? It is evident they are. Suppose, instead of the present system established among us, the French laws were to be introduced, for the good of all the colonies, should we have the same security for our lives which we now have? I presume we should not. I presume also, that a revolution in our laws might and would, gradually, take place.

* See Page 19th of your own letter.

A fondness for power is implanted, in most men, and it is natural to abuse it, when acquired. This maxim drawn from the experience of all ages makes it the height of folly to entrust any set of men with power, which is not under every possible controul: perpetual strides are made after more, as long as there is any part with-held. We ought not, therefore, to concede any greater authority to the British parliament, than is absolutely necessary. There seems to be a necessity, for vesting the regulation of our trade *there*, because, in time, our commercial interests might otherwise interfere with her's. But with respect to making laws for us, there is not the least necessity, or even propriety in it. Our legislatures are confined to ourselves and cannot interfere, with Great-Britain. We are best acquainted with our own circumstances, and therefore best qualified, to make suitable regulations. It is of no force to object, that no particular colony has power to enact general laws for all the colonies: There is no need of such general laws. Let every colony attend to its own internal police, and all will be well. How have we managed heretofore? The parliament has made no general laws, for our good; and yet our affairs have been conducted, much to our ease and satisfaction. If any discord has sprung up among us, it is wholly imputable to the incursions of Great-Britain. We should be peaceable and happy, if unmolested by her: We are not so destitute of wisdom, as to be in want of her assistance, to devise proper and salutary laws for us.

The legislative power of parliament, would at any rate be useless to us, and as utility is the prime end of all laws, that power has no reason for which it should exist. It is not even requisite for preserving the connexion, between Britain and the colonies; for that is sufficiently secured, in two ways, by being united under the same king; and by the important privilege of regulating our commerce, to which we have submitted.

That it might be prejudicial to us, no reasonable man can deny. We may trace the evils of it, through the whole administration of justice. Judicial proceedings may be so ordered, as to render our lives and properties dependent on the will and caprice of court favourites and tools. A wide field for bribery and corruption, of every kind, would be opened; and the most enormous exactions would take shelter under the garb of law. It is unnecessary to enter into a particular detail of the different methods, in which all this might be effected; every man's own imagination will suggest to him a multiplicity of instances.

Rigorous, oppressive and tyrannical laws may be thought expedient, as instruments to humble our rebellious tempers, and oblige us to submit to further exertions of authority, 'till the claim to bind us, in all cases whatsoever, be fully complied with. This no doubt would be a work of time. The steps would be gradual and perhaps imperceptible; but they would be sure and effectual. That thirst of power, which influenced the parliament to assert an unlimited authority over us, without the least plausible foundation for it (as I have clearly proved) will authorize us to apprehend the worst.

The power of legislating for us, and of raising a revenue upon the articles of commerce would be a sufficient degree of slavery. It is absurd to say, that Great-Britain could not impose heavy burthens, on our commerce, without immediately feeling the effect herself. She may enrich herself, by reducing us to the most lamentable state of penury and wretchedness. We are already forbid to purchase the manufactures of any foreign countries. Britain and Ireland must furnish us with the necessaries we want. Those things we manufacture among ourselves, may be disallowed. We should then be compelled to take the manufactures of Great-Britain, upon her own conditions. We could not, in that case, do without them. However excessive the duties, laid upon them, we shall be under an inevitable necessity to purchase them. How would Great-Britain feel the effects of those impositions, but to her own advantage? If we might withdraw our custom, and apply to other nations; if we might manufacture our own materials; those expedients would serve, as a refuge to us; and would indeed be a security against any immoderate exactions. But these resources would be cut off. There would be no alternative left us. We must submit to be drained of all our wealth, for those necessaries, which we are not permitted to get elsewhere.

As to our trade with foreign countries, the burthens imposed on that, however grievous, would, in like manner, affect Great-Britain, only by increasing her public treasure. Her own inhabitants would pay no part of them: They would fall solely upon ourselves. There is no immediate connection between her trade and ours of this kind: they are separate and independent; and, of course, the incumbrances on the one would not injure the other. The superfluity of our products must be exported to enable us to pay our debts to her; and we must submit to be loaded, at her discretion. If we look forward to a period not far distant, we shall perceive, that the productions of our country will infinitely exceed the demands, which Great-Britain and her connections can possibly have for them; and, as we shall then be greatly advanced in population, our wants will be proportionably increased. These circumstances will open an ample field, for extortion and oppression.

The legislative authority of Parliament would always be ready to silence our murmurs, by tyrannical edicts: These would be enforced, by a formidable army, kept up among us, for the purpose. The slightest struggles, to recover our lost liberty, would become dangerous and even capital. Those hated things Continental Conventions, by which there might be a communion of councils and measures, would be interdicted. Non-importation and non-exportation agreements would, in effect, be made *seditious, illegal,* and *treasonable.** No remedy would be left, but in the clemency of our oppressors; a wretched one indeed, and such as no prudent man would confide in! In whatever light, we consider the matter, we shall find, that we must effectually seal our bondage by adopting the mode you recommend.

Agreeable to your own concession, Great-Britain is abundantly recompensed for the naval protection she affords, by the *principal profits* of our trade: It can, therefore, with no colour of justice, be urged upon us, to permit her to raise a revenue through that channel.

But, after all, let us suppose, that the emolument which arises, from the simple and abstracted regulation of our trade, is inadequate to the protection, we derive, from the parent state; does it follow, that her just demands cannot be satisfied, unless we put it in her power to ruin us? When did the colonies refuse to contribute their proportion, towards defraying the expences of government? During the war, our contributions were so liberal and generous, that we were thought to have done more, than our part, and restitution was accordingly made. Massachusetts, that injured, insulted and calumniated country was foremost in displaying its loyalty; and was neither parsimonious of its men nor money. But, notwithstanding this, no

* I believe these were the epithets, bestowed upon them by General Gage.

confidence, it seems is due to our virtue, or fidelity; but every thing is to be trusted to the wisdom and disinterestedness of a British Parliament.

We do not expect, or require, that all should depend upon our integrity or generosity; but only a part: And this every rule of equity intitles us to. We have assented to the exercise of a power, which gives a certainty to Great-Britain of a vast annual income: Any further aids, that may be necessary, ought to be intrusted to our fidelity: When the circumstances of two parties will not admit of precise boundaries to the duty of each, it is not a dictate of justice to put one entirely into the power of the other. If the mother country would desist from grasping at too much, and permit us to enjoy the privileges of freemen, interest would concur with duty, and lead us to the performance of it. We should be sensible of the advantages of a mutual intercourse and connection; and should esteem the welfare of Britain, as the best security for our own. She may, by kind treatment secure our attachment in the powerful bands of self-interest. This is the conduct that prudence and sound policy point out; but alas! to her own misfortune, as well as ours, she is blind and infatuated.

If we take futurity into the account, as we no doubt ought to do, we shall find, that, in fifty or sixty years, America will be in no need of protection from Great-Britain. She will then be able to protect herself, both at home and abroad. She will have a plenty of men and a plenty of materials to provide and equip a formidable navy. She will indeed owe a debt of gratitude to the parent state, for past services; but the scale will then begin to turn in her favour, and the obligation, for future services, will be on the side of Great-Britain. It will be the interest of the latter to keep us without a fleet, and, by this means to continue to regulate our trade, as before. But, in thus witholding the means of protection, which we have, within our own reach, she will chiefly consult her own advantage, and oblige herself much more, than us. At that æra, to enjoy the privilege of enriching herself, by the direction of our commerce, and at the same time, to derive supports from our youthful vigour and strength, against all her enemies, and, thereby to extend her conquests over them, will give her reason to bless the times that gave birth to these colonies.

By enlarging our views, and turning our thoughts to future days, we must perceive, that the special benefits we receive from the British nation are of a temporary and transient nature; while, on the other hand, those it may reap from us, by an affectionate and parental conduct, will be permanent and durable; and will serve to give it such a degree of stability and lasting prosperity, as could not be expected, in the common fluctuating course of human affairs. Such reflections will teach us, that there is no propriety in making any concessions to Great-Britain, which may be at all inconsistent with our safety.

You employ several contemptible artifices to varnish and recommend your scheme. Your conduct, in every respect, affords a striking instance of the depravity of human nature. You insinuate, that the Pennsylvania Farmer admits the right of Parliament to regulate our trade, in the same sense, you do.[29] The very letter your extracts are taken from, is expressly levelled against the revenue act, with regard to paper, glass, &c. The design of that and all his subsequent papers, is to prove, that all duties, imposed upon the articles of commerce, for the purpose of raising a revenue, are to be considered, in the same light, as what you call *internal* taxes, and ought equally to be opposed.

By the "legal authority to regulate trade," he means nothing more, than what the Congress have allowed. An authority to confine us to the use of her own manufactures, to prescribe our trade, with foreign nations, and the like. This is the power he speaks of as being "lodged in the British Parliament." And as *to general duties*, he means such, as the people of Great-Britain are to pay, as well as ourselves. Duties, for the purpose of a revenue, raised upon us only, he calls *special* duties, and says, "they are as much a tax upon us, as those imposed by the stamp-act."

The following passage will shew the sentiments of this ingenious

29. Seabury had referred to the second letter of "The Pennsylvania Farmer," John Dickinson, and quoted the following: "The parliament unquestionably possesses a legal authority to regulate the trade of Great Britain, and all her colonies. Such an authority is essential to the relation between a mother country and her colonies. . . . We are but *parts of a whole*, and therefore there *must exist a power somewhere, to preside, and preserve the connection in due order:* This power is lodged in the parliament." See Seabury, *A View of the Controversy*, 15–16.

and worthy gentleman; and, at the same time, will serve to illustrate what I have heretofore said.

"If you once admit, (says he) that Great-Britain may lay duties upon her exportations to us, for *the purpose of levying money on us only* she will then have nothing to do, but to lay duties on the articles which she prohibits us to manufacture; and the tragedy of *American* liberty is finished. We have been prohibited from procuring manufactures, in all cases, any where but from Great-Britain (excepting linens, which we are permited to import, directly from Ireland). We have been prohibited, in some cases, from manufacturing, for ourselves, and may be prohibited, in others. We are, therefore, exactly in the situation of a city besieged, which is surrounded by the besiegers, in every part, but *one.* If that is closed up, no step can be taken, *but to surrender at discretion.* If Great-Britain can order us to come to her, for the necessaries we want, and can order us to pay what taxes she pleases, before we take them away, or when we land them here, we are as abject slaves as *France* and *Poland* can shew in wooden shoes, and with uncombed hair.*

"Perhaps the nature of the necessities of dependent states, caused by the policy of a governing one, for her own benefit, may be elucidated, by a fact, mentioned in history. When the Carthaginians were possessed of the island of *Sardinia,* they made a decree, that the Sardinians should not raise *corn,* nor get it any other way, than from the *Carthaginians.* Then, by imposing any duties they would upon it, they drained from the miserable *Sardinians* any sums they pleased; and, whenever that miserable and oppressed people made the least movement to assert their liberty, their tyrants starved them to death, or submission. This may be called the most perfect kind of political necessity." [30]

You would persuade us also, that Mr. *Pitt's* sentiment accords with yours, about the regulation of trade; but this is as false as the other. When he tells them "to exercise every power, but that of taking money out of our pockets," he does not mean, that they shall barely

* The peasants of *France* wear wooden shoes, and the vassals of Poland are remarkable for matted hair, which never can be combed.

30. This quotation is also from John Dickinson's second letter. In the first sentence of the quotation, which H writes "If you once admit," Dickinson actually wrote "If they once admit."

refrain from a *manual operation* upon our pockets; but that they shall exact money from us, in no way whatever. To tax the commodities, Great-Britain obliges us to take from her only, is as much taking money out of our pockets, as to tax our estates; and must be equally excluded by Mr. Pitt's prohibition.

You, all along, argue upon a supposititious [31] denial of the right of Parliament to regulate our trade. You tell us, "It will never give up the right of regulating the trade of the colonies;" and in another place "if we succeed, in depriving Great-Britain of the power of regulating our trade, the colonies will probably be soon at variance with each other. Their commercial interests will interfere; * there will be no supreme power to interpose; and discord and animosity must ensue."

I leave others to determine, whether you are most defective in memory or honesty; but, in order to shew, that you are starting difficulties, where there are really none, I will transcribe, for your perusal, part of the fourth resolve of the Congress. After asserting the right of the several provincial legislatures to an exclusive power of legislation, "in all cases of taxation and internal policy," they conclude thus: "But from the necessity of the case, and a regard to the mutual interests of both countries, we chearfully consent to the operation of such acts of the British parliament, as are *bona fide* restrained to *the regulation of our external commerce,* for the purpose of securing the commercial advantages of the whole empire to the mother country, and the commercial benefits of its respective members; excluding every idea of taxation, internal or external, for raising a revenue on the subjects in America, without their consent."

It seems to me not impossible, that our trade may be so regulated, as to prevent the discord and animosity, at the prospect of which you are so terrified, without the least assistance, from a *revenue*.

Thus have I, not only disproved the existence of that parliamentary authority, of which you are so zealous an abettor. But also shewn, that the mode you have proposed, for the acsomodation [32] of our disputes, would be destructive to American freedom. My next business is to vindicate the Congress, by a few natural inferences; and

---

* I do not see any reason to believe this would be the case, but as it is of no importance to controvert it, I shall pass it over.

31. "supposititious," in "Errata."   32. "accomodation," in "Errata."

such reflections, on the state of our commercial conexion, with the mother country, as are necessary to shew the insignificancy of your objections to my former arguments, on this head.

Since it has been proved, that the British parliament has no right, either to the legislation, or taxation of America; and since neither could be ceded, without betraying our liberties, the Congress would have acted inconsistent with their duty to their country, had they done it. Their conduct, therefore, so far from being reprehensible, was perfectly justifiable and laudable.

The regulation of our trade, in the sense it is now admitted, is the only power we can, with justice to ourselves, permit the British parliament to exercise; and it is a privilege of so important a nature, so beneficial and lucrative to Great-Britain, that she ought, in equity, to be contented with it, and not attempt to grasp at any thing more. The Congress, therefore, have made the only concession which the welfare and prosperity of America would warrant, or which Great Britain, in reason could expect.

All your clamours, therefore, against them, for not having drawn some proper line, are groundless and ridiculous. They have drawn the only line which American freedom will authorize, or which the relation between the parent state and the colonies requires.

It is a necessary consequence, and not an assumed point, that the claim of parliament to *bind us by statutes in all cases whatsoever*, is unconstitutional, unjust and tyrannical; and the repeated attempts to carry it into execution, evince a fixed inveterate design to exterminate the liberties of America.

Mr. Grenville, during his administration, was the projector of this scheme. His conduct as a minister has been severely arraigned, by his successors in office, and by the nation in general; but, notwithstanding this, a measure, which disgraces his character more, than any thing else, has been steadily pursued, ever since.

The Stamp Act was the commencement of our misfortunes;[33] which, in consequence of the *spirited* opposition made by us, was

33. H's discussion of the Stamp Act and succeeding Parliamentary acts relating to America was in reply to the "Farmer's" assertion that these had been repealed because of the opposition of the colonists and that any other Parliamentary measure detrimental to the interest of the colonies might be removed by petition and remonstrance to the King and Parliament. See Seabury, *A View of the Controversy*, 23–24.

repealed. The revenue act, imposing duties on Paper, Glass, &c. came next; and was also partly repealed on the same account: A part, however, was left to be the instrument of some future attack. The present minister, in conjunction with a mercenary tribe of merchants attempted to effect, by stratagem, which could not be done by an open undisguised manner of proceeding: His emissaries, every where, were set to work. They endeavored, by every possible device, to allure us into the snare. The act, passed for the purpose, was misrepresented; and we were assured with all the parade of pretended patriotism, that our liberties were in no danger. The advantage, we should receive, from the probable cheapness of English tea, was played off, with every exaggeration of falshood; and specious declamations, on the criminality of illicit trade, served as a gilding for the whole. Thus truth and its opposite were blended. The men, who could make just reflections, on the sanctity of an oath, were yet base enough to strike at the vitals of those rights, which ought to be held sacred by every rational being.

It so happened, that the first tea ship arrived at Boston. The Assembly of that province, justly alarmed at the consequences, made repeated applications to the consignees, for the East-India company, requesting them to send back the tea. They, as often refused to comply. The ship was detained, 'till the time was elapsed, after which the tea must have been landed, and the duties paid, or it would have been seized, by the Custom-house. To prevent this, a part of the citizens of Boston assembled, proceeded to the ship, and threw the tea into the river.*

The scheme of the ministry was disappointed, on all hands. The tea was returned from all the colonies, except South-Carolina. It was landed there; but such precautions were taken, as equally served to baffle their attempt.

This abortion of their favourite plan inflamed the ministerial ire. They breathed nothing, but vengeance against America: Menaces of punishment resounded, through both houses of parliament. The commons of Great-Britain spoke more in the supercilious tone of masters, than in the becoming language of fellow subjects. To all the

* I shall examine the justice and policy of this proceedure in some future publication.[34]

34. There is no evidence that H ever wrote an article on the Boston Tea Party.

judicious reasonings of a Burke, or Barry, no other answer was returned, than an idle tale of *lenity* and *severity*. Much was said of
their past forbearance and of their future resentment: This was the
burthen of the song. The Quixot minister too, promised to bring
America to his feet. Humiliating idea! and such as ought to be
spurned by every free-born American!

Boston was the first victim to the meditated vengeance: An act was
passed to block up her ports, and destroy her commerce, with every
aggravating circumstance that can be imagined. It was not left at
her option to elude the stroke, by paying for the tea; but she was
also to make such satisfaction to the officers of his Majesty's revenue
and others, who might have suffered as should be judged *reasonable
by the governor*. Nor is this all, before her commerce could be restored, she must have submitted to the authority claimed and exercised by the parliament.*

Had the rest of America passively looked on, while a sister colony
was subjugated, the same fate would gradually have overtaken all.
The safety of the whole depends upon the mutual protection of
every part. If the sword of oppression be permitted to lop off one
limb without opposition, reiterated strokes will soon dismember the

* This must be evident to every person, who has read the act. The prefatory
part of it is in these words. "Whereas dangerous commotions and insurrections
have been fomented and raised, in the town of Boston, &c. in which commotions and insurrections, certain valuable cargoes of tea, &c. were seized and
destroyed; and whereas, in the present condition of the said town and harbour,
the commerce of his Majesty's subjects cannot be safely carried on there, nor
the *customs* payable to his Majesty duly collected, &c."

The commotions specified are those, in which the tea was destroyed: The
commerce obstructed was that of the East-India company, and the customs
which could not be collected were those on the tea, These are the evils the
act is intended to punish, and remove; and accordingly it provides, that
"whenever it shall appear to his Majesty, in his privy council, that peace and
obedience to the laws (i.e. the laws of parliament) shall be so far restored,
in the said town of Boston, that the trade of Great-Britain, may safely be carried on there, and his Majesty's *customs* duly collected," then his Majesty
may, at his discretion, so far open the Port, as to him seems necessary. So that
until the Bostonians shall submit to let the trade of Great-Britain be carried
on, upon her own terms, and suffer his Majesty's customs (the duty upon tea,
or any other the parliament may impose) to be duly collected, they must
remain in their present distressed situation; that is, unless they resign their
freedom, and put on the ignominious yoke tendered them, by parliament, they
are never to recover their lost trade. Hence it appears, how weak, ungenerous
and contemptible that objection is, which supposes the Bostonians might have
avoided their present calamities, by paying for the tea. The truth is, they
had no alternative; but submission to all the *unjust claims of Parliament.*

whole body. Hence it was the duty and interest of all the colonies to succour and support the one which was suffering. It is sometimes sagaciously urged, that we ought to commisserate the distresses of the people of Massachusetts; but not intermeddle in their affairs, so far, as perhaps to bring ourselves into like circumstances with them. This might be good reasoning, if our neutrality would not be more dangerous, than our participation: But I am unable to conceive how the colonies in general would have any security against oppression, if they were once to content themselves, with barely *pitying* each other, while parliament was prosecuting and enforcing its demands. Unless they continually protect and assist each other, they must all inevitably fall a prey to their enemies.

Extraordinary emergencies, require extraordinary expedients. The best mode of opposition was that in which there might be an union of councils. This was necessary to ascertain the boundaries of our rights; and to give weight and dignity to our measures, both in Britain and America. A Congress was accordingly proposed, and universally agreed to.

You, Sir, triumph in the supposed *illegality* of this body; but, granting your supposition were true, it would be a matter of no real importance. When the first principles of civil society are violated, and the rights of a whole people are invaded, the common forms of municipal law are not to be regarded. Men may then betake themselves to the law of nature; and, if they but conform their actions, to that standard, all cavils against them, betray either ignorance or dishonesty. There are some events in society, to which human laws cannot extend; but when applied to them lose all their force and efficacy. In short, when human laws contradict or discountenance the means, which are necessary to preserve the essential rights of any society, they defeat the proper end of all laws, and so become null and void.

But you have barely asserted, not proved this *illegality*. If, by the term, you mean a contrariety to law, I desire you to produce the law against it, and maintain, there is none in being. If you mean, that there is no law, the intention of which may authorise such a convention, I deny this also. It has been always a principle of the law that subjects have a right to state their grievances, and petition the King for redress. This is explicitly acknowledged by an act of the first of William and Mary; and "all prosecutions and commitments for such petitioning," are declared to be illegal. So far then the Congress was a body founded in law; for if subjects have such a right they may undoubtedly elect and depute persons from among themselves to act for them.*

As to the particular agreements entered into, with respect to our commerce, the law makes no provision for, or against them: They are perfectly indifferent, in a *legal* sense. We may, or may not trade, as is most suitable to our own circumstances.

The deputies, chosen in the several provinces met at Philadelphia, according to appointment; and framed a set of resolves declarative of the rights of America, all which, I have by general arguments proved, are consonant to reason and nature; to the spirit of the British constitution and to the intention of our charters. They made the only concession (as I have also shewn) that their duty to themselves and their country would justify, or that the connection, between Britain and the colonies, demanded.

They solicited the King, for a redress of grievances; but justly concluding, from past experience, from the behaviour and declarations of the majority, in both Houses of Parliament, and from the known character and avowed designs of the Minister, that little or no dependence was to be placed upon bare entreaties, they thought it necessary to second them by restrictions on trade.

In my former defence of the measures of the Congress, I proved in a manner you never will be able to invalidate, that petitions and remonstrances, would certainly be unavailing. I will now examine your frivolous and prevaricating reply.

You answer thus: "In the commotions, occasioned by the stamp act, we recurred to petitions and remonstrances, our grievances were pointed out, and redress solicited with temper and decency. They were heard, they were attended to, and the disagreeable act repealed. The same mode of application succeeded, with regard to the duties laid upon glass, painters colours, &c: You say indeed, that our addresses on this occasion were treated with contempt and neglect. But I beseech you, were not our addresses received, read and debated

---

* All Lawyers agree, that the *spirit* and *reason* of a law, is one of the principal rules of interpretation; if so, it cannot be doubted, that when a people are aggrieved, and their circumstances will not allow them unitedly to petition in their own persons, they may appoint representatives to do it for them.

upon? And was not the repeal of those acts the consequence? *The fact you know is as I state it.* If these acts were not only disagreeable to the Americans; but were also found to militate against the commercial interests of Great-Britain, it proves what I asserted above, that duties, which injure our trade, will soon be felt in England; and then there will be no difficulty in getting them repealed."

I entirely deny the fact to be, as you state it; and you are conscious it is not. Our addresses were not heard, attended to, and the disagreeable act repealed in consequence of them: If this had been the case, why was no notice taken of them in the repealing act? Why were not our complaints assigned as the inducement to it? On the contrary, these are the express words of the first repeal, to which the second is also similar. "Whereas the continuance of the said act would be attended *with many inconveniencies; and may be productive of consequences greatly detrimental to the commercial interests of Great-Britain,* may it, therefore, please your most excellent Majesty, by and with the advice and consent, &c. that from and after the first day of May, 1766, the above mentioned act, and the several matters and things, therein contained, shall be, and is, and are, hereby, repealed, and made void, to all intents and purposes, whatsoever."

The inconveniences, and the ill-consequences to Great-Britain, are the only reasons, given for the revocation of the act. How then can you pretend to say it was in compliance with our petitions? You must think the complaisance of your readers very great, to imagine they will credit your assertions, at the expence of their own understandings.

Neither is the use you make of the assigned reason, at all just. The consequences, so detrimental to the commercial interests of Great-Britain, are not such as would have resulted from the natural operation of the act, had it been submitted to; but from the opposition made by us, and the cessation of imports, which had taken place.

A non-importation, (to which you have so violent an aversion) was the only thing, that procured us redress, on preceding occasions. We did not formerly, any more, than now, confine ourselves to petitions only; but took care to adopt a more prevailing method, to wit, a suspension of trade.

But what proves, to a demonstration, that our former petitions were unsuccessful is, that the grand object, they aimed at, was never obtained. This was an exemption from parliamentary taxation. Our addresses turned entirely upon this point. And so far were they from succeeding, that immediately upon the repeal of the stamp-act, a subsequent act was passed, declaring the right of Parliament to bind us, by statutes, in all cases whatsoever. This declaration of the unlimitted universal authority of Parliament was a direct denial of the leading claim held up in our petition; and of course a rejection of the petition itself.

The same observations are applicable to the revenue act, which, had our addresses been successful, would have been wholly not partially revoked; and we should not, at this time, have had any occasion to renew our complaints; but should have been in a state of security and tranquillity.

In my former reflections on this head, I urged many considerations to shew, that there is less reason now, than ever, to expect deliverance, by means of remonstrance and entreaty. And indeed, if we consider the vindictive spirit diffused thro' the words and actions of our oppressors, we must be convinced of this. It impeaches the understandings of the Ministry and the Parliament, in the grossest manner, to suppose they have renewed their attempts, and taken such violent methods to carry them into execution; merely, to have the pleasure of undoing the whole, in condescension to our prayers and complaints. The taxation of America is an object, too near at heart, to be resigned, unless from necessity: And, if they would not have abandoned the principle, there could be no reason to expect they would have desisted from the exercise of it, in the present instance: For the duty upon tea is, in itself, very trifling; and since that is opposed, they could not hope to vary the mode, in any way, that would be less offensive and less obnoxious, to opposition.

In answer to the instance, I produced, from the unsuccessful application of the Boston Assembly, you tell me, that "the Governor, against whom the complaint was made, was called to a public trial, before the only court where the cause was cognizable, the King in Council; but the Boston Assembly could not support their charge; and the Governor was acquitted." The truth is, their charge was extremely well supported in the eye of strict justice; but it was destitute of the mere formalities of law, and, on this score, it was rejected. They accuse him of treachery and falshood; and produced his own letters, against him. It was not admitted as a *legal* charge, or *crimen;* nor the party's letters as an evidence or *testis;* and by these evasions, the criminal escaped the punishment he deserved, and, instead of it, has been advanced to higher honours; while the complainants were unrelieved and insulted. I remember, when the particulars of this transaction were first published, there was this circumstance mentioned, that the petition, in question, was pronounced at *St. James's* to be a "*a seditious, vexatious* and *scandalous libel.*"

You tell me, "there is also this reason why we should, at least, have tried the mode of petition and remonstrance, to obtain a removal of the grievances we complain of. The Friends of America, in England, have strongly recommended it, as the most decent and probable means of succeeding." I wish you had been so kind, as to have particularised those friends, you speak of. I am inclined to believe, you would have found some difficulty in this. There have been some publications, in the news-papers, said to be extracts of letters from England; but who were the authors of them? How do you know they were not written in America? or, if they came from England, that the writers of them were really sincere friends? I have heard one or two persons named, as the authors of some of these letters; but they were those, whose sincerity we have the greatest reason to distrust. The general tenor of advice, from those, with whose integrity we are best acquainted, has been to place no dependence on the justice or clemency of Great-Britain; but to work out our deliverance, by a spirited and self-denying opposition. Restrictions, on our trade, have been expressly pointed out and recommended, as the only probable source of redress.

You say, "if the information from England be true, we have, by our haughty demands, detached most of our friends there, from our interest, and forced them to take part against us." Pray, Sir, where did you get this information? Is there any inhabitant of the invisible world, that brings intelligence to you, in a supernatural way? There have been no arrivals from England, preceding the time you wrote your letter, that have brought any account of the proceedings of the Congress being received there, or of the consequences resulting from them. Your information must have, either, come to you, in a miraculous manner, or it must be a fiction of your own imagination.

But there are other powerful reasons against trusting to petitions only, in our present circumstances. The town of Boston is in a very critical situation: Men, under sufferings, are extremely apt, either to plunge into desperation, or to grow disheartened and dejected. If the colonies, in general, appeared remiss, or unwilling to adopt vigorous measures, in order to procure the most speedy relief, the people of Massachusetts might perhaps have been hurried on to a rash and fatal conduct, or they might have become languid and lifeless. Delays are extremely dangerous in affairs of such vast consequence.

The dispute might have been spun out by ministerial artifice, till the generality of the people became careless and negligent, and, of course, fitter to be imposed upon, and less forward to assert their rights with firmness and spirit. The hand of bribery might have been stretched across the atlantic, and the number of domestic vipers increased among us. The ministry and their agents here are active and subtle. Nothing would have been neglected, that might have a tendency to deceive the ignorant and unwary, or to attract the dishonest and avaricious. How great an influence, places, pensions and honours have upon the minds of men, we may easily discover, by contrasting the former, with the present conduct of some among ourselves. Many, who at the time of the Stamp act were loudest in the cause of liberty, and the most ardent promoters of the spirited proceedings, on that occasion, have now from patriots of the first magnitude dwindled into *moderate men,* friends to order and good government, dutiful and zealous servants to the ministry.

Had our petitions failed, we should have found our difficulties multiplied much more, than we can imagine; and, since there was the highest probability of a failure, it would have been madness to have hazarded so much upon so unpromising a footing.

It betrays an ignorance of human nature to suppose, that a design formed and ripening, for several years, against the liberties of any people might be frustrated, by the mere force of intreaty. Men must cease to be as fond of power as they are before this can be the case.

I therefore infer, that, if the Congress had not concerted other more efficacious measures, they would have trifled away the liberties of their country; and merited censure, instead of approbation. Commercial regulations were the only peaceable means, from which we could have the least hope of success. These they have entered into; and these I maintain must succeed, if they are not treacherously or pusillanimously infringed.

You tell me, "I over-rate the importance of these colonies to the British empire;" and proceed to make such assertions, as must convince every intelligent person, that you are either a mortal foe to truth, or totally ignorant of the matter you undertake. The following extracts will shew whether my representations have been just or not.

"Our plantations spend mostly our *English* manufactures; and those of *all sorts* almost imaginable, in *prodigious* quantities; and employ near *two thirds* of all our English shipping; so that we have more people, in *England,* by reason of our plantations in *America.**

"We may safely advance, that our trade and navigation are *greatly* increased, by our colonies; and that they really are a source of treasure, and naval power to this kingdom, since they *work for us,* and their treasure *centers here.* Before their settlement *our manufactures were few* and those but *indifferent.* The number of English merchants very small; and the *whole shipping* of the nation much inferior to what now belongs to the northern colonies, only. *These are certain facts.*" But since their establishments, our condition has altered for the better, *almost to a degree beyond credibility.* Our manufactures are *prodigiously* increased, chiefly, by the demand for them, in the plantations, where they *at least take off one half,* and supply us with many valuable commodities for exportation, which

* Postlethwait.[35]

35. H's reference is to Malachy Postlethwayt, *The Universal Dictionary of Trade and Commerce, Translated from the French of the Celebrated Monsieur Savary, Inspector-General of the Manufactures for the King, at the Custom-house of Paris: With Large Additions and Improvements, Incorporated throughout the Whole Work; Which more particularly accomodate the same to the Trade and Navigation of these Kingdoms, And the Laws, Customs, and Usages, To which all Traders are subject* (London, Printed for John and Paul Knapton, In Ludgate-Street., 2 vols., 1751).

is as great emolument to the mother kingdom, as to the plantations themselves.*

The same author says, in another place, "before the settlement of these colonies, our *manufactures were few,* and those but indifferent. In those days, we had, not only our *naval stores,* but our *ships* from our neighbours." [37]

"I shall sum up my whole remarks (says another writer) on our *American* colonies, with this observation, that, as they are a *certain* annual revenue of *several millions sterling* to their mother country, they ought carefully to be protected, duly encouraged, and every opportunity, that presents, improved for their increment and advantage; *as every one, they can possibly reap, must at last return to us, with interest."* †

These quotations clearly prove, that the colonies are of the last importance to Great-Britain. They, not only take off vast quantities of her manufactures, but furnish her with materials to extend her trade, with foreign nations. They also supply her, with naval stores; and, in a great measure, with a navy itself. The present flourishing state of her commerce is chiefly to be attributed to the colonies, who *work for her* and whose treasure *centers with her.* How unjust therefore is it in her, not to be satisfied, with the advantages, she has hitherto received, from us; but to aim at depriving us of our freedom, and happiness! And what ruinous consequences must flow from a cessation of our trade, on which her manufactures so much depend! What prodigious numbers must be thrown out of employ, and reduced to beggary and misery!

"But she is a great nation, has vast resources, may easily supply the want of our trade, by making very small concessions to Portugal,

* Postlethwait.[36]

† Lex mercatoria.[38]

36. The material is taken from Postlethwayt's section on "Colonies" (I, 532–33). Although H put the paragraph in quotation marks, he paraphrased rather than quoted the source.

37. *Ibid.*

38. The quotation, to which H's note refers, is from [Wyndham Beawes,] *Lex Mercatoria Rediviva: or, the Merchant's Directory. Being a Complete Guide to all Men in Business, . . . Containing An Account of our Trading Companies and Colonies, with their Establishments, and an Abstract of their Charters; the Duty of Consuls, and the Laws subsisting about Alien, Naturilization and Denization. . . . By Wyndam Beawes . . .* (Second Edition, London, Printed for R. Baldwin at the *Rose,* and S. Crowder and Co. at the *Looking-Glass,* in *Pater-Noster-Row,* 1761), 657.

Russia, Turkey, &c. Should our non-importation distress her manufactures, every man may employ himself to labour on a farm; and
the price of grain would be much advanced, in France, Spain, and
the Mediterranean. Notwithstanding the present high cultivation of
the lands, in England, that kingdom is capable of being improved,
by agriculture and commerce, so as to maintain double the number
of people, that it does at present. The improvements, in Scotland,
within the last thirty years, are amazing. The enterprizing spirit of
the people has opened an easy intercourse between all parts of the
country; and they have been enriched, by commerce, to a surprizing
degree."

I can hardly prevail upon myself to give a serious answer to such
ridiculous rant; but, it may be requisite for the sake of the uninformed; and, of course, it would be improper to decline it.

The national debt is now about one hundred and forty millions
sterling; a debt unparalelled, in the annals of any country, besides. The surplus of the annual revenues, after paying the interest
of this debt, and the usual expences of the nation, is, upon an average, about one million and a quarter sterling: * so that, with all
their present resources, they would not be able to discharge the
public debt, in less, than *one hundred* and *twelve years*, should the
peace continue all that time. It is well known, that most of the
necessaries of life are, at present, heavily taxed, in Great-Britain and
Ireland. The common people are extremely impoverished, and find
it very difficult to procure a subsistence: They are totally unable to
bear any new impositions; and, of course, there can be no new internal sources opened. These are stubborn facts, and notorious to every
person, that has the least acquaintance, with the situation of the two
kingdoms: Had there been the vast resources you speak of, why
have they not been improved to exonerate the people, and discharge
the enormous debts of the nation? The guardians of the state have
been a supine, negligent, and stupid pack indeed, to have overlooked,
in the manner they have done, those numerous expedients, they
might have fallen upon for the relief of the public. It cannot be ex-

---

* See a calculation made by Blackstone. He says [in] the year [17]65, two
millions were paid, and three millions in the 3 succeeding years, i.e. 5 millions
in 4 years.[39]

39. See Blackstone's *Commentaries*, Book I ("*Of the* Rights *of* Persons"),
Ch. VIII ("*Of the* King's Revenue"), p. 330.

pected, but that a war will take place, in the course of a few years, if not immediately; and then, through the negligence of her rulers, Great-Britain, already tottering under her burthens, will be obliged to increase them, 'till they become altogether insupportable; and she must sink under the weight of them. These considerations render it very evident, that the mighty resources you set forth, in such pompous terms, have nothing, but an *imaginary* existence; or they would not have been left so uncultivated in such necessitous and pressing circumstances.

You think, you have nothing to do; but to mention the names of a few countries, Portugal, Russia, Turkey, &c. and you have found out an easy remedy for the inconveniences flowing from the loss of our trade. Yet, in truth, Great-Britain carries on, as extensive a commerce with those countries and all others, as their circumstances will permit. Her trade is upon the decline with many of them. France has, in a great measure, supplanted her in Spain, Portugal and Turkey, and is continually gaining ground. Russia is increasing her own manufactures fast, and the demand for those of Great-Britain must decrease in proportion.

"Most of the nations of Europe have interfered with *her*, more or less in divers of her *staple manufactures*, within half a century, not only in her woolen, but in her lead and tin manufactures, as well as her fisheries." *

A certain writer, in England, who has written on the present situation of affairs, with great temper, deliberation, and apparent integrity, has these observations; [41] "the condition of the great *staple manufactures* of our country is well known, those of the linen and the silk, are in the greatest distress, and the woolen and the linen are now publickly bandied and contending, against one another. One part of our people is starving at home, on the alms of their parishes; and another running abroad to this very country, that we are con-

* Postlethwait.[40]

40. The exact source of H's quotation has not been found; but the information may be found in many of Postlethwayt's articles. See, for example, the sections on "Britain" (Postlethwayt, I, 344-59), "France" (Postlethwayt, I, 808-838).

41. [Matthew Robinson-Morris, second Baron Rokeby] CONSIDERATIONS *on Measures Carrying on with respect to the* BRITISH COLONIES IN NORTH AMERICA . . . (London: Printed. Boston, Reprinted and sold by Edes and Gill, in Queen-Street. 1774), 29-30. H made some minor punctuation and word changes.

tending with. The produce of North-America used to be sent yearly to Britain, is reckoned at about four millions sterling; the manufactures of Britain, and other commodities returned from hence, at nearly the same sum; the debts due from America to the British merchants here, at about six millions, or a year and a half of that commerce.[42] Supposing, therefore, the Americans to act in this case, as they did, in the time of the stamp act; we shall then have yearly, until the final settlement of this affair, manufactures to the value of four millions sterling, left and heaped on the hands of our merchants, and master manufactures; or we shall have workmen and poor people put out of employ, and turned adrift in that proportion. There will likewise be drawn from our home consumption, and out of our general trade and traffic, North-American commodities, to the same value; and debts will to the immense sum above mentioned be withheld from private people here.[43] What effects these things will produce, considering the present state of our trade, manufactures, and manufacturers, the condition of our poor at home, and the numbers of people running abroad, it don't want many words to explain and set forth. *They were before severely felt*, for the time that they lasted, and it is apprehended, that the present situation of the public is yet more liable to the impression. These are some of the difficulties and distresses, which we are, for a trial of skill,[44] going to bring on ourselves; and which will be perpetually magnifying and increasing, as long as the unnatural contest shall continue."

From these facts and authorities, it appears unquestionable, that the trade of Great-Britain, instead of being capable of improvement among foreign countries, is rather declining; and, instead of her being able to bear the loss of our commerce, she stands in great need of more colonies to consume her manufactures.

It is idle to talk of employing those, who might be thrown out of business, upon farms. All the lands in England, of any value, have been long ago disposed of, and are already cultivated as high as possible. The laborious farmers find it an exceeding difficult task to pay their yearly taxes, and supply their families, with the bare necessaries

42. H omitted at this point this sentence: "I say, the time past must be our guide with respect to that to come."

43. H omitted at this point this sentence: "This was the train of things begun before and we must look for the like again."

44. H omitted the words "with our colonies" at this point.

of life; and it would be impracticable to give employment in agriculture to any more, than are already engaged. We can have no
doubt of this, if we consider the small extent of territory in Great
Britain, the antiquity of its settlement, and the vast number of people it contains. It is rather overstocked, with inhabitants; and were
it not for its extensive commerce, it could not maintain near the
number it does at present. This is acknowledged on all hands. None,
but yourself, would hazard the absurdity of a denial. The emigrations from Britain, particularly, from the north part of it, as well
as the most authentic accounts, prove the contrary of your representations—Men are generally too much attached to their native
countries to leave it and dissolve all their connexions, unless they are
driven to it, by necessity. The swarms, that every year come over to
America, will never suffer any reasonable man to believe, upon the
strength of your word, that the people in Scotland or Ireland, are
even in tolerable circumstances.

I cannot forbear wondering, when you talk of the price of grain
being advanced in France, Spain and the Mediterranean; and insinuate, that Britain may be able to supply them: It will be well, if she
can raise grain enough, for herself, so as not to feel the want of
those considerable quantities, she frequently gets from us. I am apt
to think, she will experience some inconvenience, on this account.

With respect to Ireland, you think yourself under no obligation
to point out, where she may find purchasers for her linens, so numerous and wealthy, as we are; but, unless you could do this, you
must leave that country in very deplorable circumstances. It is not
true, that she may do just as well with her linens, upon her hands,
as we can with our flax seed, upon ours. Linen is a staple manufacture
of hers, and the sole means of subsistence to a large part of her inhabitants. Flax seed, as an article of commerce, is comparatively of
little importance to us; but we shall stand in need of all the flax we
can raise to manufacture linens for ourselves, and therefore, shall
not lose our seed by ceasing to export it. I shall say more of this
hereafter.

Nor is it by any means a just inference, that because Ireland
formerly subsisted, without a linen manufactory, she would not
therefore severely feel any present obstruction to the sale of the
article in question. Her burthens are now much more grievous than

they formerly were; and, of course, her resources ought to be proportionably greater, or she must sink under the pressure of them. The linen manufactory is, at this time one of her most valuable resources, and could not be materially injured or impeded, without producing the most melancholy effects. The distressed condition of Ireland will not admit of any dimunition of her *means;* but pressingly demands an enlargement of them.

It is of little moment to contest the possibility, that that country might procure a sufficiency of flax seed, elsewhere, than from us; 'till it can be shewn, where she may find a mart for her linens, equal to the American; and this you are not willing even to attempt. Yet I have credible information, that she could not obtain from Holland, much more than usual (for the reasons I before assigned) and, that she has always had, as much from the Baltic, as she could conveniently get. With regard to Canada, any considerable supply from thence, would be a work of time, and no relief to her immediate exigencies.

I observed in my former pamphlet, that "the Dutch may withold their usual supplies: They may choose to improve the occasion, for the advancement of their own trade: They may take advantage of the scarcity of materials in Ireland, to increase and put off their own manufactures." You answer it by saying, "you never yet knew a Holander, who would withold any thing that would fetch him a good price." The force of my observation turns upon its being his interest to do it. You should have shewn, that it would be more profitable to him, to sell it to the Irish, than to retain it, for the purposes mentioned; otherwise that very avarice, you ascribe to him will operate, as I supposed.

You are unmercifully witty, upon what I said, concerning the West-Indies; [45] but the misfortune of it is, you have done nothing else, than "blunder round about my meaning." I will endeavour to explain myself, in a manner more level to your capacity.

The lands in the West-Indies are extremely valuable, because they produce the Sugar Cane, which is a very lucrative plant; but they

45. In the *Full Vindication*, H wrote that it would be at least ten or fifteen years before Canada could supply the needs of the West Indians. "In the mean time," he said, "the West Indians might have the satisfaction of starving." To this statement Seabury replied: "And to see them starve, I presume, would be a particular satisfaction to you." See Seabury, *A View of the Controversy*, 30.

are small, in quantity, and therefore, their proprietors appropriate only small portions, to the purpose of raising food. They are very populous, and therefore, the food raised among themselves, goes but little way. They could not afford sufficient sustenance to their inhabitants, unless they were chiefly or entirely applied to the production of necessaries; because they are so small in quantity, and so thickly inhabited.

These are truths, which every person, acquainted with the West Indies, must acquiesce in; and should they be deprived of external succours, they must either starve, or suspend the cultivation of the sugar cane. The last is the best side of the dilemma; but that would cut off an annual income of several millions sterling to Great Britain: For it cannot admit of a doubt, that the chief part of the profits of the English West-Indies, ultimately center there.

But, in order to disappoint my malice, you tell me, that Canada raises 400,000 bushels of wheat a year; and this you imagine will pretty well supply the wants of the West-Indians; but, give me leave to inform you, that it would not satisfy a tenth part of them. The single Island of Jamaica would require much more. At a moderate computation, I believe there are 400,000 people in the British West Indies only: Let us allow a pound of wheat a day, upon an average, to each; * and make a calculation accordingly.

At a pound a day, every person must be supposed to consume 365 lb. a year, that is, about twelve bushels. Now as there are as many people as there are bushels of wheat raised in Canada; and as each person would consume twelve bushels, it follows, that the quantity you mention, would not be above a twelfth part sufficient.

But can we imagine, that all the wheat of Canada would be devoted to the use of the British West Indies? If our ports were to be blocked up, would not the French and Spanish islands be in great distress for provisions? And have not the Canadians any near connexions among them? Would they not naturally sympathize with them, and do all in their power to afford relief? And could they find no means to accomplish their inclinations? The answer to these questions is easy: The Islands belonging to the French and Spaniards

---

* This allowance cannot be thought too much, if we consider, that the negroes chiefly live upon grain; and must continue to do so; because the quantity of flesh and fish would be proportionably diminished, when our supplies failed.

will be greatly distressed: The Canadians will be very ready and desirous to assist them; and they will contrive some expedients to communicate a large share of what their country yields.

What you say concerning the lumber exported from Canada, is totally false.[46] That country labours under many inconveniencies, which have hitherto prevented the exportation of that article, but in very small quantities, and of a particular kind. The places w[h]ere the lumber grows, are so far distant from the sea ports, that the expence of transportation is too great to make it worth while to ship any other than butt staves, and these must be brought quite from Lake Champlain. This disadvantage, together with the number of hands it would require, and the time necessary to enter extensively into any branch of trade, and to remove all the impediments naturally in the way, would render the situation of the West-Indians, truly pitiable, were they once necessitated to depend upon Canada only, for supplies of lumber.

The attention of Missisippi is entirely engrossed in raising Corn and Indigo: The advantage arising from these articles, is much greater than would result from lumber; and of course, the people of that country will never attend to the latter, in preference to the former.

Thus have I proved in a full, clear, and conclusive manner, that a cessation of our trade with Britain, Ireland and the West-Indies, would be productive of the most fatal consequences to them all; and that, therefore, the peace, happiness and safety of the British Empire, are connected with the redress of our grievances; and, if they are at all consulted, our measures cannot fail of success.

As to the justice of proceeding in the manner we have done, it must depend upon the *necessity* of such a mode of conduct. If the British parliament are claiming and exercising an unjust authority, we are right in opposing it, by every necessary means. If Remonstrances and Petitions have been heretofore found ineffectual, and we have no reasonable ground to expect the contrary, at present, it

46. The reference is to the following statement: "I have also the pleasure of informing you, that there is now, more lumber annually shipped from Quebec, than from any colony on the continent. This, with what would come from Mississippi, the Floridas, and what the Islands themselves afford, would be more than sufficient for all their purposes." See Seabury, *A View of the Controversy*, 30.

THE
FARMER REFUTED:
OR,
A more impartial and comprehensive
VIEW
OF THE
DISPUTE between GREAT-BRITAIN
AND THE
COLONIES,
INTENDED AS A
FURTHER VINDICATION
OF THE
CONGRESS:
IN
ANSWER TO A LETTER
FROM
A. W. FARMER,
INTITLED
A VIEW of the CONTROVERSY
BETWEEN
GREAT-BRITAIN *and her* COLONIES:
INCLUDING
A MODE of determining the present DISPUTES
FINALLY AND EFFECTUALLY, &c.

by Alexander Hamilton

Tituli remedia pollicentur; sed pixedes ipsæ venena continent. COKE.
The Title promises Remedies, but the Box itself contains Poisons.

NEW-YORK: Printed by JAMES RIVINGTON, 1775.

9.

Title page of *The Farmer Refuted*, one of Alexander Hamilton's most
famous pamphlets, printed by James Rivington, New York, 1775.

is prudent and justifiable to try other methods, and these can only be restrictions on trade. Our duty to ourselves and posterity, supersede the duties of benevolence to our fellow-subjects in Great-Britain, Ireland and the West-Indies.

You can never confute the arguments I before made use of on this head, unless you can prove the right of parliament to act as it has done, or the likelihood of succeeding by petitions; your feeble endeavours to effect this, I have sufficiently baffled. You must now collect new forces, and make a more vigorous effort, or you must quit the field in disgrace.

Such vociferation as this, is not to be admitted instead of argument, "are the Irish and West-Indians accountable for our mad freaks? Do you ex[p]ect to extend the tyranny of the congress over the whole British empire, by the legerdemain of calling it American freedom? Do you think that the Irish and West-Indians are in duty bound to enter into our non-importation, non-consumption, and non-exportation agreement, till our grievances real or pretended, are removed? And that they deserve to be starved if they do not? Enjoy your folly and malevolence if you can."

The resistance * we are making to parliamentary tyranny, cannot wear the aspect of *mad freaks* to any, but such mad imaginations as yours. It will be deemed virtuous and laudable, by every ingenuous mind. When I said, that the people of Great-Britain, Ireland, and the West-Indies, were to be considered as *politically* criminal, for remaining neutral, while our privileges were attacked; I did not mean, that they ought to enter into any of the above mentioned agreements; but, that it was their duty to signify, in a public manner, their disapprobation of the measures carrying on; and to use all their influence to have them laid aside. Had they interested themselves in the affair, with any degree of zeal and earnestness, we should not, probably, have had occasion to act as we do; and they would not have been in danger of their present calamities. Their obligation to assist us in the preservation of our rights, is of the very same nature with ours, to carry on a trade with them.

But you insist upon it, that we should not be able to live without

* I mean the general resistance. That there have been some irregularities committed in America I freely confess. It would be miraculous, and inconsistent with human nature, for a people in such critical and trying circumstances to act perfectly right.

the manufactures of Great-Britain; and that we should be ruined by a prohibition of our exports "the first winter after our English goods are consumed, we shall be starving with cold," after all our endeavours, "the requisite quantity of wool to clothe the inhabitants of this continent, could not be obtained in twenty years." As to cotton it "must come from the southern colonies, and the expence of bringing it by land, would be too great for the poor. Besides, we have nobody to manufacture our materials after we have got them." All these, you think, are insuperable obstacles; and would, if duly considered, induce us to bend our necks tamely and quietly to the profered yoke, as much less dreadful, than the evils attendant upon our measures will inevitably be.

Nature has disseminated her blessings variously throughout this continent: Some parts of it are favourable to some things, others to others; some colonies are best calculated for grain; others for flax and hemp; others for cotton; and others for live stock of every kind: By this means, a mutually advantageous intercourse may be established between them all. If we were to turn our attention from external to internal commerce, we should give greater stability, and more lasting prosperity to our country, than she can possibly have otherwise. We should not then import the luxuries and vices of foreign climes; nor should we make such hasty strides to public corruption and depravity.

Let all those lands, which are rich enough to produce flax and hemp, be applied to that purpose; and let such parts, as have been a long time settled, still continue to be appropriated to grain, or other things they are fit for. We shall want as much of the former articles as can be raised; and perhaps, as much of the latter, as may be requisite towards the due improvement of the poorer part of our soil. Let it be considered, that the colonies, which are adapted to the production of materials for manufactures, will not be employed in raising grain, but must take what they use chiefly from the other colonies; and, in return, supply their materials; by this means, and by dedicating no more of our land to the raising of wheat, rye, corn, &c. than is incapable of producing other things, we shall find no superfluity of those articles, and shall make a very beneficial use of all our lands. This is practicable; difficulties may be started, but none which perseverance and industry may not overcome.

The clothes we already have in use, and the goods at present in the country, will, with care, be sufficient to last *three years*.* During that time, we shall be increasing our sheep as much as possible. It is unfair to judge of the future from the past. Hitherto we have paid no great attention to them; we have killed and exported as fast as we could obtain a sale: When we come to attend properly to the matter, to kill but few, and to export none, we shall, in the course, of two or three years, have large numbers of sheep; and wool enough to go a considerable way towards clothing ourselves.

Flax and hemp, we should undoubtedly have in abundance. The immense tracts of new rich land, which may be planted with these articles, would yield immense quantities of them. What large supplies of seed do we annually export to Ireland! When we come to with-hold these, and make the cultivation of flax and hemp, a matter of serious attention, we shall soon procure a plenty of them. In speaking of this matter, you confine your views to the single small province of New-York. You say, "We sow already as much flax, as we can conveniently manage. Besides, it requires a rich free soil; nor will the same ground in *this* country produce flax a second time, till after an interval of five or six years. If the measures of the Congress should be carried into full effect, I confess we may in a year or two, want a large quantity of hemp, for the executioner. But I fear, we must import it. It exhausts the soil too much to be cultivated, in the old settled parts of the province."

There is land enough in the other provinces, that is rich, free and new; nor is at all liable to the objections you make. As to this particular province, and any others in the same circumstances, let only such parts as are fit, be planted, with the articles in question; and let the rest be managed as before. Much more may be produced in this, than has been hitherto; but, if it could not afford a sufficiency for itself; let it exchange its grain with other colonies, that superabound with such materials.

If we sow already as much flax, as we can conveniently manage, it is, because the chief of our attention is engrossed by other things; but the supposition is, that there will be less demand for them, and

---

* I may be thought here to contradict my former assertion, (to wit) that in eighteen months, all the goods we have among us will be consumed; but I only meant, that all the goods in the hands of the merchants would be purchased and taken off.

more for flax; and, by attending less to present objects, we shall have it in our power for the future, to sow and manage much more flax, than in the time past.

With respect to cotton, you do not pretend to deny, that a sufficient quantity of that might be produced. Several of the southern colonies are so favorable to it, that with due cultivation, in a couple of years they would afford enough to cloath the whole continent. As to the expence of bringing it by land, the best way will be to manufacture it w[h]ere it grows; and afterwards transport it to the other colonies. Upon this plan I apprehend, the expence would not be greater, than to build and equip large ships, to import the manufactures of Great-Britain from thence.

The difficulty of transportation would be attended, with one great advantage. It would give employment and bread to a number of people; and would among other things, serve to prevent there being those terrific bands of thieves, robbers and highwaymen, which you endeavor to draw up, in such formidable array, against the Congress.

It would however be hardly possible to block up our ports, in such a manner, as to cut off all communication between the colonies, by water. There would remain some avenues in spite of all that could be done, and we should not be idle in making proper use of them.

I mentioned before, the vast quantities of skins in America, which would never let us want a warm and comfortable suit. This is one of our principal resources, and this you have passed over in silence. A suit made of skins, would not be quite so elegant as one of broad cloth; but it would shelter us from the inclemency of the winter, full as well.

Upon the whole, considering all the resources we have; and the time we shall have to prepare them, before we are in actual want; there can be no room to doubt, that we may live without the manufactures of Britain, if we are careful, frugal and industrious.

But, it is said, we have no persons to manufacture our materials, after we have provided them. Among the swarms of emigrants, that have within these few years past, come to the continent; there are numbers of manufacturers, in the necessary branches. These, for want of encouragement in their own occupations, have been obliged to apply themselves to other methods of getting a living; but would be glad of an opportunity to return to them. Besides these, we should soon have a plenty of workmen, from Britain and Ireland: Numbers, who would be thrown out of employ *there*, would be glad to flock to us for subsistence. They would not stay at home and be miserable, while there was any prospect of encouragement here. Neither is there any great difficulty, in acquiring a competent knowledge of the manufacturing arts. In a couple of years many of our own people might become proficient enough, to make the coarser kinds of stuffs and linens.

But if it should be necessary, we have other resources besides all these. It will be impossible for the ships of Britain, to line the vast extended coast of this continent, in such a manner, as to preclude the admission of foreign aids and supplies. After every possible precaution against it, we shall still be able to get large quantities of goods from France and Holland.*

I shall conclude this head, with one more observation, which is this, That all such, as may be deprived of business, by the operation of our measures in America, may be employed in cultivating lands. We have enough, and to spare. It is of no force to object, that "when our exports are stopped, our grain would become of little worth." They can be occupied in raising other things, that will be more wanted, to wit; Materials for manufactures; and only a sufficiency of provisions, for their own use. In such a country as this, there can be no great difficulty in finding business, for all its inhabitants. Those obstacles, which to the eye of timidity or disaffection, seem like the *Alps* would to the hand of resolution and perseverance, become mere *hillocks*.

Once more I insist upon it, that Great-Britain can never force us to submission, by blocking up our ports; and that the consequences of such a procedure to herself, Ireland and the West-Indies, would be too fatal to admit of it. If she is determined to enslave us, it must be by force of arms; and to attempt this, I again assert, would be nothing less, than *the grossest infatuation, madness itself*.

Whatever may be said of the disciplined troops of Britain, the

---

* You may perhaps tell me here, that I contradict the sentiments I formerly delivered, respecting unlawful trade. But it is by no means the case. I despise the practice of avaricious smugglers, very heartily; but when a whole people are invaded, there can be no law of any force, against their procuring every needful succours.

event of the contest must be extremely doubtful. There is a certain enthusiasm in liberty, that makes human nature rise above itself, in acts of bravery and heroism. It cannot be expected, that America would yield, without a magnanimous persevering and bloody struggle. The testimony of past ages, and the least knowledge of mankind, must suffice to convince us of the contrary. We have a recent instance in *Corsica*, to what lengths a people will go, in defence of its liberties; and if we take a view of the colonies in general, we must perceive that the pulse of Americans beats high, in their country's cause. Let us then suppose, the arms of Britain triumphant and America mutilated, exhausted and vanquished. What situation will Britain then be in? What laurels will she reap, from her conquest? Alas! none. Every true friend to that deluded country, must shudder at the prospect of her self-destroying success. The condition, we should be left in would disable us from paying the six millions sterling, which is due, for the manufactures of Britain. Instead of the present millions, derived annually from our trade, we should be so distressed and reduced, as to be for many years to come, a burthen, and not an advantage. Millions are soon dispensed, in supporting fleets and armies. Much British treasure and blood would be expended in effecting our ruin.

This then would be the situation of Great-Britain. Her public debt would be augmented several millions. Her merchants, who are one of the principal sources of her opulence, would many of them become bankrupt, by the loss of the vast sums due them, in America. Her manufactures would stagnate and decay, and her revenues would be considerably diminished. This continent, which is now a rich source of wealth and strength, would be debilitated and depressed.

Would the ancient rivals and enemies of Britain be idle, at such a conjuncture as this? Would they not eagerly seize the opportunity to recover their former losses, and revenge the evils, they have sustained on former occasions? It will be said, this is possible, but it may not happen. I answer, causes must fail of their usual effects, if it does not. Princes and nations must cease to be ambitious and avaricious. The French from being a jealous, politic and enterprizing people, must be grown negligent, stupid and inattentive to their own interest. They never could have a fairer opportunity, or a greater temptation to aggrandise themselves, and triumph over Britain, than would be here presented. Let us imagine England immersed in a war with France, Spain, or any other potent neighbour, with her public debt increased, some of her best springs dried up, and America ruined; not only unable to afford her any assistance; but, perhaps fired with resentment and a sense of accumulated injuries, ready to throw itself into the arms of her enemies. In these circumstances, what would be the fate of this unhappy kingdom? Every man of discernment must be convinced, that ruin would be unavoidable.

But, what reason have we to believe, the arms of Britain would prevail? It will be replied, because she can send against us some of the best troops in the world, either with respect to valour, or discipline; and because we have only a raw, unexperienced militia to oppose them with. Discipline and military skill are certainly matters of great importance, and give those, to whom they belong, a vast superiority; but they do not render them invincible. Superior numbers, joined to natural intrepidity, and that animation, which is inspired by a desire of freedom, and a love of one's country, may very well overballance those advantages.

I imagine, it will be readily allowed, that Britain could not spare an army of above fifteen thousand men to send against the colonies. These would have to subdue near 600,000. The established rule of computing the number of men, capable of bearing arms in any nation, is by taking a fifth part of the whole people. By the best calculations we are supposed in America, to exceed three millions. The fifth part of three millions is 600,000. But, in order to be certain of our computation; let us suppose, there are only 500,000 fighting men in the colonies. Then there will be upwards of 30 Americans to one British soldier. A great disparity indeed! And such as never can be compensated by any discipline, or skill whatever! It will be objected, that these 500,000 cannot act together. I grant it; nor is there any occasion that they should: Forty thousand, will be a sufficient number to make head at a time, and these must be kept up by fresh supplies as fast as there is any diminution.

Let it be remembered, that there are no large plains, for the two armies to meet in, and decide the contest, by some decisive stroke, where any advantage gained, by either side, might be prosecuted, 'till a complete victory was obtained. The circumstances of our country put it in our power, to evade a pitched battle. It will be better policy, to harrass and exhaust the soldiery, by frequent skirmishes and incursions, than to take the open field with them, by which means, they would have the full benefit of their superior regularity and skill. Americans are better qualified, for that kind of fighting, which is most adapted to this country, than regular troops. Should the soldiery advance into the country, as they would be obliged to do, if they had any inclination to subdue us, their discipline would be of little use to them. We should, in that case, be at least upon an equality with them, in any respect; and as we should have the advantage, on many accounts, they would be likely to gain nothing by their attempts.

Several of the colonies are now making preparation, for the worst (and indeed the best way to avoid a civil war, is to be prepared for it.) They are disciplining men, as fast as possible; and, in a few months, will be able to produce many thousands, not so much inferior, in the essentials of discipline, as may, perhaps, be imagined. A little actual service will put them very nearly upon a footing, with their enemies. The history of the Swedes and Russians, under Charles XII, and Peter the Great, will teach us, how soon a people, possessed of natural bravery, may be brought to equal the most regular troops. The Swedes, at first, obtained very signal advantages; but, after a while, the Russians learned to defeat them with equal numbers. It is true, there was one of the greatest men, the world has seen, at the head of the latter; but there was one who emulated the Macedonian conqueror, at the head of the former. Charles was, perhaps, never surpassed by any man, in courage, or skill; and his soldiers were well worthy of such a general. There is also this important circumstance, in our favour, when compared with the Russians. They were barbarous and untractable: We are civilized and docile. They were ignorant even of the theory of war: We are well acquainted with it; and, therefore, should more easily be brought to the practice of it; and be sooner taught that order and method, which we are deficient in.

It is sometimes urged, that we have no experienced officers to command us. We labour under some disadvantage, in this respect; but not so great, as is believed. There are many, who have served in the last war, with reputation, dispersed throughout the colonies. These might have the superior direction of matters; and there are men enough of known sense, and courage, who would soon make excellent officers. During the disputes, between the unfortunate *Charles* and the parliament, many country gentlemen served, in the armies of the latter, and signalized themselves, for their military virtues. It is worthy of observation, that the present state of the army is not the most favourable. As is always the consequence of a long peace, there are many effeminate striplings, among the officers, who are better calculated to marshal the forces of *Venus,* than to conduct the sturdy sons of *Mars.* There are, comparatively, but few veterans, either among the leaders, or the common soldiers.

You ask me, what resources have the colonies to pay, cloath, arm and feed their troops? I refer you to the accounts, from Virginia and Marblehead, for an answer to this question. Our troops, on the spot, with us, will be much more easily maintained, than those of Britain, at such a distance. We are not so poor and incumbered, as to be unable to support those who are immediately employed in defending our liberties. Our country abounds in provisions. We have already materials enough among us, to keep us in cloaths, longer than Britain would have any appetite to continue her hostilities. Several of the colonies are pretty well stored with ammunition. France, Spain, and Holland would find means, to supply us with whatever we wanted.

Let it not be said, that this last is a bare *possibility,* that France and Spain have promised not to interfere in the dispute, and that Holland has long been a faithful ally to the British nation. There is the highest degree of probability, in the case. A more desireable object, to France and Spain, than the disunion of these colonies from Great-Britain, cannot be imagined. Every dictate of policy and interest would prompt them to forward it, by every possible means. They could not take any so effectual method, to destroy the growing power of their great rival. The promises of princes and statesmen are of little weight. They never bind longer, than 'till a strong temptation offers to break them; and they are frequently make,[47] with a sinister design. If we consult the known character of the French, we shall be disposed to conclude, that their present, seem-

47. "made," in "Errata."

ingly, pacific and friendly disposition is merely a piece of *finesse;* intended to dupe administration into some violent measures with the colonies, that they may improve them to their own advantage. The most that can be expected is, that they would refrain from an open rupture, with Britain. They would undoubtedly take every clandestine method to introduce among us supplies of those things, which we stood in need of to carry on the dispute. They would not neglect any thing, in their power, to make the opposition on our part, as vigorous and obstinate as our affairs would admit of.

With respect to Holland, notwithstanding express engagements to the contrary, her merchants, during the last war, were constantly supplying the French and Spaniards, with military stores, and other things, they had occasion for. The same, or perhaps, more powerful motives, would influence them to assist us, in a like manner.

But it seems to me a mark a great credulity to believe, upon the strength of their assurance, that France and Spain, would not take a still more interesting part, in the affair. The disjunction of these colonies from Britain, and the acquisition of a free trade with them are objects of too inviting a complexion, to suffer those kingdoms to remain idle spectators of the contention. If they found us inclined to throw ourselves upon their protection, they would eagerly embrace the opportunity to weaken their antagonist and strengthen themselves. Superadded to these general and prevailing inducements, there are others of a more particular nature. They would feel no small inconvenience, in the loss of those supplies, they annually get from us; and their Islands in the West-Indies, would be in the greatest distress for want of our trade.

From these reflections, it is more than probable, that America is able to support its freedom, even by the force of arms, if she be not betrayed, by her own sons. And, in whatever light we view the matter, the consequences to Great-Britain, would be too destructive, to permit her to proceed to extremities, unless she has lost all just sense of her own interest.

You say, "the grand Congress, the *piddling* committees, through the continent, have *all* disclaimed their subjection to the sovereign authority of the empire: They deny the authority of parliament, to make any laws, to bind them all. They claim an absolute independency. Great-Britain has no choice, but to declare the colonies independent states, or to try the force of arms, in order to bring them to a sense of their duty."

It is the common trick of ministerial writers to represent the Congress, as having made some new demands, which were unknown to former times; whereas, in truth, they have, in substance, acknowledged the only dependence on parliament which was ever intended, by their predecessors. Nor [is] it true, that they have claimed an *absolute independency*. It is insulting common sense, to say so when it is notorious, that they have acknowledged the right of parliament to regulate the trade of the colonies. Any further dependence on it, is unnecessary and dangerous. They have professed allegiance to the British King, and have bound themselves, on any emergency, to contribute their proportion of men and money, to the defence and protection of the whole empire. Can this be called *absolute independency?* Is it better for Britain to hazard the total loss [of] these colonies, than to hold them upon these conditions? Is it preferable to make enemies of the people of America, instead of being connected with them, by the equal tie of fellow subjects? Is it not madness, to run the risk of losing the trade of these colonies, from which the mother country, drew * "more clear profit, than Spain has drawn from all her mines," because they insist only upon all the essential rights of free men? You may call it effrontery, consummate assurance, or what you please, to say so; but every man, capable of taking a full prospect of all the probable mischiefs, which may result, from an open rupture between Britain and the colonies, will coincide with me, when I affirm, that nothing, but the most *frantic extravagance*, can influence administration to attempt the reduction of America, by force of arms.

It is sufficiently evident, from the respective charters, that the rights, we now claim, are coeval with the original settlement of these colonies. These rights have been, at different times, strenuously asserted, though they have been suffered to be violated, in several instances, through inattention, or, perhaps, an unwillingness to quarrel with the mother country. I shall decline producing any other proofs of the sense of the other provinces, than those already mentioned,

* See Shipley's Speech.[48]

48. The quotation is from Jonathan Shipley, *A Speech Intended to Have been Spoken on the Bill for Altering the Charters of the Colony of Massachusett's Bay* (London, 1774), 15.

and shall confine my self, to a few extracts, from the resolves of some assemblies of this province.

In 1691, there was an act passed by the General Assembly,[49] which contained the following clauses.*

"Be it enacted, by the Governor, Council and Representatives, met in General Assembly, and it is hereby enacted and declared, by the authority of the same, that the *supreme legislative power and authority*, under their Majesty's William and Mary, King and Queen of England, &c. shall, for ever, be and reside, in a Governor in chief, and Council appointed, by their Majesties, their heirs and successors, and the people, by their representatives, met and convened, in General Assembly.

"That no freeman shall be taken, or imprisonned, or be deprived of his freehold, or life, or liberty, or free customs, or outlawed, or exiled, or any other ways destroyed, nor shall be passed upon, adjudged, or condemned, but *by the lawful judgment of his peers and by the law of the province.*

"That no *aid, tax, talliage, custom, loan, benevolence, gift, excise, duty*, or *imposition whatsoever*, shall be laid, assessed, imposed, levied, or required, of, or on, any of their Majesty's subjects, within this province, &c. or their estates, *upon any manner of colour or pretence whatsoever*, but, by the act and consent of the Governor and Council and Representatives of the people, in General Assembly, met and convened."

This act shews clearly the sense of his Majesty's Representative, his Council and the Assembly of this province, above *eighty years* ago, which was, that the supreme legislative authority and the exclusive power of taxation should, for ever, be and reside, in a Governor in chief, and Council, appointed by their Majesties, their heirs and successors, and the people, by their representatives, met and convened, in General Assembly.

We may also infer, from hence, that the other colonies actually

---

* This act is very remarkable. It was drawn up by Mess. *Farewell* and *Emmett*,[50] two gentlemen appointed by the governor for the purpose; and remained *six years* in England, before there was a negative put upon it.

49. The reference is to the General Assembly of New York.

50. George Farewell and Thomas Emott were attorneys in the Province of New York. Farewell was attorney general of New York for a short period in 1791. See John R. Brodhead, ed., *Documents Relative to the Colonial History of the State of New-York* (Albany, 1853–1887), III, 679, 701; IV, 308, 847.

enjoyed similar privileges, at that time: For, it would have been the height of presumption, in this province, to claim such important immunities, had not the others been in possession of the like.

This act of itself confutes all, that has been said, concerning the novelty of our present claims, and proves, that the injurious reflections, on the Congress, for having risen, in their demands, are malicious and repugnant to truth.

You have produced some expressions of the Congress and Assembly of this province, in 1765, which you lay great stress upon.[51] The true meaning of them may be gathered, from the following passage, which is taken from the same piece, that contains the expressions in question: The Congress speak thus: "It is humbly submitted, whether there be not a material distinction, in reason and sound policy, at least, between the necessary exercise of parliamentary jurisdiction, in general acts, for the amendment of the common law, and the regulation of trade and commerce, through the whole empire, and the exercise of that jurisdiction, by imposing taxes, on the colonies."

They allow only a power of making *general acts* for the amendment of the *common law*, and for the general regulation of trade. As to any special laws, to bind the colonies, in particular, they never intended submission to these; nor could they intend a right to impose special duties, of any kind, for the purpose of raising a revenue, which is, to all intents and purposes, a species of taxation.

The resolves of our Assembly, the last day of December 1771, about three years afterwards, will serve as a full explanation. "As it is, not only, the common birthright of all his Majesty's subjects, but, is also essential to the preservation of the peace, strength and prosperity of the British empire, that an *exact equality of constitutional rights*, among all his Majesty's subjects, in the several parts of the empire, be uniformly and invariably maintained and supported; and as it would be inconsistent with the constitutional rights, of his Majesty's subjects, in Great-Britain, to tax them, either in per-

51. The reference is to the resolutions of the General Assembly of New York, December 18, 1765, quoted by Seabury as follows: "That they think it their indispensable duty to make a declaration of their faith and allegiance to his Majesty, King George, the Third, and their *submission to the supreme legislative power*, and at the same time to shew, that the *rights claimed by them* are in *no manner inconsistent* with either." See Seabury, *A View of the Controversy*, 11.

son, or estate, without the consent of their representatives, in Parliament assembled. It is therefore

"RESOLVED *nemine contradicente,*

"That it is the opinion of this committee, that *no tax under any name, or denomination, or on any pretence, or for any purpose whatsoever,* can, or ought to be imposed, or levied upon the persons, estates, or property of his Majesty's good subjects within this colony, *but of their free gift, by their representatives lawfully convened, in General Assembly.*

"That it is the opinion of this committee, that this colony lawfully and constitutionally has and enjoys an internal legislature, in which, the crown and the people of this colony are constitutionally represented; and that *the power and authority of the said legislature cannot lawfully or constitutionally be suspended, abridged, abrogated or annulled by any power or prerogative whatsoever,* the prerogative of the crown, ordinarily exercised, for prorogations and dissolutions, only, excepted."

A supreme authority, in the Parliament, to make any special laws for this province, consistent with the internal legislature here claimed is impossible; and cannot be supposed, without falling into that solecism, in politics, of *imperium* in *imperio.*

I imagine, Sir, I have, by this time, pretty fully and satisfactorily answered every thing, contained in your letter, of any consequence: The parts, I have left unattended to, are such as cannot operate, materially, to the prejudice of the cause I espouse; but I should not have neglected them, had it not been, that I have already taken a very ample range; and it would, perhaps, be imprudent to delay a conclusion.

Whatever opinion may be entertained of my sentiments and intentions, I attest that being, whose all-seeing eye penetrates the inmost recesses of the heart, that I am not influenced (in the part I take) by any unworthy motive—that, if I am in an error, it is my judgment, not my heart, that errs. That I earnestly lament the unnatural quarrel, between the parent state and the colonies; and most ardently wish for a speedy reconciliation, a perpetual and *mutually* beneficial union, that I am a warm advocate for limitted monarchy, and an unfeigned well-wisher to the present Royal Family.

But on the other hand, I am inviolably attached to the essential rights of mankind, and the true interests of society. I consider civil liberty, in a genuine unadulterated sense, as the greatest of terrestrial blessings. I am convinced, that the whole human race is intitled to it; and, that it can be wrested from no part of them, without the blackest and most aggravated guilt.

I verily believe also, that the best way to secure a permanent and happy union, between Great-Britain and the colonies, is to permit the latter to be as free, as they desire. To abridge their liberties, or to exercise any power over them, which they are unwilling to submit to, would be a perpetual source of discontent and animosity. A continual jealousy would exist on both sides. This would lead to tyranny, on the one hand, and to sedition and rebellion, on the other. Impositions, not really grievous in themselves, would be thought so; and the murmurs arising from thence, would be considered as the effect of a turbulent ungovernable spirit. These jarring principles would, at length, throw all things into disorder; and be productive of an irreparable breach, and a total disunion.

That harmony and mutual confidence may speedily be restored, between all the parts of the British empire, is the favourite wish of one, who feels the warmest sentiments of good will to mankind, who bears no enimity to you, and who is,   A sincere Friend to America.

N. B. The destruction of the Tea at Boston, the act for altering the government of Quebec, and the Suffolk resolves, shall be considered in some future publications.[52]

52. Of the three proposed subjects, H wrote only on the government of Quebec.

Remarks on the Quebec Bill: Part One

By the Author of
The Farmer Refuted, &c.

[New York, June 15, 1775]

In compliance with my promise to the public,* and in order to rescue truth from the specious disguise, with which it has been

Rivington's New-York Gazetteer, June 15, 1775.
* See page 78 of the Farmer Refuted, a pamphlet published last winter by James Rivington.

cloathed, I shall now offer a few remarks on the act, intitled, "An Act for making more effectual provision, for the government of the province of Quebec, In North-America" whereby, I trust, it will clearly appear, that arbitrary power, and its great engine the Popish Religion, are, to all intents and purposes, established in that province.

While Canada was under the dominion of France, the French laws and customs were in force there; which are regulated in conformity to the genius and complexion of a despotic constitution; and expose the lives and properties of subjects to continued depredations, from the malice and avarice of those in authority: But when it fell under the dominion of Britain, these laws so unfriendly to the happiness of society gave place, of course, to the milder influence of the English laws; and his Majesty, by proclamation, promised to all those who should settle there, a full enjoyment of the rights of British subjects.

In violation of this promise, the act before us declares, "That the said proclamation, and the commission, under the authority whereof, the government of the said province is at present administered, be, and the same are hereby revoked, annulled and made void, from and after the first day of May, 1775." This abolition of the privileges stipulated by the proclamation was not inflicted as a penalty for any crime, by which a forfeiture had been incurred, but merely on pretence of the present form of government having "been found, by experience, to be inapplicable to the state and circumstances of the province." I have never heard any satisfactory account concerning the foundation of this pretence: for it does not appear, that the people of Canada, at large, ever expressed a discontentment with their new establishment, or solicited a restoration to their old. They were doubtless, the most proper judges of the matter, and ought to have been fully consulted, before the alteration was made. If we may credit the general current of intelligence, which we have had respecting the disposition of the Canadians, we must conclude they are averse to the present regulation of the Parliament; and had rather continue under the form of government instituted by the royal proclamation.

However this may be, the French laws are again revived. It is enacted, "that in all matters of controversy relative to property and civil rights, resort shall be had to the laws of Canada, as the rule for the decision of the same; and all causes, that shall hereafter be instituted, in any of the courts of justice, shall, with respect to such property and rights, be determined agreeably to the said laws and customs of Canada, until they shall be varied and altered, by any ordinances, that shall, from time to time, be passed in the said province, by the Governor, Lieutenant Governor or commander in chief for the time being by and with the advice and consent of the legislative council of the same." Thus the ancient laws of Canada are restored, liable to such variations and additions, as shall be deemed necessary, by the Governor and council, and as both the one and the other are to be appointed by the King, during pleasure, they will all be his creatures, and entirely subject to his will; which is thereby rendered the original fountain of law; and the property and civil rights of the Canadians are made altogether dependent upon it; because the power communicated of varying and altering, by new ordinances, is indefinite and unlimited. If this does not make the King absolute, in Canada, I am at a loss for any tolerable idea of absolute authority; which I have ever thought to consist, with respect to a monarch, in the power of governing his people according to the dictates of his own will. In the present case, he has only to inform the governor and council what new laws, he would chuse to have passed, and their situation will ensure their compliance.

It is further provided, "that nothing contained, in the act, shall extend, or be construed to extend to prevent or hinder his Majesty, his heirs and successors, from erecting, constituting and appointing, from time to time, such courts of *criminal, civil,* and *ecclesiastical jurisdiction,* within, and for the said province of Quebec; and appointing, *from time to time,* the judges and officers thereof, as his Majesty, his heirs and successors shall think necessary, for the circumstances of the said province."

Here a power of a most extraordinary and dangerous nature is conferred. There must be an end of all liberty, where the Prince is possessed of such an exorbitant prerogative, as enables him, at pleasure, to establish the most iniquitous, cruel, and oppressive courts of criminal, civil, and ecclesiastical jurisdiction; and to appoint temporary judges and officers, whom he can displace and change, as often as he pleases. For what can more nearly concern the safety and happiness of subjects, than the wise œconomy and equitable consitiution of these courts, in which, trials for life, liberty, property and religion are to be conducted? Should it ever comport with the designs of an ambitious and wicked minister, we may see an inquisition erected in Canada, and priestly tyranny may hereafter find as propitious a soil, in America as it ever has in Spain or Portugal.

But, in order to varnish over the arbitrary complexion of the act, and to conciliate the minds of the Canadians, it is provided, that "whereas the certainty and lenity of the criminal law of England, and the benefits and advantages resulting, from the use of it, have been sensibly felt by the inhabitants, from an experience of more, than nine years; therefore, the same shall be administered, and shall be observed, as law, in the province of Quebec, to the exclusion of every rule of criminal law, which did, or might prevail, in the said province, before the year 1764."

As "it is on the goodness of criminal laws, that the liberty of the subject principally depends *," this would have been an important privilege, had it not been rendered uncertain and alienable, by the latter part of the same clause, which makes them "subject to such alterations and amendments, as the Governor, Lieut. Governor, and Commander in Chief, for the time being, by and with the advice and consent of the legislative council of the same, shall, from time to time, cause to be made therein." Under the notion of necessary alterations and amendments, the King, through the medium of his creatures, the Governor and Council may intirely new mould the criminal laws of Canada, and make them subservient to the most tyrannical views: So that, in this respect also, the principle of arbitrary power, which is the soul of the act, is uniformly maintained and preserved, in full vigour, without the least real, or effectual diminution.

It has been denied, with the most palpable absurdity, that the right of trials by juries is taken from the Canadians. It is said, that the provincial legislature of Canada may introduce them, as soon as they please; and it is expected, that they will, as "soon as the inhabitants

* *Montesquieu.*[1]

1. This is a quotation from Montesquieu's *The Spirit of Laws*, Vol. I, Book XII ("Of the Laws that form political Liberty as relative to the Subject"), Ch. II ("Of the Liberty of the Subject"), p. 261. See Charles Louis de Secondat, Baron de La Brede et de Montesquieu, *The Spirit of Laws*, trans. Mr. Nugent, 2 vols. (3d. ed.; London, Printed for J. Nourse and P. Vaillant in the Strand, 1758).

desire them, or the state of the country will admit of them." A civil right is that, which the laws and the constitution have actually conferred, not that, which may be derived, from the future bounty and beneficence of those in authority. The possibility that the legislature of Canada may hereafter introduce trials, by juries, does not imply a right, in the people, to enjoy them. For, in the same sense, it may be said, that the inhabitants of France or Spain have a right to trials by juries; because it is equally in the power of their legislatures to establish them.

Since therefore it is apparent, that a system of French laws has been re-established, in the province of Quebec, and an indefinite power vested in the King, to vary and alter those laws, as also to constitute such courts of criminal civil and ecclesiastical jurisdiction, and to introduce such a form of criminal law, as he shall judge necessary; I say since all this is deducible, from the express letter of the act; or in other words, since the whole legislative, executive, and judiciary powers are ultimately and effectually, though not immediately, lodged in the King, there can be no room to doubt, that an arbitrary government has been really instituted throughout the extensive region now comprised in the province of Quebec.

[To Be Continued.]

Remarks on the Quebec Bill: Part Two

By the Author of
The Farmer Refuted, &c.

[New York, June 22, 1775]

Having considered the nature of this bill, with regard to civil government, I am next to examine it with relation to religion, and to endeavour to shew, that the Church of Rome has now the sanction of a legal establishment, in the province of Quebec. In order to do this the more satisfactorily, I beg leave to adopt the definition given of an established religion, by a certain writer, who has taken great pains to evince the contrary. "An established religion," says he, "is a religion, which the civil authority engages, not only to protect, but to

Rivington's New-York Gazetteer, June 22, 1775.

support." This act makes effectual provision not only for the protection, but for the permanent support of Popery, as is evident from the following clause, "And for the more perfect security and ease of the minds of the inhabitants of the said province, it is hereby declared, that his Majesty's subjects professing the religion of the church of Rome in the said province, may have, hold, and enjoy, the free exercise of the religion of the church of Rome, subject to the King's supremacy, &c. and *that the clergy of the said church may hold, receive and enjoy their accustomed dues and rights, &c.*"

This is represented as a bare permission to the clergy, to enjoy the usual emoluments of their functions; and not as a legal provision for their support. Much stress seems to be laid on the word *may* which is commonly italickised. But though the phraseology be artful, yet it is easy to perceive, that it operates to the same effect, as if it had been more positive and emphatical. The clergy may hold, receive and enjoy their accustomed dues and rights. They may, if they please: It is at their option, and must depend upon their will; and consequently there must be a correspondent obligation upon their parishoners, to comply with that will and to pay those dues, when required. What the law gives us an unconditional permission to enjoy, no person can legally withold from us. It becomes our property, and we can enforce our right to it. If the legislature of this colony were to decree, that the clergy of the different denominations may hold, receive and enjoy tithes of their respective congregations, we should soon find, that it would have the same efficacy, as if it were decreed, that the several congregations should pay tithes to their respective clergy. For otherwise the legislature might confer a right, which had no co-relative obligation, and which must therefore be void and inefficacious. But this is contradictory and impossible.

"Tithes in Canada (it is said) are the *property* of the Romish Church; and permitting a tolerated church to enjoy its own property, is far short of the idea of an establishment." But I should be glad to know, in the first place, how tithes can be the *property* of any but an established church; and, in the next, how they came to be the *property* of the Romish Church, in Canada, during the intermediate space between the surrender of that province to the English and the passing of this act. Nothing can be deemed my *property*, to which, I have not a perfect and uncontrolable right by the laws. If a church have not a similar right to tithes, it can have no *property* in them; and if it have, it is plain the laws must have made provision for its support, or in other words must have established it.

Previous to the surrender of Canada, the Catholic religion was established there, by the laws of France; and tithes were on that account the legal property of the church of Rome; and could not be withheld by the laity, though eversomuch disposed to it. But, after the surrender, this circumstance took a different turn. The French laws being no longer in force, the establishment of the Romish church ceased of course, and, with it, the *property* which it before had in tithes. It is true, the clergy may have continued to receive and enjoy their customary dues; tithes and other perquisites; but they were not, for all that, the property of the church, because it had lost its legal right to them; and it was at the discretion of the laity to withhold them, if they had thought proper, or to abridge them, and place them upon a more moderate footing. Their voluntary concurrence was necessary, to give their priests a right to demand them, as before. But by the late act, this matter is again put into its former situation. Tithes are now become the *property* of the church as formerly; because it again has a legal claim to them, and the conditional consent of the people is set aside. Thus we see, that this act does not in fact, permit "a tolerated church to enjoy its own property;" but gives it a real and legal property in that, which it before held, from the bounty and liberality of its professors; and which they might withhold or diminish at pleasure. And this, in the most proper sense, converts it into an establishment.

The characteristic difference between a tolerated and established religion consist in this—With respect to the support of the former, the law is passive and improvident; leaving it to those, who profess it, to make as much, or as little provision, as they shall judge expedient; and to vary and alter that provision, as their circumstances may require. In this manner, the Presbyterians and other sects are tolerated in England. They are allowed to exercise their religion without molestation; and to maintain their clergy as they think proper. These are wholly dependent upon their congregations, and can exact no more than they stipulate and are satisfied to contribute. But with respect to the support of the latter, the law is active and provident. Certain precise dues (tithes, &c.) are legally annexed to the clerical office, independent on the liberal contributions of the people; which is exactly the case with the Canadian priests, and therefore no reasonable impartial man will doubt, that the religion of the church of Rome is established in Canada. While tithes were the free, though customary, gift of the people, as was the case before the passing of the act in question, the Romish church was only in a state of toleration. But when the law came to take cognizance of them; and, by determining their permanent existence, destroyed the free agency of the people; it then resumed the nature of an establishment, which it had been divested of, at the time of the capitulation.

As to the Protestant religion, it is often asserted, that ample provision has often been made, by the act, for its future establishment; to prove which, the writer before mentioned, has quoted a clause, in the following mutilated manner, "It is provided (says he) that his Majesty, his heirs, or successors, may make such provision out of the accustomed dues or rights, for the encouragement of the Protestant religion, and for the maintenance of a Protestant clergy, within the said province, as he, or they shall, from time to time, think necessary and expedient."

It must excite a mixture of anger and disdain, to observe the wretched arts, to which a designing administration and its abettors are driven, in order to conceal the enormity of their measures. This whole clause, in its true and original construction, is destitute of meaning; and was evidently inserted for no other end, than to deceive, by the *appearance* of a provident regard for the Protestant religion. The act first declares, "That his Majesty's subjects professing the religion of the Church of Rome may have, hold and enjoy the free exercise of their religion; and that the clergy of the said church may hold, receive and enjoy their accustomed dues and rights." Then follows this clause:

"Provided nevertheless, that it shall be lawful for his Majesty, his heirs and successors, to make such provision out of *the rest of* the said accustomed dues and rights, for the encouragement of the Protestant religion, for the maintenance and support of a Protestant clergy, within the said province, as he, or they shall, from time to time, think necessary and expedient." Thus we see, the

Romish clergy are to have, hold and enjoy their accustomed dues and rights, and the *rest*, or remainder of them is to be applied towards the encouragement of the Protestant religion, but when they have had their wonted dues, I fancy it will puzzle administration, by any effort of political chymistry, to produce the *rest* or remainder. Suppose for instance, A had made an actual settlement of an hundred pounds upon B and, by a subsequent act, should declare that B should still continue to hold and enjoy his accustomed and annual bounty, and that the *rest* of the said bounty should be given to C, it is evident, that C would have nothing, because there would be no *rest* whatever. Exactly parallel and analogous is the case in hand. The Romish Priests are to have their accustomed dues and rights; and the *rest* of the said dues and rights is to be dedicated to the encouragement of the Protestant religion.

In the above recited quotation, there is a chasm, the words *the rest of* being artfully omitted, to give the passage some meaning, which it has not in itself. With this amendment, the sense must be, that his Majesty might appropriate what portion of the customary revenues of the Romish clergy, he should think proper, to the support and maintenance of protestant churches: But according to the real words of the act, he can only devote the rest, or remainder of such revenues to that purpose, which, as I have already shewn, is nothing: So that the seeming provision in favour of the protestant religion is intirely verbal and delusory. Excellent must be the encouragement, it will derive from this source!

But this is not all: Had there been really provision made, to be applied at the discretion of his Majesty, I should still consider this act as an atrocious infraction on the rights of Englishmen, in a point of the most delicate and momentous concern. No protestant Englishman would consent to let the free exercise of his religion depend upon the mere pleasure of any man, however great or exalted. The privilege of worshipping the deity in the manner his conscience dictates, which is one of the dearest he enjoys, must in that case be rendered insecure and precarious. Yet this is the unhappy situation, to which the protestant inhabitants of Canada are now reduced. The will of the King must give law to their consciences. It is in his power to keep them for ever dispossessed of all religious immunities; and there is too much reason to apprehend, that the same motives which instigated the act, would induce him to give them as little future encouragement as possible.

I imagine, it will clearly appear from what has been offered, that "the Roman catholic religion instead of being tolerated as stipulated by the treaty of peace, is established" by the late act; and that the protestant religion has been left intirely destitute and unbefriended in Canada. But if there should be any, who think, that the indulgence granted does not extend to a perfect establishment, and that it may be justified by the terms of the treaty and the subsequent conduct of the Canadians; and if they should also be at a loss to perceive the dangerous nature of the act with respect to the other colonies, I would beg their further attention to the following considerations.

However justifiable this act may be in relation to the province of Quebec with its ancient limits, it cannot be defended by the least plausible pretext, when it is considered as annexing such a boundless extent of new territory to the old. If a free form of government had "been found by experience, to be inapplicable to the state and circumstances of the province"; and if "a toleration less generous, although it might have fulfilled the letter of the articles of the treaty, would not have answered the expectations of the Canadians, nor have left upon their minds favourable impressions of British justice and honour:" if these reasons be admitted as true, and allowed their greatest weight, they only proved, that it might be just and polite to place the province of Quebec alone, with its former boundaries, in the circumstances of civil and religious government, which are established by this act. But when it is demanded why it has also added the immense tract of country that surrounds all these colonies, to that province, and has placed the whole under the same exceptionable institutions, both civil and religious, the advocates for administration must be confounded and silent.

This act develops the dark designs of the ministry more fully than any thing they have done; and shews, that they have formed a systematic project of absolute power. The present policy of it is evidently this. By giving a legal sanction to the accustomed dues of the priests, it was intended to interest them in behalf of administration; and by means of the dominion they possess over the minds of the laity, together with the appearance of good will towards their religion, to prevent any dissatisfaction, which might arise from the loss of their civil rights, and to propitiate them to the great purposes in contemplation; first the subjugation of the colonies and afterwards that of Britain itself. It was necessary to throw out some such lure, to reconcile them to the exertions of that power, which has been communicated to the King, and which the emergencies of the times may require in a very extensive degree.

The future policy of it demands particular attention. The nature of civil government will hereafter put a stop to emigrations from other parts of the British dominions thither, and from all other free countries. The preeminent advantages secured to the Roman catholic religion will discourage all protestant soldiers of whatsoever nation: And on these accounts the province will be settled and inhabited by none, but papists. If lenity and moderation are observed in administering the laws, the natural advantages of this fertile infant country, united to the indulgence given to their religion, will attract droves of emigrants, from all the Roman catholic states in Europe; and these colonies, in time, will find themselves encompassed with innumerous hosts of neighbours, disaffected to them, both because of difference in religion and government. How dangerous their situation would be, let every man of common sense judge.

What can speak in plainer language, the corruption of the British Parliament, than its act; which invests the King with absolute power over a little world, (if I may be allowed the expression) and makes such ample provision for the popish religion, and leaves the protestant, in such dependent disadvantageous situation that he is like to have no other subjects, in this part of his domain, than Roman catholics; who, by reason of their implicit devotion to their priests, and the superlative reverence they bear to those, who countenance and favour their religion, will be the voluntary instruments of ambition; and will be ready, at all times, to second the oppressive designs of administration against the other parts of the empire.

Hence while our ears are stunned with the dismal sounds of New-England's republicanism, bigotry, and intolerance, it behoves us to be upon our guard against the deceitful wiles of those, who would persuade us, that we have nothing to fear from the operation of the Quebec act. We should consider it as being replete with danger, to ourselves, and as threatening ruin to our posterity. Let us not therefore suffer ourselves to be terrified at the prospect of an imaginary and fictitious Sylla, and, by that means, be led blindfold into a real and destructive Charybdis.

To John Jay [1]

New York Novem 26. 1775

Dear Sir

I take the liberty to trouble you with some remarks on a matter which to me appears of not a little importance; doubting not that you will use your influence in Congress to procure a remedy for the evil I shall mention, if you think the considerations I shall urge are of that weight they seem in my judgment to possess.

You will probably ere this reaches you have heard of the late incursion made into this city by a number of horsemen from New England under the command of Capt Sears, who took away Mr. Rivington's types, and a Couteau or two.[2] Though I am fully sensible how dangerous and pernicious Rivington's press has been, and how detestable the character of the man is in every respect, yet I cannot help disapproving and condemning this step.

In times of such commotion as the present, while the passions of men are worked up to an uncommon pitch there is great danger of fatal extremes. The same state of the passions which fits the multitude, who have not a sufficient stock of reason and knowlege to guide them, for opposition to tyranny and oppression, very naturally leads them to a contempt and disregard of all authority. The due medium is hardly to be found among the more intelligent, it is almost impossible among the unthinking populace. When the minds of these are loosened from their attachment to ancient establishments and courses, they seem to grow giddy and are apt more or

ALS, MS Division, New York Public Library.

1. Jay, a member of both the First and Second Continental Congresses, was in frequent correspondence with New York Patriots.

2. James Rivington was the printer of *Rivington's New-York Gazetteer.* Because of his own and his paper's Tory views, he was attacked by a mob of Patriots in May, 1775. On November 23, 1775, his shop was attacked by a group of men from Connecticut, recruited by Isaac Sears, a leader of the New York Sons of Liberty.

less to run into anarchy. These principles, too true in themselves, and confirmed to me both by reading and my own experience, deserve extremely the attention of those, who have the direction of public affairs. In such tempestuous times, it requires the greatest skill in the political pilots to keep men steady and within proper bounds, on which account I am always more or less alarmed at every thing which is done of mere will and pleasure, without any proper authority. Irregularities I know are to be expected, but they are nevertheless dangerous and ought to be checked, by every prudent and moderate mean. From these general maxims, I disapprove of the irruption in question, as serving to cherish a spirit of disorder at a season when men are too prone to it of themselves.

Moreover, New England is very populous and powerful. It is not safe to trust to the virtue of any people. Such proceedings will serve to produce and encourage a spirit of encroachment and arrogance in them. I like not to see potent neighbours indulged in the practice of making inroads at pleasure into this or any other province.

You well know too, sir, that antipathies and prejudices have long subsisted between this province and New England. To this may be attributed a principal part of the disaffection now prevalent among us. Measures of the present nature, however they may serve to intimidate, will secretly revive and increase those ancient animosities, which though smothered for a while will break out when there is a favorable opportunity.

Besides this, men coming from a neighbouring province to chastise the notorious friends of the ministry here, will hold up an idea to our ennemies not very advantageous to our affairs. They will imagine that the New Yorkers are totally, or a majority of them, disaffected to the American cause, which makes the interposal of their neighbours necessary: or that such violences will breed differences and effect that which they have been so eagerly wishing, a division and qurrelling among ourselves. Every thing of such an aspect must encourage their hopes.

Upon the whole the measure is condemned, by all the cautious and prudent among the whigs, and will evidently be productive of secret jealousy and ill blood if a stop is not put to things of the kind for the future.

All the good purposes that could be expected from such a step will be answered; and many ill consequences will be prevented if your body gently interposes a check for the future. Rivington will be intimidated & the tories will be convinced that the other colonies will not tamely see the general cause betrayed by the Yorkers. A favourable idea will be impressed of your justice & impartiality in discouraging the encroachments of any one province on another; and the apprehensions of prudent men respecting the ill-effects of an ungoverned spirit in the people of New England will be quieted. Believe me sir it is a matter of consequence and deserves serious attention

The tories it is objected by some are growing insolent and clamorous: It is necessary to repress and overawe them. There is truth in this; but the present remedy is a bad one. Let your body station in different parts of the province most tainted, with the ministerial infection, a few regiments of troops, raised in Philadelphia the Jerseys or any other province except New England. These will suffice to strengthen and support the Whigs who are still I flatter myself a large majority and to suppress the efforts of the tories. The pretence for this would be plausible. There is no knowing how soon the Ministry may make an attempt upon New York. There is reason to believe they will not be long before they turn their attention to it. In this there will be some order & regularity, and no grounds of alarm to our friends.

I am sir with very great Esteem—   Your most hum servant
                                                                A. Hamilton

To John Jay

N York Decemr. 31st. 1775

Dear Sir

It is hardly necessary to inform you that I received your favour [1] in answer to my letter on the subject of Capt Sear's Expedition; and that I shall be at all times ready to comply with your request of information concerning the state of the province, or any matters of importance that may arise. Any thing that may conduce to the public service or may serve as a testimony of my respect to you will be always gladly embraced by me.

I have much reason to suspect that the tories have it in contemplation to steal a march upon us, if they can, in respect of a New Assembly. I believe the governor will shortly dissolve the old and issue writs for a new one. The motives for it, at this time, are probably these: It is hoped the attention of the people being engaged with their new institutions, Congresses, committees and the like; they will think the assembly of little importance, and will not exert themselves as they ought to do, whereby the tories may have an opportunity to elect their own creatures. Or at least it is expected the people may be thrown into divisions and ferments, injurious to present measures.[2]

The tories will be no doubt very artful and intriguing, and it behoves us to be very vigilant and cautious. I have thrown out a hand bill or two to give the necessary alarm, and shall second them by others.

It appears to me that as the best way to keep the attention of the people united and fixed to the same point, it would be expedient that four of our Continental delegates should be candidates for this city and county;[3] Mr. Livingston[4] Mr. Alsop,[5] Mr. Lewis,[6] Mr. Jay.[7] The minds of all our friends will naturally tend to these, and the opposition will of course be weak and contemptible, for the whigs I doubt not constitute a large majority of the people. If you approve the hint, I should wish for your presence here. Absence you know is not very favorable to the influence of any person however great.

I shall give you farther notice, as I see the scheme advance to execution.

I am Dr. Sir   Your very hum servant   A Hamilton

ALS, Columbia University Libraries.
   1. Letter not found.
   2. New York's first Provincial Congress met on May 22, 1775. Although the royal governor and his Loyalist supporters still maintained that the old Assembly was the legal legislature, the Provincial Congress exercised de facto legislative power. The second Provincial Congress, elected in November, 1775, convened on December 6 and adjourned on December 22, 1775, having authorized a Committee of Safety to carry on business and to order the election of a new congress. Loyalist opposition to the measures of the Provincial Congress was vigorous. Some Loyalists (as well as the royal governor, William Tryon, who had withdrawn in October, 1775, to a British warship in New York Harbor) concluded that it might be possible to restore the power of the old Assembly. Governor Tryon dissolved the Assembly on January 2, 1776, and issued writs for a new election. Although the Assembly met on February 14, 1776, it was prorogued and accomplished nothing.

3. H here suggests the plan followed by the New York Patriots. The Assembly, elected on the basis of the writs issued by Governor Tryon, on January 2, 1776, contained a majority of men who had been members of the Provincial Congress. The four men recommended by H were among the New York delegates to the Continental Congress.

4. Philip Livingston, born and raised on the family manor, established himself as an importer in New York City. A member of the New York General Assembly in the seventeen-sixties, he subsequently served both as a delegate to the First and Second Continental Congresses and as a member of the New York Provincial Congress.

5. John Alsop, New York City merchant, was active in the politics of colonial New York. Although he early sided with the Patriots in their dispute with the English Ministry and was a New York delegate to the First and Second Continental Congresses, he eventually became a Tory.

6. Francis Lewis, born in Wales, came to the American colonies in 1735 and established mercantile houses in New York and Philadelphia. After the French and Indian War, during which he served as clothing contractor for the British troops in America, he became prominent in New York politics. A member of the Stamp Act Congress and a signer of the Declaration of Independence, he represented New York in the Continental Congress from 1775 to 1779.

7. John Jay.

1 7 7 6

To John Jay

[New York, January 4, 1776] [1]

Dear Sir

The inclosed was intended by the last post, but I was disappointed in sending it. You will find by the papers, that a proclamation has been issued for dissolving the old Assembly; writs are making out for the election of a new.

The tories seem to give out that there will be no opposition, but I suspect this as an artifice to throw the people off their guard. I doubt not however the whig Interest will prevail.

I should be glad to see you here with all convenient dispatch; though perhaps your presence may not be absolutely necessary, yet I like not to hazard any thing, or to neglect any step which may have the least tendency to insure success.

I am   Your most hum servt   A Hamilton

ALS, Mr. Frank L. Pleadwell, Honolulu, Hawaii.
    1. The endorsement, in the writing of John Jay, reads, "A. Hamilton to Mr. Jay. Lettr. Jany 1776." The letter is postmarked "N. York Jan. 4."

To Colonel Alexander McDougall [1]

[New York, March 17, 1776]

Newyork. March 17th 1776. Recived of Col. McDougall Seventy three Pounds, Nineteen Shillings and a Penny half penny for the Pay of the Commissioned Non-Commissioned officers and privates of my Company to the first Instant for which I [have] given three other receipts. [2]

£73.19.1¾   Alex: Hamilton Capt

DS, New-York Historical Society, New York City.
    1. Alexander McDougall, prominent Revolutionary War general, gained his first military experience as a commander of privateers from 1756 to 1763. After the French and Indian War, McDougall returned to New York City where he

became a successful merchant. Because of his opposition to the royal government he was dubbed the "Wilkes of America." A member of the first and second Provincial Congresses, he was among the most prominent of the radical
leaders in New York City. Appointed colonel of the First New York Regiment
in 1775, he was made a Continental brigadier general in 1776 and major general
the following year.

2. Verso is entitled: "Pay Roll of the Artillery Company of the Colony of
New York at Present under the Command of Jas. Moore, Capt Leiut, from
the time of their Inlistment to 1st March (exclusive) 1776." It is dated "10
March 1776" and signed "Jas. Moore Capt. Leiut." The payroll is printed in
Colls. of N.Y. Hist. Soc. for 1915, 338–41.

As early as the spring of 1775, H had joined the volunteers who drilled every
morning in St. George's Churchyard in New York City, and in August he had
been under fire when he assisted in the removal of cannon from the Battery.
On January 6, 1776, the Provincial Congress ordered that an artillery company
be raised for the defense of New York, and H, who had studied gunnery,
apparently sought command of it. On February 23, 1776, it was recorded in
the *Journals* of the Provincial Congress that:

"Col. McDougall recommended Mr. Alexander Hamilton for captain of a
company of artillery; Mr. James Moore for captain-lieutenant; and [Martin]
Johnson who was in service last year, and who was lately appointed by the
Committee of Safety, for first lieutenant.

"*Ordered*, That the appointment of those officers be taken into consideration
tomorrow morning" (*Journals of the Provincial Congress, of the State of New-
York*, I, 321).

There is no record of action on the day following, but on March 14, 1776,
H received his official appointment. An entry of that date in the *Journals* of
the Congress reads:

"A certificate of Stephen Badlam, capt. of artillery, was read and filed. He
thereby certifies that he has examined Alexander Hamilton and judges him
qualified to command a company of artillery.

"*Ordered*, That the said Alexander Hamilton be, and he is hereby, appointed
captain of the Provincial company of artillery of this Colony" (*Journals of
the Provincial Congress of the State of New-York*, I, 359).

From Committee of Safety of the New York Provincial Congress

[*New York, April 2, 1776*. An entry in the *Journals* of the New
York Provincial Congress under this date reads: "*Ordered* That
Capt. Hamilton be directed to place and keep a proper guard of his
company at the Records [1] until, further order." [2] *Letter not found.*]

Journals of the Provincial Congress of the State of New-York, I, 396.

1. The records were those of the colony. Anticipating the possible capture
of New York City by the British, the Provincial Congress resolved to move
the colony's records to Kingston, New York.

2. The resolution which precedes this order reads:

"WHEREAS the present guard of the first regiment of the city of New-
York, where the records of the Colony are deposited, has, by experience, been
found a very expensive Colony charge; and although the Committee are of
opinion that the guards hitherto employed in that service have great merit
and are worthy of the highest confidence, yet they conceive themselves bound

in duty to the good people of this Colony, to prevent every expense that can be saved: AND WHEREAS the Committee are fully informed that Capt. Alexander Hamilton's company of artillery raised for this Colony, now consists of so many men as that they may safely and easily perform that duty: Therefore . . ." (*Journals of the Provincial Congress of the State of New-York*, I, 396).

To Colonel Alexander McDougall [1]

[New York, April 4, 1776]

New York April 4th, 1776. Received of Colonel McDougall one hundred and seventy two pounds, three shillings and five pence half penny, for the pay of the Commissioned, Non commissioned officers and privates of my company to the first instant, for which I have given three other receipts.

£172.3.5½.   Alex Hamilton Capt

ADS, New-York Historical Society, New York City.
    1. This receipt appears at the end of "Pay Roll of the Colony Company of Artillery commanded by Alexander Hamilton from first of March to first of April 1776—Vizt." The payroll, which is in H's writing, is signed "A. Hamilton Capt." and dated April 1, 1776. The complete document has been printed in *Colls. of N.Y. Hist. Soc. for 1915*, 340-45.

Return of Captain Alexander Hamilton's Company of Artillery

[*New York*] *April 20, 1776.* The return is headed: "A Return of the Colony Company of Artillery commanded by Alexander Hamilton April 20th, 1776" and is in the form of a table showing the number of each rank present and fit for duty, sick, on furlough, on command duty, or taken as prisoner. Hamilton's company contained a total of 69 commissioned and noncommissioned officers.

AD, George Washington Papers, Library of Congress.

To the Provincial Congress of the Colony of New York

[New York, May 26, 1776]

Gentlemen,
    I take the liberty to request your attention to a few particulars, which will be of considerable importance to the future progress of

the company under my command, and I will be much obliged to you for as speedy a determination concerning them as you can conveniently give. The most material is respecting the pay. Our company, by their articles, are to be subject to the same regulations, and to receive the same pay as the Continental artillery. Hitherto, I have conformed to the standard laid down in the Journal of the Congress, published the 10th May, 1775, but I am well informed that by some later regulation the pay of the artillery has been augmented and now stands according to the following rates: captain, £10 13s. 4d.; captain-lieutenant, £8; lieutenants, each £7. 6s. 8d.; sergeants, £3 6s. 8d.; corporals, £3 1s. 4d.; bombadiers, £1s. 4d.; gunners £3; matrosses, £2 17s. 4d.; drummers and fifers, £3. By compairing these with my pay rolls, you will discover a considerable difference, and I doubt not you will be easily sensible that such a difference should not exist. I am not personally interested in having an augmentation agreeable to the above rates, because my own pay will remain the same that it now is; but I make this application on behalf of the company, as I am fully convinced such a disadvantageous distinction will have a very pernicious effect on the minds and behaviour of the men. They do the same duty with the other companies and think themselves entitled to the same pay. They have been already comparing accounts and many marks of discontent have lately appeared on this score. As to the circumstance of our being confined to the defence of the Colony, it will have little or no weight, for there are but few in the company who would not as willingly leave the Colony on any necessary expedition as stay in it; and they will not therefore think it reasonable to have their pay curtailed on such a consideration.

Capt. Beauman,[1] I understand, enlists all his men on the above terms, and this makes it very difficult for me to get a single recruit, for men will naturally go to those who pay them best. On this account I should wish to be immediately authorized to offer the same pay to all who may incline to enlist.

The next thing I should wish to know is, whether I might be allowed any actual expenses that might attend the enlistment of men, should I send into the country for that purpose; the expense would not be great, and it would enable me to complete my company at once, and bring it the sooner into proper order and discipline. Also,

I should be glad to be informed if my company is to be allowed the frock which is given to the other troops as a bounty. This frock would be extremely serviceable in summer while the men are on fatigue, and would put it in their power to save their uniform much longer.[2]

I am, gentlemen, with the greatest respect,   Your most obedient servant,   A. Hamilton, *Capt.*

The Honourable the Provincial Congress.

Journals of the Provincial Congress of the State of New-York, II, 108–09.

1. Sebastian Bauman was appointed on March 30, 1776, by the New York Committee of Safety "captain of the Continental Company of Artillery to be raised in this Colony, which Mr. Beauman is hereby authorized and requested to enlist with all possible despatch" (*Journals of the Provincial Congress of the State of New-York*, I, 392).

2. On the same day, May 26, the Provincial Congress resolved "that the artillery company of the said Captain Hamilton be allowed the same pay as the Continental artillery, and that the said Captain Hamilton receive 10s. for every man he has or shall enlist not exceeding 100 men, and that each of the men of said company be allowed a frock as a bounty" (*Journals of the Provincial Congress of the State of New-York*, I, 462).

From the Provincial Congress of the Colony of New York

[*New York, May 31, 1776.* An entry in the *Journals* of the New York Provincial Congress under this date reads: "*Ordered,* that Capt. Alexander Hamilton, or any or either of his officers, be and they are hereby authorized to go on board any ship or vessel in this harbour, and take with them such guard as may be necessary, and that they make strict search for any men who may have deserted from Captain Hamilton's company." [1] *Letter not found.*]

Journals of the Provincial Congress of the State of New-York, I, 468.

1. This order was issued after a member had "informed the Congress that some of Captain Hamilton's company of artillery have deserted, and that he has some reasons to suspect that they are on board of the Continental ship, or vessel, in this harbour, under the command of Capt. Kennedy" (*Journals of the Provincial Congress of the State of New-York*, I, 468).

To the Convention of the Representatives of the State of New-York [1]

[New York] *July 26, 1776.*

Gentlemen,

I am obliged to write you, to remove a difficulty which arises respecting the quantity of subsistence which is to be allowed my men. Enclosed you have the rate of rations which is the standard allowance of the whole Continental and even the Provincial army; but it seems Mr. Curtenius [2] can not afford to supply us with more than his contract stipulates, which by comparison, you will perceive is considerably less than the forementioned rate. My men, you are sensible, are by their articles, entitled to the same subsistence with the Continental troops; and it would be to them an insupportable discrimination, as well as a breach of the terms of their enlistment, to give them almost a third less provisions than the whole army besides receives. I doubt not you will readily put this matter upon a proper footing. Hitherto, we have drawn our full allowance from Mr. Curtenius, but he did it upon the supposition that he should have a farther consideration for the extraordinary supply. At present however he scruples to proceed in the same way, until it can be put upon a more certain foundation. [3]

I am, gentlemen, With the utmost esteem and respect, Your most obdt. and most hum. servant, A. Hamilton,

Capt. of New-York Artillery.

The Honourable the Provincial Congress.

Journals of the Provincial Congress of the State of New-York, II, 299.

1. On July 10, 1776, one day after it had approved the Declaration of Independence, the Provincial Congress of New York changed its title to "The Convention of the Representatives of the State of New York" (*Journals of the Provincial Congress of the State of New-York,* II, 519). H incorrectly addressed his letter to "The Honorable the Provincial Congress."

2. On June 2, 1775, Peter T. Curtenius, a New York City merchant, was appointed commissary for New York. Curtenius and his staff of assistants were responsible for supplying the New York troops with provisions.

3. On the same date as H's letter the Congress received a letter from Cornelius C. Roosevelt, commissary for H's troops, stating "that he had been obliged to supply Capt. Hamilton's company with a much larger quantity of

provisions than the rations stipulated for, which had enhanced the price so that each ration as by him delivered cost him 12½d. His accounts were enclosed" (*Journals of the Provincial Congress of the State of New-York,* I, 550). After referring the letters from H and Roosevelt to a committee, the Convention ordered, "That as Capt. Hamilton's company was formerly made a part of General Scott's brigade, that they be henceforth supplied with provisions as a part of that Brigade" (*Journals of the Provincial Congress of the State of New-York,* I, 550).

To the Convention of the Representatives of the State of New-York

[New York, August 12, 1776]

Gentlemen

It is necessary I should inform you that there is at present a vacancy in my company, arising from the promotion of Lieutenant Johnson to a captaincy in one of the row-gallies, (which command, however, he has since resigned, for a very particular reason.) As artillery officers are scarce in proportion to the call for them, and as myself and my remaining officers sustain an extraordinary weight of duty on account of the present vacancy, I shall esteem it a favour if you will be pleased, as soon as possible, to make up my deficiency by a new appointment. It would be productive of much inconvenience, should not the inferior officers succeed in course, and from this consideration, I doubt not, you will think it proper to advance Mr. Gilleland and Mr. Bean,[1] and fill up the third lieutenancy with some other person. I would beg the liberty warmly to recommend to your attention Thomas Thompson, now first sergeant in my company, a man highly deserving of notice and preferment. He has discharged his duty in his present station with uncommon fidelity, assiduity and expertness. He is a very good disciplinarian, possesses the advantage of having seen a good deal of service in Germany; has a tolerable share of common sense, and is well calculated not to disgrace the rank of an officer and gentleman. In a word, I verily believe he will make an excellent lieutenant, and his advancement will be a great encouragement and benefit to my company in particular, and will be an animating example to all men of merit, to whose knowledge it comes.[2]

Myself and my officers will be much obliged to the Honourable

Convention to favour us with our commissions with all convenient speed, as they may be highly requisite under some circumstances, that may possibly hereafter arise.

I am, with the utmost respect, gentlemen,   Your most obedient and most humble servant,   A Hamilton,
                                        Captain of N. Y. Artillery.

Augt. 12*th,* 1776.
The Honourable the Convention
of the State of New-York.

Journals of the Provincial Congress of the State of New-York, II, 278.
    1. James Gilleland and John Bean were lieutenants in H's artillery company. Their names were sometimes spelled "Gilliland" and "Bane" (James A. Roberts, *New York in the Revolution as Colony and State* [Albany, 1904], 65).
    2. On August 14, 1776, H's request was referred to Colonel Peter R. Livingston who was instructed to inquire into the matter and report to the Convention. Livingston, after conferring with H, reported on August 15, and it was then resolved that Thomas Thompson be promoted to the rank of lieutenant (*Journals of the Provincial Congress of the State of New-York,* I, 573–74).

To the Convention of the Representatives of the State of New York [1]

[New York, September 14, 1776]

I do hereby certify that Wm. Douglass,[2] the bearer hereof, faithfully served as a matross in my company till he lost his arm by an unfortunate accident, while engaged in firing at some of the enemy's ships. He is therefore recommended to the attention of those who have been appointed to carry into execution the late resolve of the Continental Congress, by which provision is made for all persons disabled in the service of the United States.   A. Hamilton
                                        Capt. of Artillery.
New-York, Sept. 14th, 1776.

Journals of the Provincial Congress of the State of New-York, II, 221.
    1. This is the first of two certificates written by H for Douglass. The other certificate is dated November 6, 1776.
    2. William Douglass enlisted in H's artillery company on May 28, 1776. While on duty at the Battery in New York City, June 12, 1776, he lost his right arm and had his leg broken by the explosion of a cannon. He was transferred to the Corps of Invalids and discharged September 1, 1782.

Warrant to Captain Alexander Hamilton

[*Harlem Heights, New York*] *September 29, 1776.* In George
Washington's "Warrant Book No 2" an entry for this date reads "To
Capn Hamilton for his Co Arty. Aug–774. 3/72 [dollars]."

D, George Washington Papers, Library of Congress.

Account with Alsop Hunt and James Hunt

[*New York*] *October 11, 1776.* Account between Alsop Hunt
and James Hunt and Hamilton for "Buckskin Breeches Delivered
the Soldiers of the New york Artillery" company commanded
by Hamilton. The account runs from March 5 to October 11,
1776, and was not settled until 1785. A receipt, verso, reads: "Received Payment of the within Acct. in full thereof and all other
Demands, per Alsop Hunt & Jas Hunt. March 9th 1785." The account is addressed incorrectly to "Colo. Andrew Hamilton."

AD, Hamilton Papers, Library of Congress.

Return of Captain Alexander Hamilton's Company of Artillery

[*New York, October, 1776.*] [1] The return is headed: "Return
of the Artillery Company of the State of New York commanded by
Alexander Hamilton."

AD, Massachusetts Historical Society, Boston.
1. Dated "Oct. 1776" in an unidentified handwriting and at a later date. The
return was for one of the months between May, 1776, and January, 1777, but
the correct date cannot be determined.

To the Convention of the Representatives of the State of New-York [1]

[New York, November 6, 1776]

I do hereby certify that the bearer William Douglass has lost his arm in the service of this state, having been a Matross in my company of Artillery, thereto belonging; and he is accordingly recommended to the Convention thereof, as intitled to the provision made by a late resolve of the Continental Congress, for those disabled in defence of American liberty.   A Hamilton Capt

New York Novemr. 6. 1776
Pay was drawn for the above Wm. Douglass 'till ye. first day of August   AH

ALS, MS Division, New York Public Library.
    1. This is the second of two certificates written by H for William Douglass. The other certificate is dated September 14, 1776.

Return of Two Companies of Artillery [1]

Trenton, December 5, 1776. The return is headed "Return of the States of part of two Companeys of artilery Commanded by Col Henery Knox & Capt Drury & Capt Lt Moores of Capt Hamiltons Com."

ADS, Papers of George Washington, Library of Congress.
    1. H's company had been assigned at first to General John Scott's brigade but was soon transferred to the command of Colonel Henry Knox. This return is for a part of H's company shortly before H was taken into Washington's official family. It is in the writing of and signed by Jotham Drury and dated "Trentown Decem'r 5th. 1776."

Warrant for Captain Alexander Hamilton

[Bucks County, Pennsylvania] December 19, 1776. In George Washington's "Warrant Book No. 2" an entry for this date reads: "To Capn Alexr Hamilton his pay for his Coy. Arty from 1st Sepr to 1 Decr—1562 [dollars]."

D, George Washington Papers, Library of Congress.

Alexander Hamilton's Account with the Government of the United States [1]

I [2]

A

March 7th. 1789

Army in old Emissions   Dr.
To John Pierce [3]   Pay Master General, his account
                                              old emissions

For Five thousand six hundred and twenty nine dollars 30/90 old Emissions that Lieut Col: Hamilton late aid de Camp to General Washington, credits on the settlement of his account at the Treasury the 2nd instant the specie value of which deducted from the amount in Specie .... 5.629.30 O.E.

Army in Specie   Dr. to Sundries   (specie)
For the discharge of Lieut Colo. Hamiltons account above mentioned,

To John Pierce   Pay Master General.
For Sixty dollars paid by him to said Hamilton August 81 .. $60.
To John Ross [4] cloathing stipulated for on the surrender of York. Virga.
For Sixty six dollars Sixty ninetieths of a dollar the amount of sundry articles credited by him being part of the Cloathing contracted for at the surrender of York $66.60
To Michael Hillegas [5]   Treasurer,
For a Warrant drawn the 6th. instant by the Superintendant of Finance [6] in favor of said Lieut Col Hamilton for seven hundred and five dollars Sixty nine ninetieths of a dollar Specie being part of the balance due him   705.69
To Funded debt.
For two thousand Eight hundred and twenty dollars funded being the residue of the balance due to said Hamilton & for which a Certificate was this day given by the Register,[7] pursuant to a Warrant from the Superintendant of Finance dated the 6 inst. on interest at 6 ℔ Ct. from the 4th. March 1789, & entered to the credit of said Hamilton in Aux: Books funded debt W. 13

pa. 22   2.820.

$3.652.39

Old Emission account

| Dr. | Capt. Alexr Hamilton of a Compy. of Arty. now Aid de Camp In a/c with the United States | Cr. |

1776			1785	
Octr.	To William Palfrey [9]		Dec	By Old Emissions reduced & accounted for in Specie
	For pay of his Compy. for Aug. 1776.			For this sum reduced & carried to his Specie Debit ... 7942.30
	$774 \cdot \frac{3}{72}$			By the United States for his pay & the pay of his Company to Feby 28th.
Decr.	For pay of his Co. from 1st. Septr to 1st. Decr. 76 .... 1562.			1777 .... 3522.44
Mar	For pay of his Co. for Decr 76			
	$420 \frac{9}{72}$			
	For Do. Do. to 28 Feby 77			
	$766 \frac{22}{90}$			
	$1186. \frac{31}{72}$			
1778				
Feby	For his pay in full to 31 Jany 78 .... 646.			
Aug	For his pay to 31 July 1778 360			
Nov.	For his pay to 31 Oct. 1778 .... 180.			
Decr.	For his pay for Nov & Decr. 78 .... 120.			
1779				
May	For his pay & rations to May			
	1779 .... $1007. \frac{2}{90}$			
July	To John Pierce Jr.			
	For his pay for May & June 79 200.			
1780				
Mar	For his pay & subsce. from 1 July 79 to 1 March 1780			
	$3129. \frac{30}{90}$			
May	For his pay & Sube. for Mar & April 1780 920.			
Aug	For his pay & sube. from 1 May to 1 August 1780 1380			
		11464	74		11464

The above is an Extract taken from The Books of the late Pay office now in this off
Department of War   Accountants Off
June 15th. 1809   Wm Simmon

Specie Account

r. Lt. Col. Alexr. Hamilton   In a/c with The United States.   **Cr.**

81	To Richard Lloyd [12]		By Pay of the Army	
	For this sum received of him	66.60	1785	
82	To John Pierce P.M.G.		Decr	For pay as Aid de Camp from March
	For this sum received of him for			1777 to 31 Decr. 1781 .... 3480.
	pay for Jany. & Feby. 1782	120.		Rations from 2 June 1778 to 31
	To Nicholas Fish [13]			July 1781 @ 4 per day is 4620
	For one months pay; paid him at			@ 10d. 513.30
	the Head of Elk in Aug 1781,			Ditto from 1 Aug 1781 to 31 Decr
	which he credits in his settlement			following 612 rations @ 9½d. ... 64.54
	with the Auditor	60.		For pay due him for January & Feb-
85				ruary 1782 .... 120.
ecr.	To Specie arising from old Emis-			
	sions reduced For 7942 $\frac{30}{90}$ Drs.			
	reduced to Specie ....:....	405.45		
	To United States Funded Debt			
85	For the Registers Certificate on In-			
ec	terest from 4th March 1782	2820.		
	To United States			
	For a Warrant on the Treasurer			
	received March 7th. 1782 in full ..	705.69		
		4177.84		Drs. 4177.84

The above is an Extract taken from The Books of the late Pay office now in this office
Department of War   Accountants Office
June 15th. 1809   Wm Simmons

1. The three documents, which appear below this title and are numbered I, II, and III, accompanied a petition which H's widow, Elizabeth, submitted to the Senate and House of Representatives on January 10, 1816 (LS, RG 233, Records of the Committee on Pensions, 14th Congress, National Archives). In this petition Elizabeth Hamilton stated that H had been "intitled to commutation of half pay, as provided by the Continental Congress of the United States to the officers of the Army of the Revolution, but, owing to his Situation as a member of Congress, at the time of the Provision for commutation being made, and to divest himself of all possible Interest in the question, he did, from motives of delicacy, by some note or memorandum for that purpose as your petitioner has understood relinquished the benefit of said provision." She then requested "the Honorable the Congress of the United States to restore to the Representatives of her late Husband that compensation due for the services of her husband as aforesaid."

2. D, RG 233, Records of the Committee on Pensions, 14th Congress, National Archives.

Accompanying this account was the following statement by Joseph Nourse, register of the Treasury:

"I certify that a Registered debt Certificate was issued by the Register of the Treasury on the 7 March 1782, pursuant to a Warrant of the Superintendant of Finance dated 6 March 1782 in the name of Lieut Colo Alexander Hamilton late aid de Camp to General Washington for Two thousand Eight hundred and twenty dollars on Interest from the 2nd March 1782, being the undue of the balance due to the said Hamilton on the settlement of his account at the Treasury on the 2nd March 1782, as will more fully appear from the subjoined Extract, from the original enteries on the Books of the Treasury Department marked A."

3. John Pierce of Connecticut had been appointed assistant paymaster general for the Continental Army in 1776. He was promoted to paymaster general in 1781 and remained in that position until his death in 1788.

4. John Ross was a contractor for the Army.

5. Michael Hillegas had been elected Treasurer under the Confederation in November, 1778.

6. Robert Morris had been elected Superintendent of Finance on February 20, 1781.

7. Joseph Nourse.

8. D, RG, 233, Records of the Committee on Pensions, 14th Congress, National Archives.

9. William Palfrey was paymaster general for the Continental Army from 1776 to November, 1780.

10. William Simmons was appointed accountant to the War Department in 1795.

11. D, RG 233, Records of the Committee on Pensions, 14th Congress, National Archives.

12. Presumably Captain Richard Lloyd of the Second Canadian Regiment.

13. Presumably Major Nicholas Fish of the Second New York Regiment.

1 7 7 7

From George Washington

[*Morristown, New Jersey, January 20, 1777.* A statement in George Washington's letter to Lieutenant Colonel Robert Hanson Harrison [1] of this date reads: "Be so good as to forward the Inclosed to Captn. Hamilton." [2] *Letter not found.*]

1. Before the Revolution, Harrison, who was a native of Maryland, was a lawyer in Alexandria, Virginia, where he met Washington and became his occasional legal adviser. On November 25, 1775, he was appointed aide-de-camp to Washington, and in May, 1776, he replaced Joseph Reed as Washington's secretary.
2. "Captn. Hamilton" is identified by Fitzpatrick (*GW*, VII, 519) as Alexander Hamilton. It is probable that it was in this letter that Washington asked H to join his staff as an aide-de-camp.

From The Pennsylvania Evening Post

[Philadelphia, January 25, 1777]

Captain Alexander Hamilton, of the New-York company of artillery, by applying to the printer of this paper, may hear of something to his advantage.

The Pennsylvania Evening Post, January 25, 1777.

To Hugh Knox

[*February 14, 1777.* In a letter to Hamilton dated April 31, 1777, Knox wrote: "I could not omit acknowledging the receipt of you⟨r⟩ Very Circumstantial and Satisfactory Letter of the 14th. Feby." *Letter not found.*]

General Orders, Appointing Alexander Hamilton Aide-de-Camp to General Washington [1]

Head-Quarters, Morristown [New Jersey] March 1, 1777.

Alexander Hamilton Esquire is appointed Aide-De-Camp to the Commander in Chief; and is to be respected and obeyed as such.

Extract of General Orders
Alexd Scammell   Adjt. Genl.

Facsimile, Hamilton, *Intimate Life*, 37.
1. H's copy of the General Orders has not been found. Washington's General Orders of March 1, 1777, are printed in *GW*, VII, 218.
It is not known how H came to Washington's attention or whose recommendation led to Washington's invitation to H to join his staff. For a discussion of the possibilities, see Mitchell, *Hamilton*, I, 104.

George Washington to Lieutenant Colonel Archibald Campbell [1]

Morristown [*New Jersey*] *March 1, 1777.* Seeks to mitigate severity of Campbell's imprisonment.

Df, in writing of H, George Washington Papers, Library of Congress.
1. Campbell, a member of the 71st Regiment of the British army, was a prisoner in Concord, Massachusetts.

George Washington to Major General Horatio Gates

Morristown [*New Jersey*] *March 1, 1777.* Orders investigation of fraudulent recruiting returns. Requests inoculation of two Virginia regiments.

Df, in writing of H, George Washington Papers, Library of Congress.

George Washington to
Brigadier General Benedict Arnold [1]

Morristown [New Jersey] *March 3, 1777.* Discusses Arnold's proposed attack against Rhode Island. Notes that Arnold's name was not on list of newly promoted major generals.

Df, in writing of H, George Washington Papers, Library of Congress.
1. Arnold was at this time in Providence, Rhode Island. On May 2, 1777, Arnold was promoted to the rank of major general. On August 8, 1777, he was given a new commission which stated that his rank of major general was to date from February 19, 1777. This new commission restored his seniority in rank.

George Washington to
Brigadier General George Clinton [1]

Morristown [New Jersey] *March 3, 1777.* Asks Clinton to decide location of cannon on the Hudson. Places choice of men and officers for Clinton's forces in Clinton's hands.

Df, in writing of H, George Washington Papers, Library of Congress; LS in writing of H, George Washington Photostats, Library of Congress.
1. Clinton, a brigadier general in the Continental Army, was at New Windsor, New York, in command of the Highland forts.

George Washington to
Major General William Heath [1]

Morristown [New Jersey] *March 3, 1777.* Orders Heath to relieve Major General Artemas Ward.

Df, in writing of H, George Washington Papers, Library of Congress.
1. Heath, who was in command of the Hudson River posts, was appointed Artemas Ward's successor as commander of the Eastern Department on Ward's resignation.

George Washington to
Major General Joseph Spencer

Morristown [*New Jersey*] *March 3, 1777.* Requests that proposed Rhode Island venture be undertaken only if success is certain. Discusses inoculation of troops.

Df, in writing of H, George Washington Papers, Library of Congress.

George Washington to
Major General Artemas Ward

Morristown [*New Jersey*] *March 3, 1777.* Accepts Ward's resignation. Appoints Major General William Heath to succeed Ward.

Df, in writings of H and John Fitzgerald, George Washington Papers, Library of Congress.

George Washington to
Brigadier General William Woodford

Morristown [*New Jersey*] *March 3, 1777.* Discusses Woodford's loss of seniority. Urges Woodford to accept promotion to brigadier general.

Df, in writing of H, George Washington Papers, Library of Congress.

George Washington to Lieutenant Colonel
Robert Hanson Harrison

By His Excellency George Washington Esqr.,
General and Commander in chief of all the Forces
of the Thirteen united States of America

[Morristown, New Jersey, March 4, 1777]

To Lieutenant Colonel Robert H Harrison.

Differences in opinion having arisen, between General Howe and myself, respecting the construction of a proposition, made the 30th. of July and acceded to the 1st. of August last, for the exchange of prisoners, whereby it was stipulated, that officers should be given for officers of equal rank, soldier for soldier, and citizen for citizen; for the accommodation of these differences, and to remove every just cause of complaint on the part of the enemy, if such there be; You are to meet any officer, not of inferior rank to yourself, who shall come properly authorized to treat upon the subject; and to adopt such measures as you shall deem adequate to that end.

Experience having also shewn, that the agreement above recited is not sufficiently definite to answer all the salutary purposes intended by it, nor sufficiently comprehensive to include the various cases incident to the state of prisoners, You are hereby vested with full power and authority to devise and conclude upon such improvements, in aid of the same, as shall appear necessary, for establishing a more regular and explicit mode of Exchange, as well with respect to the Prisoners who have been as those who shall be hereafter taken; making mutual provision for such an allowance of pay and necessaries as their comfort and welfare, during their captivity, may require; And finally to treat, determine and agree upon all matters whatsoever relative to Prisoners of War, on the principles of justice and humanity, and conformable to the most civilized customs and usages, for the greater ease, convenience, and security of all captives belonging to the armies under our respective command: For all which, This shall be your sufficient warrant; and your engagements, being mutually interchanged, shall be ratified and confirmed by me.

By His Excellency's	Given under my Hand and Seal
command.	at Head Quarters in Morris Town
Alexander Hamilton	this 4th. day of March 1777,
Aid De Camp	Go: Washington

LS, in writing of H and countersigned by H, George Washington Papers, Library of Congress.

To the Convention of the Representatives of the State of New-York [1]

[Morristown, New Jersey, March 6, 1777]

The change in my own circumstances and in those of your company of Artillery lately under my command make it necessary I should inform you of the present state of things, respect⟨ing⟩ it; in order that you may determine as to the future disposal of it; and I should be happy as speedily as convenient to know your pleasure on the subject.

His Excellency has been pleased to appoint me one of his Aid du Camps. Capt Lieutenant James Moore, a promising officer, and who did credit to the state he belonged to, di⟨ed⟩ the 25th of December, after a short but excruciating fit of illness. Lie⟨ut.⟩ Gilliland, from domestic inconveniences, and *other motives*, resigned his Commission to General Washington about three weeks before. There remain now only two officers Lieutenant Bean & Lieuten⟨ant⟩ Thompson.[2] Mr. Johnson[3] began the enlistment of the Compan⟨y,⟩ contrary to his orders from the convention, for the term of a year, instead of during the war; a circumstance I was unacquainted with till lately, but which, with deaths and desertions; reduces it at present to the small number of 25 men.

If you think proper to retain the company on its present establishment it will be necessary to fill up the vacanc⟨ies and⟩ make provision to have the number of men completed. In this cas⟨e I⟩ would beg leave to recommend to your attention Lieutenant Thompson, as fa⟨r⟩ as a Capt Lieutenancy; but Mr. Bean though a brave man, h⟨as⟩ *a failing* that disqualifies him for any farther preferment.[4] As to the new arrangement for the Artillery, if I am n⟨ot⟩ misinformed, the number of officers is increased to six & the pay of both officers and men is raised to ⟨a⟩ fourth part more than the other troops. As the rest ⟨of⟩ the Company can hardly answer any special good purposes to the s⟨tate I⟩ imagine you will resolve to resign it. There will be no ⟨difficulty⟩ in having it transferred to the Continental establishment.[5]

I should have advised you earlier of these ⟨changes⟩ but, am just recovered from a long and severe fit of ⟨sickness⟩.

I have the honor to be with the most sincere respect   Gentlemen
Yr. most Obedient Ser

ADf, Hamilton Papers, Library of Congress.

1. A printed version, presumably of the receiver's copy, is found in *Journals of the Provincial Congress of the State of New-York*, II, 415. Although the phraseology of the two differ, the contents are the same.

2. For a discussion by H of the officers in his artillery company, see his letter to the New York Convention, August 12, 1776.

3. Martin Johnson was a lieutenant in H's artillery company.

4. Printed version reads: "I should beg leave to recommend to your notice,

as far as a captain-lieutenancy, Mr. Thompson. Mr. Bean is so incurably addicted to a *certain failing*, that I cannot, in justice, give my opinion in favour of his preferment."

5. Printed version reads: "if you should determine to resign the company, as I expect you will, considering it as an extraordinary burthen, without affording any special advantages, the Continent will readily take it off your hands."

The Convention referred H's letter to Gouverneur Morris and Jacob Cuyler (*Journals of the Provincial Congress of the State of New-York*, I, 831). On March 17, 1777, Gouverneur Morris "requested the sense of the House relative to the artillery company lately commanded by Captain Hamilton." The House resolved "that the said company be permitted to enlist in the service of the Continent, and that Mr. Morris inform Capt. Hamilton thereof" (*ibid.*, 838).

George Washington to
Brigadier General Alexander McDougall

Morristown [New Jersey] March 6, 1777. Requests a return of troops. Questions validity of some returns and suspects fraud. Orders McDougall to have troops in readiness at Peekskill.

Df, in writing of H, George Washington Papers, Library of Congress.

George Washington to
Brigadier General William Smallwood

Morristown [New Jersey] March 8, 1777. Instructs Smallwood to order all officers and men not needed for recruiting to repair to camp.

Df, in writing of H, George Washington Papers, Library of Congress.

To Brigadier General Alexander McDougall

Head Qrs. Morris Town [New Jersey] March 10th. 1777

Dr. Sir,

Your letter of the 7th. instant to his Excellency[1] fell into my hands. He has been very much indisposed for three or four days past, insomuch that his attention to business is pronounced by the Doctor to be very improper; and we have made a point of keeping all from him which was not indispensibly necessary. I detained your express a day in hopes of a convenient opportunity to communicate your letter to him; but though he has grown considerably better than he was, I find he is so much pestered with matters, which cannot be avoided, that I am obliged to refrain from troubling him on the occasion; especially as I conceive the only answer he would give, may be given by myself.

It is greatly to be lamented that the present state of things does not admit of having the requisite number of troops at every post: on the contrary the most important, are deficient; and we are under the necessity, of calling all that can be gotten together to those places where the danger is the most pressing and imminent. 'Till matters get into a better train, it is impossible but those posts must suffer which, from their situation ought only to be the objects of a secondary attention. We have, I think, the most decisive evidence that the enemy's operations will be directed on this quarter; to this end they are drawing all their forces into the Jerseys, and as soon as the weather will permit 'tis expected they will move towards Philadelphia. Not being very numerous 'tis unlikely they should attempt such an object, without collecting their whole force; and for that reason 'tis not much to be apprehended they should make any stroke of the kind you mention, which would require a number of men they could not spare, and would proba⟨bly⟩ delay the execution of what clearly appears to be their principal intention.

The General in a letter to you of the　　instant[2] desires all the York regiments not gone to Ticonderoga to be assembled at Peeks Kill. The reason of this must be obvious to you; and for the same reason, he has requested a reinforcement of 2000 Connecticut Militia to rendesvous at the same place: Though the design is chiefly that they may be ready to join the army here; they will in the mean time, in some measure, answer the purposes you have in view.

I am Dr Sir　Yr. most Obedient servant　　　　　A Hamilton

ADfS, George Washington Papers, Library of Congress.
　1. This letter (LS, George Washington Papers, Library of Congress) discussed the scarcity of troops and inadequacy of the garrisons for the Highland forts.
　2. Washington's letter, in the writing of H was dated March 6, 1777 (Df, George Washington Papers, Library of Congress).

George Washington to
Lieutenant Colonel John Brooks [1]

Morristown [New Jersey] March 11, 1777. Transmits commission for William Hull.[2]

Df, in writing of H, George Washington Papers, Library of Congress.
1. Brooks was a Massachusetts doctor turned soldier.
2. Major William Hull, Eighth Massachusetts Regiment.

George Washington to
Major General Thomas Mifflin [1]

Morristown [New Jersey] March 11, 1777. Orders preparations for approaching campaign.

Df, in writing of Tench Tilghman, interlineation by H, George Washington Papers, Library of Congress.
1. Mifflin was the quartermaster general of the Army.

George Washington to
Brigadier General Gold Selleck Silliman

Morristown [New Jersey] March 11, 1777. Discusses British naval feints. Is not apprehensive of an attack on Connecticut and, therefore, refuses to send requested detachments.

Df, in writing of H, George Washington Papers, Library of Congress.

George Washington to
Major General Philip Schuyler [1]

Morristown [New Jersey] March 12, 1777. Discusses necessity of concentrating forces. States that Philadelphia is enemy's object. Weighs advantages of centralizing forces at Peekskill as against Ticonderoga.

Df, in writings of John Walker, George Washington, and H, George Washington Papers, Library of Congress.
1. Schuyler was at this time in Albany in command of the Northern Department.

George Washington to Connecticut and Rhode Island Colonels

Morristown [New Jersey] March 12, 1777. Requests exact return of troops. Orders colonels to send all their men to join the Army. Instructs colonels to remain behind to complete their regiments.

Df, in writing of H, George Washington Papers, Library of Congress.

George Washington to New York Colonels

Morristown [New Jersey] March 12, 1777. Requests exact return of troops. Orders recruits to Peekskill. Instructs colonels to remain behind to complete their regiments.

Df, in writing of Richard Kidder Meade, corrections by H, George Washington Papers, Library of Congress.

George Washington to Pennsylvania Colonels

Morristown [New Jersey] March 12, 1777. Requests exact return of troops. Orders men who have had smallpox to the Army, others to Philadelphia to be inoculated. Instructs colonels to remain in Philadelphia to supply their regiments.

Df, in writing of H, indorsed by H as sent to "the Committee of Safety of Pennsylvania and to Delaware State," George Washington Papers, Library of Congress.

To Major General Adam Stephen [1]

Head Quarters Morris Town [New Jersey] March 13. 1777

Sir,

In a letter Just received from Colonel Ward,[2] there appears to be an objection made against innoculating his regiment, in consequence of some former order, not to innoculate Militia 'till all the Continental troops had undergone the operation. His Excellency desires that this objection, with respect to Colonel Wards regiment, should cease; and that they may immediately be admitted to the benefit of innoculation, in the usual proportion. He begs also that the present opportunity, while the roads continue incommodious for any movements of the enemy, may be improved to the greatest advantage, as we do not know how long it may last; and shall have no time to spare, even if the utmost diligence is used. There is no need to wait precisely for the moment the Hospital becomes vacant, before the infection is communicated to others. Four or five days before one set is fit to leave it, another set may be preparing to go in; which would save a great deal of time, and forward the business exceedingly. Let this be urged upon the Doctors, and every thing else done which may be conducive to dispatch, in a matter of so great importance.

Colonel Ward has solicited a furlough: It seems hardly worth his while to ask one as his regiment will be going home in about a Month. But the General has referred him to Yourself and Gen[e]ral Maxwell [3] jointly; and if you think his reasons for desiring a furlough sufficient; and his going away compatible with the good of the service, his request is to be granted.

I am Sir   Your most humble servant   A Hamilton   ADC

ALS, MS Division, New York Public Library.
1. Adam Stephen, a Virginian, served with distinction during the French and Indian War. At the beginning of the Revolution he was given command of the Fourth Virginia Regiment. He was made a brigadier general in September, 1776, and was promoted to major general in February, 1777. When this letter was written he was stationed at Chatham, New Jersey.
2. Andrew Ward was a colonel of a Connecticut state regiment from May, 1776, to May, 1777; in June, 1777, he was appointed brigadier general of the Connecticut Militia.
3. William Maxwell of New Jersey was appointed colonel of the Western Battalion of New Jersey Continental troops in November, 1775, and at the head of that battalion he accompanied Major General Sullivan on the expedition against Canada in February, 1776. In October, 1776, he was made a brigadier general and appointed by General Washington commander of four battalions in the second establishment of New Jersey Continental troops. In the spring of 1777, he was engaged principally in harrassing the enemy in New Jersey.

To Colonel Samuel Blachley Webb

Head Quarters Morris Town [New Jersey] March 13. 1777

Dr. Sir

If General Knox has not passed through on his way here, and gotten out of your reach, you will be pleased carefully and expeditiously to convey the inclosed letter to him; as it is intended to hurry him on to Camp.[1] If he is out of reach, destroy the letter, for it will be of no consequence to return it.

The family [2] are all well; and hope soon to see you here, at the head of your bloody myrmidons.

I am Dr. sir   Your most hum servant   A Hamilton   ADC

P.S. If the General has not yet come from the Eas[t]ward, send the letter to him by express.

ALS, Yale University Library.
    1. At the time that this letter was written, Samuel Webb was colonel of a Continental regiment at Wethersfield, Connecticut, and Brigadier General Henry Knox was en route from Boston to Washington's Headquarters. On March 14, 1777, Washington wrote to Knox: "I have for some time past most earnestly expected you, to arrange matters in the Artillery department, which has in a manner lain Still since you went away. . . . I beg you will endeavour to bring forward as many of the Artillery Men, intended for this department, as you possibly can. . . . As you see how necessary your presence is here, I hope you will make as much haste as possible to Join" (George Washington Papers, Library of Congress). This may have been the enclosure to which H refers in his letter to Webb.
    2. This refers to the members of Washington's staff at Headquarters.

To Colonel Andrew Ward

[Morristown, New Jersey, March 14, 1777]

Since writing the within,[1] The General received your letter, respecting the innoculation of your regiment, and permission for yourself to go home. He has removed the difficulty in the way of innoculating your regiment, but has thought proper to refer the decision of what you request concerning yourself to Generals Stephen & Maxwell; and if they think the situation of affairs, requires your going home, your desire will be complied with. In addition to what you are called upon to explain, within; The General would be glad to know on what particular commands, the 108 men you return, are employed.

I am Sir   Your hum servant   A Hamilton   ADC

General A Ward

ALS, Yale University Library.
    1. H is referring to an enclosed letter (George Washington to Andrew Ward, March 14, 1777, ALS, Yale University Library) in which Washington

wrote Ward as follows: "In looking over the return made of your Regimt. I find that no less than 17 men are upon Furlough and 14 others discharged. By what authority Sir is this done? You know I presume that no officer under the Rank of General has a right to discharge Men & you must have known I should think, that this is no time for granting Furloughs, especially in a Regiment whose term of Service is so near expiring."

George Washington to
Brigadier General Alexander McDougall

Morristown [*New Jersey*] *March 15, 1777.* Approves of McDougall's decision to order troops to Forts Constitution and Montgomery instead of to Peekskill, New York. Approves stationing of Colonel Henry B. Livingston in Westchester to secure magazines. Urges inoculation when needed. Instructs McDougall to receive Massachusetts troops.

Df, dated March 14, 1777, in writings of Robert H. Harrison and H, George Washington Papers, Library of Congress.

George Washington to
Major General John Sullivan

Morristown [*New Jersey*] *March 15, 1777.* Exhorts Sullivan not to imagine slights. Discusses separate commands. States that the only separate command is that of the Northern Department.

Df, in writing of H, George Washington Papers, Library of Congress.

From the New York Committee
of Correspondence [1]

Kingston [New York] 17th: March 1777

Dr Sir

We are to inform you that Robt. R Livingston [2] is with us a Committee appointed by Convention to correspond with you at Head Quarters. You will give us Pleasure in the Information that his Excellency is recovered from the Illness which had seized him the Day before Messrs. Cuyler and Taylor [3] left Head Quarters. Any Occurrences in the Army which may have happened you will please to communicate.

In Answer to your Letter to the Convention of the sixth of March Instant We are to inform you that it is determined to permit that Company to join the Continental Army for which you will take the necessary Steps.[4] At the same Time you will take some Notice of the Disposition of our Guns which as you well know are all in the Continental Service & unless some little Attention is paid to them We may perhaps never see them again.

We are Sir   your most obedt. & humble Servants

Gouvr Morris
Wm Allison

LS, in writing of Gouverneur Morris, Hamilton Papers, Library of Congress.
   1. On September 17, 1776, the Provincial Convention of New York adopted the following resolution:
   "*Resolved*, That Colo. Allison, Mr. R. R. Livingston and Mr. Wisner, Senr. be and are hereby appointed a committee of correspondence. That they be and hereby are authorized to establish post riders between the Fish Kill, where this Convention now statedly sits, and Head-Quarters, for the purpose of obtaining daily intelligence, and that this Convention will make provision for defraying the expense thereof; and that the said committee be and are hereby empowered to write letters to any correspondents, and take every other proper means to obtain intelligence" (*Journals of the Provincial Congress of the State of New-York*, I, 627).
   Henry Wisner, Sr., who was also a delegate to the Continental Congress, was apparently dropped from the committee, and on March 14, 1777, Gouverneur Morris was added to it. On the same date, the Convention ordered the committee to "employ a proper person at Head-Quarters to communicate intelligence" (*ibid.*, 835).
   2. Son of Robert R. Livingston, who was a cousin of Colonel Robert Livingston, the third and last lord of Livingston Manor.
   3. Jacob Cuyler and John Taylor were both delegates to the Provincial Convention from Albany County.
   4. On March 17, 1777, the Provincial Convention adopted the following resolution: "*Resolved*, That the said company be permitted to enlist in the service of the Continent, and that Mr. Morris inform Capt. Hamilton thereof" (*Journals of the Provincial Congress of the State of New-York*, I, 838).

George Washington to John Rutledge [1]

Morristown [*New Jersey*] *March 17, 1777.* Discusses proposed expedition against St. Augustine.

Df, in writing of H, George Washington Papers, Library of Congress.
   1. Rutledge was the chief executive of South Carolina. He was referred to as both governor and president of the state.

From the New York Committee
of Correspondence

[*Kingston, New York, March 19, 1777.* On March 22, 1777, Hamilton wrote to the Committee of Correspondence: "I had the pleasure of receiving yours of the 19th. instant." *Letter not found.*]

To the New York Committee
of Correspondence [1]

[Morristown, New Jersey, March 20, 1777]

Gentlemen,

With chearfulness, I embrace the proposal of corresponding with your convention, through you; and shall from time to time as far as my leisure will permit, and my duty warrant, communicate such transactactions as shall happen, such pieces of intelligence as shall be received and such comments upon them as shall appear necessary, to convey a true idea of what is going on in the military line. Let me caution you however, that whatever opinions I shall give, in the course of our correspondence, are to be considered merely as my private sentiments; and are never to be interpreted as an echo of those of the *General;* since they will not be really so, and a construction of the kind may lead into errors and be productive of inconveniences.

The present season affords nothing of importance. There are dayly little skirmishes, arising from attempts of the enemy to forage; but which, though generally favourable to us, are attended with consequences so trifling and insignificant as to be scarcely worth mentioning. They are indeed of great service in the general scale, as they serve to harass and distress the enemy, and by keeping them from forage will put them under difficulties, as to the transportation of their baggage and cannon, whenever they shalt think of making any capital movement. One thing worthy of notice is that hardly a day passes, without some deserter coming in. The fact itself, and the accounts they concurrently give, prove that the spirit of desertion runs high; and the reason assigned for it is, that many of the regiments have been a very long time without pay, and that the men are most barbarously treated if they only dare to lisp their discontent on the score of it.

'Tis rumoured, that the Congress have received a letter from Doctor Franklin, by which he seems to be in such high spirits as to prognosticate a favourable disposition of affairs in the quarter where he is.[2] I was just now also, transiently told, that he had been received in the public character of a plenipotentiary from the American states. When it receives confirmation I will give it to you.

I shall observe your directions respecting a transferrence of the Company lately mine, to the Continental establishment; and in my next shall communicate the result of my inquiry into to the present state of your Cannon.

The General is now perfectly recovered, and added to the pleasure of returning health, enjoys the solace of his lady's company, who has lately joined the army.

I am with much respect   Gentlemen   Your most obedient servant

A Hamilton

ALS, New-York Historical Society, New York City.
    1. This letter is dated 1777 in *JCHW*, VI, 568, and is addressed to "The Honourable G: Morris, Livingston & Allison Esqrs., Members of the New York Convention."
    2. Benjamin Franklin's letter to John Hancock, President of Congress, is dated December 8, 1776. It is printed in Francis Wharton (ed.), *The Revolutionary Diplomatic Correspondence of the United States* (Washington, 1889), II, 221–22.

Warrant for
Lieutenant Colonel Alexander Hamilton

[*Morristown, New Jersey*] *March 21, 1777.* An entry in George Washington's "Warrant Book No 2" reads: "To Captain Alexr Hamilton for 1 Months Pay of the N. York Artillery to Jany. 1st —420 9/72 [dollars]." Another entry for the same date reads: "To Ditto of Do. For 2 Months Pay to 1st March—766 22/72 [dollars]."

D, George Washington Papers, Library of Congress.

To the New York Committee
of Correspondence

Head Qrs. Morris Town [New Jersey] 2[2] March 1777

Gentlemen,

Two days ago I accepted your challenge and met you for the first time in the epistolary field; since which I had the pleasure of receiving yours of the 19th. instant; [1] and as far as circumstances will permit, close with your proposal of interchanging blows twice a week.

The present time is so unfruitful of events that it affords no intelligence worth your notice, as to transactions of a military nature. I can only say, that the British army continues to decrease by the dayly loss of prisoners and deserters taken at and coming in to the different posts, which is a striking symptom, that the situation of affairs with the enemy is not so favourable as it might be; for when an army is in good humour and its affairs prosperous, desertion is a disease that seldom prevails in it.

From all the accounts they have given us, seconded by considerations that obviously present themselves; it is my opinion the enemy will make no grand movement before the beginning of May; and perhaps not then. There is no expectation in their army of their being speedily called to the field, nor the least disposition of matters that I have heard of for a sudden excursion. It will be a long time before the roads will be fit for the transportation of Artillery, which is an essential instrument in their operations; and a still longer [time] before the ground will admit of an incampment consistent with the health and comfort of the soldiers—and it would defeat their purpose to undertake any thing of importance under circumstances, that would oblige them to divide their army in order to accommodate it. It seems also to be an opinion supported by the best reasons that the main object with which they will open the Campaign, will be the capture of Philadelphia. If so, they will have a greater probability of success by co-operating both by sea and land; and the preparations for this added to the danger of making an attempt by water at too early a season will, in all likelihood, protract the execution of their project at least 'till the time I have mentioned.

I intimated that it might perhaps be later before they would move. It seems to be a pretty general idea in their army, that they will wait for reinforcements before they take the field. Should they do this, I see not from what quarters they can expect any succours worth mentioning so early as the beginning of May. But I would lay no great stress upon this, notwithstanding the idea is countenanced by their weakness in numbers, which must make their success more doubtful, and expose them to greater hazard in whatever they attempt, than can be agreeable where so much is at stake. Much will depend however upon the comparative strength of our army, and the conception they may form of it.

Though I do not doubt your discretion, which occasioned me so readily to embrace your proposal, yet such is the delicacy of my situation, that I must beg leave to repeat, what I before observed to you, that wherever I give opinions, they are merely my own and will probably, so far from being a transcript of those of the general, differ widely from them in many respects. The one I now advance is of this kind, and is besides improper to be generally circulated; for many people who have the management of affairs are of so lethargic a complexion, that they are to be kept in action only by the fear of immediate danger; and should they get it into their heads that the enemy would remain idle for six weeks, would think they had a right to dose away forty days at least.

In my last I mentioned a rumour concerning Doctor Franklin. Since that, I have seen something, said (and I believe it) to be an extract of a letter from him to Mr. Beech [2] of Philadelphia, in which he represents things to be in an excellent train in France, and uses this strong emphatical language, that a War between her & Britain "was as inevitable as death." No public advices from him, that I know of, have reached Head Quarters.

I spoke to General Knox about your cannon in the Continental service. He answered, that it would be difficult to ascertain to what particular class the pieces that have been lost belonged; but he considered the Continent at all times bound to make good the number borrowed from your state; and that he had still your six pieces in his hands. I have always looked upon the matter in the same light.

I have the honor to be Gentlemen Your most Obdt. servant

Alex Hamilton

ALS, New-York Historical Society, New York City. This letter is dated
March 2, 1777, in *JCHW*, VI, 570.
    1. Letter not found.
    2. A Richard Beach is listed as Franklin's representative on the tax rolls of
Philadelphia in 1779 (*Pennsylvania Archives*, 3rd ser., XIV, 501, 778). On the
other hand, it seems more likely that H was referring to Richard Bache, a
Philadelphia merchant and Franklin's son-in-law.

To Joshua Loring [1]

Head Quarters Morris Town [New Jersey] March 25th
1777

Sir,

His Excellency General Washington has permitted Doctor
Thomas Sendown,[2] the bearer hereof, and Mr. Laghlin McIntosh [3]
prisoners with us on parole, to go into New York to be exchanged
for two other Gentlemen of similar rank, prisoners with you. The
Gentlemen he desires should be released instead of them are Doctor
Samuel McKensie,[4] taken at Three Rivers, and Mr. Daniel Frink
Commissary, who was taken at Fort Washington.

I am Sir   Your most humble servant   A Hamilton   ADC

ADfS, George Washington Papers, Library of Congress.
    1. Loring was British commissary general of prisoners.
    2. Thomas Sandom (or Sendown), surgeon's mate, British army.
    3. Loughlin McIntosh, commissary, British army.
    4. Before his capture in March, 1776, McKenzie was a surgeon with the
Third Pennsylvania Regiment.

From Gouverneur Morris [1]

Kingston [New York] 26th. March 1777.

Sir

By unavoidable Incidents this Letter is delayed beyond the usual
Time for which I assure you I am extremely sorry. Your Favor [2] gave
great Pleasure as well to the Committee as to several Members of
the House who are much pleased with your judicious Caution to distinguish between what you sport as your private Opinion and the
weighty Sentiments of the General.

No Circumstance could have more contributed to our Happiness
than to hear of the General's Recovery which believe me gave uni-

versal Joy. Be pleased to make my most respectful Compliments of his Lady.

That the Enemy are willing to desert can hardly be doubted and a Variety of sufficient Reasons may easily be assigned. Want of Success is not among the least considerable. Add also to the Want of Pay the Want of Plunder. I think the Situation of the Enemy clearly demonstrates their Want of Political Wisdom & Knowlege of War at the Fountain Head. To pass over the Succession of other Blunders they committed from their Attempt on Long Island to their present Disposition, their Treatment of the Soldiery is a Monument of Folly. First to prevent their foreign Mercenaries from deserting they kept back Arrearages of Pay & secondly to prevent Mutiny & silence Murmurings they allowed the Plundering of a Country they intend to conquer. Here common Sense alone would have informed them had they listened to her Dictates that by irritating they could never subdue; that an Indulgence in Excesses would relax all Discipline. Taught by Experience they begin now to wind up the Cords, but as it was said of James the first they are always either too high or too low. Instead of liberal Discipline they ask servile Obedience. Would it not be wise to meet this with taunting Insult to encourage our Men in abuse of them as poor Slaves hired without pay yet not daring to vent a Complaint & contrast the differe⟨nt⟩ situations at the same Time inviting them to come and taste the Air of Freedom. The English are the proudest People on Earth.

You will hear more of a little Expedition against Peeks Kill at Head Quarters than I can tell you. I suppose it is intended as a Diversion; if so, it is a ridiculous one.

I am &c.   Gouvr. Morris

We this Instant received your second Letter which shall be answered in turn.[3]

ALS, Hamilton Papers, Library of Congress.
1. Morris wrote this letter in his capacity as a member of the New York Committee of Correspondence.
2. H to the New York Committee of Correspondence, March 20, 1777.
3. H to the New York Committee of Correspondence, March 22, 1777.

George Washington to
William Shippen, Junior [1]

Morristown [New Jersey] March 26, 1777. Discusses the problem of soldiers dismissed from hospitals.

Df, in writing of H, George Washington Papers, Library of Congress.
1. Shippen was chief physician of the Flying Camp. On April 11, 1777, he became director general of hospitals.

From Robert R. Livingston [1]

Kingston [New York] March 29th. 1777.

Sir

We received your favor of the [22] [2] Instant and am obliged to you not only for your Acceptance of a very troublesome Challenge, but for the Alacrity with which you meet us in the field. We wish it would Afford you as many Laurels, as you are like to reap elsewhere!

You have heard of the Enemy's little Excursion to Peeks ⟨Kill⟩; [3] we wish it may not encourage them, to make a more serious Attempt, mig⟨ht⟩ it not be proper to remove the Stores to a Place of greater Safety?

We are somewhat alarmed at Accounts of the Indians having left their Villages; from whence many conclude, that they have hostile Intentions; [4] tho' as they are much in our Power, we cannot be entirely of this Opinion.

Your Reasons for supposing that the Enemy will not proceed to Philadelphia 'till the beginning of May seem to be conclusive; are you equally well satisfied that they may not open their Campaign by sailing to the Northward? You have probably seen some Affidavits of People who had been to New York which were sent by Convention to his Excellency the Genl. As this does not go by our own Express we do not care to risque any thing more on this Subject, which we shall treat more at large in our next.

Time must shortly prove the truth of Mr. Franklins Conjecture, which derives great Credit from the several Accounts we daily receive of the State of Europe. You will oblige us by communicating any further Intelligence you may have received on this Subject; it's Importance renders us solicitous about the Event.

I am   Sir by Order   Your most Obedt. humble servt.

Robt R. Livingston

Colo. Alexander Hamilton

LS, Hamilton Papers, Library of Congress.
    1. Livingston wrote this letter in his capacity as a member of the New York Committee of Correspondence.
    2. This date was left blank in MS. See H to the New York Committee of Correspondence, March 22, 1777.
    3. On March 23, 1777, a British force of about 500 men attacked Peekskill, New York, and compelled Brigadier General Alexander McDougall's forces to withdraw. The British, having destroyed some provisions and stores, withdrew on the following day.
    4. Livingston's alarm arose from reports of a meeting of Indians which was held at Oneoghquaga, New York, and which was presided over by Joseph Brant.

To the New York Committee of Correspondence

[*Morristown, New Jersey, March 29, 1777.* On April 2, 1777, the New York Committee of Correspondence, writing to Hamilton, stated: "We received Your's of the 29th. Ultimo and are extream⟨ly⟩ sorry to hear of your Indisposition." *Letter not found.*]

To Hugh Knox

[*Morristown, New Jersey, March, 1777.* On December 10, 1777, Knox, writing to Hamilton, referred to "The fine, impartial, laconic & highly descriptive account you favour'd me with of the last Years Campain, in your letter of March last." *Letter not found.*]

From the New York Committee
of Correspondence

Kingston [New York] April 2d 1777

Sir

We received Your's of the 29th. Ultimo [1] and are extream⟨ly⟩ sorry to hear of your Indisposition.

In our last we expressed an Apprehension that the Enemy might possibly make Hudson's River their first Object; not only because they could open their Campaign there earlier than they could go to Pensilvania as in one Case their Army would move by land and in the other by Water; But because having the command of the River, by taking the advantage of a southerly Wind, they would have it in their Power to run up in a few Hours and by destroying the Boats that are along it's Banks render it impossible for Genl. Washington's Army to cross till they have marched to Albany; a Thing almost impracticable at this Season of the Year, considering the distance and badness of the Roads. This would enable them not only to ravage all this State but to enter Connecticut on it's Western side, where the disaffection of the People will insure them many friends. We have strained every Nerve to prepare for their reception, having vested a Power in Genl. George Clinton [2] to make whatever Drafts he may think necessary from the Militia; in consequence of which every third Man is ordered to be drawn from the Southern and every fifth Man from the Northern Counties. We are not without Apprehensions that these heavy Drafts will be dreadfully felt in the want of the necessary Supplies for the Army and Inhabitants, which can hardly be raised under such Circumstances in this State; but more remote Evils must yield to the pressures of Necessity. We enclose you by direction of Convention some Resolutions lately passed in order to render the Laws against Spies and secret Enemies more effectual. [3] You will be pleased to deliver them with our respectful Compliments to his Excellency the General.

We are happy to hear of the Arrival of the Vessel with Arms from France, [4] as no supplies can be more necessary. We flatter ourselves that it will shortly be in your Power to communicate ⟨m⟩ore important Intelligence from that Quarter.

We are with great Respect   Sir   Your most Obedient and very humble Servants.   Wm. Allison

Robt R. Livingston

Gouvr Morris

Colo. Alexander Hamilton

LS, in writing of William Allison, Hamilton Papers, Library of Congress; Df, in writing of Robert R. Livingston, New-York Historical Society, New York City.
   1. Letter not found.
   2. Clinton was in command of the Highland forts.
   3. The resolutions to which the Committee here refers read:
   "*Resolved,* That all such persons as have been or shall be apprehended in this State, without the enemy's lines, by Continental or other American troops, as spies from the enemy, or for enlisting men into their service, or for furnishing supplies or intelligence to them, be tried for the said offences by martial law, and if found guilty, suffer death or other punishment at the discretion of a general court martial of the Continental army or of the militia of this State; provided that where any person shall have been convicted by a court martial by virtue of this resolution, that the sentence shall not be executed until approved by this Convention or a future Legislature of this State.
   "Whereas a form of government will soon be established in this State, and proper courts organized for the trial of offences therein: Therefore,
   "*Resolved,* That the resolution above mentioned continue in force until the first day of July next, unless sooner repealed by this Convention or the future Legislature of this State" (*Journals of the Provincial Congress of the State of New-York,* I, 856–857).
   4. On March 17, 1777, the French ship *Mercury* arrived at Portsmouth, New Hampshire, with 12,000 firelocks, 1,000 barrels of powder, and other supplies.

To the New York Committee of Correspondence

[*Morristown, New Jersey, April 2, 1777.* On April 5, 1777, Hamilton, writing to the New York Committee of Correspondence, stated: "Since my last I have had the pleasure of receiving your reply to my two favours of 29th. Ulto. & 2d. current." *Letter of April 2, 1777, not found.*]

To the New York Committee
of Correspondence

[*Morristown, New Jersey, April 3, 1777.* On April 8, 1777, the New York Committee of Correspondence wrote to Hamilton: "Yours of the third came safe⟨ly to hand⟩ this Day." *Letter not found.*]

To the New York Committee
of Correspondence

Head Quarters,
Morristown [New Jersey] April 5th. 1777

Gentlemen,

Since my last I have had the pleasure of receiving your reply to my two favours of 29th. Ulto & 2d.[1] current. I am happy enough to be able to inform you that my indisposition, which was the occasion of my brevity when I last wrote, is now removed.

The opinion I advanced respecting the Enemy's not moving before the beginning of May seems to be Shaken, though not entirely overthrown by some present appearances. We have received information that they are embarking about three thousand men on board of transports, which are lying at the Hook, by way of Staten Island. This it is conjectured is with a view to the Delaware; and the Supposition is confirmed by the circumstance of a confederacy lately detected at Philadelphia, who among other things were endeavouring by the temptation of 50 pounds to engage persons, as pilots up that river. The extreme difficulties they must labour under for want of forage, and the infinite hazard they must run by moving with a Small body of about 5000 men, with an enemy in the rear, incapable of Sparing any Considerable body of troops to form a post behind, and be an asylum to them in case of accident. These circumstances will hardly allow me to think they will be daring enough to make the attempt at this time. But on the other hand, as they know we are

JCH Transcripts.
1. Letters not found.

in a progressive state as to numbers and other matters of importance, and as they have no prospect of early reinforcement, and are in a state of uncertainty as to any from the bustling aspect of European affairs, it is probable they may conceive a necessity of making a push at all risks. Perhaps however this embarkation is intended for some other purpose to make a diversion or execute some partizan exploit elsewhere. On the whole I find it difficult to believe they are yet ready for any Capital Operation.

As to your apprehensions of an attempt up the North River I imagine you may discard any uneasiness on that score, though it will be at all times adviseable to be on the watch against a contingency to be almost reduced to a certainty that the principal views of the enemy in the ensuing campaign will be directed towards the southward and to Philadelphia more immediately; of which idea the discovery before mentioned with respect to pilots is no contemptible confirmation. Philadelphia is an object calculated to strike and attract their attention. It has all along been the main source of supplies towards the war and the getting it into their possession would deprive us of a wheel we could very badly spare in the great political and military machine. They are sensible of this, and are equally sensible, that it contains in itself, and is surrounded by a prodigious number of persons attached to them and inimical to us, who would lend them all the assistance they could in the further prosecution of their designs. It is also a common and well grounded rule in war, to strike first and principally at the capital towns and Cities in order to the conquest of a country.

I must confess I do not see any object equally interesting to draw their efforts to the Northward. Operations merely for plundering and devastation can never answer their end; and if they could, one part of the continent would do nearly as well as another. And as to the notion of forming a junction with the northern army, and cutting off the communication between the Northern and Southern States, I apprehend it will do better in speculation than in practice. Unless the Geography of the Country is far different from any thing I can conceive, to effect this would require a chain of posts and such a number of men at each as would never be practicable or maintainable but to an immense army. In their progress, by hanging upon their rear and seizing every opportunity of Skirmishing, their Situation might be rendered insupportably uneasy.

But for fear of mistake, The General has determined to collect a considerable body of Troops at or about Peeks-Kill, which will not be drawn off 'till the intentions of the enemy have acquired a decisive complexion. These will be ready according to conjunctures, either to proceed Northerly or Southerly as may be requisite. Every precaution should be taken to prevent the boats from being destroyed, by collecting them, at the first movement of the enemy, under cover of one of the forts, or into some inlet difficult of access and easily defensible with a small number of men. The loss of them would be an irreparable disadvantage.

The Enemy's attempt upon Peeks-Kill is a demonstration of the folly of having any quantity of Stores at places so near the water and so much exposed to a Sudden inroad. There Should never be more there than sufficient to answer present demands. We have lost a good deal in this way at different times, and I hope experience will at last make us wiser.

His Excellency lately had a Visit from the Oneida Chief and five others. He managed them with a good deal of address and sent them away perfectly satisfied.[2] He persuaded them to go to Philadelphia; but they declined it, alleging their impatience to return, and remove the erroneous opinions of their Countrymen, from the misrepresentations of British emmissaries, which they were apprehensive might draw them into some rash proceedings. They parted after having

2. On March 29, 1777, Washington wrote to the President of Congress:
"Mr. [Rev. Samuel] Kirkland, the Oneida Missionary, arrived here this week, with a Chief Warrior and five other Indians of that Nation. They had been to Boston and came from thence to this place, to enquire into the true state of matters, that they might report them to a Grand Council to be shortly held. They said things were so falsely and variously represented by our Enemies thro their Agents, that they did not know what to depend on. I invited them to go to Philadelphia, but they declined it, declaring they were well satisfied with what they had seen and that they were authorized to tell their Nation, all they had heard from the Enemy was false. Being told that France was assisting us and about to join in the War, they seemed highly pleased. . . . I shewed them every civility in my power and every thing that I thought material to excite in them an Idea of our strength and independence. After staying Two days, they set off for their Nation, expressing their desire of the most speedy return to the Council and professing the most friendly Sentiments toward us" (George Washington Papers, Library of Congress).

made the most solemn protestations of friendship and good will. His Excellency has been very busy all day in dispatching the Southern Post, which has prevented me giving him your resolve. It will no doubt be very acceptable; and it is with pleasure I inform you that the zeal and abilities of the New York Convention hold the first rank in his estimation.

No news from France, save that the Congress have obtained a credit there, for which they can draw bills to the amount of £100.000.Stg. This will be extremely Serviceable in carrying on a trade with the french. The new troops begin to come in. If we can shortly get any considerable accession of Strength, we may be able to strike some brilliant Stroke.

I am Gentlemen with the greatest respect   Your most obedient Servant   A. Hamilton

We have been some time endeavouring to negotiate a regular Cartel; but it has been lately broken off, principally on account of Major General Lee. General Howe will not allow him to be comprehended under the general idea of American prisoners.[3]

3. This postscript refers to a long and complicated series of events that attended the attempts of General William Howe and Washington to draw up a mutually suitable cartel for the exchange of prisoners. Major General Charles Lee, a former officer in the British army who had joined the Continental Army at the outbreak of the Revolution, had been captured by the British at Basking Ridge, New Jersey, on December 13, 1776. For a time, it was thought that the British would try him for treason, but he was exchanged in April, 1778.

George Washington to
Brigadier General Nathaniel Heard [1]

Morristown [New Jersey] April 7, 1777. Orders Heard to see that the number of officers is in proportion to the number of men. States that brigadiers must choose a field commander and must demand an exact return of troops.

Df, in writing of H, endorsement reads "to General Herd and Wyne," George Washington Papers, Library of Congress.
    1. Heard was a brigadier general in the New Jersey Militia. "Wyne" was Brigadier General William Winds, also of the New Jersey Militia.

George Washington to Joseph Reed
or Colonel Cornelius Cox[1]

Morristown [*New Jersey*] *April* 7, *1777*. Orders release of "Mr. Smith" who had been acting as a spy for the Americans and was mistakenly arrested by Major General Benjamin Lincoln.

Df, in writing of H, George Washington Papers, Library of Congress.
   1. Joseph Reed had resigned as adjutant general and was residing in Philadelphia as a private citizen.

From the New York Committee
of Correspondence

Kingston [New York] 8th April 1777.

Sir.

Yours of the third came safe⟨ly to hand⟩[1] this Day[2] and gave us great Pleasure by certifying your Hea⟨lth. The scantiness of⟩ our Numbers will not permit the Loss of one useful ⟨citizen. It is⟩, therefore, a determined Point that sick or well, you are by no means ⟨to⟩ die.

At this Distance it is impossible to determine what the Enemy can or what they can not do. But certainly if we can bring a respectable Force into the Field previous to their Movements it must be extremely difficult for them to advance or retreat. The latter indeed may be assisted by the Works they are throwing up.

Their Attempt upon the Delaware is far from improbable. Howe is certainly a stupid Fellow but if he reasons so far the Taking of Philadelphia would give a splendid Sight to their Manœuvres in the Eyes of Europe. This would be productive of Advantage. The seizing that large City would also afford him much Benefit in the several Ways which you suggest. But would it not be wise to permit his Force to be thus divided, that one Part after another might be cut to Pieces?

Since the Affair at Peeks Kill, their Views this Way seem to be less probable. It was doubtless unmilitary to warn us of our Danger:

They will also soon learn that we are in this Quarter in a decent Posture of Defence and that may decide their fluctuating Counsels.

Perhaps after all they will find it more convenient to keep Post at Amboy with an advanced Party at Brunswick secure New York and carry on a kind of naval Partizan War till the further Aid and Order of their Masters.

You will take Care whenever you write to us Matters which ought ⟨not to be seen by all⟩, to direct to one of *us* only in a separate Letter, while that which is me⟨rely indif⟩ferent, comes under your usual Direction. The Reason is that sometimes when we do not happen to be immediately in the Way your Letters are opened by the President and altho no evil Consequences have accrued from this as yet it is nevertheless proper to guard against it.[3]

What you say relative to a Cartel reminds us of the Case of Major Edminston[4] who was taken by Genl. Schuyler at the same Time with Sir John Johnson.[5] This Gentleman as His Excellency will recollect was sent into the Enemy's Quarters with a Letter to negotiate an Exchange for one of three Majors Prisoners in their Hands. He hath since returned with a Letter from Howe to Genl. Schuyler purporting that one of those Majors shall be exchanged for him he being permitted to join his Regt. in Canada. He was three Weeks or thereabouts travelling from New York to Albany of which the Convention being informed caused him to be made Prisoner and intend sending him to Head Quarters. He is well acquainted with the Face of this Country, and the Dispositions of it's Several Inhabitants. He has sufficient Interest with the Indians to accomplish an Escape upon the whole (as it will not be prudent to confine him within this State) it is submitted whether it would not be proper to secure him elsewhere untill the Close of the present Campaign.

We are Sir your most obedient & humble Servants

Robt R Livingston
Gouvr Morris

LS, in writing of Robert R. Livingston, Hamilton Papers, Library of Congress.

1. Portions of the MS are mutilated. Bracketed material in this paragraph has been taken from interlineations made in the MS in an unidentified handwriting at a later date.

2. Letter not found.

3. Bracketed material in this paragraph has been taken from Hawks, *The Official and Other Papers of Alexander Hamilton,* 247.

4. Major William Edmonston, British Forty-eighth Regiment, overstayed his parole in New York City where he had gone to negotiate his own exchange. He failed in this attempt, and, as Livingston and Morris indicate, he was returned to Washington's Headquarters.

5. Sir John Johnson was the son of Sir William Johnson, superintendent of Indian affairs in colonial New York. In January, 1776, he gave his parole that he would take no part in the war against the colonies. In May, Major General Philip Schuyler, believing that Johnson had broken his parole, sent a detachment to arrest him. Johnson, however, escaped to Canada.

From William Smith [1]

Kingston [New York] April 9th. 1777

Sir.

The Convention on having granted a Permission to Mr. Le Roy [2] to repair to head Quarters in order to solicit leave to go to New York; And having omitted to take his Parole, they beg the favor of you to carry the enclosed Resolution [3] into execution.

I am   Sir   Your most Obedt. Servt.   By Order.

Wm Smith president P.T.

Colo. Hamilton

LS, Hamilton Papers, Library of Congress.
   1. Smith, a delegate from Suffolk, wrote in his capacity as president *pro tempore* of the Convention of the State of New York.
   2. Jacob Le Roy, a New York merchant.
   3. The resolution stated that Le Roy "do give his parol to return and appear before the Convention, or Committee of Safety of this State, within six weeks from the time of his arrival within the enemy's lines" (*Journals of the Provincial Congress of the State New-York,* I, 871–872).

To Catharine Livingston [1]

Morris Town [New Jersey] April 11th. 1777

I take pleasure in transmitting you a letter,[2] committed to my care, by your Sister Miss Suky,[3] and in executing a promise, I gave her, of making an advance towards a correspondence with you. She says you discover, in all your letters to her, a relish for politics, which she thinks my situation qualifies me better for gratifying, than would be in her power; and from a desire to accommodate you in this particular, as well as to get rid of what she calls a difficult task to herself, and to give me an opportunity of enjoying the felicity which must naturally attend it, she wishes me to engage on the footing of a political correspondent.

Though I am perfectly willing to harmonize with your inclination, in this respect, without making the cynical inquiry, whether it proceed from sympathy in the concerns of the public, or merely from female curiosity, yet I will not consent to be limited to any particular subject. I challenge you to meet me in whatever path you dare; and if you have no objection, for variety and amusement, we will even sometimes make excursions in the flowery walks, and roseate bowers of Cupid. You know, I am renowned for gallantry, and shall always be able to entertain you with a choice collection of the prettiest things imaginable. I fancy my knowlege of you affords me a tolerably just idea of your taste, but lest I should be mistaken I shall take it kind, if you will give me such intimations of it, as will remove all doubt, and save me the trouble of finding it out with certainty myself. This will be the more obliging, as, without it, I should have a most arduous task on my hands, at least, if connoisseurs in the sex say true, according to whose representations, contrary to the vulgar opinion, woman is not a *simple*, but a most complex, intricate and enigmatical being.

After knowing exactly your taste, and whether you are of a romantic, or discreet temper, as to love affairs, I will endeavour to regulate myself by it. If you would choose to be a goddess, and to be worshipped as such, I will torture my imagination for the best arguments, the nature of the case will admit, to prove you so. You shall be one of the graces, or Diana, or Venus, or something surpassing them all. And after your deification, I will cull out of every poet of my acquaintance, the choicest delicacies, they possess, as offerings at your Goddesships' shrine. But if, conformable to your usual discernment, you are content with being a mere mortal, and require no other incense, than is justly due to you, I will talk to you like one [in] his sober senses; and, though it may be straining the point a little, I will even stipulate to pay you all the rational tribute properly applicable to a fine girl.

But amidst my amorous transports, let me not forget, that I am also to perform the part of a politician and intelligencer. This however will not take up much time, as the present situation of things gives birth to very little worth notice, though it seems pregnant with something of importance. The enemy, from some late movements, appear to be brooding mischief, which must soon break out, but I hope it will turn to their own ruin. To speak plainly, there is reason to believe, they are upon the point of attempting some important entreprize. Philadelphia in the opinion of most people, is their object. I hope they may be disappointed.

Of this, I am pretty confident, that the ensuing campaign will effectually put to death all their hopes; and establish the success of our cause beyond a doubt. You and I, as well as our neighbours, are deeply interested to pray for victory, and its necessary attendant peace; as, among other good effects, they would remove those obstacles, which now lie in the way of that most delectable thing, called matrimony;—a state, which, with a kind of magnetic force, attracts every breast to it, in which sensibility has a place, in spite of the resistance it encounters in the dull admonitions of prudence, which is so prudish and perverse a dame, as to be at perpetual variance with it. With my best respects to Mr. & Mrs. Jay,[4] I beg you will believe me to be,   Your assured friend & servant

Alexr. Hamilton

ALS, Massachusetts Historical Society, Boston.
1. Catharine Livingston was the daughter of William Livingston, Revolutionary War governor of New Jersey. H had met and become well acquainted with the members of the Livingston family when he lived at Elizabethtown, New Jersey, soon after his arrival in this country.
2. This letter has not been found.
3. Susanna Livingston who subsequently married John Cleves Symmes.
4. The former Sarah Livingston who had married John Jay in 1774.

To the New York Committee of Correspondence

Head Quarters Morris Town [New Jersey]
April 12th 1777

Gentlemen,

I this day received your favour of the 8th instant.

Hurry of business prevents my entering into a particular detail of affairs, either with respect to the enemy, or ourselves; though matters remain much in the same situation, as when I last wrote. The enemy are unquestionably preparing to take the field as soon as possible; notwithstanding which, I believe it may be full as late, as I at first suggested, before they will be perfectly ready for a general movement. By several persons, who have come out of New York, within these few days, it is pretty well confirmed, that they have constructed a bridge to be laid upon boats, for the purpose, in all probability, of crossing the Delaware.

The new levies begin to come in from the southward, but not in such large numbers, as could be wished. It is to be hoped however, that we shall shortly be sufficiently re-inforced to give an effectual obstruction to their designs. The Congress have resolved, if the General approves, to form a camp on the West side of the Delaware, and have called upon Pensylvania to furnish 3000 militia to join the same. Every nerve must and will be strained to prevent Philadelphia falling into the enemy's hands. It is a place of infinite importance.

It is said, there are favourable accounts, lately received from Doctor Franklin; but we have no authentic advice of the kind; nor does the report extend to any particulars.

Your sentiments of Major Edmiston's conduct,[1] correspond with the General's ideas of it. He had given some directions to General Schuyler on the subject.[2] Besides other purposes, it might serve, the design of his going to Canada, was evidently that he might be a vehicle of instructions to General Carleton. It would be the most convenient, certain and expeditious mode, they could have fallen upon to convey them. I communicated the paragraph of your letter respecting him, to His Excellency. He wishes the Major might be sent on directly to Philadelphia. I fancy he would be glad to be saved the trouble of an interview with him.

I should be obliged to you to inform the Convention, that it is my opinion The General will not permit Mr Le Roy to go into New York. It is a determined point with him to grant no such indulgence, when any matter of the kind is referred to him, unless the person applying can assign the most substantial reasons for his request and can also produce explicit credentials of his political principles and conduct being favourable to the American cause. I conclude from my being instructed to require his parole that he cannot give satisfaction on these points. If however he should obtain permission, I will execute the resolve transmitted to me. For the future, if the convention have cogent reasons for allowing any subject of the state to go into the enemy, as they are the best judges of all the circumstances concerning him, they had better send him in, without referring the matter particularly to The General.

I take the liberty to inclose a letter to the care of Mr. Jay,[3] the delivery of which to him will be a favour conferred on   Gentlemen Your most respectful servt   A Hamilton

ALS, New-York Historical Society, New York City.
  1. See New York Committee of Correspondence to H, April 8, 1777.
  2. A draft of Washington's letter to Philip Schuyler (dated March 12, 1777) is in the George Washington Papers, Library of Congress.
  3. This is probably H to Catharine Livingston, April 11, 1777.

To the New York Committee
of Correspondence

Morris Town [New Jersey] April 12th, 1777.

Gentlemen
    His Excellency requests that you will transmit the enclosed letter to General Wayne,[1] by the first safe opportunity.
    I am, gentlemen,   Yr. most humble serv.   A. HAMILTON

Honourable the Committee of Correspondence
    of the Convention of New-York.

Journals of the Provincial Congress of the State of New-York, II, 431.
  1. George Washington to Anthony Wayne, April 12, 1777. A draft of this letter is in the George Washington Papers, Library of Congress.

From Major General William Alexander,
Lord Stirling [1]

Basking Ridge [New Jersey] April 12, 1777. ". . . the time of Capt. James Scotts [2] Company will expire the 14th. . . . I believe it will be best that I be furnished with His Excellency's dismission of them by the day. I wrote to his Excellency . . . about the Appointment of Wilcocks.[3] If he is approved of, I wish you would get both McWilliams [4] & him in orders. . . ."

ALS, Hamilton Papers, Library of Congress.

1. William Alexander, or Lord Stirling, was a native of America who in 1755 instituted legal proceedings to secure the title Earl of Stirling, to which his father had been heir presumptive before leaving Scotland for America. Although he lost the suit, he used the title and was generally known by it. At the time this letter was written, Stirling, whose home was in Basking Ridge, New Jersey, was a major general in the Continental Army.

2. James Scott, captain of a volunteer company from Virginia.

3. William Willcocks (or Wilcocks) of New York, who was appointed Stirling's aide-de-camp on April 13, 1777.

4. Major William McWilliams of Virginia, who was appointed Stirling's aide-de-camp on March 19, 1777.

To Major General William Alexander, Lord Stirling

Head Quarters Morris Town [New Jersey] April 12th 1777

My Lord

I communicated your Lordship's letter to his Excellency. He has desired me to send Capt Scott's company their dismission, which you will therefore be pleased to give them, on the expiration of their time.

General Green [1] will bring you an answer to your letter respecting Mr. Willcox's, by which you will perceive that his Excellency has approved, and that I have written to Mr. Willcox agreeable to your desire. Mr. McWilliams was appointed in general orders the 19th. of March. Mr. Willcocks shall be inserted in tomorrow's orders.

I inclose you the only order I know of, that has been lately issued, in which you division is concerned.

I am with great respect   Your Lordship's   Most humble serv.

A Hamilton   ADC

ALS, MS Division, New York Public Library.
1. Major General Nathanael Greene of Rhode Island.

George Washington to John Hancock [1]

Morristown [New Jersey] April 12, 1777. Introduces Mauduit du Plessis [2] and recommends his appointment as a captain of artillery.

LS, in writing of H, Papers of the Continental Congress, National Archives.
1. John Hancock was President of the Continental Congress.
2. Thomas Antoine, Chevalier de Mauduit du Plessis, was appointed a captain in the Continental artillery on April 15, 1777.

George Washington to Robert Morris, George Clymer, and George Walton[1]

Morristown [New Jersey] *April 12, 1777.* States objections to forming an army in Pennsylvania. Names Bristol as rendezvous. Orders Pennsylvania Militia to be kept at a distance from Continental troops until there is action. Again recommends removal of stores from Philadelphia.

LS, in writing of H, New-York Historical Society, New York City. Df, in writing of Tench Tilghman with minor changes by H, George Washington Papers, Library of Congress.

1. On December 21, 1776, Congress resolved that "Robert Morris, George Clymer, and George Walton, Esqrs be a committee of Congress, with powers to execute such continental business as may be proper and necessary to be done at Philadelphia" (*JCC*, VI, 1032).

To the New York Committee of Correspondence

[Morristown, New Jersey, April 14, 1777][1]

Gentlemen,

I take occasion to inform you, that an ⟨attempt⟩ was yesterday made to suprize Bound Brook. It partly succeeded but not to the enemy's wish. They got possession of Bound Brook, but our people eluded their design of surrounding and cutting off the whole party, and made good their retreat to the pass of the mountains in the rear. We lost however 3 field pieces, one iron 6 pounder, and 2 brass three pounders, about 30 men killed and taken; and 'tis supposed General Lincoln's[2] Aid Du Camp is among the number of the taken. Our troops had three full fires upon the enemy at a short distance, whence 'tis not improbable many of them fell; particulars not accurately ascertained. Lord Cornwallis & three or ⟨four Ma⟩jor Generals were upon the party; a division made an amusement in front, and two other divisions, came upon each of the flanks.

Besides this, we have just received a piece of disagreeable intelligence from Philadelphia. There are three or four ships in the river, with intention⟨s⟩ no doubt to interrupt our trade. A ship from france,[3] coming into the river, was attacked by them. The Comma⟨nder⟩ of her, one Anderson, defended her gallantly for two or three hours. He beat off the enemy's boats who attempted to board him, but as they persisted, ⟨finding⟩ her effectual defence impossible, he set fire to a ⟨train⟩ of powder placed for the purpose and blew her up. Unfortunately this brave man paid his life as the price of his heroism. The dispatches from France were saved, (the conten⟨ts⟩ as yet to us unknown) and a part of the Cargo was thrown on shore, consisting of Guns, Gunlocks, cloaths &c. This was so far lucky.

I am Gentlemen   Yr. most humble servant   A Hamilton

ALS, Charles Roberts Autograph Collection of the Haverford College Library, Haverford, Pennsylvania.
  1. This letter has been dated by the attack on Bound Brook which occurred on April 13, 1777, and which H mentions in his first sentence.
  2. Major General Benjamin Lincoln, who at the time of the attack was in command of the American outpost at Bound Brook.
  3. The ship was the *Morris* sailing from Nantes, under the command of Captain Anderson.

From the New York Committee
of Correspondence [1]

Kingston [*New York*] *April 17, 1777.* "We are directed by Convention to enclose a resolution [2] passed this day in addition to that of the 1st. of Apl. which we before did ourselves the honor to transmit to his Excellency. . . ." Asks Hamilton to consult with Washington on propriety of enlisting "ignorant young lads," who had joined the enemy and now wish "to enlist in our regiments."

ALS, Hamilton Papers, Library of Congress.
  1. Although this letter is signed by Robert R. Livingston, he wrote it in his capacity as a member of the New York Committee of Correspondence.
  2. The resolution reads: "*Resolved,* That the resolutions of this Convention of the first day of April instant, empowering court martials to try persons coming from the enemy as spies, enlisting men in their service, or supplying them with provisions, be extended to all such persons as shall be taken in going off privately to the enemy, and continue in force till the first day of July next, unless sooner repealed" (*Journals of the Provincial Congress of the State of New-York,* I, 885).

To the New York Committee
of Correspondence

Head Quarters Morris Town [New Jersey]
April 20th. 1777

Gentlemen.

The disposition of the Convention, with respect to the disaffected among you is highly commendable, and justified by every principle of equity and policy. The necessity of exemplary punishment, throughout the States, is become evident beyond a doubt; and it were to be wished every one of the thirteen would imitate the judicious conduct of New-York. Lenity and forbearance have been tried too long to no purpose: it is high time to discard what the clearest experience has shown to be ineffectual.

But in dispensing punishments, the utmost care and caution ought to be used. The power of doing it, or even of bringing the guilty to trial should be placed in hands that know well how to use it. I believe it would be a prudent rule to meddle with none but those whose crimes are supported by very sufficient evidence, and are of a pretty deep die. The apprehending innocent persons, or those whose offences are of so slender a nature as to make it prudent to dismiss them, furnishes an occasion of triumph, and a foundation for a species of animadversion, which is very injurious to the public cause. Persons so apprehended generally return home worse than they were; and by expatiating on their sufferings first excite the pity towards themselves and afterwards the abhorrence towards their persecutors, or those with whom they converse. I believe it would also be in general a good rule, either to pardon offenders intirely or to inflict capital and severe punishments.

The advice given by a certain general to his son, when the latter had the Roman army in his power, was certainty very politic. He advised him either to destroy them utterly or to dismiss them with every mark of honour and respect. By the first method says he you disable the Romans from being your enemies, by the last you make them your friends. So with respect to the Tories I would either disable them from doing us any injury, or I would endeavour to gain their friendship by clemency. Inflicting trifling punishments only imbitters the minds of those on whom they fall, and increases their disposition to do mischief without taking away the power of doing it.

I shall communicate your additional resolve to the General; and consult him on what you mention; [1] and shall let you know his opinion in my next. Mine however is that those who appear to be of such a character as to be susceptible of reformations should be employed; but it is a delicate point. As to News the most material is, that from intelligence received from Rhode Island it appears the enemy are abandonning it. This is a preparatory step to the intended operations of the enemy.

The other day we surprized a Lieutenants guard took 16 prisoners and killed three or four.

In a private letter from Philadelphia, I am informed that a treaty of a very particular nature is on the point of being concluded between the Court of France & the states of America. There is a prospect of opening a trade with Sweden. I hear Mr. Morris [2] of Philadelphia has a vessel arrived from thence.

I am in haste. Gentlemen   Yr. most respectful servt   A Hamilton

ALS, New-York Historical Society, New York City.
1. This refers to problem of enlisting "young lads" who had joined the enemy. See the New York Committee of Correspondence to H, April 17, 1777.
2. Robert Morris.

George Washington to
Brigadier General George Clinton

Morristown [New Jersey] April 20, 1777. Discusses whether enemy plans to attack Philadelphia or move up North River. Reminds Clinton to call out militia. Approves of placing a chain across the North River.

Df, in writing of H, George Washington Papers, Library of Congress.

To William Livingston

Morris Town [New Jersey] April 21st. 1777

Sir,

A number of disaffected persons having been taken up and brought to His Excellency, he ordered an examination into their cases to know who of them were subject to a military jurisdiction, & who came properly under the cognizance of the civil power; also to discriminate those who were innocent, or guilty of trivial offences from those whose crimes were of a more capital and heinous nature; directing that those of the former character should be dismissed; and those of the latter referred to you for further trial and punishment.

This examination (at which, I was present) has been accordingly made, and the inclosed list of names will inform you of those who have been deemed proper subjects for a legal prosecution; and who are herewith sent under guard to be disposed of as you shall direct. I have transmitted you a bundle of papers, in which you will find the information & evidence that support the charges against them; and the confessions themselves made in the course of the enquiry. Many of them have nothing against them but what is to be found in their own acknowlegements; how far these may operate in fixing their guilt you can best determine. Several of them have been taken in arms and others were beyond a doubt employed in inlisting men for the service of the enemy. You will readily concur with his Excellency in the obvious necessity of inflicting exemplary punishments, on such daring offenders, to repress that insolent spirit of open and avowed enmity to the American cause, which unhappily is too prevalent in this and some other states.

There are several papers of consequence relating to some of the Prisoners, which are in the hands of Col: Dehart,[1] who is now down at one of the out posts. I shall procure them as soon as possible and forward them to you. Among the Prisoners is a certain John Eddy,[2] who appears to be an offender of some magnitude. One Francis Miller[3] is a full evidence against him, who is at present detained to give testimony against a person, that Eddy inlisted for the enemy, who was originally a deserter from the British Army, and now belongs to Col: Hands [4] regiment. As soon as this trial is over Miller shall be dispatched to you.

Peter Hopkins [5] of Sussex, brother of Silas Hopkins,[6] who some time since went to New York, was examined among the others; but as the whole evidence against him rested solely upon the credit of Gustins [7] deposition; and as Gustin had made declarations incompatible with the tenor of what he has sworn, as appears by the affidavit of three men of good repute both in political and other respects, it was thought proper to indulge him with permission to go at large, 'till his case could be further scrutinized, and new light thrown upon it in the course of the examination of others, whose circumstances bore a near affinity to his. He was desired to wait for a releasement but disobeyed this injunction and went off without getting it, which renders him somewhat suspicious, and affords a strong argument for a further inquiry. In confronting him with his accuser, I was inclined to believe, that Gustins seemingly contradicting himself was owing to his stupidity and to Hopkins' superior cunning. This man if he is not very innocent is certainly very subtle and may be dangerous.

The examination which has been made in this instance is somewhat irregular, and out of the common order of things; but in the present unsettled state of government, the distinctions between the civil and military power, cannot be upheld with that exactness which every friend to society must wish. I flatter myself however you are convinced with me his Excellency desires to avoid nothing more than a deviation from the strict rule of propriety in this respect or the least incroachment either upon the rights of the citizen or of the Magistrate. It was necessary to make the enquiry for the sake of the discrimination beforementioned; and tenderness to the innocent to save them from long and unmerited confinement recommended the measure.

I have the honor to be with great respect, Sir Your most Obdt. servt.   AH

ADfS, George Washington Papers, Library of Congress.
    1. Lieutenant Colonel William De Hart, First New Jersey Regiment.
    2. A resident of Sussex County, New Jersey, Eddy was charged with enlisting men for the British service. Indicted for treason by a grand jury, he escaped before he could be tried.
    3. Nothing is known concerning Francis Miller, although a man of that name did live in Smiths Clove, New York, during the Revolution.

4. Edward Hand, First Pennsylvania Regiment, had been made a brigadier general on April 1, 1777.

5. A former member of the House of Assembly of New Jersey, Hopkins was presumably a Tory, for in September, 1783, he testified on oath concerning the property of a Loyalist before David Matthews, the last mayor of New York City under the Crown.

6. New Jersey Tory, who was a captain in the Fifth New Jersey Volunteers, a Loyalist unit.

7. Presumably Peter Gusden, brigade major to Brigadier General Nathaniel Heard.

To the New York Committee of Correspondence [1]

[Morristown, New Jersey, April 21–27, 1777]

It may not be amiss to hint that some sentences have been passed in persuance of this resolve,[2] which have been improper. Confiscations of the real and personal estates of offenders have been in some instances ordained, and in others, whipping. It would be best where the nature of the case would justify it, to punish capitally; or where the crimes are not of sufficient enormity, to authorise this, pecuniary mulcts or imprisonments should be substituted. An execution or two, by way of emample would strike terror, and powerfully discourage the wicked practices going on; corporal punishment inflicted on an inhabitant is apt to excite compassion and breed disgust. Confiscation of property is not cognizable by martial law. These are His Excellency's sentiments and mentioned to prevent mistakes.

A Hamilton ADC

ALS, Historical Society of Pennsylvania, Philadelphia.

1. This letter, or fragment of a letter, is undated and does not include the name of the addressee. In the light of H's remarks in his letter of April 20, 1777, to the New York Committee of Correspondence, it has been assumed that the addressee of this letter is also the New York Committee of Correspondence.

2. The resolve referred to is that of April 17, 1777 (*Journals of the Provincial Congress of the State of New-York*, I, 885).

George Washington to John Hancock

Morristown [New Jersey] April 23, 1777. Requests apprehension of a spy.

LS, in writing of H, Papers of the Continental Congress, National Archives.

From the New York Committee
of Correspondence

[*Kingston, New York, April 24, 1777.* On this date the Provincial Convention of New York adopted the following resolution: "*Resolved,* That Major Lawrence [1] and Capt. Rutgers,[2] be a committee to confer with Colonel Robert Livingston [3] on the subject of making field cannon out of wrought iron; and that the committee of correspondence be directed to write to Colonel Hamilton for his opinion on the usefulness of such artillery." *Letter not found.*]

Journals of the Provincial Congress of the State of New-York, I, 901.
    1. Presumably Jonathan Lawrence, a delegate from Queens.
    2. Anthony Rutgers, delegate from New York City, and a privateer captain in the naval service.
    3. Son of Philip Livingston, and grandson of Robert Livingston, the first lord of Livingston Manor, Colonel Robert Livingston was the third and last lord of Livingston Manor.

To the Commanding Officer of the
German Battalion at Quibbletown [1]

Head Quarters [Morristown, New Jersey] April 25th. 1777

Sir,

His Excellency desires me to inform you, that the Congress have been pleased, to appoint Monsieur Le Baron D.'Arondhl,[2] colonel of the regiment, to which you belong. He conceives both the honor and advantage of the regiment, to be [3] promoted by the appointment of a Gentleman to the command of it, so respectable by birth, the honorable Station he fill'd in the service of his Prussian Majesty, and the experience he must have acquired by the long course of Two & Twenty years service. These considerations, he doubts not, will secure him a welcome reception from the Regt. and produce that respect and cheerful obedience to him, which his own character and merits, the determination of Congress in his favor, and his Excellencies particular approbation demand. It will certainly be of great advantage to the Regiment to have a person of experience and ability at its Head. Such a Man is best fitted to gain it Credit and distinction, and to raise it into importance and ev'ry Officer will find his interest in the general weight and respectability, which the corp will derive from him.

As he is a German by birth and has so many things beside to recommend him; it is evident the Congress have paid a particular attention to the good and accommodation of the Regt. in appointing him, and the Genl. expects it will be Gratefully received. He hopes a sense of duty and interest will beget a suitable disposition both in the Officers and men of the Regt., and it is therefore unnecessary to say, that the least want of respect or obedience, will meet with his severest disapp[r]obation.

I am &c.   A. H.

All promotions under the degree of Colo. will take place in the Regimental line.

Df, in writings of H and Richard Kidder Meade, George Washington Papers, Library of Congress.

1. The German Battalion was organized under a resolution of Congress, dated May 25, 1776. It was raised in Pennsylvania and Maryland; but as it did not belong to any state, in 1777 it was considered as one of the Sixteen Additional Continental Regiments. At the time that H wrote this letter, he did not know the name of the officer who was serving as acting commander of the German Battalion. Colonel Nicholas Housegger or Haussegger, who formerly held the command, was superceded on March 19, 1777, by Baron d'Arendt.

2. H's spelling is incorrect for he was referring to Henry Leonard Philip, Baron d'Arendt, who had served in the Prussian army. D'Arendt was appointed colonel of the German Battalion, as indicated above, on March 19, 1777, was granted a leave of absence on August 18, 1778, and did not rejoin the regiment.

3. The preceding part of this letter is in the writing of H; the succeeding part is in the writing of Meade.

To Major General Benjamin Lincoln

Head Quarters
Morris Town [New Jersey] 26th. April 1777.

Sir,

It is his Excellency's desire, that you have an immediate inspection made into the state of the mens arms and accoutrements, belonging to your division; and take effectual measures to have them put into the best order possible. Also to have your men completed to their proper complement of ammunition, strictly injoining the greatest care to avoid all wanton and unnecessary waste.

I am Sir   Your most Obedt. servt   A Hamilton   ADC

General Lincoln

ALS, Maine Historical Society, Portland.

George Washington to John Hancock

Morristown [*New Jersey*] *April 26, 1777*. Gives instructions concerning pay of American prisoners. Discusses conduct and influence of Tories.

Df, in writing of H, George Washington Papers, Library of Congress.

To the New York Committee of Correspondence

Head Quarters Morris Town [New Jersey]
April 28, 1777

Gentlemen

Extreme hurry of business puts it out of my power to say but very little.

Your information concerning a piece of ordnance lately constructed at Philadelphia is true. There is such a piece at Head Quarters, weighs 227 ld, carries a three pound ball. The iron is wraught hooped and welded together. The General and others esteem it a great acquisi[ti]on. It has been fired twenty times as fast as possible, and is supposed to be thorough proof. For my part I am rather dubious of this matter, and have recommended 50 successive discharges instead of 20. If she would stand that her sufficiency would be ascertained beyond a doubt, and her value would be immense; and as it is a new experiment, we cannot take too much pains ⟨to be sure. If Mr.⟩ Livingston [1] ⟨can con⟩struct ⟨pieces of the same kind⟩ [2] and weight that will stand a similar proof, he will render the most essential service to his Country. We cannot have too respectable an artillery; and he need not doubt they will be wanted.

As to the ships opposite Fort Washington, The General first supposed they might be intended to make a descent on the Jersey side and come by surprise on our left flank; but he now considers it wholly as an amusement, while they were executing their attempt upon the stores at Danbury.[3] Of this affair, you are probably as well advised as we are.

I thank you for your promise of sending me the model of your Government[4] as soon as published. I have sanguine expectations concerning it.

Nothing new at Head Quarters but the attempt against Danbury. If the enemy do not ⟨take the field⟩[5] in a general way in a fortnight, of ⟨which except⟩ the maturity of the season, ⟨there are no new arguments since I last, entered upon the Subject, I shall begin to think with you, that they probably mean to confine themselves to a partizan war⟩ 'till they get reinforced or receive further orders.

Troops coming on from the southward. We are told there are 2000 Carolinians, far on their way to Philadelphia—a part arrived.

I am with great respect   Gentlemen   Your most Obdt servant

A Hamilton

ALS, New-York Historical Society, New York City.
1. Robert Livingston, mentioned in committee's letter to H, April 24, 1777.
2. Bracketed material in this paragraph taken from *JCHW*, VI, 576.
3. On April 26, 1777, 2,000 British troops under Governor William Tryon marched into Danbury, Connecticut, an important supply base for the Continental forces. After burning the public stores and some private dwellings, the British withdrew on April 28. They were then attacked by militia and Continentals, and in the ensuing fighting, the American casualties were approximately 100, and those of the British were approximately 150.
4. This is a reference to New York State's first constitution which was voted by the Provincial Convention on April 20, 1777.
5. Bracketed material in this paragraph is taken from a copy of this letter in the Bancroft Transcripts, MS Division, New York Public Library.

To Major General Benjamin Lincoln[1]

[Morristown, New Jersey, April 28, 1777]

It appears by your letter to his Excellency that the detachment of Marylanders under Col Spotswood,[2] have marched to your post, with the other troops. His intention and directions were, that they should remain at Princeton, as he wishes to keep the Corps united, but since the matter has fallen out differently, he desires that detachment may immediately return to Princeton.[3]

1. ALS, sold at Anderson Galleries, November 28–29, 1927, Lot 421. The draft, also in H's writing, is in the George Washington Papers in the Library of Congress. The draft is written in the first person as though prepared for Washington's signature.
2. Colonel Alexander Spotswood, Second Virginia Regiment. He resigned on October 9, 1777.
3. Text taken from extract of letter in catalogue of Anderson Galleries. Original not found.

George Washington to Brigadier General Gurdon Saltonstall [1]

Morristown [*New Jersey*] *April 28, 1777.* Refuses to comply with Saltonstall's request for back pay.

Df, in writing of H, George Washington Papers, Library of Congress. H signed this letter with his initials which he later crossed out.
1. Saltonstall, a brigadier general in the Connecticut Militia, became ill soon after arriving in camp. He returned home and never rejoined the brigade.

To William Livingston

Head Quarters Morris Town [New Jersey]
April 29. 1777

Sir,

The inclosed was intended to be sent with the prisoners mentioned in the list; but before this could be done, Mr. Sims,[1] one of the chief Justices of the State came to this town, and informed me, that the Governor and Council were upon the point of adjourning, and that the sending the prisoners to them would only be an embarrassment without answering, at present, any valuable purpose. He considered himself as authorised to take the matter under his direction, and desired a sight of the papers relating to it. After perusing them, he determined, that it was best the prisoners should remain here, until he should receive your further orders on the subject; and informs me, that a letter here-with sent you, contains a representation of their cases, as they appear to him, for the purpose of knowing your sense in what manner they shall be disposed of.

He admitted two of them, Woolverton[2] and Silas Howel,[3] to bail.

In addition to the former, I send you a second list of four others that have been lately committed to Jail. These are capital offenders and among the number of those, who, it were to be wished, could have an immediate trial and punishment, Isaac Ogden in particular is one of the most barefaced, impudent fellows, that ever came under my observation.[4] He openly acknowleged himself a subject to the King of Great Britain and flatly refused to give any satisfaction to some questions that were put to him respecting one Moses Nichols, an emissary from the enemy, alleging no other reason for his refusal, than that he had given his word to be silent.

A spirit of disaffection shows itself with so much boldness and violence, in different parts of this state, that it is the ardent wish of his Excellency, no delay might be used in making examples of some of the most atrocious offenders. If something be not speedily done to strike a terror into the disaffected, the consequences must be very fatal. Among other ill effects all security to the friends of the American cause, will be destroyed; and the natural effect of this will be an extinction of their zeal in seconding and promoting it. Their attachment, if it remain, will be a dead, inactive, useless principle. And the tories, emboldened by impunity, will be encouraged to proceed to the most daring and pernicious lengths.

On the other hand it may not be unuseful to acquaint you, that in the course of the examination made by His Excellency's order, it appeared, that private pique and resentment had had their influence in causing some innocent persons to be apprehended; and that, in many instances, there was so slight a foundation of guilt as made it highly impolitic to meddle with them. It is always injurious to apprehend those, whose cases are such as afterwards oblige us to acquit or discharge them. To the innocent and friendly it is an occasion of disgust; to the wavering and disaffected it serves as an argument for a greater defection, and affords an opportunity for triumph and declamation. Their unmerited persecution is a good topic to excite the sympathy and pity of their neighbours; and there is an easy transition from these feelings to those of abhorrence and indignation against the unjust persecutors. It would be happy could things be put upon such a footing, as that those who ought to be taken notice of, might not escape; and that the innocent, or petty offenders might not be improperly molested, just as the malignity of some and the indiscretion of others may suggest. All this is submitted with due deference to Your Excellency's judgment.[5]

I have the honor to be, with the greatest respect   Your Excellency's   Most Obedient servant   A Hamilton
A D.C.

Governor Livingston

ADfS, George Washington Papers, Library of Congress.
   1. John Cleves Symmes, associate justice of the Supreme Court of New Jersey and a colonel in the New Jersey Militia.
   2. Thomas Woolverton, a Tory from Sussex County, New Jersey, was committed to jail in 1777, and his property was advertised for sale by the commissioners of forfeited estates in 1779–80.
   3. There is no mention of Silas Howel in the lists of New Jersey Tories compiled by E. A. Jones, "Loyalists of New Jersey," *Proceedings of the New Jersey Historical Society*, XI–XII (1926–27).
   4. A New Jersey lawyer and Tory, who fled to New York City. After the Revolution he was appointed judge of the Admiralty Court in Quebec.
   5. In MS, this paragraph has been crossed out. It appears that this was done at a later date by some one other than H.

From Hugh Knox

St. Croix April 31st: 1777.

My Dear Friend,

A pretty fair opportunity Just offering for Philada., I could not omit acknowledging the receipt of you⟨r⟩ Very Circumstantial and Satisfactory Letter of the 14th. Feby.[1] The thing has Happen'd which I wish'd for. We have been amased here by vague, imperfect, & very false accts. of matters from the Continent, & I always told my friends that if you Surviv'd the Campain & had an hour of leisure to write to me, I expected a more true, circumstantial & Satisfactory Acct. of matters in your letter, than by all the public papers & private Intelligence we had received here. I have but a moment to Command at present, & have not time to remark upon your Letter. I can only inform you that, it has given high Satisfactn. to all friends here. We rejoice in your *Good Character* & *Advancemt.*, which is indeed only the just reward of merit. May you Still live to deserve more & more from the friends of America, & to Justify the Choice & merit the approbation of the Great & Good General

Washington, a name which will Shine with distinguished Lustre in the Annals of History—A name dear to the friends of the Liberties of mankind! Mark this: You must be the Annalist & Biographer, as well as the Aid de Camp, of General Washington, & the Historiographer of the American War! I take the liberty to insist on this. I hope you take Minutes & Keep a Journal! If you have not Hitherto, I pray do it henceforth. I Seriously & with all my little influence urge this upon you. This may be a new & Strange thought to You; but if you Survive the present troubles, I Aver few men Will be as well qualified to Write the History of the present Glorious Struggle. God only knows, how it may terminate. But however that may be, it Will be a most interesting Story.

I Congratulate you on your recovery from A long & dangerous Illness. It is my Own Case. I am Just Convalescent, after the Severest Attack I ever had in my life. I hope to write you more at large soon, & remain, With the tender of Every kind & friendly wish, My Dear Sir   Your Affectionate Servt.   Hugh Knox

ALS, Hamilton Papers, Library of Congress.
1. Letter not found.

George Washington to the Massachusetts Legislature

Morristown [*New Jersey*] *May 3, 1777.* Transmits congressional resolve concerning defense of Ticonderoga.

Df, in writings of Tench Tilghman and H, George Washington Papers, Library of Congress.

George Washington to Brigadier General Alexander McDougall

Morristown [*New Jersey*] *May 3, 1777.* Approves detention of Seward's [1] company. States that the sailing of British ships from Amboy, New Jersey, necessitates further attention to British movements on North River.

LS, in writing of H, The Huntington Library, San Marino, California.
1. Captain Thomas Seward, Third Continental Artillery.

George Washington to Meshech Weare [1]

Morristown [New Jersey] May 3, 1777. Transmits congressional resolve concerning defense of Ticonderoga.

Df, in writing of H, George Washington Photostats, Library of Congress.
1. Weare was president of New Hampshire.

To William Duer [1]

Head Quarters Morris Town [New Jersey]
May 6. 1777

Sir,

The bearer of this is Mr. Malmedi a french Gentleman of learning, abilities and experience.[2] I believe he thinks himself intitled to preferment and comes to Congress for that purpose. At the recommendation of General Lee [3] he was made Brigadier General by the State of Rhode Island, and filled the station to the satisfaction of his employers, as appears by a letter from Governor Cook,[4] speaking of him in the highest terms of approbation. This has led him to hope that he should be adopted by the Continent on an equal footing. But in this he will no doubt be mistaken as there are many insuperable objections to such an event. Among others it would tend to raise the expectations of Frenchmen in general, already too high, to a pitch, which it would be impossible to gratify or endure. It might not however be amiss to do whatever propriety would warrant to keep him in good humour, as he is a man of sense and merit. I think policy would justify the advancing him a step higher, than his former Continental rank.[5]

Congress in the beginning went upon a very injudicious plan with respect to Frenchmen. To every adventurer that came, without even the shadow of credentials, they gave the rank of field officers. This circumstance, seconding the aspiring disposition natural to those people, carried the expectations of those who had really any pretensions to the character of officers to a length that exceeded all bounds of moderation. As it was impossible to persue this impolitic plan, the

Congress have begun to retrench their excessive liberality; and the consequence has been universal disgust and discontent.

It would perhaps be injurious, as the French are much addicted to national punctilio, to run into the opposite extreme to that first embraced, and by that mean create a general clamor and dissatisfaction. Policy suggests the propriety of discriminating a few of the most deserving, and endeavouring to keep them in temper even by gratifying them beyond what they can reasonably pretend to. This will enable us to shake off the despicable part with safety, and to turn a deaf ear to the exorbitant demands of the many. It will be easily believed in France that their want of merit occasioned their want of success, from the extraordinary marks of favor that have been conferred on others; whereas the united voice of complaint from the whole, might make ill impressions in their own Country, which it is not our interest should exist.

We are already greatly embarrassed with the Frenchmen among us, and from the genius of the people shall continue to be so. It were to be wished that our agents in France, instead of courting them to come out, were instructed to give no encouragement but where they could not help it; that is where applications were made to them by persons, countenanced and supported by great men, whom it would be impolitic to disoblige. Be assured, Sir, we shall never be able to satisfy them; and they can be of no use to us, at least for sometime. Their ignorance of our language, of the disposition of the people, the resources and difficiencies of the country, their own habits and tempers—all these are disqualifications that put it out of their power to be of any real use or service to us. You will consider what I have said intirely as my own sentiments & believe me to be with regard Sir   Your most hum servt   A. Hamilton

ALS, Hamilton Papers, Library of Congress.
    1. Duer, a New York merchant and financier, was a delegate to the Continental Congress.
    2. François, Marquis de Malmady (or Malmedy), was made a brevet major in the Continental Army in September, 1776. He also served as a brigadier general of Rhode Island troops from December, 1776, to March, 1777.
    3. Major General Charles Lee.
    4. Nicholas Cooke, governor of Rhode Island, 1775–1778.
    5. Malmady was made a colonel in the Continental Army on May 10, 1777, and served until the end of the war.

To the New York Committee of Correspondence [1]

Head Quarters Morris Town [New Jersey]
May 7th. 1777

Gentlemen,

I thank you for the favor of the pamphlet,[2] containing your form of government, which, without flattery, I consider as far more judicious and digested than any thing of the kind, that has yet appeared among us; though I am not so unreserved in my approbation as to think it free from defects. While I view it, in the main, as a wise and excellent system, I freely confess it appears to me to have some faults, which I could wish did not exist. Were it not too late to discuss particulars for any useful end, or could my judgment have any weight in a matter, which is the work of so many far more able and discerning, than I can pretend to be, I should willingly descend to an exhibition of those parts I dislike, and my reasons for disapproving. But, in the present situation of things, it would be both useless and presumptuous.

I congratulate you on the late important arrivals to the Eastward.[3] We consider them as immense acquisi[ti]ons. Did I not suppose you must be possessed of the same particulars we have at Head Quarters, I would transmit those we have to you.

I congratulate you also on the Danbury expedition.[4] The stores destroyed there have been purchased at a pretty high price to the enemy. The spirit of the people on the occasion does them great honor—is a pleasing proof that they have lost nothing of that primitive zeal, with which they begun the Contest, and will be a galling discouragement to the enemy from repeating attempts of the kind. Such an opposition under such circumstances was not to be expected. By every account both from our friends, and from themselves, they cannot have sustained a loss of less than 500 killed, wounded and taken.[5] An honest intelligent lad, a prisoner with them, who made his escape two or three days ago, informs that he saw three vessels loaded with wounded. He was permitted to look into the hold of two of them, and affirms there could not be fewer than forty in each. He attempted to inspect the contents of the third but was hindered by the Sentries. He also informs, that there were loud wailings and lamentations among the soldiers' women on the occasion, and that the people of New York considered the affair in the light of a defeat to the British troops.

From some late appearances, my opinion is greatly shaken as to the enemy's intention to move against Philadelphia. I begin to fear they will disappoint us with a contrary movement. The General is aware of this possibility, and will do every thing he can to provide for the event; and I trust the Convention of your state will co-operate with him by every exertion in their power. By intelligence received yesterday and to day from General's Putnam and Lincoln,[6] at the out posts, we have reason to suspect the enemy will soon evacuate Brunswick and push for Amboy; whence they will no doubt embark for some expedition by water. This may either be to Philadelphia or up the North River. Or perhaps the appearances that indicate this may be only feints to perplex and deceive us. The testimony of every person, that comes from them, confirms this fact, that their horses are in such miserable condition as to render them incapable of any material operations by land. If therefore proper care be taken wherever they shall point their efforts to prevent their collecting supplies of good horses among ourselves, I know not how it will be possible for them to penetrate any distance into the Country. As far as it may depend upon them, I hope the Convention will attend to this circumstance & will take effectual measures to put it out of their power to gain such supplies in any part of your state, towards which they may direct their movements.

Nothing particular from Europe. Doctor Lee [7] indeed writes, that from the face of affairs there a war cannot be postponed longer than three months. He thinks however the English will be able to get a reinforcement this year of 8 or 10.000 Germans. If I mistake not he says they have already engaged them and sent transports to take them in.

I am with great respect   Gentlemen   Your most Obedient servant   A Hamilton

ALS, New-York Historical Society, New York City.
    1. The envelope of this letter was addressed to Gouverneur Morris, but the salutation, "Gentlemen," indicates that it was intended for all the members of the committee.

2. *The Constitution of the State of New York* (Fish-Kill, Printed by Samuel Louden, 1777).

3. This is a reference to the arrival of the *Amphitrite*, a French vessel, at Portsmouth, New Hampshire, on April 20 or 21, 1777. This vessel brought cannon desperately needed by the Continental Army.

4. H here refers to the attack by the militia and Continentals on the British forces withdrawing from Danbury, April 28, 1777.

5. "British casualties were variously estimated at figures as high as '500 or 600' and in reality ran to the substantial total of about 154 killed and wounded" (Freeman, *Washington*, IV, 410).

6. At this time Major General Israel Putnam was in command at Princeton and Major General Benjamin Lincoln was at Bound Brook.

7. Arthur Lee, one of three commissioners (Benjamin Franklin and Silas Deane were the others) appointed to seek aid from France and to negotiate a treaty with that country.

George Washington to
Major General Horatio Gates [1]

Morristown [*New Jersey*] *May 7, 1777*. Encloses letter to Brigadier General Anthony Wayne, who is needed at Headquarters.

LS, in writing of H, New-York Historical Society, New York City.
1. Gates was in command of the Northern Department.

George Washington to
Brigadier General Alexander McDougall

Morristown [*New Jersey*] *May 11, 1777*. States that Major General Nathanael Greene and Brigadier General Henry Knox will inspect posts under McDougall's command.

LS, in writing of H, The Huntington Library, San Marino, California.

From Gouverneur Morris

[*Kingston, New York, May 11, 1777*. On May 12, 1777, Hamilton wrote to Morris: "I have received the pleasure of your favour of yesterday's date." *Letter not found.*]

To Gouverneur Morris [1]

Head Quarters Morris Town [New Jersey]
May 12th 1777

Dear Sir,

I have received the pleasure of your favour of yesterday's date.[2] The reasons you assign for the interval of silence on your part are admitted as sufficient; though I regret that the principal one exists— the combination of the tories for a general insurrection. But perhaps on the scale of policy I ought rather to congratulate you on the event: That there are too many tories in your state as well as in several others is a fact too well known: That they should confederate themselves for active purposes of revolt and disaffection, when once discovered, is desireable; because it arms the vindictive justice of the state, and will justify, in the eyes of all the world, a radical blow at the faction. Were it not that we have seen so many similar instances, that only prove the temerity and folly of the Tories, I should consider this, as a presumptive argument, that the enemy intend your way.

It seems now fully the opinion of our Generals, that the last year's project for uniting the two armies by the conquest of your state, will be prosecuted this campaign. To confirm this supposition, all the latter intelligence we have received from the enemy strongly indicates an intention to evacuate the Jerseys; and 'tis thought there will be very great obstacles to an attempt upon Philadelphia, by way of the Delaware; 'tis concluded that the North River must be the object. And, upon this principle, General's Green and Knox in whom, His Excellency has great confidence, are sent to examine the situation of things with you, and in concert with General McDougall, who is in equal estimation, to adopt every proper expedient for putting you in the best state of defence. They set out this day.[3]

If the enemy do not, in fact, aim at Philadelphia, they have been very artful in throwing out appearances well calculated to deceive; and which, though they have not had so full an effect, as at any time to cause our cautious General to lose sight of the other object which 'tis now imagined they propose to themselves; yet they have so far deceived as to beget pretty universally the opinion they wished to impose. But for my own part, though I am staggered in my conjectures; yet I by no means give up my first supposition. I think it very probable they are only evacuating the Jerseys, to be out of danger of an attack from us, which they have reason to fear from the increasing strength of our army; and mean to incamp on Staten Island 'till reinforced. It would be madness in them weak as they are in numbers to risk all in any capital attempt; and I am confident they will not do it unless they have a desperate game to play and have no expectation of reinforcements. Such a conduct would be contrary to every principle of war or policy. Howe cannot take the field with more than eight thousand men; let him go where he will, the probability of a defeat will be strong; and the consequences of it would be absolutely fatal. How can he hope to penetrate so far with so small a force, and with such a miserable supply of Horses to convey his Artillery and Baggage? It seems to me too, with respect to the supposed design upon your state, if it really existed, they would have taken care to have seized your forts and other important posts, when they must have been apprized you were in no condition to defend them.

We have lately had one or two little skirmishes here. A party from Bound brook, beat up some of the enemies advanced pickets, from Brunswick. An attack was made upon their pickets near Bonum Town.[4] We have no regular account of this matter; but what we have had is to this purport: That a party under Col: Cook [5] attacked one of their pickets and drove it in: That it was reinforced and sallied out again and was beaten in a second time: That it received a second reinforcement and made a second sally; and, That General Maxwell [6] who conducted the affair; perceiving the matter growing too serious by continual succours coming to them from Brunswick and Amboy, thought it best to retire which he did in good order, the enemy keeping at a respectful distance, during the whole time of their retrogradation. Tis said we have lost between 20 & 30, killed, wounded and a few stragglers taken; and 'tis also asserted that some of our officers counted nineteen dead bodies of the enemy on the field. The Royal Highlanders had taken possession of a wood, by way of ambuscade, out of which they were expelled by our troops. Here I believe the principal loss was sustained on both sides.

I am with great regard   Sir   Your Obedient servant   A Hamilton

I thank you for the inclosures of every kind. I believe you have not received a letter I wrote a few days ago, giving my idea of your cons[ti]tution, with which on a second inspection I am better pleased than at first. You will oblige me by forward[ing] the inclosed.[7]

ALS, New-York Historical Society, New York City.
  1. This letter was addressed to Morris in his capacity as a member of the New York Committee of Correspondence.
  2. Letter not found.
  3. Major General Nathanael Greene and Brigadier General Henry Knox were sent by Washington to examine "the State and Condition of the Forts in the Highlands (especially Fort Montgomery)" (Washington to Greene, May 12, 1777, *GW*, VIII, 51). Brigadier General Alexander McDougall was in command at Peekskill, New York.
  4. Located between Brunswick and Woodbridge, New Jersey.
  5. Colonel William Cooke, Twelfth Pennsylvania Regiment.
  6. William Maxwell of New Jersey, who was a brigadier general in the Continental Army.
  7. This enclosure was probably H to Catharine Livingston, May, 1777.

George Washington to Brigadier General James Mitchell Varnum

Morristown [*New Jersey*] *May 14, 1777.* Orders Varnum to forward recruits despite the opposition of the Rhode Islanders.

LS, in writing of H, The Huntington Library, San Marino, California.

From Gouverneur Morris [1]

Kingston [New York] 16th. May 1777

Sir.

I had the Pleasure of your two Favors within two Days of each other and am very happy to find that our Form of Government meets with your Approbation. That there are Faults in it is not to be wondered at for it is the Work of Men and of Men perhaps not the best qualified for such Undertakings. I think it deficient for the Want of Vigor in the executive unstable from the very Nature of popular elective Governments and dilatory from the Complexity of the Legislature. For the first I apologize by hinting the Spirit which now reigns in America suspiciously Cautious. For the second because unavoidable. For the third because a simple Legislature soon possesses itself of too much Power for the Safety of its Subjects. God grant it may work well for we must live under it.

I cannot perswade myself that Howe[2] will either go to Philadelphia or come hither. In either Case Genl. Washington can hang upon his Rear and place him in the Light rather of a fugitive than a Conqueror. If he bends his Efforts this Way the Council of Safety you may depend upon it will exert themselves to make his Situation as uneasy as he would wish probably more so. The Spirit of the Tories we have great Reason to believe is entirely broken in this State. If it is not it will soon be so. For they shall have a few more Executions than which nothing can be more efficacious. I speak from Experience but then it is necessary to disperse the Victims of public Justice throughout different Parts of the several States for nothing but occular Demonstration can convince these incredulous Beings that we do really hang them. I wish the several States would follow our Example. Pensilvania in particular would experience many good Effects from a vigorous manly executive.

Adieu   Your most obdt.   & humble Servant   Gouvr Morris

ALS, Hamilton Papers, Library of Congress.
  1. This letter was written by Morris in his capacity as a member of the New York Committee of Correspondence.
  Although the new state constitution of New York was proclaimed on April 20, 1777, it was several months before the new government was actually established. In the interval between old and new governments, New York was run by a Council of Safety, which consisted of fifteen men elected by the Provincial Convention on May 3, 1777. The Committee of Correspondence, which had been established by the Provincial Convention, remained in existence under the Council of Safety (*Journals of the Provincial Congress of the State of New-York*, I, 910, 934).
  2. Sir William Howe, commander in chief of the British forces in America.

To Gouverneur Morris [1]

Head Quarters Morris Town [New Jersey]
May 19th. 1777

Dear Sir,

I this moment received the favour of your letter of the 16th instant.

I partly agree and partly disagree with you respecting the deficiencies of your constitution. That there is a want of vigor in the executive, I believe will be found true. To determine the qualifications proper for the chief executive Magistrate requires the deliberate wisdom of a select assembly, and cannot be safely lodged with the people at large. That instability is inherent in the nature of popular governments, I think very disputable; unstable democracy, is an epithet frequently in the mouths of politicians; but I believe that from a strict examination of the matter, from the records of history, it will be found that the fluctuation of governments in which the popular principle has borne a considerable sway, has proceeded from its being compounded with other principles and from its being made to operate in an improper channel. Compound governments, though they may be harmonious in the beginning, will introduce distinct interests; and these interests will clash, throw the state into convulsions & produce a change or dissolution. When the deliberative or judicial powers are vested wholly or partly in the collective body of the people, you must expect error, confusion and instability. But a representative democracy, where the right of election is well secured and regulated & the exercise of the legislative, executive and judiciary authorities, is vested in select persons, chosen *really* and not *nominally* by the people, will in my opinion be most likely to be happy, regular and durable. That the complexity of your legislative will occasion delay and dilatoriness is evident and I fear may be attended with much greater, evil; as expedition is not very material *in making* laws, especially when the government is well digested and matured by time. The evil I mean is, that in time, your senate, from the very name and from the mere circumstance of its being a separate member of the legislature, will be liable to degenerate into a body purely aristocratical. And I think the danger of an abuse of power from a simple legislative would not be very great, in a government where the equality and fulness of popular representation is so wisely provided for as in yours. On the whole, though I think there are the defects intimated, I think your Government far the best that we have yet seen, and capable of giving long and substantial happiness to the people. Objections to it should be suggested with great caution and reserve.

Nothing particular in the military line— The enemy still in the Jersies, though they have been some time sending away their stores baggage &c. and are raising new works of defence. All this may be preparatory to an evacuation at all events, and they may be only intended to pave the way for a retreat, in case of an attack, or any accident. Advices from the West Indies, that have an appearance of authenticity, mention a french vessel bound for the Continent, being taken by the British frigate, Perseus, and carried into Dominique; [2] and a remonstrance being made by the Governor of Martinique, threatening reprisals in case of a detention. Nay, some accounts say he has actually seized all the English vessels in the harbour of Martinique and imprisonned their seamen 'till restitution shall be made. If these accounts be true, they are important, and may be considered as an earnest of more general hostility.

Perhaps your next favour will find me at Bound brook. Head Quarters will soon be moved there. Our family seem desirous of cultivating a closer acquaintance with the enemy than we have had the pleasure of, for some time past.

With real regard, I am Sir, Your most obedt servant A Hamilton

Relying on your punctuality in favouring me with any important intelligence your way, I am likely to lose a beaver hat, which was staked against the truth of the report of the stores at St. John's being destroyed.[3] If you forget me in future, I will certainly excommunicate you.

ALS, New-York Historical Society, New York City.
    1. This letter was addressed to Morris in his capacity as a member of the New York Committee of Correspondence.
    2. The ship was the *La Seine,* one of Beaumarchais's supply ships.
    3. St. Johns, located on the Richelieu River, twenty miles southeast of Montreal, was the site of a British fort. It was at this point that the British stopped Brigadier General Richard Montgomery's advance in 1775.
    H apparently won his bet, for there is no report of the stores at St. Johns being destroyed.

George Washington to
Brigadier General Alexander McDougall

Morristown [*New Jersey*] *May 23, 1777.* Commends McDougall on his attachment to the cause. Suggests that the needed food can be obtained at Albany. Agrees that uniformity of regulations is necessary and disapproves of officers breaking parole.

LS, in writing of H, The Huntington Library, San Marino, California.

General Washington to James Warren [1]

Morristown [New Jersey] May 23, 1777. Commends Massachusetts' exertions, but states that still more effort is necessary. Lists reasons why the invasion of Massachusetts is unlikely. Discusses the necessity and advantages of a single, unified army as opposed to individual state forces. Entreats Massachusetts, therefore, not to raise local regiments. States that supernumerary regiments can remain in Massachusetts.

Df, in writing of H, George Washington Papers, Library of Congress.
1. Warren was president of Massachusetts.

From Gouverneur Morris [1]

Kingston [New York] May 24, 1777. Has no news of the destruction of stores at St. Johns. Speculates on future course of the war and discusses need for maintaining health of troops.

ALS, Hamilton Papers, Library of Congress.
1. This letter was written by Morris in his capacity as a member of the New York Committee of Correspondence.

George Washington to Charles Thomson [1]

Morristown [New Jersey] May 24, 1777. Encloses copy of plan for establishing a cavalry force.

Df, in writing of H, George Washington Papers, Library of Congress.
1. Thomson was secretary of Congress.

George Washington to Robert Morris [1]

Morristown [New Jersey] May 28, 1777. Encloses a letter from Major General Charles Lee.[2] States that he (Washington) is on his way to Bound Brook.

LS, in writing of H, George Washington Photostats, Library of Congress.
1. Morris was a member of the Committee of Foreign Affairs of the Continental Congress.
2. Lee was a prisoner of the British.

George Washington to Major General John Sullivan

Morristown [New Jersey] *May 29, 1777.* Orders Sullivan to send intelligence concerning the enemy as rapidly as possible. Repeats orders for rerouting men and wagons. States that John Parke Custis [1] is not to come by the usual road.

LS, in writing of H, postscript in the writing of George Washington, George Washington Photostats, Library of Congress.
    1. Custis was Martha Washington's son by her first marriage.

To Captain Francis Grice

[*Middlebrook, New Jersey, May 30, 1777.* By Washington's orders Hamilton wrote to Grice, assistant deputy quartermaster general, ordering the removal of all boats in the Delaware from Trenton up to Coryells.[1] *Letter not found.*]

GW, VII, 144, note 29.
    1. Coryell's Ferry, located on the New Jersey side of the Delaware River and approximately 25 miles above Trenton.

To Catharine Livingston

Head Quarters Morris Town [New Jersey]
May 1777

When I was almost out of patience and out of humour at your presumptuous delay, in not showing yourself duly sensible of the honor done you, by me, your epistle opportunely came to hand,[1] and has put all matters tolerably to rights.

As I thought it well enough written, and no discredit to you, I ventured to show it to a Gentleman of our family. He was silly enough to imagine, that I did this through vanity, and a desire to display my own importance, in having so fair and so sensible a correspondent, as he indulgently called you; but I hope you will not be so vain as to entertain a single moment, the most distant imagination of the same kind. It would be paying your self too high a compliment, and give room to suspect you are strongly infected with that extreme self-complacency, commonly attributed to your sex.

But as I have no reason to believe this Gentleman has serious thoughts of becoming my rival; to give, at once, a mortal blow to all his hopes, I will recount what passed on this occasion. After attentively perusing your letter, during which, the liveliest emotions of approbation were pictured in his face, 'Hamilton!' cries he, 'when you write to this divine girl again, it must be in the stile of adoration: none but a goddess, I am sure, could have penned so fine a letter!' As I know you have ⟨an⟩ [2] invincible aversion to all flattery and extravagance, I ⟨can⟩not be afraid, that a Quixot[e], capable of uttering hims⟨elf⟩ perfectly in the language of knight-errantry, will ev⟨er be⟩ able to supplant me in the good graces of a lady of you⟨r⟩ sober understanding.

I am glad you are sensible of the oblig⟨at⟩ions, you are under to me, for my benevolent and disinteres⟨ted⟩ conduct, in making so currageous an effort, under all the imaginary terrors you intimate, without any tolerable p⟨ros⟩pect of . . . compensation. I am very willing to continue my kindness, even though it meet with no better a return, than in the past instance; provided you will stipulate on your part, that it shall meet with no worse. But to g⟨ive⟩ a more perfect idea of what you owe me for this condesce⟨nding⟩ generosity, let me inform you, that I exercise it at the ⟨risk⟩ of being anathematized by grave censors for dedicating so much of my time, to so trifling and insignificant a toy as—woman; and, on the other hand, of being run through the body by saucy inamorato's, who will envy me the prodigious favour, forsooth, of your correspondence. So that between the morose apathy of some and the envious sensibility of others, I shall probably be in a fine way. But ALL FOR LOVE is my motto. You may make what comments you please. Now for politics.

'Tis believed by our military Connoisseurs, that the enemy are preparing to quit the Jerseys, and make some expedition by water. Many suppose up the North River. But my opinion is, that, if they abandon the Jerseys, they will content themselves with enjoying quiet quarters on Staten Island, 'till re-inforced. Perhaps, however, the appearances, which give rise to an opinion of an evacuation of the Jerseys, are only preparatory to an attack upon us. They would admit such an interpretation if an attempt of the kind were not too hazardous to be consistent with prudence. Should they leave this state, your return home would be the more safe and agreeable; but you need not be precipitate.[3]

Your sentiments respecting war are perfec⟨tly⟩ just. I do not wonder at your antipathy to it. Every finer feeling of a delicate mind revolts from the idea of shedding human blood and multiplying the common evils of life by the artificial methods incident to that state. Wer⟨e⟩ it not for the evident necessity and in defence of all that is valuable in society, I could never be reconciled to a milit⟨ary⟩ character; and shall rejoice when the restoration of pe⟨ace⟩ on the basis of freedom and independence shall put it ⟨in⟩ my power to renounce it. That my fugitive friend soon be restored to those peaceful and secure abodes she ⟨longs⟩ for, is not more her own wish, than that of—   Alexr. Hamilton

ALS, Massachusetts Historical Society, Boston.

   1. Letter not found.

   2. The material within broken brackets is taken from a transcript in the Hamilton Papers, Library of Congress.

   3. With the British occupation of Elizabethtown in 1776, William Livingston moved his family from their home, Liberty Hall. When this letter was written, Catharine Livingston was probably living in Basking Ridge, New Jersey, with her mother and sisters, although it was about this time that they moved to Parsippany, New Jersey. It is also possible that she may still have been visiting her sister Sally, who was married to John Jay. This letter may have been the enclosure in H to Gouverneur Morris, May 12, 1777.

To Major General Adam Stephen [1]

[*Morristown, New Jersey May, 1777.* "Mr. Carter who I am told is a friend of the cause has been here to complain that some persons under the Commersary's orders, insist on taking from him two labouring oxen, which he cannot possibly spare from the business of his farm. As Agriculture is as necessary to go on as anything else, as The General wishes not unreasonably to distress the inhabitants and as it often happens that those who are charged with business of this kind are incapable of weighing matters as they ought, and in some instances may act wantonly and oppressively, you will be pleased to pay some attention to this complaint, and if reasonable remove the cause." [2] *Letter not found.*]

ALS, sold at Goodspeeds, March, 1945.
   1. Stephen was stationed at Chatham, New Jersey, when this letter was written.
   2. Text taken from extract of letter in catalogue of Goodspeeds.

George Washington to
Major General William Heath

Middlebrook [New Jersey] June 1, 1777. Discusses arrival of Du Coudray.[1] Approves of removal of military stores.

LS, in writing of H, Massachusetts Historical Society, Boston.
   1. Philippe Charles Jean Baptiste Tronson du Coudray. By an agreement with Silas Deane, Du Coudray was to receive the rank of major general. Although Congress rejected this agreement, he did receive this rank in August, 1777.

George Washington to
Brigadier General Samuel Holden Parsons [1]

Middlebrook [New Jersey] June 1, 1777. Orders all troops not needed for the Long Island expedition to Peekskill, New York.

Df, in writing of H, George Washington Papers, Library of Congress.
   1. Parsons was in New Haven, Connecticut, recruiting men for the Continental Army.

To John Jay [1]

Middle Brook Camp [New Jersey]
June 2d. 1777

Dear Sir,

I received your favour per express,[2] and as the absence of my former respectable correspondents has made a change necessary, I am happy that you have been substituted in their room.

Except a body of Militia at and about Pumpton [3] and a few detachments of observation, our whole army is now collected at two points; the main body here, and a division under General Sullivan [4] at Princeton. Though this alteration of circumstances takes off in a great measure the restraints imposed upon the enemy during the Winter, gives them a more ample field to range in, and exposes the country more to their ravages; yet the measure is abundantly justified by every wise military maxim. The rigor of the season has been heretofore our chief security against those advantages which might have been taken of our dispersed state; and this dispersion was necessary, both for the conveniency of Winter Quarters, and with a view to confine and distress the enemy, which was the most capital object we could then propose to ourselves. It was also necessary by this method to second the check to that torrent of influence which their successes in the Jerseys had given them. Many other justifying reasons might be assigned which I doubt not you will easily conceive, and which it would be indiscreet to commit to paper.

But now that a more active season is arrived, and something of importance must be done on one side or the other, it becomes our business to put ourselves in the best posture both for defence and offence. Common sense dictates that the best way to effect this is to collect our strength. In a collected state we can best repel a general attack; we can best make one, if circumstances warrant it; and we can move with greater expedition to disconcert any sudden push not immediately upon us, which the enemy are likely to make. It is needless to enlarge on a subject which your own judgment will enable you, of itself, to view in a just light.

As to the designs of the enemy, appearances are so intricate, fluctuating, and seemingly inconsistent, that it is difficult to form any certain conclusion from them. Either they do not understand themselves and are very irresolute and fickle, or they very artfully manage matters to deceive us. I am rather inclined to suppose the former. This however I may say, with tolerable certainty, that my ideas of their intending to operate to the Southward, derive just support from such parts of their conduct lately as are most intelligible. We have a variety of concurring intelligence that they have lately drawn more troops into the Jerseys, that they have brought over a large number of waggons and all the boats perpared for bridges, with several other particulars of less importance—all which denote a preparation to operate this way. Persons who have been among them assert confidently that they mean to attack us. But we are divided in sentiment as to the probability of that or of their making a forced march to Philadelphia. If they act wisely they will neither attack us in our present situation, strongly posted as we are, nor will they attempt to cross a river, where they may certainly expect opposition in front, and leaving at the same time a formidable army in the rear. He should endeavour to draw us off from here and fight us upon more equal ground. But after all, if he expects any timely reinforcement, upon what rational principle can he risk his own reputation and all the hopes of his cause, in an attempt, with his present force, so extremely important and hazardous? Perhaps he only means to get every thing in readiness against the arrival of the reinforcements, looked for, that he may immediately commence his operations. Things however will hardly bear this construction.

We are told that in seventeen sail lately arrived from Europe, there were about 2000 raw recruits. This from deserters.

The enemy yesterday perpetrated a most barbarous butchery upon a Lieutenant Martin [5] of ours. He was out with a scouting party, and met some of the British light horse; his men 'tis said quitted him. But however other matters may be 'tis certain his dead body was found most horribly mangled. He had not a single bullet wound, but was hacked to pieces with the sword. He had several cuts in his head, each of which was sufficient to dispatch him, besides a number of more inconsiderable scars about his body and hands. It is evident, that the most wanton and unnecessary cruelty must have been used towards him; for the greater part of his wounds must have been given him when utterly out of a condition to resist. This may be relied on as a fact, for I saw his corps as did also every officer and soldier in camp that chose it. The General sent him down to their lines with a letter to Lord Cornwallis, as an undeniable evidence of their brutality; but the letter was taken from the flag and sent in; the flag and the body not permitted to pass their out posts. [6]

I am   Sir   With real respect & esteem   Your most Obedt servt
A Hamilton

ALS, New-York Historical Society, New York City.
1. According to J. C. Hamilton and Henry Cabot Lodge, this letter was addressed to Gouverneur Morris (*JCHW*, VI, 583; Hamilton, *History*, I, 204;

HCLW, IX, 74), while a transcript of this letter (Bancroft Transcripts, MS Division, New York Public Library) gives the addressee as Robert R. Livingston. But H's reference to the "absence of my former respectable correspondents" in the first sentence of this letter makes either assumption unlikely, while the contents of Robert R. Livingston's letter to H (June 7, 1777) indicates that John Jay was the addressee.

2. Letter not found.

3. I.e., Pompton.

4. Major General John Sullivan.

5. William Martin of New Jersey, first lieutenant, Spencer's Additional Continental Regiment. He was killed on May 31, 1777.

6. Washington's letter to Cornwallis (June 2, 1777) is found in the George Washington Papers, Library of Congress.

George Washington to Charles, Earl Cornwallis

Middlebrook [*New Jersey*] *June 2, 1777.* Remonstrates against murder of William Martin.[1]

LS, in writing of H, George Washington Photostats, Library of Congress; Df, in writing of H, George Washington Papers, Library of Congress.

1. For details of Martin's murder, see H to John Jay, June 2, 1777.

To Major General Israel Putnam [1]

Camp at Middle Brook [New Jersey]
June 2d. 1777

Sir,

By order of His Excellency, I am to acknowlege receipt of your favour of yesterday.[2]

The General is astonished at that extraordinary want of cloathing you mention; as Mr. Mease [3] informed Mr. Tilghman [4] that a full proportion of this article had been retained in Massachusetts for all its troops. It is unaccountable, that they should be ⟨so⟩ unprovided, unless the cloaths destined for them should have been sent by mistake to the Northward, as being the place for which they were first intended. On this supposition, General McDougall has been directed to inquire into the matter and if he found it so, to send up an officer from each of those regiments to bring them down. The General wishes to know what has been done on the occasion. If inquiry has not been yet made you will please to make it, and if ⟨it⟩ appears to be as is conjectured, you will persue the mode pointed out to General McDougall for obtaining a return of them, or any other more convenient mode you may think of. His Excellency desires you will speedily inform him how the matter stands, and what prospect you may have of gaining a supply in this way.

In the meantime, you can detain the cloathing arrived at Fish-Kills 'till further orders, but they must not be issued to the troops. It would be inexpedient to devote the cloathing destined for the southern troops which are in great want of them to those from the Eastward, when provision has been made for them, unless it shall prove to have been so misapplied as to render it impossible to make it answer the end.

ADf, George Washington Papers, Library of Congress.
1. Putnam had been placed in command at Peekskill, New York. Brigadier General Alexander McDougall, who had held this command, was placed under Putnam.
2. Putnam's letter is in the George Washington Papers, Library of Congress.
3. James Mease, clothier general of the Continental Army.
4. Lieutenant Colonel Tench Tilghman, aide-de-camp and military secretary to Washington.

George Washington to John Hancock

Middlebrook Camp [*New Jersey*] *June 2, 1777.* Encloses news from Northern Department. Deplores deficiency of troops. States that Colonel Elias Boudinot [1] is going to Philadelphia to discuss exchange of prisoners.

Df, in writing of H; last line and postscript in writing of Robert Hanson Harrison, George Washington Papers, Library of Congress.
1. Boudinot was commissary general for prisoners, Continental Congress.

To Major General John Sullivan [1]

Head Quarters Camp
at Middle Brook [New Jersey] June 4th. 1777

Sir

His Excellency has received your favour of this Day.[2] In answer to it he commands me to inform you that though he is exceedingly happy to hear such an animation prevails among the inhabitants, yet he can by no means, consent to put arms in their hands. This article is too much wanted for the Continental army to be spared to the militia; and experience has taught us, that there has been infinite abuse and misapplication of the public arms when confided to them. As to ammunition, [The] [3] General has no objection that a small quantity should be given them; provided it be lodged with their officers, who are to be accountable, for its being devoted to the uses intended.

I am   Dr. Sir   Yr Most Obedt serv   A Hamilton ADC

ALS, New Hampshire Historical Society, Concord.
    1. When this letter was written, Sullivan was in command at Princeton.
    2. Sullivan's letter to Washington is in neither the George Washington Papers, Library of Congress, nor the Sullivan Papers, New Hampshire Historical Society, Concord, New Hampshire.
    3. H first wrote, "I have." He then crossed out "have," and wrote "General has," making it read "I General has."

To Joseph Trumbull [1]

Head Quarters [Middlebrook, New Jersey] June 4th 1777

Sir,

His Excellency has examined your Provision report; and finds every part of it very well, except that relating to the placing a quantity at Trenton. This is the most improper place in the world; for if the enemy should move towards Philadelphia the provisions at trentown in the hurry occasioned by such an event would inevitably fall into their hands. You will therefore without loss of time have them removed much higher up the river, at least as high as Corel's; [2] a moment should not be lost in doing this.

I am Sir   Yr most Obed serv   A Hamilton ADC

ALS, Connecticut State Library, Hartford.
    1. Trumbull was commissary general of stores, Continental Army, from 1775 to June 18, 1777.
    2. Coryell's Ferry.

George Washington to James Lovell [1]

Middlebrook [New Jersey] June 4, 1777. Discusses the qualifications of Lutterloh.[2]

Df, in writing of H, George Washington Papers, Library of Congress.
    1. Lovell was a delegate from Massachusetts to the Continental Congress.

2. Major Henry Emanuel Lutterloh who was employed in the quartermaster's department.

George Washington to Charles, Earl Cornwallis

Middlebrook [*New Jersey*] *June 6, 1777.* States that all supplies for prisoners must go through Colonel Elias Boudinot's hands. Assures Cornwallis that the greatest care will be taken with these supplies. Is surprised at Cornwallis' reasoning concerning the murder of William Martin.[1]

Df, in writing of H, George Washington Papers, Library of Congress.
1. See H to John Jay, June 2, 1777.

From Robert R. Livingston [1]

7th. June 1777 Kingston [New York]

Dear Sir

With my place at Council [2] I resume the agreeable task of writing to you & answering your Letter directed to Mr. Jay.

I see with you the propriety of collecting our army to a point & have often been under apprehentions least the enemy should take advantage of our former dispersed state & the necessity that drove us into it. But they have wanted the spirit of enterprize or been deceived greatly as to our strength. I can hardly yet persuade myself that they design to go to the Southward since it appears to me an undertaking infinitely above their strength unless they are very considerably reinforced; what their prospects of being so are I have not been able to learn. I do not know how to account for their leaving a part of their troops at Rhode Island when they need their assistance in the Jersies; had they heretofore moved on rational principles I should suppose that they expected to be so far strengthened as to be able to make a divertion there, while their main body carried on its operations to the Southward; but their motions have always been so excentrick that there is no rule by which we can form a judgment of them.

If it should be true that more force has been drawn from New York into the Jerseys, might it not be worth while to alarm New York by sending down two or three thousand men who might possibly strike some bold stroke or at least oblidge the Enemy to retain a considerable part of their force at that place & proportionably weaken their army in the Jerseys? The practicability of this measure must however depend upon a variety of circumstances with which you are better acquainted than I can be. Our act of grace has had a very happy effect & numbers are daily coming in to take the benefit of it.[3] The spirit of disaffection being lower now than it has been in this State since the begining of the controversy owing to the vigilence of the government, the punishment of some capital Offenders, and above all to the weakness & langour of the enimies measures. Some very concientious persons have declared (when they took the oath to the State) that they held themselves absolved from all allegience to a power that was no longer able to protect them. Tho' I do not think such convertions greatly to be relied on, yet they are of use in stoping the progress of disaffection & giving an appearance of strength & unanimity to our government on which more depends than is generally imagined.

I am Sir   With the utmost regard & esteem   Yours &c.

ADf, New-York Historical Society, New York City; transcript, National Library of Scotland, Edinburgh.

On October 19, 1777, Charles Cochrane of the British army wrote to Andrew Stuart, a member of Parliament: "I inclose you some Letters which I found in Genl. Washingtons house after the action [Battle of September 11, 1777] the originals was given to the Genl. I wish you may be able to read them as they were copied by some private men of the company in haste." These transcripts are now found in the National Library of Scotland and the British Museum. Although the contents of this particular letter are the same as that of the draft the wording is very different.

For other letters that were seized at this time and have been preserved, see: Gouverneur Morris to H, July 4, 1777; Livingston to H, August 2, 1777; H to Livingston, August 7, 1777, and Livingston to H, August 10, 1777.

1. This letter was written by Livingston in his capacity as a member of the New York Committee of Correspondence.

2. This is a reference to Livingston's duties as a member of the New York Council of Safety. Livingston had been elected to the Council on May 3, 1777. On the same day, he was elected chancellor of the State of New York (*Journals of the Provincial Congress of the State of New-York*, I, 910).

3. On March 7, 1777, the New York Convention offered to Loyalists an oath of allegiance to the American cause. Those who took the oath were "discharged" (*Journals of the Provincial Congress of the State of New-York*, I, 827).

George Washington to
Colonel Samuel Blachley Webb

Middlebrook [New Jersey] June 7, 1777. Censures Webb for over-drafts of clothing. Orders Webb to march to Peekskill.

Df, in writing of George Washington and H, George Washington Papers, Library of Congress.

To Major General Israel Putnam

Head Quarters Camp at
Middle Brook [New Jersey] June 9th. 1777.

Sir,

His Excellency desires you will not open or distribute the Cloathing stopped at your post, 'till a Deputy Cloathier comes up to take Charge of it, who will be with you without Loss of time.

I am Sir Your most humb servt. A Hamilton ADC

Df, or contemporary copy, in writing of Caleb Gibbs, George Washington Papers, Library of Congress.

To Brigadier General George Clinton

Head Quarters Camp at
Middle Brook [New Jersey] June 10th. 1777

Sir,

By His Excellencys Command, I am to desire you will give orders upon the deputy Clothier General at Peeks-Kill, for the necessary supply of Cloathing &c. for the four companies raising under your direction. It is not however intended, that more shall be drawn than a sufficiency for the number of men actually inlisted.

I am Sir Your most Obedt servant AH ADC

ADfS, George Washington Papers, Library of Congress.

George Washington to Colonel Charles Armand [1]

[*Middlebrook, New Jersey*] *June 11, 1777.* Orders Armand to assume command of Ottendorf's [2] corps, to expand this corps to a full regiment, and in the future to take orders from Major General Benjamin Lincoln.

Df, in writing of H, George Washington Papers, Library of Congress.
1. Charles Armand-Tuffin, Marquis de la Rouerie, was generally known as Colonel Armand.
2. Nicholas Dietrich, Baron de Ottendorf, was a major of three Pennsylvania companies.

To Major General John Sullivan [1]

Head Quarters Camp at
[Middlebrook, New Jersey, June 12–25, 1777] [2]

Sir,

His Excellency has received your two last favours to day. In the first you hint the want of a reinforcement; but as the intention of your body is chiefly for observation and skirmishing and not to make any serious stand, it is the less necessary it should be powerful in numbers. It will however depend upon circumstances, how far it will be expedient to reinforce you; and as soon as any thing can be determined from them, you shall have whatever addition of strength you may stand in need of.

The information contained in your last of the enemy's being incamped on the road leading from Brunswick to Princeton about the three Mile run is not well founded. We have had parties and officers reconnoitring as far as the mile run and there is no sign of an incampment. They seem to be taking their old position with their right at Amboy and their left at Brunswick; but how long they will remain so it is hard to tell. His Excellency desires you will engage some trusty persons at South Amboy, on whom you can depend for faithful and early intelligence of the appearance of shipping in the river, or any preparations for a movement by water, that we may be, in time, prepared to counteract them.

I am with regard   Sir   Your most Obed servant

A Hamilton ADC

ALS, George Washington Papers, Library of Congress.
1. When this letter was written, Sullivan was in the Sourland Hills, New Jersey.
2. Date and place have been supplied on basis of contents of this letter. In both *JCHW*, I, 60, and *HCLW*, X, 458, this letter is dated 1778.

Discharge of Joshua Austin

Middlebrook [New Jersey] June 13, 1777. ". . . Joshua Austin, belonging to the independent company of the State of Connecticut, . . . appears to be incapable of military service. He is hereby discharged from the Continental army. . . ."

ADS, Connecticut State Library, Hartford.

George Washington to Charles Thomson

Middlebrook [New Jersey] June 13, 1777. Encloses copy of a plan for the establishment of a cavalry force.

Df, in writing of H, George Washington Papers, Library of Congress.

George Washington to
Major General Benedict Arnold

Middlebrook [New Jersey] June 17, 1777. Describes position at Middlebrook and plans of attack. Discusses probability of enemy attack on the army at Middlebrook and on Philadelphia. Orders Arnold to send on Continental troops.

Df, in writing of H, George Washington Papers, Library of Congress.

George Washington to Chevalier d'Annemours [1]

Middlebrook [New Jersey] June 19, 1777. Discusses advantages of an overt declaration of war by France. Corrects error in estimate of British losses at Danbury, Connecticut. Questions purpose of General William Howe's recent moves.

Df, in writings of Richard Kidder Meade and H, George Washington Papers, Library of Congress.
1. Charles François Adrien le Paulnier, Chevalier d'Annemours, was seeking an Army appointment which he did not receive. He was later appointed French consul to Maryland.

George Washington to
Brigadier General Alexander McDougall [1]

Middlebrook [*New Jersey*] *June 20, 1777*. Describes General William Howe's latest moves. Orders McDougall either to remain at present post or return to Peekskill.

LS, in writing of H, The Huntington Library, San Marino, California; Df, in writing of H, George Washington Papers, Library of Congress.
    1. The draft of this letter is endorsed to Alexander McDougall and Brigadier General John Glover. The receiver's copy in The Huntington Library is unaddressed.

George Washington to
Major General Israel Putnam

Middlebrook [*New Jersey*] *June 20, 1777*. Discusses General William Howe's latest movements. Reviews orders to Brigadier Generals John Glover and Alexander McDougall concerning these movements. Orders stand-by preparations in case of attack on Ticonderoga. Emphasizes need of continued intelligence from New York.

Df, in writing of H, George Washington Papers, Library of Congress.

George Washington to Colonel Thomas Elliott [1]

Middlebrook [*New Jersey*] *June 21, 1777*. Warns Elliott that any further delay in appearing at Headquarters will result in a replacement being appointed to his position in the regiment.

Df, in writing of H, George Washington Papers, Library of Congress.
    1. Elliott was a colonel, Fourth Virginia Regiment.

George Washington to
Major General Israel Putnam

Middlebrook [*New Jersey*] *June 22, 1777*. Orders Putnam to prepare for a probable British attack up the North River. States that enemy has abandoned Brunswick and will probably also leave Amboy. Orders stores to be removed from Fishkill.

Df, in writing of H, George Washington Papers, Library of Congress.

George Washington to Brigadier General Alexander McDougall

Middlebrook [*New Jersey*] *June 23, 1777.* Approves of McDougall's return to Peekskill. States that British are leaving New Jersey. Warns McDougall to expect an attack up North River.

LS, in writing of H, George Washington Photostats, Library of Congress.

George Washington to Jonathan Trumbull [1]

Middlebrook [*New Jersey*] *June 23, 1777.* Regrets inability to supply field pieces. Is pleased with report on quota of troops. Advises Trumbull on exchange of Danbury prisoners. Praises American attack on British evacuating Brunswick.

Df, in writing of Robert Hanson Harrison and H, George Washington Papers, Library of Congress.
1. Trumbull was governor of Connecticut.

From Robert R. Livingston

[*Kingston, New York, June 25, 1777.* On June 28, 1777, Hamilton wrote to Robert R. Livingston: "Yours of the 25th came to hand last night." *Letter not found.*]

George Washington to Baron d'Arendt [1]

Quibbletown [*New Jersey*] *June 25, 1777.* Grants permission for Baron d'Arendt to visit Philadelphia and advises D'Arendt to consult Congress on plan for Prussian treaty.

LS, in writing of H, Papers of the Continental Congress, National Archives.
1. Henry Leonard Philip, Baron d'Arendt, commander of the German Battalion at Quibbletown.

George Washington to
Colonel William Malcom [1]

Middlebrook [*New Jersey*] *June 27, 1777.* Appoints Malcom to the command of a regiment. Gives instructions for completion of this regiment. Orders Malcom to the field.

Df, in writing of H, George Washington Papers, Library of Congress.
    1. Malcom had been a major and then a colonel of the New York Militia. The regiment referred to in this letter was one of the Sixteen Additional Continental Regiments.

To Robert R. Livingston [1]

Head Quarters Camp
at Middle Brook [New Jersey] June 28 1777

Dear Sir.

Yours of the 25th [2] came to hand last night. Since my last addressed to Mr. Morris,[3] the enemy have been trying a second experiment to tempt us to an engagement, on equal terms of ground. Under the supposition of their intending to evacuate the Jerseys immediately, in order to keep up the idea of a persuit, and to be in a posture to take advantage of any critical moment that might present itself to give them a blow, the chief part of our army, after their retreat from Brunswick, was marched down to Quibble town, and parties detached thence further towards the enemy. Finding this disposition take place and expecting that elated by what had passed, we might be willing to venture upon a general engagement, which is Howe's only hope, he came out with his whole army from Amboy early on thursday morning and made a forced march towards our left, with design, if possible, to cut off some of our detachments, particularly one under Lord Stirling; and propably, if we were not expeditious in regaining the heights, to get there before us, by rapidly

ALS, New-York Historical Society, New York City.
    1. This letter was addressed to Livingston in his capacity as a member of the New York Committee of Correspondence.
    2. Letter not found.
    3. Letter not found.

entering the passes on our left. Lord Stirlings party was near being surrounded; but after a smart skirmish with the enemy's main body, made their retreat good to Westfield, and ascended the pass of the mountains back of the Scotch plains. The other parties after skirmishing on their flanks came off to join the main body and take possession of the heights. The enemy continued their march towards our left as far as Westfield, and there halted. In the mean time, it was judged prudent to return with the army to the mountains, lest it should be their intention to get into them and force us to fight them on their own terms. They remained at Westfield 'till the next day, and perceiving their views disappointed have again returned to Amboy, plundering and burning as usual. We had parties hanging about them in their return; but they were so much on their guard no favourable opportunity could be found of giving them any material annoyance. Their loss we cannot ascertain; and our own, in men, is inconsiderable, though we have as yet received no returns of the missing. I have no doubt they have lost more men than we, but unfortunately, I won't say from what cause, they got three field pieces from us, which will give them room for vapouring, and embellish their excursion, in the eyes of those, who make every trifle a matter of importance. It is not unlikely they will soon be out of the Jersies; but where they will go to next is mere matter of conjecture, for as you observe, their conduct is so eccentric, as to leave no certain grounds on which to form a judgment of their intentions.

I know the comments that some people will make on our Fabian conduct. It will be imputed either to cowardice or to weakness: But the more discerning, I trust, will not find it difficult to conceive that it proceeds from the truest policy, and is an argument neither of the one nor the other. The liberties of America are an infinite stake. We should not play a desperate game for it or put it upon the issue of a single cast of the die. The loss of one general engagement may effectually ruin us, and it would certainly be folly to hazard it, unless our resources for keeping up an army were at an end, and some decisive blow was absolutely necessary; or unless our strength was so great as to give certainty of success. Neither is the case. America can in all probability maintain its army for years, and our numbers though such as would give a reasonable hope of success are not such as should make us intirely sanguine. A third consideration did it exist might make it expedient to risk such an event—the prospect of very great reinforcements to the enemy; but every appearance contradicts this, and affords all reason to believe, they will get very inconsiderable accessions of strength this campaign. All the European maritime powers are interested for the difeat of the British arms in America, and will never assist them. A small part of Germany is disposed to make a market of its troops, and even this seems not over-fond of being drained any further. Many springs may be put in motion even to put a stop to this. The King of Prussia may perhaps without much difficulty be engaged to espouse views unfriendly to the Court of Britain, and a nod of his would be sufficient to prevent all future German succours. He as well as most other powers of Europe feels the necessity of Commerce and a large maritime force to be generally respectable. His situation, 'till lately, has been unfavourable to this; but the reduction of Poland and the acquisition of Dantzig in the Baltic, have put it very much in his power to persue commercial schemes; and may tempt him to be propitious to American independence. Russian assistance is still infinitely more precarious; for besides that it cannot be the true interest of that ambitious empire to put its troops to sale, it is, at present, embroiled with the turks and will want all its men to employ in its own wars. England herself, from the nature of her polity can furnish few soldiers and even these few can ill be spared to come to America in the present hostile appearance of affairs in Europe. On whatever side it is considered, no great reinforcements are to be expected to the British army in America. It is therefore Howe's business to make the most of his present strength, and as he is not numerous enough to conquer and garrison as he goes, his only hope lies in fighting us and giving a general defeat at one blow.

On our part, we are continually strengthening our political springs in Europe, and may every day look for more effectual aids than we have yet received. Our own army is continually growing stronger in men arms and discipline. We shall soon have an important addition of Artillery, now in its way to join us. We can maintain our present numbers good at least by inlistments, while the enemy must dwindle away; and at the end of the summer the disparity between us will be infinitely great, and facilitate any exertions that may be made to settle the business with them. Their affairs will be growing worse—our's better;—so that delay will ruin them. It will serve to perplex and fret them, and precipitate them into measures, that we can turn to good account. Our business then is to avoid a General engagement and waste the enemy away by constantly goading their sides, in a desultory teazing way.

In the mean time it is painful to leave a part of the inhabitants a prey to their depredations; and it is wounding to the feelings of a soldier, to see an enemy parading before him and daring him to a fight which he is obliged to decline. But a part must be sacrificed to the whole, and passion must give way to reason. You will be sensible, that it will not be adviseable to publish the sentiments contained in this letter as coming from me, because this will make the enemy more fully acquainted with our views; but it might not be amiss to have them circulated, as those which ought to govern the conduct of the army, in order to prepare the minds of the people for what may happen and take off the disagreeable impressions our caution [4] may make.

I am Dr. Sir   Your most Obed servant   A Hamilton

4. In MS reads "catition."

To Brigadier General Charles Scott [1]

Head Quarters [Middlebrook, New Jersey] June 30th. 1777

Sir,

I wrote you this moment by His Excellency's order; [2] but he is so anxious you should be acquainted with his apprehensions on the score of the enemy's leaving Amboy, with some of their stores remaining in it, that fearing a miscarriage of my former letter he desires me to write another to the same effect.

The enemy have had their own leisure to go off and carry whatever they thought proper. What then should induce them to leave any stores behind unless by way of ensnaring some party of ours that should be tempted by them to venture incautiously into the place they have quitted? This is much to be suspected, and you are strongly enjoined to reconnoitre well before you trust any part of your men into the Town. It will be the easiest matter in the world if you are not exceedingly vigilant to throw a party across the river [3] upon your rear and intercept you. You had better not send your whole Brigade in; but only send in a small party to take possession of the stores, and convey as many out as you can to some other place. For this purpose you will collect as many waggons as you can about the neighbourhood. You are, by no means, to remain in Amboy all night; but retire immediately after you have put an end to any endeavours to carry off the remaining stores. Keep parties reconnoitring from Amboy to Elizabeth Town point and take every precaution to avoid a surprise.

I have ordered down provisions to Bonum Town. You can either go that place or send for the provisions from thence.

I am Dr. sir   Your most Obed serv   A Hamilton ADC

ALS, The Andre deCoppet Collection, Princeton University Library.
   1. On June 28, 1777, Washington wrote to the President of Congress: "On thursday Morning Genl Howe advanced with his whole Army in Several Columns from Amboy, as far as Westfield. . . . I detached a Body of Light Troops under Brigadier General Scott, to hang on their Flank and to watch their Motions" (George Washington Papers, Library of Congress). On the following day he wrote: "I have two Brigades (Scott's and Conway's) now lying at and near Woodbridge, as Corps of Observation and to act as circumstances may require" (ibid.).
   2. Letter not found.
   3. Raritan River.

George Washington to the Board of War

Middlebrook [New Jersey] June 30, 1777. Discusses disposal of artillery imported in the *Amphitrite*.[1] Emphasizes need for centralized regulations for procuring supplies.

Df, in writing of H, George Washington Papers, Library of Congress.
   1. The first of Beaumarchais's supply ships.

George Washington to Tronson du Coudray

Middlebrook [New Jersey] June 30, 1777. Countermands order from Northern Department demanding guns. Discusses disposal of artillery that arrived on the *Amphitrite*. States that Tousard [1] is to return to Du Coudray, and that French engineers will be sent to Du Coudray.

Df, in writing of H, George Washington Papers, Library of Congress.
1. Lewis Tousard, captain of artillery in the French army. Later he was an aide to Lafayette.

George Washington to Brigadier General George Clinton

Middlebrook [*New Jersey*] *July 1, 1777.* Reports news of attack on Ticonderoga. Warns of probable attack on Peekskill. Orders Clinton to call out militia to defend the area around Peekskill.

LS, in writing of H, George Washington Photostats, Library of Congress.

George Washington to Jonathan Trumbull

Middlebrook [*New Jersey*] *July 2-4, 1777.* Approves of suggested exchange of prisoners, but states that Colonel Elias Boudinot must first be consulted. Refuses request for arms. Discusses probable British moves and American plans to counteract these moves.

Df, in writing of H, George Washington Papers, Library of Congress.

From Gouverneur Morris [1]

Kingston [New York] July 4 1777

Dear Sir

Your Letter [2] gave me the Pleasure of knowing with Certainty what might be depended upon among the numerous Reports circulated Thro the Country with Relation to the Several movements of the Enemy. That Howe [3] wishes to draw you to a General Action is highly Probable because certainly he hath no other Means of conquering the Country, but the time when he wishes to Engage must depend upon a General Estimate in his mind of what Forces he now hath, What Accessions he may receive, our Force and the Probability of its Increase or Decrease. To hazard a Generale Action on our Part is certainly contrary to the true Principles of the defensive War in wich we are engagd, so long as we can keep an Army in the Field. The most splended Victory would not Increase our Resources, nor while the Enemy keeps Amboy Strongly fortifyd in their Rear would it much weaken them. Whether Howe will risque an Attack upon our Strong Hold at a Distance from him is rather doubtfull. Possibly he may with a View to draw our Army out Upon a disorderly Retreat, tho this Idea is Rather too fine Spun for him. All the Difficulty with us will be to avoid an Action, and at the same Time save our Reputation. This Perhaps may require some master strokes in the Art of war. On the whole I am Inclined to think that Howe is loth to leave the Ferries with the Air of Compulsion, & Genl, Washington unwilling to let it be believed that he retires in any other way. That is to say (if we may venture to speake Philosophically upon a Subject of this Kind) they are Both Bidding for the Good Opinion of the Disaffected. Many Brave Fellow may Possibly Loose theare Lives on this Occasion which after all can be of little Importance in the General Scale. If the news from the northward be true in all the Extent wich the GENERALS seem to *apprehend* Howe will come up the River, but If as I verily believe The Truth is Carlton [4] only makes a Fient in that Quarter to Prevent an Attack on our Part then Howe must in some way or other force you to fight him or bid Adieu to the Conquest of America.

But tis in vain to Scrutinize future Events. Let us know from Time to time how many Prisoners you make and what Deserters come in that we may Puff a little. Adieu.

your most Obedient & humble Servant   Gouvr Morris

Transcript, National Library of Scotland, Edinburgh. For an explanation of the presence of this transcript in the National Library, see Robert R. Livingston to H, June 7, 1777.

1. This letter was signed by Morris in his capacity as a member of the New York Committee of Correspondence.

2. Morris may have been referring to H to Robert Livingston, June 28, 1777, or to a letter addressed to Morris which has not been found and is referred to in that letter.

3. Sir William Howe.

4. Sir Guy Carleton.

George Washington to
Major General Charles Lee [1]

Morristown [*New Jersey*] *July 4, 1777.* Discusses Drummond's [2] breach of parole.

Df, in writing of H, George Washington Papers, Library of Congress.
 1. Lee was a prisoner of the British in New York City.
 2. Lord James Drummond.

George Washington to John Rutledge

Morristown [*New Jersey*] *July 5, 1777.* Approves of Rutledge's and Brigadier General Robert Howe's decision not to attack St. Augustine. Discusses British failure to move against Philadelphia. Speculates on whether the center of the next British attack will be the Hudson River or Philadelphia. Describes American plans to counteract either move.

Df, in writing of H, George Washington Papers, Library of Congress.

To Gouverneur Morris [1]

Head Quarters Morris
Town [New Jersey] July 6th. 1777

Dear Sir,

I received your favour of the 4th, by express. If I recollect how far my last went, it did not announce the return of the enemy from Westfield to Amboy, nor their evacuation of that place since. After resting and refreshing themselves a night, they decamped the following day and proceeded to Amboy from which place they went to Staten Island as expeditiously as they could; where they still remain.

The news, from the Northward, wore so serious a face that our generals thought the enemy were about to operate in earnest against our posts in that quarter; [2] and, as supposing this the case, General Howe might certainly be expected to co-operate by way of the

North river, it was judged necessary to move the main body of the
army from Middle Brook to Morris Town—to advance a division
under General Sullivan to Pumpton—and another under General
Parsons [3] ⟨as⟩ [4] far ⟨as⟩ Peeks Kill. A Brigade at that post under General N⟨ixon⟩ [5] was ordered, so soon as Parsons' division arrived near
its destination, to proceed immediately as a reinforcement to the
Northern army. This disposition is deemed advantageous to prevent
the success of a *coup de main,* on the Highland passes, and not inconsistent with a proper attention to Philadelphia, should the Northern alarm prove nothing more than a diversion and Howe return
to the charge that way. I am loth to risk a conjecture about Mr.
Howe. He is such an untilligible Gentleman, that no rule of interpretation can possibly be found out, by which to unravel his designs.
If he acted like a man of sense, he would wait quietly on Staten
Island, and there concenter all his forces. He would draw round all
the men that could be spared from Canada, and all that are now at
Rhode Island. With these and the reinforcements he may receive
from Europe, he would make a point of forcing us by some means or
other to an action. In this his only hope lies, if he could defeat our
army, and improve the moment of success he would go very near
effecting his purpose. But let him go to the Northward or to the
Southward, every new post he takes weakens his main body, and
makes it the more liable to be ruined by our collective strength.
Any object short of our army is a bad one, and that plan is the worst,
where by a division of his forces he runs the hazard, in case of an
accident either way, of having his whole scheme overturned.

We have different accounts of the present situation of his army.
Some tell us that the whole is now incamped on Staten Island, others,
that the greater part of the Hessians are on board the Ships. By
some sailors who came from them yesterday, we are told that the
ships are taking in water and provisions for two months, and that
conveniences for transporting horses are fitting up in them. All this
is rather vague and may, or may not be true.

Their flourishes in the Jerseys, I believe, cannot have cost them
less than 6 or 700 men. We have not lost above a hundred. This is the
best way to ruin them, without risking anything.

Our present situation is embarrassing. Their ships give them a vast
advantage; and we shall probably be much puzzled when they begin

their operations again. We shall however act cautiously and do the best we can. We are anxiously waiting for Northern intelligence.

I am Dr. Sir   With great regard   Yrs. &c.   A. Hamilton

Please to forward the inclosed [6] to General Schuyler ℔ first Oppy.

ALS, New-York Historical Society, New York City.
    1. This letter was addressed to Morris in his capacity as a member of the New York Committee of Correspondence.
    2. On July 2, 1777, Washington wrote: "I last night received intelligence from Genl Schuyler that General Burgoyne is beginning to operate against Ticonderoga and its dependencies. If it is not merely a diversion, but a Serious attack, of which it bears Strongly the appearance, it is certain proof that the next Step of General Howe's Army will be towards Peekskill" (GW, VIII, 335).
    3. Brigadier General Samuel Holden Parsons, Continental Army.
    4. The material within broken brackets is taken from a copy of this letter in the Bancroft Transcripts, MS Division, New York Public Library.
    5. Brigadier General John Nixon, Continental Army.
    6. Enclosure presumably was George Washington to Major General Philip Schuyler, July 6, 1777 (George Washington Papers, Library of Congress).

To Colonel Elias Dayton [1]

Head Quarters Morris
Town [New Jersey] July 7th. 1777

Sir,

Doctor McWorter [2] has represented to His Excellency the case of a certain negro lately taken by a party of militia belonging to Mr. Caleb Wheeler.[3] This fellow, it seems, some time since, went over to the enemy, and is now detained in confinement on that account. I am ordered to desire you to inquire into the circumstances of the affair, and particularly by whom the negro was taken, for on this depends the Generals power of releasement; and if you find he was taken by any party acting under Continental authority and in Continental pay, and there is no reason for detaining him besides merely the consideration of his having joined the enemy, you are authorized, as far as it comes under His Excellency's direction to deliver him to his owner. If he was taken by a party acting merely under the authority of the state, The General has nothing to do with him, and of course you must refer his owner to the Governor or other civil magistrate impowered to take cognizance of it. If there are any particular circumstances other than those mentioned that make it improper to release him, and yet leave the matter within the reach of The General's authority, you will be pleased to explain them to him, and wait his further directions.

I am   Sir   Your most hum serv   A Hamilton ADC

ALS, Hamilton Papers, Library of Congress.
  1. Dayton, a colonel, Third New Jersey Regiment, was at Elizabethtown, New Jersey.
  2. Alexander MacWhorter of New Jersey, who in 1778 became chaplain of Knox's artillery brigade.
  3. A man with this name is listed as living in Essex County, New Jersey, in William S. Stryker, *Official Register of the Officers and Men of New Jersey in the Revolutionary War* (Trenton, 1872), 817.

To Major General John Sullivan [1]

Head Quarters Morris
Town [New Jersey] July 7th. 1777

Sir,

You will be pleased to forward the inclosed to General Putnam with all expedition, as it is of importance they should not be delayed. By His Excellency's desire, I wrote to you [2] a day or two ago, requesting that a Capt McConnel [3] & a waggon master who had taken a horse from some inhabitants abused and confined them, should be sent to Head Quarters to have an examination in to their conduct. I am ordered to make mention of it again, and to repeat the Generals desire that they may be sent as before directed. He wishes to correct and discountenance such abuses by taking proper measures with those who commit them.

I am   Sir   Your most Obedient servant   A Hamilton ADC

ALS, New Hampshire Historical Society, Concord.
  1. Sullivan was at Pompton, New Jersey. Two days after this letter was written, he was ordered to march to Peekskill.
  2. Letter not found.
  3. On July 9, 1777, Tench Tilghman, aide-de-camp and military secretary to Washington, wrote to Sullivan, "As the dispute between Capt McConnel and the Countryman is settled, you need not send him down" (Hammond, *Letters and Papers of John Sullivan*, I, 412). This order was, however, countermanded as soon as it became clear that Sir William Howe did not plan to advance up the Hudson.

George Washington to Jonathan Trumbull

Morristown [*New Jersey*] *July 7, 1777.* Speculates on purpose of attack on Ticonderoga. Warns Trumbull that British may attack eastern states rather than advance up North River. Gives permission for use of arms from Springfield arsenal if Connecticut is attacked.

Df, in writing of H, George Washington Papers, Library of Congress.

George Washington to Major General Israel Putnam

Pompton Plains [*New Jersey*] *July 12, 1777.* Orders Putnam to keep Brigadier General John Glover in readiness to march to Ticonderoga, to send Brigadier General John Nixon's men on to join their brigade, and to forward field pieces to Major General Philip Schuyler. Warns of possible attack by Sir William Howe on Peekskill.

Df, in writing of H, George Washington Papers, Library of Congress.

To John Jay

Head Quarters Pompton
Plains [New Jersey] July 13th. 1777

D Sir,

I received your favour and one from Mr. Morris [1] last night by express. The stroke at Ticonderoga is heavy, unexpected and unaccountable.[2] If the place was untenable why not discovered to be so before the Continent had been put to such an amazing expence, in furnishing it with the means of defence? If it was tenable, what, in the name of common sense could have induced the evacuation? I would wish to suspend my judgment on the matter; but certainly present appearances speak either the most abandonned cowardice, or treachery. What can be become of Sinclair [3] and the army? Did they venture to retreat without knowing where the enemy were, or what rout[e] to take? Or did they wilfully run into their mouths? All is mystery and dark beyond conjecture. But we must not be discouraged at a misfortune; we must rather exert ourselves the more vigorously to remedy the ill-consequences of it. If the army gets off safe, we shall soon be able to recover the face of affairs. I am in hope that Burgoignes [4] success will precipitate him into measures that will prove his ruin. The entreprizing spirit he has credit for, I suspect, may easily be fanned by his vanity into rashness.

The day before yesterday, Our whole army marched to this place computed to be about eighteen miles from Morris Town; as soon as the weather will permit we shall continue our march to Peeks-Kill. Howe's army we are told are all embarked. We suppose they will shortly make an excursion up the North River. If we can get there before them all will be well.

The most we have to fear is that a panic will seize the people, and disqualify them for giving their aid. It behoves their leaders to put on a chearful countenance, and combat their fears by a spirited and manly example.

I am Dr Sir   Your most Obed servant   A Hamilton

ALS, Columbia University Libraries.
  1. Neither letter has been found.
  2. On July 5, 1777, Major General Arthur St. Clair, with 3,500 men, evacuated Ticonderoga permitting General John Burgoyne to continue his advance.
  3. Arthur St. Clair.
  4. General John Burgoyne.

George Washington to Tronson du Coudray

Pompton Plains [New Jersey] July 13, 1777. Discusses disposal of the artillery imported on Amphitrite. Says that Du Coudray is wrong in assuming that Mauduit du Plessis [1] is aide-de-camp to Brigadier General Henry Knox. States that, as Du Coudray does not yet hold an official position, original arrangements for artillery will continue in effect.

Df, in writing of H, George Washington Papers, Library of Congress.
  1. Thomas Antoine, Chevalier de Mauduit du Plessis, a captain of artillery.

George Washington to
Major General Philip Schuyler

Pompton Plains [*New Jersey*] *July 13, 1777.* Discusses supplies sent to Schuyler. Is astonished that there has been no word from Major General Arthur St. Clair.

Df, in writing of H, George Washington Papers, Library of Congress.

George Washington to
Major General Joseph Spencer

Smiths Clove [*New York*] *July 17, 1777.* Is pleased with capture of Major General Richard Prescott. Will try to exchange Prescott for Major General Charles Lee. Praises conduct of Lieutenant Colonel William Barton.[1]

Df, in writing of H, George Washington Papers, Library of Congress.
1. Barton was a lieutenant colonel of the Rhode Island Militia. Congress, because of the part he played in the capture of Prescott, promoted him to the rank of colonel in the Continental Army.

From Gouverneur Morris

[*Saratoga, New York, July 18, 1777.* On July 22, 1777, Hamilton wrote to Morris: "Your favour of the 18th ⟨from Saratoga reached me⟩ yesterday." *Letter not found.*]

George Washington to
Colonel Thomas Elliott[1]

Smiths Clove [*New York*] *July 18, 1777.* Orders Elliott to appear at Headquarters.

1. Df, in writing of H, who indorsed on the verso Washington's decision: "in Six or Seven weeks from this time if he does not come on must expect to be superseded" George Washington Papers, Library of Congress.

George Washington to
Brigadier General William Smallwood

Smiths Clove [New York] July 18, 1777. Requests Smallwood to join Army at Headquarters.

Df, in writing of H, George Washington Papers, Library of Congress.

To Colonel Theodorick Bland [1]

Head Quarters Galloways
in the Clove [2] [New York] July 21st 1777

Sir

The intelligence, on which the order given you to join this army was founded, proving not to be as expected,[3] His Excellency desires you to return to your old station and there remain 'till further orders. He thinks it not improbable the enemy may take it into their heads to make some incursion into the Jerseys to plunder and distress the inhabitants, or perhaps even to endeavour to destroy our stores at Morris Town. This will be worthy of your attention and should it happen, you will give all the assistance in your power to the force, which, is or may be collected to oppose them.

Use every expedient, you can think of, to gain the exactest intelligence possible, of the movements of the enemy. Our situation and theirs are such, that it is extrem⟨ely⟩ difficult to know what they are about and we are rather in the dark with resp⟨ect⟩ to it. This occasions some embarrassment, and makes it necessary you should take the greatest pains to be well informed.

I am   Sir   Your most huml Servant   Alex Hamilton A D C

ALS, Park Collection, Morristown National Historical Park, Morristown, New Jersey.

1. Bland, colonel of the First Continental Dragoons, was stationed at Bound Brook, New Jersey.

2. Smiths Clove, Orange County, New York. Washington's Army arrived at this place on July 22, 1777, and remained there until he was certain that General William Howe's troops were not going to advance up the Hudson. On July 24, 1777, believing Philadelphia to be Howe's most likely destination, Washington started to move the major part of the main Army southward.

3. This is a reference to Washington's original belief that Howe planned to advance up the Hudson.

To Gouverneur Morris [1]

⟨Smiths Clove, New York, July 22, 1777⟩ [2]

Dear Sir,

Your favour of the 18th[3] ⟨from Saratoga reached me⟩ yesterday. Your pronouncing Fort Edward [4] among the other forts indefensible surprises me a little, as it is intirely contrary to the representations of several Gentlemen of judgment, who have had an opportunity of seeing and considering its situation, by whom we have been taught to believe, that it would be an excellent post, at least ⟨for⟩ checking and retarding Burgoigne's progress. I agree with you ⟨that⟩ our principal strength in the quarter you are will be in the ⟨forests and⟩ natural strength of the Country, and in the want of forage, ⟨provisions,⟩ carriages &c. in which the enemy may easily be thrown by ⟨taking⟩ away what there are of those articles; which you observe have ⟨never⟩ been in great abundance.

I am doubtful whether Burgoigne will attempt to penetrate far, and whether he will not content himself with harassing our back settlements by parties assisted by the savages, who, it is to be feared will pretty generally, tempted by the enemy's late successes, confederate in hostilities against us. This doubt arises from some appearances that indicate a Southern movement of General Howes army, which, if it should really happen, will certainly be a barrier against any further impressions of Burgoigne; for it cannot be supposed he would be rash enough to plunge into the bosom of the Country, without an expectation of being met by General Howe. Things must prove very adverse to us indeed, should he make such an attempt, and not be ruined by it. I confess however that the appearances I allude to do not carry a full evidence in my mind; because they are opposed by others of a contradictory kind; and because I cannot conceive upon what principle of common sense or military propriety Howe can be running away from Burgoigne to the Southward. It is much to be wished he may, even though it should give him ⟨the possession of Phila⟩delphia, which by our remoteness from it may very ⟨well happen. For⟩ in this case, we may not only if we think proper retali⟨ate by aiming a st⟩roke at New York; but we may come upon him with ⟨the greatest part of⟩ our collective force, to act against that part which is ⟨under him. We⟩ shall then be certain that Burgoigne cannot proceed, ⟨and that a small forc⟩e of Continental troops will be sufficient for that ⟨partizan War which⟩ he must carry on the rest of the Campaign. A small force will also be sufficient to garrison the fort in the highlands, and prevent any danger there; so that we shall be able to bring nearly the whole of the Continental army against Mr. Howe. The advantages of this are obvious. Should he be satisfied with the splendor of his acquisition and shut himself up in Philadelphia, we can ruin him by confinement. Should he leave a Garrison there and go forward, we can either fall upon that or his main body diminished as it will be by such a measure with our whole force. There will however be many disagreeable consequences attending such an event; amongst which the foremost ⟨is⟩ the depreciation of our currency; which from the importance in which Philadelphia is held, could not fail to ensue.

I am Dear Sir   Your most Obedient servant   Alex Hamilton

ALS, Hamilton Papers, Library of Congress.
    1. There is no indication in the MS of the addressee of this letter. H states in the first line, however, that the receiver had recently written him from Saratoga. The contents show that the letter was written to the New York Committee of Correspondence. Morris was the one member of that committee who had recently been in Saratoga.
    2. Material within broken brackets is taken from a transcript in JCH Transcripts.
    3. Letter not found.
    4. Located on the east bank of the Hudson River, approximately half way between Ticonderoga and Albany. Major General Arthur St. Clair retreated to Fort Edward after withdrawing from Ticonderoga. When this letter was written, Fort Edward was held by forces under Major General Philip Schuyler; but with the approach of General John Burgoyne's army, Schuyler withdrew.

George Washington to
Major General Israel Putnam

Smiths Clove [*New York*] *July 22, 1777.* Asks for accurate report of British movements on Long Island Sound. Requests information on posts around Kings Bridge and Fort Washington.

Df, in writing of H, George Washington Papers, Library of Congress.

George Washington to
Major General Philip Schuyler [1]

Smiths Clove [*New York*] *July 22, 1777.* Is sending Brigadier General John Glover's brigade to reinforce Schuyler.

Df, in writing of H, George Washington Papers, Library of Congress.
   1. Although the partially erased signature of H can be seen on the draft, this is without a doubt a Washington letter.

George Washington to
Major General Philip Schuyler

Ramapo [*New Jersey*] *July 24, 1777.* Is disappointed in number of militia sent to Schuyler. Regrets inability to send Schuyler more Continental troops, but believes Schuyler will be aided by eastern states. Discusses strength of enemy. Is sending Major General Benjamin Lincoln to aid Schuyler and to command militia. Approves of stationing men about the New Hampshire Grants. Suggests putting Major General Benedict Arnold in charge of Fort Schuyler.

Df, in writing of H, George Washington Papers, Library of Congress.

George Washington to Colonel Elisha Sheldon [1]

Ramapo [*New Jersey*] *July 24, 1777.* Orders Sheldon to Headquarters.

Df, in writing of H, George Washington Papers, Library of Congress.
   1. Sheldon was a colonel of the Second Continental Dragoons.

From Robert R. Livingston

[*July 25, 1777.* On July 29, 1777, Hamilton wrote to Livingston: "I have the pleasure of your favour of the 25th." *Letter not found.*]

George Washington to William Franklin [1]

Ramapo [New Jersey] July 25, 1777. Expresses sympathy with Franklin's request to see sick wife. Regrets that commanding general cannot supersede a congressional resolution, but has forwarded Franklin's letter to Congress.

Df, in writing of H, George Washington Papers, Library of Congress.
1. Franklin, the last Loyalist governor of New Jersey, was at this time imprisoned in Connecticut because of a breach of his parole.

George Washington to John Hancock

Ramapo [New Jersey] July 25, 1777. Introduces Monsieur D'Avout.

LS, in writing of H, Papers of Continental Congress, National Archives.

George Washington to
Major General Israel Putnam

Pompton Plains [New Jersey] July 25, 1777. Reports that Philadelphia is probable destination of enemy fleet. Orders Putnam to replace part of Continental troops at Peekskill with New York and Connecticut militia.

Df, in writing of H, George Washington Papers, Library of Congress.

George Washington to
Colonel Theodorick Bland

Mr. Lott's [East of Morristown, New Jersey] July 26, 1777. Orders Bland to halt at Bristol, Pennsylvania, or Trenton and then proceed to Philadelphia if enemy is in Delaware Bay.

Df, in writing of H, George Washington Papers, Library of Congress.

George Washington to
Major General William Heath

Morristown [New Jersey] July 27, 1777. Disapproves of requisition of arms for proposed St. Johns expedition. Approves of Heath's methods of dealing with deserters. Requests Heath not to send French volunteers to Headquarters, as their pretensions to office are "embarrassing." Reports that British fleet's destination is probably Philadelphia. Orders Continental troops sent to the Northern Department. States that fall of Ticonderoga could not have happened if the eastern states had complied with requests for troops.

LS, in writing of H, George Washington Photostats, Library of Congress; Df, in writing of H, George Washington Papers, Library of Congress.

George Washington to Robert Erskine [1]

Flemington [New Jersey] July 28, 1777. Offers Erskine position of geographer with the Army.

Df, in writing of H, George Washington Papers, Library of Congress.
   1. Erskine was a civil engineer operating a mine at Ringwood, New Jersey.

George Washington to
Major General Thomas Mifflin

Flemington [New Jersey] July 28, 1777. Believes that appearance of enemy fleet off Little Egg Harbor is proof that its destination is Philadelphia. Orders Mifflin to reconnoiter area around Philadelphia, and to obtain "drafts . . . of the Country." Presents possible plan for stationing of American troops. Recommends baking of large quantities of hard bread.

Df, in writing of H, George Washington Papers, Library of Congress.

To Robert R. Livingston [1]

Head Quarters Coryells [2] ferry [New Jersey]
July 29th 1777

Dear Sir,

I have the pleasure of your favour of the 25th.[3] I cannot be induced to think the enemy are so numerous as you apprehend, and
would place no dependence on what is said either by deserters or
prisoners, further than as it respects their own company, nor even
that with regard to prisoners in general who commonly have their
cue, as the phrase is, and know very well how to manufacture stories
calculated to serve the purposes of the side they belong to. If we
may judge at all from the state of the British and foreign regiments
in Howes army, or the proportion of recruits they have had this
year, we cannot but believe the representations you mention greatly
exaggerated. Though the Northern army have not suffered much by
action, they have probably suffered more by sickness than the
Southern; for many accounts agree that they have been very sickly
and particularly that there was a great mortality among them while
lying at the Isle of Noix.[4] From the estimate of the first prisoner,
they must have been greatly reduced by some means or other, for
it appears that before his company had been augmented by the 24
foreigners, it was only 26 strong; and it is very improbable it should
have had so large an augmentation, for I am morally certain the
regiments under Howe have not had fifty men each as recruits,
and I see no reason to suppose Burgoignes could have had so much
better luck. Eight companies at 26 men each amount to 208. Suppose
each regiment to have received 100 recruits, which by every rule
of comparison must be more than the truth. This brings a regiment
to about 300 men. Ten regiments at 300 each amount to 3000, the
number of British troops in Canada.

ALS, New-York Historical Society, New York City.
    1. This letter was sent to Livingston in his capacity as a member of the
New York Committee of Correspondence. Both J. C. Hamilton (*JCHW*, VI,
589) and Lodge (*HCLW*, IX, 91) give Gouverneur Morris as the addressee of
this letter.
    2. In MS, "Coyels."
    3. Letter not found.
    4. British post, situated at southern end of Richelieu River.

Again, if I am not mistaken, 4000 was the allotment of foreign troops for the Northern department. As the sickness spoken of fell chiefly upon them, they in all probability lost more in that way than they have gained in recruits. But even if this were not the case, they cannot exceed the original number, 4000 added to 3000 make 7000. Besides these there are the Grenadiers and light infantry. Of these there cannot be above eighteen companies each—which allowing them to contain every one [1]oo men amount to 1800— and this brings them to about 8.800 men in their whole force of British and foreign troops. Of these at least one sixth must be unfit for duty, by every calculation, which reduces the number of men fit for the field to about seven thousand five hundred. Part of these must be left in Canada, if it were for no other purpose than to guard their magazines, and for other duty of that kind. Nor could they with safety commit the charge of those things to the Canadians, many of whom are notoriously disaffected, and would be very likely to destroy instead of preserve them. From this view which I verily believe is too favorable to them, they cannot bring more than between six and seven thousand British & foreign troops to act out of Canada.

Out of these six or seven thousand, a considerable part must be left to Garrison Ticonderoga and secure their rear in case of accidents; for they could not without madness attempt to advance, and leave the posts behind them in a defenceless state. And they may be obliged to increase their attention to this matter by keeping a body of men somewhere about the grants [5] which has been recommended. When this last deduction is made Burgoigne cannot advance with more than between five and six thousand men, to suppose him to act with his whole collective force; except Canadians and Indians who are not by any accounts numerous.

Let us now take a view of our own force. When Glovers Brigade [6] gets up, and the recruits for the regiments there, now on their march, arrive, General Schuyler will have about five thousand Continental troops. Surely the Eastern states cannot sleep so soundly, when the

5. New Hampshire Grants, or Vermont.
6. On July 22, 1777, Washington wrote to Major General Philip Schuyler: "I have come to a resolution to send you a further reinforcement, . . . and have accordingly directed General Putnam immediately to forward General [John] Glover's Brigade to you" (GW, VIII, 450).

danger is so imminent, but that they will reinforce him with 8 or 10000 militia. If this happens and He cannot stop General Burgoigne progress it must proceed from other causes than the want of men. With about the same army last year, General Washington kept Howe with 16. or 17000 men at bay.

Perhaps it may be said there will not be time to collect this force as the enemy are advancing with very great rapidity. I am much mistaken if there will not be abundant time. The nature of the ground, the difficulty of transporting the immense quantity of baggage provisions &c. necessary to accompany an army of 5000 men penetrating an enemys country, the want of waggons for the purpose, the impediments thrown in their way by cutting up the roads—all these obstacles will retard their march much more than is at first sight imagined; and will give full time to prepare them a good reception.

On the whole I am clearly of opinion, that unless Howe cooperates with Burgoigne against your state it has very little to fear; and I even doubt, if he goes to the Southward, whether Burgoigne will attempt to penetrate far. At present there is every appearance of a Southern expedition. Seventy Sail of the enemys fleet have been seen passing by little egg harbour [7] making short tacks towards the capes of Philadelphia. Three divisions of the army are arrived here and at Howels ferry 4 miles up.[8] One is coming on by way of Princeton &c. Another coming after us by way of Morris Town. I wish this last to halt there. Two Brigades more have been ordered to cross the North River and wait further orders. We shall not however pass the Delaware 'till we hear of the arrival of the enemy in the capes of Philadelphia. Nor will those two Brigades be ordered on 'till the same event takes place. We shall act the most cautious part possible in our circumstances.

I communicated your letter to the General. He agrees with me, in point of the enemy's numbers. With respect to animating the Eastern states, he has written the most urgent letters to their several assemblies, which I am in hopes will answer the end you propose from sending persons to each of them.

It were to be wished your forts and ships were well supplied with

7. On coast of New Jersey, about fifteen miles north of Atlantic City.
8. Howell's Ferry, as H indicates, was four miles north of Coryell's Ferry on the Delaware.

Cannon; but it is wholly out of the General's line to strip the ships
to the Eastward of their cannon for that purpose. If your Convention were to make application to the Congress or board of war *it
might* succeed; but I should have very little hope of it.

I am with great esteem   Dr Sir   Your most Obedt

Alexr. Hamilton

To Major General Israel Putnam

Head Quarters Coryel[l]s ferry [New Jersey]
July 30th. 1777.

Sir,

His Excellency commands me to acknowlege the receipt of yours
of the 27th instant.[1]

The circumstance of the fleet appearing off, opposite to Blue
Point[2] does not indicate any movement to the Eastward. It was
necessary in going out of the Hook, whatever course they might
intend to steer, whether to the Southward or Eastward, to stand out
in that direction for some time, as they went out with a Westerly
wind. If however you hear any thing more of them, you will give
His Excellency the earliest notice of it.

General Clinton informs His Excellency, that he is called to attend
at Kingston and take the oath of office conformable to his appointment as Governor of the State of New York.[3] It is to be regretted
that so useful an officer is obliged to leave the posts under his
superintendency at a time like this. The General is at a loss how to
supply his place properly, without doing an injury to some other
post, where the presence of the person fit to succeed General Clinton
would be equally wanted. But as some person must be found to
succeed him, He desires me to mention to you General James Clinton,[4] who is, in his present situation, in a manner lost to the service.
This Gentleman, having been formerly stationed at those posts, is to
be supposed well acquainted with them; and he has the character of
being a brave man, but it is to be apprehended he may want activity
which will be a very essential quality. To remedy this defect I am to
suggest the stationing Col: Malcolm[5] ⟨----------⟩. The General does not mean to direct absolutely in this matter. He only means

To Robert R. Livingston [1]

Head Quarters Coryells [2] ferry [New Jersey]
July 29th 1777

Dear Sir,

I have the pleasure of your favour of the 25th.[3] I cannot be induced to think the enemy are so numerous as you apprehend, and would place no dependence on what is said either by deserters or prisoners, further than as it respects their own company, nor even that with regard to prisoners in general who commonly have their cue, as the phrase is, and know very well how to manufacture stories calculated to serve the purposes of the side they belong to. If we may judge at all from the state of the British and foreign regiments in Howes army, or the proportion of recruits they have had this year, we cannot but believe the representations you mention greatly exaggerated. Though the Northern army have not suffered much by action, they have probably suffered more by sickness than the Southern; for many accounts agree that they have been very sickly and particularly that there was a great mortality among them while lying at the Isle of Noix.[4] From the estimate of the first prisoner, they must have been greatly reduced by some means or other, for it appears that before his company had been augmented by the 24 foreigners, it was only 26 strong; and it is very improbable it should have had so large an augmentation, for I am morally certain the regiments under Howe have not had fifty men each as recruits, and I see no reason to suppose Burgoignes could have had so much better luck. Eight companies at 26 men each amount to 208. Suppose each regiment to have received 100 recruits, which by every rule of comparison must be more than the truth. This brings a regiment to about 300 men. Ten regiments at 300 each amount to 3000, the number of British troops in Canada.

ALS, New-York Historical Society, New York City.
1. This letter was sent to Livingston in his capacity as a member of the New York Committee of Correspondence. Both J. C. Hamilton (*JCHW*, VI, 589) and Lodge (*HCLW*, IX, 91) give Gouverneur Morris as the addressee of this letter.
2. In MS, "Coyels."
3. Letter not found.
4. British post, situated at southern end of Richelieu River.

Again, if I am not mistaken, 4000 was the allotment of foreign troops for the Northern department. As the sickness spoken of fell chiefly upon them, they in all probability lost more in that way than they have gained in recruits. But even if this were not the case, they cannot exceed the original number, 4000 added to 3000 make 7000. Besides these there are the Grenadiers and light infantry. Of these there cannot be above eighteen companies each—which allowing them to contain every one [1]00 men amount to 1800— and this brings them to about 8.800 men in their whole force of British and foreign troops. Of these at least one sixth must be unfit for duty, by every calculation, which reduces the number of men fit for the field to about seven thousand five hundred. Part of these must be left in Canada, if it were for no other purpose than to guard their magazines, and for other duty of that kind. Nor could they with safety commit the charge of those things to the Canadians, many of whom are notoriously disaffected, and would be very likely to destroy instead of preserve them. From this view which I verily believe is too favorable to them, they cannot bring more than between six and seven thousand British & foreign troops to act out of Canada.

Out of these six or seven thousand, a considerable part must be left to Garrison Ticonderoga and secure their rear in case of accidents; for they could not without madness attempt to advance, and leave the posts behind them in a defenceless state. And they may be obliged to increase their attention to this matter by keeping a body of men somewhere about the grants [5] which has been recommended. When this last deduction is made Burgoigne cannot advance with more than between five and six thousand men, to suppose him to act with his whole collective force; except Canadians and Indians who are not by any accounts numerous.

Let us now take a view of our own force. When Glovers Brigade [6] gets up, and the recruits for the regiments there, now on their march, arrive, General Schuyler will have about five thousand Continental troops. Surely the Eastern states cannot sleep so soundly, when the

5. New Hampshire Grants, or Vermont.
6. On July 22, 1777, Washington wrote to Major General Philip Schuyler: "I have come to a resolution to send you a further reinforcement, . . . and have accordingly directed General Putnam immediately to forward General [John] Glover's Brigade to you" (*GW*, VIII, 450).

George; and our army nearly equal in number to them were about to take post somewhere between Fort Edward and Saratoga.

The consequences of this Northern affair will depend much upon the part that Howe acts. If he were to cooperate with Burgoigne, it would demand our utmost efforts to counteract them. But if he should go towards the Southward all or most of the advantages of Burgoignes success will be lost. He will either be obliged to content himself with the possession of Ticonderoga and the dependent fortresses, and with carrying on a partizan war the rest of the Campaign, or he must precipitate himself into certain ruin, by attempting to advance in the country with a very incompetent force. Appearances lead us to suppose that Howe is fool enough to meditate a southern expedition, for he has now altered his station at Staten Island mentioned above and has fallen down to the Hook. Judging it morally certain, that there would be a cooperation of the two armies, we thought it expedient to march Northerly, and had accordingly reached within fourteen miles distance from New Windsor, the place where we could cross the North River, without danger of interruption. But this new movement of the enemy's fleet has induced us to return a few miles, and make a disposition for marching Southerly. We shall however be cautious how we proceed in that course, lest nothing more than a feint is intended, to divert us from the real object. If they go to the Southward in earnest, they must have the capture of Philadelphia in view, for there is no other sufficient inducement. We shall endeavour to get there in time to oppose them, and shall have the principal part of the Continental force and a large body of spirited militia, many of them from their services during the last campaign pretty well inured to arms, to make the opposition with. Yet I would not have you to be much suprised if Philadelphia should fall; for the enemy will doubtless go there with a determination to succeed at all hazards, and we shall not be able to prevent them without risking a general action—the expediency of which will depend upon circumstances. If the militia turn out, with that zeal, we have a right to expect from their conduct, when the enemy made their last experiment in the Jerseys and were supposed to be going to Philadelphia we may do it without much inconvenience: But If they fall materially short of it, we shall be obliged to confine ourselves to a skirmishing opposition, which we cannot expect will be effectual. It may be asked, if to avoid a general action, we give up objects of the first importance, what is to hinder the enemy from carrying every important point and ruining us? My answer is that our hopes are not placed in any particular city or spot of ground, but in the preserving a good army furnished with proper necessaries, to take advantage of favourable opportunities and waste and defeat the enemy by piece-meal. Every new post they take requires a new division of their forces, and enables us to strike with our united force against a part of thei⟨rs⟩ and such is their present situation that another Trentown aff⟨air⟩ will amount to a complete victory on our part, for they are at too low an ebb to bear another stroke of the kind. Perhaps before I may have an opportunity of sending this facts will unfold what I am now endeavouring to anticipate by conjecture.

You will expect some animadversions on the temper and views of the French-nation. I presume you are nearly as well acquainted with the assistance they are giving us as, I am; both by their intrigues in foreign courts and by supplies of every kind of war like stores and apparatus. It does not admit of a doubt that they are interested to wish us success, and their conduct plainly shows they are willing to give us every aid essential to our preservation. But it is natural they should desire to do it with as much convenience to themselves as they can; I apprehend they are not overfond of plunging themselves into a war with England, if they can avoid it and still answer the end, they have to persue; and indeed, from the evident reluctance show⟨n⟩ on the part of the latter to do any thing that may bring about such an event, it becomes extremely difficult to dra⟨w⟩ her into it. The conclusion we may make is—that France will not wish to force England into a war, unless she finds our affairs to require it absolutely, and England will not enter into one 'till she is compelled to do it.

My best respects to all friends and, I beg you will believe me to be with unabated regard Dr Sir Your most Obed servant

A Hamilton

act against that part which is ⟨under him. We⟩ shall then be certain that Burgoigne cannot proceed, ⟨and that a small forc⟩e of Continental troops will be sufficient for that ⟨partizan War which⟩ he must carry on the rest of the Campaign. A small force will also be sufficient to garrison the fort in the highlands, and prevent any danger there; so that we shall be able to bring nearly the whole of the Continental army against Mr. Howe. The advantages of this are obvious. Should he be satisfied with the splendor of his acquisition and shut himself up in Philadelphia, we can ruin him by confinement. Should he leave a Garrison there and go forward, we can either fall upon that or his main body diminished as it will be by such a measure with our whole force. There will however be many disagreeable consequences attending such an event; amongst which the foremost ⟨is⟩ the depreciation of our currency; which from the importance in which Philadelphia is held, could not fail to ensue.

I am Dear Sir   Your most Obedient servant   Alex Hamilton

ALS, Hamilton Papers, Library of Congress.
    1. There is no indication in the MS of the addressee of this letter. H states in the first line, however, that the receiver had recently written him from Saratoga. The contents show that the letter was written to the New York Committee of Correspondence. Morris was the one member of that committee who had recently been in Saratoga.
    2. Material within broken brackets is taken from a transcript in JCH Transcripts.
    3. Letter not found.
    4. Located on the east bank of the Hudson River, approximately half way between Ticonderoga and Albany. Major General Arthur St. Clair retreated to Fort Edward after withdrawing from Ticonderoga. When this letter was written, Fort Edward was held by forces under Major General Philip Schuyler; but with the approach of General John Burgoyne's army, Schuyler withdrew.

George Washington to
Major General Israel Putnam

Smiths Clove [*New York*] *July 22, 1777.* Asks for accurate report of British movements on Long Island Sound. Requests information on posts around Kings Bridge and Fort Washington.

Df, in writing of H, George Washington Papers, Library of Congress.

George Washington to
Major General Philip Schuyler [1]

Smiths Clove [*New York*] *July 22, 1777.* Is sending Brigadier General John Glover's brigade to reinforce Schuyler.

Df, in writing of H, George Washington Papers, Library of Congress.
  1. Although the partially erased signature of H can be seen on the draft, this is without a doubt a Washington letter.

George Washington to
Major General Philip Schuyler

Ramapo [*New Jersey*] *July 24, 1777.* Is disappointed in number of militia sent to Schuyler. Regrets inability to send Schuyler more Continental troops, but believes Schuyler will be aided by eastern states. Discusses strength of enemy. Is sending Major General Benjamin Lincoln to aid Schuyler and to command militia. Approves of stationing men about the New Hampshire Grants. Suggests putting Major General Benedict Arnold in charge of Fort Schuyler.

Df, in writing of H, George Washington Papers, Library of Congress.

George Washington to Colonel Elisha Sheldon [1]

Ramapo [*New Jersey*] *July 24, 1777.* Orders Sheldon to Headquarters.

Df, in writing of H, George Washington Papers, Library of Congress.
  1. Sheldon was a colonel of the Second Continental Dragoons.

From Robert R. Livingston

[*July 25, 1777.* On July 29, 1777, Hamilton wrote to Livingston: "I have the pleasure of your favour of the 25th." *Letter not found.*]

part returned already, And I am verry Sorry to say, that we have no reason to Except Any Effectual Aid from them—And what is particularly Distressing is that our own Efforts must be weakened by an Attention to the passes in the Highlands, which may be Seized at any time Unless Garrisoned by Continential Troops—Or Our Own Militia: to leave them to Connecticut Militia, even if they could be got out—would Occasion such a wast of Stores &c. As [c]ould Endanger that Safety of the posts even if they had Sufficient Spirit to Defend them, (I write Confidintialy to a friend or I should not have throne out that Sentiment). By our laste Accounts from the Norward, Burgoine was at Fort Edward And our Armey at Saragtaga, how much farther they will be under a necesaty to retreat I Know not, but I am satisfied if they get to Albany (& I see nothing to prevent it) That their Strength will be greatly increasd. by tories, together with all the wariours of the Six Nations, who will then be Under a Necessity of Joyning them. The Inhabitants & Troops in Tryon County being then cut off From the rest of the States Must fall a sacrafice— And this State be intirely Subjected.

Whether the Enemy are gone to the Southard or not is in my opinion Verry Doubtful, Should they return Sudenly to this place, they would leave Burgoine little to do. If they go elsewhere it furnishes a Strong presumtion of his being Compatent to the Conquest of this State, If they Can draw of Genl. Washington.

As this Letter is Allredy Unreasonably Long I will not add to it— I may be Mistaken in all my Conjectures but be Assured, that the Greatest Error That we can fall into, is to Undervalue Our Enemy

I am Dr. Sr. with Great   Esteem Your Most   Obedient Humble. Servt.   Robt. R. Livingston

---

Transcript, National Library of Scotland, Edinburgh. For an explanation of the presence of this transcript in the National Library of Scotland, see Robert R. Livingston to H, June 7, 1777.

1. This letter was signed by Livingston in his capacity as a member of the New York Committee of Correspondence.

2. This dash was used by the British soldier who transcribed this letter to indicate words that he could not read in the original letter.

3. Brigadier General John Glover.

George Washington to
Brigadier General Preudhomme de Borre [1]

Philadelphia, August 3, 1777. Orders De Borre to remain at Bound Brook until enemy arrives at "the Hook" and then to proceed to Peekskill. Condemns De Borre's execution of a Tory.

Df, in writing of H, George Washington Papers, Library of Congress.
1. De Borre arrived in America in March, 1777, and enlisted in the American Army as a volunteer. He resigned in the same year.

George Washington to
Brigadier General Francis Nash [1]

City Tavern [Philadelphia] August 3, 1777. Orders Nash to hold troops and vessels in readiness.

Df, in writings of Richard Kidder Meade and H, George Washington Papers, Library of Congress.
1. Francis Nash, Brigadier General in the Continental Army from North Carolina, died October 17, 1777, of wounds received at Germantown on October 4.

George Washington to
Major General Horatio Gates

[Philadelphia] August 4, 1777. Forwards Congress' appointment of Gates to the command of Northern Department.

LS, in writing of H, New-York Historical Society, New York City.

George Washington to
The New York Council of Safety

Philadelphia, August 4, 1777. Warns of danger of popular attitude toward fall of Ticonderoga and the advance of General John Burgoyne. Does not wish to aid Northern Department by weakening main Army. Laments lack of aid that has been given by the eastern

what rout[e] to take? Or did they wilfully run into their mouths? All is mystery and dark beyond conjecture. But we must not be discouraged at a misfortune; we must rather exert ourselves the more vigorously to remedy the ill-consequences of it. If the army gets off safe, we shall soon be able to recover the face of affairs. I am in hope that Burgoignes[4] success will precipitate him into measures that will prove his ruin. The entreprizing spirit he has credit for, I suspect, may easily be fanned by his vanity into rashness.

The day before yesterday, Our whole army marched to this place computed to be about eighteen miles from Morris Town; as soon as the weather will permit we shall continue our march to Peeks-Kill. Howe's army we are told are all embarked. We suppose they will shortly make an excursion up the North River. If we can get there before them all will be well.

The most we have to fear is that a panic will seize the people, and disqualify them for giving their aid. It behoves their leaders to put on a chearful countenance, and combat their fears by a spirited and manly example.

I am Dr Sir   Your most Obed servant   A Hamilton

ALS, Columbia University Libraries.
    1. Neither letter has been found.
    2. On July 5, 1777, Major General Arthur St. Clair, with 3,500 men, evacuated Ticonderoga permitting General John Burgoyne to continue his advance.
    3. Arthur St. Clair.
    4. General John Burgoyne.

George Washington to Tronson du Coudray

Pompton Plains [*New Jersey*] *July 13, 1777.* Discusses disposal of the artillery imported on *Amphitrite*. Says that Du Coudray is wrong in assuming that Mauduit du Plessis[1] is aide-de-camp to Brigadier General Henry Knox. States that, as Du Coudray does not yet hold an official position, original arrangements for artillery will continue in effect.

Df, in writing of H, George Washington Papers, Library of Congress.
    1. Thomas Antoine, Chevalier de Mauduit du Plessis, a captain of artillery.

George Washington to
Major General Philip Schuyler

Pompton Plains [*New Jersey*] *July 13, 1777.* Discusses supplies sent to Schuyler. Is astonished that there has been no word from Major General Arthur St. Clair.

Df, in writing of H, George Washington Papers, Library of Congress.

George Washington to
Major General Joseph Spencer

Smiths Clove [*New York*] *July 17, 1777.* Is pleased with capture of Major General Richard Prescott. Will try to exchange Prescott for Major General Charles Lee. Praises conduct of Lieutenant Colonel William Barton.[1]

Df, in writing of H, George Washington Papers, Library of Congress.
1. Barton was a lieutenant colonel of the Rhode Island Militia. Congress, because of the part he played in the capture of Prescott, promoted him to the rank of colonel in the Continental Army.

From Gouverneur Morris

[*Saratoga, New York, July 18, 1777.* On July 22, 1777, Hamilton wrote to Morris: "Your favour of the 18th ⟨from Saratoga reached me⟩ yesterday." *Letter not found.*]

George Washington to
Colonel Thomas Elliott [1]

Smiths Clove [*New York*] *July 18, 1777.* Orders Elliott to appear at Headquarters.

1. Df, in writing of H, who indorsed on the verso Washington's decision: "in Six or Seven weeks from this time if he does not come on must expect to be superseded" George Washington Papers, Library of Congress.

Generals Schuyler & Sinclair,[3] & given the Command to Gates, how far this will be a remedy I will not determine, but I am afraid General Gates is hardly the Man. I wish among other things he had never rendered himself Odious to your State by taking the part tis said he did with the people of the Grants, but his appointment to this Command could not be avoided. It behoves you my Dear Sir & every other Gentleman of Influence in the State to do every thing that can be done to remove the prejudices of the people, and prevent their opperating against their own Safety. In a Conversation I lately had with Mr. Jay he mentioned sending Governor Clinton with all the New York Malitia of the upper part of your State to assist in opposing Mr. Burgoine. I wish you may do this of all things. Genl Clinton is an excellent officer, the people have Confidence in him, will once act with zeal and Serve with Spirit & perseverance under him; his being wanted in the Civil line should be no Objection. It imports you more to take measures for preserving your State than for Governing what you may not long have to Govern. Governor Clinton I am persuaded can render you the most Essential Services in the way purposed. It is now better than a Week since Mr Howe has disappeared from the Capes; there are many Conjectures where he is gone but none Satisfactory; that he did not Steer for the North River seems pretty certain, from his not yet having appeared that Way, & his having had the fairest Winds to Carry him there. That he is not hovering about the Capes, with Intention to Return is pretty Evident because no Reason can be assigned why he should do it so long, Especially as there must be some Risk and Inconvenience in Coasting it with so large a Fleet. There is no object it is thought further to the Southward. And therefore it is concluded they are gone far to the Eastward—some think to Rhode Island, & thence to Boston; others immediately thither & others to portsmouth —for my own part I am weary of Conjecture. We are however bending Eastward; our heavy Baggage Marches to day towards Coryel[l]s. The *Army probably Marches* to morrow. If Burgoine *presses on as fast as some people* seems disposed to let *him, he will*

3. On July 30, 1777, the Continental Congress directed Major General Arthur St. Clair "forthwith to repair to headquarters." On August 1, 1777, Major General Philip Schuyler was also "directed to repair to headquarters" (*JCC*, VIII, 590, 596).

become the first and greatest object to this Army. I cannot conclude without saying some thing about the Enemys numbers. I still think *you* over rate *them*. Were we to count How's *force by the same* rate you do Burgoines, we should soon make him Irestable on Similar Evidence; he cannot have less than 20,000 Effective Men, but we know he has not many more than half the number; we compare & compound every circumstance, use different kinds of Calculations, & from the whole deduct a pretty acurate & certain Judgment. His prisoners tell us the same tales & concur in them as well, but this has no weight with us because we know that great care is taken by the British Officers to give the Men their Lesson & the Dogs are accute enough to profit by it. The Voluntary Examination you speak of has very little Credit with me.[4] I suspect his desiring to become a Subject of the State is all a pretence to be rid of an Irksome Confinement & get a favourable opportunity to Escape.

You say I am mistaken about the number of Foreigners destined last Campaign for the Northern department which you have been well informed were 6000 instead of 4000; but is it not a fact too well known to be doubted that all the German Troops (except the Brunswickers) came to Genl Howe, and is it not equally certain that there were only 4000 & odd of those people Contracted for. I was never more mistaken in my Life than I am now, if that was not the Case. I agree with you that there is no greater Error than that of undervaluing an Enemy, but with one Exception, which is that of over valueing them. Indeed my Dear Sir I am afraid an Extravagant Idea of their power and numbers in our General officers whose Business it is to oppose them, is of Infinite detriment to our Affairs. But be assured that the Contrary has no ill effect with us, for we plainly see & have long seen that whether the Enemys force be great or Small it too well answers their purpose, & calls for every thing we can do to give it a check, but our means are not equal to our Wishes.

I am Dear Sir with great Esteem and Regard Your most obedient Servant   A Hamilton.

4. See Livingston to H, August 2, 1777.

North river, it was judged necessary to move the main body of the army from Middle Brook to Morris Town—to advance a division under General Sullivan to Pumpton—and another under General Parsons [3] ⟨as⟩ [4] far ⟨as⟩ Peeks Kill. A Brigade at that post under General N⟨ixon⟩ [5] was ordered, so soon as Parsons' division arrived near its destination, to proceed immediately as a reinforcement to the Northern army. This disposition is deemed advantageous to prevent the success of a *coup de main*, on the Highland passes, and not inconsistent with a proper attention to Philadelphia, should the Northern alarm prove nothing more than a diversion and Howe return to the charge that way. I am loth to risk a conjecture about Mr. Howe. He is such an untilligible Gentleman, that no rule of interpretation can possibly be found out, by which to unravel his designs. If he acted like a man of sense, he would wait quietly on Staten Island, and there concenter all his forces. He would draw round all the men that could be spared from Canada, and all that are now at Rhode Island. With these and the reinforcements he may receive from Europe, he would make a point of forcing us by some means or other to an action. In this his only hope lies, if he could defeat our army, and improve the moment of success he would go very near effecting his purpose. But let him go to the Northward or to the Southward, every new post he takes weakens his main body, and makes it the more liable to be ruined by our collective strength. Any object short of our army is a bad one, and that plan is the worst, where by a division of his forces he runs the hazard, in case of an accident either way, of having his whole scheme overturned.

We have different accounts of the present situation of his army. Some tell us that the whole is now incamped on Staten Island, others, that the greater part of the Hessians are on board the Ships. By some sailors who came from them yesterday, we are told that the ships are taking in water and provisions for two months, and that conveniences for transporting horses are fitting up in them. All this is rather vague and may, or may not be true.

Their flourishes in the Jerseys, I believe, cannot have cost them less than 6 or 700 men. We have not lost above a hundred. This is the best way to ruin them, without risking anything.

Our present situation is embarrassing. Their ships give them a vast advantage; and we shall probably be much puzzled when they begin their operations again. We shall however act cautiously and do the best we can. We are anxiously waiting for Northern intelligence.

I am Dr. Sir   With great regard   Yrs. &c.   A. Hamilton

Please to forward the inclosed [6] to General Schuyler ⅌ first Oppy.

ALS, New-York Historical Society, New York City.
  1. This letter was addressed to Morris in his capacity as a member of the New York Committee of Correspondence.
  2. On July 2, 1777, Washington wrote: "I last night received intelligence from Genl Schuyler that General Burgoyne is beginning to operate against Ticonderoga and its dependencies. If it is not merely a diversion, but a Serious attack, of which it bears Strongly the appearance, it is certain proof that the next Step of General Howe's Army will be towards Peekskill" (GW, VIII, 335).
  3. Brigadier General Samuel Holden Parsons, Continental Army.
  4. The material within broken brackets is taken from a copy of this letter in the Bancroft Transcripts, MS Division, New York Public Library.
  5. Brigadier General John Nixon, Continental Army.
  6. Enclosure presumably was George Washington to Major General Philip Schuyler, July 6, 1777 (George Washington Papers, Library of Congress).

To Colonel Elias Dayton [1]

Head Quarters Morris
Town [New Jersey] July 7th. 1777

Sir,

Doctor McWorter [2] has represented to His Excellency the case of a certain negro lately taken by a party of militia belonging to Mr. Caleb Wheeler.[3] This fellow, it seems, some time since, went over to the enemy, and is now detained in confinement on that account. I am ordered to desire you to inquire into the circumstances of the affair, and particularly by whom the negro was taken, for on this depends the Generals power of releasement; and if you find he was taken by any party acting under Continental authority and in Continental pay, and there is no reason for detaining him besides merely the consideration of his having joined the enemy, you are authorized, as far as it comes under His Excellency's direction to deliver him to his owner. If he was taken by a party acting merely under the authority of the state, The General has nothing to do with him, and of course you must refer his owner to the Governor or other civil magistrate impowered to take cognizance of it. If there

I think it my duty to state things to you truly, that you may not be surprized if affairs should take a turn which we do not expect, especially as I see you have formed very fallacious Conjectures both of our Strength & of the Army.

I am Dear Sir   Your most Obedient   humble Servant

R. R. Livingston [2]

To Coll Alexr. Hamilton Aid de Camp
to General Washington
Head Quarters.

Transcript, Add. MS 35912, f 235–236, British Museum.
1. Located on the Mohawk River at the present site of Rome, New York. Built in 1758 and called Fort Stanwix, it was repaired in 1776, when its name was changed to Fort Schuyler.
2. In MS, "R. B. Levingstone."

George Washington to John Hancock

Camp near Germantown [*Pennsylvania*] *August 10, 1777.* Reports that Army has been moved to Coryells Ferry. Discusses desirability of defending Fort Island rather than Billingsport. Asks permission to have Major General Tronson du Coudray survey region between Marcus Hook and Philadelphia.

LS, in writing of H, Papers of the Continental Congress, National Archives.

George Washington to John Hancock

Camp at Cross Roads [1] [*Pennsylvania*] *August 12, 1777.* Has instructed Brigadier General Silas Newcomb to maintain New Jersey militia at Woodbury. Asks if Major General Tronson du Coudray may call on Newcomb for aid.

LS, in writing of H, Papers of the Continental Congress, National Archives.
1. Also known as Neshaminy Camp. This later became Hartsville, Pennsylvania.

George Washington to Colonel Elias Dayton

Camp at Cross Roads [*Pennsylvania*] *August 14, 1777.* Instructs Dayton to send information on strength of the enemy at Kings

Bridge and on Staten Island. Also asks Dayton to send account of number of boats available in that area.

LS, in writing of H, The Huntington Library, San Marino, California.

George Washington to John Hancock

Camp at Cross Roads [Pennsylvania] August 15, 1777. Suggests plan of defence for Fort Island based on Major General Tronson du Coudray's maps.

LS, in writing of H, Papers of the Continental Congress, National Archives.

George Washington to George Clinton

Camp at Cross Roads [Pennsylvania] August 16, 1777. Discusses importance of the two actions near Fort Schuyler. Asks for more information. Commends New York's efforts. States that a body of New Hampshire Militia under Brigadier General John Stark has joined Major General Benjamin Lincoln at Bennington, Vermont. Differs with the plan of Major General Philip Schuyler and Lincoln to unite all their forces to confront General John Burgoyne. Is sending Colonel Daniel Morgan's riflemen to Northern Department. Advises removing all boats from enemy's path.

Df, in writing of H, with postscript in writing of John Laurens, George Washington Papers, Library of Congress.

George Washington to Benjamin Franklin [1]

[Camp at Cross Roads, Pennsylvania] August 17, 1777. Acknowledges receipt of Turgot's [2] recommendation for a French volunteer. Discusses difficulty of placing French officers and advises Franklin to discourage potential candidates in France.

Df, in writing of H, George Washington Papers, Library of Congress.
1. Franklin was in France serving as United States Commissioner to that country.
2. Anne Robert Jacques Turgot, former French Minister of Finance.

your men into the Town. It will be the easiest matter in the world
if you are not exceedingly vigilant to throw a party across the river [3]
upon your rear and intercept you. You had better not send your
whole Brigade in; but only send in a small party to take possession
of the stores, and convey as many out as you can to some other place.
For this purpose you will collect as many waggons as you can about
the neighbourhood. You are, by no means, to remain in Amboy all
night; but retire immediately after you have put an end to any
endeavours to carry off the remaining stores. Keep parties reconnoitring from Amboy to Elizabeth Town point and take every precaution to avoid a surprise.

I have ordered down provisions to Bonum Town. You can either
go that place or send for the provisions from thence.

I am Dr. sir   Your most Obed serv   A Hamilton ADC

ALS, The Andre deCoppet Collection, Princeton University Library.
    1. On June 28, 1777, Washington wrote to the President of Congress: "On
thursday Morning Genl Howe advanced with his whole Army in Several
Columns from Amboy, as far as Westfield. . . . I detached a Body of Light
Troops under Brigadier General Scott, to hang on their Flank and to watch
their Motions" (George Washington Papers, Library of Congress). On the
following day he wrote: "I have two Brigades (Scott's and Conway's) now
lying at and near Woodbridge, as Corps of Observation and to act as circumstances may require" (*ibid.*).
    2. Letter not found.
    3. Raritan River.

George Washington to the Board of War

Middlebrook [*New Jersey*] *June 30, 1777.* Discusses disposal of
artillery imported in the *Amphitrite*.[1] Emphasizes need for centralized regulations for procuring supplies.

Df, in writing of H, George Washington Papers, Library of Congress.
    1. The first of Beaumarchais's supply ships.

George Washington to Tronson du Coudray

Middlebrook [*New Jersey*] *June 30, 1777.* Countermands order
from Northern Department demanding guns. Discusses disposal of
artillery that arrived on the *Amphitrite*. States that Tousard [1] is to

return to Du Coudray, and that French engineers will be sent to Du Coudray.

Df, in writing of H, George Washington Papers, Library of Congress.
1. Lewis Tousard, captain of artillery in the French army. Later he was an aide to Lafayette.

George Washington to Brigadier General George Clinton

Middlebrook [*New Jersey*] *July 1, 1777.* Reports news of attack on Ticonderoga. Warns of probable attack on Peekskill. Orders Clinton to call out militia to defend the area around Peekskill.

LS, in writing of H, George Washington Photostats, Library of Congress.

George Washington to Jonathan Trumbull

Middlebrook [*New Jersey*] *July 2–4, 1777.* Approves of suggested exchange of prisoners, but states that Colonel Elias Boudinot must first be consulted. Refuses request for arms. Discusses probable British moves and American plans to counteract these moves.

Df, in writing of H, George Washington Papers, Library of Congress.

From Gouverneur Morris [1]

Kingston [New York] July 4 1777

Dear Sir

Your Letter [2] gave me the Pleasure of knowing with Certainty what might be depended upon among the numerous Reports circulated Thro the Country with Relation to the Several movements of the Enemy. That Howe [3] wishes to draw you to a General Action is highly Probable because certainly he hath no other Means of conquering the Country, but the time when he wishes to Engage must depend upon a General Estimate in his mind of what Forces he now hath, What Accessions he may receive, our Force and the Probability of its Increase or Decrease. To hazard a Generale Action on

Morgan's corps of riflemen, are on their march for the same purpose.[3] They left Trentown yesterday morning, and as they march light and vessels are ordered to be ready waiting for them at Peeks Kill, they will soon be at the place of their destination. It has been my wish and endeavour for some time past that this corps might be sent to your assistance. I expect much from them. They are a picked corps, well used to rifles and to wood-fights, commanded by officers of distinguished bravery, and have been very serviceable in frequent skirmishes with the enemy. I dare say these people will soon chastise the forwardness of the indians, and I should not be surprized, if after a little time they make them desert their British friends. Their known inconstancy and want of perseverance, give great reasons to hope a few drubbings will exceedingly discourage them and send the greatest part of them home. From every account, I am led to believe, our misfortunes are greatly owing to a panic dread of the indians. If this be so, the presence of Morgan's corps will not fail to have the most happy effect. It would be[4] well to propagate th[r]ough the country and army, such ideas of this corps as will tend to revive the spirits of both inhabitants and soldiers. If their numbers which is about 500 were magnified it would do no harm. But of all things, my dear Sir, let every topic be carefully avoided, that may tend to breed jealousies between this Corps and the Northern troops. Such jealousies have been, are, and will be more detrimental to our affairs than anything besides.

I communicated your Letter to His Excellency.

I am with real regard and esteem   Dear Sir   Your most Obed servant   A Hamilton

Your express not calling on his return was the sole reason of your not receiving a letter from me. I had written one to go by him.

His Excellency desires his particular respects to you, and assures you that nothing in his power will be left undone for your assistance.

3. On August 16, 1777, Washington wrote to Major General Israel Putnam: "The people in the Northern Army seem so intimidated by the Indians that I have determined to send up Colo. [Daniel] Morgan's Corps of Rifle Men who will fight them in their own way. They march from Trenton to morrow Morning and will reach Peeks Kill with all expedition. You will please to have sloops ready to carry them and provision laid in, that they may not wait a moment" (George Washington Papers, Library of Congress).
4. In MS, "we."

George Washington to Baron de Holtzendorff [1]

Camp at the Cross Roads [Pennsylvania] August 18, 1777. Acknowledges receipt of the Baron's "plan of a military work." Encloses letter to Major General Nathanael Greene stating that the Baron is to be attached as a lieutenant colonel to Greene's division.

Df, in writing of H, George Washington Papers, Library of Congress.
1. Baron de Holtzendorff, commissioned a lieutenant colonel in 1776, resigned in 1778.

George Washington to Brigadier General Preudhomme de Borre

Camp at Cross Roads [Pennsylvania] August 19, 1777. Abides by Brigadier General de Borre's preference of an American as brigade major and recommends Captain Matthew McConnell of Colonel Moses Hazen's regiment.

Df, in writing of H, George Washington Papers, Library of Congress.

George Washington to John Hancock

Camp at Cross Roads [Pennsylvania] August 22, 1777. Acknowledges receipt of news that enemy is in Chesapeake Bay. Informs Hancock of orders given to Colonel Thomas Proctor, Brigadier General Francis Nash, Major General John Sullivan, and the Army at Headquarters. Approves of removal of stores from Lancaster and York.

Df, in writing of H, George Washington Papers, Library of Congress.

George Washington to Major General John Sullivan

Wilmington [Delaware] August 27, 1777. Discusses failure of Staten Island expedition. Advises Sullivan to spare health of men on march to Headquarters.

Df, in writing of H, George Washington Papers, Library of Congress.

George Washington to
Colonel William Malcom [1]

Middlebrook [*New Jersey*] *June 27, 1777.* Appoints Malcom to the command of a regiment. Gives instructions for completion of this regiment. Orders Malcom to the field.

Df, in writing of H, George Washington Papers, Library of Congress.
1. Malcom had been a major and then a colonel of the New York Militia. The regiment referred to in this letter was one of the Sixteen Additional Continental Regiments.

To Robert R. Livingston [1]

Head Quarters Camp
at Middle Brook [New Jersey] June 28 1777

Dear Sir.

Yours of the 25th [2] came to hand last night. Since my last addressed to Mr. Morris,[3] the enemy have been trying a second experiment to tempt us to an engagement, on equal terms of ground. Under the supposition of their intending to evacuate the Jerseys immediately, in order to keep up the idea of a persuit, and to be in a posture to take advantage of any critical moment that might present itself to give them a blow, the chief part of our army, after their retreat from Brunswick, was marched down to Quibble town, and parties detached thence further towards the enemy. Finding this disposition take place and expecting that elated by what had passed, we might be willing to venture upon a general engagement, which is Howe's only hope, he came out with his whole army from Amboy early on thursday morning and made a forced march towards our left, with design, if possible, to cut off some of our detachments, particularly one under Lord Stirling; and propably, if we were not expeditious in regaining the heights, to get there before us, by rapidly

ALS, New-York Historical Society, New York City.
1. This letter was addressed to Livingston in his capacity as a member of the New York Committee of Correspondence.
2. Letter not found.
3. Letter not found.

entering the passes on our left. Lord Stirlings party was near being surrounded; but after a smart skirmish with the enemy's main body, made their retreat good to Westfield, and ascended the pass of the mountains back of the Scotch plains. The other parties after skirmishing on their flanks came off to join the main body and take possession of the heights. The enemy continued their march towards our left as far as Westfield, and there halted. In the mean time, it was judged prudent to return with the army to the mountains, lest it should be their intention to get into them and force us to fight them on their own terms. They remained at Westfield 'till the next day, and perceiving their views disappointed have again returned to Amboy, plundering and burning as usual. We had parties hanging about them in their return; but they were so much on their guard no favourable opportunity could be found of giving them any material annoyance. Their loss we cannot ascertain; and our own, in men, is inconsiderable, though we have as yet received no returns of the missing. I have no doubt they have lost more men than we, but unfortunately, I won't say from what cause, they got three field pieces from us, which will give them room for vapouring, and embellish their excursion, in the eyes of those, who make every trifle a matter of importance. It is not unlikely they will soon be out of the Jersies; but where they will go to next is mere matter of conjecture, for as you observe, their conduct is so eccentric, as to leave no certain grounds on which to form a judgment of their intentions.

I know the comments that some people will make on our Fabian conduct. It will be imputed either to cowardice or to weakness: But the more discerning, I trust, will not find it difficult to conceive that it proceeds from the truest policy, and is an argument neither of the one nor the other. The liberties of America are an infinite stake. We should not play a desperate game for it or put it upon the issue of a single cast of the die. The loss of one general engagement may effectually ruin us, and it would certainly be folly to hazard it, unless our resources for keeping up an army were at an end, and some decisive blow was absolutely necessary; or unless our strength was so great as to give certainty of success. Neither is the case. America can in all probability maintain its army for years, and our numbers though such as would give a reasonable hope of success are not such as should make us intirely sanguine. A third

To Colonel Timothy Pickering [1]

Wilmington [Delaware] August 29, 1777. Sends extract from General Orders of June 18, 1777, stating that "Timothy Pickering Esquire is appointed Adjutant General in the Armies of the United States of America."

ADS, Pickering Foundation, Salem, Massachusetts.
1. Before his appointment as adjutant general, Timothy Pickering had served as colonel of a Massachusetts militia regiment.

To Major General Israel Putnam

Head Quarters Wilmington [Delaware]
Augt. 29th.[1] 1777

Sir,

By command of His Excellency, I am to request you will immediately send on Major Blackden [2] & the detachment that came with him to join this army.

I am Sir   Your most Obed serv   Alex Hamilton A.D.C.

ADfS, George Washington Papers, Library of Congress.
1. The date reads either 28 or 29, for one set of numbers has been written over the other.
2. Lieutenant Colonel Samuel Blackden or Blagden, Second Continental Dragoons.

To Gouverneur Morris [1]

Head Quarters Wilmington [Delaware]
September 1st 1777

Dear Sir,

Agreeable to the intention of the Council [2] I have delivered their inclosed letter [3] to His Excellency who after perusing it has sealed and forwarded it to Mr. Hancock.[4]

The relieving Fort Schuyler [5] is a very happy and important event, and will concur with the two happy strokes given by Harkemar and Stark to reverse the face of affairs and turn the scale against Mr Burgoigne. I hope Capt Montgomery's [6] suggestions may be right as to his being obliged to advance; but I fancy if he once thinks it unsafe he will not be bound by such an empty punctilio to risk the destruction of his army. As General Howe is now fairly sat down to the Southward, the Eastern states, no longer under any apprehensions from him, ⟨will⟩ [7] be disposed, I am in hopes, to exert their whole force, and if they do, I shall wonder at it if Mr. Burgoigne advances with impunity.

Before this reaches you, you will have heard of General Howes ⟨com⟩ing into Chesapeak bay; where he has landed his whole army within about four miles from the head of Elk; a day or two, after his landing, he marched from his first position and extended his van as far as Grey⟨'s⟩-Hill. He still lies there in a state of inactivity; in a great measure I believe from the want of horses, to transport his baggage and stores. It seems he sailed with only about three weeks provendor and was six at sea. This has occasioned the death of a great number of his horses, and has made skeletons of the rest. He will be obliged to collect a supply from the neighbouring country before he can move, unless he should be disposed to make a more hazardous movement, than he would ever be able to justify, unless by a degree of success he has no right to expect.

The main body of our army is incamped on the heights of Wilmington so as to cover the town; we have strong parties of light troops and militia advanced towards the enemy who have ⟨frequent⟩ skirmishes with them, of little consequence, and often ⟨pick up a few⟩ prisoners. We have taken ⟨at least⟩ 70 since they landed & have had 30 deserters. This Country does not abound in good posts. It is intersected by such an infinity of roads, and is so little mountainous that it is impossible to find a spot not liable to capital defects. The one we now have is all things considered the best we could find, but there is no great depindence to be put upon it. The enemy will have Philadelphia, if they dare make a bold push for it, unless we fight them a pretty general action. I opine we ought to do it, and that we shall beat them soundly if we do. The Militia seem pretty generally stirring. Our army is in high health & spirits. We shall I hope have twice the enemy's numbers. I would not only fight them, but I would attack them; for I hold it an established maxim, that there is three to one in favour of the party attacking.

I am in haste Dr Sir Your most Obed servant   A Hamilton

George Washington to Colonel Charles Armand [1]

[*Middlebrook, New Jersey*] *June 11, 1777.* Orders Armand to assume command of Ottendorf's [2] corps, to expand this corps to a full regiment, and in the future to take orders from Major General Benjamin Lincoln.

Df, in writing of H, George Washington Papers, Library of Congress.
  1. Charles Armand-Tuffin, Marquis de la Rouerie, was generally known as Colonel Armand.
  2. Nicholas Dietrich, Baron de Ottendorf, was a major of three Pennsylvania companies.

To Major General John Sullivan [1]

Head Quarters Camp at
[Middlebrook, New Jersey, June 12–25, 1777] [2]

Sir,

His Excellency has received your two last favours to day. In the first you hint the want of a reinforcement; but as the intention of your body is chiefly for observation and skirmishing and not to make any serious stand, it is the less necessary it should be powerful in numbers. It will however depend upon circumstances, how far it will be expedient to reinforce you; and as soon as any thing can be determined from them, you shall have whatever addition of strength you may stand in need of.

The information contained in your last of the enemy's being incamped on the road leading from Brunswick to Princeton about the three Mile run is not well founded. We have had parties and officers reconnoitring as far as the mile run and there is no sign of an incampment. They seem to be taking their old position with their right at Amboy and their left at Brunswick; but how long they will remain so it is hard to tell. His Excellency desires you will engage some trusty persons at South Amboy, on whom you can depend for faithful and early intelligence of the appearance of shipping in the river, or any preparations for a movement by water, that we may be, in time, prepared to counteract them.

I am with regard   Sir   Your most Obed servant

A Hamilton ADC

ALS, George Washington Papers, Library of Congress.

1. When this letter was written, Sullivan was in the Sourland Hills, New Jersey.

2. Date and place have been supplied on basis of contents of this letter. In both *JCHW*, I, 60, and *HCLW*, X, 458, this letter is dated 1778.

Discharge of Joshua Austin

Middlebrook [*New Jersey*] *June 13, 1777.* ". . . Joshua Austin, belonging to the independent company of the State of Connecticut, . . . appears to be incapable of military service. He is hereby discharged from the Continental army. . . ."

ADS, Connecticut State Library, Hartford.

George Washington to Charles Thomson

Middlebrook [*New Jersey*] *June 13, 1777.* Encloses copy of a plan for the establishment of a cavalry force.

Df, in writing of H, George Washington Papers, Library of Congress.

George Washington to Major General Benedict Arnold

Middlebrook [*New Jersey*] *June 17, 1777.* Describes position at Middlebrook and plans of attack. Discusses probability of enemy attack on the army at Middlebrook and on Philadelphia. Orders Arnold to send on Continental troops.

Df, in writing of H, George Washington Papers, Library of Congress.

George Washington to Chevalier d'Annemours [1]

Middlebrook [*New Jersey*] *June 19, 1777.* Discusses advantages of an overt declaration of war by France. Corrects error in estimate of British losses at Danbury, Connecticut. Questions purpose of General William Howe's recent moves.

Df, in writings of Richard Kidder Meade and H, George Washington Papers, Library of Congress.

1. Charles François Adrien le Paulnier, Chevalier d'Annemours, was seeking an Army appointment which he did not receive. He was later appointed French consul to Maryland.

here this morning; but as you have not done it, I send you the letters, that they may be immediately forwarded by express. No time should be lost in the matter [3] as it is a point of the most urgent necessity.

I am Sir   Your most Obed serv   A Hamilton ADC

ALS, Harvard College Library.
   1. Stewart was commissary general of issues.
   2. Christopher Ludowick, superintendent of bakers.
   According to John Bakeless "General Washington himself dealt with a few secret agents directly. One of these was probably the German baker—and specialist in fancy gingerbread—Christopher Ludwick, who, as "Baker General" of the Continental Army, supplied such bread as he could to the troops at Valley Forge. German born, long in business in Philadelphia, he was the ideal agent to encourage German troops to desert and could hardly help mingling espionage with these duties" (John Bakeless, *Turncoats, Traitors and Heroes* [Philadelphia, 1959], 207). Washington wrote to Ludowick on September 5, 1777 (George Washington Papers, Library of Congress).
   3. This is a reference to Washington's demand that more bread be provided for the Army.

George Washington to Christopher Ludowick

Wilmington [*Delaware*] *September 5, 1777.* Orders Ludowick to Camp by way of Pittstown and Coryells Ferry. Asks Ludowick to send bread from these places to Camp, and to set up as many ovens as possible in Philadelphia for baking hard bread.

Df, in writing of H, George Washington Papers, Library of Congress.

George Washington to Brigadier General William Maxwell

Wilmington [*Delaware*] *September 5, 1777.* Encloses two letters for Lord Richard Howe and General William Howe. Orders Maxwell to apologize to Howe if there is any truth in report that an enemy flag was fired upon. Requests information concerning situation of enemy.

Df, in writing of H, George Washington Papers, Library of Congress.

George Washington to
Brigadier General William Maxwell

Wilmington [*Delaware*] *September 5, 1777.* Asks if Maxwell is prepared to make a secret foray against enemy. Gives instructions concerning proper guides and return route.

Df, in writing of H, George Washington Papers, Library of Congress.

George Washington to
Major General Philemon Dickinson[1]

Near Germantown [*Pennsylvania*] *September 14, 1777.* Forwards to Dickinson steps taken to counteract the enemy in New Jersey. Is confident of Dickinson's cooperation and assistance.

Df, in writing of H, George Washington Papers, Library of Congress.
1. Dickinson was a major general in the New Jersey Militia from June 6, 1777, to the close of the war.

George Washington to John Hancock

Near Germantown [*Pennsylvania*] *September 14, 1777.* Is directing Major General Israel Putnam to send a second detachment of one thousand men to camp.

LS, in writing of H, George Washington Papers, Library of Congress.

George Washington to
Major General William Heath

Near Germantown [*Pennsylvania*] *September 14, 1777.* Orders Heath to send all Continental troops in Massachusetts to join the main Army. Relays information concerning engagement at Brandywine Creek.

LS, in writing of H, Massachusetts Historical Society, Boston.

is too much wanted for the Continental army to be spared to the militia; and experience has taught us, that there has been infinite abuse and misapplication of the public arms when confided to them. As to ammunition, [The] [3] General has no objection that a small quantity should be given them; provided it be lodged with their officers, who are to be accountable, for its being devoted to the uses intended.

I am   Dr. Sir   Yr Most Obedt serv   A Hamilton ADC

ALS, New Hampshire Historical Society, Concord.
    1. When this letter was written, Sullivan was in command at Princeton.
    2. Sullivan's letter to Washington is in neither the George Washington Papers, Library of Congress, nor the Sullivan Papers, New Hampshire Historical Society, Concord, New Hampshire.
    3. H first wrote, "I have." He then crossed out "have," and wrote "General has," making it read "I General has."

To Joseph Trumbull [1]

Head Quarters [Middlebrook, New Jersey] June 4th 1777

Sir,

His Excellency has examined your Provision report; and finds every part of it very well, except that relating to the placing a quantity at Trenton. This is the most improper place in the world; for if the enemy should move towards Philadelphia the provisions at trentown in the hurry occasioned by such an event would inevitably fall into their hands. You will therefore without loss of time have them removed much higher up the river, at least as high as Corel's; [2] a moment should not be lost in doing this.

I am Sir   Yr most Obed serv   A Hamilton ADC

ALS, Connecticut State Library, Hartford.
    1. Trumbull was commissary general of stores, Continental Army, from 1775 to June 18, 1777.
    2. Coryell's Ferry.

George Washington to James Lovell [1]

Middlebrook [New Jersey] June 4, 1777. Discusses the qualifications of Lutterloh.[2]

Df, in writing of H, George Washington Papers, Library of Congress.
    1. Lovell was a delegate from Massachusetts to the Continental Congress.

2. Major Henry Emanuel Lutterloh who was employed in the quartermaster's department.

George Washington to Charles, Earl Cornwallis

Middlebrook [*New Jersey*] *June 6, 1777.* States that all supplies for prisoners must go through Colonel Elias Boudinot's hands. Assures Cornwallis that the greatest care will be taken with these supplies. Is surprised at Cornwallis' reasoning concerning the murder of William Martin.[1]

Df, in writing of H, George Washington Papers, Library of Congress.
1. See H to John Jay, June 2, 1777.

From Robert R. Livingston [1]

7th. June 1777 Kingston [New York]

Dear Sir

With my place at Council[2] I resume the agreeable task of writing to you & answering your Letter directed to Mr. Jay.

I see with you the propriety of collecting our army to a point & have often been under apprehentions least the enemy should take advantage of our former dispersed state & the necessity that drove us into it. But they have wanted the spirit of enterprize or been deceived greatly as to our strength. I can hardly yet persuade myself that they design to go to the Southward since it appears to me an undertaking infinitely above their strength unless they are very considerably reinforced; what their prospects of being so are I have not been able to learn. I do not know how to account for their leaving a part of their troops at Rhode Island when they need their assistance in the Jersies; had they heretofore moved on rational principles I should suppose that they expected to be so far strengthened as to be able to make a divertion there, while their main body carried on its operations to the Southward; but their motions have always been so excentrick that there is no rule by which we can form a judgment of them.

If it should be true that more force has been drawn from New York into the Jerseys, might it not be worth while to alarm New York by sending down two or three thousand men who might possi-

These two boats will convey 50 men across at a time so that in a few hours they may throw over a large party, perhaps sufficient to overmatch the militia who may be between them and the city. This renders the situation of Congress extremely precarious if they are not on their guard; my apprehensions for them are great, though it is not improbable they may not be realized. The most cogent reasons oblige me to join the army this night or I should have waited upon you myself. I am in hopes our army will be up with the enemy before they pass Schulkill. If they are, something serious will insue.

I have the honor to be with much respect   Sir Your Most Obedt servt   A Hamilton

ALS, Charles Roberts Autograph Collection of the Haverford College Library, Haverford, Pennsylvania.
  1. The date and time were taken from note on verso by H.
  2. Swedes' Ford was on the Schuylkill on the site of what is now Norristown, Pennsylvania.
  3. Daverser's (or Daviser's) ferry, on the Schuylkill, was the place where the flour, which Captain Henry Lee and H were sent to destroy, was stored.

George Washington to
Brigadier General Alexander McDougall

[Reading Furnace, Pennsylvania] September 19, 1777. Orders McDougall to join main Army.

LS, in writing of H, George Washington Photostats, Library of Congress.

Major General John Sullivan to
Lieutenant Colonels Alexander Hamilton
and John Laurens [1]

[September 20, 1777. On September 21, 1777, Hamilton and Laurens wrote to Sullivan: "We have just received your favour of Yesterday." Letter not found.]

  1. Laurens, like H, was an aide-de-camp of Washington. A native of South Carolina and the son of Henry Laurens, John Laurens was H's closest friend in Washington's official family.

Bill for Expenses of George Washington's Staff

[Potts Grove, Pennsylvania, September 21, 1777]
paid at Christiana [1] for family's [2] breakfast, horses &c.— £6.5
paid on the road from thence to Wilmington for lodging
&c—   6.
paid for breakfast the morning we crossed brandywine—[3]   1.12
pd.   1.12
                                                               ———
                                                               15.9

Received the above from Capt Gibbs [4]
Sepr. 21st 1777   A. Hamilton

ADS, Hamilton Papers, Library of Congress.
  1. Town on creek of same name, which flows into the Delaware near Wilmington.
  2. I.e., Washington's staff.
  3. The American forces crossed Brandywine Creek on September 9, 1777.
  4. Caleb Gibbs, Washington's aide-de-camp, and captain and commander of a company of Washington's Guards.

Lieutenant Colonels Alexander Hamilton and John Laurens to Major General John Sullivan

Head Quarters [Potts Grove, Pennsylvania] Septr 21: 1777

Dear Sir

We have just received your favour of Yesterday,[1] desiring from us a Testimony of your Conduct, so far as it fell under our Observation, the day of the Battle on the Brandywine.[2]

As we had not the pleasure of seeing you in the fore part of that Action when the Line at large was Engaged, We are unable from our own Knowledge, to say any thing of your Conduct at that time. But we can chearfully testify in justice to Your Reputation, that when we had an opportunity of seeing you, it was in circumstances which did you Honour. This was from the time you rode up, and joined Genl: Weedon's Brigade [3] 'till your Horse was wounded. You were employed in animating and encouraging the Men, to their duty, both by your Words and example; and in every Respect behaved, with becoming bravery, and Activity.

We have the Honour to be   Sir   Your most Obedt Servts.

A Hamilton
John Laurens

Major Genl. Sullivan

Copy, New Hampshire Historical Society, Concord.
    1. Letter not found.
    2. At the time that this letter was written, a court of inquiry was investigating Sullivan's conduct of a raid against Staten Island in August. At the same time he was being severely criticized in Congress and the Army for his part in the Battle of Brandywine (September 11, 1777). In this battle, in which he had commanded the right wing of the American Army, he had permitted his forces to be outflanked by the British. In an attempt to clear his name, he asked various officers for testimonials concerning his conduct. The present letter by H and Laurens is in reply to such a request by Sullivan.
    3. Brigadier General George Weedon was in command of a brigade of Major General Nathanael Greene's division, which had been sent to re-enforce Sullivan during the Battle of Brandywine.

From George Washington

[Potts Grove, Pennsylvania, September 21, 1777] [1]

Sir,

The distressed situation of the army for want of blankets and many necessary articles of Cloathing, is truly deplorable; and must inevitably be destructive to it, unless a speedy remedy be applied. Without a better supply than they at present have, it will be impossible for the men to support the fatigues of the campaign in the further progress of the approaching inclement season. This you well know to be a melancholy truth. It is equally the dictate of common sense and the opinion of the Physicians of the army as well as, of every officer in it. No supply can be drawn from the public magazines. We have therefore no resource but from the private stock of individuals. I feel, and I lament, the absolute necessity of requiring the inhabitants to contribute to those wants which we have no other means of satisfying, and which if unremoved, would involve the ruin of the army, and perhaps the ruin of America. Painful as it is to me to order and as it will be to you to execute the measure, I am compelled to desire you immediately to proceed to Philadelphia, and there procure from the inhabitants, contributions of blankets and Cloathing and materials to answer the purposes of both; in proportion to the ability of each. This you will do with as much delicacy and discretion as the nature of the business demands; and I trust the necessity will justify the proceeding in the eyes of every person well affected to the American cause; and that all good citizens will chearfully afford their assistance to soldiers, whose sufferings they are bound to commisserate, and who are eminently exposed to danger and distress, in defence of every thing they ought to hold dear.

As there are also a number of horses in Philadelphia both of public and private property, which would be a valuable acquisition to the enemy, should the city by any accident fall into their hands, you are hereby authorised and commanded to remove them thence into the Country to some place of greater security and more remote from the operations of the enemy.

You will stand in need of assistance from others, to execute this commission with dispatch and propriety; and you are therefore impowered to employ such persons as you shall think proper to aid you therein. Given

Df, in writing of H, George Washington Papers, Library of Congress.
1. In *GW*, IX, 248–49, this letter is dated September 22, 1777. H in his letter to John Hancock on September 22, 1777, states, "I left camp last evening." Since these instructions are in H's writing, it is more probable that they were written before he left Headquarters on September 21, 1777.

To John Hancock

Philadelphia Sepr. 22d. 1777

Sir,

I left camp last evening and came to this city to superintend the collection of blankets and cloathing for the army. Mr. Lovel [1] sends to inform me there is an express going off to Congress, and I do myself the honor to communicate a brief state of things, when I left camp. The enemy moved yesterday from where they lay opposite to valley forge &c. higher up the river on their old scheme of gaining our right. I dont know precisely where they halted; but our army was preparing to move up also to counteract them. I am this morning told they marched about twelve oClock at night for that purpose. The general opinion was that the enemy would attempt crossing [2] this day. Every appearance justified the supposition.

We had intelligence that the enemy had the night before last surprised Generals Smallwood and Wayne and consequently dispersed them, after a small opposition.[3] The loss tis said was not great; and our troops were reassembling fast at the Red Lion.[4] This seems to have been a bad look-out and is somewhat disconcerting.

By a letter from General McDougall received this morning, it appears he was, on the 20th in the morning, at Second River [5] just setting out on his march towards Woodbridge.[6] He is pressing forward with all possible expedition.

I have the honor to be   With much Respect   Sir   Your most Obed servt   A Hamilton ADC

PS The troops were pretty well refreshed & in good spirits.

ALS, The Huntington Library, San Marino, California.
1. Presumably James Lovell, a delegate from Massachusetts to the Continental Congress.
2. I.e., crossing the Schuylkill River.
3. Washington on September 19, 1777, recrossed the Schuylkill at Parker's Ford, but left on the southern, or British, side of the stream Brigadier General William Smallwood's brigade and Brigadier General Anthony Wayne's division. Smallwood and Wayne were to harass the enemy's flank and rear and attempt to cut off the enemy's baggage. On the evening of September 20–21, 1777, three British regiments attacked and routed Wayne's force, which was encamped near Paoli, Pennsylvania.
4. Presumably, the Red Lion Tavern, in the vicinity of Wilmington, Delaware.
5. Passaic River.
6. Brigadier General Alexander McDougall was en route from Peekskill, New York, with re-enforcements for Washington's Army.

From George Washington

Camp on Reading Road 28 Miles from Philadelphia
Sept 22d. 1777.

Dr. Sir

I have order'd eight or Ten light Horse more to your assistance, and if you should find a further force necessary to facilitate the business you are upon, there are fifty or sixty dismounted No Carolinians attach'd at present to Colo. Nicholas Corps.[1] These must be subject to your order. I have been just now inform'd, that there are not less than three thousand pair of Shoes in the hands of three or four Persons in Philadelphia—a Peter January himself is said to have 140 Pair. You will make the most diligent inquiry upon this Head; you know our distresses and will collect ev'ry pair you possibly can. I refer you to Mr J Mease for proper information,[2] being told that he knows where they are. I do not wish your exertions to be solely directed to obtaining shoes & Blankets; extend them to evry other article, you know to be material for the Army; your own prudence will point out the least exceptionable means to be pursued in these instances; but remember, that delicacy and a strict adherence to the ordinary modes of application must give place to our necessity's. We must if possible, accommodate the Soldiery with such articles as they stand in need of or we shall have just reasons to apprehend the most injurious & alarming consequences from the approaching season. As fast as you collect Shoes & Blankets you will send them off by some interior middle road, that they may be secure, with peremptory orders to those who shall have em in charge, not to delay a moment in getting them to the Army. The business you are upon I know is disagreable, & perhaps in the execution, you may meet with more obstacles than were at first apprehended & also with opposition to the parties I have mention'd; call in such a number of Militia as you may think necessary, observing however over the conduct of the whole, a strict discipline, to prevent evry species of rapine & disorder. If Mr Mease has any under Jackets & stockings, he should order a supply to be forwarded to the Army as soon as possible. This you will tell him.

I am Dr Sr   Yr &c.   GW

ps I doubt not but Mr Mease has remov'd all the clothing 'ere this but you'll mention the propriety of doing it immediately, in case of accidents.

To Colo Hamilton.

Df, in writing of Richard Kidder Meade, George Washington Papers, Library of Congress.
1. Lieutenant Colonel George Nicholas, Eleventh Virginia Regiment.
2. James Mease, clothier general of the Continental Army.

To William Livingston

Philadelphia Sepr. 22d 1777

Sir,

I am in Philadelphia on some business of great importance to the army; to execute which I stand in need of a party of about 100 men which are not readily to be procured here. If Your Excy. will be pleased to order over such a party under good active officers, you will equally serve the public & oblige.   Yr. Excy's   Most Obed servt.

A Hamilton ADC

ALS, Massachusetts Historical Society, Boston.

To ————

[Philadelphia, September 23, 1777]

by Virtue of powers from His Excellency General Washington I do hereby Authorise you to require from the inhabitants, contributions of Blankets and Cloathing of every kind and to take whatever materials you know will be useful to the Army that you may find in the Stores keeping an account of the same and giving receipts.[1]

ADS, sold by Stan V. Henkels, March 9, 1904, Lot 1150.
    1. Text taken from extract of a letter in Stan V. Henkels' catalogue.

To Lieutenant Colonel Anthony Walton White[1]

[Philadelphia, September 23, 1777]

Sir,

In consequence of orders received from His Excellency General Washington, I desire you will press all the horses in this city & neighbourhood in order to be conveyed thence to some place more remote from the present seat of the war, except such as come under the following description: Those which are the property of poor needy persons, whose livelihood depends upon them, and those which belong to transient persons, or persons who are on the point of leaving the city, and will want their horses for the purpose. This is the general outline of your duty: such deviations as particular circumstances may require are left to your discretion.

I am Sir   Your most Obedt serv   A Hamilton ADC

Sep: 23d. 1777
To Lt Col: White

ALS, Mr. A. Philippe von Hemert, New York City.
1. White was lieutenant colonel, Fourth Continental Dragoons.

George Washington to the Board of War

Pennypackers Mill [Pennsylvania] September 28, 1777. Asks Board of War to order the militia "from the Southward" to join the main Army.

Df, in writing of H, George Washington Papers, Library of Congress.

George Washington to Major General William Heath

Skippack [Pennsylvania] September 30, 1777. Approves of Heath's action in supplying Continental frigates with needed ammunition and is pleased with the capture of prizes. Sends news of successes in North and of British occupation of Philadelphia. Repeats orders to forward three regiments from Massachusetts.

LS, in writing of H, George Washington Photostats, Library of Congress.

George Washington to Colonel Jonathan Mifflin [1]

[Skippack, Pennsylvania] October 1, 1777. Orders Mifflin to remove stores from Trenton.

Df, in writing of H, George Washington Papers, Library of Congress.
1. Mifflin was deputy quartermaster general of the Continental Army.

George Washington to Jonathan Trumbull

[*Skippack, Pennsylvania*] *October 1, 1777.* Discusses promotion of Colonel Return Jonathan Meigs and sends news of fall of Philadelphia.

Df, in writing of H, George Washington Papers, Library of Congress.

To Count Casimir Pulaski [1]

[Worcester Township,[2] Pennsylvania, October 2, 1777]

Monsieur,

Son Excellence vous desire d'assembler toute la cavalerie le plutot possible prés de ses quartiers, ou vous trouverez de place propre pous les accommoder, ceux qui sont utilement employé excepté. Vous informerez son Excellence dés le moment de votre arrivé. I'l n'y a pas du temps a perdre.

J suis   Votre serveteur tres hum   A Hamilton

Peter Wentz, Worcester Township
Octor. 2d. 1777

ALS, Maine Historical Society, Portland.
    1. Count Casimir Pulaski, a Polish officer who on September 15, 1777, had been appointed by Congress to the newly-created post of "Commander of Horse."
    To this letter H appended the following translation: "Sir, His Excellency desires you immediately to collect all the horse, except those on necessary duty and repair to some place as near his quarters as you possibly can, consistent with the accommodation of the horses. Inform him when you have done this and lose no time in doing it. Yrs. A Hamilton"
    The following notes, in Pulaski's hand, also appear on the letter: "I Receive now contrarys orders of his excellency as you will see, and I pray you to joigne me in the army as quick as you can.
    "p.S. As soon as you meet the encampement, you will send me a orderly Light horse to warn me of your poste.
    "You will order, to the men of my guard that I have send before you to the same place where you are; to follow you and joigne me in the army."
    2. This town in Pennsylvania was the site of Washington's Headquarters during part of October. While there, he apparently established his Headquarters at the house of Peter Wentz.

General . Orders [1]

[*Worcester Township, Pennsylvania, October 3, 1777.*] Describes order of march for attack on Germantown.

D, in writing of H, George Washington Papers, Library of Congress.
1. Although the manuscript is undated it is endorsed by George Washington "Order of March and Battle German Town 4th Oct. 1777."

George Washington to John Hancock

Near Pennypackers Mill [*Pennsylvania*] *October 5, 1777.* Describes the "unfortunate" attack on Germantown.

Df, in writings of Robert Hanson Harrison and H, George Washington Papers, Library of Congress.

George Washington to Sir William Howe

[*Near Pennypackers Mill, Pennsylvania*] *October 6, 1777.* Returns a lost dog belonging to General Howe.

Df, in writing of H, George Washington Papers, Library of Congress.

George Washington to John Hancock

Near Pennypackers Mill [*Pennsylvania*] *October 7, 1777.* Reports American losses at Germantown and estimates British losses. Intends to rest the men and wait for reinforcements. Reports on naval forces on the Delaware. Asks for more general officers. Recommends Brigadier General Alexander McDougall for promotion. Urges speedy completion of inquiry into Major General Arthur St. Clair. Reports arrival of British ships at Verplanks Point.

Df, in writings of Robert Hanson Harrison and H, George Washington Papers, Library of Congress.

George Washington to Brigadier General James Mitchell Varnum [1]

Pawlins Mill [Pennsylvania] October 7, 1777. Orders Varnum to "the Baptist meeting House in Montgomery Township" to meet main Army.

Df, in writing of H, Papers of George Washington, Library of Congress.
   1. Fitzpatrick dates this letter October 8, 1777 (*GW*, IX, 333).

George Washington to Major General John Armstrong [1]

[Pawlins Mill, Pennsylvania] October 8, 1777. Instructs Armstrong to send Brigadier General James Potter and six hundred men to intercept British communications between Philadelphia and Chester. Expects to be informed of Potter's actions.

Df, in writing of H, George Washington Papers, Library of Congress.
   1. Armstrong was a major general, Pennsylvania Militia.

George Washington to Colonel Christopher Greene [1]

[Pawlins Mill, Pennsylvania] October 8, 1777. Orders Greene's regiment and that of Colonel Israel Angell to Red Bank as a special detachment with Greene in command.

Df, in writing of H, George Washington Papers, Library of Congress.
   1. H dated this letter October 7 at the beginning and October 8 at the end. Greene was a colonel, First Rhode Island Regiment.

George Washington to William Livingston

[Pawlins Mill, Pennsylvania] October 8, 1777. Asks Livingston to send a large portion of New Jersey Militia to Major General Israel

Putnam. States that precarious situation in the Highlands can undo the good that has been achieved in New York.

Df, in writing of H, George Washington Papers, Library of Congress.

To Brigadier General Silas Newcomb [1]

Head Quarters [Towamencin, Pennsylvania] October 10th. 1777

Sir,

I am desired by His Excellency, to inform you that, on a second consideration, it has been thought inexpedient to send as many Continental troops to Red-bank,[2] as was at first intended; and that the number, now on their march for that place, will be rather insufficient for the defence of it. He therefore requests you will, in addition to the Continental troops, furnish from a 100 to 150 of your Militia, to complete the number necessary for the security of a post of such essential consequence; and that you will hold the rest of the troops under your command, in constant readiness to cooperate with the Garrison, whenever the enemy shall make an attempt upon it.

I am &c   AH ADC

ADfS, George Washington Papers, Library of Congress.
    1. Newcomb was a brigadier general of the New Jersey Militia.
    2. Red Bank, situated below Philadelphia on the New Jersey shore of the Delaware River, was the site of Fort Mercer. At the time this letter was written, the Americans, holding both Fort Mercer and Fort Mifflin on the Delaware, were seeking to prevent General William Howe from receiving supplies by way of the Delaware. The British, for their part, were attempting to reduce both forts.

George Washington to Major John Jameson [1]

[*Skippack Camp, Pennsylvania*] *October 11, 1777.* Orders Jameson to collect horses, clothing, and other supplies for Army.

Df, in writing of H, George Washington Papers, Library of Congress.
    1. Jameson was a major of the Second Continental Dragoons.

George Washington to
Brigadier General Edward Hand

[*Towamencin, Pennsylvania*] *October 12, 1777.* Discusses conditions at Fort Pitt and orders Eighth Pennsylvania Regiment to join main Army.

Df, in writing of H, George Washington Papers, Library of Congress.

George Washington to
Colonel Christopher Greene

[*Towamencin, Pennsylvania*] *October 14, 1777.* Orders Greene to send sufficient men to replace deserters in Commodore John Hazelwood's fleet and to assist Lieutenant Colonel Samuel Smith.

Df, in writing of H, George Washington Papers, Library of Congress.

George Washington to
Lieutenant Colonel Samuel Smith

[*Towamencin, Pennsylvania*] *October 14, 1777.* Hopes that Smith will be more successful in the future in gaining control of enemy's batteries. Has ordered Colonel Christopher Greene to assist Smith.

Df, in writing of H, George Washington Papers, Library of Congress.

To Colonel Christopher Greene [1]

Head Quarters [Towamencin, Pennsylvania] Octor. 15th. 1777. 11 OClock PM.

Sir

His Excellency is persuaded by intelligence from different Quarters that the Enemy are determin'd to endeavour, by a speedy & vigorous effort to carry Fort Mifflin, and for this purpose are preparing a con-

This view of New York City includes Kings College, where in 1774 Alexander Hamilton was a student.

siderable force. Their attempt will probably be sudden & violent as they are hardly in a situation to delay a matter so essential to them as that of removing the River obstructions. It is of infinite importance to disappoint their intentions in this instance, as their keeping or evacuating Philadelphia materially depends upon their having the communication with their shipping immediately opened, & it is not unlikely they may dispair of effecting it, if they should fail in the push which is imagin'd they are now about to make. Colo Smiths[2] present force is not as great as could be wish'd, & requires to be augmented to put him in a condition to make an effectual opposition. The Genl would therefore have you to detach immediately as large a part of your force as you possibly can in aid of his garrison. He cannot well determine what proportion; this must be regulated by circumstances & appearances, but his present idea is that the principal part should go to his assistance: To enable you the better to spare a respectable reinforcement, He has directed Genl Newcomb to send his Brigade of Militia to Red Bank or as many of them as he can prevail upon to go. Colo Angell[3] will also March tomorrow morning to join you with his Regt. The Garrisons & Fleet may be inform'd of these succours by way of keeping up their spirits. It will not be adviseable to trust to the houses in the Neighbourhood of your Post, as these in case of an investiture will fail you, which makes it prudent to have a sufficient Number of huts before hand prepar'd within the Fort. He hopes & doubts not you will keep fully in mind the prodigious importance of not suffering the Enemy to get entire possession of the Delaware & will spare no pains nor activity to frustrate their efforts for that purpose. He begs you to be watchfull on ev'ry Quarter & industrious in stopping ev'ry avenue by which you are assailable, cautious not to pay too much attention to any one part of your works, & neglect the others, but take ev'ry precaution to strengthen the whole, for otherwise the greatest danger may be where you least expect it.

I am &c.   AH ADC

To Colo Green

Df, in writings of Richard Kidder Meade, George Washington Papers, Library of Congress.

1. The receiver's copy of this letter, also in Meade's writing, is printed in *GW*, IX, 375–76. The draft, written in the third person, was prepared for H's signature while the receiver's copy, written in the first person, was prepared

for Washington's signature. The receiver's copy contains the following post-script: "N.B. The above letter was written by His Excellency's orders; but as he went to bed before it was finished it will be handed you without his signature."

Greene, a colonel of the First Rhode Island Regiment, had been sent to Red Bank, New Jersey, to help defend Fort Mifflin and Fort Mercer.

2. Lieutenant Colonel Samuel Smith was in command of the American forces at Fort Mifflin.

3. Colonel Israel Angell, Second Rhode Island Regiment, was on his way to Red Bank, New Jersey, to help defend Fort Mifflin and Fort Mercer.

From Marquis de Fleury [1]

[*Fort Mifflin on Mud Island in the Delaware River*] *October 15–19, 1777.* Discusses defences of Fort Mifflin and the British attack on the fort.

Copy in writing of John Laurens, George Washington Papers, Library of Congress. MS which is headed "Substance of Captain Fleury's Letter to Col. Hamilton" can be found in a journal kept by Fleury from October 15 to November 8, 1777.

1. François Louis Teisseydre, Marquis de Fleury, a veteran of the French army, was appointed "Brigade Major to The Count Pulaski, Brigadier General of the Light Dragoons" on October 3, 1777 (*GW*, IX, 305).

George Washington to
Colonel Christopher Greene

[*Worcester, Pennsylvania*] *October 18, 1777.* Informs Greene that Baron d'Arendt will assume command of Fort Mifflin and that Lieutenant Colonel John Green, with reinforcements, is on the way to the fort. Sends news of surrender of General John Burgoyne.

Df, in writing of Richard Kidder Meade, last sentence in writing of H, George Washington Papers, Library of Congress.

George Washington to
Lieutenant Colonel Samuel Smith

[*Worcester, Pennsylvania*] *October 18, 1777.* Informs Smith that Baron d'Arendt will assume command of Fort Mifflin and that Lieutenant Colonel John Green, with reinforcements, is on the way to the fort. Sends news of the surrender of General John Burgoyne. Suggests a plan to prevent British from preparing floating batteries.

Df, in writings of Tench Tilghman and H, George Washington Papers, Library of Congress.

George Washington to
Brigadier General David Forman [1]

[*Whitpain Township, Pennsylvania*] *October 21, 1777.* Believes that British will attack Red Bank. Requests Forman to collect as many militiamen as possible and go to aid of that post. Has asked Brigadier General Silas Newcomb to do the same.

Df, in writing of H, George Washington Papers, Library of Congress.
1. Forman was a brigadier general in the New Jersey Militia and a colonel in one of the Sixteen Additional Continental Regiments.

George Washington to
Commodore John Hazelwood [1]

[*Whitpain Township, Pennsylvania*] *October 21, 1777.* Announces that Baron d'Arendt will assume command of Fort Mifflin. Hopes that there will be complete cooperation between Hazlewood and D'Arendt.

Df, in writing of H, George Washington Papers, Library of Congress.
1. Hazelwood was a commodore in the Pennsylvania navy.

[*From George Washington*] [1]
[Whitpain Township, Pennsylvania, October 21, 1777]

The Magazine of History, VI (November, 1907), 294.
1. This letter is listed here because it is attributed to H in *The Magazine of History*. Actually it was written by Robert Hanson Harrison for Washington to Brigadier General James Potter and is printed in *GW*, IX, 408–09.

George Washington to John Hancock

[*Whitpain Township, Pennsylvania*] *October 22, 1777.* Regrets that Hancock is forced to retire as President of Continental Congress because of poor health and the pressure of private affairs.

LS, in writing of H, George Washington Photostats, Library of Congress.

George Washington to Major General William Heath

Whitpain Township [*Pennsylvania*] *October 22, 1777.* Discusses distribution of newly arrived supplies. Sends news of General John Burgoyne's defeat. Describes recent movements of enemy.

Df, in writing of H, George Washington Photostats, Library of Congress.

George Washington to Colonel Christopher Greene

[*Whitpain Township, Pennsylvania*] *October 24, 1777.* Congratulates Greene on defeat of enemy on October 22, 1777, and orders that all prisoners be sent to Morristown.

Df, in writing of H, George Washington Papers, Library of Congress.

George Washington to Major General John Sullivan

[*Whitpain Township, Pennsylvania*] *October 24, 1777.* Answers questions concerning Sullivan's conduct at Brandywine.

Df, in writing of H, George Washington Papers, Library of Congress.

George Washington to Dragoon Commanders

[*Whitpain Township, Pennsylvania*] *October 25, 1777.* Deplores manner in which horses have been acquired from disaffected persons. Rescinds former instructions. States that anyone found meddling with private property does so "on pain" of "militiary execution."

Df, in writing of H, George Washington Papers, Library of Congress.

Baron d'Arendt to Lieutenant Colonels Alexander Hamilton and John Laurens [1]

Fort Mifflin [*on Mud Island in the Delaware River*] *October 26* [*1777*]. Discusses plans for defence of Fort Mifflin.

ALS, MS Division New York Public Library.
  1. This letter is in French. There is no addressee on the MS. In unidentified handwriting on the last page the following is written, "Col Hamilton Col John Larens." The contents of the letter indicate that it was written to someone at Headquarters who was to relay the information to Washington. Aside from the above notation there is no evidence that the letter was written to H.
  Henry Leonard Philip, Baron d'Arendt, had been made colonel of the German Battalion in March, 1777. He was placed in command of the troops at Fort Mifflin on October 18, 1777.

From Marquis de Fleury

[*Fort Mifflin on Mud Island in the Delaware River*] *October 26, 1777.* Describes the situation at Fort Mifflin. Expects an assault.

Copy, in writing of John Laurens, George Washington Papers, Library of Congress. John C. Fitzpatrick in his *Calendar of the Correspondence of George Washington with the Officers*, I, 448, states that this letter was written to H. See also De Fleury to H, October 15–19, 1777.

George Washington to General Officers

[*Whitpain Township, Pennsylvania*] *October 26, 1777.* Lists questions to be considered at a council of war.

One set of questions, addressed to Brigadier General Anthony Wayne and in writing of H, is in the Historical Society of Pennsylvania, Philadelphia. Another set, unaddressed and in writing of H, is in The Huntington Library, San Marino, California.

From Marquis de Fleury

[*Fort Mifflin on Mud Island in the Delaware River*] October 28, *1777*. Expects an attack on the Fort. Describes the victory of October 23, 1777.

Copy in writing of John Laurens, George Washington Papers, Library of Congress. Fitzpatrick in his *Calendar of the Correspondence of George Washington with the Officers*, I, 450, states that this letter was written to H. See also De Fleury to H, October 15–19, and 26, 1777.

George Washington to Lieutenant Colonel John Green

[*Whitpain Township, Pennsylvania*] October 28, *1777*. States that in Baron d'Arendt's absence, Fort Mifflin is to be under command of Lieutenant Colonel Samuel Smith.

Df, in writing of H, George Washington Papers, Library of Congress.

George Washington to Brigadier General James Mitchell Varnum

[*Whitpain Township, Pennsylvania*] October 28, *1777*. Orders Varnum to Woodbury to cooperate with those already there for the relief of Fort Mifflin and the garrison at Red Bank.

LS, in writing of H, George Washington Photostats, Library of Congress.

Council of War

Whitpain Township [*Pennsylvania*] October 29, *1777*. Hamilton recorded the minutes of this meeting.

D, in writing of H, George Washington Papers, Library of Congress.

From George Washington [1]

Head Quarters Philada: County 30th: October 1777

Dear Sir

It having been judged expedient by the Members of ⟨a⟩ [2] Council of War [3] held yesterday, that one of the Gentlemen of my family should be sent to Genl: Gates in order to lay befor⟨e⟩ him the State of this Army; and the Situation of the Ene⟨my⟩ and to point out to him the many happy Consequences that will accrue from an immediate rein-forceme⟨nt⟩ being sent from the Nothern Army; I have thought ⟨it⟩ proper to appoint you that duty, and desire that yo⟨u⟩ will immedi-ately set out for Albany, at which pla⟨ce⟩ or in the neighbourhood, I imagine you will find ⟨Genl:⟩ Gates

You are so fully acquainted with the two princip⟨al⟩ points on which you are sent, namely the state of ⟨our⟩ Army and the Situation of the Enemy, that I Sha⟨ll not⟩ enlarge on those Heads; what you are chiefly to at⟨tend⟩ to, is to point out in the Clearest and fullest manner ⟨to⟩ Genl: Gates the absolute necessity that there is for ⟨his⟩ detaching a very considerable part of the Army at pre⟨sent⟩ under his Command to the reinforcement of this; a measure that will in all probability reduce Genl: H⟨owe⟩ to the same situation in which Genl: Burgoine now ⟨is⟩ should he attempt to remain in Philadelphia with⟨out⟩ being able to remove the obstructions in Delaware, & open⟨ing⟩ a free communication with his Shipping.

The force which the Members of the Counc⟨il⟩ of War judge it safe and expidient to draw down at prese⟨nt⟩ are the three New Hampshire, and Fifteen Massachus⟨setts⟩ Regiments, with Lee's [4] and Jacksons,[5] two of the 16 adition⟨al⟩. But it is more than proba-ble that Gen Gates may ha⟨ve des⟩tined part of those Troops to the reduction of Ticondero⟨ga⟩ should the Enemy not have evacuated it, or to the garriso⟨nning⟩ of it. If they Should, in that case, the reinforcement will vary according to Circumstances; but, if possi-ble, let it be made up to the same Number out of other Corps.

If upon your meeting with Genl: Gates, you should find that he intends in Consequence of his Success to employ the Troops under his Command upon some expedition by the prosecution of which the common cause will be more benefitted than by their being sent down to reinforce this Army, it is not my wish to give any interruption to the plan. But if he should have nothing more in contemplation than those particular objects which I have mention'd to you, and which it is unnecessary to commit to paper, in that case you are to inform him that it is my desire that the reinforcements before mentioned, or such part of them as can be safely spared, be immediately put in motion to join this Army.

I have under stood that Genl: Gates has already detached Nixons [6] & Glovers [7] Brigades to join Genl: Putnam,[8] and Genl: Dickinson [9] informs me Sr: Henry Clinton has come down the River with his whole force. If this be a fact, you are to desire Genl: Putnam to send the two Brigades forward with the greatest expedition, as there can be no occasion for them there.

I expect you will meet Colo: Morgans Corps [10] upon their way downe, if you do, let them know how essential their services are to us, and desire the Colo. or Commanding Officer to hasten their March as much as it is consistent with the health of the Men, after their late fatigues.

Let me hear from you when you reach the North River, and upon your arrival at Albany. I wish you a pleasent Journey And am   Dr: Sir   Your most obt. Servant   Go: Washington

P.S. I ordered the detatchments belonging to Genl. Mcdougalls Division to come forward. If you meet them direct those belonging to Green's,[11] Angell's,[12] Chandlers [13] and Durgees [14] Regt. not to cross Delaware but to proceed to Red Bank.

LS, in writing of George Lewis (except for postscript, which is in writing of Tench Tilghman), Hamilton Papers, Library of Congress.

1. H's mission, as described in this letter, was one of the most delicate and important in his entire military career. Following the defeat of General John Burgoyne, Major General Horatio Gates's popularity was enormous, and he also continued to enjoy the support of most of the leading New England politicians. At the same time, the mutual dislike of Gates and Washington had already become apparent.

H left for Gates's headquarters soon after receiving this letter and did not return to Washington's headquarters until the end of December.

2. All bracketed material was taken from a transcript in JCH Transcripts.

3. Proceedings printed in *GW*, IX, 461–64.

4. William R. Lee, colonel of one of the Sixteen Additional Continental Regiments.

5. Henry Jackson, colonel of one of the Sixteen Additional Continental Regiments.

6. Brigadier General John Nixon, Continental Army.

7. Brigadier General John Glover, Continental Army.

8. At this time Major General Israel Putnam was stationed at Fishkill, New York.

9. Major General Philemon Dickinson, New Jersey Militia.

10. On October 18, Colonel Daniel Morgan's regiment had marched from Saratoga, New York, to join Washington.

11. Colonel Christopher Greene, First Rhode Island Regiment.

12. Colonel Israel Angell, Second Rhode Island Regiment.

13. Colonel John Chandler, Eighth Connecticut Regiment.

14. Colonel John Durkee, Fourth Connecticut Regiment.

To George Washington [1]

Head Quarters Fish Kill [New York]
Novemr. 2d. 1777

Dear Sir,

I lodged last night in the neighbourhood of New Windsor. This morning early, I met Col: Morgan with his corps about a mile from it, in march for Head Quarters. I told him the necessity of making all the dispatch he could so as not to fatigue his men too much, which he has promised to do.

I understood from Col: Morgan that all the Northern army were marching down on both sides the River, and would probably be to-morrow at New Windsor and this place; and that General Putnam had held a council for the general disposition of them, in which it was resolved to send you 4000 men, and to keep the rest on this side the River. I came here in expectation that matters were in such a train as to enable me to accomplish my errand without going any farther; unless it should be to hasten the troops that were on their march. But on my arrival, I learn from Mr Hughes [2] and Aid De Camp of General Gates, that the following disposition of the Northern army had taken place.

General Patersons,[3] Glovers & Nixons brigades, & Col. Warners [4] mountain boys to remain in and about Albany; barracks building for them.

General Poor's [5] Brigade marching down this side of the River to join General Putnam; will probably be here tomorrow. General Larned's [6] brigade, Morgan's corps, Warn⟨er's⟩ Brigade of Massachusettes militia & some Regimen⟨ts⟩ of N York militia—on their march on the West side of the River.

I have directed General Putnam, in your name, to send forward with all dispatch to join you, the two Continental brigades & Warner's Militia brigade. This last is to serve 'till the latter end of this month. Your instructions did not comprehend any militia; but as there are certain accounts here that most of the troops from New York are gone to reinforce General Howe, and as so large a proportion of the Continental troops have been detained at Albany, I concluded you would not disapprove of a measure calculated to strengthen you, though but for a small time, and have ventured to adopt it, on that presumption. Being informed by General Putnam, that General Wynds,[7] with 700 Jersey militia were at Kings ferry,[8] with intention to cross to Peeks-Kill, I prevailed upon him to relinquish that idea & send off an immediate order for them to march towards Red-bank. It is possible however, unless your Excellency supports this order by an application from yourself, he may march his men home instead of to the place he has been directed to repair to. Neither Lee's Jackson's Regiments, nor the detachments belonging to General McDougall's division have yet marched. I have pressed their being sent, and an order has been dispatched for their instantly proceeding.

Col: Hughes[9] is pressing some Fresh horses, for me. The moment they are ready I shall recross the River in order to fall in with the troops on the other side, and make all the haste I can to Albany to get the three brigades there sent forward.

Will your Excellency permit me to observe, that I have some doubts under present circumstances and appearances of the propriety of leaving the regiments proposed to be left in this quarter? But if my doubts on this subject were stronger than they are I am forbid by the sense of Council from interfering in the matter.

I have the honor to be With the warmest esteem & respect Your Excelly. most Obedt serv.   A. Hamilton

General Poor's Brigade is just arrived here. They will proceed to join you with all expedition. So strongly am I impressed with the importance of endeavoring to crush Mr. Howe, that I am apt to think it would be adviseable to draw off all the Continental troops. Had this been determined on, General Warner's 1600 militia might have been left here.

ALS, Hamilton Papers, Library of Congress.

1. For background to this letter, see Washington to H, October 30, 1777.
2. Lieutenant Peter Hughes of Pennsylvania who had resigned as aide to Gates on January 1, 1777.
3. Brigadier General John Paterson, Continental Army.
4. Colonel Seth Warner of one of the Sixteen Additional Continental Regiments.
5. Brigadier General Enoch Poor, Continental Army.
6. Brigadier General Ebenezer Learned, Continental Army.
7. Brigadier General William Winds, New Jersey Militia.
8. Ferry between Stony Point and Verplancks Point.
9. Colonel Hugh Hughes, assistant quartermaster general.

From Marquis de Fleury

[*Fort Mifflin on Mud Island in the Delaware River*] *November 2–3, 1777.* Describes the erection of a battery on the British ship *Augusta*. Complains of his lack of authority at the fort.

Copy in writing of John Laurens, George Washington Papers, Library of Congress. This MS is entitled "Major Fleury's Journal and Letter to Colonel Hamilton." Fitzpatrick in his *Calendar of the Correspondence of George Washington with the Officers*, I, 455–56, states that H was the recipient of this letter. See also De Fleury to H, October 17–19, 26, and 28, 1777.

From Marquis de Fleury

[*Fort Mifflin on Mud Island in the Delaware River*] *November 4–8, 1777.* Acknowledges receipt of "His Excellencys order authorizing me to exercise the functions of Engineer at Fort Mifflin."

Copy in writing of John Laurens, George Washington Papers, Library of Congress. Fitzpatrick in his *Calendar of the Correspondence of George Washington with the Officers*, I, 460, states that H was the recipient of this letter. See also De Fleury to H, October 17–19, 26, and 28 and November 2–3, 1777.

To Major General Horatio Gates [1]

Albany, Novemr. 5th. 1777

Sir,

By inquiry, I have learned that General Patterson's brigade, which is the one you propose to send is, by far, the weakest of the three now here, and does not consist of more than about 600 rank and file fit for duty. It is true there is a militia regiment with it of about 200, but the term of service for which this regiment is engaged is so near expiring, that it would be past by the time the men could arrive at the place of their destination, and to send them would be to fatigue the men to no purpose. Under these circumstances, I cannot consider it either as compatible with the good of the service or my instructions from His Excellency General Washington, to consent, that that brigade be selected from the three, to go to him; but I am under the necessity of requiring, by virtue of my orders from him, that one of the others be substituted instead of this; either General Nixons or General Glover's, and that you will be pleased to give immediate orders for its embarkation.

Knowing that General Washington wished me to pay great deference to your judgment, I ventured so far to deviate, from the instructions he gave me as to consent, in compliance with your opinion that two brigades should remain here instead of one. At the same time permit me to observe that I am not myself sensible of the expediency of keeping more than one here, in conjunction with the detached regiments in the neighbourhood of this place; and that my ideas coincide with those of Gentlemen, whom I have consulted on the occasion, whose judgment I have more reliance upon than my own and who must be supposed to have a thorough knowlege of the circumstances, necessary to enter into the question. Their opinion is, that one brigade with the regiments before mentioned would amply answer the purposes of this post. When I preferred your opinion to other considerations, I did not imagine you would pitch upon a brigade little more than half as large as the others; and finding this to be the case I indispensibly owe it to my duty, to desire in His Excellency's name, that another brigade may go instead of the one intended. As it may be conducive to dispatch, that Genl. Glovers brigade should be the one; if agreeable to you; you will give directions accordingly.

I have the honor to be With real respect & esteem Sir Your most Obedt serv   Alex Hamilton ADC

If you think proper to order Glovers brigade and will be pleased to send your orders to me, I will have them immediately forwarded.

ALS, New-York Historical Society, New York City; ADf, Hamilton Papers, Library of Congress.
　1. For background to this letter, see Washington to H, October 30, 1777.

To Major General Israel Putnam

[*Albany, November 5–8, 1777.* On November 9, 1777, Hamilton wrote to Putnam: "I wrote to you from Albany." *Letter not found.*]

To George Washington [1]

Albany, November [6] [2] 1777

Dr Sir,

　I arrived here yesterday at Noon and waited upon General Gates immediately on the business of my mission; but was sorry to find his ideas did not correspond with yours for drawing off the number of troops you directed. I used every argument in my power to convince him of the propriety of the measure, but he was inflexible in the opinion that two Brigades at least of Continental troops should remain in and near this place. His reasons were, that the intelligence of Sir Harry Clinton's having gone to join Burgoigne was not sufficiently authenticated to put it out of doubt; That there was therefore a possibility of his returning up the River which might expose the finest arsenal in America (as he calls the one here) to destruction should this place be left so bare of troops as I proposed; And That the want of conveniences and the difficulty of the roads would make it impossible to remove the Artillery & stores here for a considerable time; That the New England States would be left open to the depredations & ravages of the enemy; That it would put it out of his power to entreprise any thing against Ticonderoga, which

ALS, Hamilton Papers, Library of Congress.
　1. For background to this letter, see Washington to H, October 30, 1777.
　2. Day of month not given in MS, but on November 6, 1777, Jonathan Trumbull, Jr., wrote to Jonathan Trumbull from Albany, "Yesterday arrived in town Colo Hamilton, Aid to Genl Washington" (*Collections of the Massachusetts Historical Society*, 7 ser., II [1902], 185). This corresponds to H's statement at beginning of this letter. This letter is dated in both *JCHW*, I, 41, and *HCLW*, IX, 106, as November, 1777.

he thinks might be done in the Winter, and which he considers it of importance to undertake.

The force of these reasons did by no means strike me, and I did everything ⟨in⟩ my power to show they were unsubstantial; but all I could effect was to have one Brigade dispatched in addition to those already march⟨ed⟩. I found myself infinitely embarrassed ⟨and⟩ was at a loss how to act. I felt the importance of strengthening you as much as possible, ⟨but⟩ on the other hand, I found insuperable inconviences in acting diametrically opposite ⟨to⟩ the opinion of a Gentleman, whose successes have raised him into the highest importance. General Gates has won the intire confidence of the Eastern States; if disposed to do it by addressing himself to the prejudices of the people he would find no difficulty to render a measure odious; which it might be said, with plausibility enough to be believed, was calculated to expose them to unnecessary danger, not withstanding their exertions during the campaign had given them the fullest title to repose and security. General Gates has influence and interest elsewhere; he might use it, if he pleased, to discredit the measure there also. On the whole it appeared to me dangerous to insist on sending more troops from hence while General Gates appeared so warmly opposed to it. Should any accident or inconvenience happen in consequence of it, there would be too fair a pretext for censure, and many people are too-well-disposed to lay hold of it. At any rate it might be considered as using him ill to take a step so contrary to his judgment in a case of this nature. These considerations and others which I shall be more explicit in when I have the pleasure of seeing you determined me not to insist upon sending either of the other brigades remaining here. I am afraid what I have done may not meet with your approbation as not being perhaps fully warranted by your instructions; but I ventured to do what I thought right, hoping that at least the goodness of my intention will excuse the error of my judgment.

I was induced to this relaxation the more readily, as I had directed to be sent on two thousand militia, which were not expected by you, and a thousand Continental troops out of those proposed to be left with General Putnam; which I have written to him since I found how matters were circumstanced here, to forward to you with all dispatch. I did this for several reasons; because your reinforcemt. would be more expeditious from that place than from this; because two thousand Continental troops at Peeks-Kill will not be wanted in its present circumstances; especially as it was really necessary to have a body of Continental troops at this place for the security of the valuable stores here, and I should not, if I had my wish, think it expedient to draw off more than two of the three brigades now here. This being the case, one of the ends you proposed to be answered by leaving the ten Regiments with General Putnam will be equally answered by the troops here; I mean that of covering and satisfying the Eastern states; and 1000 Continental troops, in addition to the militia collected and that may be collected there, will be sufficient in the Highlands for covering the Country down that way and carrying on the works necessary to be raised for the defence of the River.

The troops gone and going to reinforce you are near 5000 Rank & file Continental troops & 2500 Massachusettes and New Hampshire militia. These and the seven hundred Jersey militia will be a larger reinforcement than you expected, though not quite an equal number of Continental troops; nor exactly in the way directed. General Lincoln tells me the militia are very excellent; and though their times will be out by the last of this month, you will be able if you think proper to order the troops still remaining here to join you by the time their term of service expires.

I cannot forbear being uneasy, lest my conduct should prove displeasing to you; but I have done, what considering all circumstances, appeared to me most eligible and prudent.

I have the honor to be with   great esteem & respect   Your Excellencys   Most Obed Serv   Alex Hamilton

Vessels are preparing to carry the brigade to New Windsor, which will embark this evening. I shall this afternoon set out on my return to Camp, and, on my way, shall endeavor to hasten the troops forward.

To Major General Israel Putnam [1]

Head Quarters New Windsor [New York] Novr. 9th. 1777 [2]

Sir,

I cannot forbear Confessing that I am astonishd. and Alarm'd beyond measure, to find that all his Excellency's Views have been hitherto flustrated, and that no single step of those I mention'd to you has been taken to afford him the aid he absolutely stands in Need of, and by Delaying which the Cause of America is put to the Utmost conceivable Hazard.

I so fully explaind to you the Generals Situation, that I could not entertain a Doubt you would make it the first object of your Attention to Reinforce him with that speed the exigency of affairs demanded; but I am sorry to say, he will have too much Reason to think other Objects, in Comparison with that Insignificant, have been Uppermost. I speak freely, and emphatically, because I tremble at the Consequences of the Delay has hap[pe]ned. General Clintons Reinforcement is prob[ab]ly by this time with Mr. Howe; this will give him a Decicive superiority over our Army. What may be the Issue of such a state of things, I Leave to the feelings of every friend to his Country capable of foreseeing Consequences. My Expressions may prehaps have more Warmth than is altogether proper: But they proceed from the overflowing of my heart in a matter where I conceive this Continent essentially Interested. I wrote to you from Albany,[3] desired you would send a thousand Continental Troops of those first proposed to be left with you. This I Understand has not been done; how the Non Complyance can be answered to Genl. Washington you can best Determine.

I now Sir, in the most explicit terms, by his Excellency's Authority, give it as a positive Order from him, that all the Continental Troops under your Command may be Immediately marched to Kings Ferry, there to Cross the River and hasten to Reinforce the Army under him.

The Massachusetts Militia are to be detaind instead of them, untill the Troops coming from the Northward arrive. When they do, they will replace them, as far as I am Instructed the Troops you shall send away, in Consequence of this Requisition.

The Generals Idea of keeping troops this way does not extend farther than Covering the Country from any little uruptions of Small parties and carrying on the Works Necessary for the Security of the River. As to attacking New York, that he thinks ought to be out of the Question at Present. If men could be spared from the other Really Necessary Objects he would have no objections to attempting a divertion by way of New York, but nothing further.

As the times of the Massachusetts and New Hampshire Militia will soon expire, it will be proper to Call in time for a Reinforcement from Connecticut. Governor Clinton will do all in his power to promote objects, in which the state he Commands in is so Immediately Concernd.

General Glovers and Pattersons Brigades are on their way down. The Number of Continental Troops Necessary for this Post, will be furnished out of them.

I cannot but have the fullest Confidence, you will Use Your Utmost exertions to execute the Business of this Letter and am

with great Respect   Sir   Your Mos. Obt Servt   A Hamilton ADC

To Major Genl Putnam

Copy, George Washington Papers, Library of Congress. This letter was enclosed in Putnam to Washington, November 14, 1777.
1. For background to this letter, see Washington to H, October 30, 1777.
2. Lodge incorrectly dates this letter December 9, 1777 (*HCLW*, IX, 120).
3. Letter not found.

To George Washington [1]

New Windsor [New York] Novemr 10 ⟨1777⟩ [2]

Dear Sir,

I arrived here last night from Albany. Having given General Gates a little time to recollect himself I renewed my remonstrances on the necessity and propriety of sending you more than one Brigade of the three he had detained with him, and finally prevailed upon

ALS, Hamilton Papers, Library of Congress.
1. For background to this letter, see Washington to H, October 30, 1777.
2. All material within broken brackets has been taken from Hawks, *The Official and Other Papers of Alexander Hamilton*, 283-87.

him to give orders for Glover's in addition to Patterson's brigade to march this way. As it was thought conducive to expedition to send the troops by water, as far as it could be done, I procu⟨red⟩ all the vessels that could be had at Albany fit for the purpose; but could not get more than sufficient to take in Pattersons brigade. It was embar⟨ked⟩ the 7th instant and I expected would have been ⟨there⟩ before this; but the wind has been contrary, though they must in all probability be here to day. General Glover's brigade marched at the sa⟨me⟩ time on the East side of the river, the roads be⟨ing⟩ much better there, than on this side. I am ⟨at this⟩ moment informed, that one Sloop with a part ⟨of⟩ Patterson's is arrived and that the others are ⟨in⟩ sight. They will immediately proceed by wa⟨ter⟩ to Kings ferry and thence take the shortest ⟨route⟩ to you.

I am pained beyond expression ⟨to⟩ inform your Excellency that on my arrival ⟨here⟩ I find everything has been neglected and de-⟨ranged⟩ by General Putnam, and that the two brigades Poor's and Learned's still remained here and on the other side the River at Fish-Kill. Col: Warner's Militia, I am told, have been drawn to Peeks-Kill to aid in an expedition against New York which it seems is at this time the Hobby horse with General Putnam. Not the least atten-tion has been paid to my order in your name for a detachment of 1000 men from the toops hitherto stationed at this post. Every thing is sacrificed to the whim of taking New York.

The two Brigades of Poors & Learneds it appears would not march for want of money and necessaries, several of the Regts. having received no pay for 6 or 8 months past. There has been a high mutiny among the former on this account, in which a Capt. killed a man, and was shot himself by his comrade. These difficulties for want of proper management have stopped the troops from proceeding. Gov-ernor Clinton has been the only man, who has done any thing toward removing them; but for want of General Putnam's coopera-tion has not been able to effect it. He has only been able to prevail with Larned's brigade to agree to march to Goshen; in hopes by getting them once on the go, to get them to continue their march. On coming here, I immediately sent for Col: Bailey [3] who now com-mands Larned's Brigade, and have gotten him to engage for carrying the Brigade on to Head Quarters, as fast as possible. This he expects

3. Colonel John Bailey, Second Massachusetts Regiment.

to effect by means of 5 or 6000 Dollars which Governor Clinton was kind enough to borrow for me; and which Col: Bailey thinks will keep the men in good humour 'till they join you. They marched this morning toward Goshen.

I shall as soon as possible see General Poor and do every thing in my power to get him along. I hope I shall be able to succeed.

The plan I before laid having been totally deranged, a new one has become necessary. It is now too late to send Warne⟨r's⟩ militia. By the time they got to you their term of service would be out. The motive for sending them, which was to give you a speedy reinforcem⟨ent⟩, has by the past delay been superceded. By Governor Clinton's advice, I have sent an ⟨order⟩ in the most emphatical terms to General Putnam, immediately to dispatch all the Continental troops under him to your assistance; and to detain the militia instea⟨d⟩ of them. My opinion is that the only presen⟨t⟩ use for troops in this quarter is to protect the country from the depredations of little plunder⟨ing⟩ parties and for carrying on the works necess⟨ary⟩ for the defence of the River. Nothing more ought to be thought of. Tis only wasting time and misapplying men, to employ them in a farcical parade against New York; for in this it will undoubtedly terminate. (New York is no object if it could be taken; and to take it would require more men than could be spared from more substantial purposes.) Governor Clintons ideas coincide with mine. He thinks that there is no need of more Continental troops here than a few to give a spur to the militia in working upon the Fortifications. In persuance of this, I have given the directions before mentioned; if General Putnam attends to them, the troops under him may be with you nearly as early as any of the others (though he has unluckily marched them down to Tarry Town); and General Glover's brigade when it gets up will be more than sufficient to answer the true ends of this post.

If Your Excellency agrees with me in opinion it will be well to send instant directions to General Putnam to persue the objects I have mentioned; for I doubt whether he will attend to any thing I shall say, notwithstanding it comes in the shape of a positive order. I fear, unless you interpose the works here will go on so feebly for want of men, that they will not be completed in time; whereas it appears to me of the utmost importance it should be pushed with the utmost vigor. Governor Clinton will do every thing in his power. I wish Genera⟨l⟩ Putnam was recalled from the command of this post,[4] and Governor Clinton would accept it. The blunders and caprices of the form⟨er⟩ are endless.

Beleive me Sir nobody can be more impressed with the importance of forwarding the reinforcements coming to you with all speed, nor could any body have endeavoured more to promote it than I have done but the *ignorance* of some and the *design* of others have been almost insuperable obstacles. I am very unwell;[5] but I shall not spare myself to get things immediately in a proper train, and for that purpose intend, unless I receive other orders from you, to continue with the troops in the progress of their march. As soon as I get General Poor's brigade in march I shall proceed to General Putnam at Peeks Kill.

I have the honor to be   With much regard & respect   Yr. Excelly's   Most Obed serv   A Hamilton ADC

4. Although neither Major General Israel Putnam nor H were aware of the fact, Congress on November 5, 1777, had relieved Putnam of his command and ordered him to join the main Army under Washington at White Marsh, Pennsylvania.
5. On November 12, 1777, H wrote to Washington that he was suffering from "a fever and violent rheumatic pains throughout my body."

From Brigadier General Enoch Poor

[*Fishkill, New York, November 11, 1777.* On November 12, Hamilton wrote to Washington: "By a letter . . . of yesterday, General Poor informs me. . . ." *Letter not found.*]

To George Washington [1]

New Windsor [New York] November 12th 1777

Dear Sir,

I have been detained here these two days by a fever and violent rheumatic pains throughout my body. This has prevented my being active in person for promoting the purposes of my errand, but I have taken every other method in my power, in which Governor Clinton has obligingly given me all the aid he could. In answer to my pressing application to General Poor for the immediate marching of his brigade, I was told they were under an operation for the itch, which made it impossible for them to proceed till the effects of it were over. By a letter however of yesterday, General Poor informs me [2] he would certainly march this morning. I must do him the justice to say, he appears solicitous to join you; and that I beleive the past delay is not owing to any fault of his, but is wholly chargeable on General Putnam. Indeed Sir, I owe it to the service to say that every part of this Gentleman's conduct is marked with blunders and negligence, and gives general disgust.

Parson's brigade will join you I hope in five or six days from this. Larned's may do the same. Poors will, I am persuaded, make all the haste they can for the future, and Glovers may be expected at Fish Kill tonight, whence they will be pushed forward as fast as I can have any influence to make them go; but I am sorry to say, the disposition for marching in the officers and men in general of these troops, does not keep pace with my wishes or the exigency of the occasion. They have unfortunately imbibed an idea that they have done their part of the business of the campaign and are now intitled to repose. This and the want of pay make them averse to a long march at this advanced Season.

A letter from you to General Putnam of the 9th. fell just now into my hands.[3] As it might possibly contain something useful to me, I took the liberty of opening it and after reading it, immediately dispatched it to him. If he has paid any attention to my last letters to him, things will be in a right train for executing the order in yours; but whether he has or not is a matter of doubt. In a letter from him just now received by Governor Clinton, he appears to have been the 10th. Instant at Kings street, at the White-plains. I have had no answer to my last applications.

The enemy appear to have stripped New York very bare. The people there (that is the tories) are in a very great fright. This adds to my anxiety, that the reinforcements from this quarter to you, are not in greater forwardness and more considerable.

I have written to General Gates, informing him of the accounts of the situation of New York, with respect to troops, and the probability of the force gone to Howe being greater than was at first ex-

pected—to try if this will not *extort* from him a further reinforcement. I don't however expect much from him; as he pretends to
have in view an expedition against Ticonderoga, to be undertaken
in the Winter; and he knows, that under the sanction of this idea,
calculated to catch the Eastern people, he may without ⟨cen⟩sure [4]
retain the troops. And as I shall be ⟨under⟩ a necessity of speaking
plainly to Y⟨our⟩ ⟨Excellen⟩cy when I have the pleasure of seeing
⟨you,⟩ I shall not hesitate to say, I doubt whethe⟨r⟩ you would
have had a man from the Northern Ar⟨my⟩ if the whole could have
been kept at Albany, with any decency. Perhaps you will think me
blameable in not having exercised the powers you gave me, and
given a positive order. Perhaps I have been so; but deliberately
weighing all circumstances, I did not and do not think it advisable
to do it.

I have the honor to be   With Unfeigned esteem & regard   Yr.
Excellys.   Most Obed servt   A Hamilton

ALS, Hamilton Papers, Library of Congress.
    1. For background to this letter, see Washington to H, October 30, 1777.
    2. Letter not found.
    3. This letter is in the George Washington Papers, Library of Congress.
    4. Material within broken brackets in this paragraph is taken from *JCHW*,
I, 49.

To Major General Horatio Gates [1]

Fish Kill [New York] Novemr. 13. 177⟨7⟩

Sir,
    Since my arrival in this quarter, I have been endeavouring to col-
lect the best idea I could, of the state of things in New York in order
the better to form a judgment of the probable reinforcement gone
to General Howe. On the whole, these are facts well ascertained,
that New York has been stripped extremely bare; That in consequence of this the few troops left there and the inhabitants are under
so strong apprehensions of an attack as almost to amount to a *panic
dread;* That to supply the deficency of men, every effort is making
to excite the citizens to arms in defence of the city; And for this purpose, the public papers are full of addresses to them that speak plainly
the alarm prevailing on the occasion.
    I infer from hence, that a very formidable reinforcement is gone

to General Howe. The calculations made by those who have had the best opportunities of judging make the number from 6 to 7000. If so, the number gone and going to General Washington is far inferior —5000 at the utmost. The militia were all detained by General Putnam 'till it became too late to send them.

The state of things I gave you when I had the pleasure of seeing you was, to the best of my knowledge, sacredly true. I give you the present information, that you may decide whether any further succour can with propriety come from you.

The fleet with the troops on board sailed out of the Hook the 5th. Instant. This circumstance demonstrates beyond a possibility of doubt, that it is General Howe's fixed intention to endeavour to hold Philadelphia, at all hazards, and removes all danger of any further operations up the North River this winter: otherwise this movement at so advanced a season is altogether inexplicable.

If you can with propriety afford more aid, the most expeditious mode of conveying it will be to acquaint General Putnam of it that he may send on the troops with him to be replaced by them. You Sir best know the uses to which the troops with you are destined and will determine accordingly; I am certain, it is not His Excellency's wish to interrupt any plan you may have formed for the benefit of the service so far as it can possibly be avoided, consistent with a due attention to more important objects.

I am with Respect   Sir   Your most Obed serv

                                        Alex Hamilton ADC

ALS, New-York Historical Society, New York City; ADfS, Hamilton Papers, Library of Congress. The draft, which is dated November 12, 1777, varies in minor details from the receiver's copy. In both *JCHW*, I, 49, and *HCLW*, IX, 117, this letter is dated November 12, 1777.

1. For background to this letter, see Washington to H, October 30, 1777.

To George Washington [1]

Peeks Kill [New York] November 15. 1777
Mr. Kennedy's house [2]

Sir

I arrived at this place last night and unfortunately find myself unable to proceed any further. Imagining I had gotten the better of my complaints while confined at Governor Clinton's & anxious to be about, attending to the march of the troops, the day before yesterday I crossed the ferry in order to fall in with General Glover's brigade which was on its march from Poughkepsie to Fish Kill. I did not however see it myself but received a letter from Col. Shepherd,[3] who commands the Brigade informing me he would be last night at Fish Kill and this night at Kings Ferry. Waggons &c. are provided on the other side for his accomodation so that there need be no delay but what is voluntary, and I believe Col. Shepherd is as well disposed as could be wished ⟨to hasten⟩ [4] his march. General Poors Brigade crossed the ferry the day before yesterday. ⟨Two⟩ york regiments, Cortlands [5] & Livingstons,[6] are with them. They were unwilling to be separated from the Brigade and the Brigade from them. General Putnam was unwilling to keep them with him, and if he had consented to do it, the regiments to replace them would not ⟨join you⟩ six days as soon as these. The troops ⟨now⟩ remaining with General Putnam ⟨will amount⟩ to about the number you intended, though ⟨they⟩ are not exactly the same. He has ⟨detached⟩ Col. Charles Webbs [7] regiment to you. ⟨He⟩ *says* the troops with him are not in a ⟨condition⟩ to march being destitute of shoes, stockings ⟨and⟩ other necessaries; but I believe the true ⟨reasons⟩ of his being unwilling to persue the mo⟨de pointed⟩ out by you were his aversion to the Yor⟨k troops,⟩ and his desire to retain General Par⟨sons [8] with⟩ him.

I am with much respect ⟨and esteem⟩   Yr. Excellys.   Most Obed. servt.   A Hamilton

ALS, Hamilton Papers, Library of Congress.
    1. For background to this letter, see Washington to H, October 30, 1777.
    2. This was the home of Dennis Kennedy. "The Kennedy House, now known as the Mackey House, is still standing. It is a large, barn-like structure on the north side of the King's Ferry Road between Montrose and Verplanck's" (Emma L. Patterson, *Peekskill in the American Revolution* [Peekskill, 1944], 77).
    3. Colonel William Shepard, Fourth Massachusetts Regiment. Letter not found.
    4. All material within broken brackets is taken from *JCHW*, I, 51.
    5. Colonel Philip Van Cortlandt, Second New York Regiment.
    6. Colonel Henry Beekman Livingston, Fourth New York Regiment.
    7. Colonel Charles Webb, Second Connecticut Regiment.
    8. Brigadier General Samuel Holden Parsons, Continental Army.

From George Washington [1]

Head Quarters [Whitemarsh, Pennsylvania] 15th. Novemr. 1777

Dear Sir

I have duly received your several favours from the time you left me to that of the 12th. inst. I approve intirely of all the Steps you have taken, and have only to wish that the exertions of those you have had to deal with had kept pace with your Zeal and good intentions. I hope your health will before this have permitted you to push on the Rear of the whole reinforcement beyond New Windsor. Some of the Enemy's Ships have arrived in the Delaware, but how many have Troops on board I cannot exactly ascertain. The Enemy have lately damaged Fort Mifflin considerably, but our people keep possession and seem determined to do so to the last extremity. Our loss in Men has been but small. Capt Treat [2] is unfortunately among the killed.

I wish you a safe return and am   Dear Sir   Your most obt Servt.
Go. Washington

LS, in the writing of Tench Tilghman, Hamilton Papers, Library of Congress.
1. For background of this letter, see Washington to H, October 30, 1777.
2. Captain-Lieutenant Samuel Treat, Second Continental Artillery, who was killed on November 15, 1777.

From Hugh Knox [1]

St Croix Decr. 10th. 1777

Dear Hamilton

The fine, impartial, laconic & highly descriptive account you favour'd me with of the last Years Campain, in your letter of March last,[2] excited in me, & many of your other friends here, an earnest desire of farther accounts from your pen of the succeeding fortunes of the Great American War; A War which will, one day,

ALS, Hamilton Papers, Library of Congress.
1. This letter was enclosed in a letter which Cornelius Durant, a St. Croix merchant, wrote to H on March 27, 1778.
2. Letter not found.

shine more illustriously in the historic page, than any which has happened since the times of Nimrod & the Giants. And deservedly, on account of the Goodness of the Cause, the grandeur of the Object, the eclat of the Generals, the bravery of the troops & (alas! that I should be obliged to add) of the cruelty & ferocity which has marked the route of yr. Enemies, & the tons of brother's blood which have been shed on the unhappy Occasion!

I wrote two Answers[3] to your Obliging letter, both of which, I hope, have reached you, & in both of which I have urged it upon you to make & Collect such memoires, as the Urgency of your affairs will permit you, which may furnish Materials for an Accurate history of the War, when you ⟨shall⟩[4] have leisure to fill up & Embellish Such a Skeleton, with ⟨all⟩ that eligance & dignity of which your fine pen is Capable. The Honourable post you hold under the Great Gen: Washington & so near his person, will give you a peculiar advantage for delineating his Character, both in his Amiable private Virtues & military abilities. And depend upon it the Very Minutiæ of that incomparable man Will be read with Avidity by posterity. You know me too well, I hope, to Suspect me of Superstition. Yet I feel myself, at times, under a strong Impulse, to *prophesy* that *Washington* was born for the Deliverance of America; that that Providence who has raised & trained him up for that Very purpose will watch over his *Sacred* life with a paternal & solicitious Care, will Shield his head in every Day of Battle, *Will Guide* him to See America *free, flourishing* & *happy*, and *Will* Adorn his fame, among latest posterity, with a Garland of Laurel more Verdant, blooming & enviable, than ever adorn'd the brow of A *Marlborough!*

The Bearer of this line (if he shall be indeed so fortunate as to put it into your Hand) is our worthy friend Mr. Cornelius Durant, who is possessed of an ardent desire of having the Honour of a Short Interview With General Washington, principally, that he may have it to say that he has seen & Spoken to *the Greatest Man of this Age;* &, indeed, Considering Mr. Durant's Personal Worth, his uncommon Zeal for & attachment to the American Cause, the losses he has Sustain'd in attempting to assist her, & his extraordinary Admiration

---

3. Perhaps one of the missing letters is Knox to H, April 31, 1777.
4. Material within broken brackets is taken from Hawks, *The Official and Other Papers of Alexander Hamilton,* 294–97.

of & love to the General's Character & person, few men more richly merit this Indulgence. If you Still exist, & exist near the General's person (And I have not Yet Seen your Name Among the lists of the Slain, or the disgraced!), you can easily procure him this Honour. And I trust you will.

We are now blessed with, & Certified of the Glorious News of Burgoine's Surrender to the *Immortal Gates;* another bright Star in the Constellation of American Heroes. And we are momently Expecting to hear that Gen: Washington has done Something like the Same by Gen: Howe!—but we Yet tremble in Suspence; & it is indeed a *painful one.* Probably before this letter goes, we shall hear more of the matter. Our general accts. are favourable; and while the Cheveaux de fries are defended, who have no fears about Philada. May this campain decide the matter!

By the time this reaches you, you will be (if you are at all) ⟨in wi⟩nter Quarters, & perhaps may be at leisure to write me a ⟨ha⟩lf-folio, of which Mr. Durant will take Care to write ⟨me⟩ duplicates or triplicates for fear of miscarriage.

A Piece of mine, Intitled "An Address to America, by a friend in a foreign Government," [5] has been sent to the Congress, for publicatn. (if approv'd). I know not yet its fate. It is at least an honestly designed & animating piece, but written incorrectly & in a hurry. If you have seen it, pray give me your sentiments about it. But let it be on a loose paper inclosed in your letter, for the Knowledge of my being the Author must be a profound Secret here.

My Wishes Are that the God of Armies may defend & protect You, & Cause You happily to survive, & to hand down to posterity, the present important Scenes. Numbers here esteem you & would join me in declaring themselves, as I do,   Dear Hamilton,   Your ever Affectionate friend   & Servt.   Hugh Knox

5. There is no record of this pamphlet in Charles Evans, *American Bibliography* (New York, 1910–1934), or Joseph Sabin, *Bibliotheca Americana* (New York, 1868–1936).

To George Clinton

Peekskill, [New York] Decr. 22d. 1777

Dear Sir,

During my stay in this place, I have received intimations that certain officers high in command in this quarter have been guilty of practices, equally unjust, disgraceful to the Army, and injurious to the common cause; I mean seizing the property of the inhabitants of this State, and converting it to their own use, without any compensation either to the right owners, or to the State. A particular instance, among others, I have heard mentioned is, that at the time of some incursion of the enemy this way, a great number of cattle belonging to the inhabitants were driven off—sold at a kind of mock auction by order of a general officer—sent into Connecticut, and no kind of account rendered of the proceeds. Such enormities, if real, are evidently of the most mischievous tendency; a timely stop ought by all means to be put to them, and the perpetrators brought to an exemplary punishment. When I heard of them, I determined to make a careful scrutiny into the matter, in order to furnish myself with proper materials to lay before General Washington, as a foundation for an inquiry into it. But my slow recovery [1] and my impatience to get home will not allow me leisure nor opportunity to pursue my intention, and gain the necessary information. My feelings however, on the occasion, induced me to mention the matter to you, and to take the liberty to suggest, that in my opinion, every consideration makes it well worth while to have facts ascertained, and if they are found to be such as I am told, to prosecute those who are guilty. I know General Washington, if proper representations came before him, would take effectual measures to show his abhorrence of such iniquitous conduct.

Thank God! I am now so far recovered that I promise myself, if the weather is good, to begin my journey to Head Quarters tomorrow.

Accept my respectful acknowledgments for the interest you took in the restoration of my health, and in the safety of my person during my illness; and believe me to be with real regard and esteem, Yr. Excell'y's most obedt. Servant,   A. Hamilton

Capt. Gibbs [2] desires me to offer his respectful compliments.

Transcript, Sparks Transcripts, Harvard College Library.

1. When H had visited Governor George Clinton at the latter's home for two or three days earlier in the month, Clinton asked Doctor John Jones to attend H. But Jones was also ill, and H had no doctor. For the best account of H's illness see Mitchell, *Hamilton*, I, 140.

2. Captain Caleb Gibbs, one of Washington's aides-de-camp and a commander of a company of Washington's Guards, accompanied H on this trip.

From George Clinton

[*December 22–23, 1777.* On December 28 Clinton wrote to Hamilton: "I was favoured with the Receipt of your Letter of the 22d Instant some Days since and returned a short Answer to it by the Express who brought it." *Letter not found.*]

From Edward Stevens

Edinburgh Decem: 23rd. 1777

My Dear Hamilton

Tho' I have written you so repeatedly since my Arrival in Scotland, without having ever received an Answer, and 'tho' I am, at present, uncertain whether you have escaped those Dangers, to which you have been so long exposed in Defence of the glorious Cause in wh: you are engaged; yet so anxious am I to hear Something concerning you, and to convince you that I still retain the most sincere and disinterested Friendship for you, that I have determined to hazard this Letter at least, by the Way of France, the only possible mode of Conveyance to the continental Army, which the *present State* of Affairs allows of. If you have ever had any Reason, my dear Hamilton, to beleive the Sincerity of my Friendship, you may readily conceive the disagreeable Sensations I felt at my Departure from New York,[1] and those which I still continue to experience from the anxious and uncertain State in which I remain concerning my Friends in that Part of the World. Why have you not written me a single Line since our Separation? Has your Anxiety for publick Affairs entirely eradicated from your Mind all remembrance of your private Concerns? Or have you forgotten those Vo⟨ws⟩ of eternal Friendship, which we have so often mutually exchanged? I am perfectly at a Loss I assure you, my Dr: Hamilton, to account for your Silence. I have written you frequently, and, as I know that you was at a Distance from New York, enclosed your Letters to some of our common Friends in that City, and requested them to transmit them to you. But I have not been able to collect the least Intelligence concerning you from any Quarter, untill very lately your Friend Dr: Knox informed me, that he had heard from you, that you was perfectly well, and that you had been exalted to the Rank of Col: and Aid de Camp to general Washington. You may be certain I received these Accounts with the most unfeigned Pleasure, especially as I was perfectly convinced that they were the Rewards of essential Services. Write me my Dear Hamilton by the first opportunity, and direct to me at this University. I was lately honoured with the Degree of M.D.,[2] and hope soon to have the Pleasure of seeing you, as I shall take the first opportunity that offers, let the Consequence be what it will. I congratulate you my Dr: Friend on the late Successes of the united States against their tyrannical adversaries. I never read any Thing that gave me more Pleasure, than the accounts, which have been lately published concerning the Capitulation of Gen: Burgoyne. Why did you grant *the Puffer, the Boaster, the Savage* (⟨as⟩ his Proclamation proves him to be) such favorable Terms? I am glad you have humbled his Pride, and with his, *that* of his Directors, Advocates and Abettors. The Inhabitants of great Britain begin to despond ⟨and if⟩ the provincial Forces are but strenuous in their ⟨oppo⟩sition, they have nothing now to fear. The ⟨time is ap⟩proaching, when I hope to see America ⟨one of the⟩ most flourishing Republics in the World. ⟨Nothing can⟩ now prevent it from being so, but the volun⟨tary submis⟩sion of its Inhabitants, which Pray God avert. Excuse this hasty, wild Scrawl, as I have been obliged to write in the utmost Hurry, and beleive me to be

My Dr. Ham   *Yours inviolably*

AL, Hamilton Papers, Library of Congress.

1. Stevens received his bachelor's degree from King's College in 1774 and began his medical studies at the University of Edinburgh in 1775.

2. Stevens had received his degree in medicine on September 12, 1777, with the thesis "*De alimentorum concoctine.*"

From George Clinton

Poughkeepsie [New York] 28th. Decr. 1777.

Dear Sir,

I was favoured with the Receipt of your Letter of the 22d Instant some Days since and returned a short Answer to it by the Express who brought it; but as I have Reason to believe you had left Peeks' Kill before he got there I conclude my Letter has not been received.[1] I have not a Doubt but that there have been such unjust and dishonorable Practices committed on the Inhabitants as you mention nor have I Reason to believe they were without the Knowledge of the Commanding Officer of the Department. Complaints have been exhibited to him of Cattle the property of the Inhabitants of this State living near Colo Robinsons [2] being drove off by Parties of the Continental Troops and sold at Vendue in New England without any Account being rendered to the Proprietors. And if I am rightly informed an Officer with a Party took sundry Articles from Robinsons, sent them off & sold them in like Manner in Connecticut & has not accounted with the State for the Proceeds of this. I informed Genl Putnam and desired that an Inquiry might be made into the Conduct of the Officer commanding the Party to which I was more particularly induced as I found he had given an Order on the Quarter Master General for the Payment of the Teams employed in carrying off those effects: but I have Reason to believe he has paid no Regard to my Request. Of this I am fully convinced that the Soldiery claim as lawful Prize every Thing they take within the Enemy's Lines tho the Property of our best Friends, and whatever is taken beyond our Advanced Posts by a generous Construction comes within the above Predicament. On this Principle the several Articles taken at & near Robinsons were sold because the Enemy's Shipping were then in the River near that Place and on the same Principle indiscriminate Plunder might have taken Place on both Sides of the River as high up as the Manor of Livingston. Little good can be expected of an Army whose Interest it is to suffer a Country to be abandoned to the Enemy thereby to Justify Plundering the Inhabitants. Perhaps, & I dont know that it woud be uncharitable to suppose, that it is this Trade that makes People so very fond of little Expeditions.

I have long thought to ascertain these Facts and seek redress not only for the Parties immediately injured but the public; but my Time has been so fully imployed of late about ⟨other matters that I have been obliged⟩ to neglect it. I am now ⟨however determined to set about⟩ it & wish therefore to ⟨have the particular instructions you⟩ allude to. I mean the ⟨– – – – –⟩ Circumstances as far as ⟨– – – –⟩ as this may afford me ⟨– – – – –⟩ full discovery. I won⟨– – – – –⟩ pretend to justify ⟨– – – – –⟩ of last Winter ⟨– – – – –⟩ be considered Plunder ⟨– – – – –⟩

I am ⟨– – – – –⟩ your Health as to be able ⟨– – – – –⟩ you my Dr Sir to be ⟨– – – – –⟩ yourself ⟨too soon you should occasion⟩ in ⟨all⟩ probability ⟨would prove⟩ fatal. May I expect a Line from you whenever you have Liesure; be assured it will always be most kindly received ⟨though⟩ perhaps not quite so punctually answered by Your   Most Obed Servt   G W Clinton

My Respects to Capt Gibbs & young Livingston

ALS, Hamilton Papers, Library of Congress.
    1. Letter not found.
    2. Beverley Robinson, colonel of the Loyal (i.e., Tory) American Regiment raised in New York. His house, situated two miles south of West Point on the east bank of the Hudson River, was confiscated early in the war and was used as headquarters by the American generals who successively commanded in the Highlands. Both Robinson and his house figured prominently in Major General Benedict Arnold's treason.

Pay Book of the State Company of Artillery [1]

[1777] [2]

The Continent of Europe is 2600 miles long and 2800 miles broad.[3]
The Dutch in the Greenland fishery have from 150 to 200 sail and ten thousand seamen.

It is ordered that in their public prayers they pray that it would please God to bless the government, the Lords, the states, and their great & small fisheries.[4]

The Dutch were computed by Sir Walter Raleigh to have 3000 ships & fifty thousand seamen employed in the herring fishery; 8000 [5] more ships & 150.000 seamen more in exporting and vending—the province of Holland in the whole having 20.000 ships.[6]

Glass is a compound of sand or stone and vegetable salts—100 ld [7] of sand will produce 150 ld of glass. The kind of sand or stone is of that species called tarso—the white, chrystalline and flinty. The salt

AD, Hamilton Papers, Library of Congress.

1. The title page of this document reads: "New York—August 31th—1776—Pay Book of the State Company of Artillery Commanded By Alexr. Hamilton."
The "Pay Book" is divided into three sections. The first section consists of the accounts of H's company of artillery; the second section contains his notes on a wide variety of subjects; and the third section is composed of a few pages of weekly returns of the artillery company. The second section, which contains H's notes, has been printed in its entirety.

2. The date 1777 is assigned on the assumption that H's notes were written after the accounts in the "Pay Book" were closed. The last date on which entries were made was May 23, 1777. H probably did not begin to use the blank pages for his notes until after that date.

3. Almost all the material for the first part of H's notes in the "Pay Book" was taken from Malachy Postlethwayt, *The Universal Dictionary of Trade and Commerce*. For full title see "The Farmer Refuted," February 23, 1775, note 35.

H either paraphrased Postlethwayt or quoted him without bothering to use quotation marks. The first sentence in the "Pay Book," for example, was taken from Postlethwayt, "Europe," *Universal Dictionary*, I, 737. The location of other material taken by H from Postlethwayt is indicated in subsequent notes. Unless otherwise indicated, each note citing Postlethwayt refers to all the material in the "Pay Book" between that note and the preceding note.

4. Postlethwayt, "Fisheries," *Universal Dictionary*, I, 783.

5. "9,000," according to Postlethwayt.

6. Sir Walter Raleigh's computation was made in 1618. Postlethwayt, "Fisheries," *Universal Dictionary*, I, 783-84.

7. Pounds.

is produced from a sea weed called Kali, or for want of this from wormwood, woad, alga, common thistle, bramble, hops, and the whole leguminous tribe.

The proportion for chrystal glass is 200 pounds of tarso to 130 of salt.

These are put into an oven or reverbatory furnance and calcined for five hours when it becomes frit.

The frit is put into melting pots with a kind of blackish stone called Manganese to render it more clear and azure.[8]

ASIA MINOR

Pamphylia produces a great number of goats whose hair make excellent camblets.[9]

Greece is a fertile Country now divided into Macedonia, Albania, Epirus, Thessaly and Achaia. Macedonia has rich mines of gold.

Achaia produces rice cotton tobacco.

Greece in general has plenty of corn wine and oil. Several parts produce silk—its wool is coarse and bad.

Salonica or Thessalonica [10] is one of the principal cities and best ports in Greece; it has near 300.000 people. Constantinople is near it.[11]

Smyrna, the most considerable town in Asia Minor, has one of the best ports in the Levant and the greatest trade of this part of the Turkish dominions.

The River Pactolus remarkable for its golden sands runs through Lydia in Asia minor.

The country about Tocat produces a great variety of excellent plants and particularly some Fossilia, or subterraneous vegetations of surprising beauty. They are something like our flints, inclosed in matrices, which when broken display some of the finest chrystalliza-tions that can be imagined.

The High Chain of Mountains in Capadocia called Antitaurus have mines of silver copper iron allum &c.

8. Postlethwayt, "Glass," *Universal Dictionary*, I, 896–97.
9. Postlethwayt, "Anatolia," *Universal Dictionary*, I, 60.
10. In MS, "Salonichi or Thessalonicha."
11. All material on Greece taken from Postlethwayt, "Greece," *Universal Dictionary*, I, 914–15.

There is a great deal of saffron and fine marble in several parts of Asia Minor.[12]

Postlethwait

BRITAIN

Lies Between 50 & 59 d[egrees] N L. Long from 5 to 600 Miles. Greatest breadth 300.

Chief productions of England:

Corn	Cheese	Rock salt	Fullers earth
Timber	Hides	Alum	Pipe &
Cattle	Beer & Malt	Copperas	Potters clay
Horses	Spirits	Lapis Calaminary	
Sheep	Cyder	Stones of divers sorts	
flax	Tin	for building paving &c.	
wool	Copper	Slate	
Salt	Lead	Oker	
Tallow	Iron		
butter			

Manufactures of Woll Hair & Cotton
{
Cloth of several sorts
Serges perpets says shallons
Stuffs of various kinds
Bays flannels dimities fustians
Camblets mohairs grograms &c
Blankets, rugs carpets
}

Manufacturers of Silk
{
Lace
Velvets
Brocades
Sattins
Taffeties
Damasks
Lutestrings
Mantuas
Sarsenets
}

12. Postlethwayt, "Anatolia," *Universal Dictionary*, I, 59–60.

Manufacturers of Flax & Hemp
- Linnens [13] of various sorts
- Lace [14]
- Thread
- Cordage
- Paper

Manufacturers of Timber
- Ships & vessels of all sorts
- Casks of all kinds

Manufacturers of Metal
- Artillery
- cannon, Mortars
- Bullets boms &c.
- Coin & wrought plate — Gold, Silver, copper
- Bells of all sizes of mixed metals
- Coppers
- Caldrons
- Furnaces
- Statues of Brass or lead
- Ballustres or Pallisadoes
  - Pipes & Vessels for culinary and other domestic uses of Iron, brass Copper Pewter lead silver
- Edged tools
- Engines
- Weapons
- Armour of all sorts
  - Iron, Brass, Steel — Wire — Gold, Silver, Copper, Iron, Brass, Steel

Manufacturers of Skins & Hair of beasts
- Parchment
- vellum
- Leather of which are made furs for Cloathing
- Hats & Caps Shoes & Boots
- Saddles harness & furniture for horses
- Gloves & garments coaches & chairs. Houshold stuffs Covers of books

13. In MS, "Linnerns."
14. In MS, "Lacie."

Products & Manufactures of Scotland & Ireland much the same except for timber plaiding & striped muslins peculiar to the former.

The Coal trade an immense trade; employs near 1500 sail of shipping & seamen in proportion, besides watermen lightermen &c. You may see 600 Colliers before the city of London at a time.

Another Branch of the coastry trade: Tin from Cornwall, rock salt from Lancashire, Cheese & Lead from Cheshire, culm from Swansey in Ways.[15] The whole employs 300 sail Ships. These and several other branches of coasting trade for corn, fish, copper, glass &c. are computed to employ 100.000 persons.

The Hard ware manufactures Birmingham & Sheffield.[16] The latter employs 40.000 people.

The woolen manufactors employs a milion of people. The consumption at home amounts to a million Sterling ℔ yr.

Their fisheries a large branch—consist of herrings, Pilchards, mackarel, oysters, lobsters—Salmon taken on the severn.

Scotland produces grain which it sends partly to Spain, Holland, Norway. Fir trees of an immense size. A great number of black Cattle. Wool which goes Chiefly to England.

A fine manufacture of worsted stockings at Aberdeen. Large linnen manufactures & fine fisheries in Scotland.

Scotland has a fine salt manufacture & exports great quantities annually to Germany, Norway & the Baltic.

Irland is chiefly a country of Grazing though they have also a good deal of corn. They have a great many quarries of fine stone slate marble; and sea coal but their principal fuel is turf. They have some glass works the sand for which comes from England.

Their exports consist in cattle, hides, furs, tallow, butter, cheese, honey, wax, salt, hemp, linnen Cloth, timber, pipe staves, wool, and woolen Cloth, coarse rugs, and shag mantles, freezes, ratteens,[17] camblets, salmon, herring &c—some lead tin and iron.

The Irish have immense quantities of Excellent Wool. They sheer their sheep twice a year. The Irish from the restraint on their manu-

15. "From Swanzey to Wales," in Postlethwayt, "Britain," *Universal Dictionary*, I, 346.

16. Postlethwayt states, "The manufactures of hard-ware are carried on principally at Birmingham in Warwickshire, and at Sheffield in Yorkshire" (*Universal Dictionary*, I, 346).

17. In MS, "rateens."

factures clandestinely export great quantities of unwrought wool to France.

They trade a great deal with Flanders and the low countries especially for butter tallow & leather.

They carry on a great trade for beef with France.

They have a large herring fishery which they send to Spain & Portugal.

The Ballance of Trade with the Portuguese not so considerable in favour of the English as is imagined. Trade with Spain declined latterly by the interference with the French. No large ballance in favour of England.[18]

The Ballance with Italy against England.

Trade with Turkey rather advantageous in the light of giving rise to new manufactury by the raw silk imported thence.

Among other articles exported to Germany are *tobacco, ginger, Sugar*. Hamburgh and Germany has a ballance against England. They furnish her with large quantities of linnen.

In the trade with Holland a considerable ballance in favour of England.

Trade with France greatly against England.

The Trade with Flanders in favour of England.

A large ballance in favour of Norway & Denmark.

Ballance in favour of Sweden.

Great Ballance in favour of Russia.

Indian trade very advantageous upon the whole. A vast quantity of raw silk brought from thence.[19]

18. Postlethwayt wrote: "Formerly a great ballance from them in bullion; but, since the house of *Bourbon* has filled the *Spanish* throne, and introduced French stuffs and *French* fashions, we have very great reason to believe the ballance is but very small in our favour." ("Britain," *Universal Dictionary*, I, 350).

19. All material on Britain taken from Postlethwayt, "Britain," *Universal Dictionary*, I, 344–59.

RATE OF EXCHANGE
WITH THE SEVERAL NATIONS IN 52 [20]

To Venice for a ducat [21] 51*d* ¾.   Par 49*d*. .492. ⟨*dec.*⟩ [22]

                                            Loss   4½ ⑭ Ct.

Leghorn for a dollar   50 ⟨*d.*⟩   do. 51 ⟨*d.*⟩.69 ⟨*dec.*⟩

                                            Gain   1⅔ ⑭ Cent

Genoa in favour of England not mentioned.

Lisbon for a milree   5/5 ⅞.   Par 67*d*.166 ⟨*dec.*⟩.

                                    Gain not 2 ⑭ Cent

To Antwerp a £ Stg.   for 36/.5.⟨*d.*⟩   Par 35/. 17 ⟨*dec.*⟩.

                                    Gain   3⅜ ⑭ Cent

Amsterdam do.   for 35[*s*].4.2⟨*d.*⟩ Par 36/ 59 ⟨*dec.*⟩

                                    Loss   3½ ⑭ Cent

Hamburgh do.   for 33[*s*].5.⟨*d.*⟩ Par 35/. 17 ⟨*dec.*⟩

                                    Loss   5   ⑭ Cent

Exchanges with Norway Sweden, Russia & most parts of Germany are carried on through Amsterdam & Hamburgh at an equal disadvantage.

To Madrid for a piece 8/8 [23] 40 ⟨*d*⟩ ⅜. Par 43⟨*d.*⟩ 2 ⟨*dec.*⟩

                                    Gain above 6½ ⑭ Cent

To Paris for the Crown of three livres 31*d* ⁷⁄₁₆ Par 29*d*.149 ⟨*dec.*⟩

                                    Loss above 7⅛ ⑭ Cent

Postlethwaite supposes the quantity of Cash necessary to carry on the circulation in a state one third of the rents to the land proprietors for ⅑ the whole Product of the lands. See the articles Cash & Circulation.[24]

20. These rates of exchange, also taken from Postlethwayt's discussion of Britain, were designed to show "that many branches of our foreign trade are now carried on to the disadvantage of the nation, which a few years since were greatly for its benefit, is certain from the courses of exchange." Postlethwayt's information was taken from Lloyd's List of April 21, 1752, and Sir Isaac Newton's Tables (*Universal Dictionary*, I, 352).

21. I.e., "London gave to Venice for the ducat banco. . . ." The phrase "London gave to" is implied before each of the places which H lists.

22. All material within broken brackets in table appears in Postlethwayt, but was not copied by H.

23. A piece of eight.

24. Postlethwayt, "Cash," *Universal Dictionary*, I, 464.

FRANCE

Has an immense inland commerce carried on principally by rivers the chief of which are the Seine, the Loire, the Soane, the Rhone and the Garonne. There are five rivers [that] empty into the Seine not far from Paris and near eighty large cities that have a direct commerce with it by water. Tis supposed to contain near a million of inhabitants and the villages in the neighbourhood half a million more.

Lyons—situated at the confluence of the Soane & Rhone—the second city of France—is to the Southern provinces what Parris is to the Northern. It drives an immense inland commerce chiefly by water communications. By means of the Rhone it communicates with Geneva and All switserland and hence by the River Aar with the Rhine and several parts of Germany. By the Durance a large River but rapid it trades through piedmont with italy and brings home the productions of that Country. It is supposed to contain 200.000 people.

Marseilles in the Mediterranean is one of the principal sea ports of France.

Toulon is the best Harbour of France it has immense naval Magazines and arsenals a very large foundery for cannon. At the time it was besieged by the confederates in 1707, it had fifty four French ships of the line from 1st to fourth rates in the harbour.

Lewis the fourteenth was fifteen years with vast labour and expence uniting the Calabrian with the Mediterranean sea by a canal.

The French have a considerable smuggling trade of wool from England by way of Bologne, at the entrance of the Soane from whence passing to Amiens and Rouen it gives rise to flourishing woollen manufactures in imitation of those of England.

Marigolante produces cinnamon trees.

St Domingo (belonging to F[rance] & S[pain]) is 400 miles long and 120 broad—400 leagues in circumference. It is the largest of the Antilles. It has large forests of palms, elms, oaks, pines, juniper, caramite, acajou—great abundance of cattle and horses—well watered with navigable rivers full of fish—and the coast has a great number of crocodiles and tortoises. Its commodities are hides, sugar, rum, indigo, cotton, cocoa, coffee, ginger, tobacco, salt wax, hon[e]y ambergrease and various kinds of drugs and dying woods. It has mines of gold silver and copper not now cultivated.

In 1690 France had a fleet in the port of Brest superior to the united naval force of England & Holland.

At a certain period the French navy consisted of 115 sail of the line from 1st to fourth rates and 24 frigates &c. the whole having 7.080 ps. of Cannon—20618 sailors and 10904 marines.

Lewis the 14th. in June 1700 established the Council of Commerce consisting of some of the principal officers of state and twelve merchants chosen & paid by the principal trading towns, to represent all things relative to trade and manufactures and propose regulations &c. Infinite good has resulted to France from this institution. The salaries are about 400 £ Stg ₩ annum.[25]

AUSTRIA

Produces corn, wine, iron, steel, salt, parts of it fruit, cattle, horses. Great quantity of saffron.

It has a port in the Adriatic sea called Trieste with a good harbour; the chief export is iron and some salt. A good deal of wine is raised in the neighbourhood.

At Tirol there are mines of Iron silver and copper which produce a good revenue to government. Schwatz is noted for mines of silver. Halle the second city of Tyrol is famous for the produce of Salt. 40 years before Post[lethwayt,] according to Addison, it made 3,200.00 weight and gave a revenue to the Emperor of 200.000 crowns. A great quantity of Specie is coined here.

At Roveredo is a considerable manufacture of silk.[26]

THE NETHERLANDS

Have valuable woolen manufactures but their chief manufactures are lace, cambricks, lawns and linnen. They have valuable manufactures of silk as well in the Austrian as in the French Netherlands.

Bruges (part of Aust[rian] N[etherlands]) has the most foreign trade of any town in Flanders. It sits about eight Miles from Ostend. The Emperor attempted here at the instance of some English

25. Postlethwayt, "France," *Universal Dictionary*, I, 808–38.
26. Postlethwayt, "Austria," *Universal Dictionary*, I, 157–61,

Merchants to establish an East India Company which appeared to be in a thriving way. He made an alliance with Spain to support his project; but a counter alliance being formed between France, England, Prussian Holland and Hanover which at length obliged him to renounce it.

The Austrian Netherlands export annually in fine thread, bone, lace, linnen, lawns, and Cambrick to amounts of near two millions Sterling besides which the[y] export considerable quantitys of tapistry, woolen stuff, cotton, silk &c.[27]

The Kingdom of Bohemia is divided into Three parts—Bohemia proper, Silesia and Moravia. It is bounded by Austria, Brandenburgh & Lusatia, Bavaria, Saxony and Poland. Its revenues are computed at 12 or 14.00.000 £ one year with another. It has the best mines in Europe both for gold and precious stones besides its mines of silver copper tin, iron lead, sulphur and nitre. The precious stones are carbuncles, emeralds, amethysts, jasper, sapphire and some others. They make salt and alum in abundance. The soils produces a great deal of saffron. They have plenty of horses and Cattle, a great deal of beer but little wine. Prague is the principal city of Bohemia, the principal part of the commerce of which is carried on by the Jews. Carelsbadt another town is famous for baths and medicinal waters. It has a good many manufactures in iron.[28]

Hungary [is] in longitude 16 to 23 latitude [29] 45 to 49 North; bounded by the Carpathian mountains, which divide it from Poland on the North, by Transylvania and Wallachia on the East, by the River Drave which separtes it from Sclavonia on the South, and by Austria and Moravia on the West.

It possesses a very fruitful soil great abundance of horses and Cattle —corn six times as cheap as in England. It is rich in mines of gold silver and all other metals except tin. Produces a plenty of excellent wines particularly the celebrated Tockay. In some places are found even diamonds and other precious stones. It has great plenty of white red and black marble and some fine porphyry. It has a good breed of buffaloes which are made use of in husbandry. The peasants in tilling the ground find grains of gold. It has few other manufac-

27. Postlethwayt, "Austrian Netherlands," *Universal Dictionary*, I, 158–61.
28. Postlethwayt, "Bohemia," *Universal Dictionary*, I, 302–03.
29. In MS, "latituded."

tures than those of copper and other hard wares, though some late attempts have been made to introduce others and with an appearance of success. This country abounds with salutary hot baths and fountains of vitriolic petrifying and other peculiar qualities; its rivers abound with fish; a thousand carp have been sold for a crown.

Chremnitz has the finest gold mine in Europe which has been worked near a thousand years. It extends nine or ten miles in length. It has also a mine of vitriol not far from the gold mine.

Schemnitz has six silver mines which also afford Gold. Hewsol and Hermgrant have abundance of rich copper mines from which are also extracted silver with several sorts of vitriol. There is said to be in the last two springs of vitriolic water which have the singular faculty of turning iron into copper. There are many fine medicinal baths.[30]

AMERICA

Its boundaries yet unascertained. The part known little less in extent than all the other three parts together [31] contains the greatest part of their [32] productions and a variety of others peculiar to itself.

After the Spaniards (says Postlethwaite) the English have the most flourishing colonies, both with regard to the multitude of the inhabitants, the number of ships they send thither every year and the rich and precious commodities they draw from them, above half the trade and navigation of Great Britain being reasonably supposed to depend on her American settlement.[33]

Mesnager [34] in his secret memoirs says that when he returned with an account to Lewis 14th. that the spaniards would not come into his project for attacking Jamaica, the Monarch was most chagrined at their refusal and said "They were the most stupid wise people in the world." [35]

30. Postlethwayt, "Hungary," *Universal Dictionary*, I, 962–63.
31. The sentence in Postlethwayt of which this is a paraphrase reads: "The Spaniards gave it the name of the *New World* and not improperly, it being such an immense tract that it exceeds any of the other three parts of the old one, and, indeed, is little less in extent than all the three parts put together" (Postlethwayt, "America," *Universal Dictionary*, I, 54–55).
32. I.e., European.
33. Postlethwayt, "America," *Universal Dictionary*, I, 54–56.
34. In MS, "Mesnagers."
35. Postlethwayt, "British America," *Universal Dictionary*, I, 377.

ASIA

Productions: all those in Europe with the addition of many either in greater abundance than there or not produced there at all.

There is a great abundance of diamonds, pearl, coral, gold, silver, copper, iron, sulphur, red earth, salt peter, allum, quicksilver, potters earth (of which is made the porcelain), raw silk, cotton, tea, sago coffee, nutmegs, mace, cloves, cinnamon, peppers, indigo, china root, aquila wood, rhubarb, musk, vermillion, sticklack, borax, *lapis lazuli*, dragon's blood, cubebs, frankincense, saffron myrrh, manna, ambergrease and many other of the valuable drugs and gums.

There is an immense canal in China 1000 Miles long which traverses the whole Chinese empire from Canton to Pekin. There is an immense wall of 600 leagues long that is a barrier against the tartars.[36]

ASIA MINOR ISLANDS

Tenedos is famed for its excellent Muscadine wines.

Lesbos since called Mytillene besides corn, wine, fruit, has quarries of Jasper and several sorts of marble.

Chios now sico—the rendezvous of the ships that go [to] Constantinople or from thence to Syria Egypt &c. It has corn wine and fruit—variety of gums—some silk and other manufactures.

Samos, extremely fertile, produces Muscadine wine—raw silk saffron Minerals drugs of different sorts—badly inhabitated at present.

Icaria, Now Nicaria has no great advantages either physical or improved.

Patmos has the best port in the Archipelago; nothing else remarkable.

Claros nothing worth notice.

Leria produces aloes.

Coos or Cos—one of the most flourishing of these Islands produces plenty of corn wine, olives and oil. Has a pretty good port.

Astypata, now Stampalia, not worth notice.

Carpathus, now Scarpanto. Nothing remarkable here but a plenty of marble.

Rhodes, in as flourishing a state now as Turkish Government will permit. Besides the usual productions of corn wine oil &c. it has

36. Postlethwayt, "Asia," *Universal Dictionary*, I, 120-22.

iron copper and other minerals. Its manufactures are soap, camblets & tapestry, damasks and other silk stuffs. It has vermillion &c.

Cyprus was formerly flourishing & among other things produced sugar. This has now ceased. They have the best manufactures of cotton & wool of all the East.[37]

POSTLETHWAITE ON FUNDS

"It is computed (says he) by the British Merchant that out of 49.000.000 £ expended and consumed by our people at home, not more than four millions are of foreign commodities. There remain therefore 45.000000 £ for an annual expence and consumption in home product and manufactures. Of these the land owner can expend and consume no more than his rents, and they are computed at no more than 14.000.000 of £. Sterling; therefore above two parts in three in home product and manufactures are expended and consumed by all other denominations of our people." He infers that the farmer and trader pay three fourths of the public taxes.

The circulation was about thirty millions at this time twelve in specie, eighteen in paper. The same British Merchant in 1713 computed the imports of Great Britain at 5000000 £; its exports at 7000.000.[38]

LABOUR

"It has been judged by experience that labour of 25 persons is nearly sufficient to provide meat drink apparel housing and generally all the necessaries of life for 100 persons." [39]

The par between land and labour is twice the quantity of land whose product will maintain the labourer. In France one acre and a half will maintain one; in England three owing to the difference in the manner of living.[40]

37. Postlethwayt, "Asia Minor Islands," *Universal Dictionary*, I, 122–23.
38. Postlethwayt, "Funds," *Universal Dictionary*, I, 879–80.
39. Postlethwayt, "Labour," *Universal Dictionary*, II, 6.
40. The paragraph in Postlethwayt, here paraphrased by H, reads: ". . . the labour of a working man corresponds to more or less land in different countries, according to the different customs of living used in the said countries; and that, if the labour of a peasant in France be worth the produce of their acres, and that of an English countryman, who drinks beer, wears woolen cloth, eats meat pretty often, and consequently consumes the produce of more land, is worth in England from six to eight acres" (*Universal Dictionary*, II, 2)

EGYPT

Produces in abundance corn, wine, rice, dates, senna, cassa, baulm, physical drugs, plants &c.

Alexandria is now Called Scanderic by the turks. It has a considerable manufacture of striped and coarse linnen.

Damietta has a very flourishing manufacture of fine linnen Cloth of all colors.

Maquilla carries on several kinds of linnen and cotton manufactures. Makes great quantities of sal armoniac.

Cairo is the capital of Egypt; formerly a place of great trade; the medium of all the commerce between Europe and the East Indies. It now carries [on] a good many manufactures, particularly one of Turkey carpets.

Fium a large and populous city; its principal commerce consists in linnen plain and striped; fine leather, carpets, the finest mats in all Egypt, figs, raisins, oranges, lemons and other fruits.

Upper Egypt among other things produces Rice.

Minio, famous for an earthern manufacture of water pots curiously wrought and said to give a peculiar freshness to the water.

Aboutic produces vast quantities of black poppies from which the best opium is made and spread over the whole turkish dominions.[41]

VENICE

The revenues of the state of Venice were 4.000.000 ounces of silver per annum. All transactions for above a certain value were invalid if not paid in Bank.[42]

The Azores belong to the Portuguese. 7 in number, they produce corn wine fruits of every sort. Lie in the Alantic ocean between 37 & 40 N.L.[43]

The Canaries belong to Spain—twelve in No. of which Teneriff [44] [is] one. They produce wine corn & a variety of fruits but not enough corn for their subsistence. This is the rendezvous of the Galleons &c. from South America.[45]

41. Postlethwayt, "Egypt," *Universal Dictionary*, I, 697–98.
42. Postlethwayt, "Banking," *Universal Dictionary*, I, 193–97.
43. Postlethwayt, "Azores," *Universal Dictionary*, I, 163.
44. In MS, "Teneriffe."
45. Postlethwayt, "Canaries," *Universal Dictionary*, I, 444–45.

Amyanthus [46] a kind of incumbustible stone said to be found in the Isle of Cyprus and in the Pyrrhennes whose fibres resemble cotton and may be manufactured. It is pretended that the ancients made their bays in which they used to burn their dead of this stone, and that they also made paper of it which being put into the fire lost the stain of former writing. The Caravansiers in travelling through the burning deserts of Lybia have stockings and drawers of this. Some assert that it is a tree. It is also called Abestos and is found in several other parts of the world—in India, Japan, China, Egypt, Negro pont, Corsica, Liguria, Bavaria, Wales &c.

In some experime[n]ts before the Royal society, it was found to be diminshed by fire; it has been vitrified by a burning glass but it cannot be consumed or calcined. It appears to be a kind of half mineral half vegetable. Grows in our highlands. [47]

Florence in Italy subject to the Duke of Tuscany. It produces abundance of wines, citrons, lemons, oranges, olives &c., corn, rice, saffron, honey, wax, wood, flax, hemp, silk, copper, iron, allum, marble, prophyry and other fine stone. It manufactures serges and several other kinds of woolen cloths, silks, linnen, tapestries, gilt leather, earthen ware and perfumes.

From England it takes pepper, cloves, mais, indico, callicoes, lead, tin, Cloths, bays, perpetuanas, herring white and red, pickled sammon—New found land fish, pilchards, calf skins &c. [48]

LANDED INTEREST

Maitland in his history of London says in the year 961 land sold at 1/. per acre. In the year 1000 an ox sold for 2/6, a cow for 2/, a sheep for 1/, & a hog for 8d.

"It is agreed by the best authers of Political Arithmetic that the rents of lands houses and mines are not more than ⅜ [49] of the an-

46. In Postlethwayt, "Amiantus."

47. Postlethwayt, "Amiantus," *Universal Dictionary*, I, 56; Postlethwayt, "Asbestos," *Universal Dictionary*, I, 119-20; Postlethwayt, "Allum," *Universal Dictionary*, I, 43-44.

48. Postlethwayt, "Florence," *Universal Dictionary*, I, 799.

49. In the MS, H changed the fraction from "¾" to "⅜." In Postlethwayt the sentence reads: "for it is agreed by the best authors of political arithmetic, that the rents of lands, houses, and mines, are not more than ¼ part, and half of the annual expences of the nation" (Postlethwayt, "Landed Interest," *Universal Dictionary*, II, 12).

nual expences of the nation." Davenant calculates them at 14 Millions Stg.

Sir William Petty supposes every person in England upon an average spends 7 £ a head which supposing the nation to be 7 million makes the whole expence & consumption 49 Millions.[50]

Aristotles politics Chap 6 definition of money. "As all useful things (says he) could not without great difficulty be transported from place to place, it was resolved, by common consent, that in bartering commodities they should reciprocally give and receive some substance, which being in its nature applicable to the purposes of life, might at the same time be easily carried about." [51]

The proportion of Gold & Silver as settled by Sir Isaac Newtons proposition was 1 to 14. It was generally throughout Europe 1 to 15. In China I believe it is 1 to 10.[52]

It is estimated that the labour of 25 persons on an average will maintain an hundred in all the necessaries of life.[53]

Postlethwaite in his time supposes six millions of people in England.

"The ratio of increase has been found by a variety of observations to be that 100.000 people augment annually one year with another to 100.175."

Mr. Kerseboom agreeing with Doctor Halley makes the number of people thirty five times the number of births in a year.

Postlethwaite makes the Nobility, Gentry, Merchants, Farmers, Manufacturers and others which composed the increasing stock of the nation at . . .   3.052.083

> The common soldiers, seamen,
> Labouring people and outservants,
> Cottagers, paupers, vagrants,
> beggars &c.
}   2.947.917

————————
6.000.000 [54]

Spain produces corn, wine, oil, all the fruits of Europe and America, the finest wool in the world and silk in abundance, of which two

---

50. *Universal Dictionary*, II, 10–16.
51. Quoted in Postlethwayt, "Money," *Universal Dictionary*, II, 282.
52. Although the figures do not correspond exactly, H probably took this information from Postlethwayt's section on "Coins," *Universal Dictionary*, I, 523–32.
53. Postlethwayt, "Labour," *Universal Dictionary*, II, 6.
54. Postlethwayt, "People," *Universal Dictionary*, II, 438.

articles there are valuable manufactures. She has mines of Gold, silver, copper, iron, lead & Mercury & allum—marble in abundance, and several precious stones. Some provinces produce rice and Sugar.[55]

The mines of South America according to the registers of the Council of Trade are said in the first hundred years to have yielded in gold, silver, diamonds, pearls and other precious stones to the amount of 50.00.000.000. of money. Arragon, Valencia, Estramadura & Granada are earthly paradises.[56]

Portugal is in its greatest extent from North to South 300 Miles; from East to West 120. Not very fertile in general. Does not afford a sufficiency of corn for its own consumption. Produces wine and oil—the latter not good. Has mines of allum, white marble, white allum, and alabaster and great quantities of salt. They have some woolen manufactures but of no value. Some silk but of inferior quality.[57]

Russia commodities for exportation are Pitch Tar, in great quantity, [and]

Honey & bees wax
Russia leather, deer, bear and elk skins
Pot-ash, timber and plank, iron, and some copper
Hemp & flax, Linseed the best in Europe
Linnen & Linnen yarn, Russia linnen
Furrs such as sable, black fox, ermine, rain deer, martins, beaver
Raw silk by the wolga
Persian, Indian & Chinese goods
Deals, firr timber, Masts
Corn, Sturgeon & Caviar
Diaper
Sail Cloth, Canvas and duck,
Pot-ash
Tobacco—in plenty from Circassia—
Salt—very rich mines.

The Russian general export from Petersburgh estimated at three millions of which two by British subjects. The English had a million ballance against them.[58]

55. Postlethwayt, "Spain," *Universal Dictionary*, II, 750–51.
56. Postlethwayt, "Spanish America," *Universal Dictionary*, II, 761.
57. Postlethwayt, "Portugal," *Universal Dictionary*, II, 506–07.
58. Postlethwayt, "Russia," *Universal Dictionary*, II, 642–49.

The native Exports of Portugal are Wine, lemons, oranges, figs, raisins, almonds, salt, oil, cork, shumac, tunny fish, and other small articles. Some wool is also exported though prohibited.

The commodities they bring from their foreign dominions are diamonds of brazil and India, Sugar, tobacco, brazil wood, cocoa nuts, coffee, cotton, pepper, drugs, some inferior spices, whale bone, raw and tanned hides, elephants teeth, arrac, orchella, citrons and occasionally china-ware, India silks and cotton piece goods, Silver and gold, the former by permission obtaining licence, the latter c[l]andestinely.[59]

Venice has the largest state of any in the Mediterranean. She possesses Dalmatia [60] & several Islands in the Neighbourhood of the Morea. Her land is not very abundant in its productions nor has she many manufactures but she is the mart of that part of the world. She has a large Inland Commerce by the River Po, the Adige [61] Adda &c. She has some silk manufactures. She has some mines of Iron & lead, all sorts of naval stores. She imports great quantities of drugs from her neighbours, which she sells again to the rest of the world. She had the finest glass manufactories in the world but was rivalled by France who has been since rivalled by England. There is a good deal of luxury at Venice, which is of service to her, by an influx of strangers.[62]

EXTRACTS FROM DEMOSTHENES ORATIONS

Philippic I. "As a general marches at the head of his troops, so ought wise politicians, if I dare to use the expression, to march at the head of affairs; insomuch that they ought not to wait the *event*, to know what measures to take; but the measures which they have taken, ought to produce the *event*." [63]

"Where attack him it will be said? Ah Athenians war, war itself will discover to you his weak sides, if you seek them." Sublimely simple. Vide Long: Ch. 16 [64]

59. Postlethwayt, "Portugal," *Universal Dictionary*, II, 512–13.
60. In MS, "Dalmation."
61. In MS, "Addige."
62. Postlethwayt, "Venice," *Universal Dictionary*, II, 819–20.
63. Demosthenes, *First Phillippic*, 39–40.
64. Demosthenes, *First Phillippic*, 44. This passage from Demosthenes was quoted, as H indicated, in Dionysius Longinus, *On the Sublime*. H's reference to this work is in error. The passage appeared in Ch. XVIII rather than XVI.

TO BE ATTENDED TO

Are the limits of the several states & the acts on which they are founded ascertained and are our ministers provided with them?

What intelligence has been given to Congress by our ministers of the designs, strength by sea & land, actual interests & views of the different powers in Europe?

These notes are selected more for their singularity than use— though some important facts are comprehended.[65]

PLUTARCHS LIVES [66]

Vol. 1.

Theseus: Ægeus (his father) "being desirous of Children consulted the oracle at Delphi and received that celebrated answer which forbad him the use of any woman before his return to Athens." It was in these words:

"The *mystic* vessel must
untouched remain
'Till thou to Athens shalt
return again." [67]

Page 11 [68]   Procrustes, a robber of Attica slain by Theseus in the same manner he used to put to death those who fell into his hands.

He had beds of several sizes and when he lit upon a traveller if he was too tall he would cut off a part of his legs, if too short he would extend him by machines to fit his bed.

Minos the King of the Cretans reduced the Athenians so low that by advice of the oracle they bound themselves every ninth year to pay a tribute of seven young men and seven virgins, who the fable says were put into a subterraneous place and there devoured by an animal called the Minotaur. Soon after Theseus arrived at Athens, the time of the tribute came about. He went a volunteer contrary to

---

65. This is an introductory remark by H to the succeeding notes.

66. The edition, used by H and to which the subsequent notes refer, was *Plutarch's Lives, in six volumes: Translated from the Greek. With Notes, Explanatory and Critical, from Dacier and others. To which is prefix'd the Life of Plutarch, Written by Dryden* (London, Printed for J. and R. Tonson in the Strand, 1758).

67. *Plutarch's Lives,* I, 4.

68. The numbers which H wrote in the margin refer to the pages of Plutarch from which his information was taken. These references are to the paragraph or paragraphs succeeding.

the persuasions of his father Ægeus; and by the assistance of Ariadne the daughter of Minos who fell in love with him, he slew the minotaur and returned with the young men and virgins triumphant to Athens, bringing off Ariadne with him. It is added that if he returned safe, there was a Convential signal to be hoisted on the vessel, which in the hurry of his joy was omitted. Ægeus, in sorrow for the imagined loss of his son, precipitated himself from a rock into the sea.[69]

26   Theseus is said to have instituted games at Delos and to have been the introducer of the custom of giving palms to victors.

33   Hercules in honor of Jupiter instituted the Olympian games; in imitation of him Theseus instituted the Isthmian games in honor of Neptune.

He was the first that divided the commonwealth into three ranks: the nobles, the husbandmen and Artificers; to the first he committed the care of religion, the choice of Magistrates, the interpreting and dispensing the laws.

"Theseus was the first, as Aristotle says, who out of inclination to popular government parted with the regal power."

Castor and Pollux were two brothers whose sister having been ravished by Theseus took Athens in his absence. They were worshipped afterwards as gods for the care they took of the city. His [70] tomb was placed near the gymnasium and is a sanctuary for servants and others in distress, thereby signifying that while living he was the patron of the poor and afflicted.

In his absence from Athens his wife Phædra fell violently in love with his son Hyppolitus who was banished by his father in consequence of the resentment of Phædra and was devoured by a sea Monster. This fable has given rise to the Tragedy of Phædra by Euripides, imitated by Racine, the conduct and execution of which piece are as admirable as the subject is monstrous disgusting and absurd.[71]

The Athenians Sacrifice to Theseus the eight day of every

69. *Plutarch's Lives*, I, 12–26.
70. I.e., Theseus.
71. This sentence is H's comment on the fable. Plutarch's comment is: "As to the calamities which befel *Phædra* and *Hippolytus*, since none of the historians have contradicted the tragic poets that have written of them, we must suppose they happened, as all the poets have described them" (*Plutarch's Lives*, I, 38–39).

month, in the same manner as they do to Neptune whose reputed son he was. The mystical meaning of this sacrifice is "because the number 8 being the first cube of an even number and the double of the first square, seemed to be an emblem of the immoveable power of this god, who has the names of *Asphalius* and Gaieochus, the establisher and supporter of the earth." [72]

ROMULUS

52   One of the accounts of his origin is that Tarchetius, King of Alba, saw in his own house the apparition of the God Priapus issuing out of the Chimny Hearth, and having consulted the oracle, was told that some young virgin should accept the embraces of the God and that she should have a son eminent for strength valour and good fortune. He commanded one of his own daughters to entertain the lover, but she thinking it an indignity sent her servant maid in her place who some-time after brought her two sons Romulus and Remus &c. &c. The most received [73] is the story of the vestal virgin, well known &c.

54   The Romans call the Tutelar goddess of young Children Rumilia and in sacrificing to her use milk instead of wine in their libations.

54   "The Keeper of Hercules's temple, having it seems little else to do, proposed to his deity a game at dice on condition that if he won he should have something valuable of the god, and if he lost he would provide him with a good supper and a pretty girl. Having lost he kept his word and Larentia was the woman to whom as the mistress of a god sacred honors were afterwards paid."

The vulture was a favourable omen with the ancients because, says Plutarch, "it is the least hurtful of any animal; it preys only upon carrion and never kills or molests any living animal; and as for birds it touches not them, though dead, as being of its own species." [74]

64   The city being built, Romulus enlisted all that were able to bear arms into military companies of 3000 footmen and 300 horse; which were called legions because they were the choicest and most

72. *Plutarch's Lives,* I, 34–48.
73. According to Plutarch, "the account which obtains most credit" (*Plutarch's Lives,* I, 52).
74. *Plutarch's Lives,* I, 60.

select of the people. "An hundred of the most eminent men he chose for his counsellors who were styled patricians and the whole body of them the senate which signifies a consistory of old men."

The senate were afterwards called *patres* and then *patres conscripti* to distinguish them from the populace. A relation was established between the nobles and the common people in this manner: the former were styled patrons and the latter clients. Every common man chose some nobleman for his client and a reciprocity of good offices was established.

The Patrons were the counsellors and pleaders for their clients in law suits, their advocates when under prosecution, their advisers and directors in all affairs. These in return were warmly attached to their patrons, not only showed them great respect and deference, but supported their interests and in case of poverty helped them to portion their daughters and pay their debts. No law could oblige a patron to be witness against his client or the client against his patron.

78   When the accommodation took place between Romulus and Tatius, uniting the Romans and Sabins, an hundred sabin senators were elected and the legions were increased to 6000 foot and 600 horse; the whole people were divided into three tribes, each tribe containing ten curiae or wards.

The commentator says [75] plutarch was mistaken in the number of the Legion, and asserts from Livy's authority that during the reign of romulus it never consisted of more than three thousand foot 300 horse; that after the Kings they were augmented to 4000 foot, again to 5000, and lastly by Scipio Africanus to 6000, and the horse to 600.

Romulus adopted the use of the Sabin shields instead of the small Roman targets. The feasts and sacrifices of both nations were united and new ones introduced, the Matronalia and Carmentalia; the former in honor of the women for having put an end to the war. Carmenta is thought by some to be the destiny who presides over Child-birth. By others she is said to have been a priestess who delivered her oracles in verse.

75. *Plutarch's Lives*, I, 78, note 4. This is a reference to the notes in this edition of Plutarch. They were written, according to the title page, by "Dacier and others."

In the feasts of the Lupercalia two young noblemen were produced, a bloody knife was applied to their foreheads and the blood was afterward wiped off by wool dipped in Milk. Then the two young men run about naked and with thongs of goat skin whipped all they met. The young married women were glad of this kind of whipping as they imagined it helped conception.

Some say that Romulus instituted the order of vestals, though the most received account of his birth makes his mother a vestal. Others ascribe the institution to Numa. Romulus as Pontifix maximus had a lituus or rod used in describing the four quarters of the heavens in auguries from the flight of birds. This lituus, after Rome was sacked and burnt by the Gauls, is pretended to have been found unhurt amongst the ruins, a trick of Camillus's to encourage the citizens to rebuild the city instead of going to Veii as they wanted.[76]

A husband might put away his wife for three causes: adultery, poisoning her children, and counterfeiting his keys.

It is said that Romulus having taken the city of Fidenae made it a Roman Colony and sent there *2500 inhabitants*.

Having soon after overcome the Camerians he removed those who survived to Rome and soon after sent back double the number. This was 16 years after the foundation.

Romulus after having subdued all his enemies abroad grew haughty and affected absolute government. He established the lictors who preceded him with rods and leather thongs to bring whom he should direct.[77]

92   Plutarch speaking against the translation of human bodies to heaven adopts the sentiment of Pindar in these lines:

> Our bodies shrink to dust by
> deaths decree
> The soul survives and fills
> eternity.

He says, "We must, not contrary to nature, send the bodies with the souls of good men to heaven; but then we must readily believe, that both from their nature and the divine constitution virtuous souls are exalted from men into heroes, from heroes into demigods,

76. *Plutarch's Lives*, I, 80–83. The last half of the last sentence is not from Plutarch's essay on Romulus; it is found in his essay on Camillus (*Plutarch's Lives*, I, 357)
77. *Plutarch's Lives*, I, 83–85, 87–88.

and after that, if they are perfectly purified as in the sacred initia-
tions, and refined from all the passions which attend mortality, they
are raised to consummate felicity and enrolled amongst the gods not
by the vote of a people but by the just and established order of
nature."

Hesiod is said to have originated these four distinctions. Plato has
similar ideas in that philosophic fiction of a regular gradation of
beings from nothing to infinite; a scheme as inconsistent with fact
as sublime in theory. Shaftesbury among the moderns revived it,
and Pope has erected a delightful poem upon this foundation.[78]

⟨"For a Prince's first concern ought to be the preservation of the
government itself; and in order to do this he should neither claim
more authority than is his due, nor on the other hand⟩ [79] give up any
part of his prerogative. Whoever gives up his right, or extends
his claim too far, is no more a king, but either a slave to the people
or a tyrant, and so becomes odious or contemptible to his subjects.
The one seems to be the fault of easiness and good nature, the other
of pride and severity." [80] A false sentiment; it would often be praise
worthy in a prince to relinquish a part of an excessive prerogative
to establish a more moderate government, better adapted to the
happiness or temper of his people! [81] Plutarch pronounces a very
hard sentence upon Theseus, on the occasion of his having omitted
to hoist the signal agreed upon by his father, though the omission
was only an inadvertency. He says,

98   "But Theseus in his forgetfulness of the command concerning the flag can scarcely in my opinion by any excuses, or before
the mildest judges, avoid the imputation of Paricide." This shows in
how high veneration the commands of a father were held.

LYCURGUS

107   He met with the works of Homer in Ionia and transcribed
and collected them. He is said to have [82] been the first that brought

78. The first sentence of this paragraph is from *Plutarch's Lives*, I, 92, note
7. H interpolated the remaining information.
79. Page or pages missing. The material within broken brackets is from
Plutarch's Lives, I, 96.
80. *Plutarch's Lives*, I, 96–97.
81. H's interpolation.
82. In MS, "him."

them into general reputation. In his travels to see the government and manners of different countries, he passed into Egypt and "being much pleased with their way of separating their soldiery from the rest of the people he resolved to imitate them at Lacedaemon; and this distinction of the military men from those of low and mechanical employments rendered the constitution much more regular and beautiful."

Lycurgus being returned to Sparta resolved to new model the commonwealth and, having consulted the oracle concerning it, the prophetess called him "beloved of the gods and rather a god than a man" assuring him that the laws he should establish would make the commonwealth which observed them the most famous in the world.

Sparta had originally two Kings. Archelaus, one of them, said of his partner when he heard him highly extolled for his goodness "How can Charilaus be a good man who cannot be severe even to the worst of men." [83]

109 "Amongst the many Alterations, which Lycurgus made, the first and most important was the establishment of the Senate, which having a power equal to the Kings in matters of consequence did (as Plato expresses it) foster and qualify the imperious and fiery genius of Monarchy, by constantly restraining it within the bounds of equity and moderation. For the state before had no firm basis to stand upon, leaning sometimes towards an absolute monarchy and sometimes towards a pure demockracy; but this establishment of the senate was to the commonwealth what the ballast is to a ship and preserved the whole in a just equilibrium. For they always adhered to the Kings so far as to oppose a democracy, and on the other side assisted the people to prevent tyranny."

The having two Kings, the senate and the Ephori are considered by Aristotle as the causes of the duration of the Spartan government.[84] The first circumstance would be in modern times a source of endless confusion and distraction.[85]

The principal regulations of the Spartan government were the

83. *Plutarch's Lives*, I, 109.
84. Plutarch said the statement was made by Plato. See *Plutarch's Lives*, I, 110, note 7.
85. H's, not Plutarch's, comment.

ordinances of the oracles called Rhetræ. One of them is in the following terms: "After you have built a temple to Jupiter the Syllanian and to Minerva the Syllanian, and after you have divided the people into tribes and classes, you shall establish a council of thirty senators in the number of which the two Kings shall be comprised and you shall from time to time call the people to an assembly betwixt Babyca & Cnaicon and they shall have the supreme powers of determination."

The senate proposed and the people adopted or rejected; they could not alter or add. Finding they departed from this rule, a Rhetra was procured decreeing, "That if the peop[l]e should alter or pervert any law, then the senate and Kings should reject it."

However careful Lycurgus was to temper the constitution, it is said the power of the Kings and senate was found to be too great and sometimes oppressive, which induced Theopompus, one of their Kings, to establish the Ephori. These were five in number chosen among the people for a year. Their authority was very extensive. Theopompus, when his Queen upbraided him one way that he would leave the regal power to his children less than he had received it from his ancestors, replied that he would leave it greater because more durable. For the prerogative being thus kept within reasonable bounds were secured both from envy and dangers.

The most arduous and dangerous thing attempted by Lycurgus was the division of property which when he began was very unequal. The lands and money were in the hands of a few and there were a great number of necessitous people. "Therefore that he might banish out of the commonwealth, luxury and arrogance and envy and fraud, together with those more fatal and inveterate distempers of a state, wealth and poverty, he persuaded the people to reduce the whole Country to a common stock to consent to a new division of the land, and live all in perfect equality allowing the pre-eminence to virtue only, and considering no other difference or inequality between one man and another, but what the disgrace of doing base actions or credit of doing worthily created." He divided the whole country of Laconia into thirty thousand shares and the territory of the city of Sparta into 9 thousand and made the distribution. A lot was so much as to yield one year with another seventy bushels of grain for the master of the family and twelve for his wife with a proportion of wine and fruits. The whole population this ground could support could not much exceed 600.000.[86]

To destroy avarice he cried down all the gold & silver and made only iron current.

"He instituted public tables at which every citizen was obliged to eat. There were different messes. No man could be admitted into any mess but by unanimous consent."

The Rich were so enraged at Lycurgus that a tumult arose one day and a young man run after him and knocked out one of his eyes. He carried the young man home with him and instead of punishing him as he was authorised to do made him one of his most zealous partizans by kindness.

The principal dish of the Lacedemonians was a kind of black-broth which the old men fed solely upon by preference. A King of Pontus sent for a Lacedæmonian cook, to make him some black broth. Finding it very disagreeable on tasting it, the cook observed to him, "Sir to make this broth relish, you must first bath yourself in the Eurotas."

By one of his Rhetræ Lycurgus forbid his laws being written, imagining that the impressing would be more lasting and efficacious by obliging the citizens to depend on their memory, than by referring them to a written code.

Another of the Rhetræ ordained that only the saw and the ax should be used in their buildings. This was to prevent luxury in building furniture &c. For as Epaminondas afterwards said of his table, "Treason will never come to such a dinner as this;" so Lycurgus thought that such houses would never be the receptacles of luxury and superfluity.

Another Rhetra ordained that they should not make war often or long with the same enemy for fear of instructing them in the art of war.

To make the women more robust and more capable of a vigorous offspring, he ordered them to practice several of the athletic exercises, and to destroy an excessive delicacy he ordained that at certain solemn feasts and sacrifices the virgins should go naked as well as the young men and in this manner dance in their presence.

The women of these occasions used to praise or rally the young

86. This sentence was interpolated by H.

men who had done any honorable or dishonorable action, which was a great incitement to emulation.

To promote marriage those who continued batchelors beyond a certain age were made infamous by law. They were excluded from the public spectacles and the magistrates sometimes made them dance naked through the market place singing a song to their own disgrace.

124   When a couple were to be married the husband carried off the bride by force. She who was charged with the management of the wedding shaved the head of the bride, dressed her in mens cloaths and left her at the place of rendezvous where after the usual supper the Bride groom came secretely in quest of her, untied her girdle and carried her to another bed. The intercourse between them continued [for] some time privately.

125   To prevent jealousy a man might lend his wife. "Lycurgus allowed a man who was in years and had a young wife to recommend some virtuous handsome young man that she might have a child by him, who might inherit the good qualities of such a father. On the other side a worthy man, who was in love with a married woman, *on account of her modesty* and the beauty of her children, was at liberty to beg of her husband admission to her, that thus by planting in a good soil he might raise a generous progeny to possess all the valuable qualifications of their parents." [87]

127–128   It was ordained that deformed and sickly children should be cast into the place called Apothetæ, a deep cavern near the mountain Taygetus; to prove the strength of their constitutions the women used to bathe the new born children in wine instead of water; imagining that epyleptic and weakly children would die in the operation and only the vigorous and healthy survive. The principle was that it was neither for the good of the public nor of the Child itself that it should be preserved when nature [88] had denied it the means of happiness, health, and strength. A horrid practice mentioned with no marke of disapprobation.

Every lad had a lover or friend who took [89] care of his education and shared in the praise or blame of his virtues or vices. It was the same with the women.

87. *Plutarch's Lives*, I, 111–125. The quotation is from p. 125.
88. In MS, "natured."
89. In MS, "take."

129   The Youth were educated to theft, to give them habits of courage and address. If taken in the fact, the person was severely whipped for his negligence and want of dexterity.

The youth were accustomed to spare diet to stimulate their enterprise in this way and promote their health.

Plutarch has this remark: "But there was another subordinate intention which was to make them grow tall; for the vital spirits not being overburthened and oppressed by too great a quantity of nourishment (which necessarily extends itself into thickness and breadth) do by their natural lightness and activity mount upwards so that the body while it is pliable and yielding must necessarily increase in length" [90]—a kind of jargon which only shows [91] the ignorance of the times in the science of the human frame.

130   Tis said that a young Lacedæmonian having stolen a fox, and put it under his cloak, suffered it to tear out his bowels rather than be detected in the fact.

It was primitively a custom to sacrifice a man to Diana Taurica [92] every year, which sacrifice was abolished by Lycurgus and her Goddessship was obliged to content herself with the blood of the boys who had been whipped round her altar.

The Lacedæmonians were remarkable for a laconic, sententious way of speaking. Among other sayings recorded of Lycurgus are these: Being consulted how best to oppose an invasion of their enemies, he replied by continuing poor and one not coveting to have more than another. Being again consulted whether it were requisite to inclose the city with a wall he sent back word, "That city is best fortified which has a wall of men instead of brick." [93]

A stranger once said to Theopompus that he was so remarkable for his love to the Lacedæmonians as to be called from thence Philolacon (a lover of the La–d–s). Theopompus replied that it had been more for his honor to have been called Philopolites (a lover of his own countrymen).

An Orator at Athens asserting that the Lacedæmonians were an illiterate and ignorant people, Plistonax, the son of Pausanias, told

90. *Plutarch's Lives*, I, 126–129. The quotation is from p. 129.
91. In MS, "shoes."
92. In Plutarch, "Diana, surnamed Orthia" (*Plutarch's Lives*, I, 130).
93. *Plutarch's Lives*, I, 133.

him: "You say true for we only of all the Grecians have learned none of your ill qualities."

A spartan being asked to go to hear a man who exactly counterfeited the voice of the Nightingale replied: "I have heard the Nightingale itself."

The Lacedæmonians erected a temple to the Muses and cultivated poetry and music with success making them subservient to moral and political purposes.

When the Spartans were at war their exercises were more moderate and their fare better; so that war to them was the season of repose and enjoyment. They always advanced to battle with a hymn to Castor. When they routed the enemy, they persued them no further than 'till they were assured of the victory; then they sounded a retreat, thinking it base to destroy those who made no resistance. This was not the practice in remote antiquity. "This conduct did not only show their magnanimity, but had an advantage in it too; for the enemy knowing that they killed only those who resisted and gave quarter to the rest, generally thought it their best way to consult their safety by flight." [94]

138   The Spartans despised all labour and mechanic arts; arms were the only honorable profession. The Helots [95] tilled the ground and paid their masters the revenues already mentioned. "A certain Lacedæmonian happened to be at Athens when the Courts of justice were sitting, and hearing that a citizen who had been fined for idleness came home much discontented, and attended by his friends who were greatly concerned for his disgrace, the Lacedæmonian desired the company to show him the man who was condemned for living like a Gentleman." [96]

The Spartans were so far from being morose that Lycurgus dedicated a little statue to the god of laughter and great pleasantry prevailed in conversation.

Xenophon says it was the custom for the Ephori to appoint three officers and each of these were to pick out an hundred of the best men in the city, and it was a point of great emulation to be one of 140   these three hundred. Padaretus, having been refused admit-

---

94. *Plutarch's Lives*, I, 134–37. The quotation is from p. 137.
95. In MS, "helotis."
96. *Plutarch's Lives*, I, 135.

tance into this list returned home well pleased saying "he rejoiced to find that there were in Sparta three hundred men better than himself." [97]

The senate were chosen for life out of men not under sixty; a wise institution. The elections were made by shoutings, and persons were placed apart to number the frequency and loudness of those for each candidate.

The person chosen had two portions of food allowed him at the public tables, one of which he gave to the woman he esteemed most; a great mark of distinction.

Lycurgus banished all strangers who could not give a very good account of themselves to prevent a corruption of morals and the introduction of customs repugnant to the constitution.

143 "Hitherto (says Plutarch) I for my part can see no sign of injustice in the laws of Lycurgus (though some who allow that they are well contrived for making men good soldiers, yet censure them as defective in civil justice and honesty). Perhaps it was the Cryptia or Ambuscade, if this were one of Lycurgus's institutions, as Aristotle says it was, that gave Plato likewise the same opinion both of the law giver and his government. The thing was this: The Magistrates dispatched from time to time some of the ablest of the young men into the Country, where they dispersed themselves, being armed only with their daggers and taking a little necessary provision with them. In the day time they hid themselves in the thickets and clefts, but in the night they issued out into the highways and killed all the helots they could light upon; sometimes they set upon them by day, as they were at work in the fields and murdered the ablest and stoutest of them. And Thucidydes in his history of the Pelponnesian war, tells us that such of them as the Lacedæmonians had singled out for their valour were crowned as persons infranchised and went about to all the temples in token of freedom, but that soon after they all disappeared of a sudden, being about the number of 2000, and no man either then or since could give any account how they were destroyed. Aristotle particularly says, that the Ephori as soon as they entered into their office used to declare war against them that they might be massacred [98] under pretence of law. In other respects, too,

97. *Plutarch's Lives*, I, 140.
98. In MS, "massachered."

the Spartans dealt very hardly with them; for they often forced them to drink to excess and led them in that condition into their public halls, that their children might see what a contemptible vice drunkenness was. They made them sing such songs and dance such dances as were vulgar and ridiculous, forbidding them to meddle with any that were liberal and graceful. Upon this account when the Thebans invaded Laconia and took a great number of Helots Prisoners, they could by no means persuade them to sing the odes of Terpander, Alcman, or Spendin the Lacedæmonian, because they said that they were forbidden by their masters." [99]

After Lycurgus thought his institutions had acquired stability, he took an oath of the whole nation to observe them 'till his return, and set out to consult the oracle of Delphi: "Whether the laws he had established were sufficient to make a city virtuous and happy." The oracle replied "That his laws were excellent and that the city should continue in the highest renown while it observed the polity of Lycurgus." He wrote down this answer and sent it to Sparta and then that his countrymen might never be released from their oath it is said he put an end to his own life by a total abstinence from food.

The Government established by him remained in vigor about five hundred years 'till a thirst of empire tempted the Spartans to entertain foreign troops and introduce Persian gold to maintain them; then the institutions of Lycurgus fell at once and avarice and luxury were introduced.[100]

NUMA POMPILIUS

155–156   After the death of Romulus, the Romans and Sabins not being able to agree on the choice of another King, came to this determination—that each senator should exercise the regal power by turns six hours by day and six hours by night to prevent all jealousy, and this kind of Government was called an Interregnum. But the people clamouring through envy and jealousy, the Senate were obliged to come to the determination of choosing a King and

99. *Plutarch's Lives*, I, 141, 143-45.

100. *Plutarch's Lives*, I, 145-48. MS reads "avarice and luxury were ~~introduced succeeded~~."

they adopted the wise expedient of one party choosing out of the body of the other. The choice was left to the Romans who pitched upon Numa and sent an embassy to him in his retirement to persuade him to accept the royalty. He was prevailed upon with great difficulty.[101] His answer to the ambassadors, page 160, is full of very sensible reflections. He was a wise Prince and went a great way in civilizing the romans. The chief engine he employed for this purpose was religion, which could alone have sufficent empire over the minds of a barbarous and warlike people to engage them to cultivate the 157   arts of peace. "Numa (says Plutarch) judging that it was no slight undertaking to civilize the furious and unruly spirit of this people called in the assistance of religion and chiefly by the sacrifices, processions, and religious dances, which he appointed [and] at which he officiated in person and in which an agreeable amusement was mixed with their solemn devotion, he soothed the minds of the people and rendered their fiery martial temper more cool and sedate. Sometimes he filled their imaginations with religious terrors pretending that ⟨strange apparitions were seen, and dreadful voices heard; whereby he⟩ [102] subdued their minds and rendered them submissive by superstition. It is not improbable says Plutarch that God, who places not his affections on horses or birds but on mankind, should be pleased to dwell with such as are eminently virtuous and not disdain to converse with the wise and good, though it be altogether irrational to believe that any god or Dæmon is capable of a sensual love for a human bodily form or beauty; and yet the Egyptians make a distinction which seems not very absurd; they suppose that a divine spirit may possibly approach a woman and produce in her the principles of generation; but on the other side that it is impossible for a man to have any such intercourse with a goddess; but at the same time they do not consider that there can be no mixture without a mutual communication."

Speaking of Zaleucus, Minos, Zoraster, Lycurgus, Numa and others, he says: "What if we should suppose that the gods make it

101. In the margin of this page of the "Pay Book" next to the above paragraph H wrote: "Every generation consists of thirty years an olympiad of forty."

102. The material within broken brackets, illegible in MS, is taken from *Plutarch's Lives*, I, 164.

a serious business to inspire such men with great and noble designs, and that if they ever converse with poets and musicians, they do it merely to divert themselves?" [103]

165   It is said that Pythagoras had tamed an eagle which in pronouncing certain words would come down to him; sometimes when the people were assembled at the Olympic games he would show them a golden thigh upon which Timon the Philiasian wrote this distich:

> The Samian juggler of applause so proud
> Who tries with solemn words to cheat the crowd.

In like manner Numa feigned that a certain Goddess or Mountain nymph was in love with him and frequently met him in private.

165   "Pythagoras supposed that the supreme being was not an object of sense or capable of any suffering or infirmity, but was incorruptible, invisible, and to be comprehended only by the mind. And Numa forbad the romans to represent God in the form of man or beast; nor was there any picture or statue of a deity admitted among them formerly; for during the space of the first hundred and seventy years, they built temples and erected chapels but made no images, thinking that it was a great impiety to represent the most excellent beings by things so base and unworthy, and that it was by the understanding only that men could form any conception of the deity."

167   The first institution of Chief Priests called Pontifices is ascribed to Numa.

The [104] Numa is ascribed the institution of the sacred fire and the Vestal Virgins. If by any accident the fire became extinct it was relighted by burning glasses. The number of vestal virgins were six who were obliged to preserve their chastity thirty years; a violation of which subjected them to being buried alive.

"It is said also that Numa built the temple of Vesta, intended for a repository of the holy fire, in an orbicular form, not with a design to represent the figure of the earth, but the frame of the Universe, in the center of which the Pythagoreans place the element of fire, giving it the name of Vesta or Unity; but they do not hold that the earth is immoveable, or that it is situated in the middle of the world,

103. *Plutarch's Lives*, I, 154–64.
104. In Plutarch, "for to Numa" (*Plutarch's Lives*, I, 168).

but that it has a circular motion about the central fire. Nor do they count the Earth among the chief or primary elements. And this they say was the opinion of Plato, who in his old age, held that the earth was placed at a distance from the center, for that being the principal place was reserved for some more noble and refined body."

172   Numa instituted the Priests called Fetiales [105] whose office it was to judge of the merits of a war before it was entered upon and to accommodate differences. When the Romans received any injuries from their neighbours, they dispatched these priests to represent their grievances and obtain amicable redress, which being refused they denounced war. It is remarkable that the decrees of these priests upon different occasions were very consistent with un-biassed justice, and that when their advice was not followed, the Romans generally had cause to repent it.

Numa pretended that a certain Target fell from heaven which while it was preserved would render the romans invincible. He had el[e]ven others made exactly like it, and the whole deposited in different temples, the true one in that of Minerva near her statue. These Targets were called *Ancylia*.

It is said that Numa having invited a number of citizens to an entertainment told them that the Goddess with whom he conversed was coming in and all of a sudden the whole room was changed into a more splendid and better furnished apartment.

Numa built a temple to Faith and to Terminus, the god of bounds, and taught the Romans that to swear by faith was the most solemn of all oaths. This was to teach them to respect their engagements [106] and the boundaries of their neighbours.

Numa encouraged the citizens much to Agriculture and for this purpose distributed the lands into Pagi or boroughs appointing over-seers to them. He would himself survey the lands, reward the in-dustrious, and reprove the indolent. The people were then divided into two classes, Romans and Sabins. Productive of great incon-veniences. He thru them into companies.[107]

105. In MS, "Feciales."
106. In MS, "enagements."
107. *Plutarch's Lives*, I, 172–82.

DOCTOR HALLEYS TABLE OF OBSERVATIONS EXHIBITING THE PROBABILI-
TIES OF LIFE, CONTAINING AN ACCOUNT OF THE WHOLE NUMBER OF
PEOPLE AT BRESLAU CAPITAL OF SILESIA, AND THE NUMBER OF THOSE
OF EVERY AGE FROM ONE TO AN HUNDRED.[108]

Ages	Persons	Ag[es]	Per[sons]	Ag[es]	Per[sons]	Ages	Persons
1	1000	8	680	15	628	7	5547
2	855	9	670	16	622	14	4584
3	798	10	661	17	616	21	4270
4	760	11	653	18	610	28	3964
5	732	12	646	19	604	35	3604
6	710	13	640	20	598	42	3178
7	692	14	634	21	592	49	2709
	5547		4584		4270	56	2194
						63	1694

Ages	Persons	Ages	Persons	Ages	Persons		
22	586	29	539	36	481	70	1204
23	579	30	531	37	472	77	692
24	573	31	523	38	463	84	253
25	567	32	515	39	454	100	107
26	560	33	507	40	445		34000
27	553	34	499	41	436		
28	546	35	490	42	427		33893
	3964		3604		3178		

Ages	Persons	Ages	Persons	Ages	Persons
43	417	50	346	57	272
44	407	51	335	58	262
45	397	52	324	59	252
46	387	53	313	60	242
47	377	54	302	61	232
48	367	55	292	62	222
49	357	56	282	63	212
	2709		2194		1694

Ages	Persons	Ages	Persons	Ages	Persons
64	202	71	131	78	58
65	192	72	120	79	49
66	182	73	109	80	41
67	172	74	98	81	34
68	162	75	88	82	28
69	152	76	78	83	23
70	142	77	68	84	20
	1204		692		253 [109]

From 84 to 100 are—107

108. Postlethwayt, "Annuity," *Universal Dictionary*, I, 69.
109. The totals at the bottom of the preceding columns are not in Postlethwayt.

From this table it will appear there are 18053 persons between 18 and 56, half of whom are fencible men,[110] more than ¼ of the whole.

According to the tables of deathes and births in the same city drawn up monthly by Doctor Newman [111] for the course of five years, it appears that upon an average there were born annually 1238

$$\text{Buried} \underline{\hspace{3cm}} 1174$$

$$\text{Difference} \overline{\hspace{2cm} 64}$$

By the same tables it appears that 348 of the births die in first year, and that in 5 years afterwards 193 more die so that only 692 children survive six years.

Table of deaths of different ages, the first column representing the ages, the second the number of persons who die.[112]

Ages	7	8	9	14	18	21	27	28	35
Persons	11	11	6–5½	2–3½	5–6	4½–6½	9	8–7	7

Ages	36	42	45	49	54	55	56	63
Persons	8–9½	8–9	7	7–10	11	9	9–10	12–9½

Ages	70	71	72	77	81	84	90	91	98	99
Persons	14	9	11–9	6–7	3–4	2–1	1	1	0	⅓

Ages	100
Persons	⅔

The average of human life by these tables appears to be about 28½ or 29 years.

Doctor Halley has calculated the value of lives on the following scale: [113]

110. The sentence from Postlethwayt ("Annuity," *Universal Dictionary*, I, 69), of which this is a paraphrase, reads: "At least one half thereof are males, or 9027: So that the whole force this city can raise of fencible men, as the *Scotch* call them, is about 9000."
The two pages of the "Pay Book" following the "Table of Observations" consist of figures, obviously H's computations based on Halley's tables.
111. Caspar Neuman (1648–1715), German philosopher and theologian. H was referring to Neuman's "Reconstruirte Tafeln über die Geborenen und Gestorbenen in Breslau von 1687 bis 1691" (J. Graetzer, *Edmund Halley und Caspar Neumann. Ein Beitrag zur Geschichte der Bevölkerungs-Statistik* [Breslau, 1883], 49–75).
112. In Postlethwayt ". . . number of persons of that age *dying* yearly" (*Universal Dictionary*, I, 68).
113. In Postlethwayt, "Dr. *Halley* . . . has formed the following table; which shews the value of annuities for every fifth year of age, to the 70th, as follows: . . ." (*Universal Dictionary*, I, 6).

Age	Years Purchase	Age	Years Purchase	Age	Years Purchase
1	10.28	25	12.27	50	9.21
5	13.40	30	11.72	55	8.51
10	13.44	35	11.12	60	7.60
15	13.33	40	10.57	65	6.54
20	12.78	45	9.91	70	5.32

It has been found by experience that the total number of the inhabitants of the Country is to the births as 35 to 1, and in England for a number of years the males and females born have been as 18 to 17. Women in every period have been observed to live three or four years longer than men.

In England the proportion in 100.000 people has been estimated as follows:

Married men and women 34.500
Widowers 1.500
Unmarried youth & Children 45.000
Servants 10.000
Travellers strangers &c. . . . . 4.000 [114]

Short Rule to determine the average interest per annum for any sum of money for a given term of years at a given rate, discharging annually an equal proportion of the principle. Example: Suppose A should borrow of B 1.200.000 £ payable in twenty years, one twentieth part or 60,000 £ annually, interest at 8 per Cent ℔ annum, what would be the average sum each year to pay off the whole interest in twenty years? Answer 50.400 £.

Process and rule:
Sum borrowed 1.200.000
find the amount of the interest for one year
say . . . £ 96.000—
take the mean of the number of years
that is of 20—10½
Multiply the interest of the whole sum for one year with this mean of 10½, divide the product by 20, the number of years, and the quotient will be the sum required— £ 50.400 [115]

Quere? Would it not be adviseable to let all taxes, even those imposed by the states, be collected by persons of Congressional ap-

114. *Universal Dictionary*, I, 73.
115. The source of this was not found in Postlethwayt.

pointment and would it not be adviseable to pay the collectors so much per Cent on the sums collected?

Money Coined in England from the Reign of Queen Elizabeth to that of George 1st inclusive that is from the Year 1558 to 1727.

169 years

		£.		
In	Elizabeths Reign	5.513.711.11	17	
	James 1st	5.432.351.13	9	
	Charles 1st	12.096.220—		
	Charles 2d	7.899.434	2	1⟨¼⟩
	James— 2d	2.631–955	8	1⟨¾⟩

Great Recoinage amounted
to £ 6. 435. 039. 14. 9½

Kings Williams regign . . .	10.511.963	17.	11⟨¾⟩	
Queen Annes	2.691.626.	6	8⟨½⟩	
George 1st	8.725.921.15.	6		

55.503.184.15   38 [116]

When you can get more of foreign Coin, coin for your native exchange is said to be high & the reverse low. For instance, when for a bill of one crown of three livres in france on Holland, you can get 60 gros,[117] exchange is high; when only fifty it is low. The par is 54. That is, when the native money is worth more than the par in foreign exchange is high, when worth less it is low.[118]

AMERICA

Wool may become an article of trade. We may raise Goats in the Southern colonies for the Skin and hair.[119]

116. Postlethwayt, "Gold," *Universal Dictionary*, I, 910-12. As the MS is mutilated, the material within broken brackets is supplied from Postlethwayt.
117. In MS, "gross."
118. Postlethwayt, "Exchange," *Universal Dictionary*, I, 742. H's statements are based on this paragraph in Postlethwayt: "When money of the same standard and weight in France yields money of the same standard and weight in Holland, it is said that the exchange is at par. In the actual state of specie, which was in 1744, the par was nearly at 54 gros to the French crown of three livres. When the exchange is above 54 gros, the French say it is high; when beneath, they say it is low."
119. Postlethwayt, "America," *Universal Dictionary*, I, 54-56. On the next page of the "Pay Book" H wrote in no apparent order the names of certain products and regions. The remaining pages of the "Pay Book" are either blank or contain brief entries of the accounts of H's artillery company.

1 7 7 8

Account of Expenses of Lieutenant Colonel Alexander Hamilton and Captain Caleb Gibbs, October 30, 1777–January 20, 1778 [1]

[Valley Forge, January 20, 1778]

Account of Expences of. Colo. Hamilton. & Captain Gibbs. to Albany & back again—set off from Skippack road, 15. miles from Phila: Returnd. to Valley Forge—
Sent by His Excelly. Genel. Washington on public service.

1777.

October	30th.	Cash paid at Corrells. ferry Lodgg—Sup. horses—		£ 1.19. 6
	31	at Crossroads N. Jersey		6. 6
Novr—	1—	at Chester.—	1. 17.4—2d at N. Windsor ferry 8/6	2. 5.10.
	4	at Paukeepsey— 19/—at Rhynbeck— 25/6.		2. 4. 6
	5th.	at Clauverick— 16/8.—gave a guide—9/		1. 5. 8.
		at Kinderhook— 16/—at Albany ferry 6/.		1. 2—
	8th.	at Cosockett [2] 19/6—at Wells's ferry—5/.		1. 4. 6
		at Pools landing 24/6—9th on the road to Clauvierck 10/		1.14. 6
	10th.	at Clauverick— 14/—at Tatias tavern dinner &c. 12/		1. 6.
	11th.	at the flatts 18/6—at paukeepsey 10/6		1. 9—
	12th.	at Fish Kill— 30/—at New windsor ferry 10/.		2.—
	14th.	at Goshen— 20/—at Chester— 27/.		2. 7—
	16th.	at Pompton— 14/		14. £ 19. 5. 0

On the road to PeeksKill when Colo. Hamilton was taken sick from Morris Town

	22d.	at Ramapaugh 13/—at Cacaat [3]— 16/8		1. 9. 8.
	23	at Kings ferry— 11/—gave the ferry man 5/.		.16—

Cash paid at Peeks Kill when Colo. Hamilton was sick
25th. to 3 quarters mutton @ 8/24 gave the doctr. 6/   1.10—

Decembr— 4th. to 12 fouls—for the whole 5 dollars—   1.17. 6

      7   to Cash for Oranges & Shrub 15/; 10th. to
          potatoes 10/   1. 5—

   12th to 3 dozen Eggs @ 5/ To 15/; 19th.
          To potatoes 5/   1—

   21   to quails—   5/ —To a partridge 2/6   7.6

   23d. To Mr. Kennedys Bill—£ 12.0.—To Cash
          for a bed 45/   £ 14. 5—
          To washing &c.—   15/   15—

Expices to Head Quarters from Peeks Kill—

Decembr—23d. at Kings ferry 8/ —at Cacaat horse. Lodgd.
          Breakft—&c   6.13. 4
                                         £ 30.13. 0

Decembr—24th: Cash paid at Ramapaugh dinig horses &c—   1.12. 6.
      25th. at Pompton— 37/6 at Hardoorits   1.17. 6.

1778
January—   5th: Paid Coach for his Expences to Peeks Kill—   3.15—

   8   at Cross Roads New Jersey—   3. 9

   12th: at White house tavern 47/6 at—   2. 7. 6.

   13th. at Oakhams near Deleware—   1.17. 6.

   15th at Latharams—   5—

17-18-19th 20   To Cash paid between Newton & Schuylkill —   3.15—
                                Total   £ 115. 9. 9.[4]

Errors. Excepted
    𐐝. C. Gibbs

ADS, George Washington Papers, Library of Congress.

1. This expense account, which was written and signed by Gibbs, is the only extant record of H's itinerary of his journey to New York State to confer with Major General Horatio Gates and Major General Israel Putnam.

2. Coxsackie, twenty miles south of Albany, on the west bank of the Hudson River.

3. Kakiate, approximately half way between Suffern and Stony Point, New York.

4. This total should read £65.11.9. The manuscript of this document consists of two pages. Gibbs totaled the first page and carried that sum (£49.18.0) over to the second page. In totaling the second page he added in error the sum £49.18.0 twice, once as a carry-over and once as one of the items on the second page.

From Major Nicholas Fish [1]

Valley Forge, January 22, 1778. Requests written discharge for Captain Barent J. Ten Eyck, Second New York Regiment.[2]

LS, RG 93, Miscellaneous Records, National Archives.
    1. Fish, a major in the Second New York Regiment, subsequently became a close friend of H and a prominent New York Federalist.
    2. At the end of this letter, H wrote: "One of the Gentlemen below is requested to transact the business of this letter. AH."

To George Washington

[Valley Forge, before January 29, 1778] [1]

There are still existing in the army so many abuses absolutely contrary to the military constitution, that, without a speedy stop is put to them, it will be impossible even to establish any order or discipline among the troops.

I would, therefore, propose the following Regulations; submitting to His Excellency the Commander-in-Chief, to distinguish such as may be published under his own authority in General Orders, and such as will require the sanction and authority of the committee of Congress now in camp.[2]

Hawks, *The Official and Other Papers of Alexander Hamilton*, I, 315–26; also printed in *JCHW*, II, 176–183.
    1. On January 29, 1778, Washington presented to the congressional committee at Camp a long letter or report on the Army. Two incomplete drafts of Washington's letter and the final copy (see the calendar of this final copy below) are in the writing of H. The drafts are located in the Hamilton Papers, Library of Congress. The latter half of what appears to be the earlier draft reads as though it were used as the basis of the document printed here. Sometime late in 1777 Washington had requested the general officers to give their observations on a proposed new establishment and regulation of the Army. The answers to this request are found in the George Washington Papers, Library of Congress, among the letters for the period of December, 1777, through January, 1778. Fitzpatrick states that Washington used these letters as a basis for his report (*GW*, X, 403, note 39). The document here printed was evidently written by H during the same period and submitted to Washington for the same purpose. Both Francis L. Hawks and J. C. Hamilton print this document without date.
    2. Francis Dana, Joseph Reed, Nathaniel Folsom, John Harvie, Charles Carroll, and Gouverneur Morris.

1stly.—Every officer or soldier who acts contrary to the Regulations for the order and discipline of the army, established by Congress, shall be tried and punished for disobedience of orders.

2ndly.—Every officer who absents himself from his regiment without leave, shall be tried and punished. If he remain absent three weeks, he shall be ordered to join by a notification in General Orders, and in the public newspapers. And in case of his absence three weeks afterward, such notification shall be repeated. And should he not return in three weeks from the last notification, he shall, by the sentence of a court martial, be cashiered and rendered incapable of ever holding a commission in the armies of the United States.

3rdly.—Every officer on furlough, who remains absent ten days longer than the time allowed him, shall be tried by a court martial. And in case of his being, by sickness or any other cause, detained from his regiment six days above the time allowed in his furlough, he shall inform the comanding officer of his regiment of the reasons that prevent his returning. In default of such information, he shall be notified, tried, and punished, agreeably to the second article.

4thly.—It being permitted, for the care and convenience of the Generals, and other officers of the army, to take servants from the regiments, many abuses have resulted therefrom. To remedy which, the following Regulations are to take place for the future:

Each Major-General is permitted to take from the division which he commands, four men. Each Brigadier-General, three men. Each Colonel, or Lieutenant-Colonel-Commandant, two men. Each Lieutenant-Colonel, or Major, one man, and a second man, who is to be exempted from ordinary duty, but to turn out in time of action. Each Captain, two men, to be exempted from ordinary duty only. Each Subaltern, one man, who is to mount guard with the officer he serves. Those Generals, and other officers, who are not attached to any particular division or brigade, to take their servants from the line.

No officer in a civil department, shall be permitted to take a soldier from any regiment to serve him: nor is any Colonel, or commanding officer, to suffer a soldier of their regiment to be detained by any such officer.

Those who may be permitted to have servants from the line, are to apply to the Quarter-Master-General, who will take them from the regiments, and distribute them to whom he thinks proper.

5thly.—Great quantities of arms and ammunition have been destroyed, by being in the possession of men who do not use them in time of action. To prevent this, for the future, no arms, accoutrements, or ammunition, is to be delivered to those under the following description, viz: General and staff officers, waiters, waggoners, camp colour men, and all those who do not bear arms in time of action. Such of those as have arms, are immediately to deliver them to their Captains, who will deliver them to the Conductor, that they may be returned to the Field Commissary.

6thly.—Abolition of standing guards, though of great consequence to the order and discipline of the army, has not yet taken place. The soldiers on these guards, being separated from their regiments, are often employed as servants. They become ignorant of the service, and lose and destroy their arms and clothing. Therefore, for the future, no standing guard shall be permitted to any General, or other officer, on any pretence whatever.

Those guards which cannot be relieved every twenty-four hours, must be relieved at least every three days; for which the Inspectors and Majors of Brigade are to be answerable. All guards or pickets, for more than three days, shall be called detachments.

7thly.—The multiplicity of small guards, for the stores and baggage of the army, being unnecessary, and diminishing the strength of the regiments; it will be necessary to repeat the order given at Smith's Clove, the 25th of June last, relative to this object. It should therefore be ordered, that

The order given at Smith's Clove the 25th of June last, relative to the guard usually furnished for the Quarter-Master's, and other stores, is to be carried into execution with the greatest rigour, and is to be regarded as a standing order.

8thly.—It being very improper and hurtful to the service, that guards should be sent too far from the corps to which they belong; it is ordered,

That the general officers shall have their guard from the divisions and brigades to which they belong: and those who have no division or brigade, shall be furnished with a guard from the line, by detail from the Adjutant-General.

No General shall take his guard above ten miles from camp, without the express leave of the Commander-in Chief.

9thly.—Nothing being more disgraceful to the service, nor dangerous for the army, than for the advanced posts to be surprised by the enemy; it is necessary that every possible precaution should be taken, to prevent an accident so dishonourable to the officer who commands at such a post. And as the instruction given in the chapter on the service of the guard, in the Regulations, is not full and explicit, it is thought necessary to add the following article:

As soon as an officer, commanding a detachment, arrives at the post he is to occupy, he must endeavour to procure some inhabitant on whom he can depend, to show him all the roads, footpaths, and other avenues leading to the post. These he must himself reconnoitre, and then determine the number of guards necessary for his security, as well in front, as on the flanks and in the rear of the post. He must then divide his detachment into three parts, one of which must be always on guard; another, act as reserve picket; and the third, be off duty.

The part destined for guard, must be divided into as many guards as the officer may think necessary: always observing, that the guards are so proportioned as that one-third of each guard may always be on sentry at the same time.

These guards should be posted at three or four hundred paces from the main post, and the sentinels form a chain round it. They must be within sight of each other during the day, and within call during the night.

The commanding officer having himself posted these guards and sentinels, and well instructed the officers and sergeants in their duty, will fix the place where he means to defend himself in case of an attack; as a house, a height, or behind some bridge or fence, which he will strengthen as much as possible, by an abatis ditch, or anything his genius may direct him for that purpose.

The reserve pickets are on no account to stir from the main post, or take off their accoutrements; but must be ready to parade under arms at any moment of the day or night; though, during the day, they may be permitted to lay down and sleep. Every man must have his haversack under his head; and if the post is dangerous, his arms in his hand.

The Reserve will furnish a guard of a sergeant and from six to twelve men, to furnish from two to four sentinels round the house, or wherever they are posted, to give notice of all that approach, or of any alarm. One of these sentries must always be before the arms.

That part of the detachment off duty, may undress and repose themselves. They must cook for the guard and picket, and fetch the wood and water necessary for the post; but they must not do this before the roll-call in the morning, when the commanding officer receives the reports of all the guard. If the post is near the enemy, this part of the detachment must not undress during the night.

As the guard form a chain of sentinels round the post, no soldier must pass the chain without a non-commissioned officer; nor any stranger be permitted to enter, without being conducted to, and examined by, the commanding officer.

After roll-call in the evening, no soldier must be permitted to go more than forty paces from the place of arms. The officers, it is expected, always remain with their men.

As soon as a sentry perceives the enemy, he must fire his piece to alarm the other guards and the main body. The guards immediately parade, and follow the rules prescribed in the Regulations. The picket parades immediately, and the other part joins it as fast as it can get ready. The commanding officer will immediately detach one-third of the picket, with orders to march toward the guard attacked, and lay in ambuscade behind some house, barn, or in a wood on the road leading from them to the main post. And when the guard attacked, retreat, and are followed by the enemy, they must fall in the rear of the enemy, and keep up a scattered fire. This manœuvre, especially in the night, will not fail to disconcert the enemy, and cause a failure of their enterprise.

The guard are, in every respect, to observe the rules laid down in the Regulations.

The part on guard is to be relieved by the part off duty; and the guard take the reserve picket.

No part of the service is more important, nor more neglected, than this of the guard; notwithstanding the duties are so particularly described in the Regulations.

It is very seldom a guard turn out for a General officer of the day; and even when they turn out, they are seldom or ever drawn up in the order prescribed. Therefore, for the future, the Generals, and Field officers of the day, are ordered to pay the greatest attention, that the service of the guard is performed strictly conformable to the Regulations. For which purpose, they must visit the guards of sentinels at different hours, and arrest or confine any officer, or non-commissioned officer, whose guard is not already paraded in order at his arrival. A guard which is surprised by an officer of the day, may, with the same facility be surprised by the enemy. If the sentinel before the guard-house, is not sufficient, others must be added, who can see around the environs of the post, and give notice of all that approach.

For the more effectual preservation of the arms, accoutrements, and ammunition, each regiment shall be charged with the arms, &c., now in their possession, agreeably to the returns made at the last inspection. And for the future, none of those articles shall be drawn from the Field Commissary, but by returns signed by the Inspector of the Division, or, in his absence, by the Major of Brigade, doing his duty. And the Inspector and Major of Brigade, are to pay the strictest attention, that the Regulations, with respect to this object, are strictly carried into execution; examining and comparing the Regimental Returns with those of the Conductors.

In the Returns of the army, a great number of men are reckoned, who have been sick, or otherwise absent, a long time, without any account of them having been sent to their regiments.

Orders must be given to the officers superintending the hospitals, to send their Returns regularly every month; and the Majors of Brigade must take an extract of those of their Brigades returned in the several hospitals, to compare with the Returns of the inspection.

For those men who are sick in the country at private houses, certificates must be produced every two months, signed by a justice of the peace: and without such certificates, the men must no longer be returned; though the regiment may keep an account of them, that they be reclaimed if ever found.

The army, even at this day, is much reduced, by a considerable number of men being permitted to retire on furlough and extra service. I would therefore recommend the following Regulations:

That from the first of May till the campaign closes, no officer have leave of absence for more than eight days, unless by permission from the Commander-in Chief, or officer commanding at a separate post: and that no non-commissioned officer, nor soldier, be furloughed, during the aforesaid period, unless by his Major-General, or officer commanding at a separate post; and that, for only six days, and on the most special account. That during the army's continuance in winter quarters, not more than six men of a hundred, be absent on furlough at the same time; these to have leave of absence from the officers commanding the regiments to which they belong.

That every officer, non-commissioned officer, and soldier, now on furlough, or on the recruiting service, be ordered to join their respective corps, by the first of June; the commanding officers of regiments to be answerable that they be notified of this order.

Notwithstanding the General Order [3] lately issued, respecting men on extra service, many are still improperly absent. It is therefore ordered, that they join by the first of June; the commanding officers of the regiments to which they respectively belong, to be answerable that they be notified of this order. That for the future, none be suffered to go on such employ, except by order of the Commander-in-Chief, officers commanding at a separate post, or the Quarter-Master-General.

The Marechaussie Corps,[4] though raised at a great expense, has been found not to answer the purpose for which it was raised: and as, by its composition, it is not fit to be employed on the lines; in order that they may not be useless to the army, I would propose the following.

Arrangement for the Marechaussie.

That the name they at present bear, be changed into that of General-Staff-Dragoons; and that they be employed in the following manner:

To furnish a guard for the Commander-in-Chief, of such a number as he shall please to order.

To furnish Orderly dragoons to Major-Generals and Brigadeers; when their divisions and brigades are separated from the army, or when the Commander-in-Chief shall think them necessary. To fur-

3. In late December, 1777, there were several orders respecting absent officers and men (December 20 and December 27, 1777).

4. A provost corps (Maréchaussé) had been organized in January, 1776, to which William Marony was appointed provost marshal. This may have been the corps to which H was referring.

nish, also, Orderly dragoons to the Quarter-Master-General, and Inspector-General of the Army, and commanding officers of separate departments.

The Inspector who has the department of the Cavalry, to have the direction of this corps; to furnish the guards and Orderly dragoons, agreeably to the orders he may receive from the Commander-in-Chief, without whose orders no dragoons shall be detached from the troop.

To prevent the abuses which have arisen, with respect to Orderly dragoons, the following Order should be rigorously observed:

No Orderly dragoons to be employed on any but military duty, nor sent express more than twenty miles; their duty being only to carry the orders of the General in writing, whenever they may be ordered: nor are they to follow the Aids, or any other officer, but the General to whom they are Orderly; who will himself consult the preservation of the horses as much as possible, by employing them only in cases of necessity.

No person whatever is to ride the dragoon horses but the dragoons themselves: and any dragoon is to inform the Inspector, of any breach of this order; and the Inspector will immediately inform the Inspector-General thereof; that the person who made use of the horse, may be punished. And in case any dragoon neglects to inform the Inspector as aforesaid, he shall receive one hundred lashes for such neglect.

George Washington to the Committee of Congress with the Army [1]

[*Valley Forge, January 29, 1778.*] Discusses proposed changes in military establishment. Submits questions concerning foreign officers, use of Indians to fight British, Colonel Daniel Morgan's Riflemen, use of Negroes as wagoners, pay for prisoners, and proper gradation of punishments.

LS, in the writing of H, George Washington Papers, Library of Congress; two drafts in writing of H, Hamilton Papers, Library of Congress.

1. Fitzpatrick states "the original report . . . seems to have been left with Washington by the committee" (*GW*, X, 403, note 39). This report is signed by George Washington and endorsed by Francis Dana. For another document bearing on this letter, see H to George Washington, dated "before January 29, 1778."

Receipt to George Washington

[*Valley Forge*] *January 29, 1778*. Receipt for payment of $100 by Washington to Hamilton for Hamilton's expenses at Morristown.

DS, George Washington Papers, Library of Congress.

From Colonel Alexander Scammell [1]

[Valley Forge, January, 1778]

Dear Sir,

Enclosed [2] is the remaining part of the Instructions first given to the Officers superintending Hospitals when the[y] were sent off, which I forgot to give you last Evening, when I gave you the first part. The additional Instructions which I gave last evening are all copied off, ready to be sent to the Office⟨rs⟩ at the several Hospitals.

Please to inform me, whether they are agreable to the Genl or whether he has any thing further to insert.

Yr Very Humble   Servt   Alexd Scammell AGl

ALS, George Washington Papers, Library of Congress.
1. This letter is addressed to "Colo Hamilton or [Lieutenant Colonel Robert Hanson] Harrison."
Scammell had been appointed adjutant general of the Continental Army on the staff of Washington on January 5, 1778.
2. The enclosure, a contemporary copy consisting of three MS pages and located in the George Washington Papers, Library of Congress, gives regulations for patients, equipment, deaths, and recoveries. This enclosure is printed in *GW*, X, 405–07 and is dated January [30?] 1778.

Remarks Concerning the Office of Inspector General [1]

[*Valley Forge, January–March, 1778.*] Describes purpose and proposed organization of the department of inspector general. Recommends Baron von Steuben for inspector general and suggests other men as assistants.

D, in writing of H, Papers of the Continental Congress, National Archives.
1. This document is found undated among the letters of April, 1781. Fitzpatrick dates it January, 1778, and states that "it seems to be a statement made

by Washington to the Congress Committee then at Valley Forge in January, 1778" (*GW*, XXVII, 548, note 91). The first mention of the office of inspector general by Washington is found in a list of questions put to the council of war, October 26, 1777. The issue again arose when Major General Thomas Conway was appointed inspector general in late 1777. Washington in a letter to the President of Congress, Henry Laurens, on January 2, 1778, concerning Conway, mentioned the earlier list of questions and stated that he had intended to recommend Baron d'Arendt for the position. On January 29, 1778, in a long report to the Committee of Congress with the Army there is a short paragraph mentioning the need of an inspector general and assistants. However, beginning March 17, 1778, Washington wrote a series of letters and orders using the material contained in the document printed above. Then, in a letter to the President of Congress, Henry Laurens, on April 30, 1778, he recommended the creation of the office of inspector general and suggested the appointment of Baron von Steuben to that office. J. C. Hamilton prints this as an H document and dates it May 5, 1778 (*JCHW*, II, 153–55), but since H probably wrote this in the capacity of aide-de-camp, it is calendared as such in this volume.

George Washington to William Livingston

[*Valley Forge*] *February 2, 1778.* Discusses detection of plot to assassinate Livingston.

Df, in writing of H, George Washington Papers, Library of Congress.

George Washington to Thomas Bond, Junior [1]

Valley Forge, February 3, 1778. Refuses Bond's request that Bond's father be permitted to visit in territory held by enemy.

Df, in writing of H, George Washington Papers, Library of Congress.
   1. Thomas Bond was the son of Dr. Thomas Bond, a Philadelphia physician who had helped to found the Pennsylvania Hospital.

To Commodore John Hazelwood [1]

Head Quarters Valley forge
February 5th 1778

Sir,

It is his Excellency's desire, that you have all the public boats below the falls,[2] removed as expeditiously as possible to Coryells ferry, or higher, as you may think necessary for their safety. Their present situation exposes them to being destroyed or taken without much difficulty, and we should feel the loss of them.

I am Sir   Your most Obd Serv   Alex Hamilton ADC

ALS, George Washington Papers, Library of Congress.
1. Hazelwood was a commodore in the Pennsylvania navy. At this time he was in charge of all American military vessels on the Delaware.
2. H is referring to the falls in the Delaware at Trenton.

George Washington to Henry Champion [1]

[*Valley Forge*] *February 7, 1778.* Discusses Army's need for meat. Instructs Champion to purchase all that is available. Has directed Major General Israel Putnam to use salt provisions available but to send on all cattle.

Df, in writing of H and Robert Hanson Harrison, George Washington Papers, Library of Congress.
1. Champion was deputy commissary general of purchases.

George Washington to Brigadier General John Nixon

[*Valley Forge*] *February 8, 1778.* Asks Nixon to send return of Connecticut troops to Jonathan Trumbull.

Df, in writing of H, George Washington Papers, Library of Congress.

George Washington to Major General Israel Putnam

[*Valley Forge*] *February 8, 1778.* Asks Putnam to send return of Connecticut troops to Jonathan Trumbull.

Df, in writing of H, George Washington Papers, Library of Congress.

To Elias Boudinot [1]

Head Quarters [Valley Forge] feby. 9th. 1778

Dear Sir,

General Howe has just made a proposition, towards a general exchange of prisoners, or rather has acceded to our former propositions on that subject. His Excellency commands me to inform you of this and to desire your *immediate* attendance at Camp, which is indispensably necessary.

I am with great regard   Dr Sir   Your most Obdt serv

AH: ADC

ADfS, George Washington Papers, Library of Congress.
1. Boudinot was commissary general of prisoners. Although elected a delegate to Congress from New Jersey on November 20, 1777, he did not attend that body until July 7, 1778.

To George Clinton

Head Quarters [Valley Forge] Feb'y 13, 1778.

Dear Sir,

I did myself the honor of writing to you, immediately after my arrival at Head Quarters, in answer to two letters I found here, from you.[1]

There is a matter, which often obtrudes itself upon my mind, and which requires the attention of every person of sense and influence, among us. I mean a degeneracy of representation in the great council of America. It is a melancholy truth Sir, and the effects of which we dayly see and feel, that there is not so much wisdom in a certain body, as there ought to be, and as the success of our affairs absolutely demands. Many members of it are no doubt men in every respect, fit for the trust, but this cannot be said of it as a body. Folly, caprice a want of foresight, comprehension and dignity, characterise the general tenor of their actions. Of this I dare say, you are sensible, though you have not perhaps so many opportunities of knowing it as I have. Their conduct with respect to the army especially is feeble indecisive and improvident—insomuch, that we are reduced to a more terrible situation than you can conceive. False and contracted views of economy have prevented them, though repeatedly urged to it, from making that provision for officers which was requisite to interest them in the service; which has produced such

Public Papers of George Clinton (New York and Albany, 1900), II, 860–64.
1. The letter from H to George Clinton has not been found. George Clinton to H, December 28, 1777, may be one of the two letters that Clinton wrote to H. The other letter has not been found.

carelessness and indifference to the service, as is subversive of every officer-like quality. They have disgusted the army by repeated instances of the most whimsical favouritism in their promotions; and by an absurd prodigality of rank to foreigners and to the meanest staff of the army. They have not been able to summon resolution enough to withstand the impudent importunity and vain boasting of foreign pretenders; but have manifested such a ductility and inconstancy in their proceedings, as will warrant the charge of suffering themselves to be bullied, by every petty rascal, who comes armed with ostentatious pretensions of military merit and experience. Would you believe it Sir, it is become almost proverbial in the mouths of the French officers and other foreigners, that they have nothing more to do, to obtain whatever they please, than to assume a high tone and assert their own merit with confidence and perserverance? These things wound my feelings as a republican more than I can express; and in some degree make me contemptible in my own eyes.

By injudicious changes and arrangements in the Commissary's department, in the middle of a campaign, they have exposed the army frequently to temporary want, and to the danger of a dissolution, from absolute famine. At this very day there are complaints from the whole line, of having been three or four days without provisions; desertions have been immense, and strong features of mutiny begin to show themselves. It is indeed to be wondered at, that the soldiery have manifested so unparallelled a degree of patience, as they have. If effectual measures are not speedily adopted, I know not how we shall keep the army together or make another campaign.

I omit saying any thing of the want of Cloathing for the army. It may be disputed whether more could have been done than has been done.

If you look into their conduct in the civil line, you will equally discover a deficiency of energy dignity and extensiveness of views; but of this you can better judge than myself, and it is unnecessary to particularise.

America once had a representation, that would do honor to any age or nation. The present falling off is very alarming and dangerous. What is the cause? or how is it to be remedied? are questions that the welfare of these states requires should be well attended to.

The great men who composed our first council; are they dead, have they deserted the cause, or what has become of them? Very few are dead and still fewer have deserted the cause;—they are all except the few who still remain in Congress either in the field, or in the civil offices of their respective states; far the greater part are engaged in the latter. The only remedy then is to take them out of these employments and return them to the place, where their presence is infinitely more important.

Each State in order to promote its own internal government and prosperity, has selected its best members to fill the offices within itself, and conduct its own affairs. Men have been fonder of the emoluments and conveniences, of being employed at home, and local attachment, falsely operating, has made them more provident for the particular interests of the states to which they belonged, than for the common interests of the confederacy. This is a most pernicious mistake, and must be corrected. However important it is to give form and efficiency to your interior constitutions and police; it is infinitely more important to have a wise general council; otherwise a failure of the measures of the union will overturn all your labours for the advancement of your particular good and ruin the common cause. You should not beggar the councils of the United States to enrich the administration of the several members. Realize to yourself the consequences of having a Congress despised at home and abroad. How can the common force be exerted, if the power of collecting it be put in weak foolish and unsteady hands? How can we hope for success in our European negociations, if the nations of Europe have no confidence in the wisdom and vigor, of the great Continental Government? This is the object on which their eyes are fixed, hence it is America will d[e]rive its importance or insignificance, in their estimation.

Arguments to you Sir, need not be multiplied to enforce the necessity of having a good general council, neither do I think we shall very widely differ as to the fact that the present is very far from being such.

The sentiments I have advanced are not fit for the vulgar ear; and circumstanced as I am, I should with caution utter them except to those in whom I amy place an entire confidence. But it is time that men of weight and understanding should take the alarm, and excite each other to a proper remedy. For my part, my insignificance, allows me to do nothing more, than to hint my apprehensions to those of that description who are pleased to favour me with their confidence. In this view, I write to you.

As far, as I can judge, the remarks I have made do not apply to your state nearly so much as to the other twelve. You have a Duane a Morris and may I not add a Duer? [2] But why do you not send your Jay and your R. R. Livingston? I wish General Schuyler was either explicitly in the army or in the Congress. For yourself Sir, though I mean no compliments you must not be spared from where you are.

But the design of this letter is not so much that you may use your influence, in improving or enlarging your own representation, as in, discreetly, giving the alarm to other states, through the medium of your confidential friends. Indeed Sir it is necessary there should be a change. America will shake to its center, if there is not.

You and I had some conversation when I had the pleasure of seeing you last with respect to the existence of a certain faction. Since I saw you, I have discovered such convincing traits of the monster, that I cannot doubt its reality in the most extensive sense. I dare say, you have seen and heard enough to settle the matter, in your own mind. I believe it unmasked its batteries too soon and begins to hide its head; but as I imagine it will only change the storm to a sap; all the true and sensible friends to their country, and of course to a certain great man, ought to be upon the watch, to counterplot the secret machinations of his enemies. Have you heard any thing of Conway's [3] history? He is one of the vermin bred in the entrails of this chimera dire, and there does not exist a more villainous calumniator and incendiary. He is gone to Albany on a certain expedition.

I am with great regard & respect, Sir, Your most Obed. servant

Alex. Hamilton

His Excellency Governor Clinton, Poughkeepsie.

2. James Duane, Gouverneur Morris, and William Duer.

3. Major General Thomas Conway an Irish born Frenchman who through the recommendation of Silas Deane came to this country in April, 1777. On May 13, 1777, he was appointed a brigadier general in the Continental Army. In spite of Washington's opposition, Congress, on December 14, 1777, promoted him to major general and appointed him inspector general.

George Washington to
Lieutenant Colonel Henry Haskell [1]

Valley Forge, February 13, 1778. Orders Haskell to rejoin regiment.

Df, in writing of H, George Washington Papers, Library of Congress.
1. Haskell, Fifteenth Massachusetts Regiment, was in Massachusetts on furlough.

George Washington to Colonel Morgan Lewis [1]

[Valley Forge] February 13, 1778. Asks for a return of stores in Lewis's department.

Df, in writing of H, George Washington Papers, Library of Congress.
1. Lewis was deputy quartermaster general of the Northern Department.

George Washington to
Major General Horatio Gates [1]

[Valley Forge] February 14, 1778. Regrets inability to "ratify" sentence of court-martial held by Gates's order, but will leave ultimate decision to Gates's judgment.

Df, in writing of H, George Washington Papers, Library of Congress.
1. Gates was at this time president of the Board of War.

George Washington to
Lieutenant Colonel Adam Hubley [1]

[Valley Forge] February 14, 1778. States that proceedings of the court-martial sent to Headquarters by Hubley are illegal. Encloses the proper authority to retry the accused.

Df, in writing of H, George Washington Papers, Library of Congress.
1. Hubley was a lieutenant colonel of the Tenth Pennsylvania Regiment.

George Washington to George Clinton

Valley Forge, February 16, 1778. Describes sufferings at Camp because of lack of food and clothing. Asks Clinton to do all that is possible to forward supplies.

Df, in writing of H, George Washington Papers, Library of Congress.

George Washington to
Colonel Henry Hollingsworth [1]

Valley Forge, February 16, 1778. Asks Hollingsworth to aid Captain Henry Lee in securing supplies from Head of Elk and Dover.

Df, in writing of H, George Washington Papers, Library of Congress.
   1. Hollingsworth was deputy forage master general.

George Washington to William Livingston

[Valley Forge] February 16, 1778. Is sending Lieutenant Colonel Tench Tilghman to Livingston to present picture of distressing state of the Army. Repeats request to Livingston to help relieve situation by sending goods stored in New Jersey.

Df, in writing of H, George Washington Papers, Library of Congress.

George Washington to
Brigadier General John Lacey, Junior [1]

[Valley Forge] February 18, 1778. Suggests methods to stop communication between Philadelphia and surrounding countryside.

Df, in writing of H, George Washington Papers, Library of Congress.
   1. Lacey was a brigadier general in the Pennsylvania Militia.

George Washington to the Inhabitants of New Jersey, Pennsylvania, Maryland, and Virginia

Valley Forge, February 18, 1778. Asks inhabitants to supply cattle. Promises a "bountiful price."

Df, in writings of Gouverneur Morris and H, George Washington Papers, Library of Congress.

George Washington to Patrick Henry [1]

Valley Forge, February 19, 1778. Describes distressing situation of Army. States that unless effective measures are taken, another campaign may prove impossible. Requests Henry to send all available supplies to Army.

Df, in writing of H, George Washington Papers, Library of Congress.
1. Henry was governor of Virginia.

George Washington to the Board of War [1]

Valley Forge, February 21, 1778. Asks that artillery at Farmington and Albany be forwarded to Camp.

Df, in writing of H, George Washington Papers, Library of Congress.
1. The draft is indorsed to "Genl. Horatio Gates, President of the Board."

George Washington to William Duer [1]

Valley Forge, February 21, 1778. Discusses impossibility of an enemy attack on Valley Forge.

Df, in writing of H, George Washington Papers, Library of Congress.
1. Duer was a delegate from New York to Congress.

George Washington to
Brigadier General Henry Knox

Valley Forge, February 21, 1778. Discusses disposal of the artillery at Albany and Farmington. Instructs Knox to send the artillery to Camp as soon as weather permits. Hopes that Knox will soon return to Camp.

Df, in writing of H, George Washington Papers, Library of Congress.

George Washington to
Brigadier General William Smallwood

Valley Forge, February 21, 1778. Discusses method for obtaining shoes for Smallwood's men. States difference between intended and attempted desertion and proper punishment for each.

Df, in writing of H, George Washington Papers, Library of Congress.

George Washington to William Livingston

Valley Forge, February 22, 1778. Commends New Jersey's efforts. States that a change of method is needed in handling supplies.

Df, in writing of H, George Washington Papers, Library of Congress.

George Washington to the Board of War

Valley Forge, February 23, 1778. Approves mode suggested to gain redress for Daniel Heister.[1] Will comply with congressional regulations for ordinance department. Asks about possibility of securing stores and ordinance needed for the next campaign. Asks for apprehension of John Robinson.[2]

Df, in writing of H, George Washington Papers, Library of Congress.
1. Daniel Heister, Jr., of Pennsylvania had been seized by the British.
2. Robinson was a Loyalist.

George Washington to
Captain-Lieutenant Jonas Symonds [1]

Valley Forge, February 24, 1778. Instructs Symonds to obtain artillery from Captain Charles Alexander and to bombard British shipping near Philadelphia.

Df, in writing of H, George Washington Papers, Library of Congress.
1. Jonas Symonds was a captain-lieutenant in the Fourth Continental Artillery Regiment.

George Washington to
Major General John Sullivan

Valley Forge, February 26, 1778. Instructs Sullivan on methods, sources, and routes to be used in procuring clothing.

Df, in writing of H, George Washington Papers, Library of Congress.

George Washington to
Captain Stephen Chambers [1]

Valley Forge, February 27, 1778. Instructs Chambers to cut communications between Philadelphia and the surrounding country and to protect supplies coming into Camp.

Df, in writing of H, George Washington Papers, Library of Congress.
1. Chambers was a captain in the Twelfth Pennsylvania Regiment.

George Washington to James Mease [1]

Valley Forge, February 27, 1778. Instructs Mease to supply Major General Israel Putnam with clothing.

Df, in writing of H, George Washington Papers, Library of Congress.
1. Mease was clothier general of the Continental Army.

George Washington to Officers
Sent to the Hospitals

Valley Forge, February 28, 1778. Requests complete and accurate return of the hospitals, patients, equipment, and employees. Orders all who have recovered and are fit for duty to return to Camp.

This letter, which is written in the third person in an unidentified writing, is in the George Washington Papers, Library of Congress. It is endorsed, in the writing of H, "All right and approved—no addition except an interlineation of a few words on the other side—Youl please to return this. A Hamilton."

George Washington to
Captain-Lieutenant Jonas Symonds

Valley Forge, February 28, 1778. Instructs Symonds to act under Brigadier General Anthony Wayne's orders.

LS, in writing of H, George Washington Photostats, Library of Congress.

George Washington to
the Committee of Congress [1]

[Valley Forge] February 29, 1778.[2] States that inadequacies of armorer's department will soon result in a shortage of arms for the Army.

LS, in writing of H, Papers of the Continental Congress, National Archives.
1. The Committee of Conference consisted of Francis Dana, Joseph Reed, Nathaniel Folsom, John Harvie, Charles Carroll, and Gouverneur Morris.
2. This letter should have been dated either February 28 or March 1, as there was no February 29 in 1778.

General Officers Wanted and Proportioned
to the Several States [1]

[Valley Forge] February, 1778. Heading reads: "In the present arrangement of the Army, there will be wanted 11 Major Generals

& 25 Brigadiers. 3 Maj: Generals to act as Lt Generals, eight to command divisions—22 Brigades—for the Regiments of the line and 3 for light troops." There then follows lists of major generals and other officers who "May be counted on."

AD, George Washington Papers, Library of Congress.
1. On verso, in Washington's writing, is written: "Genl. Officers wanted & Proportioned to the several States. Feby. 1778."
This document was prepared by H for Washington, probably for the use of the Committee of Congress then at Headquarters.

To Colonel Henry E. Lutterloh [1]

[Valley Forge, February, 1778]

Dr. Sir

You are hereby Authorised by order of His Excellency General Washington to impress any number of Waggons you stand in need of in the neighbourhood of the Camp—you don't say what number you expect in tomorrow. General Green [2] & Coll. Bidle [3] write, that they meet with the greatest difficulty in foraging for want of Waggons. The General begs you to give them all the assistance you can. For Gods sake, my Dear Sir, exert yourself upon this occasion, our distress is infinite.

Yrs.   A Hamilton A D C

To Coll. Lutterloh

Copy, Pennsylvania Historical and Museum Collection, Harrisburg, Pennsylvania.
1. This letter is included in another letter, which concerns the impressment of wagons for the Army and which was written by James Young, wagon-master general of Pennsylvania, to Timothy Matlock, secretary to the Supreme Executive Council of Pennsylvania. Young's letter is dated February 21, 1778. At the end of his transcription of H's letter to Lutterloh, Young wrote: "I have transcribed the above Copys that you may be a better Judge of the Wants of the Army."
Lutterloh was deputy quartermaster general of the Continental Army.
2. Major General Nathanael Greene, who became quartermaster general on March 2, 1778.
3. Clement Biddle, commissary general of forage.

George Washington to the Pennsylvania Navy Board

Valley Forge, March 2, 1778. Advises that the stores be removed from the galleys and the ships sunk.

LS, in writing of H, George Washington Photostats, Library of Congress.

From George Clinton

Poughkeepsie [New York] 5th March 1778.

Dear Sir,

I have received your Favour of the 13th Feb'y last. Your other Letter has not reached me. I am so Circumstanced at present so much to do & no Body to assist me that I can hardly steal a Moment to write to my Friends tho their Letters always afford me the greatest Pleasure. May I then hope Sir that you will continue to write me frequently tho I shoud not prove a very punctual Correspondent. When I shall have more Leisure I hereby promise to pay the Debt with Interest. I wish the Defects of a certain great Body were less apparent. Even their Want of Wisdom but too Evident in most of their Measures woud in that Case be less Injurious. A New Mode of doing Business by Proxy is very Fashionable whenever any alarming Difficulties arise they are referred to the New B of W [1] & by them to the Executive Powers of the different States; this alone is a glaring Evidence of Weakness & Incapacity. Coud our Soldiery subsist on Resolves, they woud never want Food or Cloathing. Resolves are most Powerful Expedients. They are to fill to Cloath to Feed & pay our Armies at least this is the Language which the late Conduct of our Masters speak.

I need not ask you who contrived & planned the Northern Expedition, I have seen the Marquis's Instructions.[2] They are a Curiosity indeed. They suppose the Enemy are to be pannic Struck & fly on the Approach of our Army. Our Army you may be assured were to take the advantage of this pursue them & take Possession of Montreal with all the public Stores & Cloathing therein &ca. &ca. What a Pitty we had not Men sufficient to have carried all this into Execution that those we had were not cloathed or paid that Provissions & Forrage had not been provided in Season.

I wish Jay or Livingston [3] or both in Congress tho they coud be illy spared from here, but this cant be at present. I am D'r Sir &c.

(G. C.)

I take for granted that Military Men burn Confidential Letters for fear of accidents as soon as they are read.

Public Papers of George Clinton, II, 865–66.

1. A new Board of War, with Major General Horatio Gates as president, had been established by Congress in November, 1777.

2. This is a reference to a plan considered by the Board of War for the invasion of Canada. The Marquis de Lafayette was to be in titular command of this expedition, but Major General Thomas Conway, Washington's principal critic and opponent, also hoped to become the leader of the expedition. Clinton's remark on "who contrived & planned the Northern Expedition" is presumably a reference to Gates.

3. Robert R. Livingston.

To James McHenry [1]

Head Quarters [Valley Forge] March 5th 1778

Sir,

It gives me pleasure to inform you that Mr Boudinotte [2] has been able to effect your exchange for a Doctor Mentzes.[3] Allow me to congratulate you on the event.

We are again on the business of a general cartel with Mr Howe He seems inclined to meet us on fair ground. Commissioners from us meet an equal number from him the 10th instant.[4] One great and preliminary point to be settled is the proportion of prisoners that we ought to account for. To assist our judgment in this point we shall be much obliged to you by the return of this express, and without a moment's loss of time to send us your deposition, to the best of your knowlege, on the actual state of the prisoners sent out at the time of their delivery; and whatever else may serve to throw light upon the subject.

I am Sir Your most Obedt   A Hamilton ADC

ALS, James McHenry Papers, Library of Congress.

1. McHenry, surgeon of the Fifth Pennsylvania Regiment, had been taken prisoner at Fort Washington, New York, November 16, 1776.

2. Elias Boudinot, commissary general of prisoners.

3. McHenry had been paroled on January 27, 1777, and was exchanged on March 5, 1778.

4. Four commissioners were appointed by Washington to negotiate a cartel with the British. They were, in addition to H, Elias Boudinot, Lieutenant Colonel Robert Hanson Harrison, and Colonel William Grayson, a former aide to Washington.

George Washington to Major Warham Parks [1]

[*Valley Forge*] *March 5, 1778*. Urges Parks to remain in service in spite of temporary disability.

Df, in writings of John Laurens and H, George Washington Papers, Library of Congress.

1. Parks was a major of the Fourth Massachusetts Regiment.

From George Clinton

[*Poughkeepsie, New York, March 6, 1778*. On March 12, 1778, Hamilton wrote to Clinton: "Capt. Coleman delivered me your two letters of the 5th & 6th, instant." *Letter of March 6 not found.*]

George Washington to Sir William Howe

[*Valley Forge*] *March 9, 1778*. Asks that meeting of commissioners for the exchange of prisoners be delayed until March 31, 1778. Is disturbed that, although Major General Richard Prescott was sent to New York City in exchange for Major General Charles Lee, Lee has not yet been sent out of New York City. Asks that Howe immediately order Lee's release.

Df, in writing of H, George Washington Papers, Library of Congress.

To George Clinton

Head Quarters [Valley Forge] March 12th 1778.

Sir,

Capt. Coleman [1] delivered me your two letters of the 5th & 6th,[2] instant.

The pleasure, I have, in corresponding with you, will dispose me, whenever I have any thing to communicate, that may be worth your attention, or that appears to me so, to trouble you with my sentiments: But I shall not expect you to make an equal return either in quantity or frequency. You will, in this, intirely consult your own convenience.

I had previously flattered myself, that your ideas and mine would correspond, in a certain matter, and I am glad to find I was not mistaken. I doubt not the defects of a certain synod,[3] will appear to you not the subject of speculation only; but as disorders in the state, that require a remedy, and will, as far, as your influence, reaches, contribute to it. Shall I speak what seems to me a most melancholy truth? It is this—that with the most adequate means to ensure success in our contest, the weakness of our councils will, in all probability, ruin us. Arrangements on which, the existence of the army depends, and almost the possibility of another campaign, are delayed in a most astonishing manner; and I doubt whether they will be adopted at all.

A late resolve directs G. W. to fix the number of men under which G. H. shall not send any parties out of his lines, on pain of being treated as marauders. The folly of this is truly ridiculous; but as there is perhaps nothing but folly in it, it may be excused in them. Another resolve made for punishing Kidnappers or persons who aid the enemy in carrying off the peaceable inhabitants has a retrospective view to those, who have assisted, as well as a perspective one to those who shall assist in such practices. Thus we have gotten

Public Papers of George Clinton, III, 30–33.

1. Presumably Captain-Lieutenant Whitehead Coleman, First Continental Artillery.
2. Letter of March 6, 1778, not found.
3. This is apparently a reference to the Board of War.

into the spirit of making *ex post facto laws,* or rather violating all
law. Another resolve, by plain implication, acknowledges a thing
not founded in fact, which is very injurious to us—to wit, that we
have inlisted prisoners of war. This silences all our complaints against
the enemy for a similar practice, and furnishes them with a damning
answer to any thing we can say on the subject. This is at least an
instance of folly and inconsideration, and serves to prove the general charge.

These men seem also to have embraced a system of infidelity.
They have violated the convention of Saratoga; and I have reason
to believe the ostensible motives for it were little better than pre-
tences, that had no foundation. I have lately seen some letters from
Burgoigne on the subject. There was however a strong temptation
for this, and it may be excused, though I cannot say the measure
is to my taste. Lately, a flag, with provisions and cloathing for the
British prisoners, with G. W.'s passport was seized at Lancaster. The
affair was attended with circumstances of violence, and mean[n]ess
that would disgrace hottentots. Still more lately, G. W. engagements with G.H., for an exchange of prisoners, has been most
shamefully violated. C—s have resolved that no exchange shall take
place 'till all accounts are settled and the ballance due the U: S:
paid. The beauty of it is—on a fair settlement we shall without
doubt be in Mr. Howe's debt; and in the meantime we detain his
officers and soldiers, as a security for the payment. The operation of
this resolve, though it does not plainly appear upon the face of it,
is to put off an exchange, perhaps forever. At any rate it cannot take
place all next summer.

It is thought to be bad policy to go into an exchange; but admitting this to be true it is much worse policy to commit such frequent
breaches of faith, and ruin our national character. Whatever refined
politicians may think, it is of great consequence to preserve a national character; and if it should once seem to be a system in any
state to violate its faith whenever it is the least inconvenient to keep
it, it will unquestionably have an ill-effect upon foreign negociations
and tend to bring Government at home into contempt, and of course
to destroy its influence. The general notions of justice and humanity
are implanted in almost every human breast; and ought not to be
too freely shocked. In the present case, the passions of the country

and army are on the side of an exchange; and a studied attempt to avoid it will disgust both, and serve to make the service odious. It will injure drafting and recruiting, discourage the militia & increase the discontents of the army. The prospect of hopeless captivity cannot but be very disagreeable to men constantly exposed to the chance of it. Those, whose lot it is to fall into it, will have little scruple to get rid of it by joining the enemy.

It is said, not to be our present interest to exchange, because we should endeavour, by and by, to take advantage of the enemy's weakness to strike some decisive blow. If we should fail in this, which I believe we shall, when they get reinforced we shall not think it our interest to add to the strength of an enemy, already strong enough and so on ad infinitum.

The truth is, considered in the mere view of barter, it never can be our interest to exchange; the constitution of our army, from the short term of inlistment the dependence we are obliged to place in the militia, are strongly opposed to it; and if the argument of present interest be adhered to, we never can exchange. I may venture to assert, there never can be a time more proper than the present, or rather a month or two hence; and go about it as soon as we please the previous negociations necessary and other circumstances, will, of course, procrastinate it for some time. And I would ask, whether in a republican state and a republican army; such a cruel policy as that of exposing those men who are foremost in defence of their country to the miseries of hopeless captivity, can succeed?

For my own part I have so much of the milk of humanity in me, that I abhor such *Neronian* maxims; and I look upon the old proverb, that *honesty is the best policy* to be so generally true, that I can never expect any good from a systematical deviation from it; and I never can adopt the reasonings of some *American* politicians deducible from their practice, that no regard is to be paid to national character, or the rules of good faith.

I dwell upon the faults of Congress because I think they strike at the vitals of our opposition and of our future prosperity, and with this idea I cannot but wish that every Gentleman of influence in the country should think with me.

We have nothing new in camp, save that Capt. Barry,[4] late of

4. Captain John Barry, American Navy.

a Continental frigate, has destroyed with a few gunboats two large ships belonging to the enemy, laden with forage from Rhode Island. He also took an armed schooner, which he has since been obliged to run on shore, after a gallant defence.[5] 'Tis said he has saved her cannon & stores—among the ordnance four brass howitzers. Some acco'ts say the enemy are preparing to evacuate Philadelphia. *Sed credat Judaeus Apella, non ego.*

I have the honor to be With unfeigned esteem & respect Sir Your most Obed't   A. Hamilton

5. Barry's biographer describes this exploit as follows: "So one night in February, 1778, with twenty-seven men in four row boats, he came down from above Burlington, and, succeeding in passing Philadelphia unmolested by its British occupants. He went as far as Port Penn in the lower Delaware, and there on February 26th, 1778, captured two vessels, the *Mermaid* and the *Kitty,* and their convoy of 10 guns, the *Alert,* all laden with forage and supplies for the British army. After stripping the two ships he burned them, and sent their supplies northward through New Jersey. But British cruisers . . . discovered Barry at work and attacked him. He was obliged to run the schooner ashore, but held possession of her, however" (Martin I. J. Griffin, *Commodore John Barry* [Philadelphia, 1903], 70–71).

George Washington to Major General William Heath

Valley Forge, March 14, 1778. Instructs Heath to demand liberation of Daniel Heister and the return of Heister's papers and effects.

LS, in writing of H, Massachusetts Historical Society, Boston.

George Washington to Henry Laurens [1]

Valley Forge, March 16, 1778. States that command of Forts Montgomery and Clinton should be placed under general command of the Highlands. Has appointed Major General Alexander McDougall to that general command. Sees no prospect of carrying out intended expedition against Canada.

LS, in writing of H, Papers of the Continental Congress, National Archives.
    1. Laurens had succeeded John Hancock as President of Congress.

George Washington to
Major General Alexander McDougall

Valley Forge, March 16, 1778. Instructs McDougall to set up court of inquiry to investigate Major General Israel Putnam's alleged responsibility for fall of Forts Montgomery and Clinton. Appoints McDougall to command of the Highlands.

Df, in writing of Tench Tilghman, with postscript in writing of H, George Washington Papers, Library of Congress.

To Major Samuel French [1]

[Valley Forge, March 20, 1778]

Sir,

His Excellency has received good information, that there is a number of arms and spare Bayonets, at Bordin Town in New Jersey. This he thinks a very improper depositary for them, and desires you will have them removed thence, without delay to one of the Laboratories on this side the Delaware, Allen Town, Lebanon or elsewhere.

I am Sir   Your most hum serv   A Hamilton ADC

Head Quarters Valley
Forge March 20th. 1778

ADfS, George Washington Papers, Library of Congress.
1. French was commissary of military stores.

George Washington to Sir William Howe

[Valley Forge] March 22, 1778. Demands exchange of Lieutenant Colonel Ethan Allen for Lieutenant Colonel Archibald Campbell and release of Captains Isaiah Robinson and Nathaniel Galt. Informs Howe that Elias Boudinot, Colonel William Grayson, and Lieutenant Colonels Alexander Hamilton and Robert Hanson Harrison have

been appointed as commissioners for negotiating an exchange of prisoners.

Df, in writings of Robert Hanson Harrison and H, George Washington Papers, Library of Congress.

To Colonel Israel Shreve [1]

[Valley Forge, March 25, 1778]

Sir,

His Excellency desires me to inform you, that he, has given directions for the party stationed at the Salt works, which Col: Forman is raising,[2] to join and act with you, 'till further orders.

I am Sir   Your hum serv   A Hamilton ADC

Head Quarters Valley
Forge March 25th, 1778

ADfS, George Washington Papers, Library of Congress.
    1. Shreve was a colonel of the Second New Jersey Regiment.
    2. Colonel David Forman, of one of the Additional Sixteen Continental Regiments, was in charge of the erection of a salt works at Barnegat, New Jersey.

George Washington to Colonel David Forman

Valley Forge, March 25, 1778. Orders Forman to leave salt works and join Colonel Israel Shreve's regiment.

Df, in writing of H, George Washington Papers, Library of Congress.

George Washington to William Livingston

Valley Forge, March 25, 1778. Asks Livingston to have Mr. Jacob Bankson watched as a suspected spy.

Df, in writings of Robert Hanson Harrison and H, George Washington Papers, Library of Congress.

MARCH 1778 445

George Washington to Colonel Stephen Moylan [1]

Valley Forge, March 25, 1778. Orders transfer of horses to Iveham and Springfield if this will improve their quarters and forage.

Df, in writing of H, George Washington Papers, Library of Congress.
1. Moylan was a colonel of the Fourth Continental Dragoons.

From Cornelius Durant

Boston, March 27, 1778. Encloses letter from Hugh Knox [1] and requests Hamilton to write to Knox.

ALS, Hamilton Papers, Library of Congress.
1. Hugh Knox to H, December 10, 1777.

From Major Nicholas Fish

Valley Forge, March 27, 1778. Requests discharge for Ensign Robert Wood, Second New York Regiment.

ALS, RG 93, Miscellaneous Records, National Archives.

Commission to Colonel William Grayson, Lieutenant Colonels Robert Hanson Harrison and Alexander Hamilton, and Elias Boudinot [1]

[Valley Forge, March 28, 1778]

By His Excellency, George Washington Esquire, General and Commander in Chief of all the Forces of the United States of America.

To Colonel William Grayson, Lieutenant Colonels Robert Hanson Harrison and Alexander Hamilton and Elias Boudinot Esquire Commissary General of Prisoners

Whereas a proposition was made, by me, on the 30th day of July 1776, to His Excellency General Sir William Howe, and acceded to, by him, on the first day of August following, stipulating an exchange of Prisoners "officer for officer of equal rank, soldier for soldier and citizen for citizen": And Whereas differences have arisen on the construction and execution of this agreement; and it has been found by Experience to be inadequate to all the desireable purposes for which it was intended, not being sufficiently extensive and definite to comprehend the diversity of circumstances incident to the state of Captivity, or to ascertain the various modes of relief applicable to all:

In order to adjust all such differences, to prevent others, in future, so far as may be practicable, and to fix the exchange and accommodation of Prisoners of War, upon a more certain, liberal, and ample foundation; You are in virtue of full powers to me delegated, to meet such Commissioners of suitable rank, as are, or shall be appointed on the part of General Sir William Howe, at German Town, on the last day of this month, and who shall come duly authorised to treat on the subject:

With them to confer, determine and agree upon a Treaty and Convention for the Exchange of Prisoners of War, and for all matters whatsoever, which may be properly contained therein, on principles of justice, humanity and mutual advantage, and agreeable to the customary rules and practice of war among civilized nations: For all which, this shall be your sufficient warrant, and your engagements being mutually interchanged, shall be ratified and confirmed by me.

Given under my hand and seal

By His Excellency's ⎫
   Command ⎬
  John Laurens
  Aide de Camp

at Head Quarters, Valley Forge, this 28th day of March 1778

Df, George Washington Papers, Library of Congress.

1. This document is in writing of H and is countersigned by John Laurens, an aide-de-camp to Washington.

To Colonel Stephen Moylan

[Valley Forge, March 29, 1778]

Sir

It is His Excellency's desire that you immediately send to camp a good active vigilant officer with twenty horse. Let both horses and men be picked, as the service they are intended for will require able horses and trusty men who will not desert. They are wanted to relieve Capt Lee,[1] and perform the duties his parties did. Be pleased to have it done without delay.

Dr Col: Yrs. with regard   A Hamilton ADC

Head Quarters
March 29th. 1778

ALS, Historical Society of Pennsylvania, Philadelphia.
  1. Captain Henry (Light Horse Harry) Lee, First Continental Dragoons. When this letter was written, Washington was considering making Lee an aide-de-camp. Lee, however, remained with the cavalry; and on April 7, 1778, Congress promoted him to the rank of major commandant in command of a separate corps.

Charles Thomson to Colonel William Grayson, Lieutenant Colonels Robert Hanson Harrison and Alexander Hamilton, and Elias Boudinot [1]

In Congress [York, Pennsylvania] March 30th. 1778

Whereas Congress concur in opinion with General Washington that there are some Ambiguities characterizing the Measures taken by Genl. Howe respecting General Lee,[2] which justify alarming surmises, notwithstanding all that has passed to the contrary.

Resolved That General Washington be informed that it is the intention of Congress that it should be a preliminary in the proposed Cartel for a general Exchange of prisoners that Major General Lee be absolutely exchanged for Major Genl. Prescot, and if refused, that no exchange take place till the further order of Congress.

That it be proposed to exchange Lt. Colo. Ethan Allen [3] for Lieut.

Colo. Campbell or Lieut. Colo. Anstruther and if not acceded to that Lieut. Colo. Campbell be sent back to the State of Massachusets Bay.

That General Washington be further directed to instruct the Commissioners to be careful not to contravene, in setting the proposed Cartel, any of the Resolutions of Congress particularly that of the 30th Decemr. respecting such of the Citizens of these States as may voluntarily join the Enemy and be taken in Arms against these States.

That if the Enemy will not consent to exempt Citizens from Capture agreeable to the law of Nations the Commissioners be instructed positively to insist on their exchange without any relation to Rank.

That General Washington be directed not to permit any Article of the proposed Cartel to be finally concluded without his express approbation and that the president be directed to inform him accordingly.

Extract from the Minutes   Chas: Thompson Secy.

D, George Washington Papers, Library of Congress.
   1. This document is a contemporary copy of the original. Although addressed to the commissioners, it was sent by Thomson to Washington, who, in turn, enclosed it in his letter to the commissioners, April 1, 1778.
   Thomson was secretary of the Continental Congress.
   2. Major General Charles Lee, who had been taken prisoner at Basking Ridge, New Jersey, on December 13, 1776.
   3. Allen, commander of the Green Mountain Boys of Vermont, had been taken prisoner at Montreal on September 25, 1775.

To Baron von Steuben [1]

[Valley Forge, March–April, 1778] [2]

Voila votre reponse mon Cher Baron!

Par le camp De Bound Brook, Je suppose que vous voulez dire le Camp de Middle Brook, lequel est tres pres de Bound Brook, et nous n'avons point eu de camp la. C'est une position infiniment avantageuse a tous egards, situé sur une montagne fort escarpé, les approaches en front et par les flancs extremement difficile, couvert de bois &c. Le retraite en est bien facile &c.

Nous n'avons point de vaisseau a Burlington; mais nous avons des batteaux a Coryels ferry. Je ne scais pas le nombre, mais il y en a assez pour transporter notre armé a travers du Delaware, dans tres peu de tems.

Le terrein entre Trenton &c. n'est pas beaucoup coupé par des bois; les chemins sont bons; il y a, si je me souviens bien, deux ou trois petits creeks.

Je crois voir le raison de ces questions. Vous voulez faire faire a l'armee un mouvement dans les Jerseys. C'est une chose beaucoup as desirer, si nous avions assez de waggons pour transporter non seulement l'armee, mais nos malades, magazins &c.; mais nous n'avons pas assez pour cela.

AL, New-York Historical Society, New York City.
1. Frederick William Augustus Henry Ferdinand, baron von Steuben had arrived in this country from Germany in the autumn of 1777 after serving as one of Frederick the Great's titular aides. He first appeared at Valley Forge on February 23, 1778. On March 28, 1778, Washington appointed him volunteer inspector general.
2. There is no date on the MS, but the mention of boats at Coryell's Ferry indicates that it was probably written some time in the spring of 1778.

George Washington to Colonel William Grayson, Lieutenant Colonels Robert Hanson Harrison and Alexander Hamilton, and Elias Boudinot [1]

Head Quarters, Valley Forge 1st: April 1778

Gentlemen

The inclosed Resolutions of Congress [2] came to my hand this instant, and as they are essentially necessary for your Government I have sent them immediately by Express.

The first four Resolves are absolute and therefore you are obliged to insist upon the terms therein directed. But do not let the last embarrass you or impede your Business. I have so perfect a reliance upon your judgment and upon your prudence that you may depend upon my confirming whatever you may agree to.

I am with the greatest Regard   Gentlemen   Yr. most obt. Servt.

Go: Washington

LS, in writing of Tench Tilghman, George Washington Papers, Library of Congress.
1. For background to this letter, see "Commission," March 28, 1778.
2. Printed above under date of March 30, 1778.

Colonels Charles O'Hara and Humphrey Stephens, and Captain Richard FitzPatrick to Colonel William Grayson, Lieutenant Colonels Robert Hanson Harrison and Alexander Hamilton, and Elias Boudinot [1]

Philadelphia
April 1st: 1778

Gentlemen

We have reported to Sir Wm. Howe your observations on his Commission to us for settling a Cartel for the Exchange of Prisoners; therefore if it will not be inconvenient, We will beg the favor of you to stay in German Town 'till ten o'clock, at which time We will do ourselves the honor of waiting on you to lay before you Sir Wm: Howe's Sentiments on that matter.

We are Gentlemen With due respect Your very Obedient Servants

Chas: OHara
Humphy. Stephens
Richard FitzPatrick

To
Colonel Grayson
Lt Col: Harrison
Lt Col: Hamilton
Elias Boudinot Esqr.

We hope to have the favor of your answer.

LS, in writing of Humphrey Stephens, George Washington Papers, Library of Congress.

1. O'Hara, Stephens, and FitzPatrick were the British commissioners appointed to negotiate with the American commissioners for an exchange of prisoners. For background to this letter, see "Commission," March 28, 1778.

Colonel William Grayson, Lieutenant Colonels Robert Hanson Harrison and Alexander Hamilton, and Elias Boudinot to Colonels Charles O'Hara and Humphrey Stephens, and Captain Richard FitzPatrick [1]

[Germantown, Pennsylvania] April 2nd. 1778.

Gentlemen

We have the honor of your favor per flag;

Having inform'd General Washington of the message delivered yesterday from Sir W. Howe, & of our intentions to return to camp immediately, in consequence of it; [2] we do not think ourselves at liberty, to use so much delay, as would afford us the pleasure of the interview proposed.

We are   Gentlemen with due respect   yr. Very hble servts.

To	Willm. Grayson
Colo. O'hara	R. H. Harrison
Colo. Stephens	A. Hamilton
Capt. Fitzpatrick.	Elias Boudenot

Df, or copy, in writing of William Grayson, George Washington Papers, Library of Congress.

1. For background to this letter, see "Commission," March 28, 1778.

2. On April 4, 1778, Washington wrote to Howe: "I was sorry to learn an objection had been made to the residence of my Commissioners at German Town, during the continuance of the negotiation, as it served to give interruption to a business, which we are mutually interested should proceed without more delay, than the nature of it requires. I had no idea, but that the Gentlemen on both sides were to remain constantly at German Town 'till the conclusion of the treaty" (George Washington Papers, Library of Congress).

To Major General Nathanael Greene

[Valley Forge, April 3, 1778]

Dr. General,

We have to request, you will order a couple of very good teams to be got ready to proceed to the enemy's lines for General Lee's baggage. He is to come out on parole, on Sunday morning.[1] You will judge when they ought to set out from here—suppose tomorrow noon, so as to get in the neighbourhood of Vandeering's Mill [2] by tomorrow night. When they are ready to set out tomorrow let them make report to Head Quarters and passports will be given.

Yr hum serv   A Hamilton ADC

Head Quarters
April 3

Major General Greene   QMG

ALS, New York Society Library, New York City.
  1. Following his parole, Major General Charles Lee was exchanged on May 6, 1778.
  2. Vandeern's Mill, in Wiscohicon (or Wissahichon) district of Philadelphia.

To Colonel Stephen Moylan

Head Quarters [Valley Forge] April
3d. 1778

Sir,

By command of His Excellency, I am to desire, you will send a corporal and six dragoons, with a Trumpeter to Head Quarters, without loss of time. They are wanted to escort the Commissioners on our part who are to meet on the subject of a general Cartel.[1] You need not be told they must be picked men and horses—must make the best possible appearance—must be very trusty and very intelligent. They should also be of the same regiment.

The General reminds you again of the necessity of keeping your officers close to their quarters and duty; and of letting no attention be wanting to put the cavalry, under your command, on the best footing you can, both with respect to condition and discipline.

There is a certain Mr Bankson, late of the Continental marines, who has a family at Princeton. We suspect him to be a spy to Mr Howe, though he offers himself as one to us.[2] We wish to find out his true history. He left this camp the 24th of March, on pretence of making a visit to his family, and is now returned with renewed offers of service. It is doubted whether he has not, in the mean time, been at Philadelphia. The General wrote some days since to Governor Livingston, requesting he would take measures to explore Mr Banksons conduct and views. He directs you immediately to see the Governor and learn from him, if he has been able to make any discovery, and to take cautious methods to ascertain whether Bankson has been at home, since he left camp—how long—and when he left home—in short any thing that may throw light upon his designs.

Let him hear from you as soon as possible on the subject. Manage the business with caution and address.

Yrs. Affecty   A H. ADC

ADfS, George Washington Papers, Library of Congress.

    1. See "Commission," April 4, 1778.

    2. On June 1, 1778, Washington wrote to Governor William Livingston of New Jersey: "The Christian name of Bankson, who I begged the favor of you to keep an eye upon, is Jacob, but as I am now satisfied concerning him, you need not trouble yourself further in the matter" (George Washington Papers, Library of Congress).

    John Bakeless describes this incident as follows: "Another of General Washington's personal spies was the ex-marine captain, Jacob Bankson, whose first offer to enter Philadelphia as a secret agent led to strong suspicion that he was a British spy. The ex-marine had always been able to go in and out of British-occupied Philadelphia in some mysterious way of his own. This uncanny ability or something else made General Washington so suspicious that, in the spring of 1778, he asked Governor William Livingston, of New Jersey, to have the captain watched. Four days later, Livingston put a counter-intelligence agent on the suspect's trail, which on that very day led—straight to General Washington's headquarters! Still unconvinced, the general had Alexander Hamilton check the man's background in Princeton. Fully cleared of all suspicion in a few more days, Bankson was twice paid $100 for secret service, April 11 and May 1, 1778, though what he did remains unknown" (Bakeless, *Turncoats, Traitors and Heroes*, 207).

George Washington to Henry Laurens

Valley Forge, April 3, 1778. Recommends that Captain Henry Lee be promoted.

Df, in writing of H, George Washington Papers, Library of Congress.

Colonel William Grayson, Lieutenant Colonels Robert Hanson Harrison and Alexander Hamilton, and Elias Boudinot to George Washington [1]

[Valley Forge, April 4, 1778]

To His Excellency George Washington Esquire, General and Commander in Chief of the Forces of the United States of America.

We, the Commissioners appointed by Your Excellency, "to confer, determine and agree upon a Treaty and Convention, for the exchange of Prisoners of War, and for all matters whatsoever, which may be properly contained therein" beg leave to report—

That in pursuance of Your Excellency's orders, on the 31st day of March, we met at German Town, the Commissioners appointed by General Sir William Howe, for the purposes, as expressed in their commission, "of taking into consideration all past transactions, relative to the exchange of prisoners, to adjust the differences, that have so long subsisted in regard to them, to remove all difficulties that may arise, in carrying into execution a general exchange of prisoners, with both parties at this time, and finally to establish a regular and explicit cartel, for the future."

We produced our respective powers and interchanged copies for further examination; after which a proposition was made to us, to take up the business of our meeting, in the form of a general Cartel, and to make the discussion of past transactions a secondary object; in doing which, it was to be understood, that nothing was to be final or obligatory, 'till the whole Treaty should be concluded. To this we readily agreed, as the mode appeared eligible in itself, and consonant with the intention of our commission. These preliminaries being adjusted, a paper was submitted to our consideration, containing a number of articles, relative to the subject of our negociation which we promised to peruse and deliver our sentiment concerning.

General Howe's commissioners proposed to adjourn 'till the next day, and expressed a desire of returning that evening to Philadelphia, to which we did not then think proper to object.

Having met the next morning, we, in a cursory manner, pointed out some imperfections in General Howe's commission: An essential one was, that it contained no recital of the authority, by which he acted; whereas your Excellency's commission expressly specifies, that it is, 'in virtue of full powers to you delegated.' His commissioners promised to communicate our objections, and receive his further instructions.

We proceeded, in the mean time, to a comparison of ideas on the paper abovementioned, and made rough minutes of the result; agreeing, that whatever might be adopted should only be considered, as a concurrence in some general principles, which were to be modified, explained, enlarged and applied, as should be, afterwards determined.

It was then proposed to digest what had been done into a more regular and explicit form, and to prepare any new propositions which might occur; but as this would necessarily require time, it was agreed to defer our next interview, to Friday the 3d: of April.

The Commissioners, from General Howe, then informed us, that it was expected by him, the Commissioners on both sides were always to retire, after the business of the day, within their respective lines, and that the neutrality of German Town was only to continue, during the time of actual negotiation; as on account of the proximity of that place to Philadelphia, many inconveniences might attend our constant residence there. This proposal was equally unexpected and surprising:—We conceived it to be contrary to the tenor of the correspondence, communicated to us, which had passed between your Excellency and General Howe, for the appointment of a place of Treaty. It could not but produce much unnecessary delay in the negociation, the distance between your camp and German Town being [more than seventeen miles] [2] and tended to impose a new and burthensome condition on us by obliging us to perform a journey of twice that distance every day. In point of propriety and for the dispatch of business, we thought it necessary, the commissioners should remain constantly together. These motives and an apprehension, that something might be implied, in the objection, unfavourable to our personal honor, determined us to suspend the negociation 'till we had reported to Your Excellency the terms required and received your directions in consequence. We declared our resolution

and reasons to General Howe's commissioners and have returned
to Camp accordingly.

Willm. Grayson.

Camp Valley forge   Rob. H. Harrison

Alex Hamilton

April 4th. 1778   Elias Boudinot

DS, in writing of H, George Washington Papers, Library of Congress; Df,
in writing of Robert Hanson Harrison, George Washington Papers, Library
of Congress.
1. For background to this letter, see "Commission," March 28, 1778.
2. Bracketed material is in unidentified handwriting.

Commission to Colonel William Grayson, Lieutenant Colonels Robert Hanson Harrison and Alexander Hamilton, and Elias Boudinot

[Valley Forge, April 4, 1778]

By His Excellency George Washington Esquire General and Com-
mander in chief of all the Forces of the United States of America
To Colonel William Grayson, Lieutenant Colonels Robert Hanson
Harrison and Alexander Hamilton, and Elias Boudinot Esquire
Commissary General of prisoners.

Whereas a proposition was made by me on the 30th: day of July
1776, to His Excellency General Sir William Howe, and acceded
to by him, on the first day of August following, stipulating an exchange of prisoners, "Officer for Officer of equal rank, Soldier for
Soldier, and Citizen for Citizen;" And whereas differences have arisen
on the construction and execution of this agreement; and it has been
found by experience to be inadequate to all the desirable purposes
for which it was intended, not being sufficiently extensive and definite to comprehend the diversity of circumstances incident to the
state of Captivity, or to ascertain the various modes of relief applicable to all.

In order to adjust all such differences, to prevent others in future,
so far as may be practicable, and to fix the Exchange and accommodation of prisoners of War, upon a more certain, liberal and
ample foundation; You are, in virtue of full powers to me delegated,

to meet such Commissioners of suitable rank as are or shall be appointed on the part of General Sir William Howe, and who shall come duly authorised to treat on the subject, at Newtown in the County of Bucks on the sixth day of this month and such place afterwards as shall be mutually agreed upon— With them to confer, determine and agree upon a Treaty and Convention for the exchange of prisoners of War and for all matters whatsoever which may be properly contained therein on principles of Justice, Humanity and mutual advantage, and agreeable to the customary rules and practice of war among civilized nations For all which this shall be your sufficient Warrant and your engagements being mutually interchanged shall be ratified and confirmed by me.

Given under my hand and seal
By His Excellency's ⎱   at Head Quarters, Valley Forge
  Command ⎰   this fourth day of April 1778.
  John Laurens   Go: Washington
  Aide de Camp

DS, in writing of Tench Tilghman, George Washington Papers, Library of Congress; Df, in writing of John Laurens, George Washington Papers, Library of Congress.

George Washington to Sir William Howe

[*Valley Forge*] *April 4, 1778.* Discusses change of meeting place for commissioners from Germantown to Newtown.

Df, in writings of Robert Hanson Harrison and H, George Washington Papers, Library of Congress.

Permit for Lieutenant Colonel Alexander Hamilton to Pass British Lines [1]

Head Quarters, Philadelphia, 5th. April, 1778.

Until further Orders, advanced Posts and Patrols are not to prevent all persons, having Passports Signed by two of the following Officers, to pass unmolested, Viz.: Cols. O'Hara and Stephens, and Capt. Fitzpatrick, of the British; Col. Gregson, Lieut.-Col. Hamilton, and Mr. Boudinot (Commissary of Prisoners), belonging to the Enemy.

Colls. of the N.Y. Hist. Soc. for 1883 (New York, 1884), 564.
   1. For background to this document, see "Commission," April 4, 1778.

George Washington to Mrs. Mary Pemberton [1]

[*Valley Forge*] *April 5, 1778.* Cannot comply with Mrs. Pemberton's request, but is forwarding it to Thomas Wharton, Jr.,[2] who will no doubt approve the application.

Df, in writing of H, George Washington Papers, Library of Congress.
   1. Mrs. Pemberton had applied for a passport for wagons carrying supplies to her husband who was a prisoner.
   2. Wharton was president of the Supreme Executive Council of Pennsylvania.

George Washington to Thomas Wharton, Junior

[*Valley Forge*] *April 5, 1778.* Encloses letter from Mary Pemberton. Has refused her request but will convey the wagons requested, if Wharton agrees.

LS, in writing of H, George Washington Photostats, Library of Congress.

Colonel William Grayson, Lieutenant Colonels Robert Hanson Harrison and Alexander Hamilton, and Elias Boudinot to Colonels Charles O'Hara and Humphrey Stephens, and Captain Richard FitzPatrick [1]

[Newtown, Pennsylvania, April 10, 1778]

The Commissioners appointed by His Excellency General Washington to confer, determine and agree upon a Treaty and Convention for the Exchange of Prisoners of War, and for all matters whatsoever, that may be properly contained therein—

Having examined the powers on the part of General Sir William Howe to his Commissioners and compared them with their own, observe a difference, which, in their apprehension, [is] [2] very essential and important: General Washington in his commission, expressly declares it to be given in virtue of full powers to him delegated; General Sir Wm. Howe, in his commission, makes no acknowlegement of any authority by which he acts.

It appears to be the intention of the respective Generals, mutually expressed [3] in their powers, to do an extensive and permanent act, which shall not only effect a settlement of past differences, and a General Exchange of prisoners for the present, but shall extend to the establishment of a *regular* and *explicit* cartel, in *future*. The objects of this cartel will not be wholly of a military nature, but will include matters of very interesting civil concern. It is apprehended, that the power of entering into a Treaty of such importance is not naturally inherent in military command, and that it cannot be exercised by either of the Generals, as an official act, merely, in virtue of their military capacities; but must be founded on special authority delegated for the purpose. This authority according to reason and universal practice, ought to be declared, otherwise it will not appear, nor have the least efficiency, or operation.

That, if this authority does not exist, the negociation can have no sufficient foundation, It must rest solely on the footing of personal confidence. The public faith cannot be considered as pledged for the performance of any engagements in consequence of it, and these may, of course, be overruled at pleasure. Could the credit of individuals be supposed great enough, in preservation of personal honor, to prevent the interference of superior authority, their influence could not at any rate extend beyond their own [4] command, and should the casualties of War remove them, their successors would not be, in any manner, bound by their agreements.

In fine, it is conceived, there would be a manifest impropriety, in conducting a business of this nature on personal ground, as such a measure would be destitute of that validity, which the solemnity of a public act alone can give, and which the magnitude of the objects, it is intended to comprehend, indispensibly requires. Personal confidence, or the mutual credit of individuals is too slender and

unsubstantial a basis, for concerns of so great variety and extent as
the Treaty in contemplation must necessarily involve.

                                    Signed   Willm Grayson

New Town April 10th. 1778   Rob: H: Harrison
                                             Alexr Hamilton
To   Elias Boudinot
Colonel Charles O Hara
Colonel Humphry Stephen
Capt: Richard Fitzspatrick

Transcript, PRO: C.O., part 5, vol. 95.
    1. For background to this document, see "Commission," April 4, 1778.
    2. In MS "a."
    3. In MS "expresses."
    4. In MS "on."

Questions Concerning a Proposed Cartel for the Exchange of Prisoners of War [1]

[Newtown, Pennsylvania, April 10–11, 1778]

1st. Qre? . . . In what light are the prisoners sent out by General
       Howe to be considered?

2d . . . How far and for what proportion are we bound to ac-
       count?

3d . . . When and upon what terms are the British and foreign
       prisoners in our hands to be returned? Who are to be con-
       sidered as citizens on both sides?

4th . . . Are Americans, who join the enemy, when not in cap-
       tivity, and taken in Arms to be considered as other prisoners
       and liable to be exchanged?

5th. Is not the agreement for the exchange of prisoners now sub-
       sisting to continue?

6th. Is any further mode of Exchange to be adopted, such as giving
       a number of inferior officers or privates for one of superior
       rank, or estimating officers and privates at a price, when an

AD, Historical Society of Pennsylvania, Philadelphia.
    1. These questions were prepared by H, presumably for the consideration
of his fellow commissioners appointed for the exchange of prisoners.

exchange can't be effected according to the Agreement now in force? If a further mode is to be adopted, what shall be the proportion of inferior officers or privates? At what price are officers and privates to be estimated, how it is to be paid & in what specie?

7th. In what time are exchanges to be made, having regard to the situation of the armies as to distance from each other?

8th. Should not regular returns of prisoners be transmitted by the Commissaries of each army, or persons authorised for that purpose, of all prisoners in their possession and how often?

9th.—Who shall do the first act in exchanges? Shall the party indebted make the first return of prisoners? Or shall he give notice of the time, place, number and quality of the prisoners to be exchanged, and then and there receive a like number in return?

10th. What rations or supplies of provision, or money in lieu of them, shall be furnished prisoners? Should they be in provision? How shall the balance be estimated and when and how paid? Should not accounts be regularly transmitted and how often?

11th— Are the respective commanders to advance prisoners, in their possession, any, and what pay?

12— Are prisoners to be furnished with cloaths and medecine and how to be accounted for?

13— Are rations and other accounts already incurred to be adjusted; when and how?

14— How is the difference between gold, silver and paper currency to be considered in settling accounts?

15th. Shall prisoners taken in future be allowed to inlist?

16— Are there any and what persons in the army, who should not be considered as prisoners of War though taken, and who should be immediately released, without receiving others of the same condition in return?

Hospitals

17.—Is the Cartel proposed to be settled to comprehend officers & sailors in the marine line, supposing the officer appointed to nogociate on the part of General Howe will agree to it? If it is, are they only to be exchanged for officers in the sea service, and upon principles of equality in number and in rank? Or may they be exchanged for land officers where an exchange in the marine line cannot be effected, having regard to difference of rank?

Passports for purveyors or commissaries to Hospitals to carry or purchase provisions, where they shall happen to be in the neighbourhood.

Are Chaplains, Physicians, surgeons & all their attendants to be considered as Prisoners or not? Are the sick & wounded in hospitals?

Notes on a Proposed Cartel for the Exchange of Prisoners of War [1]

[Newtown, Pennsylvania, April 10–11, 1778]

MEMORANDUMS

Arts:

All officers and soldiers, prisoners of war on either side shall be exchanged on the terms and in the manner following.

Those first captured shall be first exchanged.

Every officer shall be exchanged for one of equal rank, as far as number will apply, except when there are officers, who have been longer in captivity, that cannot be so exchanged; in which case, these shall have a preference, and be exchanged on the principle of composition, according to the succeeding rule.

When officers cannot be exchanged for those of equal rank, two or more inferior officers shall be given for a

superior, in order to which, all officers
bearing rank shall be estimated thus:

General & Commander in chief	. 89
Lieutenant General	. 55
Major General	. 34
Brigadier	. 21
Col:	. 13
Lieut Colonel	8
Major	5
Captain	3
Lieutenant	2
Ensign	1

If there should remain any officers
on either side, who cannot be exchanged in the foregoing modes, privates may be given for officers at the
rate of five for an ensign and progressively in the above ratio.

(What shall
be the rate and maner of ransom for
money?)

Staff officers bearing rank shall be
exchanged for each other or for those
of the line of similar rank: Such as have
none shall be exchanged for each other
only, in the same or in different departments, either on the principle of
equality of station or composition;
and shall be estimated thus:

Quarter Master General	12
Deputy	6
Assistant deputy	3

AD, George Washington Papers, Library of Congress.
1. In addition to these notes made by H, there is another set in Robert Hanson Harrison's writing in which there are a few minor changes. Both sets are
based on a draft in Harrison's writing. The draft probably was used as a basis for
a conference among the American commissioners, as there are marginal notes on
the draft in the writing of Boudinot, Grayson, and H. Both the draft and
Harrison's notes are in the George Washington Papers, Library of Congress.

Commissary General of
    Provisions 6
Deputy 3
Ass: Deputy 1
Pay Master General 6
Deputy 3
Clerk 1
Commissary of Military Stores . 6
Deputy 3
Ass: deputy or conductor . . 1
Commissary of forage . . . 6
Deputy 3
Ass: deputy 1
Muster Master 6
Deputy 3
Waggon Master 3
Deputy or Conductor . . . 1
Capt of Guides 3

Officers on both sides to be returned on parole in   [2] days after captivity,

Citizens whether in or out of office how to be exchanged?—

Deserters, or persons, who bearing arms on either side, in the present war leave it, and enter into the opposite army, not to be deemed prisoners of war nor exchangeable.

Citizens of whatsoever class or denomination, whether in or out of office, and wheresoever taken to be exchanged for each other according to parity of number only.

Exchanges to be made every   [3] or sooner, if circumstances will permit.

Registers to be kept of all Prisoners taken specifying their names ranks and corps and the places of their confinement, and monthly returns, accounting for differences, shall be interchanged. When prisoners are to be returned, on either side, notice shall be given of the time and place, that proper persons may be appointed to

2. Space left blank in MS.   3. Space left blank in MS.

receive them. A list of their names ranks and corps shall be delivered with them; a duplicate of which shall be signed by the officer receiving as a voucher for the delivery.

Permission shall be allowed by both parties to purchase provisions, in aid of the stipulated rations—and cloathing and other necessaries, under proper restrictions.

Permission shall be granted to either party to send in provisions cloathing money and other necessaries for the use of prisoners, by land or water, and passports when required shall be given accordingly.

Commissaries to be mutually stationed.

to be enlarged

Surgeons & Medecines &c.

Proposed to hire instead of sending in.

Commissioned officers shall be permitted to visit the prisoners in their different stations at stated periods, and upon previous notice, under proper restrictions.

Hospitals—

Ration to be defined

Settlement of Accounts how?

Prisoners shall not be permitted to inlist or on any pretence be transported beyond sea?

Prisoners not to be thrown into dungeons or other unnecessarily rigorous confinement; but for a flagrant breach of the laws of war and nations.

All private property stolen by deserters to be returned.

Passports to be granted to Purveyors of Hospitals to provide necessaries for their use, within certain limits according to circumstances.

Draft of a Proposed Cartel for the Exchange of Prisoners of War [1]

[Newtown, Pennsylvania, April 10–11, 1778]

A Treaty and Convention for the Exchange and Accommodation of Prisoners of War, made between the Armies of The United States of America and The Kingdom of Great Britain; and for other purposes therein specified.

Whereas on the 30th. day of July, in the year 1776, a proposition was made by His Excellency General Washington to His Excellency General Sir William Howe, and acceded to by him, on the first day of August following, for an exchange of Prisoners—officer for officer of equal rank, soldier for soldier and citizen for citizen—And Whereas differences have arisen on the construction and execution of the said agreement, and it has been found by experience, to be, not fully competent to all the purposes of the exchange and accomodation of prisoners, To settle those differences and prevent the like in future, to provide more effectual and extensive relief, for captivity, in its various circumstances, and to obviate, as far as possible, every unnecessary distress and rigor of war,

We William Grayson Colonel, Robert Hanson Harrison and Alexander Hamilton Lieutenant Colonels, and Elias Boudinot, Commissary General of Prisoners, in the Armies of the United States

Being there unto duly authorised by His Excellency, George Washington Esquire, General and Commander in Chief of the same, and in virtue of the full powers to him given

Stipulate and declare, that the following articles shall have full force and effect, between the Belligerent armies, according to their true intent and meaning; and that, if any doubt or difficulty shall arise, it shall be decided, conformable to the natural import and design of this convention, and agreeable to the custom and usage of war among civilized nations.

ADf, George Washington Papers, Library of Congress.
1. This draft of a cartel, drawn up by H, is a summary of the views of the American commissioners.

Article 1st

All officers and soldiers, prisoners of war, on either side shall be exchanged on the terms and in the manner following:

Those first captured shall be first exchanged.

Every officer shall be exchanged, for one of equal rank, as far as number will apply; except when there are officers, who have been longer in captivity, that cannot be so exchanged, in which case, these shall have a preference and be exchanged on the principle of composition, according to the succeeding rule,

When officers cannot be exchanged for those of equal rank, two or more inferior officers shall be given for a superior in order to which all officers bearing rank shall be estimated thus:

General and commander in Chief	192
Lieutenant General, commanding in a separate department	96
Lieutenant General	48
Major General	24
Brigadier	12
Colonel	6
Lieut. Colonel	5
Major	4
Captain	3
Lieutenant	2
Ensign	1

If there should remain any officers on either side, who cannot be exchanged in the foregoing modes, it shall be at the option of the debtor, to give privates for officers, at the rate of five for an ensign, and progressively in the above ratio.

Staff officers bearing rank shall be exchanged for each other, or for those of the line of similar rank: Such as have none shall be exchanged for each other only; in the same, or in different departments, either on the principle of equality or of composition, and shall be estimated thus:—

Quarter Master General	12
Deputy	6
Assistant deputy	3
Commissary General of Provisions	6

Deputy	3
Assistant deputy	1
Pay Master General	6
Deputy	3
Clerk	1
Commissary of Military stores	6
Deputy	3
Assistant deputy or conductor	1
Commissary of forage	6
Deputy	3
Assistant deputy	1
Muster Master	6
Deputy	3
Waggon Master	3
Deputy or conductor	1
Capt of Guides	3

Officers of horse, foot, and artillery and Engineers shall be exchanged for each other indiscriminately: Dragoons, foot soldiers, matrosses, artificers, sappers and miners shall be exchanged for each other, in like manner.

Any officer, who may not be specifically comprehended in the preceeding articles, shall be exchanged for any other of similar station or degree, if such can be found; or some other mode shall be agreed on between the respective generals, favourable to the prisoner, which shall be an obligatory precedent for future exchanges of the same nature, and become a part of this cartel.

Retainers to, or persons serving in either army, in the most inferior capacities, not particularly enumerated, shall be exchanged for those of similar quality and description, so far as it can be done and the residue for private soldiers.

Officers shall be exchanged according to the highest rank they hold.

Exchanges shall be made every two months, or sooner, if circumstances will permit.

Officers, on both sides, shall be returned on parole in ten days after captivity; to remain so 'till regularly exchanged.

Registers shall be kept of all prisoners taken, specifying their names, ranks and corps, and monthly returns, accounting for differences, shall be interchanged. When prisoners are to be returned, on either side, notice shall be given of the time and place, that proper persons may be appointed to receive them. A List of their names, ranks and corps, shall be delivered with them; a duplicate of which shall be signed by the officer receiving, as a voucher for the delivery.

Article II

No person shall be considered, as an officer, or soldier, who is not at the time of capture, in military pay and service.

Article III

Physicians, Surgeons, Apothecaries, Purveyors and all attendants and guards on hospitals, Chaplains, Auditors of accounts, Clothiers, the Commissary General of Prisoners and his deputies, the Judge Advocate and his deputies, the Provost Marshal and his corps and all suttlers and servants, not soldiers, shall be exempt from captivity.

Hospitals should be sacred, everything they contain; the sick and wounded and stores of every kind, shall not be liable to capture or any species of violence.

Article 4th

Citizens of whatsoever class or denomination, whether, in or out of office, and wheresoever taken shall be exempt from captivity.

as exchanged on parity of number

Article V

A ration shall consist of one pound of bread and one pound of beef, fresh or salt, or three quarters of a pound of salt pork, averdupois. One ration, per day, shall be furnished to every prisoner, by the party to whom he is in captivity.

Article VI

Permission shall be granted for Commissaries to be stationed by the respective Generals with their officers, soldiers and others in captivity, to receive the rations stipulated by the preceding article, inspect their quantity and quality, and distribute them to the Prisoners. Their receipts to be vouchers for the delivery. They shall be permitted to visit the prisoners of all kinds dayly and to purchase where they reside for gold and silver, being the common medium of commerce among nations, such further necessaries (cloathing included) as may be requisite more effectually for relieving the necessities of the prisoners.

Each party shall have liberty to send its commissaries, all kinds of succours, cloathing, provisions and medecine, by land or water; for which purpose, passports shall be granted when required; and full permission shall be given such Commissaries, to sell at the market prices, where they are stationed *without restriction,* provisions or other articles sent them, the better to procure relief for the prisoners.

All practicable care shall be taken of sick and wounded prisoners; and medecine and all other necessaries shall be furnished by those in whose power they are, as far as the circumstances and condition of the parties will admit. Permission shall be mutually allowed to hire and employ doctors nurses and other attendants at the places where prisoners are confined to superintend the treatment and be intrusted with the care of the sick.

Settlements shall be made of ration accounts once every month, in which rations shall stand against rations, as far as they will extend, and the ballance shall be paid at the election of the debtor, either in provisions, or in gold and silver at the rate of twelve pence per ration, estimating spanish milled dollars at 4/6. Accounts of medicines and other necessaries, furnished the sick, shall be adjusted and paid, in like manner. These articles to be rated according to their real cost to the party furnishing them.

Article VII

All payments, in money, shall be made in gold and silver at the rate of 4/6 for each Spanish milled dollar, and 36/ for a half Johannes weighing 9 oz. 3 gr. and other coin in the same proportion.

Art: VIII

Prisoners shall not be permitted to inlist, or on any pretence be transported beyond sea.

Art IX

No officer, soldier, or other person subject to captivity by this Treaty and Convention shall be thrown into dungeons, or other kinds of unnecessarily rigorous confinement, unless for committing some flagrant violation of the laws of war and nations; in which case authentic vouchers of the crime shall be immediately transmitted to the Commissary of Prisoners of the Army, to which such offender may belong.

Art X

Passports shall be granted to Purveyors of Hospitals, to procure necessaries for their use, within certain limits, according to circumstances.

Art: XI

All private property stolen and carried off by deserters, shall be restored to the owner on application, within four days after their desertion. For this purpose, they shall be stopped at the first posts to which they come, carefully searched, and a list taken of the effects found in their possession, which they shall not be permitted to dispose of 'till the forementioned time shall be elapsed.

Art XII

In persuance of this agreement, the prisoners now actually in captivity, shall, in the first place, be exchanged in proportion to their respective numbers, within the term of two months from the date hereof, each party without delay returning an equal number of those delivered by the other, from time to time.

To adjust and remove the difference hitherto subsisting, as well with respect to the Exchange of Major General Lee, Lt. Colonel Ethan Allen, Capts. Van Dyke,[2] Vanzandt,[3] Whitlock,[4] Sullivan,[5] Bliss,[6] Ebenezer Greene,[7] Stevens,[8] Lieutenants Skinner,[9] Smock,[10]

2. Captain Abraham C. Van Dyke, New York Militia, was taken prisoner at Fort Washington, November 16, 1776.

3. Captain Viner Van Zandt. There is no record of when he was taken prisoner.

4. Presumably Major James Whitlock, New Jersey Militia, who is recorded as having been taken prisoner at an unspecified time and place. See F. B. Heitman, *Historical Register of Officers of the Continental Army* (Washington, 1893), 433.

5. Captain Ebenezer Sullivan, Continental Infantry, was taken prisoner at The Cedars, May 20, 1776.

6. Captain Thomas Theodore Bliss, Fifteenth Continental Regiment, was taken prisoner at The Cedars, May 20, 1776.

7. Captain Ebenezer Green, New Hampshire Rangers, was taken prisoner at The Cedars, May 19, 1776.

8. Captain John Stevens, Connecticut State Regiment, was taken prisoner at The Cedars, May 19, 1776.

9. Lieutenant Abraham Skinner, First Continental Infantry, was taken prisoner at Germantown, Pennsylvania, October 4, 1777.

10. Presumably, Lieutenant Henry Smock, New Jersey Militia.

and Doctor Minime,[11] or any other officers, that have been the objects of particular exception, as with respect to the proportion to be accounted for, of those Prisoners, which were sent out on parole by General Sir William Howe, between the month of November 76 and the month of April following, and which remain yet unexchanged: We do hereby specially stipulate and declare, that the aforesaid officers shall be immediately exchanged on the terms of this cartel, for any officers of equal rank, or others by way of equivalent or composition; which have been or shall be delivered in lieu of them; and that [12] private soldiers shall be returned by General Washington to General Sir William Howe, to be accepted by him as a full settlement and compensation for all prisoners heretofore in dispute.

Article XIII

To liquidate and settle all accounts, relating to prisoners, commissioners shall be mutually appointed within one month from the date of this Cartel, who shall meet on or before the [13] day of July next; and whatever ballance shall be found due from either party, shall be punctually paid and discharged within [14] after such liquidation and settlement of accounts; 'till the performance of which, it shall be at the will and choice of the party to which such ballance may be due, to make, or not to make any future exchange, besides those mentioned in the preceding twelvth article, the natural operation of this cartel being so far, and so far only, suspended.

Art. XIV

This Treaty and Convention shall be and continue in full force during the present war.

11. Daniel Memena, Surgeon, Second New York Regiment. There is no record of his being prisoner. Above "Doctor Minime," H wrote, "dead."
12. Space left blank in MS.
13. Space left blank in MS.
14. Space left blank in MS.

Colonels Charles O'Hara and Humphrey Stephens, and Captain Richard FitzPatrick to Colonel William Grayson, Lieutenant Colonels Robert Hanson Harrison and Alexander Hamilton, and Elias Boudinot [1]

New Town [Pennsylvania] 11th April *1778*

The Commissioners appointed by His Excellency Sir William Howe to take into Consideration all past Transactions relative to the Exchange of Prisoners, to adjust the differences that have so long subsisted in regard to them, to remove all Difficulties that may arise in carrying into Execution a General Exchange of Prisoners with both Parties at this Time, & finally to establish a regular & explicit Cartel for the future, Having received the Objections made to the Commission under which they act, from the Commissioners appointed to meet them for similar purposes by General Washington, are much concerned to find they are likely to prove an Obstruction to the Execution of so desirable a purpose. They conceive the Powers delegated to them by their Commission to be sufficient and ample, for effectually accomplishing the purposes therein contained, and hereby declare themselves ready and desirous of immediately entering upon a Treaty with the Commissioners appointed by General Washington for carrying in Execution the different Objects of their Commission.

Charles O'Hara
Humphy Stephens
Richd. Fitz Patrick

To
Col: Grayson
Lt. Col: Harrison
Lt Col: Hamilton
Elias Boudinot Esqr.

Transcript, PRO: C.O., part 5, vol. 95.

1. The points at issue, mentioned in this letter, are fully explained in the report of the American commissioners to Washington, April 15, 1778.

Colonel William Grayson, Lieutenant Colonels Robert Hanson Harrison and Alexander Hamilton, and Elias Boudinot to Colonels Charles O'Hara and Humphrey Stephens, and Captain Richard FitzPatrick [1]

[Newtown, Pennsylvania, April 11, 1778]

The Commissioners, appointed by His Excellency General Washington, "to confer, determine and agree upon a Treaty and Convention, for the exchange of prisoners of war, and for all matters whatsoever, that may be properly contained therein," are inexpressibly concerned, to find, that the Commissioners on the part of General Sir William Howe should think it necessary to make the objections stated to their powers, and supported, as they apprehend, by the most conclusive reasons—an insurmountable obstacle to the progress of a negotiation, intended to answer the most benevolent and estimable purposes. As General Sir William Howe must be supposed fully impowered to enter into the Treaty, his commission imports, they can conceive no sufficient reason, for not declaring his powers, and would flatter themselves that nothing can be easier, than to remove the cause of their objections, and to proceed in the business, on admissible terms. They are ready and solicitous to treat on fair, proper, and equal ground such as will give efficacy to their proceedings, and place a public act, on the foundation of public authority.

Willm. Grayson

Newton April 11th. 1778

Rob: H. Harrison

Alex Hamilton

To

Elias Boudinot

Colonel Chs. O Hara
Colonel Humphery Stephens
Capt. Richard Fitz Patrick

LS, in writing of H, The Andrew deCoppet Collection, Princeton University Library.

1. The points at issue, mentioned in this letter, are fully explained in the report of the American commissioners to Washington, April 15, 1778.

From Richard Kip, Junior [1]

Pompton [New Jersey] April 15th 1778.

Sir, Last Decm'r a Twelvemonth a Small Box was Taken at or Near Princetown And Deposited in an Amunition Cart [2] & Supposed to be Taken From thence by Capt. Crane.[3] I can Assure you that I have Seen a Box in Crane's Possession That answers the Description & Since the Discovery he is prepareing to Leave the Continent. He Now Resides in Clarks Town, Orange County. A Line to Collo. Gilbert Coper [4] at Kakeate with Direction to Detect Or Apprehend In haste May Still Serve to Recover the Money &c. for those Justly Entitled to the Same. In haste I Rem'n S'r your V H S.

Rich'd Kip, Jun'r., Ass. D.Q.M.G.

To Collo. Hammilton.

Public Papers of George Clinton, III, 173.
1. This letter was enclosed in George Washington to George Clinton, April 24, 1778.
2. On April 24, 1778, Washington wrote to Clinton: "In the affair of Princetown the winter before last, a box was taken from the enemy, which by appearances was supposed to contain a quantity of hard money" (George Washington Papers, Library of Congress).
3. Washington was more explicit, for he stated that "there was some suspicions at the time against one [Joseph] Crane, a Capt. Lieutenant in . . . [Knox's Continental Artillery], who it was imagined had converted the box and its contents to his own use," Washington to Clinton, April 24, 1778 (George Washington Papers, Library of Congress).
4. Lieutenant Colonel Gilbert Cooper (or Cuyper), Orange County Militia of New York.

Colonel William Grayson, Lieutenant Colonels Robert Hanson Harrison and Alexander Hamilton, and Elias Boudinot to George Washington

[Valley Forge, April 15, 1778]

To His Excellency George Washington Esquire General and Commander in chief of the Forces of the United States of America.

We the Commissioners appointed by Your Excellency, "to confer, determine and agree upon a Treaty and Convention for the exchange of Prisoners of War, and for all matters whatsoever which may be properly contained therein," beg leave to report—

That, agreeable to Your Excellency's orders, on monday the 6th of April, we met at New Town, in Bucks County, the Commissioners appointed by General Sir William Howe, for the purposes, as expressed in their commission, "of taking into consideration all past transactions, relative to the exchange of prisoners, to adjust the differences that have so long subsisted in regard to them, to remove all difficulties, that may arise, in carrying into execution a general exchange of prisoners, with both parties, at this time, and finally to establish a regular, and explicit cartel for the future."

The next day, we entered upon business. The Commissioners, on the part of General Howe, opened it, by informing us, that he had been made acquainted with our objection to his commission; but that he would not consent to the alteration, we had proposed, respecting an insertion of the powers, under which he acted: That he meant the Treaty to be of a personal nature, founded on the mutual confidence and honor of the contracting Generals; and had no intention, either of binding the nation, or extending the cartel beyond the limits and duration of his own command. They declared themselves ready to treat with us on this footing, and with their present powers, which they deemed adequate to the purposes of our meeting.

In answer, we assigned them our reasons at large, for thinking there was a material defect, in their powers, which must render any Treaty, we could form, nugatory and unequal; nugatory, because the private faith of an individual could not in the nature of things be a competent, or proper security for a treaty of public import; and unequal, because, on the one hand, from the express terms of our powers, the public faith would be plighted for our engagements, and on the other, General Howe alone would be bound for the performance of theirs.

The Commissioners from General Howe, in the course of the discussion, intimated an impropriety in treating with us, on a national ground, in a contest of such a nature as the present, which might imply an acknowlegement inconsistent with their claims. We observed to them, that if there was any inconsistency at all, it would operate equally against the forming a cartel, on any principle whatever, and against the whole business of exchange; but that the measure was calculated for mutual advantage, and must justify itself on its expediency and necessity. We supported our observation, by precedents, drawn from practice, in like cases; and in order to obviate every scruple, and to remove, as far as was in our power, every impediment to the execution of our commission we proposed, that a clause should be admitted into the cartel, declaring, that no expressions contained in it, should be construed to affect the political claims of either country, in any thing, not directly necessary to the due and faithful observance of the Treaty. This, we thought a good expedient for reconciling difficulties on both sides.

We agreed to come to a final determination the next day.

We met accordingly, and after some mutual explanations, we informed General Howe's commissioners, that on the most mature deliberation, we found ourselves obliged to adhere to our objections to their commission, and could by no means think ourselves authorised to treat with them, unless their powers were made correspondent to our own. They then proposed, that two of their number should immediately proceed to Philadelphia, to consult General Howe again upon the subject. This proposal we chearfully assented to, in hopes, that he would ultimately put it in our power to answer the desireable purposes of our appointments.

On the return of these Gentlemen from Philadelphia, they informed us, that General Howe persisted in the idea, of a personal treaty, on his part, and refused to enlarge his powers, by the declaration required, on ours. We then proposed to state our objections, in writing, and to receive their answer in the same manner: The former, we did, as follows— . . .[1]

In return, the commissioners, on the part of General Howe, delivered us a paper, containing a writing, as follows, . . .[2]

We immediately prepared a reply to the foregoing writing, which

DS, in writing of H, George Washington Papers, Library of Congress; Df, in writing of Robert Hanson Harrison, George Washington Papers, Library of Congress.

1. This letter has been omitted from the text. For its contents, see Grayson, Harrison, Hamilton, and Boudinot to O'Hara, Stephens, and FitzPatrick, April 10, 1778.

2. This letter has been omitted from the text. For its contents see O'Hara, Stephens, and FitzPatrick to Grayson, Harrison, Hamilton, and Boudinot, April 11, 1778.

we offered to General Howe's commissioners; but they refused to read it alleging, that if we could not meet them on the commission they now had, the negociation was at an end. We then read to them the reply, we had prepared, to the following effect— . . .[3]

We shall be happy if our conduct on this occasion meets with Your Excellency's approbation. We were fully sensible of your solicitude for the success of a Treaty designed to provide an effectual and durable remedy, for those calamities, with which the state of captivity has been hitherto afflicted. We are sorry the views of General Sir William Howe were so far different from yours as to render them impracticable. Your powers to us were the standard, by which we were to judge of the sufficiency of his. The former are founded on the broad basis of national faith; the latter, on the narrow one of private faith. A dissimilarity, in so material a point, appeared to us a solid, and on our part, an insuperable objection. We considered the formation of a Treaty, by which such momentous concerns would be affected, with no other sanction, than the personal honor and interest of an individual—not only as incompatible with our commission; but as repugnant to reason, to the nature of the business, and to common usage, in similar cases. A Treaty so formed would, in our conception, be merely nominal, or at best of temporary operation, certainly ceasing with personal command—liable, at any time, to be violated by public authority, without the imputation of public dishonor, and highly derogatory to the dignity of these United States.

Camp Valley Forge
April 15th. 1778

Willm. Grayson.
Rob: H: Harrison
Alex Hamilton
Elias Boudinot

3. This letter has been omitted from the text. For its contents see Grayson, Harrison, Hamilton, and Boudinot to O'Hara, Stephens, and FitzPatrick, April 11, 1778.

To Colonel Henry E. Lutterloh

[*Valley Forge*] *April 19, 1778.* States that a horse not fit for service should be returned to a Mr. Sellers, its owner. Signed "A Hamilton ADC."

The Pennsylvania Magazine of History and Biography, XVI (1892), 196.

George Washington to the General Officers

[*Valley Forge*] *April 20, 1778*. Lists three plans for next campaign, with possible modes of execution for each plan. Asks officers for opinions.

LS, in writing of H, George Washington Papers, Library of Congress.

George Washington to Major General John Armstrong

Valley Forge, April 24, 1778. Invites Armstrong to council of war.

Df, in writing of H, George Washington Papers, Library of Congress.

George Washington to George Clinton [1]

Valley Forge, April 24, 1778. States that a box of "hard" money taken from British at Princeton in winter of 1777 is suspected to be in the hands of a Captain–Lieutenant Joseph Crane of Orange County. Asks Clinton to investigate matter.

Df, in writing of H, George Washington Papers, Library of Congress.
    1. An enclosure in this letter was Richard Kip, Jr., to H, April 15, 1778.

George Washington to Major General Thomas Mifflin

Valley Forge, April 24, 1778. Invites Mifflin to council of war.

Df, in writing of H, George Washington Papers, Library of Congress.

To James Mease

[Valley Forge, April 26, 1778]

Sir,

By command of His Excellency, I inclose you a letter to him from the officers of the German batalion. There appears, by the representation, to be something particular in the circumstances of that batalion, with respect to cloathing, which deserves attention. You will do whatever can be done with propriety to put them upon an equal footing with other Regiments.

I am Sir   Your most Obed Serv   A Hamilton ADC

Head Quarters
April 26th. 1778

ADfS, George Washington Papers, Library of Congress.

George Washington to Major General William Tryon [1]

Valley Forge, April 26, 1778. States that the British conciliatory handbills have had free circulation among the troops. Asks Tryon to circulate among Tory troops copies of a resolution of Congress concerning the pardoning of those who have levied war against the states.

Df, in writing of H, George Washington Papers, Library of Congress.
    1. Tryon was the Loyalist governor of New York.

George Washington to Thomas Wharton, Junior

[Valley Forge] April 26, 1778. Asks for information concerning the militia available for next campaign.

Df, in writings of John Laurens and H, George Washington Papers, Library of Congress.

George Washington to Samuel Chase [1]

[Valley Forge] April 27, 1778. Discusses British practice of seizing and imprisoning civilians.

Df, in writing of H, George Washington Papers, Library of Congress.
    1. Chase was a member of the Continental Congress from Maryland.

George Washington to Thevenau Francy [1]

[*Valley Forge*] *April 30, 1778.* Encloses letter to be transmitted to Mr. Penet.[2]

Df, in writing of H, George Washington Papers, Library of Congress.
  1. Jean Baptiste Lazarus Thevenau Francy was an agent of Beaumarchais in America.
  2. Pierre Penet, who was in Nantes, France.

George Washington to Pierre Penet

Valley Forge, April 30, 1778. Thanks Penet for gifts.

Df, in writings of George Washington and H, George Washington Papers, Library of Congress.

George Washington to Henry Laurens

Valley Forge, May 3, 1778. Discusses reasons for lack of Indian aid. Thinks the United States should continue to try to counteract British overtures to Indians.

LS, in writing of H, Papers of the Continental Congress, National Archives; Df, in writing of H, George Washington Papers, Library of Congress.

George Washington to Major General Nathanael Greene

[*Valley Forge*] *May 5, 1778.* Reviews situation in Europe and discusses possible enemy movements.

Df, in writing of H, Hamilton Papers, Library of Congress.

To Lieutenant Colonel William De Hart [1]

[Valley Forge, May 7, 1778]

Sir,
  By command of His Excellency, I am to desire, You will immediately march with your Regiment by the safest and most convenient

route into the Jerseys, and there join, and put yourself under the command of, Col: Shrieve.[2] You may regulate the march of your baggage, and *the transportation* of your sick in such manner as shall appear to you most elegible, either by giving them an upper route or making them accompany the Regiment. The former would perhaps be the safer method.

I am   Sir   Your most Obd serv   AH ADC

Head Qrs. Valley
Forge May 7th 1778

Lt Col: De Hart

ADfS, George Washington Papers, Library of Congress.
   1. De Hart was a lieutenant colonel, Second New Jersey Regiment. At the time that this letter was written De Hart was at Valley Forge.
   2. Colonel Israel Shreve, Second New Jersey Regiment.

To Major General Nathanael Greene [1]

[Valley Forge, May 7, 1778]

Dr Sir

I am sadly distressed for want of a good saddle &c; and such is my situation, that I have no opportunity of procuring for myself. The one I got by your order the other day was of a coarser kind that would only do for my servant.

As you are in the way of procuring matters of this kind, you will oblige me much, if you will give orders for purchasing a good saddle bridle holsters &c. for me. These things are on my private account, and whenever I can be made acquainted with their cost will be paid for.

I am Sir   Yr most hum   A Hamilton

Hd Qrs.
May 7th. 1778

ALS, William L. Clements Library of the University of Michigan.
   1. Greene was quartermaster general of the Continental Army.

From John Jay

Albany 8 May 1778

Dear Sir,

An opinion of your Benevolence leads me to address this Letter to you. Accident has introduced me to Monsr Lewis de Celoron,[1] we happen to lodge in the same House. His modesty & decent manners made an impression upon me, and induced me to make some inquiries into his History and Character. The Gentlemen of this Place say handsome things of him. He is the son of a Major General who fell last war at Ticonderoga. The family is still in Canada and one of the most respectable in that Country. He was sent to France when five years old and there educated. He came out with some French troops to Martinico, and by their General as well as Mr. Bingham [2] was recommended to Congress. They gave him a Brevet for a Captains' Commission. He served last campaign as a Volunteer, first with General ⟨Fermoy⟩,[3] and afterwards with Col Morgan. To me he appears to have been neglected. It seems he did not descend to the adulation lately fashionable & perhaps acceptable in this department. While Effrontery and Arrogance even in our virtuous and enlightened days are giving rank & Importance to men whom Wisdom would have left in obscurity; I am persuaded you will be happy in an opportunity of exploring as well as cherishing modest merit. I think Monsr. de Celoron is not without it & under this impression recommend him to your notice as a Probationor. Tell me in your future Letters whether he deserves the favorable opinion I am inclined to entertain of him.

Your obedient servant   John Jay

JCH Transcripts.
1. Captain Louis de Celeron, Pulaski's Legion, was taken prisoner at Charleston, South Carolina, in May, 1780, and resigned from the service in July, 1782.
2. William Bingham of Philadelphia, one of the richest men in America, served during most of the Revolution as Continental agent in the West Indies.
3. Matthias Alexis Roche de Fermoy, a brigadier general in the Continental Army. He resigned January 31, 1778. This space was left blank in the MS.

From Edward Stevens [1]

London May 8th 1778

Mon cher Ami,

Comment vous portez vous? & comment vous êtes vous porté depuis que je n'ai eu le plasir de vous voir? Si vous êtes en bonne santé tout est bien avec vous; j'en suis sûre. Qui pourrait avoir imaginé mon Ami qu'un homme de votre *grandeur*, de votre délicatesse de constitution, & de votre tranquillité aurait brillé tant, & en si peu de tems, dans le Champ de Mars, que vous l'avez fait. Je vous assure mon Colonel que je me suis tourmenté beaucoup par rapport à votre santé, la quelle m'a été toujours tres chere depuis le commencement de notre connaissance. Je ne sais pas comment vous pourrez soutenir les duretés, & les fatigues d'une campagne dhiver, en Amerique. Assurément votre constitution n'aurait jamais soutenue de telle sévérité sans l assistance de quelque chose fort extraordinaire. Que ce que ce cette chose extra.? Je ne saurais vous dire, si ce n'est pas ce grand homme W––n, dont l exemple est si singulier, dont la fermeté est si in ébranlable, dont la Persévérance est si inouie, dont les moeurs sont si douces, dont la moderation est si extraordinaire, dont la clemence & si frappant, & dont les actions, en général, sont si eclatants que toute l'Europe en est etonné. En verité mon Cher Hamilton quand on pense à toutes ses choses la, &, en même tems, à ce qu on m'a dit que vous etes l'Aid de camp d'un tel homme ce n'est pas tout-a-fait si difficile à concevoir comment vous vous etes soutenu jusque le present. Quand Je pense aux actions de Monr W––n, & quand je les compare aux actions d'Annibal, d'Alexandre, ou de César; la comparison me paraît indigne, & je vois Wn. dans une elévation trop haute pour etre ranger avec eux. Quand on considere la Marche d'Annibal au travers les Alpes, on ne peut sempêcher de l admirer. Mais quand on envisage vos campagnes d'hiver, & l'Armée que vous aviez à vous combattre, l'expédition d'Annibal ne parait que petite. J'espere quelque jour d'avoir l'honneur de connaitre votre General, que j'estime, & que je regard comme le liberateur de son Patrie. Le Roi de Prusse l'a honoré l'autre jour, en disant, ma foi ce Monr Was––n doit être un homme bien singulier, pour avoir résister si long tems a toute la force d'Angleterre; la quelle dans la derniere guerre faisait tremblé à toute l'Europe.

Peutêtre souhaiteriez vous quelque chose des politiques; mais, en verité, je ne suis pas disposer a écrire sur ces sujets la, á present. Je dirai seulement, vous devez vous souvenir de mes sentiments quand nous nous somme quittés l'un l'autre; ils ont été toujours les mêmes. Notre Ami S. est encore à Edinbourg ou il a devenu un fort *Galant* homme.

Souvenez mois à Messrs Troup, Fish,[2] & Lewis [3] tres sincerement, & croyez moi Affectueusement votre a⟨mi⟩.

PS   Je partirai d ici pour la N.Y. dans tres peu de jours ou j'attends de vous voir avant six mois. Excusez la liberté que je prends à vous écrire en francais; ce n'est pas, soyez sûre, pour vous montré que je sait écrire *pitoyablement* cette Langue difficile, mais c'est pour vous montré que je desire de retenir ce que j'en sais: & qu'en l'ecrivant à un homme qui la sais parfaitement j'espere de profiter par ses correction. Adieu. Portez vous bien & ⟨—⟩ te extera sumes. Attendez de mes nouvelles aussi tot⟨—⟩ que.

AL, William L. Clements Library of the University of Michigan.
  1. This is an intercepted letter, which is now in the Sir Henry Clinton Papers at the William L. Clements Library. Although this letter has no signature, both the handwriting and the contents clearly indicate that Stevens was the writer.
  2. Robert Troup and Nicholas Fish had been students at Kings College with Stevens and H. Both, moreover, were to be close friends of H for the rest of his life.
  3. This may be a reference to Morgan Lewis, who was a New York lawyer. During the Revolution he held the rank of colonel in the Continental Army.

George Washington to the Council of War

Valley Forge, May 8, 1778. Describes distribution of enemy forces. Discusses possibilities of acquiring reinforcements, ordnance, and provisions.

Df, in writing of H, George Washington Papers, Library of Congress.

To Brigadier General William Maxwell

[Valley Forge, May 10, 1778]

Sir

His Excellency has received yours from Horsam meeting House.[1] He is a good deal surprized that you left your Artillery behind as one principal aim of the detachment was to protect the Vessels in the River in which Cannon would be essential. His Question to you on the subject was rather intended to indicate his desire that you should take cannon with your Party.[2]

He desires you will immediately march towards the River opposite BordenTown and there act according to circumstances. Though you may not be able to do any thing without Cannon, the approach of a body of men whom the Enemy will suppose to be provided with Artillery may possibly alarm and induce them to return. Perhaps by throwing a part of your men on the heights the opposite side of the river, you may be able to give them some Annoyance. This you will best judge of when you get to the Place. A detachment of 200 men will march to join you immediately with two pieces of Artillery and some Provisions. They will take their rout to the Cross roads;[3] you will be pleased to leave at that place an Officer with directions how to conduct them to you

I am Sir   Your most humble Servt.

Head Quarters
May 10th. 1778

Df, in writing of Peregrine Fitzhugh, George Washington Papers, Library of Congress.

1. Presumably the same as present-day Horsham, a village in Montgomery County, Pennsylvania.

2. On May 7, Washington had written Maxwell: "The detachment under your comd. is designed to answer the following purposes; become a security to this Camp, and the Country between the Schuylkill and Delaware; interrupt the communication with Philadelphia; obtain intelligence of the motion, and designs of the enemy; and, aided by the Militia, prevent small parties of the Enemy from patrolling, to cover the market people; whilst large Parties, especially if any attempt should be made on this side the Delaware to destroy the Vessels above Bristol, are to be harassed as much as possible, till notice thereof can be communicated to me" (George Washington Papers, Library of Congress.)

3. Cross Roads subsequently became Hartsville, Pennsylvania.

George Washington to Thomas Wharton, Junior

[*Valley Forge*] *May 11, 1778.* Is disappointed that so few militiamen are available. Asks that a plan be devised to keep the militia in constant readiness for the field, and that 400 militiamen be kept between the Delaware and the Schuylkill.

Df, in writing of H, George Washington Papers, Library of Congress.

Oath of Allegiance [1]

[Valley Forge, May 12, 1778]

I *Alexander Hamilton Lieutenant Colonel and Aide De Camp to His Excellency The commander in Chief* do acknowledge the UNITED STATES OF AMERICA, to be Free, Independent and Sovereign States, and declare that the people thereof owe no allegiance or obedience to George the Third, King of Great-Britain; and I renounce, refuse and objure any allegiance or obedience to him; and I do *swear* that I will to the utmost of my power, support, maintain and defend the said United States, against the said King George the Third, his heirs and successors and his or their abettors, assistants and adherents, and will serve the said United States in the office of *Aide De Camp* which I now hold, with fidelity, according to the best of my skill and understanding.[2]

Sworn, before me, Camp Valley   *Alex Hamilton*
Forge May 12th 1778
Stirling [3] Major Genl.

DS, RG 93, Oaths of Allegiance, vol. 165, National Archives.
1. This document is a printed form with the exception of the signature of William Alexander, Lord Stirling, and the italicized words which are in H's writing.
2. The oath was taken as a result of a congressional resolve of February 3, 1778, which read: "*Resolved,* That all officers of the army shall take and subscribe the foregoing oath or affirmation before the commander in chief, or any major general or brigadier general" (*JCC,* X, 115).
3. William Alexander, Lord Stirling.

George Washington to
Lieutenant Colonel Morgan Connor [1]

Valley Forge, May 12, 1778. Discusses courts-martial.

Df, in writing of H, George Washington Papers, Library of Congress.
  1. Connor was a lieutenant colonel of one of the Sixteen Additional Continental Regiments.

George Washington to
Major General Philip Schuyler [1]

Valley Forge, May 15, 1778. Discusses Indian relations. Asks Schuyler to stop Lieutenant Colonel Jean Baptiste Gouvion and his party of Indians before they start for Camp. Presents arguments that might be used to explain why Indians are no longer needed. Will send notice of Schuyler's trial as soon as it is received.

Df, in writing of H, George Washington Papers, Library of Congress.
  1. Schuyler was one of the commissioners for Indian affairs.

George Washington to James Mease

Valley Forge, May 16, 1778. Orders Mease to Camp.

Df, in writing of H, George Washington Papers, Library of Congress.

To Colonel Daniel Morgan

[Valley Forge, May 17, 1778]

Sir,

His Excellency is sending a considerable detachment towards the enemy's lines, which will march tomorrow morning. He desires you to select 50 men of your corps, under good officers, and send them to join that detachment. It will be at White marsh tomorrow afternoon where your party will be expected. A party of Indians will join the party to be sent from your corps, at White marsh and act with them.

I am Sir   Your most Obed serv   Alex Hamilton AD

Head Quarters Valley
Forge May 17th. 1778

ALS, MS Division, New York Public Library.

George Washington to Ezekiel Cheever [1]

Valley Forge, May 17, 1778. Instructs Cheever to rush forward arms that are en route from Springfield, Massachusetts, to Lebanon, Pennsylvania.

Df, in writing of H, George Washington Papers, Library of Congress.
   1. Cheever was commissary of military stores at Springfield, Massachusetts.

George Washington to
Major General Nathanael Greene

[*Valley Forge*] *May 17, 1778.* Instructs Greene to prepare for possible movement of Army and to set up magazines along routes to North River.

Df, in writings of Richard Kidder Meade and H, George Washington Papers, Library of Congress.

George Washington to Marquis de Lafayette

[*Valley Forge*] *May 18, 1778.* Sends instructions.

Df, in writing of H, George Washington Papers, Library of Congress.

George Washington to
Brigadier General William Smallwood

Valley Forge, May 19, 1778. Discusses crimes and court-martial of Jetson, a Loyalist. Denies request to send flour to supporters of Revolution in Philadelphia.

Df, in writing of H, George Washington Papers, Library of Congress.

George Washington to
Brigadier General William Smallwood

Valley Forge, May 22–23, 1778. Orders removal of stores from the Elk and urges Smallwood to be on continual guard against enemy. In postscript states the enemy is preparing an offensive move.

Df, in writings of James McHenry and H, George Washington Papers, Library of Congress. The postscript is dated May 23, 1778.

George Washington to Elias Boudinot

[Valley Forge] May 23, 1778. Is pleased with the improved treatment of prisoners by British. Requests Boudinot to come to Camp immediately as there is to be a general exchange of prisoners. States that Colonel Francis Johnston has been nominated to succeed Boudinot as commissary of prisoners.

Df, in writing of H, George Washington Papers, Library of Congress.

George Washington to Colonel Israel Shreve

Valley Forge, May 23, 1778. Discusses case of William Hamet, a Loyalist; disposition of the Jersey drafts; and reinlistment of Lieutenant Jonathan Rhea. Gives instructions in case enemy should evacuate Philadelphia.

Df, in writing of H, George Washington Papers, Library of Congress.

George Washington to
Brigadier General William Maxwell

Valley Forge, May 25, 1778. Orders Maxwell to secure all available information concerning enemy and to remain in readiness to march.

Df, in writing of H, George Washington Papers, Library of Congress.

To John Dixon and William Hunter [1]

Head Quarters Valley
Forge May 29th 1778

The Commander in chief positively requires all officers, absent from camp, belonging to the Troops of the State of Virginia, except those who are detained on Public service, by his Excellency the Govr of that State, or any Genl officer of the same, or those who may have furloughs not yet expired—immediately to join their respective Corps.

By his Excellys Command   Alex Hamilton Aide De Camp

The several Printers of the State of Virginia are desired to Publish the above in their respective news Papers   AH.

Df, George Washington Papers, Library of Congress.
   1. Dixon and Hunter were publishers of the *Williamsburg Gazette*, Williamsburg, Virginia.

George Washington to the Board of General Officers

[*Valley Forge*] *May 29, 1778*. Submits case of Lieutenant Colonel Pierre Regnier's rank.

LS, in writing of H, George Washington Papers, Library of Congress.

George Washington to Lieutenant Colonel James Innes [1]

Valley Forge, May 29, 1778. Orders Innes to return to Camp.

Df, in writing of H, George Washington Papers, Library of Congress.
   1. Innes was lieutenant colonel of the Fifteenth Virginia Regiment.

George Washington to Colonel Josiah Parker [1]

Valley Forge, May 29, 1778. Orders Parker to return to Camp.

Df, in writing of H, George Washington Papers, Library of Congress.
    1. Parker was colonel of the Fifth Virginia Regiment. He resigned July 12, 1778.

George Washington to the Board of General Officers

Valley Forge, June 2, 1778. Submits for the Board's decision Lieutenant Colonel Mauduit du Plessis's claim to rank.

LS, in writing of H, George Washington Papers, Library of Congress.

George Washington to the Board of General Officers

Valley Forge, June 2, 1778. Submits for the Board's decision the case of a suspected spy.

LS, in writing of H, George Washington Papers, Library of Congress.

From George Washington [1]

Head Quarters [Valley Forge]
4th. June 1778.

Sir.

Mr. Loring having been sent by Sir Henry Clinton to meet Mr. Boudinot or any other person appointed by me for the purpose of effecting an exchange of prisoners; I have therefore to desire you (Mr. Boudinot being absent from Camp) to hear any proposals Mr. Loring may have to offer on this subject; and to do definitively whatever may be necessary towards the execution of a general exchange of prisoners: And I hereby assure you that your proceedings in this instance will be ratified by me.

I am Sir, your very hble servant.   Go: Washington

Lieut. Col. Hamilton.

LS, in writing of James McHenry, Hamilton Papers, Library of Congress; Df, in writing of James McHenry, George Washington Papers, Library of Congress.

1. For background to this letter, see "Declaration on Prisoners," June 4, 1778, note 1.

Declaration on Prisoners [1]

[Valley Forge, June 4, 1778]

In the Name of His Excellency General Washington and by virtue of His authority to me, I declare, that on his being properly notified of time and place, he will appoint a person then and there to receive all Prisoners of War, in possession of the enemy, at present in the city of Philadelphia, and that He will return as speedily as possible an equal number of prisoners of war, in lieu of them, now in the power of the United States, of similar rank quality and description to those who shall be delivered as abovementioned, at such post of the British army as shall be most convenient and conducive to dispatch. Those American Prisoners, who, on account of wounds and sickness cannot be included in the general delivery, when the hospitals or places in which they are lodged shall be no longer in possession of the enemy, being left under the protection of a flag, shall be received by us and exchanged in like manner, with the prisoners aforesaid. Any hospital stores or utensils, that may be necessarily left with them shall be paid for, at such reasonable rates, as shall be mutually agreed on, by persons appointed for the purpose, or returned in kind. The Prisoners comprehended in this declaration, now in Philadelphia by Mr Loring's [2] report, amount to about 120 Commissioned officers and 670 Non Comd. Officers and privates; about 80 of whom are sick and in hospital. These Prisoners, when delivered, shall be considered as under parole and incapable of military service 'till regularly exchanged.

I do further declare, on the part of His Excellency General Washington that he will at such convenient time and place, as shall be agreed on between General Sir Henry Clinton and himself, appoint and impower proper persons to meet others duly authorised by Sir Henry Clinton to discuss and settle the difference, so long subsisting, with respect to the proportion to be accounted for, of those prisoners who were sent out by General Sir William Howe, in the Winter of 76, on just and reasonable terms.

Alex Hamilton [3]

ADS, The Andrew deCoppet Collection, Princeton University Library; ADfS, George Washington Papers, Library of Congress.

1. On May 23, 1778, Washington wrote to Elias Boudinot, American commissary of prisoners, the following: "By a resolve of Congress of the 21st., in consequence of a late proposal from General Howe, a general exchange of prisoners is to be carried into execution; This renders your *immediate* presence at Camp necessary, which I therefore request" (George Washington Papers, Library of Congress). Since Washington did not receive an answer from Boudinot and since Sir Henry Clinton, who had replaced William Howe, showed signs of evacuating Philadelphia, Washington again wrote to Boudinot on June 2, 1778, urging him to hasten "here with all possible dispatch" (George Washington Papers, Library of Congress). On June 4, 1778, Joshua Loring, British commissary of prisoners, arrived at Headquarters. Washington directed H to negotiate with Loring in Boudinot's absence (see George Washington to H, June 4, 1778)

The document printed here was probably presented to Loring at this time.

2. Joshua Loring, British commissary of prisoners of war.

3. The following postscript, which is in writing of H and is crossed out, appears at the end of this document:

"The substance of the resolve of Congress is, That as Sir Wm. Howe has it in his power to exchange the officers under the convention, they cannot consent to an equivalent of privates for Officers.

"That a General exchange shall take place of all officers and soldiers in the actual possession of the respective parties, and of such other officers & soldiers as in the opinion of General Washington are fit subjects of exchange. AH."

The congressional resolve referred to was dated May 21, 1778.

From Joshua Loring [1]

Phila June 5th 1778

Sir

Upon my Report to His Excellency Sir Henry Clinton of our meeting yesterday at the Sorrel Horse for the Purpose of settling an exchange of Prisoners—

I am directed to acquaint you that all our Prisoners in Philadelphia agreable to the enclosed Return shall be sent out on the 12th Inst under a proper Escort to the two miles stone on the Lancaster Road over Schuylkill, provided you agree to meet us There on that day with the like number of British Prisoners of equal Rank to be then & there exchanged for the same and you will be so good as to fix the hour.

I am Sir your most obedient   Humble Servant

      Josa Loring   Commissy Genl Prisoners

Col. Hamilton

Jane J. Boudinot (ed.), *The Life, Public Services, Addresses and Letters of Elias Boudinot* (Boston, 1896), I, 122.

 1. For background to this letter, see "Declaration on Prisoners," June 4, 1778.

George Washington to
Major General Nathanael Greene

[*Valley Forge*] *June 8, 1778*. Instructs Greene to find a new camp site.

Df, in writing of H, George Washington Papers, Library of Congress.

To Colonel Henry Jackson [1]

        [Valley Forge, June 9, 1778]

Sir

His Excellency desires you will put a stop, by every mean in your power to the above practice. Any officer who shall be found impressing this man's horses without proper authority will be most severely dealt with.

I am Sir   Yr. Most Obedt   A Hamilton   Aide De Camp

Hd. Quarters
June 9th. 1778

ALS, Coburn Library, Colorado College, Colorado Springs.

 1. No addressee is given in the MS, but this letter was presumably addressed to Colonel Henry Jackson, who at the time was in command at "the Gulph" or "Gulph Mills," the present site of West Conshohocken, Pennsylvania.

 H's letter is written at the bottom of the same page on which is written a petition by John Johnston to Washington. Johnston describes himself as a farmer "of Upper Merion near the Gulph Mills." In his petition Johnston wrote: ". . . the Guards at the Gulph or Some of them make a Common Practice of taking my horses out of the Gears from me, & riding them about two or three days, & never less than One day & night, by which Severe hard usage my horse are not able to Do my own Work; neither can I keep them one Whole day together at home."

From Captain Jacob Weiss [1]

Valley Forge, June 9, 1778. States that last October he delivered missing chest containing army papers to Easton, Pennsylvania.

ALS, George Washington Papers, Library of Congress.
   1. Weiss was a captain in the Maréchaussée corps.

George Washington to Colonel Lewis Nicola [1]

Valley Forge, June 9, 1778. Instructs Nicola to admit John Woelper of German Battalion as a captain in Corps of Invalids.

Df, in writing of H, George Washington Papers, Library of Congress.
   1. Nicola was a colonel in the Corps of Invalids.

From Brigadier General Henry Knox

Artillery Park [Valley Forge] June 12, 1778. Requests discharge of "Mr. Le Brune a second Lieutenant."

ALS, RG 93, Miscellaneous Records, National Archives.

George Washington to Council of War

Valley Forge, June 17, 1778. Presents probable British plans for evacuation of Philadelphia and relative strength of American and enemy forces. Asks for opinions in writing concerning measures to be taken in the event of evacuation of Philadelphia.

Df, in writing of H, George Washington Papers, Library of Congress.

To Elias Boudinot

[Valley Forge, June 18, 1778]

Dr Sir

The General has received your Billet per horseman.[1] He thanks you for your intelligence and begs you will continue to advise him of what passes. If the enemy are really gone, try to get some of the inhabitants, on whom, you can depend to pass the Delaware, to watch their motions and convey intelligence.

Caution should be used by you all in entering the city, before you are very certain how matters stand.

Yrs   Alex Hamilton

Hd. Qrs.
June 18th. 1778

ALS, Massachusetts Historical Society, Boston.
   1. On June 18, 1778, Boudinot wrote to Washington concerning the route of the British through New Jersey (George Washington Papers, Library of Congress).

To William Duer [1]

Hd Qrs. [Valley Forge] June 18, 1778

Dear Sir,

I take the liberty to trouble you with a few hints on a matter of some importance. Baron Steuben, who will be the bearer of this waits on Congress to have his office arranged upon some decisive and permanent footing.[2] It will not be amiss to be on your guard. The Baron is a Gentleman for whom, I have a particular esteem;

ADf, Hamilton Papers, Library of Congress. In *JCHW*, I, 56, this letter is dated 1778.
   1. This letter was written to Duer in his capacity as a delegate from New York to the Continental Congress.
   2. Baron von Steuben had arrived in this country from Germany in the autumn of 1777 after serving as one of Frederick the Great's titular aides. He first appeared at Valley Forge on February 23, 1778. On March 28, Washington appointed him volunteer inspector general, and on May 5, Congress appointed him major general and inspector general, Continental Army.

and whose real intelligence and success the consequence of both intitle him to the greatest credit. But I am apprehensive, with all his good qualities, a fondness for power and importance natural to every man may lead him to wish for more extensive prerogatives in his department, than it will be for the good of the service to grant. I should be sorry to ex[c]ite any prejudice against him on this account—perhaps I may be mistaken in my conjecture. The caution, I give, will do no harm, if I am. If I am not it may be useful. In either case, The Baron deserves to be considered as a valuable man, and treated with all the deference which good policy will warrant.

In the first institution of his office, The General allowed him to exercise more ample powers, than would be proper for a continuance. They were necessary in the commencement, to put things in a train with a degree of dispatch, which the exigency of our affairs required. But it has been necessary to restrain them even earlier than was intended. The novelty of the office excited questions about its boundaries. The extent of its operation alarmed the officers of every rank for their own rights. Their jealousies and discontents were rising fast to a height that threatened to over turn the whole plan. It became necessary to apply a remedy. The General has delineated the functions of the Inspectorship, in general orders,[3] a copy of which will be sent to Congress. The plan is good and satisfactory, to the army in general. It may be improved; but it will be unsafe to deviate essentially from it. It is, of course, the General's intention, that whatever regulations are adopted by him should undergo the revision and receive the sanction of Congress, but it is indispensible in the present state of our army, that he should have the power from time, to time, to introduce and authorise, the reformations necessary in our system. It is a work which must be done by occasional and gradual steps and ought to be intrusted to a person on the spot, who is thoroughly acquainted with all our defects and has judgment sufficient to adapt the progressive remedies they require. The plan established by Congress, on a report of the Board of War when Conway[4] was appointed appears to me exceptionable in many respects.[5] It makes the Inspector independent of[6] the Commander in Chief, confers powers, which would produce universal

3. See *GW*, XII, 66–68.
5. See *JCC*, IX, 1023–26.

4. Major General Thomas Conway.
6. In MS "on."

opposition, in the army, and by making the previous concurrence of the Board of War requisite to the introduction of every regulation which should be found necessary opens such a continual source of delay as would defeat the usefulness of the institution. Let the Commander in Chief introduce, and the legislature afterwards ratify or reject, as they shall think proper. Perhaps you will not differ much from me, when I suppose, that so far as relates to the Board of War, the former scheme was a brat of faction, and therefore ought to be renounced.

There is one thing which the Baron has much at heart, which in good policy he can by no means be indulged in. It is the power of enforcing that part of discipline which we understand by subordination or an obedience to orders. This power can only be properly lodged [7] with the commander in chief, and would inflame the whole army if put into other hands. Each Captain is vested with it in his company, each Colonel in his Regiment, each General in his particular command, and The Commander in Chief in the whole.

When I began this letter, I did not intend to meddle with any other subject than the Inspectorship; but one just comes into my head, which appears to me of no small importance. The goodness or force of an army depends as much, perhaps more, on the composition of the corps which form it, as on its collective number. The composition is good or bad, not only according to the quality of the men, but in proprortion to the completeness or incompleteness of a corps in respect to numbers. A Regiment for instance with a full complement of officers and fifty or sixty men, is not half so good as a company with the same number of men. A Colonel will look upon such a command as unworthy [of] his ambition and will neglect and despise it. A captain would pride himself in it and take all the pains in his power to bring it to perfection. In one case we shall see a total relaxation of discipline, and a negligence of every thing that constitutes military excellence; in the other, there will be attention energy and every thing that can be wished. Opinion, whether well or ill founded, is the governing principle of human affairs. A corps much below its establishment comparing what it is with what it ought to be, loses all confidence in itself, and the whole army loses that confidence and emulation which are essential to suc-

7. In MS "logded."

cess. These and a thousand other things, that will occur to you, make it evident, that the most important advantages attend the having complete corps, and proporti[on]al disadvantages the reverse. Ten thousand men distributed into 20 imperfect regiments will not have half the efficiency of the same number in half the number of regiments. The fact is, with respect to the American army, that the want of discipline and other defects we labour under are as much owing to the skeleton state of our regiments as to any other cause. What then?

Have we any prospect of filling our regiments? My opinion is that we are nearly arrived to our *ne plus ultra.* If so, we ought to reduce our number of corps, and give them that substance and consistency which they want, by incorporating them together so as to bring them near their establishment. By this measure the army would be infinitely improved & the State would be saved the expence of maintaining a number of superfluous officers. In the present condition of our regiments, they are incapable even of performing their common exercises without joining two or more together, an expedient reluctantly submitted to by those officers, who see themselves made second in command of a batalion instead of first as their commission imports, which happens to every younger colonel, whose regiment is united with that of an elder?

What would be the inconveniencies? While the officers who remain in command and who might be selected from the others on account of superior merit would applaud themselves in the preference given them and rejoice at a change which confers such additional consequence to themselves, those who should be excluded by the measure would return home discontented and make a noise, which would soon subside and be forgotten among matters of greater moment. To quiet them still more effectually, if it should be thought necessary they might be put upon half pay for a certain time.

⟨If on considering this matter, you should agree with me in sentiment, it were to be wished the scheme could be immediately adopted, while the arrangement now in hand is still unexecuted. If it is made, it will be rather inconvenient, immediately after, to unhinge and throw the whole system again afloat.

When you determined on your last arrangement, you did not know what success the different States might have had in draughting and recruiting. It would then have been improper to reduce the number of corps, as proposed. We have now seen their success: we have no prospect of seeing the regiments filled; we should reduce them.

Believe me to be, with great esteem and regard, Dear Sir, your obedient servant, A Hamilton) [8]

8. Material within broken brackets is taken from *JCHW*, I, 59–60.

To Brigadier General Anthony Wayne

[Valley Forge, June 18, 1778]

Sir,

His Excellency desires you will have the division commanded by General Mifflin [1] prepared to march at two OClock. You know it consists of the 1st & 2d Pennsylvania, and the Brigade late Conways.

Yr. Obed ser   Alex Hamilton   Aide De Camp

Head Quarters
June 18th.

ALS, Historical Society of Pennsylvania, Philadelphia.
    1. Major General Thomas Mifflin had served as an aide-de-camp to Washington until August 14, 1775, when he was appointed quartermaster general of the Continental Army. He resigned as quartermaster general in November, 1777.

George Washington to
Major General Philemon Dickinson

[*Valley Forge, June 18, 1778.*] States that enemy is crossing Delaware and orders Dickinson to obstruct enemy as much as possible.

Df, in writing of H, George Washington Papers, Library of Congress.

George Washington to James Mease

[*Valley Forge*] *June 18, 1778.* Instructs Mease to send agent to purchase available articles from inhabitants of Philadelphia and to seize public stores left behind by enemy.

Df, in writing of H, George Washington Papers, Library of Congress.

George Washington to
Major General Benedict Arnold

[*Doctor Shannon's, near Valley Forge*] *June 19, 1778*. Instructs Arnold to proceed to Philadelphia and to take command of troops there.

Df, in writing of H, George Washington Papers, Library of Congress.

George Washington to
Major General Horatio Gates

Coryells Ferry [*New Jersey*] *June 21, 1778*. Informs Gates of movements of American and enemy forces.

LS, in writing of H, New-York Historical Society, New York City.

George Washington to
Major General Philemon Dickinson

Coryells Ferry [*New Jersey*] *June 22, 1778*. Acknowledges receipt of Dickinson's letters. Is sending Colonel Daniel Morgan's corps to assist Dickinson.

Df, in writings of James McHenry and H, George Washington Papers, Library of Congress.

George Washington to
Major General Philemon Dickinson

Hopewell Township near the Baptist Meeting [*New Jersey*] *June 23, 1778*. Requests information concerning movements of enemy.

Df, in writing of H, Hamilton Papers, Library of Congress.

George Washington to
Brigadier General Charles Scott

Hopewell Township, New Jersey, June 24, 1778. Orders Scott to Allentown to harass enemy.

Df, in writing of H, George Washington Papers, Library of Congress.

Council of War to George Washington [1]

Hopewell Township [New Jersey] June 24, 1778. The council decided against a general action against the British.

Df, in writing of H, George Washington Papers, Library of Congress.
1. The questions asked of the council are printed in *GW*, XII, 115–17.

To Marquis de Lafayette [1]

[Cranbury Town, New Jersey, June 25, 1778]

Sir,

We find on our arrival here,[2] that the intelligence received on the road is true. The enemy have all filed off from Allen Town on the Monmouth road. Their rear is said to be a mile Westward of Lawrence Taylor's Tavern, six miles from Allen Town. General Maxwell is at Hyde's Town,[3] abt. three miles from this place. General Dickinson is said to be on the enemy's right flank, but where cannot be told. We can hear nothing certain of General Scott but from circumstances he is probably at Allen Town. We shall agreeable to your request consider and appoint some proper place of rendesvous, for the union of our force, which we shall communicate to General Maxwell & Scot and to yourself. In the mean time, I would recommend to you to move towards this place as soon as the convenience of your men will permit. I am told Col Morgan is on the enemy's right flank. He had a slight skirmish with their rear this forenoon at Robert Montgomery's, on the Monmouth road leading from Allen Town. We shall see General Maxwell immediately, and you will hear from us again.

I am Yr Obedt ser

send this to the General
after reading it.   Alex Hamilton

Doctor Stile's House [4]
Cranbury Town 9 OClock.

We are just informed that General Scot passed by Hopper's Tavern, 5 miles from Allen Town this afternoon at 5 OClock

ALS, George Washington Papers, Library of Congress.
1. The British forces, under the command of Howe's successor, Sir Henry Clinton, evacuated Philadelphia and were in New Jersey by June 18, 1778. By June 21, Washington and some of his forces were on the Jersey side of the Delaware.
The letter printed here deals with the disposition of the American forces in pursuit of the British and the maneuvers that were to culminate on June 28 in the Battle of Monmouth.
2. H, who had been assigned to Lafayette as a liaison officer, had gone ahead to Cranbury. Soon after H wrote this letter, Lafayette arrived in Cranbury. Lafayette enclosed this letter in one to Washington, June 25, 1778 (Louis Gottschalk, ed., *The Letters of Lafayette to Washington, 1777-1799* [New York, 1944], 48).
3. Hightstown, New Jersey.
4. Dr. Hezekiah Stiles, whose house was used as headquarters by some of the American forces until at least June 27, 1778.

To George Washington [1]

Robins Tavern
8 Miles from Allen Town [New Jersey]
12 OClock [June 26, 1778]

Sir,

We have halted the troops at this place. The enemy, by our last reports, were four miles from this (that is their rear) and had passed the road which turns off towards South Amboy, which determines their rout[e] towards Shrewsbury. Our reason for halting is the extreme distress of the troops for want of provisions. General Wayne's detachment is almost starving and seem both unwilling and unable to march further 'till they are supplied. If we do not receive an immediate supply, the whole purpose of our detachment must be frustrated. This morning we missed doing any thing from a deficiency of intelligence. On my arrival at Cranbury yesterevening, I proceeded by desire of ye Marquis immediately to Hides Town [2] and Allen Town to take measures for cooperating with the different parts of the detachment and to find what was doing to procure intelligence. I found every precaution was neglected—no horse was near the enemy, or could be heard of 'till late in the morning; so that before we could send out parties and get the necessary information, they were in full march and as they have marched pretty expeditiously we should not be able to come up with them during the march of this day; if we did not suffer the impediment we do on the score of provisions. We are intirely at a loss where the army is, which is no inconsiderable check to our enterprise; if the army is wholly out of supporting distance, we risk the total loss of the detachment in making an attack. If the army will countenance us we may do something clever. We feel our personal honor as well as the honor of the army and the good of the service interested and are heartily desirous to attempt whatever the disposition of our men will second and prudence authorise. It is evident the enemy wish to avoid not to engage us.

Desertions I imagine have been pretty considerable to day; I have seen 8 or 10 deserters and have heard of many more. We have had some little skirmishing by detached parties—one attacked their rear guard with a degree of success killed a few and took seven prisoners.

I am with great respect & regard   Sir   Yr Obedt ser.   A Hamilton

Marquis & Gen Dickenson send their compliments. My writing makes theirs unnecessary.

An officer just comes in who informs that [he] left the enemy's rear five miles off, still in march about half an hour ago. To ascertain still more fully their route I have ordered a fresh party on their left towards the head of their column   They have three Brigades in rear of their baggage.

ALS, George Washington Papers, Library of Congress; copy, Hamilton Papers, Library of Congress.
   1. When this letter was written, Washington was at Cranbury, New Jersey. H was with Lafayette, to whom he had been assigned and who was in command of the advanced American forces.
   2. Hightstown, New Jersey.

To George Washington

[Robins Tavern, near Allentown, New Jersey, June 26, 1778] [1]

Sir,

The result of what I have seen and heard concerning the enemy is, that they have incamped with their van a little beyond Monmouth Court House and their rear at Manalapans [2] River abt. seven miles from this place. Their march to day has been very judiciously conducted—their baggage in front and their flying army in the rear, with a rear guard of 1000 men about 400 paces from the main body. To attack them in this situation, without being supported by the whole army would be folly in the extreme. If it should be thought adviseable to give the necessary support, the army can move to some position near the enemy's left flank which would put them in a very awkward situation, with so respectable a body in their rear and would put it out of their power to turn either flank should they be so disposed. Their left is strongly posted and I am told their right is also. By some accounts one part of his army lies on the road leading from the Monmouth road to South Amboy. It is not improbable that South Amboy may still be the object.

I had written thus far when your letter to the Marquis arrived. [3] This puts the matter on a totally different footing. The detachment will march tomorrow Morning at three oClock to English Town.

I am with great regard & esteem Yr Obed ser   A Hamilton

ALS, George Washington Papers, Library of Congress; copy, Hamilton Papers, Library of Congress.

1. J. C. Hamilton (*JCHW*, I, 122) and Lodge (*HCLW*, IX, 139) both misdate this letter June 28. Fitzpatrick (*GW*, XII, 123n) misdates it June 27.

2. Also known as Penelopen; situated between Hightstown and Monmouth Court House.

3. On June 26, Washington wrote Lafayette four different letters. The one to which H refers presumably is that which ordered Lafayette to Englishtown, New Jersey, and warned him against surprise (Df, George Washington Papers, Library of Congress).

To Brigadier General Charles Scott

[Robins Tavern, near Allentown, New Jersey, June 27, 1778]

Sir,

This part of the troops marches instantly. We are to join in the Monmouth road one mile this side of Taylor's Tavern. You will govern yourself accordingly. If you can find Morgan let him be desired again to keep close to the enemy and attack when we attack.

I am sir   Yr Obed serv.   Alex Hamilton   Aide De Camp

You will endeavour to keep up a communication of intelligence.

ALS, New York Public Library.

George Washington to Brigadier General Louis Le Bèque Du Portail

Englishtown [*New Jersey*] *June 30, 1778.* Orders Du Portail to Philadelphia to study city's defenses.

Df, in writing of H, George Washington Papers, Library of Congress.

George Washington to Marquis de Lafayette

New Brunswick [*New Jersey*] *July 3, 1778.* States that Colonel Charles Armand can raise a new corps only under sanction of Congress.

Df, in writing of H, George Washington Papers, Library of Congress.

Proceedings of a General Court-Martial for the Trial of Major General Charles Lee [1]

[New Brunswick, New Jersey, July 4, 1778]

Lieutenant Colonel Hamilton being sworn,

Q. Did you deliver General Lee any orders from General Washington the 27th or 28th of June, respecting his attacking the enemy?

A. I wrote General Lee a letter the evening of the 27th of June,[2] by General Washington's order, a copy of which I have not; but it was conceived in the spirit, as I understood, of former orders that had been given by him to General Lee, and was occasioned by an apprehension (as declared to me by General Washington) that the enemy might move off either at night or very early in the morning, and get out of our reach, so that the purpose of an attack might be frustrated: To remedy this, the order directed that General Lee should detach a party of 6 or 800 men to lie very near the enemy, as a party of observation, in case of their moving off, to give the earliest intelligence of it, and to skirmish with them so as to produce some delay, and give time for the rest of the troops to come up: It also directed that he should write to Colonel Morgan, desiring him (in case of the enemy being on their march) to make an attack on them, in such manner as might also tend to produce delay, and yet not so as to endanger a general rout of his party, and disqualify them from acting in concert with the other troops, when a serious attack should be made: This, I understood from General Washington, was in pursuance of his intention to have the enemy attacked, and conformable to the spirit of previous orders he had given General Lee for that purpose. This letter was sent off by a light-horseman, and the foregoing is the purport of it, to the best of my recollection.

General Lee's question. What hour was the letter sent off to me?

A. It was rather late in the evening. I went to bed soon after.

Captain Mercer [3] being sworn.

Q. What hour was the letter received from Colonel Hamilton by General Lee?

A. To the best of my recollection, it was past one o'clock in the morning of the 28th of June.

Captain Edwards [4] being sworn,

Q. What hour was the letter received from Colonel Hamilton by General Lee?

A. When the express came I got up and looked at the watch, and think it was near two o'clock by the watch; I then immediately wrote to Colonel Morgan, General Dickinson, and Colonel Grayson, to comply with the contents of the letter that General Lee received from Colonel Hamilton, and sent off the light-horsemen to them.

Q. to Colonel Hamilton. Did you conceive General Washington's orders, or the spirit of them, to General Lee, were to attack the enemy at all events?

A. I do not. I can't conceive that General Washington could mean to give orders so extremely positive, but that circumstances, which had been unforeseen, might arise, to leave the officer, who had the execution of them, liberty to deviate; but, from everything I knew of the affair, General Washington's intention was fully to have the enemy attacked on their march, and that the circumstances must be very extraordinary and unforeseen, which, consistent with his wish, could justify the not doing it.

General Lee's question to Colonel Hamilton. Did you, either by letter to me, or in conversation with me, communicate this idea of General Washington's intention as fully and clearly as you have done it to the Court?

A. I do not recollect that I ever did.

General Lee's question. Was your idea of General Washington's intention that I should attack the enemy, had I found them in the situation which General Dickinson's intelligence assured me they were; that is, the whole arranged in order of battle, at or near [the] Courthouse?

A. I knew nothing of General Dickinson's intelligence; but were the enemy's whole army drawn up in order of battle near the Court-house, I do not conceive it was General Washington's intention to have them attacked by your detachment.

The Court adjourn till tomorrow morning at 8 o'clock.

1. *Proceedings of a General Court Martial for the Trial of Major General Lee*, 5–6.
  This court-martial concerned Lee's conduct at the Battle of Monmouth.
2. Letter not found.
3. John Francis Mercer of Virginia was aide-de-camp to Major General Charles Lee as of June 8, 1778.
4. Evan Edwards of Pennsylvania was aide-de-camp to Major General Charles Lee.

To Elias Boudinot [1]

[New Brunswick, New Jersey, July 5, 1778]

My dear Sir,

You will by this time imagine that I have forgotten my promise of writing to you, as I have been so long silent on an occasion, which most people will be fond of celebrating to their friends. The truth is, I have no passion for scribbling and I know you will be at no loss for the fullest information. But that you may not have a right to accuse me of negligence, I will impose upon myself the drugery of saying something about the transactions of the 28th, in which the American arms gained very signal advantages; and might have gained much more signal ones.

Indeed, I can hardly persuade myself to be in good humour with success so far inferior to what we, in all probability should have had, had not the finest opportunity America ever possessed been fooled away by a man, in whom she has placed a large share of the most ill judged confidence. You will have heard enough to know, that I mean General Lee. This man is either a driveler in the business of soldiership or something much worse. To let you fully into the silly and pitiful game he has been playing, I will take the tale up from the beginning; expecting you will consider what I say, as in the most perfect confidence.

When we came to Hopewell Township, The General unluckily called a council of war, the result of which would have done honor to the most honorab[le] society of midwives, and to them only. The purport was, that we should keep at a comfortable distance from the enemy, and keep up a vain parade of annoying them by detachment. In persuance of this idea, a detachment of 1500 men was sent off under General Scot to join the other troops near the enemy's lines. General Lee was *primum mobile* of this sage plan; and was even opposed to sending so considerable a force. The General, on mature reconsideration of what had been resolved on, determined to persue a different line of conduct at all hazards. With this view,

ALS, Historical Society of Pennsylvania, Philadelphia.

1. When this letter was written, Boudinot was a member of the Continental Congress from New Jersey.

A Plan of the City of NEW YORK & its ENVIRONS to Greenwich, on the North or Hudson's River, and to Crown Point, on the East or Sound River, Shewing the Several Streets, Publick Buildings, Docks, Fort & Battery, with the true Form & Course of the Commanding Grounds, with and without the Town. Surveyed in the Winter 1775.

To the Honble Thos. Gage, Esqr. Major General and Commander in Chief of his MAJESTY'S Forces in North America, and Colonel of the 22 Regiment of Foot, ——— This PLAN is Most humbly Inscribed by his Obedient Servant John Montresor Engineer.

NORTH OR HUDSON'S RIVER

EAST OR SOUND RIVER

A. Fort George.
B. Batteries.
C. Military Hospital.
D. Secretary's Office.
E. Powder Magazine.
F. Soldiers' Barracks.
G. Ship-Yards.
H. City Hall.
I. Exchange.
J. Jail.
K. Work-House
L. College.
M. Trinity Church.

N. St. George's Chapel.
O. St. Paul's Chapel.
P. Garden Street Church.
Q. Middle Dutch Church.
R. North Dutch Church.
S. Lutheran Church.
T. German Reformed Church.
U. French Protestant Church.
V. First Presbyterian Church.
W. Quaker Meeting-House.
X. Jews' Synagogue.
Y. Baptists' Meeting-House.
Z. Moravian Meeting-House.

1. New Lutheran Meeting-House
2. Methodist Meeting-House.
3. Free School.
4. The Theatre.
5. Fresh-water Pump, from which the Town is supplied.
6. Statue of George III.
7. Oswego Market.
8. Fish Market.
9. Old Slip Market.
10. Fly Market.
11. Peck's Market.
12. Fraunce's Tavern.
13. Walton Mansion.

This plan of the City of New York in 1775 shows places familiar to Alexander Hamilton.

he marched the army the next morning towards Kingston[2] and there made another detachment of 1000 men under General Wayne; and formed all the detached troops into an advanced corps under the command of the Marquis De la fayette. The project was, that this advanced corps should take the first opportunity to attack the enemy's rear on the march, to be supported or covered as circumstances should require by the whole army.

General Lee's conduct with respect to the command of this corps was truly childish. According to the incorrect notions of our army his seniority would have intitled him to the command of the advanced corps; but he in the first instance declined it, in favour of the Marquis. Some of his friends having blamed him for doing it, and Lord Stirling having shown a disposition to interpose his claim, General Lee very inconsistently reasserted his pretensions. The matter was a second time accommodated; General Lee and Lord Stirling agreed to let the Marquis command. General Lee a little time after, recanted again and became very importunate. The General, who had all along observed the greatest candor in the matter, grew tired of such fickle behaviour and ordered the Marquis to proceed.

The enemy in marching from Allen Town had changed their disposition and thrown all their best troops in the rear; this made it necessary, to strike a stroke with propriety, to reinforce the advanced corps. Two brigades were detached for this purpose, and the General, willing to accommodate General Lee, sent him with them to take the command of the whole advanced corps, which rendezvoused the forenoon of the 27th at English Town, consisting of at least 5000 rank & file, most of them select troops. General Lee's orders were, the moment he received intelligence of the enemy's march to persue them & to attack their rear.

This intelligence was received about five oClock the morning of the 28th. and General Lee put his troops in motion accordingly. The main body did the same. The advanced corps came up with the enemys rear a mile or two beyond the court House; I saw the enemy drawn up, and am persuaded there were not a thousand men; their front from different accounts was then ten miles off. However favourable this situation may seem for an attack it was not made; but after changing their position two or three times by

2. Three and a half miles northeast of Princeton.

retrograde movements our advanced corps got into a general con-
fused retreat and even route would hardly be too strong an expression. Not a word of all this was officially communicated to the
General; as we approached the supposed place of action we heard
some flying rumours of what had happened in consequence of which
the General rode forward and found the troops retiring in the
greatest disorder and the enemy pressing upon their rear. I never
saw the general to so much advantage. His coolness and firmness
were admirable. He instantly took measures for checking the enemy's
advance, and giving time for the army, which was very near, to
form and make a proper disposition. He then rode back and had
the troops formed on a very advantageous piece of ground; in which
and in other transactions of the day General Greene & Lord Stirling
rendered very essential service, and did themselves great honor.
The sequel is, we beat the enemy and killed and wounded at least
a thousand of their best troops. America owes a great deal to General Washington for this day's work; a general route dismay and
disgrace would have attended the whole army in any other hands
but his. By his own good sense and fortitude he turned the fate of
the day. Other officers have great merit in performing their parts
well; but he directed the whole with the skill of a Master workman.
He did not hug himself at a distance and leave an Arnold to win
laurels for him; [3] but by his own presence, he brought order out
of confusion, animated his troops and led them to success.

A great number of our officers distinguished themselves this day.
General Wayne was always foremost in danger. Col Stewart [4] &
Lt Col Ramsay [5] were with him among the first to oppose the
enemy. Lt Col Olney [6] at the Head of Varnum's [7] Brigade made
the next stand. I was with him, got my horse wounded and myself
much hurt by a fall in consequence. Col Livingston [8] behaved very

3. This is, of course, a reference to Gates's behavior at Saratoga.
4. Colonel Walter Stewart, formerly of the Thirteenth Pennsylvania Regiment, had been transferred to the Second Pennsylvania Regiment on July 1,
1778.
5. Lieutenant Colonel Nathaniel Ramsay, Third Maryland Regiment, was
wounded and taken prisoner at Monmouth.
6. Lieutenant Colonel Jeremiah Olney, Second Rhode Island Regiment.
7. Brigadier General James M. Varnum, Continental Army.
8. Colonel Henry Beekman Livingston, Fourth New York Regiment.

handsomely. Our friend Barber [9] was remarkably active; towards the close of the day, he received a ball through his side—which the doctors think will not be fatal. Col: Silly,[10] & Lt Col: Parker [11] were particularly useful on the left—Col Craig,[12] with General Wayne, on the right. The Artillery acquitted themselves most charmingly. I was spectator to Lt Col: Oswalds [13] behaviour, who kept up a gallant fire from some pieces commanded by him, uncovered and unsupported. In short one can hardly name particulars without doing injustice to the rest. The behaviour of the officers and men in general was such as could not easily be surpassed. Our troops, after the first impulse from mismanagement, behaved with more spirit & moved with greater order than the British troops. You know my way of thinking about our army, and that I am not apt to flatter it. I assure you I never was pleased with them before this day.

What part our family acted let others say. I hope you will not suspec[t] me of vanity when I tell you that one of them Fitsgerald,[14] had a slight contusion with a Musket ball, another, Laurens, had a slight contusion also—and his horse killed—a third, Hamilton, had his horse wounded in the first part of the action with a musket ball. If the rest escaped, it is only to be ascribed to better fortune, not more prudence in keeping out of the way. That Congress is not troubled with any messenger-aids to give swords and other pretty toys to, let them ascribe to the good sense of the Commander in Chief, and to a certain turn of thinking in those about him which put them above such shifts.

What think you now of General Lee? You will be ready to join me in condemning him: And yet, I fear a Court Martial will not do it. A certain preconceived and preposterous opinion of his being

9. Lieutenant Colonel Francis Barber, Third New Jersey Regiment, had been H's teacher at Elizabethtown, New Jersey, and a friend of Boudinot whose home was in Elizabethtown.

10. Colonel Joseph Cilley, First New Hampshire Regiment, was one of the witnesses at Lee's court martial.

11. H may have been referring to Lieutenant Colonel John Parke (or Park), who at the Battle of Monmouth was in temporary command of Colonel John Patton's Continental Regiment during Patton's absence.

12. Colonel Thomas Craig, Third Pennsylvania Regiment.

13. Lieutenant Colonel Eleazer Oswald, Second Continental Artillery Regiment.

14. Lieutenant Colonel John Fitzgerald, an aide-de-camp to Washington.

a very great man will operate much in his favour. Some people are very industrious in making interest for him. Whatever a court Martial may decide, I shall continue to believe and say—his conduct was monstrous and unpardonable.

I am Dr Sir   Yrs. Affecty   Alex Hamilton

Brunswick
July 5th. 78

One wing of the army marched this morning towards the North River, another goes tomorrow. The enemy by our last accounts were embarking their baggage. They lie three miles below Middletown. French importunity cannot be resisted. I have given two frenchmen letters to you. I am very serious about Mr. Toussard,[15] and as far as a Majority in some Corps Armands,[16] Pulaskis or such like, would wish you to interest yourself for him. The Marquis De Vienne,[17] I am so far in earnest concerning, that if his pretensions are moderate and he can be gratified I should be glad of it, but I fear they will be pretty high.

15. Lewis Tousard (usually written incorrectly as Louis Toussard), a former captain of artillery in the French army, who joined the Continental Army as a volunteer of 1777.
16. Charles Armand, a former French officer, was colonel of the Third Cavalry, Pulaski Legion.
17. On July 15, 1778, the Continental Congress adopted the following resolution:
"The Marquis de Vienne, a major in the service of the King of France, having served with reputation as a volunteer in the American army during the present campaign, and having requested Congress to honor him with the brevet commission of a colonel, without any pay annexed to the said rank:
"*Resolved*, That the request of the Marquis de Vienne be complied with, and that a brevet commission of colonel in the service of the United States be conferred on him" (*JCC*, XI, 692).

To Colonel Stephen Moylan [1]

[New Brunswick, New Jersey, July 7, 1778]

Sir,

It is His Excellency's pleasure, that you collect the *whole of the cavalry*, without delay, as well the unarmed as the armed, and after a little refreshment, and getting the horses shod &c. proceed moderately towards the North river to join the army. He has received advice from General Heath [2] of the arrival of accoutrements for the cavalry to the Eastward which he has ordered immediately on. These will meet us shortly, it is to be hoped on the North River and will serve to supply deficiencies.

I am Dr Col.   Your most Obedt   A Hamilton   A D C

Brunswick July 7th. 1778

ADfS, George Washington Papers, Library of Congress.
    1. When this letter was written, Moylan was at Elizabethtown, New Jersey.
    2. Major General William Heath who was in command of the Eastern Department with headquarters in Boston.

George Washington to Henry Laurens

[*New Brunswick, New Jersey*] *July 7, 1778.* States that American forces have advanced to North River. Asks that Committee for Arranging the Army begin operations at once.

Df, in writings of Robert Hanson Harrison and H, George Washington Papers, Library of Congress.

From Elias Boudinot

Philadelphia July 8 1778

My dear Sir

I had concluded your Laurels had produced a forgetfulness of your old friend, but am now rejoicing in my disappointment having your obliging & very entertaining favour of the 5th. Inst. just handed me. With the utmost sincerity I congratulate you & my Country on the kind Interposition of Heaven in our favour on the 28 Ultmo. It seems as if on every Occasion we are to be convinced that our political Salvation is to be as through the fire. I scarcely know whether I am more distressed that any Person engaged in the Cause of America & to whom she *has entrusted her Safety* could be capable of betraying her Interest in the critical moment of decision, or more really gratifyed & pleased that the supreme disposer of human Events is continually baffling not only the formidable & open force of our Enemies, but also the more dangerous & secret Efforts of false or lukewarm Friends. The General I allways revered & loved ever since I knew him, but in this Instance he has rose superior to himself. Every Lip dwells on his Praise for even his pretended Friends (for none dare to acknowledge themselves his Enemies) are obliged to croak it forth. The share that his family (for whom I retain a real friendship) has in the Honors of the day has afforded me real Pleasure, and among the rest none more than that of your Lordship.

The Congress have not made a House 'till yesterday. I am afraid I shall have my Hands full here, and I am not greatly elated at the Prospect.

We have undoubted Intelligence of the sailing of a French Fleet for this Country, under the Command of Vice Admiral Count de Estang consisting of 12 Ships of the Line, 6 frigates & two xebeques. I have reason to believe the French Ambassador is on Board; an English fleet lay at St. Helena ready to follow them, consisting of Eleven Ships—1 of 90— 9 of 74— and one of 64 Guns.[1]

I am sorry to inform you that there is also intelligence of the Settlement of Wyoming being cut off by Coll Buttler with about 1000 Indians Tories & British Troops.[2] It is supposed that Carlisle will soon be the frontier of this State as the Inhabitants are flying in from all Quarters. About 200 Inhabitants were Scalped.

I must beg the favour of your presenting my most respectfull Compliments of Congratulations to his Excellency and the family, especially my worthy friend Harrison.

I am Dr Sir &c

Coll. Hamilton

ADf, Historical Society of Pennsylvania, Philadelphia.

1. On July 12, 1778, formal announcement was made in Congress of the arrival of the French fleet off the Delaware (*JCC*, XI, 684).

2. John Butler was one of the leading Tories of Tryon County, New York, throughout the Revolution. On July 3–4, 1778, Butler's Rangers and their Indian allies laid waste the Wyoming Valley and carried out one of the cruelest and most devastating massacres in the American Revolution. At this time Butler was a major. He was commissioned lieutenant colonel in August, 1779.

George Washington to Henry Laurens

Paramus [*New Jersey*] *July 11, 1778.* Acknowledges receipt of Laurens's congratulations on Battle of Monmouth.

Df, in writing of H, George Washington Papers, Library of Congress.

George Washington to William Henry Drayton [1]

Paramus [New Jersey] July 12, 1778. Acknowledges receipt of Drayton's congratulations on Battle of Monmouth.

Df, in writing of H, George Washington Papers, Library of Congress.
  1. Drayton was a member of the Continental Congress from South Carolina.

Proceedings of a General Court-Martial for the Trial of Major General Charles Lee [1]

[New Brunswick, New Jersey, July 13, 1778]

Lieutenant-Colonel Hamilton,

Q. What was the strength of the corps under the command of General Lee the 28th of June?

A. To the best of my knowledge the strength of the corps under his immediate command at English Town was about five thousand rank and file; besides these, Colonel Morgan, with about six hundred men, and General Dickinson at the head of a body of militia, as I understood, of eight hundred men, were subject to his orders for the purposes of co-operation.

Q. Did you fall in with the troops under the command of General Lee the 28th of June?

A. I had been sent by General Washington to reconnoitre the intermediate country between him and the advance corps under the command of General Lee, which I fell in with at some distance beyond the Court-house.

Q. What was the situation of General Lee's troops when you fell in with them?

A. They were issuing out of a wood on the left of the Court-house in two or three small columns, so near to each other as, in my opinion, to be incapable of displaying, to which also their situation in the woods was an impediment. These columns were in an oblique direction with respect to the enemy, rather towards their

  1. *Proceedings of a General Court Martial for the Trial of Major General Lee,* 19-21.

right, and within cannon shot. I heard several questions about artillery, of which there seemed to be a deficiency, and some confusion appeared to exist with respect to their situation and circumstances. I think I understood from General Lee, that some troops had been advanced through the woods towards the enemy right. I rode up to the front of the columns, from whence I perceived the situation of the enemy, and observed their cavalry were filing off towards their left, as if with design to attempt something on the right of General Lee's troops; this I informed him of, and submitted to him whether it would not be proper to send some troops to counteract that manœuvre of theirs, and turn their left flank; he approved the suggestion, and authorized me to give orders for that purpose to a column on the right. The Marquis de la Fayette led this column, to whom I delivered the orders accordingly, which were to wheel by his right, gain and attack the enemy's left flank. After this I was under the necessity of returning to report to General Washington what I had done in the execution of his orders. To explain more particularly the situation of General Lee's troops, I would mention some circumstances that I have omitted: There appeared to be a continuation of the wood, out of which the columns were issuing towards the enemy's right; the ground in front of the columns as far as the enemy, seemed plain and open, without any material obstacles; that which was more immediately occupied by General Lee's troops was something lower than that which was occupied by the enemy, but the difference in my apprehension was not so material as to be any considerable impediment to an attack, and the distance between the enemy and advanced corps was such, that it appeared to be extremely dangerous to change the position by a retrograde movement in the face of the enemy.

Q. What was the situation of the enemy, and numbers?

A. The enemy were drawn up with their right near a wood, their left on open ground covered by their cavalry, and forming an obtuse angle with the Court-house; the whole force I saw at that time did not exceed eight hundred infantry and cavalry to the best of my judgment, if there were so many.

Q. Was any disposition made by General Lee for attacking the enemy that you saw?

A. Only the one I have mentioned, the sending off troops to

attack their left flank, and the one of which I believe I was told by
General Lee, of sending off troops to attack their right flank. I
saw no co-operation with these movements by any general disposition
of the remaining troops.

Q. Did you fall in with General Lee's troops afterwards?

A. I came up with them in their retreat, a little time before the
stand was made, by which the enemy received their first check.
I heard General Washington say to General Lee, that it would be
necessary for him (General Washington) to leave the ground and
form the main body of the army, while I understood he recommended to General Lee to remain there, and take measures for
checking the advance of the enemy; General Lee replied he should
obey his orders, and would not be the first man to leave the field.
I was some little time after this near General Lee, during which,
however, I heard no measures directed, nor saw any taken by him
to answer the purpose above-mentioned. I understood a body of
our troops commanded by General Wayne, and under him Colonel
Stewart, and Lieutenant-Colonel Ramsay had been previously
thrown into a wood on the left, in front of where I found General
Lee, which I was afterwards told had been done by direction of
General Washington. On the right I saw some pieces of artillery
pretty advantageously posted, but destitute of covering and support.
Myself and others observed this to General Lee; no troops were
sent that I know of by his direction to supply the defect, but on
its being suggested, that the cannon would certainly be lost, if left
there in so unsupported a condition. General Lee ordered them to
be drawn off. Previous to that, I believe I rode towards Colonel
Livingston,[2] who was at the head of a detachment of troops, and
strongly advised him to march to the succour of the artillery; this
he did not immediately do, but after some conversation between us,
I saw him, when at a small distance, marching his detachment to do
what I had recommended to him. I now lost sight of General Lee,
and rode towards the rear, where I found Colonel Olney retreating
with a part of General Varnum's brigade; I pressed him to form
his troops along a fence which was near him, which he immediately
performed, and had a smart conflict with the enemy. These were
all the measures I knew of, taken by any part of the advanced corp

2. Colonel Henry Beekman Livingston.

to check the progress of the enemy after my coming the second time to General Lee.

Q. Were the troops, when you fell in with them the second time, retreating in order or disorder, and in what particular manner?

A. The corps that I saw were in themselves in tolerable good order, but seemed to be marching without system or design, as chance should direct, in short, I saw nothing like a general plan, or combined disposition for a retreat; in this, however, the hurry of the occasion made it very difficult to have a distinct conception.

Q. Was there any body drawn up in their rear to cover their retreat that you saw?

A. I saw no such thing.

Q. Were the orders that you heard General Lee give that day, given distinct and clear?

A. I recollect to have heard General Lee give two orders, at both times he seemed to be under a hurry of mind.

Q. Did General Lee to your knowledge advise General Washington of his retreat?

A. He did not to my knowledge.

Q. What was General Washington's intelligence concerning the disposition of the enemy previous to the orders given to General Lee?

A. When the Marquis de la Fayette first went out with his detachment, I accompanied him. The next day after we received intelligence, that the enemy had changed their disposition, and as they were presenting their rear to us had composed it of the flower of their army, consisting of their whole grenadiers, light infantry, and chasseurs of the line. This intelligence I communicated by letter to General Washington the 26th of June, in the evening; which letter, I have since understood by some gentleman of the family, was received by him.

Question by the Court. What became of the troops of the advanced corp, after the time you saw Colonel Livingston moving to the succour of the cannon?

A. It was after this that I assisted in forming the troops under Colonel Olney. In the action they had with the enemy, my horse received a wound, which occasioned me a fall, by which I was considerably hurt. This and previous fatigue obliged me to retire, and prevented my knowing what became of the detachments of the advanced corp after that circumstance.

Question by the Court. How far from Monmouth Court-house to the place the troops made the first stand?

A. The several events I have related passed so rapidly, that I could not at the time form any accurate judgment as to the relative distances of places, and was prevented by indisposition from seeing them after the action.

General Lee's question. I should be glad to know from what point of action, you mean, that you thought it would be dangerous to make a retrog[r]ade manœuvre?

A. In the first situation I found the troops beyond Monmouth Court-house, where I first fell in with them, and where (I believe) they first came in view of the enemy.

General Lee's question. Do you recollect who commanded the two pieces of cannon which you have mentioned were left unsupported, and were afterwards supported (as you say) by your advice?

A. I was not near enough to know the officers; but from what I have since heard, I am led to suppose that Captain Cook commanded them.

General Lee's question. Did you hear me address myself in person to Colonel Livingston's detachment, intreating them to draw off either to the right or left, from before the cannon, in order to give them the means of firing upon the enemy's cavalry, which was ranged exactly in front, and presented a very fine object?

A. I heard nothing of the kind; for I was not with that regiment at the time it got up with the artillery.

General Lee's question. Did you not express in the field an idea diametrically reverse of my state of mind, from what you have before mentioned in your testimony?

A. I did not. I said something to you in the field expressive of an opinion, that there appeared in you no want of that degree of self-possession, which proceeds from a want of personal intrepidity. I had no idea in my present evidence of insinuating the most distant charge of this nature, but only to designate that there appeared a certain hurry of spirits, which may proceed from a temper not so calm and steady as is necessary to support a man in such critical circumstances.

To Major General William Alexander, Lord Stirling [1]

[Paramus, New Jersey, July 14, 1778]

Sir,

Since the giving my evidence at the Court Martial, I have been endeavouring to recollect more particularly the import of the conversation between General Lee and myself, that happened in the field the day of the action and which was the subject of discussion yesterday, before the Court. My memory will not serve me on the occasion, in so clear a manner, as I could wish; but I have been able to form some more distinct ideas, than those expressed when I was interrogated by General Lee, which I communicate to you to make what use of them you think proper. On my making some remarks to General Lee which I now forget, he asked me the following questions, or others to the same effect, and I think partly in the same words. "Do I appear to you to have lost my senses, do I not possess myself?" My answer to these questions I do not perfectly recollect; but I remember that it was a favourable one, though I am unable to determine to what extent. It will be readily conceived that so singular and unexpected a question was not a little embarrassing; and it is possible, I may have replied in terms of less reserve and caution, than I should have done at a moment of greater tranquillity and cooler reflection. I perfectly remember what passed in my mind upon the occasion, with respect to General Lee's conduct, and from the most deliberate and unbiassed retrospect of it, my judgment intirely coincides with what I then thought. His answers to what was said to him were pertinent; and his behaviour had not the least appearance of concern on the score of personal security. So far he possessed himself and could not be said to have lost his senses, according to his own expressions. But he certainly did not appear to me to be in that collected state of mind or to have that kind of self-possession, which is an essential requisite of *the General*, and which alone can enable him, in critical emergencies, to take his measures with the promptitude and decision they require. A certain indecision improvidence and hurry of spirits were apparent.

These were my thoughts to the best of my recollection at the time, and it is natural for me to believe, that what I replied to General Lee could not be inconsistent with them.

This letter I mean as explanatory to my testimony of yesterday founded upon my reflections since; and if it can be done with propriety I shall be glad it may be admitted by the Court as such.

I am with regard   Sir   Your most Obedt Serv

ADf, Hamilton Papers, Library of Congress.
 1. Although the name of the addressee is not given by H, it seems likely that this letter was intended for Lord Stirling, president of the court-martial for the trial of Major General Charles Lee.

George Washington to
Lieutenant Colonel Francis Barber

Paramus [*New Jersey*] *July 14, 1778.* Thanks Barber for information concerning the enemy. Discusses compensation of John Hendricks, an American spy.

Df, in writing of H, George Washington Papers, Library of Congress.

George Washington to
Major General Horatio Gates

Paramus [*New Jersey*] *July 14, 1778.* Informs Gates that Army is marching to Haverstraw.

Df, in writing of H, George Washington Papers, Library of Congress.

George Washington to Jonathan Trumbull

[*Paramus, New Jersey, July 14, 1778.*] Reports arrival of French fleet. Suggests that eastern states gather available vessels and attempt to intercept an enemy fleet which is expected to arrive momentarily.

Df, in writing of H, George Washington Papers, Library of Congress.

George Washington to Comte d'Estaing [1]

[*Haverstraw, New York, July 15, 1778.*] Is sending "a small quantity of livestock" and has directed commissary to supply D'Estaing with whatever supplies may be needed.

Df, in writing of H, George Washington Papers, Library of Congress.
    1. Charles Henri Hector, comte d'Estaing, vice admiral of the French fleet.

To Patrick Dennis [1]

[Haverstraw Bay, New York, July 16, 1778]

D Sir

A considerable fleet of french men of war, chiefly ships of the line, has just arrived at Sandy Hook, under the command of Admiral Count D'Estaing. As the Admiral is a stranger, and is come for the purpose of co-operating with us against the Enemy, it is absolutely necessary that he should be attended by some Gentlemen of intelligence and who possess an accurate knowledge of the Coast and harbours. His Excellency General Washington is persuaded you answer this description in every part; and I am directed by him to request you in his name, if circumstances will permit, to go on board the Admiral as early as possible. Your services may be the most important and interesting and such as will give you a just claim to the thanks and notice of your Country. If you can remain with the fleet during their operations in this Quarter it will be infinitely desireable; but if you can not, it will still be of importance for you to see the Count D'Estaing as you may inform him of several points which he may wish to know. His Excellency would have written to you himself upon this subject, but he was under the necessity of leaving Head Qrs early this morning, to visit the posts above on the River. This letter, shewn to the Count D'Estaing will be, I trust a sufficient introduction of you.

    I am D Sir   Yr: Most Obed. Servant

                        Alex Hamilton   Aid de Camp

Head Qrs. Haverstraw Bay   July 16: 1778
Capt Dennis
in the Neighbourhood of Baskinridge Jersey

Df, in writing of Robert Hanson Harrison, George Washington Papers, Library of Congress.

1. Dennis was a sea pilot, who, as this letter indicates, was to serve as a pilot for the French fleet.

Receipt to Joseph Wickers [1]

[New Brunswick, New Jersey, July 19, 1778]

Received of Mr. Joseph Wickers two horses on public service.

A Hamilton, ADC

Brunswick
July 19th 1778

ADS, George Washington Papers, Library of Congress.
1. H was at this time en route from Washington's Headquarters at Haverstraw to Black Point, New Jersey, to confer with Admiral d'Estaing.

To George Washington [1]

[Black Point, New Jersey, July 20, 1778]

Sir,

Inclosed I transmit your Excellency a letter from the Count Destain.[2] He has had the River sounded and finds he cannot enter. He will sail for Rhode Island tomorrow evening; in the mean time he is making demonstrations to deceive the enemy and beget an opinion that he intends to operate in this quarter. He would sail immediately but he waits the arrival, or to hear, of a frigate which carried Mr Gerard [3] to Delaware, and which he appointed to meet him at Sandy Hook, so that he fears, his sudden and unexpected departure, before she arrives might cause her to be lost. He will not however wait longer than 'till tomorrow evening. We have agreed, that five cannon fired briskly shall be a signal of his arrival by day, and the same number, with five sky rockets a signal by night. In communicating this to General Sullivan,[4] the Count wishes not a moment may be lost, and that he may be directed to have persons stationed on the Coast and intermediate expresses to facilitate the Communication between them. Pilots will be a material article. He begs every thing may be forwarded as much as possible; and as many troops collected as may be. He would be glad a detachment could march from your army, or could be sent by water, for which purpose he would send covering ships, and some vessels he has taken by way of transports; but he cannot think of losing so much time as seems necessary. If the water scheme could shorten it, it would be a happy circumstance. He recommends it to your attention, and that you would take measures if the end can be better answered in this; and meet him with information of the part he may have to act to execute the plan. I perceive he can with difficulty debark 4000 troops but he will try to do it.

I am Sir   Yr. most Respectful & Obedt servant   Alex Hamilton

Black Point
July 20th. 1778

I hope your Excellency will excuse my not being myself the bearer of these particulars; the end may be answered by letter. Mr. Neville [5] is anxious to get on. I just have heard of dispatches arrived from you; I don't know but they may contain something new which may make the Count to wish a good conveyance to return an answer. My stay till tomorrow morning may answer that end. I shall not delay coming forward.

ALS, George Washington Papers, Library of Congress.
    1. On July 18, 1778, Washington had sent H to Black Point, New Jersey, to show D'Estaing a proposal for an attack on Rhode Island.
    2. This letter, written in French with a translation by H and dated July 20, 1778, is in George Washington Papers, Library of Congress.
    3. Conrad Alexandre Gérard, French Minister to the United States, who arrived with D'Estaing and presented his credentials to Congress on August 6, 1778.
    4. At this time Major General John Sullivan was in command of the American forces in Rhode Island.
    5. Major Presley Neville, aide-de-camp to Lafayette.

Pay Order for Hire of a Horse [1]

Piscataway [*New Jersey*] *July 22, 1778.* Orders that John Langstaff be paid "the usual hire for a mare of his impressed the morning of the 19th. and returned in the evening of the 22d. . . ." Signed "Alex Hamilton, Aide De Camp."

ADS, George Washington Papers, Library of Congress.
    1. On verso is written: "Received ten dollars of Colonel Hamilton on account of the within order. John Langstaff."

To George Washington

Newark [New Jersey] July 23rd. One oclock [1778]

Sir,

I wrote to your Excellency the evening of the 20th. by Major Neville. I remained in the neighbourhood of Black Point 'till the afternoon following. The Count had received his expected dispatches from Congress and was to sail, as I mentioned before, the first fair wind. At Brunswick yesterday, Mr Caldwell [1] joined me. He was immediately from the Point and brought intelligence that the fleet got under way yesterday morning. The wind unfortunately has been much against them, which is so much the more to be regretted, as they are rather in want of water. I need not suggest to your Excellency that an essential part of the Rhode Island plan, is to take every possible measure to watch the enemys motions and to establish expresses from place to place to give the Count instant information of any movement among their fleet. This will enable him to be in time to intercept them should they attempt to evacuate New York, while he is at Rhode Island, and will in general facilitate the intercourse and cooperation between him and your Excellency.

I have nothing new to communicate; besides what was sent by Major Neville and what I now send. All the ideas interchanged between the Count and myself were such as were familiar before I left Head Quarters. He was to go to Rhode Island and in conjunction with General Sullivan endeavour to possess himself of the enemy ships and troops there; if on his arrival he had good reason to think it could be effected without further assistance. If not he will be glad of a reinforcement from you in the most expeditious manner possible. What manner you think will be most expeditious you will adopt and if his aid may be useful he will afford it, as soon as he is informed of it.

This being the case my immediate presence at Head Quarters is the less necessary as to this business; and I hope your Excellency will indulge me, if [I] do not make all the dispatch back, which a case of emergency would require; though I do not mean to delay more than a moderate attention to my frail constitution may make not improper.

AL, George Washington Papers, Library of Congress; copy, Hamilton Papers, Library of Congress.

1. This may be a reference to James Caldwell, Springfield, New Jersey, who was chaplain of the New Jersey Brigade and assistant quartermaster general.

To Elias Boudinot

Head Quarters [White Plains, New York] July 26th. 1778

Dr. Sir,

I have had the pleasure of receiving your favour of the [1] instant. Baron Steuben will do me the honor to deliver you this. He waits upon Congress in a temper, which I very much regret—discontented with his situation—and almost resolved to quit the service.[2] You know we have all the best opinion of this Gentleman's military merit, and shall of course consider his leaving the army as a loss to it. Whether any expedient can be adopted, to reconcile difficulties, and retain him in the service at the same time, that no disgust is given to others, who ought not to be disgusted I cannot certainly determine. But I should conceive it would not be impossible to find such an expedient. You have no doubt heard while you were with the army, of the obstacles thrown in his way by many of the General officers, excited to it by Lee and Miffling [3] as I believe, in the execution of the Inspectorship; and you have, it is equally probable, heard, of the arrangement the General was in a manner obliged to adopt, to silence the clamours which existed among them, and place the Inspectorate upon a footing more conformable to their ideas. The opposition the Baron met with in this case was one cause of dissatisfaction to him. In our march from Brunswick, as the Baron was unemployed and there was a great deficiency of General officers, not withstanding the ideas of the army are against giving a command in the line to a person vested with an office similar to that held by him, The General ventured to give him the temporary command of a division, during the march, in consequence of which the command of a wing devolved upon him. This was a source of offence to many. When we came near the White plains, The General thanked him in general orders for his services, and requested he would resume the exercise of his former office. To this, on account of the opposition he had already met with, and from the original plan for the Inspectorship being mutilated, he discovered very great disinclination, and expressed a desire to preserve a command in the line, and from some conversation we have had together I apprehend, he means to resign his present ap-' pointment if he cannot have a command suited to his rank annexed to it. You will see by the General's letters what are his sentiments both with respect to the duties of the Inspectorship and the Barons holding a command in the line.[4] Far be it from me to wish to contravene his views; you may be assured they cannot be essentially departed from without very serious inconvenience. But if any thing could be done consistent with them to satisfy the Baron, it would be extremely desireable. Perhaps the principle on which the General's arrangement is formed may be preserved and at the same time, the objects of the Inspectorship enlarged, so as to render it a more important employment. Perhaps a resolution of Congress giving the Baron a right to be employed on detachments, might, for the present, compensate for the want of a permanent command in the line, and might not be disagreeable to the officers. You can sound him on these heads. I need not caution you, that this is a matter of great delicacy and importance, and that every step taken in it ought to be well considered.[5]

I am with the greatest regard and esteem   Dear Sir   Your Most Obedt   A Hamilton

ALS, Mrs. Arthur Loeb, Philadelphia.
   1. Left blank in MS. H is referring to Boudinot to H, July 8, 1778.
   2. Baron von Steuben's grievances and troubles as inspector general were numerous enough to fill a book. H tells some of the story in this letter. Other details can be found scattered through *GW*, XI–XII.
   3. Major General Charles Lee and Major General Thomas Mifflin.
   4. For Washington's opinion of Steuben at this time, see his letter to the President of Congress, July 26, 1778 (George Washington Papers, Library of Congress).
   5. For Congressional action on this problem, see *JCC*, XI, 819–22. In brief, Congress, on August 20, 1778, regularized the position of inspector general and appointed Steuben to the post.

George Washington to Henry Laurens

White Plains [*New York*] *July 26, 1778*. Regrets Baron von Steuben finds it necessary to resign.

Df, in writing of H, George Washington Papers, Library of Congress.

George Washington to Marquis de Lafayette

White Plains [*New York*] *July 27, 1778*. Introduces Major General Nathanael Greene who is to cooperate with Lafayette in campaign against Rhode Island.

Df, in writing of H, George Washington Papers, Library of Congress.

Expenses for Trip from Haverstraw, New York, to Black Point, New Jersey [1]

[White Plains, New York, July 28, 1778]

	Dollars
Received from Capt Caleb Gibbs of the public money in his hands_____137 Dollars_____	137
Paid the expences of travelling for myself five pilots, horses & servants from Head Quarters, to Black Point, so far as vouchers were kept, which are herewith £ 19.4.9_____	48
Ballance	89

due from A Hamilton to be charged to his private account
Head Quarters July 28. 1778   A Hamilton

ADS, George Washington Papers, Library of Congress.
   1. On July 18, Washington had sent H to Black Point, New Jersey, to show D'Estaing a proposal for an attack on Rhode Island.
   Enclosures to this letter, which are not printed, consist of bills paid by H en route.

To the Commissary of Clothing
from the State of Virginia

Head Quarters White
Plains [New York] July 30th. 1778

Sir,

His Excellency is informed, that there is a quantity of state-cloathing coming on under your direction for the use of the Virginia troops. It has been hinted to him that measures are taking to get particular regiments fully supplied to the disadvantage of others, which certainly would be altogether inequitable and improper. He desires you will make a point whatever partial applications may be made, to observe one general equal rule in distributing the Cloathing, that every regiment may have a due proportion according to its numbers and wants. This, with proper care you will have it in your power to effect and justice and the good of the service essentially demand the most exact adherence to it.

I am Sir Your most Obedt serv

Alex Hamilton Aide De Camp

ADfS, George Washington Papers, Library of Congress.

George Washington to
Brigadier General James Clinton

White Plains [*New York*] *July 31, 1778.* Instructs Clinton to move to Kings Bridge in order to gain information about unfriendly inhabitants in area and to protect surveyors while they reconnoitre.

Df, in writings of George Washington and H, George Washington Papers, Library of Congress.

From Brigadier General Louis Le Bèque Du Portail [1]

[*July–November, 1778.*] Asks Hamilton to assist the Chevalier de Villefranche.[2]

ALS, Hamilton Papers, Library of Congress.
1. This letter is in French.
In *JCHW*, I, 198 this letter is dated 1780. This very vague undated letter discusses a dispute in which the Chevalier de Villefranche was involved. Du Portail thought that Washington was not doing all that was possible for the Chevalier and therefore asked H to speak to Washington. In the very last line of the letter the Marquis de Chouin, messenger for Comte d'Estaing, is mentioned. Since the Marquis was in the United States, as far as it can be ascertained, only during Comte d'Estaing's stay (July 13 to November 4, 1778), the above letter has been given the inclusive date of July–November 1778.
2. Jean Louis Ambroise de Genton, Chevalier de Villefranche, was a major of Continental Engineers.

To Brigadier General James Clinton [1]

Head Qrs White plains [New York] Augt 1st 1778

Sir

The General has received a letter written by Mr Erskine [2] by your desire at half past Nine oClock this morning; by which he perceives there are parties of the Enemy hovering about you. He desires you will take the most effectual measures to ascertain what force they are in; and be particularly watchful, that while they may be amusing you in front, they may not throw a force superior to yours on your right flank & rear, and perhaps cut off your detachment. You will remember that it is not the object of it, to effect any thing material against the Enemy; and therefore you will be pleased carefully to avoid any untoward accidents happening to it. If the Enemy should be near you, in any considerable force, you will fall back upon the Army.

I am Sir   Yr Most Obed: sert   Alexr Hamilton   Aide de Camp

To Brigr. Genl Jas Clinton

Df, in writing of Robert Hanson Harrison, George Washington Papers, Library of Congress.
1. Clinton, the brother of Governor George Clinton, and a brigadier general,

Continental Army, was in the vicinity of Kings Bridge, New York, when this letter was written.

2. Presumably Robert Erskine, geographer and surveyor to the Army of the United States.

George Washington to the Board of War

White Plains [*New York*] *August 3, 1778.* Discusses proposed attacks against Indians.

Df, in writing of H, George Washington Papers, Library of Congress.

George Washington to Comte d'Estaing

White Plains [*New York*] *August 8, 1778.* Regrets hardships that D'Estaing has had to face. Informs D'Estaing of movements of British fleet.

Df, in writing of H, George Washington Papers, Library of Congress.

George Washington to Major General John Sullivan

White Plains [*New York*] *August 8, 1778.* Asks Sullivan to deliver enclosed letter to D'Estaing.

Df, in writing of H, George Washington Papers, Library of Congress.

George Washington to Henry Laurens

White Plains, New York, August 9, 1778. Discusses desirability of forming a corps consisting of Hessian deserters.

Df, in writing of H, George Washington Papers, Library of Congress.

George Washington to
Major General John Sullivan

White Plains [*New York*] *August 10, 1778*. Regrets "the tardiness of the militia." Informs Sullivan of foraging movements of enemy on Long Island.

LS, in writing of H, George Washington Photostats, Library of Congress.

George Washington to Comte d'Estaing

White Plains [*New York*] *August 12, 1778*. States again that British fleet has left "the Hook."

Df, in writing of H, George Washington Papers, Library of Congress.

George Washington to Colonel Peter Gansevoort [1]

White Plains [*New York*] *August 13, 1778*. Instructs Gansevoort to hold Samuel Gake, who has been found guilty by a court-martial, as a witness against Major Jury Hammell.

LS, in writing of H, George Washington Photostats, Library of Congress.
   1. Gansevoort was a colonel of the Third New York Regiment.

George Washington to Henry Laurens

White Plains [*New York*] *August 13, 1778*. Encloses a letter from Major General John Sullivan. Asks for papers concerning Major General Arthur St. Clair, whose trial is about to commence.

LS, in writing of H, Papers of the Continental Congress, National Archives.

To Colonel William Malcom [1]

[White Plains, New York, August 17, 1778]

Sir,

You will appoint a genteel sensible Officer to go to Fish Kill the 19th. instant, where he will receive orders from the Governor or

the commissioners for conducting in character of a flag some inhabitants who are to [be] sent to New York. You will caution him
to treat the persons in his charge with decency and politeness. It
will be necessary to be very exact as to the time; and so to order it
that the officer may be at Fish Kill the night before or early in the
morning.

I am Sir   Your most Obed ser   Alex Hamilton   Aide De Camp
Head Quarters White Plains Aug 17. 1778

ADfS, George Washington Papers, Library of Congress.
   1. Malcom, a colonel of one of the Sixteen Additional Continental Regiments,
was stationed at West Point.

George Washington to
Major General John Sullivan

White Plains [*New York*] *August 19, 1778.* Acknowledges receipt of Sullivan's news concerning Rhode Island.

Df, in writing of H, George Washington Papers, Library of Congress.

George Washington to
Major General John Sullivan

[*White Plains, New York*] *August 19, 1778.* Introduces the Chevalier de la Neuville [1] who wishes to serve with Sullivan in proposed
expedition. Has been serving as inspector general with northern
army.

Df, in writing of H, George Washington Papers, Library of Congress.
   1. Louis Pierre Penot Lombard, Chevalier de la Neuville.

George Washington to
Major General John Sullivan

White Plains [*New York*] *August 19, 1778.* Introduces Colonel
Lewis de la Radière of the Corps of Engineers.

LS, in writing of H, George Washington Photostats, Library of Congress.

Proclamation by George Washington

White Plains [*New York*] *August 21, 1778.* Pardons certain prisoners.

Df, in writings of Robert Hanson Harrison and H, George Washington Papers, Library of Congress.

George Washington to Major General John Sullivan [1]

White Plains [*New York*] *August 22, 1778.* Sends information concerning position of enemy fleet in the Sound.

LS, in the writing of H, New-York Historical Society, New York City.
    1. The letter is endorsed as follows in writing of H:
                The expresses are positively ordered to ride
                day & night without fail.
                Head Quarters   Alex Hamilton
                Augt. 22d. 78   Aide De Camp

To Brigadier General Anthony Wayne

                    Hd Qrs. [White Plains, New York] Aug 24. 78

Sir

Capt Nelson [1] complains at Head Quarters, that he has been eight or nine months in arrest by order of Col Nagle [2] without being brought to trial. This carries upon the face of it the appearance of a great grievance, but as the General has not an opportunity of ascertaining facts himself, he will be obliged to you to inquire fully into the circumstances of the affair, and make a report of the measures which appear to you necessary to be taken. It seems to be a complicated business. I am
        Sir   Yr most Obed ser   A Hamilton   Aide de Camp

ALS, Historical Society of Pennsylvania, Philadelphia.
    1. Captain John Nelson, Ninth Pennsylvania Regiment.
    2. Colonel George Nagle, Tenth Pennsylvania Regiment, formerly a lieutenant colonel, Ninth Pennsylvania Regiment.

From Marquis de Lafayette

a Rhode Island ce 26. aoust 1778

J'ai recu votre lettre,[1] cher colonel, et j'y aurois repondu plutôt si l'absence de la flotte ne m'avoit pas mis hors d'etat de vous parler d'autre chose que de ma bonne volonté, dont je ne crois pas avoir besoin de vous assurer. Mais j'ai vu Mr le Cte d'estaing, et je puis à present vous parler en son nom. La veneration, la tendresse qu'il a pour notre cher general, joint au sentiment que vous lui avés inspiré, car j'ai mis en avant votre nom dans cette affaire, rendirent inutile l'interet que j'y apportois; j'en ai temoigné cependant beaucoup comme vous pouvés imaginer, et quoique nous eussions un grand sujet à traiter, j'ai terminé celui dont vous m'avés chargé autant que j'ai pu le comprendre.

S'il avoit été dans le pouvoir de l'amiral de donner au Clel fitzgerald[2] le titre de Consul pour tout ce qui se transacteroit au nom du roi dans le sud il l'auroit fait de tout son coeur, mais cela depend de l'ambassadeur auquel il faut en ecrire; quant aux ventes des vaisseaux pris par lui, il ne demande pas mieux; ainsi je suis chargé de vous dire en son nom que tout ce qui depend de lui sur cet article doit etre regardé comme fait. La situation ou il est à present le met hors d'etat d'avoir des prises de quelques jours. Ecrivés moi encore quelle est la forme dans laquelle vous aimés le mieux que la chose soit faite et ecrite, et je vous la renverrai avec la signature de Mr le Cte d'Estaing. Je joins ici une lettre de credit de deux mille louis que Mr. fitzgerald m'a demandé, je vous l'adresse parceque je crains qu'il ne soit parti et que d'ailleurs je remets au premier ordinaire de lui ecrire; faites lui en mes excuses. Je suis si pressé que je ne peux pas ajouter deux mots de plus que ceux que je crois necessaires; il me parle de securités, je ne m'entends pas en affaires, mais vous pourriés arranger cela avec lui, ou avec le general.

AL, Hamilton Papers, Library of Congress.

1. Letter not found.

2. This may be a reference to Lieutenant Colonel John Fitzgerald, an aide to Washington. There is, however, no record of Fitzgerald having done any work for the French. Lafayette may have been in error and meant to write Lieutenant Colonel John Laurens, aide-de-camp to Washington, who had acted as liasion officer to Admiral d'Estaing at Sandy Hook.

Ne soyés pas ettonné si je ne vous ai pas ecrit le même jour que
la flotte est allée à boston; il m'en coute pour condamner mes amis
les americains. J'hesite à juger, même une partie du peuple qui
deshonoreroit par ses sentiments la nation à laquelle elle appartient.
C'est avec peine que je dirai même à vous que j'ai vu un nombre de
nos *compatriotes adoptifs* reunis ensemble, et que je les ai vu pour
la plupart injustes, ingrats, egoïstes, manquant non seulement aux
egards de la politesse mais à toutes les impulsions de l'honneteté la
plus commune. Je sais bien qu'il y a des exceptions; j'ai dans mes
mains une lettre du Gnl Greene qui en fait foi. Plusieurs americains
sont venus rougir ici pour la conduite de leurs freres: mais ce n'est
pas general, et si vous voulés vous en convaincre, lisés ma lettre au
gnl Washington.

La flotte a été un moment malheureuse, non par le sort de guerre,
les francais ne le sont jamais à force egale, mais par un coup de vent
auquel le pouvoir des hommes ne peut pas resister.[3] La victoire düe
à leur bravoure leur echappe, et cette bravoure seule sauve quelques
vaisseaux sans mâts sans gouvernaïl separés du reste de la flotte. Ils
reviennent cependant ici parcequ'ils l'ont promis; mais l'ordre du
roi, la nouvelle d'une flotte superieure donnée par le Gnl Sullivan
lui même, le manque de provisions, les representations vives de toute
la flotte, de tous les Capitaines, enfin tout ce qui peut forcer un
homme à faire une demarche qui lui deplait, ont obligé Mr le Cte
d'estaing à partir pour boston. J'etois avec lui; j'ai vu ce qui lui en
a couté, et j'enrage de voir qu'une troupe d'imbecilles s'avisent de
juger un homme que j'admire comme un grand homme, et que j'aime
comme un ami tendre parcequ'il a fait ce qu'il ne pouvait pas empêcher—du moins à ce qu'il croyoit.

Vous avés trop de discernement pour ne pas voir que je m'efforce
de cacher au general la moitié de tout ce que j'ai souffert, et des
horreurs dont j'ai été témoin. Le croiriés vous que moi, moi qui ai
l'honneur d'appartenir à la premiere nation du monde, a une nation

3. The remarks in this and the following paragraph refer to the differences
and bitterness that developed between Major General John Sullivan and Comte
d'Estaing. Relations between the two men had been strained from the outset,
but matters were made worse when D'Estaing's fleet sailed from Rhode Island
for Boston on the night of August 21–22, 1778. D'Estaing's side of the story is
given in this letter by Lafayette. Sullivan's version can be found in Hammond,
Letters and Papers of John Sullivan, II, 225ff.

qui peut etre enviée, mais qui est admirée et respectée de toute l'europe, j'ai été exposé à entendre presque moi-même le nom francais prononcé sans respect, peut-etre avec mepris, par un troupeau d'yankey's de la nouvelle angleterre.

Ce n'est pas comme particulier que je suis faché de cela. Je vois cette affaire beaucoup plus en grand; elle pouvoit avoir des suites funestes. Vous me demanderés ce qu'il faut faire, le voici.

Que le Congress approuve la conduite de la flotte, et en presente les remerciments à l'amiral; que mon cher clel hamilton employe son habile plume pour rammener les esprits yankeys. Que le gal washington prenne deux mille hommes choisis (non pas comme grenadiers mais en choisissant les Regiments); qu'il vienne ici, que toute cette milice qui cependant ne vaut pas le diable, fasse semblant de se ranger sous les drapeaux; alors Mr le Cte d'estaing fera le tour, et si vous me donnés deux mille hommes pour appuyer son attaque du côté de la mer, si le gal washington est sur l'isle, je vous reponds du succés sur ma tête.

Dans tous les cas, cher colonel, je pense qu'il faut faire quelque chose qui put etablir sur le champ entre les deux nations cette confiance si necessaire. Mr d'estaing me paroit avoir une infinité de projets, Newport, hallifax, St Augustin &c. &c. et pour l'année prochaine le Canada. Je suis faché qu'il ait si peu de troupes, mais il depend de lui d'en avoir un nombre respectable pour l'autre campagne. *Raison de plus pour le menager et le satisfaire.* Quant à cette année ici, mandés moi ce que vous croyés qu'il vaudroit le mieux comprendre, sans oublier les isles angloises; et mandés moi ce que vous me conseilleriés de lui proposer pour entrer dans le vües du general. Mr d'estaing regrette tous les jours d'avoir si peu de troupes.

Les officiers generaux de Rhode island me prient de faire un voyage à boston: je suis prêt à tout, et je ferai tout ce qui dependra de moi pour le succés de leurs desirs et du bien commun. J'aime l'amerique. J'en aime surtout le sauveur et le protecteur; ce n'est pas contre l'amerique que je suis en colere, c'est contre ceux qui la deshonorent par des sentiments qui ne sont faits que pour les torys.

Je suis persuadé qu'il n'y a rien de si aisé que d'etablir l'intelligence entre les deux nations. Que si j'avois des troupes americaines et francaises ensemble comme je le devois sur cette isle j'etablirois la meilleure union. Il est piquant de voir tout cela manquer par maladresse, et c'est pour cela que je desire le general. Cependant je ferai ce que je pourrai pour engager Mr le Cte d'estaing à venir tout de suite, et il le fera, j'en reponds, si c'est possible. Je voudrois que le gal washington lui envoyat un courier. Je vous ecrirai de boston ou vous sentés que je ne resterai pas longtems. Adieu

George Washington to Brigadier General Louis Le Bèque Du Portail

White Plains [*New York*] *August 27, 1778.* Instructs Du Portail to examine fortifications of Highlands and to execute instructions given him relative to the plan for defense of Delaware River and Philadelphia.

Df, in writing of H, George Washington Papers, Library of Congress.

George Washington to George Clinton

[*White Plains, New York*] *August 28, 1778.* Asks Clinton to call out militia and states that French fleet has departed for Boston.

Df, in writing of H, George Washington Papers, Library of Congress.

George Washington to Major General William Heath

White Plains [*New York*] *August 28, 1778.* Advises, for reasons of policy, that removal of French fleet from Rhode Island be attributed to damages caused by a storm. Asks Heath to use his influence to obtain assistance for fleet.

Df, in writing of H, George Washington Papers, Library of Congress.

From Elisha Boudinot [1]

[White Plains, New York, August 29, 1778]
Saturday Morng. 5 oClock

The Person I mentioned to you came over last Night and informs me, that General Clinton with his whole Army has set off for Rhode

Island. They are gone up the Sound and across the East End of Long Island. There are only a small Guard left in the City. Not a Canoe is suffered to pass up the East River least it should be known, they moved with the utmost secrecy. As it might be you have not heard of this movement I send this by Express.

I am, with Esteem Yours as ever   Elisha Boudinot

Col. Hamilton

ALS, George Washington Papers, Library of Congress.
  1. Elisha Boudinot was the brother of Elias Boudinot, who was a member of the Continental Congress from New Jersey. Elisha was a Newark lawyer who had served as clerk of the circuits since February 2, 1778.

George Washington to
Major General John Sullivan

[*White Plains, New York*] *August 29, 1778*. Sends information [1] concerning maneuvers of British fleet in the Sound.

Df, in writing of H, George Washington Papers, Library of Congress.
  1. This was probably the news sent in Elisha Boudinot to H, August 29, 1778.

From Captain John Copp [1]

[*White Plains, New York*] *September 1, 1778*. Requests Hamilton's intercession to prevent Copp's discharge from service.

ALS, RG 93, Miscellaneous Records, National Archives.
  1. Copp was a captain of the First New York Regiment.

From Marquis de Lafayette

A Yorktown [1] [Rhode Island] ce 1er Septembre 1778

Ne suis je pas bien malheureux, cher colonel, on me pousse pour aller à boston, on me chasse de Rhode island, ils n'ont ni repos ni patience que je ne sois parti, et le même jour que je m'absente est le seul où j'aurois du, où j'aurois voulu etre dans l'isle. Le diable en veut dans ce moment à tous les francois; heureusement que je viens de l'attrapper car à force de courir je suis arrivé à tems pour l'evacuation dont il vouloit encore me priver. Le malheur de ne pas etre à la premiere affaire m'a fait la peine la plus vive, et je ne m'en consolerai jamais quoique ce soit bien loin d'etre ma faute. Ces deux retraites font honneur aux troupes et au general Sullivan qui s'y est conduit parfaitement, elles en font peu aux anglois, et à leurs generaux qui n'ont montré ni activité ni genie du moins à ce qu'il me paroit.[2]

Le malheureux Mr tousard a eu le bras emporté au milieu d'une des actions les plus valeureuses qui ait été faite. C'est un homme aussi brave qu'il est honnête. Je crains d'embarrasser le general en lui mandant ce que je voudrois qu'on fit pour lui; mais la commission de Major ne pourroitelle pas se changer en celle de lieutenant colonel; il avoit fait un arrangement avant de partir, *le grand arrangement de Mr du Coudray* ou en cas de la perte d'un membre ils devoient avoir une pension de tant. Cet arrangement-là qui comme vous savés n'a pas été accepté, ne pourroit-il pas se renouveller en sa faveur.[3]

Il faut que vous me rendiés un grand service; c'est me mander le plus de details possibles sur la flotte de lord howe, les troupes qui restent à New York &c. &c. Mr d'estaing a beaucoup de raisons de croire qu'il est arrivé quelques vaisseaux d'angletterre, entre autres le Cornwall. Mandés-moi, mon cher hamilton dans une longue lettre, ce que vous pensés sur ce qui a été fait, ce qui va se faire, et ce qui pourroit etre fait dans la suite. Votre depêche me trouvera à warren petite ville près de la providence où je vais m'occuper à garder beaucoup de pays avec peu de troupes, et où sans reponde d'empêcher une descente des ennemis, je ferai le moins mal possible. A forces egales je tacherai de les battre. On me flatte que le general viendra ici lui même; dieu le veuille. Les affaires sur lesquelles je vous ai ecrit mes complaintes s'appaisent un peu mais pour prendre Rhode island il nous faut le gal washington.

J'attends de vos nouvelles par Mr de pontgibault [4] et finirai simplement ma lettre en vous assurant de mon tendre attachement.

Lafayette

Faites un million de compliments à toute la famille et a Mr de Chouin.[5]
Il y a dans l'armée deux epées pour moi envoiées par Mr carmichale [6]

et dont l'aide de camp de Mr de Kalb [7] doit savoir des nouvelles.
Envoyés-les-moi par un exprés.

ALS, Hamilton Papers, Library of Congress.
1. Yorktown Manor, located in what is now the township of East Green-wich, Rhode Island.
2. On August 29, 1778, Sullivan's forces attacked the British garrison and then withdrew. Both sides suffered approximately 250 casualties.
3. Philip Charles Jean Baptiste Tronson du Coudray was one of the many French officers who was promised numerous privileges by Silas Deane and who made life miserable for Washington. Although Congress rejected the agreement made by Du Coudray and Deane, Du Coudray on August 11, 1777, was made a major general. A month later, however, he was drowned in the Schuylkill River.
4. Charles-Albert, Comte de Moré de Pontgibaud, aide to Lafayette.
5. André Michel Victor, Marquis de Choin (frequently misspelled Chouin), a major of French infantry, who had served as D'Estaing's messenger to Washington.
6. William Carmichael, who when this letter was written was a member of Congress, had formerly served as secretary to the commission seeking to obtain French assistance and had been instrumental in sending Lafayette to America.
7. Johann Kalb, who styled himself Baron de Kalb and was known by that title, was a brigadier in the French army before his arrival in America in the spring of 1777 with a promise from Silas Deane that he would be given the rank of major general. He was given that rank in September, 1777.

George Washington to Comte d'Estaing

White Plains [New York] September 2, 1778. Regrets effects of a storm on French fleet, but assures D'Estaing of every assistance possible to repair damages. Sends news of movements of British fleet.

Df, in writing of H, George Washington Papers, Library of Congress.

George Washington to Jean Baptiste de Ternant [1]

[White Plains, New York] September 2, 1778. Discusses Ternant's rank.

Df, in writing of H, George Washington Papers, Library of Congress.
1. Ternant was a subinspector. On September 25, 1778, he was commissioned lieutenant colonel and inspector in the Continental Army.

To Charles Pettit [1]

[White Plains, New York, September 3, 1778]

Sir,

Two things I am charged by the General to write to you upon. One is to prevent any more wood being cut on Mr. Jay's farm. Another is, to begin to cast about for providing materials for building Winter Quarters in case we should be obliged to winter in this part of the country—⟨– – – –⟩ [2] boards tools &c.

I am sir   Yr. humb ser   Alex Hamilton   Aide De Camp
Head Quarters White Plains Sep. 3d. 1778

ALS, facsimile in *Isographie des Hommes Celebres* (Paris, 1843), II, n.p.
  1. Pettit was deputy quartermaster general.
  2. Approximately half of a line of MS is obliterated.

George Washington to Comte d'Estaing

White Plains [*New York*] *September 3, 1778*. Sends news of arrival of four British ships of war at "the Hook" and encloses a New York newspaper stating arrival of Admiral Hyde Parker with six ships of the line.

Df, in writing of H, George Washington Papers, Library of Congress.

From Cornet Larkin Dorsey [1]

[*September 4, 1778*]. Resigns his commission.

ALS, RG 93, Miscellaneous Records, National Archives.
  1. Dorsey was a cornet, Fourth Continental Dragoons.

George Washington to Colonel William Malcom

[*White Plains, New York*] *September* [*7–8*] *1778*. Instructs Malcom and Colonel Thaddeus Kosciuszko to cooperate with Brigadier General Du Portail in examination of fortifications of Highlands.

Df, in writing of H, George Washington Papers, Library of Congress.

To Elias Boudinot [1]

Head Quarters [White Plains, New York] Sepr 8th. 78.

My Dear Sir,

It is a long time since I have had either the pleasure of writing to you or of hearing from you. The long letter you promised me through Colonel Harrison, which was to come by Baron Steuben has not made its appearance. I imagine you must have changed your mind.

You are not to expect when you see this letter, that I have anything worth your attention to say to you; I write merely to show you that I continue mindful of my promise and my friends; and when I began, I had scarcely digested a single idea which was to be the subject of my epistle.

But just at this moment one matter comes into my recollection, which is of some importance to the public; and which you as a member of Congress, are in a peculiar manner interested in. You know the feuds and discontents which have attended the departure of the French fleet from Rhode-Island. You are probably not uninformed of the imprudent conduct of General Sullivan, on the occasion—particularly in the orders he issued charging our allies with refusing to assist us.[2] This procedure was the summit of folly and has made a very deep impression upon the minds of the Frenchmen in general, who naturally consider it as an unjust and ungenerous reflection on their nation. The stigmatizing an ally in public orders and one with whom we mean to continue in amity was certainlly a piece of absurdity without parallel. The Frenchmen expect the state will reprobate the conduct of their General, and by that means, make atonement for the stain he has attempted to bring upon French honor. Something of this kind seems necessary and will in all likelihood be expected by the Court of France; but the manner of doing it suggests a question of great delicacy and difficulty, which I find myself unable to solve.

The temper with which General Sullivan was actuated was too analogous to that which appeared in the generality of those concerned with him in the expedition, and to the sentiments prevailing among the people. Though men of discression will feel the impropriety of his conduct; yet there are too many who will be ready to make a common cause with him against any attempt of the public authority to convince him of his presumption, unless the business is managed with great address and circumspection. The credit universally given him for a happy and well conducted retreat, will strengthen the sentiments in his favour, and give an air of cruelty to any species of disgrace, which might be thrown upon a man, who will be thought rather to deserve the esteem and applause of his country. To know how to strike the proper string will require more skill, than I am master of; but I would offer this general hint, that there should be a proper mixture of the *sweet* and *bitter* in the potion which may be administered.

I am sure it will give you pleasure to have heard, that our friend Greene did ample justice to himself on this expedition; and that Laurens was as conspicuous as usual. But while we celebrate our friends and countrymen, we should not be forgetful of those meritorious strangers, who are sharing the toils and dangers of America. Without derogating from the merit of the other French Gentlemen who distinguished themselves, Mr. Toussard may be justly allowed a preheminent place. In the enthousiasm of heroic valour, he attempted single and unseconded, to possess himself of one of the enemy's field pieces, which he saw weakly defended. He did not effect it and the loss of his arm was the price of his bravery; his horse was shot under him at the same time; but we should not the less admire the boldness of the exploit, from a failure in the success. This Gentleman has now in another and more signal instance justified the good opinion I have long entertained of him, and merited by a fresh testimony of his zeal as well as a new stroke of misfortune the consideration of Congress.[3] The splendid action he has now performed, and for which he has paid so dear, should neither be concealed from the public eye, nor the public patronage. You are at liberty to commit this part of my letter to the press.

I am my Dear Sir   With the most Affecto Attachm   Yr. Obedt servt
                                                    Alex Hamilton

ALS, Historical Society of Pennsylvania, Philadelphia.

1. Incomplete versions of this letter are printed in *JCHW*, I, 495, and *HCLW*, IX, 149. In each instance the letter begins with the second sentence of the third paragraph and is dated "September, 1778."

2. In his General Orders for August 24, 1778, Sullivan stated: "The General

cannot help lamenting the sudden and unexpected departure of the French fleet, as he finds it has a tendency to discourage some who placed great dependence on the assistance of it. . . . He yet hopes the event will prove America able to procure with her own arms that her Allies refused to assist her in obtaining" (General John Glover's Orderly Book, Essex Institute, Salem, Massachusetts).

3. See Lafayette to H, September 1, 1778.

To Major General Horatio Gates [1]

[White Plains, New York, September 8, 1778]

Sir,

His Excellency desires me to inform you that having received information of the enemy's being out advanced this side of Wards House,[2] He thought it prudent to put the troops quietly under arms and has sent orders to the several Brigades for this purpose. This is the second note, I have written, the first the horsemen lost.

I am Sir   Yr. most Obed servant   Alex Hamilton   Aide De Camp

Head Quarters
Sepr. 8th. 78

ALS, New-York Historical Society, New York City.
    1. When this letter was written, Gates, like H, was in Camp at White Plains.
    2. Home of Stephen Ward, located on White Plains Road, in Eastchester. Ward was a former member of the New York Provincial Congress and a leading Westchester Patriot.

George Washington to
Major General Horatio Gates

White Plains [New York] September 10, 1778. Instructs Gates to march to Danbury.

LS, in writing of H, New-York Historical Society, New York City.

To————

[White Plains, New York, September 12, 1778]

Sir,

Mr. Chouin the French Gentleman who lives at Head Quarters informs he has heard you had a bear-skin, which you would part with; and requests me to inquire if it is so. I told him I thought it very improbable you should have any but what you wanted for your own use; but for his satisfaction would inquire how the matter stands.

I am Sir   Yr most Obed ser   A Hamilton
Sepr. 12th.

ALS, MS Division, New York Public Library.

To Major General Horatio Gates

[White Plains, New York] 12. Sept. 1778

Sir,

His Excellency commands me to inform you, that he has received advice, that the enemy, who had made a debarkation at Bedford, after burning the little town, had reimbarked their troops and were hovering about the Coast. He does not think it expedient that you should advance too far from the army and therefore desires, that you will halt near Bedford 'till you hear further from him.

I am Sir   Your most Obed   servant A Hamilton   Aide De Camp

Head Quarters
Sepr. 12h, 1778

ALS, New-York Historical Society, New York City.

George Washington to Henry Laurens

White Plains [*New York*] *September 12, 1778*. Transmits a copy of report of "a Board of Officers" on proposed Canadian expedition. Discusses importance of project and problems involved.

LS, in writing of H, Papers of the Continental Congress, National Archives.

George Washington to
Major General William Heath

White Plains [*New York*] *September 13, 1778*. Orders that clothing be forwarded from Boston to Springfield and Hartford.

LS, in writing of H, Massachusetts Historical Society, Boston.

George Washington to
Major General Nathanael Greene

White Plains [*New York*] *September 14, 1778*. States that clothing is to be forwarded from Boston to the Army. Asks Greene to cooperate with Major General William Heath to assure safe and quick delivery of clothing.

Df, in writing of H, George Washington Papers, Library of Congress.

George Washington to Baron de Kalb

[*White Plains, New York*] *September 15, 1778*. Sends marching orders. De Kalb is to be under command of Major General Israel Putnam until Croton Bridge and under command of Lord Stirling thereafter.

Df, in writing of H, George Washington Papers, Library of Congress.

George Washington to
Major General Charles Lee

[*White Plains, New York*] *September 15, 1778*. Grants Lee's request to go to Philadelphia.

Df, in writing of H, George Washington Papers, Library of Congress.

George Washington to
Major General Alexander McDougall

[*White Plains, New York*] *September 15, 1778*. Orders McDougall to march to Danbury and put himself under command of Major General Horatio Gates.

Df, in writing of H, George Washington Papers, Library of Congress.

George Washington to
Major General Israel Putnam

[*White Plains, New York*] *September 15, 1778.* Orders Putnam to march to West Point to reinforce garrisons in Highlands.

Df, in writing of H, George Washington Papers, Library of Congress.

George Washington to the
Quartermaster General [1]

[*White Plains, New York*] *September 15, 1778.* Sends order of the march.

Df, in writing of H, George Washington Papers, Library of Congress.
   1. Major General Nathanael Greene, who was quartermaster general, was at this time in Boston. Lieutenant Colonel Udny Hay, deputy quartermaster general, carried out these orders.

George Washington to
Major General Israel Putnam

West Point, September 19, 1778. Orders Putnam to camp on east side of the Hudson River, to dismiss Connecticut and New York militia, and to send parties to aid in work on the garrisons.

Df, in writing of H, George Washington Papers, Library of Congress.

To Major General William Alexander,
Lord Stirling [1]

[Fredericksburg, New York, September 20, 1778]

My Lord
   His Excellency finds the relative situation of the country hereabouts something different from what his information led him to conceive and that Fredericksburgh is not quite that intermediate

Point between Danbury and the Highlands, which would answer his views but is too far Northerly. He therefore desires you will halt on the ground this will find you upon 'till further orders. He will have a post reconnoitred and give you directions to move to it. I am with great regard

    Yr. Lordships   Most obd ser   A Hamilton   Aide De Camp

Head Qrs. Freds.
Sepr. 20th. 1778

ALS, MS Division, New York Public Library.
   1. Washington, on September 15, 1778, had sent orders to Stirling to begin the march from White Plains to Fredericksburg, New York, on the following day (George Washington Papers, Library of Congress).

From James McHenry

[Fredericksburg, New York, September 21, 1778]

Sir,

In order to get rid of your present accumulations you will be pleased to take the pills agreeable to the directions; and to prevent future accumulations observe the following table of diet.

This will have a tendency also to correct your wit.

I would advise for your breakfast two cups of tea sweetened, with brown sugar, and coloured with about a teaspoonful of milk. I prefer brown sugar to loaf because it is more laxitive, and I forbid the free use of milk until your stomach recovers its natural powers. At present you would feel less uneasiness in digesting a pound of beef than a pint of milk.

You will not drink your tea just as it comes out of the pot; let it have time to cool. The astringency of the tea is more than counterbalanced by the relaxing quality of the hot-water.

For your dinner, let me recommend about six ounces of beef or mutton, either boiled or roasted, with eight or ten ounces of bread. Cut the meat from the tenderest part with little or no fat & use the natural juice, but no rancid oily gravy whatsoever. For some time I would prefer the beef, because it contains more of a natural animal stimulii than mutton. Once or twice a week you may indulge in a thin slice of ham. Your best condiment will be salt.

You must not eat as many vegitables as you please; a load of vegitables is as hurtful as a load of any other food. Besides the absurdity
of crouding in a heap of discordant vegitables with a large quantity
of meat [is] too much of itself for the digestive powers. You may
eat a few potatoes every day.

Water is the most general solvent—the kindliest diluent, and the
best assister in the process of digestion. I would therefore advise it
for your table drink. When you indulge in wine let [it] be sparingly
—never go beyond three glasses—but by no means every day.

I strictly forbid all eatables which I do not mention principally
because a formula of diet for your case should be simple and short.

Should this table be strictly observed, it will soon become of little
use, because you will have recovered that degree of health, which
is compatible with the nature of your constitution. You will then
be your own councellor in diet, for the man who has had ten years
experience in eating and its consequences is a fool if he does not
know how to choose his dishes better than his doctor.

But in case you should fall into a debauch, you must next day
have recourse to the pills. I hope however that you will not have
recourse to them often. The great Paracelsus [1] trusted to his pill to
destroy the effects of intemperance, but he died (if I forget not)
about the age of 30 notwithstanding his pill. Lewis Cornaro [2] the
Italian, was wiser; he trusted to an egg, and I think lived to above
ninety.

For Colonel Hamilton   Septr.$\frac{21}{1778}$ McHenry.

ALS, The Huntington Library, San Marino, California; Df, The Huntington
Library.

1. Philippis Aureolus Paracelsus, a sixteenth century physician and philosopher.

2. Luigi Cornaro was a Venetian nobleman who after an illness at the age of
forty ate very little. In his later life his only solid food consisted of one egg
a day. He died at the age of ninety-eight in 1566.

George Washington to Comte d'Estaing

Fredericksburg [New York] September 22, 1778. Reports that
Major de Choin will explain to D'Estaing the situation of both the
enemy and the American army.

Df, in writing of H, George Washington Papers, Library of Congress.

George Washington to
Major General Nathanael Greene

Fredericksburg [New York] September 22, 1778. States that provisions for the French fleet have not arrived. Asks Greene to see "that every possible expedient may be embraced to promote" the forwarding of supplies.

Df, in writing of H, George Washington Papers, Library of Congress.

To Baron de Kalb

HQ Fredericksburgh [New York]
Sepr. 24. 1778

Sir,

His Excellency has received advice, that the enemy have made an incursion into the Jerseys and that another body of troops has advanced beyond Kings bridge. Though He apprehends the object of these parties can only be a forage; it is *possible* they may intend something against the Highlands. He therefore thinks it necessary to give you this intimation, that you may hold yourself in readiness to march at the shortest notice; but You will not proceed until you hear further from him, or until you get such advice from General Putnam as was mentioned in His letter of the 22d,[1] in which case you will do as there directed.

I am Sir   Your most Obedt serv   A Hamilton ADC

ADfS, George Washington Papers, Library of Congress.
   1. George Washington to Baron de Kalb, September 22, 1778 (George Washington Papers, Library of Congress).

From Colonel William Malcom

[*West Point, September 24, 1778.* On September 25, 1778, Hamilton wrote to Malcom: "I received your letter of yesterday." *Letter not found.*]

George Washington to George Measam [1]

Fredericksburg [New York] September 24, 1778. Orders Measam to Hartford and Springfield to supervise repacking of clothing that is being forwarded from Boston.

Df, in writing of H, George Washington Papers, Library of Congress.
1. Measam was deputy clothier general of the Army.

To Colonel William Malcom

[Fredericksburg, New York, September 25, 1778]

Dr. Sir,

I received your letter of yesterday [1] and have procured a warrant from His Excellency for 2000 dollars, the money for which I should receive and transmit; but it seems the Pay Master General has none at present in hand. I therefore inclose the warrant.

His Excellency commands me to acknowledge the receipt of your favour of the 23d.[2] He hopes your future supply of men will be regular and ample and depends on your exertions for forwarding the works with all possible dispatch.

Our accounts from various quarters correspond with your idea that the enemy are about to evacuate; but I am sorry that appearances do no[t] yet seem to me so decisive as might be wished. Any intelligence you can procure, that may serve to throw light upon their designs, will be very acceptable to His Excellency.

Dr Sir   Your most Obedt serv   A Hamilton   Aide De Camp

Head Quarters
Sepr. 25th 1778

ADfS, George Washington Papers, Library of Congress.
1. Letter not found.
2. Writing from Fort Clinton, Malcom discussed the building of huts, his need of money, and the expected evacuation of New York by the British (Malcom to Washington, George Washington Papers, Library of Congress).

George Washington to Colonel George Baylor [1]

Fredericksburg [New York] September 27, 1778. Instructs Baylor to join brigade that Major General Israel Putnam is sending to Clarkstown.

Df, in writing of H, George Washington Papers, Library of Congress.
   1. Baylor was a colonel of the Third Continental Dragoons.

George Washington to Baron de Kalb

Fredericksburg [New York] September 27, 1778. Instructs De Kalb to send a brigade to Fishkill to replace a division that Major General Israel Putnam is sending to New Jersey.

Df, in writing of H, George Washington Papers, Library of Congress.

To Major General William Alexander, Lord Stirling

[Fredericksburg, New York, September 28, 1778.] Orders Stirling to New Jersey to take command of troops there.

Df, in writing of H, George Washington Papers, Library of Congress.

To Major General William Alexander, Lord Stirling

Fredericksburg [New York] September 28, 1778. Sends instructions for Stirling's command in New Jersey.

Df, in writing of H, George Washington Papers, Library of Congress.

To Charles Pettit

[Fredericksburg, New York, September 29, 1778]

Sir

In answer to your favor of this morning, His Excellency desires me to inform you, that the matter in question between the officers & you, involves considerations too delicate to admit of his interference.[1] It should be the subject of compromise between yourselves; He wishes some mode could be agreed upon mutually satisfactory, and thinks as far as the public service will justify it, a liberal price should be allowed.

Yrs &c   A H. ADC

Hd Qrs. 29th. Sept 78

Df, in writing of Richard Kidder Meade, George Washington Papers, Library of Congress; also L, St. Croix Museum, St. Croix, Virgin Islands.

1. Pettit wrote to George Washington concerning a dispute over the valuation of horses offered for sale to the Army by officers (George Washington Papers, Library of Congress). Pettit was deputy quartermaster general of the Continental Army.

George Washington to Major General William Heath

Fredericksburg [New York] September 29, 1778. Introduces Brigadier General Du Portail who is to examine the fortifications at Boston.

LS, in writing of H, Massachusetts Historical Society, Boston.

George Washington to Marquis de Vienne [1]

Fredericksburg [New York] September 29, 1778. Reports that De Vienne's request for a furlough has been sent to Continental Congress.

Df, in writing of H, George Washington Papers, Library of Congress.

1. Marquis de Vienne was a major in the French army and a brevet lieutenant colonel in the Continental Army.

George Washington to
Major General Horatio Gates

Fredericksburg [*New York*] *September 30, 1778.* Sends news of enemy's movements in New Jersey.

LS, in writing of H, New-York Historical Society, New York City.

Pay Order

[*Fishkill, New York*] *October 2, 1778.* Directs Paymaster to send pay to Godlip Danroth of the German Regiment.

ADS, RG 93, Miscellaneous Records, National Archives.

George Washington to Comte d'Estaing

Fishkill [*New York*] *October 2, 1778.* Sends news of enemy's movements in New Jersey. Regrets that no reinforcements can be sent to Boston.

Df, in writings of John Laurens and H, George Washington Papers, Library of Congress.

George Washington to
Brigadier General Anthony Wayne

Fishkill [*New York*] *October 2, 1778.* Orders repair of road from Bulls Iron Works to Litchfield.

Df, in writing of H, George Washington Papers, Library of Congress.

George Washington to the Director of Clothing
at Hartford and Springfield

Fishkill [*New York*] *October 2, 1778.* Orders shoes, stockings, and blankets for Army.

Df, in writing of H, George Washington Papers, Library of Congress.

George Washington to
Brigadier General Jacob Bayley [1]

Fishkill [New York] October 3, 1778. Discusses problem of supplies for expedition against Canada.

Df, in writing of H, George Washington Papers, Library of Congress.
   1. Bayley was a brigadier general in the New York Militia.

George Washington to Henry Laurens

Fishkill [New York] October 3, 1778. Sends information concerning enemy's movements in New Jersey.

LS, in writing of H, Papers of the Continental Congress, National Archives.

George Washington to
Major General William Alexander, Lord Stirling

[Fishkill, New York] October 4, 1778. Requests daily reports on situation in New Jersey.

LS, in writings of John Laurens and H, The Huntington Library, San Marino, California.

George Washington to Otis and Andrews [1]

Fishkill [New York] October 4, 1778. Orders Otis and Andrews to supply Major General John Sullivan's troops with coats.

Df, in writing of H, George Washington Papers, Library of Congress.
   1. Otis and Andrews, a Boston firm, was appointed collector of clothing for the Continental forces in November, 1777.

George Washington to Major Richard Howell [1]

Fishkill [New York] October 5, 1778. Orders Howell to check on rumor that British fleet has sailed in search of French fleet.

Df, in writing of H, George Washington Papers, Library of Congress.
   1. Howell was a major of the Second New Jersey Regiment.

George Washington to
Lieutenant Colonel Samuel Smith

[*Fishkill, New York*] *October 5, 1778.* Regrets that Captain Edward Norwood cannot be reinstated.

Df, in writing of H, George Washington Papers, Library of Congress.

George Washington to
Major General John Sullivan

Fishkill [*New York*] *October 5, 1778.* Discusses procuring clothing for Sullivan's men.

Df, in writing of H, George Washington Papers, Library of Congress.

George Washington to the Committee of
Arrangement from Congress

Fishkill [*New York*] *October 6, 1778.* Discusses problem of enlisting deserters and prisoners.

Df, in writing of H, George Washington Papers, Library of Congress.

George Washington to
Colonel Goose Van Schaick [1]

Fishkill [*New York*] *October 6, 1778.* Thanks Van Schaick for removing boats at Kings Ferry.

Df, in writing of H, George Washington Papers, Library of Congress.
1. Van Schaick was a colonel of the First New York Regiment.

George Washington to
Major General Horatio Gates

[*Fishkill, New York*] *October 7, 1778.* Discusses probable British moves. Instructs Gates to repair certain roads to the eastward.

LS, in writing of H, New-York Historical Society, New York City.

George Washington to Baron de Kalb

[*Fishkill, New York*] *October 8, 1778.* States that "the former directions given you respecting the objects of your division and the conduct you are to observe with regard to the Highland post still continue in force."

Df, in writing of H, George Washington Papers, Library of Congress.

To Major John Bigelow [1]

Head Quarters Fredericks-
burgh [New York] October 9th. 1778

Sir,

By His Excellency's command, I am to request, you will immediately furnish him with an exact return of all the cloaths and materials for cloathing, you have provided in consequence of orders from Congress or the Board of War. This return must also show, what you have delivered, when and to whom, and what now remains in yr. possession. You will be pleased to be as accurate as possible.

I am Sir   Your most Obedt. servant

Alex Hamilton   Aide De Camp

You will also make a return of any state cloathing you may have provided, but will let it be distinct from the other.

ALS, American Antiquarian Society, Worcester, Massachusetts; ADfS, George Washington Papers, Library of Congress.
1. Bigelow was the assistant clothier at Hartford, Connecticut.

George Washington to George Measam

Fredericksburg [*New York*] *October 9, 1778.* Asks that clothing be repacked and delivered immediately.

Df, in writing of H, George Washington Papers, Library of Congress.

George Washington to
Major General Horatio Gates

Fredericksburg [New York] October 11, 1778. Thanks Gates for intelligence concerning sailing of British fleet.

LS, in writing of H, New-York Historical Society, New York City.

From Brigadier General Henry Knox

[Fredericksburg, New York] October 12, 1778. States desire of Captain-Lieutenant Daniel Gano, Second Continental Artillery, to resign.

ALS, RG 93, Miscellaneous Records, National Archives.

George Washington to Comte d'Estaing

Fredericksburg [New York] October 13, 1778. Sends British account of naval battle in which Comte d'Orvillier commanded French fleet. Reports that English fleet is still at "the Hook."

Df, in writing of H, George Washington Papers, Library of Congress.

George Washington to
Lieutenant Colonel Eleazar Oswald [1]

Fredericksburg [New York] October 14, 1778. Discusses Oswald's rank and regrets Oswald's decision to resign.

Df, in writing of H, George Washington Papers, Library of Congress.
1. Oswald was a lieutenant colonel of the Second Continental Artillery.

George Washington to the Major and
Brigadier Generals

Fredericksburg [New York] October 14, 1778. Asks for opinions on winter quarters for Army.

Df, in writing of H, George Washington Papers, Library of Congress.

From Charles Pettit

Fredericksburg [New York] October 16, 1778. Describes "Preparations made and making for the Building of Barracks on Hudson's River."

ALS, George Washington Papers, Library of Congress.

Publius Letter, I [1]

[Poughkeepsie, New York, October 16, 1778]

Mr. HOLT,[2]

There are abuses in the State, which demand an immediate remedy. Important political characters must be brought upon the stage, and animadverted upon with freedom. The opinion I have of the independence of your spirit, convinces me you will ever be a faithful guardian of the liberty of the press; and determine me to commit to you the publication of a series of letters, which will give you an opportunity of exemplifying it. The following is by way of prelude. You may depend I shall always preserve the decency and respect, due either to the government of the United States, or to the government of any particular State; but I shall not conceive myself bound to use any extraordinary ceremony with the characters of corrupt individuals, however exalted their stations.

Poughkeepsie, October 16, 1778.

To the PRINTER of the New-York JOURNAL

SIR,

While every method is taken to bring to justice those men, whose principles and practices have been hostile to the present revolution; it is to be lamented, that the conduct of another class, equally criminal, and, if possible, more mischievous, has hitherto passed with impunity, and almost without notice—I mean that tribe—who, taking advantage of the times, have carried the spirit of monopoly and extortion, to an excess, which scarcely admits of a parallel. Emboldened by the success of progressive impositions, it has extended to all the necessaries of life. The exorbitant price of every article, and the depreciation of our currency are evils, derived essentially from this source. When avarice takes the lead in a State, it is commonly the forerunner of its fall. How shocking is it to discover among ourselves, even at this early period, the strongest symptoms of this fatal disease?

There are men in all countries, the business of whose lives it is, to raise themselves above indigence, by every little art in their power. When these men are observed to be influenced by the spirit I have mentioned, it is nothing more than might be expected, and can only excite contempt. When others, who have characters to support, and credit enough in the world to satisfy a moderate appetite for wealth, in an honorable way, are found to be actuated by the same spirit, our contempt is mixed with indignation. But when a man, appointed to be the guardian of the State, and the depositary of the happiness and morals of the people—forgetful of the solemn relation, in which he stands—descends to the dishonest artifices of a mercantile projector, and sacrifices his conscience and his trust to pecuniary motives; there is no strain of abhorrence, of which the human mind is capable, nor punishment, the vengeance of the people can inflict, which may not be applied to him, with justice. If it should have happened that a Member of C-----ss has been this degenerate character, and has been known to turn the knowledge of secrets, to which his office gave him access, to the purposes of private profit, by employing emissaries to engross an article of immediate necessity to the public service; he ought to feel the utmost rigor of public resentment, and be detested as a traitor of the worst and most dangerous kind.

PUBLIUS.

The New-York Journal, and the General Advertiser, October 19, 1778. In both *JCHW*, II, 156, and *HCLW*, I, 199, this essay is dated October 19, 1778.

1. This is the first of H's three "Publius" letters, in which he attacked Samuel Chase, a delegate from Maryland to the Continental Congress. As a delegate, Chase had known of Congress' secret plan for securing flour to supply the French fleet. He relayed this information to associates who planned to profit by cornering the supply of flour and raising its price. The other two "Publius" letters are dated October 26 and November 16, 1778.

2. John Holt was the printer and proprietor of *The New-York Journal, and the General Advertiser.*

Council of War

Fredericksburg [New York] October 16, 1778. Describes state of American forces and of those of enemy. Asks opinion of officers on disposition of troops in winter quarters and advisability of sending a detachment to Boston.

D, in writing of H, George Washington Papers, Library of Congress.

George Washington to George Clinton

Fredericksburg [New York] October 17, 1778. Discusses details of expedition against Anaquaga, New York.

Df, in writing of H, George Washington Papers, Library of Congress.

George Washington to Brigadier General James Clinton

[Fredericksburg, New York, October 17, 1778.] States that Colonel Goose Van Schaick is to relieve Colonel Peter Gansevoort and that Colonel Philip Van Cortlandt is to make an expedition to the frontier.

Df, in writing of H, George Washington Papers, Library of Congress.

George Washington to George Clinton

Fredericksburg [New York] October 18, 1778. Again sends information of expedition to Anaquaga.

Df, in writing of H, George Washington Papers, Library of Congress.

George Washington to Comte d'Estaing

Fredericksburg [New York] October 18, 1778. Acknowledges receipt of D'Estaing's letters. Encloses extracts of information concerning the enemy.

Df, in writing of H, George Washington Papers, Library of Congress.

George Washington to Brigadier General Edward Hand

Fredericksburg [New York] October 19, 1778. Orders Hand to Albany and sends details of the proposed expedition against Anaquaga.

Df, in writing of H, George Washington Papers, Library of Congress.

George Washington to Brigadier General John Stark

Fredericksburg [New York] October 19, 1778. Orders Stark to Providence.

Df, in writing of H, George Washington Papers, Library of Congress.

George Washington to Major General William Alexander, Lord Stirling

Fredericksburg [New York] October 21, 1778. Asks Stirling to investigate existing "commerce" between enemy and inhabitants of New Jersey.

LS, in writing of H, The Huntington Library, San Marino, California.

George Washington to Henry Laurens

Fredericksburg [New York] October 21, 1778. Introduces Lieutenant Colonel Mauduit du Plessis, who wishes to leave country.

Df, in writing of H, George Washington Papers, Library of Congress.

George Washington to Comte d'Estaing

Fredericksburg [New York] October 22, 1778. Sends news of departure of British fleet, which is presumably bound for West Indies.

Df, in writing of H, George Washington Papers, Library of Congress.

George Washington to
Colonel Charles Mynn Thurston [1]

Fredericksburg [New York] October 22, 1778. Regrets that Thurston must resign from Army.

Df, in writing of H, George Washington Papers, Library of Congress. The draft was first dated October 23 and then changed to October 22.
   1. Thurston had been a colonel of one of the Sixteen Additional Continental Regiments.

George Washington to
Major General Horatio Gates

Fredericksburg [New York] October 24, 1778. Reports that troops have been ordered eastward. Orders Gates to area threatened by British in the event of a British landing.

Df, in writing of H, George Washington Papers, Library of Congress.

George Washington to
Major General Alexander McDougall

Fredericksburg [*New York*] *October 24, 1778.* Informs McDougall that Major General Horatio Gates has been given instructions about proceeding to the danger area.

Df, in writing of H, George Washington Papers, Library of Congress.

George Washington to
Major General John Sullivan

Fredericksburg [*New York*] *October 24, 1778.* Asks Sullivan to send news of arrival of British fleet to Major General Horatio Gates and to Headquarters.

Df, in writing of H, George Washington Papers, Library of Congress.

George Washington to Comte d'Estaing

Fredericksburg [*New York*] *October 25, 1778.* Was in error in last letter in that British troops that had embarked were not on board ship that sailed.

Df, in writing of H, George Washington Papers, Library of Congress.

Publius Letter, II [1]

LETTER II.
The Honorable * * * _____ * Esq;

[Poughkeepsie, New York, October 26, 1778]

SIR,

The honor of being the hero of a public panegeric, is what you

The New-York Journal, and the General Advertiser, October 26, 1778.
1. This is the second of the three "Publius" letters by H, attacking Samuel Chase of Maryland. The other two letters are dated October 16 and November 16, 1778.

could hardly have aspired to, either from your talents, or from your good qualities. The partiality of your friends has never given you credit for more than mediocrity in the former; and experience has proved, that you are indebted for all your consequence, to the reverse of the latter. Had you not struck out a new line of prostitution for yourself, you might still have remained unnoticed, and contemptible—your name scarcely known beyond the little circle of your electors and clients, and recorded only in the journals of C——ss. But you have now forced yourself into view, in a light too singular and conspicuous to be over-looked, and have acquired an indisputed title to be immortalised in infamy.

I admire the boldness of your genius, and confess you have exceeded expectation. Though from your first appearance in the world, you gave the happiest presages of your future life, and the plainest marks of your being unfettered by any of those nice scruples, from which men of principle find so much inconvenience; yet your disposition was not understood in its full extent. You were thought to possess a degree of discretion and natural *timidity*, which would restrain you from any hazardous extremes. You have the merit both of contradicting this opinion and discovering, that notwithstanding our youth and inexperience as a nation, we begin to emulate the most veteran and accomplished states in the arts of corruption. You have shown that America can already boast at least one public character as abandoned as any the history of past or present times can produce.

Were your associates in power of a congenial temper with yourself, you might hope, that your address and dexterity, upon a late occasion, would give a new and advantageous impression of your abilities; and recommend you to employment in some important negociation, which might afford you other opportunities of gratifying your favourite inclination, at the expence of the public. It is unfortunate for the reputation of Governor Johnstone,[2] and for the

2. George Johnstone had served as governor of West Florida from 1763 to 1767, and in 1768 he had been elected to Parliament. In 1778 he was appointed one of the British commissioners with the Earl of Carlisle to negotiate for peace with representatives of the United States. In the course of the negotiations he attempted to bribe one of the American negotiators who reported the event to Congress. On August 11, 1778, Congress passed a resolution stating that representatives of the United States could no longer negotiate with Johnstone.

benevolent purposes of his royal master, that he was not acquainted
with the frailties of your character, before he made his experiment
on men, whose integrity was above temptation. If he had known
you, and had thought your services worth purchasing, he might
have played a sure game, and avoided the risk of exposing himself
to contempt and ridicule. And you, Sir, might have made your fortune at one decisive stroke.

It is matter of curious inquiry, what could have raised you in the
first instance, and supported you since, in your present elevation.
I never knew a single man, but was ready to do ample justice to
your demerit. The most indulgent opinion of the qualifications of
your head and heart, could not offend the modest delicacy of your
ear, or give the smallest cause of exultation to your vanity. It is your
lot to have the peculiar privilege of being universally despised. Excluded, from all recourse to your abilities or virtues, there is only
one way in which I can account for the rank you hold in the political scale. There are seasons in every country, when noise and
impudence pass current for worth; and in popular commotions
especially, the clamours of interested and factious men are often mistaken for patriotism. You prudently took advantage of the commencement of the contest, to ingratiate yourself in the favour of the
people, and gain an ascendant in their confidence—by appearing
a zealous assertor of their rights. No man will suspect you of the
folly of public spirit; a heart notoriously selfish, exempts you from
any charge of this nature and obliges us to resolve the part you took,
into opposite principles. A desire of popularity, and a rivalship with
the ministry, will best explain them. Their attempt to *confine* the
sale of a lucrative article of commerce, to the East-India company;
must have been more unpardonable in the sight of a *monopolist*,
than the most daring attack upon the public liberty. There is a
vulgar maxim, which has a pointed emphasis in your case, and has
made many notable patriots in this dispute.

It sometimes happens, that a temporary caprice of the people,
leads them to make choice of men, whom they neither love nor
respect; and that they afterwards, from an indolent and mechanical
habit, natural to the human mind, continue their confidence and
support, merely because they had once conferred them. I cannot
persuade myself, that your influence rests upon a better foundation,

and I think the finishing touch you have given to the profligacy of your character, must rouse the recollection of the people, and force them to strip you of a dignity which sets so aukwardly upon you, and consign you to that disgrace, which is due to a scandalous perversion of your trust.

When you resolved to avail yourself of the extraordinary demand for the article of flour, which the wants of the French fleet must produce, and which your official situation, early impressed on your attention—to form connections for monopolizing that article, and raising the price upon the public more than an hundred per cent.— when by your intrigues and studied delays, you protracted the determination of the C----tt----e of C-----ss, on the proposals made by Mr. W---sw---th, C----ss---y G---n---l,[3] for procuring the necessary supplies for the public use—to give your agents time to complete their purchases—I say when you were doing all this, and engaging in a traffic infamous in itself, repugnant to your station, and ruinous to your country—did you pause and allow yourself a moment's reflection on the consequences? Were you infatuated enough to imagine you would be able to conceal the part you were acting? Or had you conceived a thorough contempt of reputation, and a total indifference to the opinion of the world? Envelopped in the promised gratification of your avarice, you probably forgot to consult your understanding, and lost sight of every consideration that ought to have regulated the man, the citizen, or the statesman.

I am aware, that you could never have done what you have without first obtaining a noble victory over every sentiment of honor and generosity. You have therefore nothing to fear from the reproaches of your own mind. Your insensibility secures you from remorse. But there are arguments powerful enough to extort repentance, even from a temper, as callous as yours. You are a man of the world, Sir, Your self-love forces you to respect its decisions and your utmost credit with it, will not bear the test of your recent enormities, or skreen you from the fate you deserve.

3. Jeremiah Wadsworth, commissary general of purchases.

George Washington to
Major General Horatio Gates

Fredericksburg [New York] October 27, 1778. Speculates on British intentions. Instructs Gates to obtain clothing for men and to return old clothing to deputy clothier general.

LS, in writing of H, New-York Historical Society, New York City.

George Washington to George Measam

Fredericksburg [New York] October 27, 1778. Instructs Measam to supply Major General Horatio Gates with new clothing.

Df, in writing of H, George Washington Papers, Library of Congress.

George Washington to Comte d'Estaing

Fredericksburg [New York] October 27, 1778. Is pleased that D'Estaing will soon be able to put to sea.

Df, in writing of H, George Washington Papers, Library of Congress.

Cloth for Uniforms

Headquarters near Fredericksburg [New York] October 28, 1778. Certificate of color of cloth drawn for uniforms for the various regiments by Hamilton and seven other aides to Washington. Lottery held to prevent soldiers of various regiments from complaining about color or quality of uniforms.

DS, George Washington Papers, Library of Congress.

George Washington to George Measam

Fredericksburg [*New York*] *October 28, 1778.* Orders that all clothing be forwarded to Headquarters.

Df, in writings of Tench Tilghman, George Washington, and H, George Washington Papers, Library of Congress.

George Washington to Major General Horatio Gates

Fredericksburg [*New York*] *October 29, 1778.* States that Congress has ordered Gates to Boston to assume command there. Advises recall of militia at Boston.

Df, in writing of H, George Washington Papers, Library of Congress.

George Washington to Major General William Heath

[*Fredericksburg, New York*] *October 29, 1778.* Has forwarded to Congress Heath's requisition for flour.

Df, in writing of H, George Washington Papers, Library of Congress.

George Washington to Major General John Sullivan

Fredericksburg [*New York*] *October 29, 1778.* Reports that British troops that embarked did not sail. Encloses copy of a congressional resolve.

Df, in writing of H, George Washington Papers, Library of Congress.

Examination of a Hessian Deserter

[Fredericksburg, New York, October 31, 1778]

Trech—from the Corps of yagers [1]—deserted ye 30th—yagers lie between the second and third redoubt with a creek running along their right; a regiment of Hessians lies between the first and second redoubts. Emericks [2] corps lies between Fort Independence [3] and redoubt No. 3—Pensylvaina Rangers behind them. No other troops on this side the Bridge [4] except guards, that mount dayly in the redoubts—does not know the number of guards.

On the other side of the Bridge, are on a hill on the left in coming towards the Bridge, a batalion of Hessian Grenadiers—not quite a mile from the new Bridge; behind that batalion at a small distance is a British regiment; and behind them at nearly the same distance the Highlanders—about a mile from the parting of the road—a Hessian regiment encamped on the Hill on the right of the road near the Block House—2 batalions of Hessian Grenadiers in the rear of Fort Washington [5] about two miles on the right of the road. None but Hessians between Fort Washington and New York; supposes nearly all the Hessians are there. No troops that he knows of on Spiten Devil Hill; [6] a small guard of twenty or thirty men on the right of those Hills in a red⟨oubt.⟩ A triangular redoubt on the left towards the ⟨North⟩ River with embrasures to the North River and to Harlem Creek—a Hessian regiment behi⟨nd⟩ that redoubt, which he did not recollect before; a small guard at the parting of the road leading to the Bridge and some small block Houses on the left.

Nearly on the flank of the Redoubt in the North River there are three ships of twenty and upward each & two small armed vessels. They keep out guard boats every night when he has been on guard; he has heard them rowing about and crying *all's well*. There are other small vessels in the River nearer New York. General Knephaussen [7] comm⟨ands⟩ at the Bridge &c—his quarters are at Morris's. [8]

D, in writing of H, George Washington Papers, Library of Congress.
1. The Jägers were a corps of Hessian riflemen.
2. Lieutenant Colonel Andress Emmerick, who commanded a Loyalist corps.
3. Located at the juncture of the Hudson and Harlem Rivers in what is now the Riverdale section of the Bronx.

4. Kings Bridge joining Manhattan to the Bronx.

5. Located between 181 and 186 Streets, New York City.

6. In the northern end of Manhattan Island.

7. Lieutenant General Wilhelm, Baron von Knyphausen, a German in command of British troops in New York.

8. The home of Colonel Roger Morris. Subsequently known as the Jumel Mansion, it is still located in Washington Heights, Manhattan Island.

George Washington to Comte d'Estaing

Fredericksburg [New York] October 31, 1778. Acknowledges receipt of news of sailing of British vessels. Agrees that seaport towns should be fortified. Is awaiting arrival of John Holker.[1]

Df, in writing of H, George Washington Papers, Library of Congress.

1. H notes in an endorsement that enclosed in the letter was: "an extract from a letter of Lord Stirling of the 29th. with one inclosed from a Spy signed L. dated 25th. another of the 30th and another of Major Lee of the same date."

George Washington to Brigadier General Louis Le Bèque Du Portail

Fredericksburg [New York] October 31, 1778. Acknowledges receipt of plan for fortification of Boston. Has forwarded this information to Major General Horatio Gates who will take command at Boston.

Df, in writing of H, George Washington Papers, Library of Congress.

George Washington to Brigadier General Charles Scott

[Fredericksburg New York] October 31, 1778. Is doubtful about plans of the British. Asks Scott to obtain information concerning British plans for forage and wood. Regrets Scott finds it necessary to resign.

Df, in writing of H, George Washington Papers, Library of Congress.

George Washington to
Major General Israel Putnam

Fredericksburg [*New York*] *November 2, 1778.* Orders Putnam to assume command of division lately under command of Major General Horatio Gates.

Df, in writing of H, George Washington Papers, Library of Congress.

From Colonel Goose Van Schaick

[*November 3, 1778.* On November 4, 1778, Hamilton wrote to Van Schaick: "I have received your favour of Yesterday." *Letter not found.*]

From Major General Alexander McDougall

[*Near Milford, Connecticut, November 4, 1778.* On November 8, 1778, Hamilton wrote to McDougall: "I have received your favor of the 4th." *Letter not found.*]

To Colonel Goose Van Schaick

[Fredericksburg, New York, November 4, 1778]

Sir

I have received your favour of Yesterday. His Excellency desires me to inform you, that you are to march Immediately on receiving your Clothing to Fort Schuyler.[1] He wishes you to Arrive there as speedily as possible. This you will pleas[e] to communicate to General Clinton[2] and Act accordingly.

I am sir   Your most Obedient   servant

Head Quarters   Alex. Hamilton   Aide de Camp
Novbr. 4th 1778

Copy, MS Division, New York Public Library.
   1. Van Schaick had been ordered to Fort Schuyler to relieve Colonel Peter Gansevoort.
   2. Brigadier General James Clinton.

From Colonel Charles Armand

[*Near Fredericksburg, New York*] November *5, 1778*. Needs equipment and money with which to pay troops. Asks for certificate of service from Washington.

ALS, George Washington Papers, Library of Congress.

George Washington to Comte d'Estaing

Fredericksburg [*New York*] *November 5, 1778*. Reports that British ships have sailed from Sandy Hook.

Df, in writing of H, George Washington Papers, Library of Congress.

To Major General Nathanael Greene

[Fredericksburg, New York, November 8, 1778]

Sir

His Excellency requests you will direct a couple sets of tools provided and sent to General McDougall to blow up rocks which greatly impede his carting &c.

I am Sir   Yr. Most Obedt   A Hamilton   Aide De Camp

Hd. Qrs
Novr. 8th. 1778

ALS, Library of the American Philosophical Society, Philadelphia.

To Major General Alexander McDougall

[Fredericksburg, New York, November 8, 1778]

Dr Sir,

I have received your favor of the 4th,[1] and shall with pleasure communicate the intelligence we have at Head Quarters. On the

ALS, New-York Historical Society, New York City.
    1. Letter not found.

morning of the 3d. one hundred and eight sail of vessels sailed out of the Hook, supposed from the best calculations to contain 7 or 8000 men. They first steered to the Eastward; but soon after changed their course and bore S.E with the wind at NW. The general accounts from New York speak of three distinct embarkations —one for the West Indies another for Halifax another for St Augustine. One division which seems to be best ascertained contains ten or twelve British regiments and most of the new levies, which probably went in the abovementioned fleet. This much is pretty certain, that the embarkation has continued since the departure of that fleet, which is a strong circumstance in favour of a general evacuation. All their vessels the least out of repair are drawn up to the different Ship-yards & their repairs are going on with all possible vigor. Whether the merchants are packing up or not is a point still too much *in dubio;* though we have several accounts that look like it; but they are not so precise and certain, as could be wished. Several bales of goods have been seen on the wharfs marked for particular ships. A deserter indeed, lately from the city insists that he saw Coffin and Anderson [2] packing up. This, if true, would be decisive; for this is a very considerable house particularly attached to the army.

One of our spies, a trusty one too, writes the 31st of October, that the principal part of the sick from the hospitals had embarked; but this stands almost wholly upon its own bottom. The capture of Jamaica seems to be a mere rumour; there are several others, respecting St Kitts Monserat & Grenada. The two former are said to have been taken by surprise on a temporary absence of their guard ships; but these stories were not improbably suggested by a late sudden and very considerable rise in the prices of rum and molasses —the former being as high as fourteen or fifteen shillings ℔ Gallon. Large purchases have been made of these articles as sea stores for the troops and the speculators in the city have been bidding against the commissaries; which better accounts for the increased prices.

It is a question very undecided in my mind whether the enemy will evacuate or not. Reasoning *a priori* the arguments seem to be strongest for it, from the exhausted state of the British resources,

2. Coffin and Anderson was a merchant firm in New York City that dealt mainly with the British army.

the naked condition of their dominions every where, and the possibility of a Spanish War. But on the other hand naval superiority must do a great deal in the business. This, I think, considering all things appears clearly enough to be on the side of Britain. The sluggishness of Spain affords room to doubt her taking a decisive part. The preserving posts in these States will greatly distress our trade and give security to the British West India trade. They will also cover the West Indies, and restrain any operations of ours against the British dominions on the Continent. These considerations and the depreciated state of our currency, will be strong inducements to keep New York and Rhode Island, if not with a view to conquest with a view to temopary advantages, and making better terms in a future negotiation.

From appearances—the great delay which attends the embarkation, the absolute tranquillity of the post at Rhode Island, where there is no kind of preparation, for leaving it, and some other circumstances, seem to indicate an intention to remain. On the other hand besides the general appearances I have already mentioned—the inattention to the petition of the refugees,[3] and the not raising new works are strong additional reasons for going away. I think it most probable, if they were determined to continue a garrison, that they would give the most explicit assurances to their friends in order to encourage their proposal and engage them to aid in maintaining it. I think also they would contract their works to be better proportioned to the number of the garrison and of course more defensible, by throwing a chain of fortifications across the narrow part of the Island.

Nothing has yet been decided that we know of with respect to the sentences you mention. General Lee's case [4] by our last advices was on the eve of a final descision. It seems he has made a strong

3. This was a petition from "The Refugees in New York to the [British Peace] Commissioners." Washington had received a copy of this Tory petition from Brigadier General Charles Scott. He forwarded a copy to Comte d'Estaing and another to Henry Laurens, President of the Continental Congress, stating, "You may depend upon the authenticity of it, as it is taken from a New York paper. It should seem by this that they are extremely sollicitous and anxious to know whether New York is to be garrisoned . . ." (George Washington to Henry Laurens, October 18, 1778, George Washington Papers, Library of Congress).

4. See "Proceedings of a General Court-Martial for the Trial of Major General Charles Lee," July 4, 13, 1778.

party in Congress and is very confident of having the sentence annulled. S Clairs trial[5] was ordered to be printed for the separate consideration of the members.

The depreciation of our Currency really casts a gloom on our prospects; but my sentiments on this subject are rather peculiar. I think bad as it is, it will continue to draw out the resources of the country a good while longer; and especially if the enemy make such detachments, of which there is hardly a doubt, as will oblige them to act on the defensive. This will make our public expenditures infinitely less and will allow the states leisure to attend to the arrangement of their finances as well as the country tranquillity to cultivate its resources.

Any letters that may come to Head Quarters for you will be carefully forwarded.

I am with the most respectful attachment   D Sir   Yr. Obed serv

A Hamilton

Hd. Qrs.

Novemr. 8th. 1778

5. Major General Arthur St. Clair had been court-martialed for his conduct at Ticonderoga and Mount Independence.

George Washington to Henry Laurens

Fredericksburg [*New York*] *November 13, 1778.* States that Baron von Steuben waits upon Congress on the subject of the inspectorship.

Df, in writing of H, George Washington Papers, Library of Congress.

George Washington to Henry Laurens

Fredericksburg [*New York*] *November 14, 1778.* Discusses advantages and disadvantages of proposed Canadian expedition.

Df, in writing of H, George Washington Papers, Library of Congress.

Publius Letter, III [1]

LETTER, III.

The Honorable S————l C————e, Esq;

[Poughkeepsie, New York, November 16, 1778]

SIR,

It may appear strange, that you should be made a second time the principal figure of a piece intended for the public eye. But a character, insignificant in every other respect, may become interesting from the number and magnitude of its vices. In this view you have a right to the first marks of distinction; and I regret that I feel any reluctance to render you the liberal tribute you deserve: But I reverence humanity, and would not wish to pour a blush upon the checks of its advocates; were I inclined to make a satire upon the species, I would attempt a faithful description of your heart. It is hard to conceive, in theory, one of more finished depravity. There are some men, whose vices are blended with qualities that cast a lustre upon them, and force us to admire—while we detest!—yours are pure and unmixed, without a single solitary excellence, even to serve for contrast and variety.

The defects however, of your private character, shall pass untouched. I shall not trace you back to those licentious scenes, in which the unthinking levity of youth might plead your excuse, tho' the maturer habits of the present period, exhibit fresh proofs of the same byass in your disposition? Nor shall I presume to accompany you through the mysterious labyrinths of your profession, or show how much you excelled in the legerdemain of the bar? This is a field in which your personal enemies may expatiate with pleasure. I find it enough to consider you in a public capacity.

The station of a member of C——ss, is the most illustrious and important of any I am able to conceive. He is to be regarded not only as a legislator, but as the founder of an empire. A man of virtue and ability, dignified with so precious a trust, would rejoice that

The New-York Journal, and the General Advertiser, November 16, 1778.

1. This is the third and last of H's "Publius" letters attacking Samuel Chase of Maryland. The other two letters are dated October 16 and October 26, 1778.

fortune had given him birth at a time, and placed him in circumstances so favourable for promoting human happiness. He would esteem it not more the duty, than the privilege and ornament of his office, to do good to mankind; from this commanding eminence, he would look down with contempt upon every mean or interested pursuit.

To form useful alliances abroad—to establish a wise government at home—to improve the internal resources, and finances of the nation would be the generous objects of his care. He would not allow his attention to be diverted from these to intrigue for personal connections, to confirm his own influence; nor would be able to reconcile it, either to the delicacy of his honour, or to the dignity of his pride, to confound in the same person the representative of the Commonwealth, and the little member of a trading company. Anxious for the permanent power and prosperity of the State, he would labour to perpetuate the union and harmony of the several parts. He would not meanly court a temporary importance, by patronising the narrow views of local interest, or by encouraging dissentions either among the people or in C-----ss. In council, or debate, he would discover the candor of a statesman, zealous for truth, and the integrity of a patriot studious of the public welfare; not the cavilling petulance of an attorney, contending for the triumph of an opinion, nor the perverse duplicity of a partisan, devoted to the service of a cabal. Despising the affectation of superior wisdom, he would prove the extent of his capacity, by foreseeing evils, and contriving expedients to prevent or remedy them. He would not expose the weak sides of the State, to find an opportunity of displaying his own discernment, by magnifying the follies and mistakes of others. In his transactions with individuals, whether foreigners or countrymen, his conduct would be guided by the sincerity of a man, and the politeness of a gentleman, not by the temporising flexibility of a courtier, nor the fawning complaisance of a sycophant.

You will not be at a loss, sir, in what part of this picture, to look for your own resemblance, nor have I the least apprehension, that you will mistake it on the affirmative side. The happy indifference with which you view those qualities, most esteemed for their usefulness to society, will preserve you from the possibility of an illusion of this kind. Content with the humble merit of possessing qualities, useful only to yourself, you will contemplate your own image, on the opposite side, with all the satisfaction of conscious deformity.

It frequently happens, that the excess of one selfish passion, either defeats its own end, or counteracts another. This, if I am not mistaken, is your case. The love of money and the love of power are the predominating ingredients of your mind—*cunning* the characteristic of your understanding. *This,* has hitherto carried you successfully through life, and has alone raised you to the exterior consideration, you enjoy. The natural consequence of success, is temerity. *It* has now proceeded one step too far, and precipitated you into measures, from the consequences of which, you will not easily extricate yourself; your avarice will be fatal to your ambition. I have too good an opinion of the sense and spirit, to say nothing of the virtue of your countrymen, to believe they will permit you any longer to abuse their confidence, or trample upon their honour. Admirably fitted, in many respects for the meridian of St. James, you might there make the worthy representative of a venal borough; but you ought not to be suffered to continue to sully the majesty of the people in an American C-----ss.

It is a mark of compassion, to which you are not intitled, to advise you by a timely and voluntary retreat, to avoid the ignominy of a formal dismission. Your career has held out as long as you could have hoped. It is time you should cease to personate the fictitious character you have assumed, and appear what you really are—lay aside the mask of patriotism, and assert your station among the honorable tribe of speculators and projectors. Cultivate a closer alliance with your D---s---y and your W--t, the accomplices and instruments of your guilt, and console yourself for the advantage you have lost, by indulging your genius, without restraint, in all the forms and varieties of fashionable peculation.

PUBLIUS.

George Washington to Henry Laurens

Fredericksburg [New York] November 16, 1778. States that Brigadier General Du Portail, since his furlough from France expires soon, wishes to be employed by Congress.

LS, in writing of H, Papers of the Continental Congress, National Archives.

George Washington to Henry Laurens

Fredericksburg [New York] November 16, 1778. Transmits news of attack on Cherry Valley. Believes that only way to prevent such attacks is to carry on an offensive war against Indians.

LS, in writing of H, Papers of the Continental Congress, National Archives.

George Washington to Major General Alexander McDougall

Fredericksburg [New York] November 17, 1778. Orders McDougall to Danbury.

Df, in writing of H, George Washington Papers, Library of Congress.

George Washington to Henry Laurens

Fredericksburg [New York] November 19, 1778. States that Colonel Armand wishes Congress to commission officers who served in his corps, and that Armand intends to leave for France.

Df, in writing of H, George Washington Papers, Library of Congress.

George Washington to Major General Alexander McDougall

[Fredericksburg, New York] November 19, 1778. Orders McDougall to halt with the two Connecticut brigades and to send Brigadier General John Nixon on to Danbury.

Df, in writing of H, George Washington Papers, Library of Congress.

From Jeremiah Wadsworth [1]

Camp Fredg [New York] Novr 20th: 1778

Sir.

I will be at Hd. Quarters tomorrow morning & take his Excys directions—have no doubt, I shall be able to prevent any very great evil from the misconception you believe to have happened. I cannot believe as Colo Bland doth that the officer commanding the Connecticut Militia has been honestly engaged to bring them on; and am satisfyed my Countrymen have too much pride not to follow when they are led by an honest man.

I am Sir Your most obed. Jere Wadsworth CGP.

Colo Hamilton
Hd Quarters

LC, Connecticut Historical Society, Hartford.
1. Wadsworth was commissary general of purchases and a resident of Connecticut.

This letter is concerned with the plans for the transfer of the Convention troops (i.e., the British troops who surrendered under General John Burgoyne at Saratoga) from Massachusetts to Virginia. Colonel Theodorick Bland was the officer in charge of the transfer of these troops. Under the proposed plans the Convention troops were to be escorted across each state by the respective state militias. Bland apparently feared that during the march across Connecticut the state's militia would not be reliable and would not (or could not) prevent the Convention troops from deserting. Bland was also disturbed by the very real possibility that the Connecticut Militia would not cross the state line and would abandon their responsibilities at Sharon, Connecticut, before being relieved by other troops.

George Washington to Colonel Clement Biddle [1]

Fredericksburg [New York] November 20, 1778. Orders Biddle to impress forage for troops.

LS, in writing of H, Historical Society of Pennsylvania, Philadelphia.
1. Biddle was commissary general of forage.

George Washington to Baron de Kalb

Fredericksburg [New York] November 20, 1778. Sends instructions regarding escort of Convention troops during their march to the Delaware.

Df, in writing of H, George Washington Papers, Library of Congress.

George Washington to Colonel William Malcom

Fredericksburg [New York] November 20, 1778. Asks Malcom to delay trip to Headquarters in order to help guard the Convention troops.

Df, in writing of H, George Washington Papers, Library of Congress.

George Washington to
Major General Philip Schuyler [1]

Fredericksburg [New York] November 20–21, 1778. Discusses details of proposed Canadian expedition. Asks for information about geography of area involved.

Df, in writings of George Washington and H, George Washington Papers, Library of Congress.
1. Although the letter is dated November 20, 1778, there is a postscript dated November 21, 1778.

From Lieutenant Colonel Richard Kidder Meade [1]

Col Blands Quarters
Sharon [Connecticut] near 8 oClock
at night [November 21, 1778]

Dr. Hamilton,

I arrived here a few minutes after four Oclock, when I immediately agreeably to the Genls. orders called on the officer commanding the Militia Guard here, who discovered every disposition to proceed at least to the next halting place. As the matter rests with the men, & he is gone to consult them I must give you their determination at the end of my letter. They are rather dispers'd to night, so that I hardly expect a decisive answer until they parade in the morning, to which time I shall wait, in case they go on, that I may prevent Genl. Waynes Troops,[2] should it be necessary from passing Beldings.[3] I must however urge the utmost dispatch in these, as you may depend, *should* the militia go on to the next stage, *Govr. Trumbull himself*[4] could not detain them there many hours; Col. Bland observes that it may be well to let the continental Escort come up in succession as the several divisions of the Convention Troops may arrive. I think it will be well, as a smaller number may be in readiness sooner than a larger & can march much quicker. This however the Genl will decide. The road is exceedingly good to Beldings; & I think if a division could get off even by 12 oClock tomorrow, they would arrive in tolerable time. Colo. Bland has given the Genl. the route which I was instructed to transmit with this.

½ after 9 oClock.

The officer this instant returned but makes no certain report, though he is in high expectation of succeeding. He has directed the men to assemble at Sun rise when I shall attend & sett off immediately after.

I am Dr. Hamilton Yrs &c　　　　　　　　　　R K Meade, ADC

ALS, MS Division, New York Public Library; copy, George Washington Papers, Library of Congress.

1. Because of the factors mentioned in the footnote in Jeremiah Wadsworth to H, November 20, 1778, Washington had sent Meade to supervise the transfer of the Convention troops from the Connecticut Militia to the Continental troops.

2. Wayne had sent Continental troops to relieve the Connecticut Militia.

3. Town in south central portion of Dutchess County, New York.

4. Jonathan Trumbull, governor of Connecticut.

George Washington to Henry Laurens

Fredericksburg [New York] November 21, 1778. Requests Congress to promote Pierre Penet's brother to captain by brevet.

Df, in writing of H, George Washington Papers, Library of Congress.

George Washington to the Commanding Officers of Militia in the Counties of Loudoun, Fauquier, Culpeper, and Orange

Fredericksburg [New York] November 23, 1778. Asks for militia to guard the Convention troops as they pass through various counties en route to Charlottesville.

LS, in writing of H, George Washington Papers, Library of Congress.

George Washington to Colonel Theodorick Bland

Fredericksburg [New York] November 23, 1778. Sends instructions for marching of Convention troops to Virginia.

Df, in writings of George Washington and H, George Washington Papers, Library of Congress.

George Washington to Brigadier General Louis Le Bèque Du Portail

[Fredericksburg, New York] November 24, 1778. Instructs Du Portail to send request for cannon for West Point to Congress.

Df, in writing of H, George Washington Papers, Library of Congress.

George Washington to Lieutenant Colonel William Smith Livingston [1]

[Fredericksburg, New York] November 24, 1778. Regrets that Livingston finds it necessary to resign.

Df, in writing of H, George Washington Papers, Library of Congress.
1. William Smith Livingston was a lieutenant colonel of Webb's Additional Continental Regiment.

George Washington to
Major General Alexander McDougall

[*Fredericksburg, New York*] *November 24, 1778.* Instructs Mc-Dougall to take command in Highlands. Describes extent of command and gives instructions for this command.

Df, in writing of H, George Washington Papers, Library of Congress.

George Washington to Count Casimir Pulaski

Fredericksburg [*New York*] *November 24, 1778.* Approves of Pulaski's position at Rosecrantz. Approves Pulaski's reasons for wishing to leave country.

Df, in writing of H, George Washington Papers, Library of Congress.

Examination of Two British Deserters
from Halifax

[Fredericksburg, New York, November 25, 1778]

Jacob Harman, of the Royal Highland Emigrants, formerly in Col Smallwoods [1] Maryland regiment—from Halifax which he left the first of May.

When he left Halifax there was only the corps he belonged to consisting of about 300 & the marines about 700—1000 in all. He went from Halifax to the River St Johns on the bay of fundy which he left six weeks ago where he heard three thousand recruits were arrived at Halifax. There were scarcely any fortifications at Halifax when he came away; but he has heard since they have been very industrious in fortifying. They had when he left it:

On Sideral Hill which commands the Harbour, on the West side —a block house with 6 Cannon, six pounders—with 6 or 8 four and twenty pounders on a battery outside. Sideral Hill is very high and steep—a quarter of mile from the Channel; towards the foot of this hill nearer the water was another small battery of five four and twenty pounders, and below that again another battery on the waters edge of 7 heavy cannon.

A mile from ye Hill Back of the town were two forts, *Neidham* and *Good*, half a mile distant from each other—3 heavy cannon in the former two in the latter, with a block House in each.

Heard a report since he left it that the 7 Gun battery above-mentioned was enlarged to one of 28—and the five to one of 26.

He also heard that George's Island lying in the harbour and commanding the channel on both sides had also been fortified, and had near a hundred cannon upon it.

He hea[r]d that a battery had also been raised on the East side of the entrance of the harbour opposite Sideral Hill but did not learn the force.

A fort had been built at St Johns River with a block House inside with 4 Cannon, and barracks sufficient for 400 men and a couple of Cannon in the fort.

Martin Carstithers left Halifax at the same time &c. confirms the other's intelligence so far as he goes; but is not intelligent.

D, in writing of H, George Washington Papers, Library of Congress.
1. Brigadier General William Smallwood, Continental Army, formerly colonel of a Maryland regiment.

George Washington to Brigadier General Edward Hand

Fredericksburg [*New York*] *November 26, 1778*. Gives directions for distribution of troops on Hand's arrival at Minisink.

LS, in writing of H, George Washington Papers, Library of Congress.

George Washington to Count Casimir Pulaski

[*Fredericksburg, New York*] *November 26, 1778*. Repeats instructions concerning troops, cavalry, and forage.

Df, in writing of H, George Washington Papers, Library of Congress.

To Royal Flint [1]

[Fredericksburg, New York, November 27, 1778]

Dr Sir

Col Harrison and myself are to meet two Gentlemen of the British army at Amboy monday week.[2] We shall be obliged to feed them and their attendants as well as our own, while there, and must therefore request your assistance to have some handsome provision made there for us by that time. We shall probably be together only a few days and shall have sixteen or eighteen to feed. Let us have both victuals and drink enough. If you send any person of your department there be pleased also to give him directions to engage a couple of the best houses there; one for them—the other for us. The houses must be inhabited and the genteeler the families the better—if Whigs better and better still. This last I know is not in your line; but if it can be made one trouble of it will be preferable. If not, I beg you to mention the matter to General Greene or one of his assistants in my name.

I am with regard   Sir   Your obed serv
                                    Alex Hamilton   Aide De Camp
Head Qr. Novemr. 27. 1778

ALS, Connecticut Historical Society, Hartford.
    1. Flint was assistant commissary of purchases.
    2. On November 10, 1778, Sir Henry Clinton wrote to Washington concerning the exchange of prisoners. On November 27, Washington wrote to John Beatty, commissary general of prisoners, Continental Army, that he had selected H and Lieutenant Colonel Robert Hanson Harrison as the American commissioners to negotiate with the British commissioners for the exchange of prisoners (George Washington Papers, Library of Congress).

George Washington to Henry Laurens

Fredericksburg [*New York*] *November 27, 1778.* Acknowledges receipt of copies of treaties with France. States that commissioners have been appointed for exchange of prisoners. Discusses plans for winter quarters.

Df, in writing of H, George Washington Papers, Library of Congress.

George Washington to
Major Benjamin Tallmadge [1]

Fishkill [New York] November 29, 1778. Discusses arrangements for obtaining information from Samuel Culper.[2]

Df, in writing of H, George Washington Papers, Library of Congress.
   1. Tallmadge, a major in the Second Continental Dragoons, managed the secret service of the Army around New York City from 1778 until the end of the war.
   2. Abraham Woodhull of Setouket, Long Island, who used the fictitious name of Samuel Culper, Sr., was a spy for Washington.

Commission to Lieutenant Colonels
Robert Hanson Harrison and Alexander Hamilton [1]

[Fishkill, New York, November 30, 1778]

By His Excellency George Washington Esquire, General & Commander in chief of the Forces of the United States of America.

To Lieut Colonel Rob Hanson Harrison
Lieut Colonel Alexander Hamilton

His Excellency Sir Henry Clinton having by a letter to me of the 10th Instant, made a proposition to the following effect, Viz, "to exchange the Officers of our Army who are prisoners on parole or otherwise in his possession, for Officers & Men of the Troops of the Convention, according to the customary proportion, or according to such proportion as might be determined, by Commissioners appointed on both sides".

And the Honorable the Congress having authorized me, by an Act passed the 19th Instant, "to appoint Commissioners to confer with such as are or may be appointed by Sir Henry Clinton, on the exchange proposed by him—and directed that Officers of equal rank be first exchanged, after which, if it should be necessary, an equivalent of inferior for Superior Officers; and if agreably to such equivalent all the Officers of the Enemy shall be exchanged and a balance of prisoners remain in their hands, then an equivalent of privates to be settled according to the customary proportion or such proportion as may be agreed on".[2]

In virtue of these powers, you the said Robert Hanson Harrison and Alexander Hamilton are appointed and I do hereby appoint you Commissioners, to repair to Amboy in the State of New Jersey on Monday the 7 of December, then and there, or at such other place as shall be afterwards mutually agreed on, to confer, agree and determine with the Commissioners nominated or to be nominated and who shall be properly authorised, upon an exchange of prisoners, agreable to the terms of the said recited Act: for which this shall be your Warrant; and your engagements being mutually interchanged, shall be ratified and confirmed by me.

Given under my hand & Seal at
Head Quarters this 30th day of Novr 1778.

By His Excellency's command

Df, in writing of Robert Hanson Harrison, George Washington Papers, Library of Congress; copy, enclosed in Sir Henry Clinton to Lord Germain, December 16, 1778, William L. Clements Library of the University of Michigan; copies PRO: C.O., part 5, vol. 97; and copy, Papers of the Continental Congress, National Archives.

1. For background to this document see H to Royal Flint, November 27, 1778.

2. See *JCC*, XII, 1145-46.

George Washington to Colonel William Malcom

Fishkill [*New York*] *November 30, 1778.* Will not be able to stop at West Point as intended. States that Brigadier General Alexander McDougall is to assume command of Highlands.

Df, in writing of H, George Washington Papers, Library of Congress.

George Washington to Baron de Kalb

Elizabethtown [*New Jersey*] *December 4, 1778.* Reports advance of British vessels up North River. Gives instructions for countering British move.

Df, in writings of Tench Tilghman and H, George Washington Papers, Library of Congress.

From Lieutenant Colonel John Laurens

[Philadelphia, December 5, 1778]

My Dear Hamilton:

You have seen, and by this time considered, General Lee's infamous publication.[1] I have collected some hints for an answer; but I do not think, either that I can rely upon my own knowledge of facts and style to answer him fully, or that it would be prudent to undertake it without counsel. An affair of this kind ought to be passed over in total silence, or answered in a masterly manner.

The ancient secretary[2] is the Recueil of modern history and anecdotes, and will give them to us with candor, elegance, and perspicuity. The pen of Junius is in your hand; and I think you will, without difficulty, expose, in his defence, letters, and last production, such a tissue of falsehood and inconsistency, as will satisfy the world, and put him for ever to silence.

I think the affair will be definitively decided in Congress this day. He has found means to league himself with the *old faction*, and to gain a great many partisans.

Adieu, my dear boy. I shall set out for camp tomorrow.

John Laurens.

"The Lee Papers," *Colls. of the N.Y. Hist. Soc.*, VI, 273.

1. This is a reference to General Charles Lee's "Vindication to the Public," *The Pennsylvania Packet* or *The General Advertiser*, December 3, 1778, which was a defense of his behaviour at Monmouth and a reply to the hostile witnesses at his court-martial.
2. I.e., Robert Hanson Harrison.

From James McHenry

[*Paramus, New Jersey, December 6, 1778*. ". . . desire Colo. Harrison to write to Genl. Greene on the subject of his Letter respecting a change of ground for hutting. He may tell Genl. Greene, that the situation marked out in the first instance seems to His Excellency the most eligible; but that Genl. Greene must be a more competent judge, to which place the preference should be given. . . . We are informed by a Major of Militia that the Enemy's Vessels are near

King's ferry, and it is said that a body of about 2,000 men are as high up as Tarrytown. Their Object would appear forage and provision to be collected between Kingsbridge and the posts at the Highlands. Genl Wayne is ordered to Sufferans; Genl. Muhlenberg to the same place; we shall move that way immediately. . . ."]

The original of this letter has not been found. The extract quoted above was taken from Robert Hanson Harrison to Nathanael Greene, December 6, 1778 (*GW*, XIII, 369).

From Baron von Steuben

[*Philadelphia, December 6, 1778.* On December 19, 1778, Hamilton wrote to von Steuben: "I snatch a hasty moment My Dear Baron to acknowledge the receipt of yr. obliging favour of the 6th." *Letter not found.*]

Colonels Charles O'Hara and West Hyde to Lieutenant Colonels Robert Hanson Harrison and Alexander Hamilton

[Amboy, New Jersey] 12th. December 1778

Gentlemen

We cannot sufficiently lament, that the Purposes of our Meeting, you will pardon us for observing, have been defeated, by a less generous and extensive Construction of the Resolutions of Congress of the 19th. November,[1] than the View in which we had considered them.

Every Sense of Honor, Justice and Humanity, make it impossible to acquiesce in a Proposal, which might lead to seperate the Officers from the Private Soldiers, by exchanging the former, and suffering the latter to remain in Captivity. Companions in their more fortunate Hours, they must be equally Sharers of Affliction. Such cruel and unprecedented Distinctions, between Men who have equally a Claim upon the Favor and Protection of their Country, we are certain, your own Feelings as Officers and Men would condemn. You will consequently not be surprised, that we cannot assent to the partial Mode of Exchange proposed.

We beg leave therefore to acquaint you, that we intend returning to New York tomorrow, to make our Report to Sir Henry Clinton. Let us flatter ourselves, that some Expedient may be immediately embraced by both Parties, upon such honorable, humane and disinterested Principles, as may give the most speedy & ample Relief, to every Order of unfortunate Men concerned.

We are Gentlemen, &ca   Charles O'Hara
                                                West Hyde.

To Lieutt. Colonels Harrison and Hamilton.

Copy, enclosed in Sir Henry Clinton to Lord Germain, December 16, 1778, William L. Clements Library of the University of Michigan; copy, PRO: C.O., part 5, vol. 97.

1. The resolution reads:
"*Resolved,* That General Washington be empowered and directed to appoint commissioners, and fix the time and place of their meeting, to confer with the commissioners appointed or to be appointed by Sir Henry Clinton, or other the commander in chief of the British forces in America, on behalf of his Britannic majesty, on the exchange proposed by Sir Henry Clinton in his letter to General Washington of the 10th instant, of the officers in the service of these states, now prisoners in the actual possession of the enemy, or out on parole, for the officers and men of the troops of the convention, according to their ranks and number; officers of equal rank to be first exchanged; after which, if it shall be necessary, an equivalent of inferior for superior officers, and, if agreeably to such equivalent, all the officers of the enemy shall be exchanged, and a balance of officers remain in their hands, then an equivalent of privates to be given in exchange for such officers, shall be settled according to the customary proportion, or such proportion as may be agreed on. The commissioners so to be appointed, by virtue hereof, to make report of their proceedings to General Washington, who is hereby fully authorized and empowered finally to ratify the terms of the said exchange on behalf of these United States" (*JCC*, XII, 1145–46).
The nature of the dispute between the British and American commissioners is fully explained in Harrison and H to Washington, December 15, 1778.

Lieutenant Colonels Robert Hanson Harrison and Alexander Hamilton to Colonels Charles O'Hara and West Hyde [1]

Amboy [New Jersey] December 12th: 1778

Gentlemen,

We have read the Letter, with which you were pleased to favor us, this Afternoon.

We join with you in lamenting, that the purpose of our meeting have been frustrated, and we assure you, that it is to us matter of equal concern and surprise to find, that there should be a difference in our respective constructions of the Resolve, to which you refer. Persuaded, as we were, that the terms of that Resolve were too simple and precise to admit of more than one interpretation; we did not even suspect it possible to differ about its meaning; and the objects of our meeting having been delineated, in a manner, which appeared to us perfectly clear and explicit, we had no expectation of the difficulty, which has occured, in carrying them into execution.

You will not be surprised, that this should have been the case, when you recur to the circumstances, that produced our meeting. We beg leave to recal[l] them to your view. Sir Henry Clinton in His Letter of the 10th. of November proposed to General Washington an Exchange of our Officers prisoners in his hands, for Officers and Men of the Convention Troops. General Washington replied, that he did not think himself authorised to accede to the proposal, but would refer it to Congress and communicate their decision. In a subsequent Letter of the 27th., he transmitted the Resolve in question as an "answer to the proposition contained in Sir Henry's Letter of the 10th;" at the same time, announcing our appointment as Commissioners, "to negociate an Exchange on the Principles therein mentioned." The Language of the Resolve was literally this —to exchange "the Officers in the Service of the United States, prisoners in the actual possession of the Enemy, or out on parole, for the Officers and Men of the Troops of Convention, according to their Rank and number: Officers of equal Rank to be first exchanged, after which, if it shall be necessary, an equivalent of inferior for superior Officers—and if, agreeably to such equivalent, all the Officers of the Enemy shall be exchanged and a balance of prisoners remain in their hands, then an equivalent of privates shall be settled according to the customary proportion or such proportion as may be agreed on." Sir Henry Clinton in his letter of the 2d. Instant acknowledged the receipt of the foregoing and consented "in consequence" to a meeting of Commissioners at the time and place appointed.

This, Gentlemen, you will be sensible could not be considered by us otherwise, than as an acquiesence with the terms of the Resolve: and we appeal to your own candor, for their perspicuity and natural import. It could not, therefore, but appear strange, that at first sight of our powers, without any comment, or explanation; though they were expressed, not only in the Spirit, but in the letter of the Resolve; You, at once, objected to them, and declared, the purpose of our meeting had been misunderstood. As the one was only a transcript of the other, we conceived, from the manner in which the objection was raised, that it applied, not to any *construction* given to the Resolve, but to the Resolve itself.

How far the feelings of honor, justice and humanity may be repugnant to a compliance with the proposal, which has been made, you only can determine for yourselves; though we think it a question, which might have merited an earlier consideration. We believe however it is not very customary to exchange Officers for privates, when there is a sufficient number of Officers on both sides to exchange for each other; but that this is rather a secondary expedient, made use of only when there are Officers, on one side, and none, on the other. In the present War, the practice of exchanging Officers for private Men, in any case whatever, has not yet been known; and if exchanges, conducted without reference to this principle, have heretofore been thought consistent with justice and humanity, we can perceive no sufficient reason why a different opinion should be entertained, at this time.

With respect to any inconveniences, which you think might attend the exchanging all the Officers of the Convention Troops, we take the liberty to repeat what we mentioned in our interview, this morning—that we are willing to exchange as many of them, as you may judge proper, for others of equal rank, as far as numbers will extend.

We beg leave to assure you, that we should be happy to be afforded an opportunity of concurring with you, to the utmost of our power, in measures, for extending relief, as far as the circumstances of the parties will permit, to every order of captivity, on principles of humanity and mutual advantage.

We are, Gentlemen, Your Most Obedient Humble Servants
Rob: H: Harrison
Colonels O Hara & Hyde.   Alex: Hamilton.

Copy, enclosed in Sir Henry Clinton to Lord Germain, December 16, 1778, William L. Clements Library of the University of Michigan; copy, PRO: C.O., part 5, vol. 97.
  1. For background to this document, see H to Royal Flint, November 27, 1778.

Lieutenant Colonels Robert Hanson Harrison and Alexander Hamilton to George Washington [1]

[Middlebrook, New Jersey, December 15, 1778]

Report of Lieutenant Colonels, Robert Hanson Harrison & Alexander Hamilton Commissioners &ca. To His Excellency General Washington—

We, the Commissioners appointed by your Excellency for the purposes specified in the powers to us given on the 30th of November last—Beg leave to Report—

That in pursuance of your instructions, we repaired to Amboy on Monday the 7th instant at 11 oClock; where we continued till friday evening the 11th before we were met by the Commissioners on the part of His Excellency Sir Henry Clinton, who had been detained 'till that time by impediments of weather.

That the next day we had an interview with them on the business of our commission; in which they immediately objected to our powers, as not extending to the purposes they had in view—declared the object of our meeting had been misunderstood, and after a short conversation, put an end to the conference.

That their intention, as communicated to us, was that the exchange of each of their officers should necessarily involve the exchange of certain number of *their* privates also; and consequently that the *whole* of our officers, prisoners in their hands, should be exchanged for a *part* only of the Officers of the Convention troops, with the proportion of private men to discharge the balance in their favour; whereas the line of conduct proscribed to us, both by the resolution of Congress and your Excellency's powers founded thereon, was, "that Officers of equal rank should be first exchanged, after which if it should be necessary, an equivalent of inferior for superior Officers; and if agreeably to that equivalent all the Officers of the Enemy should be exchanged, and a balance of Prisoners remain in their hands, then an equivalent of privates was to be settled, according to the customary proportion or such proportion as might be agreed on."

That the British Commissioners in the course of the conference having urged certain inconveniences, which in their opinion would result from the separation of *all* the officers of the Convention troops from the men, by a general exchange, in order effectually to obviate that objection, we thought ourselves authorised by our instructions to make them an offer, which we accordingly made, to exchange whatever part of the Convention Officers, they might think proper, for an equal number of our Officers in their possession of equal rank, as far as the relative state of numbers would permit. This proposal, however, they totally declined.

That after the interview, We received a Letter from the British Commissioners containing reasons, which they had before assigned verbally, for their refusal to conduct the negotiation on the terms proposed in our instructions; a copy of which letter and of our answer, we beg leave to subjoin for your Excellency's perusal. . . .[2]

This put an end to the business of our meeting and we have taken the earliest opportunity to return to Camp and report our proceedings to Your Excellency; which we hope will meet with your approbation.

Rob: H: Harrison
Alexr Hamilton

Camp Decr 15th   1778

Copy, Papers of the Continental Congress, National Archives.
   1. For background to this letter, H to Royal Flint, November 27, 1778.
   2. These two letters have been omitted in the printed text. For their contents, see O'Hara and Hyde to Harrison and H, December 12, 1778; and Harrison and H to O'Hara and Hyde, December 12, 1778.

George Washington to Major General Alexander McDougall

[*Middlebrook, New Jersey*] *December 16, 1778.* Asks for McDougall's opinion on kind and number of ships necessary to destroy enemy's naval force on Lake Ontario.

Df, in writings of George Washington and H, George Washington Papers, Library of Congress.

George Washington to
Major General Philip Schuyler

Middlebrook [*New Jersey*] *December 18, 1778.* Congratulates Schuyler on acquittal. States that a winter campaign is now impossible. Agrees that reduction of Niagara is important and has made plans for that move. Has advised quartermaster general to confer with Schuyler on this matter.

Df, in writings of George Washington and H, George Washington Papers, Library of Congress.

To Baron von Steuben

[Middlebrook, New Jersey, December 19, 1778]

I snatch a hasty moment My Dear Baron to acknowledge the receipt of yr. obliging favour of the 6th.[1] It came here while I was absent in an interview with some British Commissioners on the subject of an exchange of prisoners; and was not delivered me 'till two days ago. I am sorry that your business does not seem to make so speedy a progress as we all wish; but I hope it will soon come to a satisfactory termination.[2] I wish you to be in a situation to employ yourself usefully and agreeably and to contribute to giving our military constitution that order and perfection, which it certainly wants. I have not time now to enter upon some matters, which I shall take another opportunity to give you my sentiments concerning.

I have read your letter to Lee, with pleasure.[3] It was conceived in terms, which the offence merited, and if he had had any feeling must have been felt by him. Considering the pointedness and severity of your expressions, his answer was certainly a very modest one and proved that he had not a violent appetitite, for so close *a tete a tete* as you seemed disposed to insist upon. His evasions, if known to the world, would do him very little honor.

I dont know but I shall be shortly at Philadelphia; if so, I shall have the honor of personally assuring you of the perfect respect and esteem, with which *I am*

My Dear Baron   Yr most Obed serv   Alex Hamilton

Hd. Qrs. Decr. 19 1778

ALS, New-York Historical Society, New York City.
    1. Letter not found.
    2. This is a reference to von Steuben's efforts to have the inspector general-ship placed upon a "decided footing" and upon a footing mutually agreeable to von Steuben and the Army (*GW*, XIII, 253, 437). When von Steuben received the above letter from H, he was in Philadelphia attempting to induce Congress to regularize the position of inspector general.
    3. Von Steuben's letter (December 2, 1778), challenging Major General Charles Lee to a duel for allegedly derogatory remarks made about von Steu-ben's courage by Lee during the latter's trial can be found in "The Lee Papers," *Colls. of the N.Y. Hist. Soc.*, VI, 253. Lee wrote in reply that he had not ques-tioned von Steuben's courage, but that he was "ready to satisfy you in the manner you desire." Von Steuben accepted Lee's explanation, and the matter was dropped (John R. Alden, *General Charles Lee* [Baton Rouge, 1951], 260–61).

George Washington to Jonathan Trumbull

Middlebrook [*New Jersey*] *December 19, 1778*. Regrets that plans for winter quarters cannot be altered.

Df, in writing of H, George Washington Papers, Library of Congress.

George Washington to Baron von Steuben

[*Middle Brook, New Jersey*] *December 19, 1778*. Will support the inspector general's department when it is fully established.

Df, in writing of H, George Washington Papers, Library of Congress.

To Colonel Clement Biddle

Headquarters [*Middle Brook, New Jersey*] *December 20* [*1778*]. Requests minutes of trials of Charles Lee and Arthur St. Clair so that they can be published in general orders.[1]

ALS, Historical Society of Pennsylvania, Philadelphia.
    1. Lee was "suspended from any command in the Armies of the United States of North America for the term of twelve months." St. Clair was acquitted (*GW*, XIII, 449–50).

George Washington to Major General William Alexander, Lord Stirling

[*Middlebrook, New Jersey*] *December 21, 1778.* Instructs Stirling to take command at Headquarters during Washington's absence in Philadelphia. Gives general directions for administration of Camp.

Df, in writing of H, George Washington Papers, Library of Congress.

George Washington to William Livingston

Middlebrook [*New Jersey*] *December 21, 1778.* Reports arrest of John Smith Hatfield on charge of treason.

Df, in writing of H, George Washington Papers, Library of Congress.

Account of a Duel between Major General Charles Lee and Lieutenant Colonel John Laurens [1]

[Philadelphia, December 24, 1778]

NARRATIVE OF AN AFFAIR OF HONOR
BETWEEN GENERAL LEE AND COL LAURENS

General Lee attended by Major Edwards [2] and Col Laurens attended by Col Hamilton met agreeable to appointment on Wednesday afternoon half past three in a wood situate near the four mile stone on the Point no point road. Pistols having been the weapons previously fixed upon, and the combatants being provided with a brace each, it was asked in what manner they were to proceed. General Lee proposed, to advance upon one another and each fire at what time and distance he thought proper. Col Laurens expressed his preference of this mode, and agreed to the proposal accordingly.

They approached each other within about five or six paces and exchanged a shot almost at the same moment. As Col Laurens was preparing for a second discharge, General Lee declared himself wounded. Col Laurens, as if apprehending the wound to be more serious than it proved advanced towards the general to offer his support. The same was done by Col Hamilton and Major Edwards under a similar apprehension. General Lee then said the wound was inconsiderable, less than he had imagined at the first stroke of the Ball, and proposed to fire a second time. This was warmly opposed both by Col Hamilton and Major Edwards, who declared it to be their opinion, that the affair should terminate as it then stood. But General Lee repeated his desire, that there should be a second discharge and Col Laurens agreed to the proposal. Col Hamilton observed, that unless the General was influenced by motives of personal enmity, he did not think the affair ought to be persued any further; but as General Lee seemed to persist in desiring it, he was too tender of his friend's honor to persist in opposing it. The combat was then going to be renewed; but Major Edwards again declaring his opinion, that the affair ought to end where it was, General Lee then expressed his confidence in the honor of the Gentlemen concerned as seconds, and said he should be willing to comply with whatever they should cooly and deliberately determine. Col. Laurens consented to the same.

Col Hamilton and Major Edwards withdrew and conversing awhile on the subject, still concurred fully in opinion that for the most cogent reasons, the affair should terminate as it was then circumstanced. This decision was communicated to the parties and agreed to by them, upon which they immediately returned to Town; General Lee slightly wounded in the right side.

During the interview a conversation to the following purport past between General Lee and Col Laurens—On Col Hamilton's intimating the idea of personal enmity, as beforementioned, General Lee declared he had none, and had only met Col. Laurens to defend his own honor—that Mr. Laurens best knew whether there was any on his part. Col Laurens replied, that General Lee was acquainted with the motives, that had brought him there, which were that he had been informed from what he thought good authority, that General Lee had spoken of General Washington in the grossest and most opprobrious terms of personal abuse, which He Col Laurens thought himself bound to resent, as well on account of the relation he bore to General Washington as from motives of personal friendship, and respect for his character. General Lee acknowleged that he had given his opinion against General Washingtons military character to his particular friends and might perhaps do it again. He said every man had a right to give his sentiments freely of military characters, and that he did not think himself personally accountable to Col Laurens for what he had done in that respect. But said he never had spoken of General Washington in the terms mentioned, which he could not have done; as well because he had always esteemed General Washington as a man, as because such abuse would be incompatible with the character, he would ever wish to sustain as a Gentleman.

Upon the whole we think it a piece of justice to the two Gentlemen to declare, that after they met their conduct was strongly marked with all the politeness generosity coolness and firmness, that ought to characterise a transaction of this nature.

Alex Hamilton

Philad Decemb. 24th 1778   E Edwards

ADS, Hamilton Papers, Library of Congress. This document is in writing of H and is signed by H and Evan Edwards.
    1. The duel, which H describes here, originated when Laurens charged that Lee had cast aspersions upon Washington's character. Laurens then insisted that he would hold Lee accountable for his derogatory remarks about Washington and issued a challenge for a duel. Lee accepted the challenge, and the two men, with their seconds, met on the edge of a wood near Philadelphia on the afternoon of December 23, 1778.
    2. Major Evan Edwards, Eleventh Pennsylvania Regiment, who had been Lee's aide in 1777.

George Washington to Sir Henry Clinton

Philadelphia, December 26, 1778. Asks Clinton to place Brower and Lozier, who were accused of killing a Loyalist, on same footing with other prisoners of war.

Df, in writing of H, George Washington Papers, Library of Congress.

George Washington to Marquis de Lafayette

Philadelphia, December 29, 1778. Reports that plans for Canadian expedition have been set aside. Wishes Lafayette a safe passage on return voyage to France.

Df, in writings of George Washington and H, George Washington Papers, Library of Congress.

George Washington to John Jay [1]

[Philadelphia] December 31, 1778. Asks if Congress is going to continue to employ Brigadier General Du Portail and if it intends to adopt Du Portail's plan of defense.

Df, in writing of H, George Washington Papers, Library of Congress.
1. Henry Laurens had resigned as President of the Continental Congress on December 9, 1778, and John Jay was elected to that position on the following day.

George Washington to Major General Philip Schuyler

Philadelphia, December 31, 1778. Asks Schuyler to take command of Northern Department and to investigate Lieutenant Colonel Daniel Whiting's request for relief of Colonel Ichabod Alden's regiment.

Df, in writing of H, George Washington Papers, Library of Congress.

INDEX

COMPILED BY JEAN G. COOKE

	DATE DUE	